U0856297

湖北统计年鉴

HUBEI STATISTICAL YEARBOOK

2016

（总第32期）

湖　北　省　统　计　局
国家统计局湖北调查总队　编

©中国统计出版社 2016
版权所有。未经许可，本书的任何部分不得以任何方式在世界任何地区以任何文字翻印、拷贝、仿制或转载。

©2016 China Statistics Press
All rights reserved. No part of the publication may be reproduced or transmitted in any form or by any means, electronic or mechanical, including photocopying, recording, or any information storage and retrieval system, without written permission from the publisher.

图书在版编目（C I P）数据

湖北统计年鉴. 2016：汉英对照 / 湖北省统计局，国家统计局湖北调查总队编. -- 北京 ：中国统计出版社，2016.8
ISBN 978-7-5037-7847-6

Ⅰ. ①湖… Ⅱ. ①湖… ②国… Ⅲ. ①统计资料—湖北省—2016—年鉴—汉、英 Ⅳ. ①C832.63-54

中国版本图书馆 CIP 数据核字(2016)第 161729 号

湖北统计年鉴-2016

作　　者/ 湖北省统计局　国家统计局湖北调查总队
责任编辑/ 佘竞雄
封面设计/ 刘亚非
出版发行/ 中国统计出版社
地　　址/ 北京市丰台区西三环南路甲 6 号　邮政编码/100073
电　　话/ 邮购（010）63376909　书店（010）68783171
网　　址/ http://www.zgtjcbs.com
印　　刷/ 武汉市委印刷厂
经　　销/ 新华书店
开　　本/ 890mm×1240mm　1/16
字　　数/ 1240 千字
印　　张/ 39
版　　别/ 2016 年 8 月第 1 版
版　　次/ 2016 年 8 月第 1 次印刷
定　　价/ 380.00 元

本书附同版本 CD-ROM 一张，光盘内容以书面文字为准。

如有印装差错，由本社发行部调换。

编 者 说 明

一、《湖北统计年鉴—2016》是一本信息密集的资料工具书。通过大量数据，全面地分析、记载和反映了湖北省2015年经济、社会、科技、文化等方面的发展情况。具有信息量大、权威性强、适用性广等特点。

二、本年鉴包括综合、人口、从业人员和职工工资、固定资产投资、能源生产和消费、物价指数、人民生活、资源和环境、城市概况、农业、工业、建筑业、运输和邮电、国内贸易、对外经济和旅游、财政、金融和保险业、教育、科技和文化、体育、卫生、社会福利、湖北省开发区主要经济指标、武汉城市圈、鄂西生态文化旅游圈、县域经济、附录等23个部分。

三、2016年的湖北统计年鉴，篇章结构与《中国统计年鉴》保持一致，参照执行了国家统计局《省级统计年鉴指标体系目录》，采用了最新的国民经济行业分类标准和指标口径，并对英文注释和指标解释进行了全面修订。

四、本年鉴对过去发表的统计资料重新予以审核，凡与本年鉴资料有出入的，均以本年鉴为准。本年鉴中统计公报的数据为初步数，若与年鉴数据不一致，请以年鉴数据为准。

五、年鉴中指标的使用要结合文中的指标解释，以及注解合理使用，以免发生错误。

六、《湖北统计年鉴》公开出版以来，受到国内外读者的爱护与支持，对本年鉴的内容和编辑工作提出了许多宝贵意见，为此，我们特表谢意。由于水平有限，编辑工作中难免有疏误之处，竭诚欢迎读者批评指正。

COMPLIERS NOTES

I.*Statistical Yearbook of Hubei* 2016 is an information–intensive data reference book. Through a large amount of data, comprehensive analysis, records and reflects the Hubei province 2015 economy, society, science and technology, culture and other aspects of development. With a large amount of information, authoritative, wide applicability and so on.

II. The Yearbook includes comprehensive, population, practitioners and staff salaries, fixed assets investment, energy production and consumption, price index, the life of people and natural resources and the environment, city situation, agriculture, industry, construction, transportation, post and telecommunications, domestic trade, foreign economy and tourism, finance, banking and insurance, education, science and culture, sports, public health, social welfare, Hubei Province Development Zone of main economic norms, Wuhan city circle ,ecological cultural tourism circle of Western Hubei, county economy, Appendix 23 departments, city of part of the Department of city information, not including the city administer county.

III. In 2016 statistical yearbook of Hubei, discourse structure and "China Statistical Yearbook" remain the same, with reference to the implementation of the "provincial statistics index system directory". The statistic of yearbook adopted the lastest standard and diameter range. And the English version and the interpretation of indicators were revised thoroughy.

IV. The Yearbook of the past published statistical data to examine every and the almanac data discrepancies, refer to this yearbook prevail. The Yearbook of statistics data for the initial count, if the Yearbook text data are not consistent, please refer to the text data is accurate.

V. In the annals of indicators are used to combine the interpretation of indicators, as well as annotations and reasonable use, so as to avoid mistakes.

VI. *Statistical Yearbook of Hubei* published since, by domestic and foreign readers to care and support, the Yearbook content and editorial work put forward a lot of valuable advice, for this, we express our gratitude. Because the level is limited, in the editing work of unavoidable errors, we welcome suggestions and criticisms.

《湖北统计年鉴-2016》

编委会和编辑工作人员

编委会

主　　任： 李克勤　王跃新

副 主 任： 郑新华　叶　青　吴中志　张　静　蔡受清
黄承喜　崔永红　程良世　梁　冰　陈小清
胡大华　程正华　朱小明　王建刚

编　　委： （以姓氏笔划为序）
丁善兵　马泽民　王　博　王行刚　尹汉华　叶福生
卢玉廷　卢　薇　龙江舫　乐友来　刘　洪　刘　荣
刘水国　刘国强　许晓红　李团中　李良华　李明星
李昌文　汪　军　陈志明　张　晓　张利阳　张小青
张必洪　张永云　张在金　时明国　吴晓秦　杜云波
明　峰　金　锐　周家庆　胡先红　贺　宾　盛少华
龚其民　谢民义　谢余强　蒋宇飞　舒振斌　魏尚平

编辑工作人员

总 编 辑： 李团中　许晓红

副总编辑： 邓有成

编辑人员： （以姓氏笔划为序）
王　道　王喜峰　王静敏　刘　通　刘洪涛　李　川
李　景　李现厂　朱　焰　汪文华　闵胜男　苏　畅
何良伟　余　南　余佑玲　陆小红　陈彬彬　柯　超
陶　禹　徐　菁　徐晓颖　章　玲　曹　珣　黄　蓉
谢　涛　董胜男　韩立友　程文懿　樊喜珍

责任编辑： 王　道　徐晓颖　胡　艺

英文翻译： 王　道　徐晓颖　董　正

封面设计： 刘亚非

光盘设计： 王立群　刘金成　熊　威　罗　浩

Hubei Statistical Yearbook -2016

EDITORIAL BOARD AND STAFF

I. Editorial Board

Chairman: Li Keqin Wan Yuexin

Vice- chairman: Zheng Xinhua Ye Qing Wu Zhongzhi Zhang Jing
Cai Shouqing Hua Chengxi Cui Yonghong
Cheng Liangshi Liang Bing Chen Xiaoqing Hu Dahua
Cheng Zhenghua Zhu Xiaoming Wang Jiangang

Editorial Board: (in order of the number of strokes of the Chinese character of the surname)
Ding Shanbing Ma Zemin Wang Bo Wang Xinggang
Yin Hanhua Ye Fusheng Lu Yuting Lu Wei
Long Jiangfang Le Youlai Liu Hong Liu Rong
Liu Shuiguo Liu Guoqiang Xu Xiaohong Li Tuanzhong
Li Lianghua Li Mingxing Li Changwen Wang Jun
Chen Zhiming Zhang Xiao Zhang Liyang Zhang Xiaoqing
Zhang Bihong Zhang Yongyun Zhang Zaijin Shi Mingguo
Wu Xiaoqin Du Yunbo Ming Feng Jin Rui Zhou Jiaqing
Hu Xianhong He Bin Sheng Shaohua Gong Qimin Xie Mingyi
Xie Yuqiang Jiang Yufei Shu Zhenbin Wei Shangping

II. Editorial Staff

Editor-in-chief: Li Tuanzhong Xu Xiaohong

Associate Editors-in-chief: Deng Youcheng

Editorial Straff: (in order of the number of strokes of the Chinese character of the surname)
Wang Dao Wang Xifeng Wang Jingmin Liu Tong LiuHongtao
Li Chuan Li Jing Li Xianchang Zhu Yan Wang Wenhua
Min Shengnan Su Chang He Liangwei Yu Nan Yu Youling
Lu Xiaohong ChenBinbin Ke Chao Tao Yu Xu Jing
Xu Xiaoying Zhang Ling Cao Xun HuangRong Xie Tao
Dong Shengnan Han Liyou ChengWenyi Fan Xizhen

Coordinators: Wang Dao Xu Xiaoying HuYi

English Translators: Wang Dao Xu Xiaoying Dong Zheng

Cover Designer: Liu Yafei

CD-ROM Designer: Wang Liqun Liu Jincheng Xiong Wei Luo Hao

目　　录
CONTENTS

特 载

SPECIAL LOAD

1 综 合

GENERAL SURVEY

4 固定资产投资

INVESTMENT IN FIXED ASSETS

6 能 源

ENERGY

7 财政、金融、保险

GOVERNMENT FINANCE, BANKING AND INSURANCE

8 价 格

PRICE

9 居民生活

PEPOLE'S LIVELIHOOD

10 城市概况

CITY OVERVIEW

11 资源和环境

RESOURCES AND ENVIRONMENT

12 农 业

AGRICULTURE

13 工 业

INDUSTRY

14 建筑业

CONSTRUCTION

15 交通运输、邮电

TRANSPORTATION, POSTAL AND TELECOMMUNICATIONS SERVICES

16 国内贸易

DOMESTIC TRADE

17 科技和教育

SCIENCE, TECHNOLOGY AND EDUCATION

18 卫生和社会服务

HEALTH AND SOCIAL SERVICES

19 文化和体育

CULTURE AND SPORTS

20 公共管理及其他

PUBLIC ADMINISTRATION AND OTHER

21 开发区主要经济指标

MAJOR ECONOMIC INDICATORS OF DEVELOPMENT ZONE

22 “两圈”主要经济指标

MAJOR ECONOMIC INDICATORS OF "TWICE"

23 县域经济主要指标

ECONOMY OF CITIES AND COUNTIES

附录 全国分省主要指标

MAJOR INDICATORS BY REGION

2015年湖北省国民经济和社会发展统计公报

湖 北 省 统 计 局
国家统计局湖北调查总队

2015年，面对少有的严峻复杂形势，在党中央、国务院和省委、省政府的坚强领导下，全省上下以党的十八大精神为指引，深入贯彻习近平总书记系列重要讲话精神，积极适应经济发展新常态，全面落实"竞进提质、升级增效"总要求，努力践行"绿色决定生死、市场决定取舍、民生决定目的"三维纲要，在应对国际金融危机持续影响和经济下行压力中，克难奋进，稳步前行，经济社会发展呈现"总量跨越、质效提升、位次前移"的竞进态势，为"五个湖北"建设和"建成支点、走在前列"奠定了良好的基础。

一、综合

2015年，全省完成生产总值29550.19亿元，增长8.9%。其中：第一产业完成增加值3309.84亿元，增长4.5%；第二产业完成增加值13503.56亿元，增长8.3%；第三产业完成增加值12736.79亿元，增长10.7%。三次产业结构由2014年的11.6:46.9:41.5调整为11.2:45.7:43.1。在第三产业中交通运输仓储和邮政业、批发和零售业、住宿和餐饮业、金融业、房地产业、营利性服务业及非营利性服务业增加值分别增长4.4%、7.8%、7.1%、16.6%、6.5%、13.7%和12.6%。

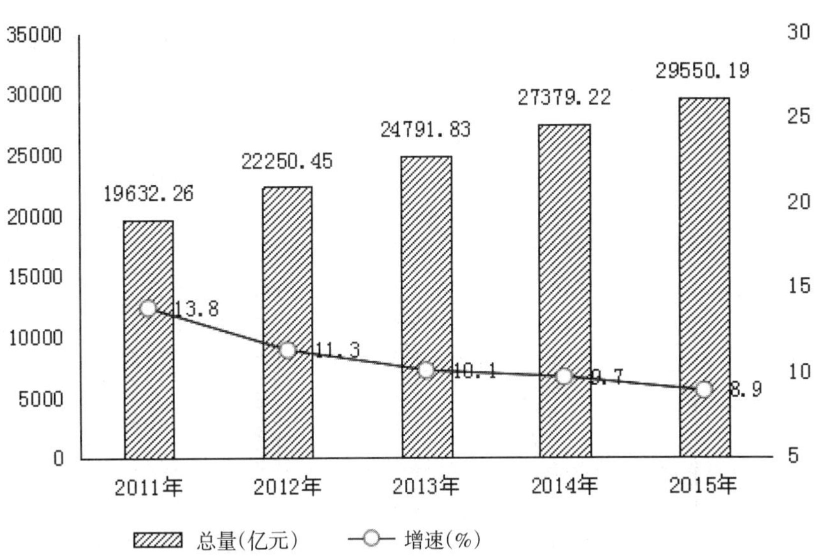

图1 2011-2015年湖北生产总值及增速

全省居民消费价格水平上涨1.5%，其中：城市上涨1.4%，农村上涨1.7%。分类别看，食品上涨2.2%，烟酒及用品上涨2.6%，衣着上涨2.7%，家庭设备用品及维修服务上涨0.6%，医疗保健及个人用品上涨1.7%，交通和通信下跌0.2%，娱乐教育文化用品及服务上涨1.3%，居住上涨0.6%。全年农业生产资料价格上涨0.4%。工业生产者出厂价格下降3.3%，工业生产者购进价格下降7.2%。

市场主体发展加快。全省新登记市场主体94.43万户，其中:新登记私营企业16.19万户，新登记个体工商户75.97万户。

就业保持稳定。年末全省城镇登记失业率为2.64%，比上年末下降0.46个百分点。

劳动生产率稳步提高。全省全员劳动生产率为8.15万元/人，比上年提高9.8%。

二、农业

全年全省农林牧渔业增加值3417.42亿元，按可比价格计算，比上年增长5.2%。粮食种植面积4466.03千公顷，比上年增加

95.69千公顷;棉花种植面积264.74千公顷,减少8.01千公顷;油料种植面积1545.52千公顷,增加3.01千公顷。粮食总产量2703.30万吨,比上年增产119.14万吨,增长4.6%,实现了历史性突破;棉花总产量27.89万吨,减产8.11万吨,下降22.4%;油料产量345.22万吨,增产3.41万吨,增长1.0%。

畜牧、水产业稳步增长。全年全省生猪出栏4363.20万头,下降2.5%;水产品产量达到455.50万吨,增长5.2%。

表1　　2015年全省主要农产品产量　　单位:万吨

产品名称	产　量	比上年增长(%)
粮 食	2703.30	4.6
棉 花	27.89	-22.4
油 料	345.22	1.0
#花 生	70.81	2.5
油菜籽	258.62	0.6
茶 叶	26.33	5.1
水 果(不含果用瓜)	615.94	0.3
蔬 菜	3848.64	4.8

三、工业和建筑业

工业生产保持稳定增长。全省全部工业增加值11532.63亿元,增长8.5%。年末全省规模以上工业企业达到15894家,比上年净增1052家,增长7.1%。规上工业增加值增长8.6%。其中:国有及国有控股企业增长3.7%;集体企业增长1.2%;股份合作企业增长2.4%;外商及港澳台投资企业增长7.1%;其他经济类型企业增长8.3%。轻工业增长9.8%;重工业增长7.8%。

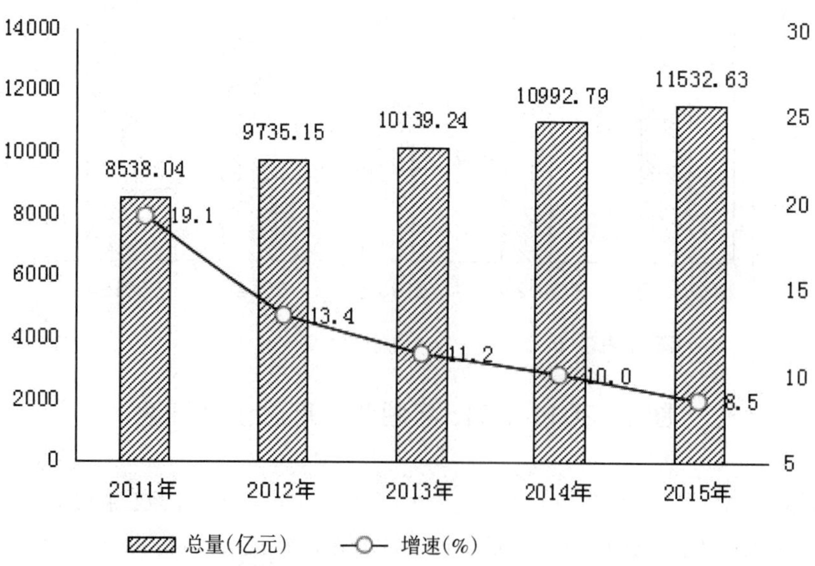

图2　2011-2015年工业增加值及增速

制造业增长9.5%,快于规上工业0.9个百分点。高技术制造业增长12.5%,快于规上工业3.9个百分点,占规模以上工业增加值的比重达8.0%,对规上工业增长的贡献率达10.9%。

全年规上工业完成销售产值44123.2亿元,增长7.6%。产品销售率为97.3%,实现出口交货值1931.2亿元,增长8.7%。全省千亿元产业增加到17个,较上年增加3个。全年规上工业企业实现利润2233.09亿元,增长2.1%。

表2　　2015年主要工业产品产量

产品名称	单位	产　量	比上年增长%
纱	万 吨	355.2	7.0
布	亿 米	79.9	-3.5
化学纤维	万 吨	35.4	17.6
卷 烟	亿 支	1389.4	-1.3
家用电冰箱	万 台	286.2	17.5
房间空气调节器	万 台	1213.0	-15.9
原 油	万 吨	71.0	-10.1
发电量	亿千瓦小时	2301.4	-2.1
#水电	亿千瓦小时	1290.0	-6.3
粗 钢	万 吨	2919.8	-4.5
钢 材	万 吨	3421.2	-0.1
十种有色金属	万 吨	96.2	-9.4
#精炼铜	万 吨	50.5	-3.1
水 泥	万 吨	11288.9	-3.2
硫 酸	万 吨	780.1	12.9
纯 碱	万 吨	159.5	13.2
烧 碱	万 吨	106.8	4.0
化 肥(折100%)	万 吨	1408.1	6.8
发电设备	万千瓦	119.7	36.2
汽 车	万 辆	196.8	12.8
# 轿 车	万 辆	85.0	11.7
移动通信手持机	万 台	5475.7	13.8

建筑业发展步伐加快。全年全省资质以内建筑企业完成施工产值10592.86亿元，增长5.3%；实现利润425.24亿元，增长8.8%；税金354.08亿元，增长3.5%。新开工房屋建筑施工面积31344.24万平方米，增长4.3%。

四、固定资产投资

全省完成固定资产投资(不含农户) 28250.48亿元，增长16.2%，其中房地产开发投资完成4249.23亿元，增长6.7%，商品房销售面积6244.55万平方米，增长11.5%，实现商品房销售额3661.37亿元，增长18.6%。按产业划分，全省一、二、三次产业投资分别为687.26亿元、12146.51亿元和15416.71亿元，分别增长28.2%、13.2%、18.3%。全省292个在建重点建设项目全年完成投资2442.73亿元，占固定资产投资的比重为8.6%。

全省亿元以上新开工项目3569个，其中：第一、二和三产业亿元以上新开项目分别为131个、2034个和1404个。亿元以上新开工项目完成投资7785.01亿元，增长3.6%。

五、国内贸易

全年全省实现社会消费品零售总额13978.05亿元，增长12.3%。分城乡看，城镇实现零售额11754.20亿元，增长12.0%；乡村实现零售额2223.85亿元，增长13.8%。其中，限额以上企业(单位)实现消费品零售额8283.65亿元，增长11.8%。

六、对外经济

全年全省实现外贸进出口总额2838.8亿元，增长7.3%，其中：进口1021.7亿元，增长1.4%；出口1817.1亿元，增长11.0%。新批外商直接投资项目301个。全年外商直接投资89.48亿美元，增长12.9%。

七、交通运输、邮电通信和旅游

全年全省完成货物周转量5902.19亿吨公里，增长1.7%；旅客周转量1514.56亿人公里，增长5.1%。公路营运里程252980公里，增长6.8%；高速公路里程6204公里，增长21.7%。

全省邮电业务总量962.66亿元，增长33.6%。长途光缆线路总长度达到3.14万公里；局用交换机达到917.20万门；固定电话用户872.50万户；移动电话用户达到4650.60万户；全省电话普及率为94.4部／百人；计算机宽带互联网用户858.60万户。

全省国内旅游人数5.07亿人次，增长12.7%；国内旅游收入4206.02亿元，增长14.3%。入境旅游人数311.76万人次，增长12.5%。国际旅游外汇收入16.72亿美元，增长35.0%。

八、财政、金融和保险

全年全省完成财政总收入4705.28亿元，增长14.9%，其中地方公共财政预算收入3005.39亿元，增长17.1%。在地方公共财政预算收入中，税收收入2086.36亿元，增长11.4%。全年财政支出6094.21亿元，增长23.5%。

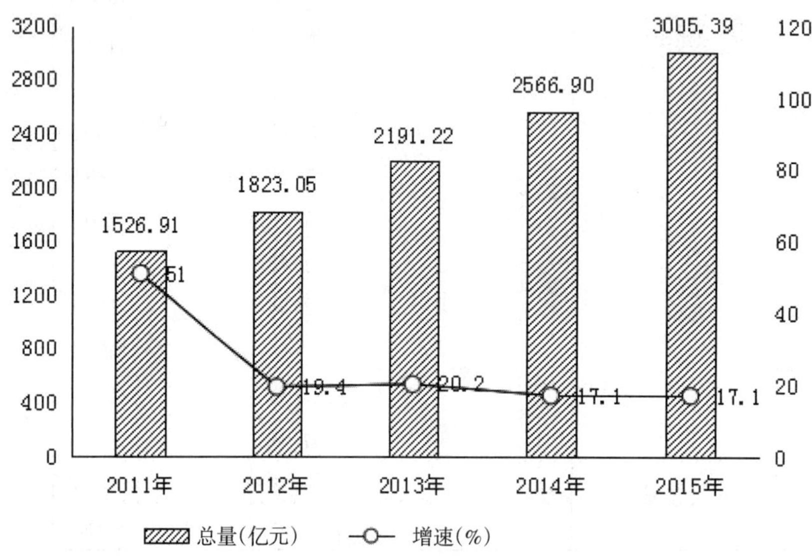

图3　2011-2015年地方公共财政预算收入及增速

年末全省金融机构本外币各项存款余额41345.88亿元，比年初增加4511.50亿元。其中：住户存款19680.14亿元，增加1877.63亿元。金融机构各项贷款余额29514.57亿元，比年初增加4217.02亿元。其中：住户贷款7364.00亿元，增加1056.55亿元；非金融企业及机关团体贷款21278.99亿元，增加2765.33亿元。

全年实现保费收入843.63亿元，增长20.5%。其中，财产险公司实现保费收入256.59亿元，增长17.0%；人身险公司保费收入587.03亿元，增长22.1%。支付各类赔款及给付283.34亿元，增长22.9%，其中，财产险公司赔款支出127.12亿元，增长15.3%；人身险公司赔付支出156.22亿元，增长29.8%。

九、教育和科学技术

2015年末，全省普通高等教育本专科招生39.18万人，在校生141.06万人，毕业生38.92万人；研究生招生4.06万人，在校研究生11.99万人，毕业生3.47万人；各类中等职业教育招生16.73万人，在校生45.43万人，毕业生15.57万人；普通高中招生27.86万人，在校生87.6万人，毕业生31.69万人；普通初中在校生136.53万人，小学在校生335.81万人，幼儿园在园幼儿162.58万人。

科学研究和技术开发取得新的成果。全年共登记重大科技成果1933项。其中，基础理论成果16项，应用技术成果1875项，软科学成果42项。全年共签订技术合同22787项，技术合同成交金额830.07亿元，合同金额比上年增长37.95%。

全省科学研究与实验发展(R&D)经费支出565亿元，增长10%，占全省生产总值的1.91%。围绕光电子器件、集成电路、平板显示、创新创业、重大科技基础设施建设等领域，加大项目策划和争取力度，共争取国家高技术和战略性新兴产业相关项目40个，争取国家资金71.2亿元。

全省具备向社会出具检测报告的产品质量监督检验机构有123个，其中国家产品质量监督检验中心26个。全省通过CNAL认可的检测/校准实验室128家。累计有8456家企业通过ISO9000体系认证；企业获得强制性认证证书11968张。法定计量技术机构有150个，强制检定计量器具660万台件。

全省天气雷达观测站点有14个，卫星云图接受站点17个。地震遥测台网3个，地震台站47个。

十、文化、卫生和体育

2015年末，全省共有国有艺术表演团体86个，群艺馆、文化馆122个，公共图书馆112个，博物馆140个。电影放映管理机构87个，放映单位1551个。广播电台6座，电视台8座，广播电视台76台，有线电视用户1105万户。全年出版全国性和省级报纸17.59亿份，各类期刊2.56亿册，图书2.53亿册。

全省共有医疗卫生机构36097家，其中医院770家，基层医疗卫生机构34516家，专业公共卫生机构703家；全省共有卫生计生人员总数44.71万人，其中执业（助理）医师12.86万人，注册护士15.46万人；全省共有医疗卫生机构床位33.85万张，其中医院床位24.22万张，社区卫生服务机构床位1.23万张，卫生院床位7.24万张。

全年全省运动健儿在国际比赛中共获得冠军29项次、亚军32项次、季军5项次，其中奥运会项目最高水平比赛冠军14项次、亚军11项次、季军3项次；在各类全国比赛中，获冠军75项次、亚军78项次、第三名85项次，其中，全运会项目全国最高水平比赛中冠军27项次、亚军27项次、第三名21项次。全年销售体育彩票36.7亿元。

十一、人口、居民生活和社会保障

年末全省常住人口5851.50万人，其中：城镇3326.58万人，乡村2524.92万人。城镇化率达到56.85%。全年出生人口62.65万人，出生率为10.74‰；死亡人口34.01万人，死亡率为5.83‰，人口自然增长率为4.91‰。

城乡居民收入继续增加。全省居民人均可支配收入20026元，增长9.5%，其中，城镇常住居民人均可支配收入27051元，增长8.8%；农村常住居民人均可支配收入11844元，增长9.2%。

社会保障进一步加强。年末全省参加城镇职工基本养老保险1315.66万人，其中：在职职工875.09万人，离退休人员440.57万人；参加城乡居民基本养老保险2214.96万人；参加城镇职工基本医疗保险949.41万人；参加城镇居民基本医疗保险1022.73万人；参加工伤保险640.09万人；参加生育保险500.21万人；参加失业保险人数528.38万人，全年累计领取失业保险金人数11.29万人。

全年全省城镇居民最低生活保障对象84.6万人，农村居民最低生活保障人数159.6万人，国家抚恤、补助各类优抚对象47.6万人。社会福利事业不断发展。年末全省各类社会福利收养床位30万张，城镇社区服务中心、站共计5265个。全年销售社会福利彩票93.91亿元。

十二、节能降耗、资源环境

全省继续大力推进节能降耗工作，单位GDP能耗继续保持下降态势，可望超额完成年初确定下降2%的目标。工业企业吨粗铜综合能耗比上年下降3.76%，吨钢综合能耗下降1.65%，单位烧碱综合能耗下降2.33%，吨水泥综合能耗下降1.12%，每千瓦时火力发电标准煤耗下降0.67%。

长江干流总体水质状况为优。监测的15个断面水质符合Ⅱ～Ⅲ类的比例为100%。

全省累计已发现矿种149种，累计已查明资源储量的矿种92种。2015年国土资源调查及地质勘查新增查明矿产地大型8处，中小型29处。

全省自然保护区达到76个，其中国家级自然保护区18个，省级自然保护区28个，自然保护区面积109.9万公顷。

2014年第九次全国森林资源清查结果显示，全省森林面积736万公顷，森林覆盖率39.61%。活立木总蓄积39580万立方米，森林蓄积36508万立方米。天然林面积486万公顷，天然林蓄积28671万立方米；人工林面积197万公顷，人工林蓄积7837万立方米。

注：1.本公报所列数据为快报数。

2.地区生产总值、规模以上工业增加值及分类项目增长速度按可比价格计算；其他指标除特殊情况外，按现价计算。

Hubei Province's National Economy and Society Development Statistical Communiqué 2015

Hubei Provincial Bureau of Statistics
Hubei Investigation Team of National Statistical Bureau

In 2015, Hubei has encountered rare, severe and complicated situation, under the leadership of the Central Committee of the Communist Party of China (CPC), the State Council, the provincial Party committee and government, guided by the spirit of the 18th CPC National Congress, all the people of Hubei have thoroughly applied the spirit of President Xi Jinping's important speeches, actively adapted to the new normal in economic development, comprehensively implemented the general requirements of " improve quality through competition, increase efficiency through upgrade", diligently practiced the three-dimensional outline of "green determines the survival, market determines the choice, livelihood determines the purpose", despite continuous influence of the international financial crisis and economic downward pressure, we have worked hard to overcome obstacles, pressed ahead with a steady manner, our economic and social development has shown a competitive and progressive trend of "a leap forward in gross value, a raise in quality and efficiency, and a forward lead in ranking", and we have laid solid foundation for the construction of "Five Hubei" and "build a fulcrum, at the forefront".

I. General Outlook

In 2015, Hubei's gross domestic product (GDP) was 2955.019 billion yuan, an increase of 8.9%. The output of primary industry was 330.984 billion yuan, grew by 4.5%; secondary industry, 1350.356 billion yuan and 8.3%; tertiary industry, 1273.679 billion yuan and 10.7%. Structure of the three industries has changed from 11.6:46.9:41.5 in 2014 to 11.2:45.7:43.1. In the tertiary industry, transport and storage and postal services, wholesale and retail, accommodation and catering, finance, real estate, profitable service and nonprofit services have risen by 4.4%、7.8%、7.1%、16.6%、6.5%、13.7% and 12.6%, respectively.

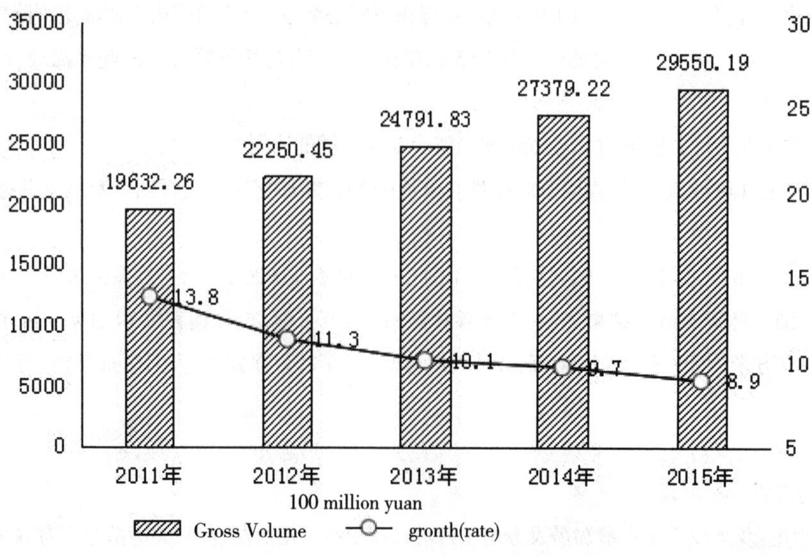

Figure I Hubei's GDP and its growth rate during 2011-2015

The consumer price index increased by 1.5%. In city it rose 1.4%% and in rural area, 1.7%. For different kinds of goods, the price of food grew by 2.2%; cigarette and wine, 2.6%; clothing, 2.7%; household facilities articles and maintenance services, 0.6%; medical care and personal items, 1.7%; transportation and communication, minus 0.2%; recreational, educational, cultural products and services, 1.3%; residence, 0.6%. Means of agricultural production's price increased by 0.4%. The PPI fell by 3.3%, while IPI decreased by 7.2%.

Development of market subject accelerated. Over the province, newly registered market players were 944, 300. Newly registered private enterprise contributed 161, 900 to the total number; while newly registered individual business accounted for another 759,700.

Employment rate remained steady. At the end of the year, the rural registered unemployment rate was 2.64%, decreased by 0.46%.

Our labor productivity rose in steady manner. The province's overall labor productivity was 81, 500 yuan per person, increased by 9.8%.

II. Agriculture

This year, our province's total output value of agriculture, forestry, animal husbandry and fishery industry was 341.742 billion yuan, in comparable price, a 5.2% increase by last year. Grain acreage was 4,466,030 hectares, grew by 95, 690 hectares; cotton plantation area was 264, 740 hectares, reduced by 8,010 hectares; oilseed acreage was 1,545,520 hectares, grew 3,010 hectares. The total grain output was 27,033,000 tons, 1,191,400 tons larger than the previous year, increasing 4.6%, this was a historic breakthrough; total cotton output was 278,900 tons, decreased by 81,100 tons, fell 22.4%; total oilseed output was 3,452,200 tons, increased by 34,100 tons, grew 1.0%.

Livestock breeding and aquaculture grew steadily. In this year, live pig output was 43,632,000, fell by 2.5%; aquatic product output was 4,555,000 tons, grew 5.2%.

Table 1 2015 Major Agricultural Products Unit: 10,000 ton

Product name	Out put	Increased over 2014
Grain	2703.30	4.6
Cotton	27.89	-22.4
Oil-bearing Crops	345.22	1.0
# Peanuts	70.81	2.5
Rapeseed	258.62	0.6
Tea	26.33	5.1
Fruits (melon not included)	615.94	0.3
Vegetables	3848.64	4.8

III. Industry and Construction

Industrial production maintained a steady growth. The overall output of industry was 1153,263 billion yuan, an increase of 8.5%. At the end of the year, Hubei's total number of above-scale industrial enterprises was 15,894, 1052 more than previous year, grew by 7.1%. State-owned and state-holding enterprises grew 3.7%; collective enterprises increased 1.2%; joint-stock cooperative enterprises increased 2.4%; foreign, Hong Kong and Macao investment enterprises increased 7.1%; other economic enterprises grew 8.3%. Light industrial grew 9.8%; heavy industrial grew 7.8%.

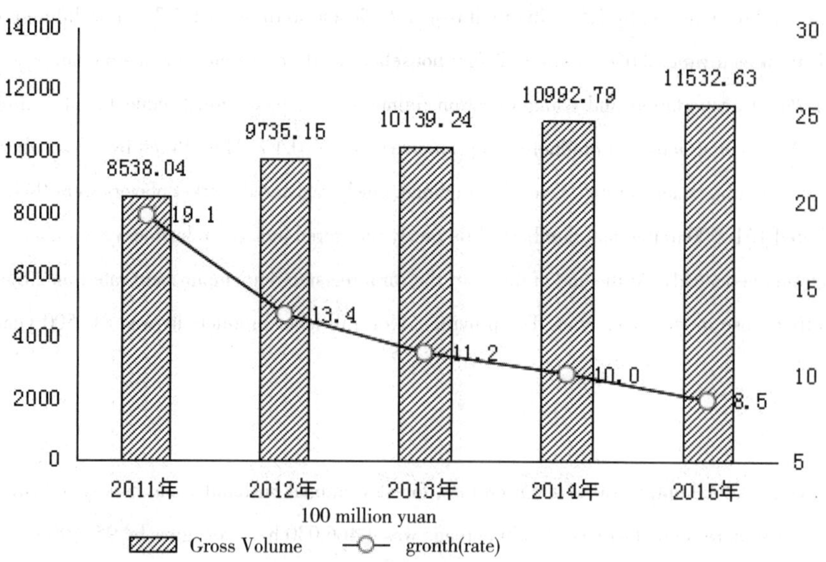

Figure II Hubei's industrial output value and its growth rate during 2011-2015

Manufacturing industry increased 9.5%, 0.9% faster than above-scale industry. High-tech manufacturing grew 12.5%, 3.9% faster than above-scale industry, took up 8.0% of above-scale industry, contributed 10.9% to the growth of above-scale industry.

In 2015, sales value of above-scale industry was 4412.32 billion yuan, increased by 7.6%. 97.3% of the products were sold, value of export delivery was 193.12 billion yuan, grew 8.7%. Over the province, there were 17 industries which output more than 100 billion yuan per year, 3 industries more than last year. Profit of the above-scale industrial enterprises was 223.309 billion yuan, rose 2.1%.

Table 2: Output of Major Industrial Products 2015

Name of the product	Unit	Out put	Increased over 2014
Yarn	10,000 tons	355.2	7.0
Cloth	million meters	79.9	-3.5
Chemical Fiber	10,000 tons	35.4	17.6
Cigarettes	100 million units	1389.4	-1.3
Household Friddge	Units	286.2	17.5
Air Conditioner	units	1213.0	-15.9
Crude Oil	10,000 tons	71.0	-10.1
Power generation	100 million KWH	2301.4	-2.1
# Hydropower	100 million KWH	1290.0	-6.3
Crude Steel	10,000 tons	2919.8	-4.5
Rolled Steel	10,000 tons	3421.2	-0.1
Ten Kinds of Nonferrous Metal	10,000 tons	96.2	-9.4
# refined copper	10,000 tons	50.5	-3.1
Cement	10,000 tons	11288.9	-3.2
Sulfuric Acid	10,000 tons	780.1	12.9

续表

Name of the product	Unit	Out put	Increased over 2014
Sodium Carbonate	10,000 tons	159.5	13.2
Caustic Soda	10,000 tons	106.8	4.0
Chemical Fertilizer(100% equivalent)	10,000 tons	1408.1	6.8
Power Generating Equipment	10,000 KW	119.7	36.2
Automobile	10,000 units	196.8	12.8
# Car	10,000 units	85.0	11.7
Mobile Phones	10,000 units	5475.7	13.8

Development of construction industry accelerated. Qualified construction enterprises outputted 1059.286 billion yuan, grew 5.3%; their profit reached 42.524 billion yuan, increased 8.8%; 35.408 billion yuan's taxes was levied from this industry, a 3.5% increase. 313, 442,400 square meters' new houses have been under construction, grew by 4.3%.

IV. Investment in Fixed Assets

The investment in fixed assets (rural households not included) was 2825.048 billion yuan, increased 16.2%. Real estate investment contributed 424.923 billion yuan to the total number, grew 6.7%. The total sold area of commodity house was 62,445,500 square meters, grew 11.5%. The total sales value of commodity house was 366.137 billion yuan, grew 18.6%. According to the industries, the provincial investment in primary, secondary and tertiary industries were 68.726, 1214.651 and 1541.671 billion yuan, respectively; accordingly grew by 28.2 %、13.2%、18.3 %. Over the province, 292 key projects under construction have totally invested 244.273 billion yuan, accounting for 8.6% of total fixed assets investment.

There were 3569 newly-commenced projects in the province, primary, secondary and tertiary industries contributed 131, 2034 and 1404 projects respectively. The newly-commenced projects with more than 100 million yuan's total investment have invested 778.501 billion yuan, increased by 3.6%.

V. Domestic Trade

The social consumable total retail sales was 1397.805 billion yuan, grew 12.3%. In Urban areas, retail sales was 1175.42 billion yuan, increased 12.0%; in rural areas, retail sales was 222.385 billion yuan, grew 13.8%. In particular, retail sales of businesses above designated scale accumulated to 828.365 billion yuan, up by 11.8%.

VI. External Economy

The total foreign trade value was 283.88 billion yuan, grew 7.3%. Import was 102.17 billion yuan, grew 1.4%; export was 181.71 billion yuan, increased 11.0%. 301 of foreign direct investment projects were approved. Total amount of FDI was 8.948 billion dollars.

VII. Transportation, Post, Telecommunications and Tourism

The provincial annual tonnage mileage was 590.219 billion ton kilometers, grew 1.7%; the volume of passenger transport was 151.456 billion passenger kilometers, grew 5.1%. Road operating mileage was 252,980 km, increased by 6.8%; while highway operating mileage was 6,204 km, increased by 21.7%

The annual income of post and telecommunications services was 962.66 billion yuan, up by 33.6%. Long distance optical cable lines reached a total length of 3,1300 km; the capacity of office telephone exchanges reached 9.172 million lines; there were 8.725 million fixed phone users and 46,506 million mobile phone users; the provincial telephone penetration rate was 94.4 units/100 people; broadband Internet users reached 8.586 million.

The number of domestic tourists was 507 million person–times, grew by 12.7%; earnings from domestic tourism was 420.602 billion yuan, up by 14.3%. The number of inbound tourism was 3.1176 million person–times, grew by 12.5%. Foreign exchange earnings from tourism reached 1.672 billion dollars, increased by 35.0%.

VIII. Finance, Banking and Insurance

The provincial annual general finance revenue was 470.528 billion yuan, a growth of 14.9%. In particular, the local public finance budget revenue was 300.539 billion yuan, grew 17.1%. In local public finance budget revenue, tax income accounted for 208.636 billion yuan, grew 11.4%. The annual fiscal expenditure was 609.421 billion yuan, up by 23.5%.

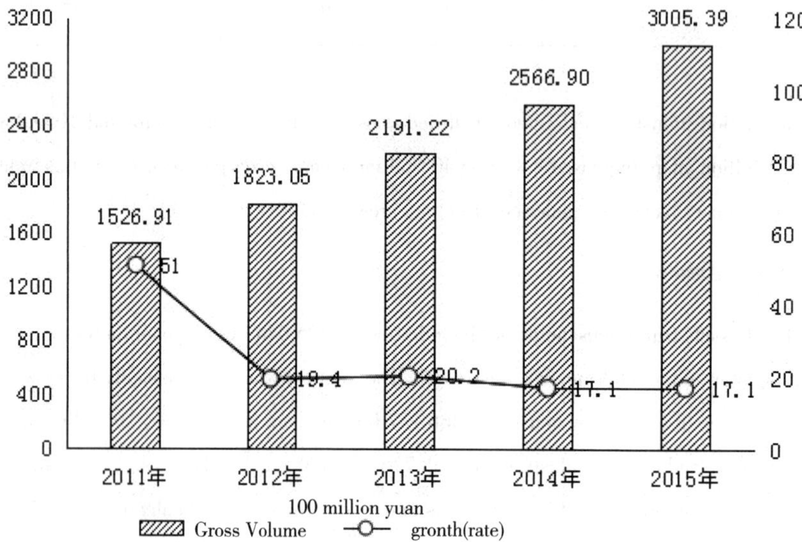

Figure III Hubei's local public finance budget revenue and its growth rate during 2011–2015

At the end of 2015, the savings deposit in Renminbi and foreign currencies in all items of financial institutions totaled 4134.588 billion yuan, 451.15 billion yuan more than at the beginning of the year. Personal deposit was 1968.014 billion yuan, an increase of 187.763 billion yuan. Loans in all items of financial institutions reached 2951.457 billion yuan, 421.702 billion yuan more than that at the beginning of the year. In particular, households' loans were 736.4 billion yuan, an increase of 105.655 billion yuan; non–financial business and government institutions loans were 2127.899 billion yuan, increased 276.533 billion yuan.

The annual premium income was 84.363 billion yuan, grew 20.5%. Property insurance companies contributed 25.659 billion yuan to the total number, increased 17.0%; personal insurance companies' premium income was 58.703 billion yuan, grows 22.1%. Payment of various indemnities was 28.334 billion yuan, grew 22.9%. In particular, property insurance companies paid 12.712 billion yuan, increased 15.3%%; personal insurance companies paid 15.622 billion yuan, grows 29.8%.

IX. Education, Science and Technology

At the end of 2015, the total number of regular higher education enrolled is 391,800 undergraduate and specialized students, the number of students at school was 1.4106 million, and the number of graduates was 389,200. Postgraduate enrollment number was 40,600, in–school postgraduate student number was 119,900, and 34,700 graduated; number of enrollment for medium vocational education was 167,300, the number at school was 454,300, and the number graduated was 155,700, For regular high school the number of enrollment was 278,600, the number at school was 876,000, and the number graduated was 316,900. There were 1.3653 million middle school students, 3.3581 million pupils and 1.6258 million kindergarten infants.

Scientific research and technology development have made new achievements. There were 1933 registered major technical achievements. In particular, 16 were about basic theory, 1875 were about application and 42 are about soft science. 22787 technological contracts were signed, with 83.007 billion yuan's volume of transactions, up by37.95%.

The scientific research and experimental development (R&D) expenditure achieved 56.5 billion yuan, grew by 10%, occupying 1.91% of provincial gross domestic product. The province increased project scheming and worked hard to bring in key projects in fields of optoelectronic device, integrated circuit, panel display, Innovation and Entrepreneurship, major scientific and technological base facilities' construction, etc, 40 national high technology and strategic emerging industry projects were brought in, with a national investment of 7.12billion yuan.

There were 123 product quality supervision and inspection institutions that are capable of issuing product quality report and 26 of them are of national level. 128 testing and calibration laboratories were certified by CNAL. 8456 enterprises have received ISO9000 certification and 11968 China Compulsory Certifications were issued. The number of authorized technical institution of metrology was 150 and they compulsorily inspected 6.6 million measurement instruments.

The number of weather radar observation stations was 14. The number of satellite cloud images receiving stations was 17. There are together 3 seismic network and 47 seismic stations.

X. Culture, Public Health and Sports

At the end of 2015, in Hubei province, there were 86 state-owned art performance troupes, 122 community art centers and cultural centers, 112 public libraries and 140 museums. There were 87 film supervision institutions and 1551 showing units. There were 6 broadcasting stations, 8 television stations, 76 radio and television stations, and 11.05 million cable television subscribers. 1.759 billion copies of national and provincial newspapers, 256 million journals and 253 million books were published.

In Hubei Province, there were 36097 health institutions, including 770 hospitals, 34516 health care institutions at grass-root level and 703 specialized public health institutions. There were 447,100 medical technical personnel, there are 128,600 licensed (assistant) doctors and 154,600 registered nurses; the number of beds in health care institutions was 338,500, among which, 222,400 were hospital beds, 12,300 beds were in community health service centers, and 72,400 beds in health centers.

In international sports competitions, our athletes won the first, second and third place for 29, 32 and 5 times, respectively, in particular, in Olympic Games the numbers were 14, 11 and 3 times respectively; in all types of nationwide competitions, the numbers were 75, 78 and 85 times respectively, among which, in China National Sports Mass Meeting, they won 27, 27 and 21 times respectively. Annual sales value of sports lottery tickets was 3.67 billion yuan.

XI. Population, Living Conditions and Social Security

At the end of 2015, the provincial resident population was 58.515 million, including 33.2658 million in urban area and 25.2492 million in rural area. Our urbanization rate was 56.85%. The newly-born population was 626,500, a birth rate of 10.74‰; death population was 340,100, a death rate of 5.83‰, the natural population growth rate was 4.91‰.

Income of urban and rural residents continued to increase. The Provincial residents' per capita disposable income was 20026 yuan, an increase of 9.5%, urban residents per capita disposable income was 27051 yuan, up by 8.8%; for rural residents, the number was 11844 yuan, grew by 9.2%.

Social security was further strengthened. At the end of the year, 13.1566 million urban employees bought basic endowment insurances. Among them, 8.7509 million were on-the-job and 4.4057 million were retired; there were 22.1496 million urban and rural residents bought basic endowment insurance; there were 9.4941 million urban employees bought basic medical care insurance; there were 10.2273 million urban residents bought basic medical care insurance; 6.4009 million workers bought employment injury insurance; 5.0021 million bought maternity insurance; 5.2838 million bought unemployment insurance; the number of person receiving unemployment insurance was 112,900.

There were 846,000 urban minimal living standard protection objects and 1.596 million rural minimal living standard protection objects, 476,000 people were comforted and compensated by the government. Social welfare continued to develop. At the end of the year, social welfare institutions of various types provided 300,000 beds, 5265 social service centers were operation in urban area. The sales value of welfare lottery was 9.391 billion yuan.

XII. Energy-saving, Resources and Environment

The province continued to vigorously advance energy saving, our energy consumption per GDP maintained a trend of decline, expecting to outperform the goal of a 2% decrease decided at the beginning of this year. Comprehensive energy consumption of industrial enterprises for producing one ton of crude copper was 3.76% lower than last year, for crude steel the number was 1.65% lower, 2.33% lower for caustic soda, 1.12% lower for cement, 0.67% for thermal power generation.

Water quality of the main stream of Yangtze River was generally good. 15 water quality monitoring sections showed that 100% achieved grade II~III.

Inside the province, 149 types of mineral have been found. Accumulatively 92 kinds were identified as resource reserve. In 2015's territorial resources and geological survey, 8 large, 29 middle and small ore fields were found.

The province has 76 natural protection areas, including 18 of national level and 21 of provincial level, covering a total area of 1,099, 000 hectares.

According to results of the ninth national forest resources inventory in 2014, our forestry area was 7,36 million hectares, with a forest coverage rate of 39.61%.Standing tree stock volume was 395.8 cubic meters, forest stock volume was 365,08 cubic meters. Natural forest area was 4.86 million hectares, natural forest stock volume was 286,71 cubic meters; man-made forest area was 1.97 million hectares, man-made forest stock volume was 78.37 cubic meters.

Note:

Ⅰ.All figures in the Communiqué are preliminary statistics.

Ⅱ.GDP, added value of above-scale industries and increasing speed of classification items is counted in comparable price; other indexes are counted in current price except special situation.

1 综　合

General Survey

综 合
General Survey

从数字看2015年的湖北
Statistic about Hubei in 2015

湖 北 的 地 位
Position of Hubei in the Country

地区生产总值29550.19亿元	Gross Domestic Production: 2955.02 billion yuan	占全国的4.37%
#第三产业12736.79亿元	Tertiary Industry: 1273.68 billion yuan	占全国的3.73%
人均地区生产总值50654元	Per Capita Regional GDP:50654 yuan	相当于全国的102.64%
全社会固定资产投资总额29191.06亿元	TotaL Investment in Fixed Assets: 2919.11 billion yuan	占全国的5.19%
社会消费品零售总额14003.24亿元	Total Retail Sales of Social Consumption: 1397.81 billion yuan	占全国的4.65%
进出口总额455.86亿美元	Total Imports and Exports: 45.59 billion yuan	占全国的1.15%
#出口总额292.14亿美元	Total Exports: 29.21 billion yuan	占全国的1.28%
实际外商直接投资89.48亿美元	Actual Foreign Direct Investment: 8.95 billion dollars	占全国的7.09%
粮食产量2703.28万吨	Grain: 27.03 million tons	占全国的4.35%
钢产量2919.77万吨	Rolled Steel: 29.20 milliom tons	占全国的3.63%
发电量2301.40亿千瓦小时	Electricity: 230.14 billion kwh	占全国的3.96%
城镇居民人均可支配收入27051元	Per Capita Disposable Income of Urban Residents: 27051 yuan	相当于全国的86.72%
农村居民人均可支配收入11844元	Per Capita Net Incomes of Rural Residents:11844 yuan	相当于全国的103.70%

湖 北 的 人 口
Population of Hubei

常住人口	Population of Permanent Residents	5851.50万人
从业人员	Employment	3658.00万人
#在岗职工人数	Staff and Workers	980.01万人
出生人口	Birth Population	62.65万人
死亡人口	Death Population	34.01万人
城镇人口	Urban Population	3326.58万人
乡村人口	Rural Population	2524.92万人
人口密度	Density of Population	315人/平方公里

湖 北 的 经 济 发 展
Economic Development of Hubei

		79-2015年平均增长(%)
地区生产总值	Regional Gross Production	10.7
第一产业	Primary Industry	4.7
第二产业	Second Industry	12.7
第三产业	Tertiary Industry	12.6
全社会固定资产投资	Investment in Fixed Assets	19.7
财政收入	Government Revenue	13.1
货物运输量	Cargo Transport Volume	7.7
社会消费品零售总额	Total Retail Sales of Social Consumption	15.9
出口总额	Total Exports	15.1

湖 北 的 一 天
One Day in Hubei

地区生产总值	Gross Domestic Product	80.96亿元
第一产业	First Industry	9.07亿元
第二产业	Second Industry	37.00亿元
第三产业	Tertiary Industry	34.90亿元
地方公共财政收入	Local Government Public Finance Income	8.23亿元
货物运输量	Freight Traffic	439.43万吨
竣工房屋面积	Floor Space of Building Completed	62.99万平方米
社会消费品零售总额	Total Retail Sales of Social Consumption	38.37亿元
出口总额	Total Exports	8003.84万美元
出版报纸	Newspapers Published	423.39万份
邮寄函件	Letters and Correspondents Delivered	18.51万件

1-1 土地面积与行政区划
LAND AREA AND ADMINISTRATIVE DIVISION

项目	单位	Item	unit	2000	2005	2010	2013	2014	2015
常住人口	(万人)	Population of the Whole Province	(10 000 persons)	5960	5710	5724	5799	5816	5852
土地面积	(万平方公里)	Land Area	(10 000 sq.km)	18.59	18.59	18.59	18.59	18.59	18.59
耕地面积	(千公顷)	Cultivated Area	(1000 hectares)	3283	3161.2	3323.9	3409.9	3420.5	3436.2
行政区划		Adinimisrtative Division							
省辖市	(个)	Municipality	(unit)	12	12	12	12	12	12
自治州	(个)	Autonomous	(unit)	1	1	1	1	1	1
林区	(个)	Forest Zone	(unit)	1	1	1	1	1	1
县级市	(个)	City	(unit)	24	24	24	24	24	24
省辖行政单位	(个)	Adinimistrative Units under the Jurisdiction of Province	(unit)	3	3	3	3	3	3
县	(个)	County	(unit)	41	39	40	40	39	39
乡政府	(个)	Local Government	(unit)	476	217	201	175	170	168
镇政府	(个)	Township Government	(unit)	853	737	742	757	761	761
办事处	(个)	Office	(unit)	145	163	211	300	302	304
村民委员会	(个)	Village Community	(unit)	32400	26678	26018	25955	25606	25343
村民小组	(个)	Village Groups	(unit)	259250	212587	209598	210108	208966	208546

1-2 市、州行政区划

ADMINISTRATIVE DIVISION OF MUNICIPALITIES AND PREFECTURE

单位：个　　(2015年底)(by the End of 2015)　　(unit)

地区	Region	县级市 Cities	县 Counties	区 Districts	乡政府 Village Government	镇政府 Township Government	村民委员会 Village Community	村民小组 Village Groups
全 省	Total	24	39	39	168	761	25343	208546
武汉市	Wuhan			13	3	3	1902	16948
黄石市	Huangshi	1	1	4	1	27	797	7563
十堰市	Shiyan	1	4	3	34	72	1848	10274
荆州市	Jingzhou	3	3	2	13	89	2261	20200
宜昌市	Yichang	3	5	5	20	67	1385	8213
襄阳市	Xiangyang	3	3	3	4	74	2345	14820
鄂州市	Ezhou			3	3	18	316	4027
荆门市	Jingmen	1	2	2	2	50	1347	9986
孝感市	Xiaogan	3	3	1	23	72	2924	23372
黄冈市	Huanggang	2	7	1	16	99	4287	37400
咸宁市	Xianning	1	4	1	12	52	903	10006
恩施自治州	Enshi	2	6		34	49	2360	23213
随州市	Suizhou	1	1	1		37	875	8513
仙桃市	Xiantao	1				15	626	4474
天门市	Tianmen	1			1	21	747	6453
潜江市	Qianjiang	1				10	353	2752
神农架林区	Shennongjia				2	6	67	332

注：乡政府、镇政府、村民委员会、村民小组数只涉及农村生产经营单位数

Note: The number of village government, township government, village community and village groups only refers to the number of units run by village production operation.

1-3 全省法人、产业活动单位数(2015)

指 标 名 称	Item	合计 Total
总 计	Total	678388
一、按地区分组	**Grouped by Region**	
武汉市	Wuhan	209747
黄石市	Huangshi	26339
十堰市	Shiyan	40344
宜昌市	Yichang	71119
襄阳市	Xiangyang	72027
鄂州市	Ezhou	13624
荆门市	Jingmen	28613
孝感市	Xiaogan	34699
荆州市	Jingzhou	34479
黄冈市	Huanggang	47323
咸宁市	Xianning	23036
随州市	Suizhou	16415
恩施州	Enshi	33308
仙桃市	Xiantao	9150
潜江市	Qianjiang	7994
天门市	Tianmen	8098
神农架	Shennongjia	2073
二、按国民经济行业门类分组	**Grouped by Sector**	
农、林、牧、渔业	Farming, Forestry, Animal husbandary and Fishery	57477
采矿业	Mining	4740
制造业	Manufacturing	83367
电力、热力、燃气及水生产和供应业	Power, Gas and Water Production and Supply	3968
建筑业	Construction	31366
批发和零售业	Transportaation, Storage and Post	183288
交通运输、仓储和邮政业	Information Transmission, Computer Service and software	18409
住宿和餐饮业	Wholesale and Retail Sale	13308
信息传输、软件和信息技术服务业	Hotel and Catering	19146
金融业	Banking	4114
房地产业	Real Estate	22570
租赁和商务服务业	Leasing and Commerical Service	68232
科学研究和技术服务业	Scietific Research, Polytechnical Service and Geological Prospecting	30688
水利、环境和公共设施管理业	Water Conservancy, Environment and Public Facility Management	6110
居民服务、修理和其他服务业	Resident Service and Others	15666
教育	Education	20637
卫生和社会工作	Health Care, Social Security and Social Welfare	12415
文化、体育和娱乐业	Culture, Sports and Recreation	12279
公共管理、社会保障和社会组织	Public Management and Social Organization	70608

NUMBER OF CORPORATIONS, INDUSTRIAL ACTIVITIES UNITS(2015)

法人单位数(个) Corporation Units			产业活动单位数(个) Number of Economic Activities Units	
单产业法人单位 Single-Industry Corperation Units	多产业法人单位 Multi-Industry Corperation Units	规模、资质或限额以上单位 Unit of Scale, Qualification or Above	合计 Total	多产业法人所属的产业活动单位 Economic Activities Units under Multi-Industry Corperation Units
651464	26924	39003	781747	130283
205267	4480	8890	227408	22141
25094	1245	1839	31013	5919
38097	2247	2344	48557	10460
68604	2515	4143	80337	11733
69758	2269	4594	81251	11493
13212	412	835	15688	2476
27072	1541	2236	33690	6618
32733	1966	2206	42280	9547
32178	2301	2832	42193	10015
44571	2752	2921	60101	15530
22134	902	1716	26620	4486
15461	954	1290	20743	5282
31795	1513	1403	38715	6920
8636	514	697	10874	2238
7679	315	475	9753	2074
7164	934	527	10069	2905
2009	64	55	2455	446
57247	230		59310	2063
4602	138	724	5029	427
81874	1493	15327	85430	3556
3690	278	325	5780	2090
30387	979	3718	33562	3175
180193	3095	8178	206611	26418
17636	773	1171	22908	5272
12910	398	2479	17368	4458
18909	237	308	22604	3695
3515	599		14080	10565
21506	1064	4514	24531	3025
67329	903	781	72520	5191
29994	694	571	32911	2917
5843	267	195	7369	1526
15474	192	169	16894	1420
18268	2369	189	24391	6123
11255	1160	157	31878	20623
12086	193	197	13241	1155
58746	11862		85330	26584

1-3　续表1 continued

指 标 名 称	Item	合计 Total
总计	Total	678388
三、按登记注册类型分组	**Grouped by Type of Registration**	
内资	Inner Funded	674530
国有	State-owned	56233
集体	Collective-owned	8966
股份合作	Share Holding Cooperative	1758
联营	Joint Funded	1175
国有联营	State Joint owned	234
集体联营	Collective Joint-owned	522
国有与集体联营	State - owned and Collective Joint-owned	106
其他联营	Other Joint-owned	313
有限责任公司	Co. Ltd	157547
国有独资公司	State-owned Solely Funded Co.	913
其他有限责任公司	Other Co. Ltd	156634
股份有限公司	Share Holding Co.Ltd.	6513
私营	Private - owned Enterprises	297259
私营独资	Private Solely Funded Enterprises	100806
私营合伙	Private Partnership Enterprises	13137
私营有限责任公司	Private Co. Ltd	176804
私营股份有限公司	Private Share Holding Co.Ltd.	6512
其他内资	Others	145079
港澳台商投资	Hongkong, Macao and Taiwan Funded Enterprises	1355
与港澳台商合资经营	Joint Venture with Hongkong, Macao and Taiwan	500
与港澳台商合作经营	Cooperate with Hongkong, Macao and Taiwan Funded	43
港澳台商独资	Enterprises Solely Funded by Hongkong, Macao and Taiwan	706
港澳台商投资股份有限公司	Share Holding Co.Ltd. with Hongkong, Macao and Taiwan Investment	70
其他港、澳、台商投资	Other Hongkong, Macao and Taiwan Investment	36
外商投资	Foreign Funded Enterprises	2503
中外合资经营	Sino - Foreign Joint Funded Enterprises	610
中外合作经营	Sino - Foreign Cooperative Funded Enterprises	39
外资企业	Foreign Solely Funded Enterprises	591
外商投资股份有限公司	Foreign Funded Share Holding Co.Ltd.	62
其他外商投资	Other Foreign Investment	1201
四、按机构类型分组	**Grouped by Type**	
企业	Enterprise	522901
事业单位	Public Institution	41718
机关	Government Agency	9873
社会团体	Mass Organization	13493
民办非企业单位	Private Non Enterprise Unit	12592
基金会	Foundation	77
居委会	Neighborhood Committee	4214
村委会	Village Committee	26457
其他组织机构	Others	47063

注：规模、资质或限额以上单位不包括省属重点服务业和投资专业法人单位

法人单位数(个) Corporation Units			产业活动单位数(个) Number of Economic Activities Units	
单产业法人单位 Single-Industry Corperation Units	多产业法人单位 Multi-Industry Corperation Units	规模、资质或限额以上单位 Unit of Scale, Qualification or Above	合计 Total	多产业法人所属的产业活动单位 Economic Activities Units under Multi-Industry Corperation Units
651464	26924	39003	781747	130283
647853	26677	37790	776088	128235
48855	7378	969	87771	38916
8404	562	401	17674	9270
1643	115	51	2757	1114
1119	56	15	1942	823
217	17	1	484	267
497	25	4	812	315
98	8	6	191	93
307	6	4	455	148
153696	3851	14966	168500	14804
762	151	427	1152	390
152934	3700	14539	167348	14414
5762	751	1388	13730	7968
292984	4275	19290	313265	20281
100258	548	1299	105393	5135
13009	128	136	13927	918
173403	3401	17022	186738	13335
6314	198	833	7207	893
135390	9689	710	170449	35059
1240	115	598	2334	1094
464	36	240	847	383
40	3	11	66	26
638	68	321	1109	471
62	8	24	202	140
36		2	110	74
2371	132	615	3325	954
554	56	317	773	219
36	3	9	48	12
536	55	258	1075	539
56	6	20	138	82
1189	12	11	1291	102
512076	10825	38652	579523	67447
37146	4572	44	62853	25707
7575	2298		14831	7256
13354	139		15173	1819
12366	226	141	12366	
76	1		87	11
3546	668		4321	775
18496	7961		27865	9369
46829	234	166	64728	17899

1-4 国民经济和社会发展总量与速度指标

指 标	Item	总 量 指 标		
		1978	1990	2000
人口与就业	**Population and Employment**			
人口 (万人)	**Population** (10 000 persons)			
年末人口	Population at Year-end	4574.91	5439.29	5950.89
城镇人口	Urban	690.23	1551.51	2408.49
乡村人口	Rural	3884.68	3887.78	3542.40
就业 (万人)	**Employment** (10 000 persons)			
就业人数	Employment	1910.37	3040.40	3384.90
职工人数	Staff and Workers	457.34	698.55	677.96
#国有单位	State-owned Units	371.56	524.12	506.11
宏观经济	Marcoeconomy			
国民核算 (亿元)	**National Accounting** (100 million yuan)			
地区生产总值	Gross Domestic Products	151.00	824.38	3545.39
第一产业	First Industry	61.11	289.45	662.30
第二产业	Second Industry	63.71	313.39	1437.38
第三产业	Tertiary Industry	26.18	221.54	1445.71
支出法地区生产总值	Gross Domestic Expenditures			
#最终消费	Final Consumption Expenditures	81.70	535.49	2030.07
居民消费	Resident Consumption	74.70	434.62	1594.08
政府消费	Government Consumption Expenditures	7.00	100.87	436.00
资本形成总额	Gross Capital Formation	43.11	261.95	1882.47
固定资本形成	Fixed Capital Formation	31.40	147.13	1451.85
存货增加	Changes in Stock	11.71	114.82	430.62
固定资产投资 (亿元)	**Investment in Fixed Assets** (100 million yuan)			
全社会固定资产投资总额	Total Investment in Fixed Assets	33.58	144.44	1421.55
#国有单位	State-Owned Units	33.19	100.35	857.01
集体单位	Collective-owned Units	0.39	15.59	128.32
#房地产开发	Real Estate Development		5.94	134.63
财政 (亿元)	**Public Finance** (100 million yuan)			
地方公共财政收入	Local Public Financial Revenue	31.38	77.85	214.35
地方公共财政支出	Local Public Financial Expenditures	29.98	84.82	368.77
物价(上年=100)	**Price (preceding year = 100)**			
商品零售价格总指数	General Retail Price Index	100.50	102.90	97.80
居民消费价格指数	General Consumer Price Index	100.30	104.20	99.00
利用外资 (亿美元)	**Utilization of Foreign Capital** (100 million dollars)			
实际外商直接投资	Actual Foreign Direct Investment		0.29	9.44
产 业	**Industry**			
农业	**Agriculture**			
乡村从业人员 (万人)	Rural Employment (10 000 persons)	1525.14	1791.30	1781.70
农林牧渔业总产值 (亿元)	Gross Output Value of Farming, Forestry, Animal Husbandry and Fishery (100 million yuan)	84.46	402.23	1125.64
主要农产品产量 (万吨)	Output of Major Farm Products (10 000 tons)			
粮食	Grain	1725.63	2475.03	2218.49
棉花	Cotton	36.67	51.73	30.43
油料	Oil-Bearing Crops	23.71	95.75	269.98
糖料	Sugar Crops	8.73	34.66	101.66
蚕茧	Silkworm Cocoons	0.47	0.79	1.22
肉类产量	Output of Meat	64.00	146.85	271.19
水产品	Aquatic Products	11.00	70.98	234.34

注:1.人口数除1982年、1990年、2000年、2010年是以人口普查为基数推算外,1982年及以后为人口抽样调查推算数。
2.2000年以前数据是总人口数,2001年以后数据为常住人口数。

AGGREGATE INDICATORS OF NATIONAL ECNONOMIC AND SOCIAL DEVELOPMENT, THEIR INDICES AND GROWTH RATES

Aggregate Data			速度指标 Indices and Growth Rates								
			2015年比下列各年增长(%) Increases					年平均增长(%) Average Annual Growth Rate			
2010	2014	2015	1978	1990	2000	2010	2014	1979~2015	1991~2015	2001~2015	2011~2015
5723.77	5816.00	5851.50	27.9	7.6	−1.7	2.2	0.6	0.7	0.3	−0.1	0.4
2844.95	3237.80	3326.58	382.0	114.4	38.1	16.9	2.7	4.3	3.1	2.2	3.2
2878.82	2578.20	2524.92	−35.0	−35.1	−28.7	−12.3	−2.1	−1.2	−1.7	−2.2	−2.6
3645.00	3687.50	3658.00	91.5	20.3	8.1	0.4	−0.8	1.8	0.7	0.5	0.1
685.21	968.77	980.01	114.3	40.3	44.6	43.0	1.2	2.1	1.4	2.5	7.4
277.60	252.43	260.27	−30.0	−50.3	−48.6	−6.2	3.1	−1.0	−2.8	−4.3	−1.3
15967.61	27379.22	29550.19	4209.7	1358.7	419.4	66.6	8.9	10.7	11.3	11.6	10.7
2147.00	3176.89	3309.84	452.0	189.1	96.7	25.1	4.5	4.7	4.3	4.6	4.6
7767.24	12852.40	13503.56	8317.0	2357.5	585.2	77.1	8.3	12.7	13.7	13.7	12.1
6053.37	11349.93	12736.79	7898.4	1701.8	426.0	68.5	0.7	12.6	12.3	11.7	11.0
7389.80	12562.76	13799.70	3204.0	931.4	358.5	61.3	8.4	9.9	9.8	10.7	10.0
5136.78	9124.48	10167.87	2476.7	786.9	329.8	70.9	10.0	9.2	9.1	10.2	11.3
2253.02	3438.28	3631.83	10565.2	1607.2	458.2	39.1	4.0	13.4	12.0	12.1	6.8
8511.17	16109.59	17418.40	8330.0	2659.7	532.6	88.1	8.9	12.7	14.2	13.1	13.5
8200.40	15442.86	16757.35	4418.7	1723.6	220.2	87.4	9.3	10.8	12.3	8.1	13.4
310.77	666.73	661.05	789.4	93.4	−27.1	108.1	1.9	6.1	2.7	−2.1	15.8
10802.69	25001.77	29191.06	86829.9	20109.8	1953.5	170.2	16.8	19.7	23.8	22.0	22.8
3768.95	5829.79	6983.99	20942.5	6859.6	714.9	85.3	19.8	15.3	19.0	14.1	10.8
602.80	820.75	754.53	193369.2	4739.8	488.0	25.2	−8.1	23.6	18.3	13.0	7.8
1618.24	3983.79	4249.23		71435.9	3056.2	162.6	6.7		31.4	27.1	23.9
1011.20	2566.90	3005.53	9477.9	3760.7	1302.2	197.2	17.1	13.1	15.7	19.2	24.3
2501.40	4934.15	6132.84	20356.4	7130.4	1563.1	145.2	24.3	15.5	18.7	20.6	19.6
103.10	100.90	100.50	374.7	142.0	32.0	11.9	0.5	4.3	3.6	1.9	2.3
102.90	102.00	101.50	600.0	238.8	48.3	15.9	1.5	5.4	5.0	2.7	3.0
40.50	79.28	89.48		30755.2	847.9	120.9	12.9		25.8	16.2	17.2
2154.44	2308.72	2300.88	50.9	28.4	29.1	6.8	−0.3	1.1	1.0	1.7	1.3
3501.99	5452.80	5728.56	6682.6	1324.2	408.9	63.6	5.1	12.1	11.2	11.5	10.3
2315.80	2584.16	2703.28	56.7	9.2	21.9	16.7	4.6	1.2	0.4	1.3	3.1
47.18	35.95	29.83	−18.7	−42.3	−2.0	−36.8	−17.0	−0.6	−2.2	−0.1	−8.8
311.80	341.73	339.60	1332.3	254.7	25.8	8.9	−0.6	7.5	5.2	1.5	1.7
32.36	30.41	32.03	266.9	−7.6	−68.5	−1.0	5.3	3.6	−0.3	−7.4	−0.2
0.71	0.64	0.67	42.8	−15.1	−45.0	−5.5	4.9	1.0	−0.7	−3.9	−1.1
379.42	440.44	431.93	574.9	194.1	59.3	13.8	−1.9	5.3	4.4	3.2	2.6
353.09	433.30	455.80	4043.6	542.2	94.5	29.1	5.2	10.6	7.7	4.5	5.2

Note: a)Data of 1982,1990,2000.and 2010 are based on population census Data of other years are based on sampling survey
b)Data before 2000 refer to total population. Data after 2001 refer to permanent residents

1-4 续表 1 continued

指 标	单位	Item	unit	总量指标 1978	1990	2000
工业		**Industry**				
主要工业产品产量	(万吨)	Output of Major Industrial Products	(10000 tons)			
粗 钢		Steel		307.97	629.25	895.92
成品钢材		Rolled-Steel		184.63	533.07	811.10
发电量	(亿千瓦小时)	Electricity	(100 million kWh)	91.64	340.39	538.11
原煤		Coal		644.01	924.26	389.34
农用化肥(折 100%)		Chemical Furtilizers		27.62	132.07	221.11
化学农药		Chemical Pesicide		2.97	1.07	5.18
水泥		Cement		328.65	987.00	2460.92
化学纤维		Chemical Fiber		0.48	2.48	9.82
布	(亿米)	Cloth	(100 million meter)	6.70	14.09	17.15
汽车	(万辆)	Automobile	(10000 Units)	0.80	11.38	19.57
建筑业		**Construction**				
建筑业企业职工平均人数	(万人)	Average Number of Employed Persons	(10000 persons)	25.94	41.88	82.76
建筑业总产值	(亿元)	Gross Output Value	(100 million yuan)	11.11	49.30	454.35
施工房屋面积	(万平方米)	Floor Space of Building Under Construction	(10 000 sq.m)	596.00	1684.90	6256.50
竣工房屋面积	(万平方米)	Floor Space of Building Completed	(10 000 sq.m)	297.40	785.90	3150.10
交通运输		**Transportation**				
货运量	(万吨)	Freight Traffic	(10 000 tons)	10199.08	10916.10	9345.19
#铁路		Railway		3342.00	3901.00	3857.00
公路		Highway		3382.00	2941.00	2228.00
水运		Waterway		3096.00	3784.00	3255.00
客运量	(万人)	Passenger Capacity	(10000 persons)	12009.20	32145.93	31593.00
#铁路		Railway		2854.00	2107.00	3469.00
公路		Highway		7429.00	27333.00	27184.00
水运		Waterway		1722.00	2693.00	679.00
港口货物吞吐量	(万吨)	Volume of Freight Handled at Seaports	(10 000 tons)			4113.46
邮电通信业		**Postal Telecommunication Services**				
邮电业务总量	(亿元)	Total Business Revenue	(100 million yuan)	0.56	4.80	116.60
函件	(亿件)	Number of Letters Delivered	(100 million pieces)	1.18	2.39	3.62
年末移动电话用户	(万户)	Number of Local Telephone Users	(10 000 units)			
国际互联网用户	(万户)	Internet Users	(10 000 units)			
农村电话用户	(万户)	Rural Telephone Users	(10 000 units)	4.13	7.07	180.00
国内商业		**Domestic Commerce**				
社会消费品零售总额	(亿元)	Total Retail Sales of Consumer Goods	(100 million yuan)	59.84	326.36	1789.35
对外经济贸易和旅游		**Foreign Trade and Tourism**				
进出口总额	(亿美元)	Total Imports and Exports	(100 million ollars)	1.73	11.90	32.10
进口		Imports		0.14	1.18	12.79
出口		Exports		1.59	10.72	19.31
入境旅游人数	(万人次)	Number of Tourists Received	(10 000 persons)	1.01	15.57	45.08
金融保险	**(亿元)**	**Banking and Insurance**	**(100 million yuan)**			
金融机构存款		Deposits of Banking System		42.16	406.56	3037.22
金融机构贷款		Loans of Banking System		96.78	732.77	3147.77
国内保险保费收入		Domestic Premium			6.19	60.53

Aggregate Data			速 度 指 标 Indices and Growth Rates								
			2015年比下列各年增长(%) Increases					年平均增长(%) Average Annual Growth Rate			
2010	2014	2015	1978	1990	2000	2010	2014	1979~2015	1991~2015	2001~2015	2011~2015
2498.67	3056.43	2919.77	848.1	364.0	225.9	16.9	-4.5	6.3	6.3	8.2	3.2
2894.72	3429.01	3421.22	1753.0	541.8	321.8	18.2	-0.2	8.2	7.7	10.1	3.4
2028.67	2344.81	2301.43	2411.4	576.1	327.7	13.4	-1.9	9.1	7.9	10.2	2.6
1291.71	890.40	758.39	17.8	-17.9	94.8	-41.3	-14.8	0.4	-0.8	4.5	-10.1
899.08	1209.02	1408.13	4998.2	966.2	536.8	56.6	16.5	11.2	9.9	13.1	9.4
19.71	24.36	25.39	754.9	2272.9	390.2	28.8	4.2	6.0	13.5	11.2	5.2
8982.87	11669.93	11288.92	3334.9	1043.8	358.7	25.7	-3.3	10.0	10.2	10.7	4.7
11.66	26.15	35.35	7264.6	1325.4	260.0	203.2	35.2	12.3	11.2	8.9	24.8
46.38	82.4	79.85	1091.8	466.7	365.6	72.2	-3.1	6.9	7.2	10.8	11.5
172.29	174.46	196.85	24506.3	1629.8	905.9	14.3	12.8	16.0	12.1	16.6	2.7
170.71	206.37	232.85	797.6	456.0	181.4	36.4	12.8	6.1	7.1	7.1	6.4
4344.39	10059.60	10591.71	95234.9	21384.2	2231.2	143.8	5.3	20.4	24.0	23.4	19.5
25046.72	62227.88	62195.32	10335.5	3591.3	894.1	148.3	-0.1	13.4	15.5	16.5	20.0
12813.44	24867.30	26825.22	8919.9	3313.3	751.6	109.4	7.9	12.9	15.2	15.3	15.9
97006.94	154736.00	160393.06	1472.6	1369.3	1616.3	65.3	3.7	7.7	11.3	20.9	10.6
10145.60	7681.30	6579.00	96.9	68.6	70.6	-35.2	-14.4	1.8	2.1	3.6	-8.3
71020.00	116280.00	121466.43	3491.6	4030.1	5351.8	71.0	4.5	10.2	16.0	30.5	11.3
15832.00	30765.00	32338.00	944.5	754.6	893.5	104.3	5.1	6.5	9.0	16.5	15.4
105415.50	103671.80	106732.59	788.8	232.0	237.8	1.2	3.0	6.1	4.9	8.5	0.2
7281.30	14302.70	15083.90	428.5	615.9	334.8	107.2	5.5	4.6	8.2	10.3	15.7
96873.00	87804.00	89996.46	1111.4	229.3	231.1	-7.1	2.5	7.0	4.9	8.3	-1.5
375.80	533.80	570.10	-66.9	-78.8	-16.0	51.7	6.8	-2.9	-6.0	-1.2	8.7
18782.67	28969.15	32949.52			701.0	75.4	13.7			14.9	11.9
1028.09	720.35	962.66	171803.6	19955.4	725.6	-6.4	33.6	22.3	23.6	15.1	-1.3
1.00	0.67	0.68	-42.7	-71.7	-81.3	-32.4	0.8	-1.5	-4.9	-10.6	-7.5
3454.70	4606.80	4650.60				34.6	1.0				6.1
459.40	869.70	983.50				114.1	13.1				16.4
355.70	294.40	240.00	5711.1	3294.6	33.3	-32.5	-18.5	11.6	15.1	1.9	-7.6
7013.90	12449.27	14003.24	23301.1	4190.7	682.6	99.6	12.5	15.9	16.2	14.7	14.8
259.07	430.64	455.86	26250.3	3730.8	1320.1	76.0	5.9	16.3	15.7	19.3	12.0
114.65	164.18	163.72	116842.9	13774.6	1180.1	42.8	-0.3	21.0	21.8	18.5	7.4
144.42	266.46	292.13	18273.0	2625.1	1412.8	102.3	9.6	15.1	14.1	19.9	15.1
181.74	277.07	311.76	30767.3	1902.3	591.6	71.5	12.5	16.8	12.7	13.8	11.4
21568.31	36153.65	40896.52	96903.1	9959.2	1246.5	89.6	13.1	20.4	20.3	18.9	13.7
14136.58	24239.96	28338.90	29181.8	3767.4	800.3	100.5	16.9	16.6	15.7	15.8	14.9
500.33	700.23	843.63	#DIV/0!	13528.9	1293.7	68.6	20.5		21.7	19.2	11.0

1-4 续表 2 continued

指 标	单位	Item	unit	1978	1990
教育、科技、文化		**Education, Science and Technology,Culture and**			
教育		**Education**			
高等学校本专科在校学生	(万人)	Students Enrollment in Institutions of Higher Eduction	(10 000persons)	4.94	13.04
中等专业学校在校学生	(万人)	Students Enrollment in Specialized Secondary Schools	(10 000persons)	5.36	1458.00
普通中学在校学生	(万人)	Students Enrollment in Regular Secondary Schools	(10 000persons)	372.38	211.56
小学在校学生	(万人)	Students Enrollment in Primary Schools	(10 000persons)	765.73	623.06
文化		**Culture**			
图书出版量	(亿册)	Books Published	(100 million copies)	1.62	4.02
杂志出版量	(亿册)	Magazines Issued	(100 million copies)	0.09	0.73
报纸出版量	(亿份)	Newspaper Issued	(100 million copies)	1.97	6.24
家庭、生活、环境		**Family, People's Livelihood and Environment**			
家庭		**Family**			
城镇居民平均每户家庭人口	(人)	Average Household size in Urban Areas	(person)	4.32	3.47
农村居民平均每户常住人口	(人)	Average Household size in Rural Areas	(person)	6.02	4.67
居住		**Housing**			
城镇居民人均住房建筑面积	(平方米)	Per Capita Net Floor Space of Urban Residents	(sq.m)		9.80
农村居民人均住房面积	(平方米)	Per Capita Net Floor Space of Rural Residents	(sq.m)		25.73
生活		**People's Livelihood**			
城镇居民人均可支配收入	(元)	Per Capita Annual Disposbale Income of Urban Residents	(yuan)	325.00	1427.20
农村居民人均可支配收入	(元)	Per Capita Annual Disposbale Income of Rural Residents	(yuan)	110.52	670.80
居民储蓄存款余额	(亿元)	Saving Deposit	(100 million yuan)	6.96	244.38
工资		**Wages**			
工资总额	(亿元)	Total Wages of Staff and Workers	(100 million yuan)	25.89	131.24
职工平均工资	(元)	Average Wages of Staff and Workers	(yuan)	581.00	1903.00
卫生		**Health Care**			
卫生机构数	(个)	Number of Health Care Organizations	(unit)	5940	10472
#医院		Hospitals		1817	2024
床位数	(万张)	Number of Hospital Beds	(10 000 units)	11.52	16.34
#医院		Hospitals		10.34	13.16
卫生技术人员数	(万人)	Number of Medical Technical Personels	(10 000 persons)	14.06	20.92
#职业(助理)医师		Professional(assitant)Doctors		5.82	8.68
环境		**Environment**			
污染治理项目本年完成投资	(亿元)	Investment for the Pollusion Treatment projects Completed	(100 million yuan)		1.81
本年施工污染治理项目数	(个)	Number of Pullution Treatment Project Under Construction	(unit)		1545
工业废水排放量	(亿吨)	Volume of Industrial Waste Water Discharged	(100 million tons)		16.23

总量指标 Aggregate Data				速度指标 Indices and Growth Rates								
				2015年比下列各年增长(%) increases					年平均增长(%) Average Annual Growth Rate			
2000	2010	2014	2015	1978	1990	2000	2010	2014	1979~2015	1991~2015	2001~2015	2011~2015
34.66	129.69	141.97	140.87	2751.6	980.3	306.4	8.6	−0.8	9.5	10.0	9.8	1.7
27.86	90.38	37.26	36.49	580.8	−97.5	31.0	−59.6	−2.1	5.3	−13.7	1.8	−16.6
350.93	341.83	229.49	224.13	−39.8	5.9	−36.1	−34.4	−2.3	−1.4	0.2	−2.9	−8.1
667.74	365.55	321.16	335.81	−56.1	−46.1	−49.7	−8.1	4.6	−2.2	−2.4	−4.5	−1.7
2.88	2.75	2.72	2.63	62.3	−34.6	−8.7	−4.4	−3.3	1.3	−1.7	−0.6	−0.9
2.20	3.01	2.81	2.51	2691.7	244.2	14.2	−16.5	−10.6	9.4	5.1	0.9	−3.5
13.42	18.17	19.11	15.39	681.3	146.7	14.7	−15.3	−19.5	5.7	3.7	0.9	−3.3
3.14	2.93	2.85	2.85	−34.0	−17.9	−9.2	−2.7		−1.1	−0.8	−0.6	−0.6
4.11	3.98	2.87	2.88	−52.2	−38.3	−29.9	−27.6	0.3	−2.0	−1.9	−2.3	−6.3
13.90	33.20	41.90	43.18		340.6	210.6	30.1	3.1		6.1	7.8	5.4
30.11	40.99	54.78	55.61		116.1	84.7	35.7	1.5		3.1	4.2	6.3
5524.50	16058.37	24852.30	27051.47	8223.5	1795.4	389.7	68.5	8.8	12.7	12.5	11.2	11.0
2268.50	5832.27	10849.06	11843.89	10616.5	1665.6	422.1	103.1	9.2	13.5	12.2	11.6	15.2
1908.80	9851.00	17820.7	19566.1	281022.1	7906.4	925.0	98.6	9.8	23.9	19.2	16.8	14.7
405.34	1870.51	4147.69	4582.41	17599.5	3391.6	1030.5	145.0	10.5	15.0	15.3	17.5	19.6
7565.00	28092.00	43217.00	47320.00	8044.6	2386.6	525.5	68.4	9.5	12.6	13.7	13.0	11.0
11065	10305	36084	36173	509.0	245.4	226.9	251.0	0.2	5.0	5.1	8.2	28.5
2041	603	771	869	−52.2	−57.1	−57.4	44.1	12.7	−2.0	−3.3	−5.5	7.6
14.96	20.07	31.83	34.38	198.4	110.4	129.8	71.3	8.0	3.0	3.0	5.7	11.4
12.99	13.51	22.20	24.66	138.5	87.4	89.8	82.5	11.1	2.4	2.5	4.4	12.8
23.88	25.16	33.98	36.76	161.5	75.7	53.9	46.1	8.2	2.6	2.3	2.9	7.9
10.30	9.95	12.61	13.60	133.7	56.7	32.0	36.7	7.9	2.3	1.8	1.9	6.4
8.52	27.74	26.29	15.79		772.6	85.4	−43.1	−39.9		9.1	4.2	−10.7
851	226	127	199		−87.1	−76.6	−11.9	56.7		−7.9	−9.2	−2.5
10.67	9.46	8.17	8.08		−50.2	−24.3	−14.6	−1.0		−2.8	−1.8	−3.1

1-5 国民经济和社会发展结构指标
STRUCTURAL INDICATORS ON NATIONAL ECONOMIC AND SOCIAL DEVELOPMENT

单位:% (%)

指 标	Item	1978	2000	2005	2010	2013	2014	2015
人口与就业	**Population and Employment**							
人 口	**Population**							
城乡结构	Urban and Rural Structure							
城镇	Urban	14.6	40.2	43.2	49.7	54.5	55.7	56.9
乡村	Rural	85.4	59.8	56.8	50.3	45.5	44.3	43.1
性别结构	Sexual Structure							
男	Male	51.3	52.1	51.8	51.4	51.3	51.2	52.0
女	Female	48.7	47.9	48.2	48.6	48.7	48.8	48.0
就 业	**Employment**							
产业结构	Industrial Structure							
第一产业	First Industry	77.0	48.0	47.7	46.4	42.9	40.3	38.4
第二产业	Second Industry	14.1	20.8	20.5	20.7	21.5	22.6	22.8
第三产业	Tertiary Industry	8.9	31.2	31.8	32.9	35.7	37.1	38.8
经济类型结构	Structrues by Ownership							
城镇单位从业人员	Staff and Workers Employed in Urban Units							
国有单位	State-Owned	81.2	74.7	62.1	40.4	26.8	26.3	26.9
城镇集体单位	Collective-Owned	18.8	14.3	8.0	3.1	1.5	1.5	1.3
其他单位	Others		11.0	29.9	56.5	71.7	72.2	71.8
宏观经济	**Macroeconomy**							
国民核算	**National Accounting**							
地区生产总值产业结构	Industrial Structure							
第一产业	First Industry	40.5	18.7	16.4	13.4	12.2	11.6	11.2
第二产业	Second Industry	42.2	40.5	43.3	48.7	47.6	46.9	45.7
第三产业	Tertiary Industry	17.3	40.8	40.3	37.9	40.2	41.5	43.1
地区生产总值支出结构	Domestic Expenditures							
最终消费	Total Consumption	54.0	54.0	55.9	45.7	43.9	43.7	44.2
居民消费	Residents Consumption	49.4	42.4	42.7	31.7	31.7	31.8	32.6
政府消费	Government Consumption Expenditures	4.6	11.6	13.2	13.9	12.2	12.0	11.6
资本形成总额	Gross Capital Formation	28.5	50.0	45.1	52.6	56.0	56.1	55.8
固定资本	Fixed Capital Formation	20.8	38.6	43.0	50.7	53.9	53.8	53.7
存货增加	Changes in Stock	7.7	11.4	2.1	1.9	2.1	2.3	2.1
净出口	Net Exports	17.4	-4.0	-1.0	1.7	0.1	0.2	0.0
投 资	**Investment**							
经济类型结构	Structrues by Ownership							
国有经济	State-Owned	98.8	60.3	38.7	34.9	24.4	23.3	23.9
集体经济	Collective-Owned	1.2	9.0	2.8	5.6	4.0	3.3	2.6
其他	Others		30.7	58.5	59.5	71.6	73.4	73.5
资金来源结构	Structure of Funded Sources							
国家预算资金	State Budget	77.2	10.0	9.0	8.0	4.3	4.4	4.6
国内贷款	Domestic Loans	0.4	17.2	16.7	16.4	13.1	11.5	10.0
利用外资	Foreign Investment		2.0	2.5	1.4	0.3	0.3	0.2
自筹资金	Fundraising	18.0	54.9	52.7	62.1	71.4	74.9	77.0
其他投资	Others	4.3	15.9	19.1	12.2	10.9	8.8	8.2

1-5 续表 1 continued

指 标	Item	1978	2000	2005	2010	2013	2014	2015
财 政	**Finance**							
地方公共支出结构	Local Public Financial Expenditure Structure							
#一般公共服务	#General Public Service				12.6	12.5	12.1	10.1
教育	Education				14.7	15.8	15.7	14.9
社会保障和就业	Social Security and Employment				14.7	13.9	14.5	14.0
利用外资	**Foreign Investment**							
实际外商直接投资结构	Actual Foreign Direct Investment							
合资经营企业	Joint Venture		63.4	40.8	35.3	32.5	38.0	36.8
合作经营企业	Cooperation		3.0	4.8	1.6	0.5	0.1	0.5
独资经营企业	Sole Proprietorship Business		33.6	34.5	63.1	64.2	55.6	61.3
外商投资股份制企业	Joint-stock Enterprises with Foreign Investment			0.9		2.8	4.5	1.0
产业经济	**Industrial Economy**							
农 业	**Agriculture**							
农林牧渔业产值结构	Agricultural Output Value Structure							
农业	Agriculture	77.3	54.7	52.5	54.9	51.9	50.6	48.5
林业	Forestry	4.9	3.6	2.1	1.9	2.4	2.9	3.2
牧业	Animal Husbandry	12.8	30.1	30.7	26.4	27.0	26.2	26.2
渔业	Fishery	0.8	11.6	13.3	13.1	14.5	15.5	16.1
农林牧渔服务业	Agriculture,Animal Husbandry and Fishery service			1.4	3.8	4.2	4.8	6.0
工 业	**Industry**							
工业产值按经济类型分	Industrial Output by Type							
#国有企业	#State-owned Enterprises	77.3	35.3	25.3	21.0	9.3	7.5	6.1
集体企业	Collective Enterprises	22.7	18.4	1.8	0.9	0.4	0.3	0.3
港澳台商投资企业	Hong Kong, Macao And Taiwan Invested Enterprises		4.2	4.3	5.1	5.1	4.9	4.5
外商投资企业	Foreign-invested Enterprises		6.8	18.3	15.0	11.3	10.9	10.1
工业产值按轻重分	Industrial Output Divided by Weight							
轻工业	Light Industry	47.1	38.4	24.8	27.5	34.2	35.4	36.7
重工业	Heavy Industry	52.9	61.6	75.2	72.5	65.8	64.6	63.3
建筑业	**Building Industry**							
建筑业总产值结构	Gross Output Value Structure							
国有经济	State-owned Economy	88.6	58.6	57.6	52.6	46.5	47.3	44.3
地方	Local	42.8	23.5	19.9	9.5	8.9	9.2	10.1
中央	Central	45.6	35.1	37.7	43.1	37.5	38.1	34.2
城镇集体经济	Urban Collective Economy	11.4	27.2	5.2	1.4	0.8	0.7	0.7
其它经济	Other Economic		14.3	37.3	45.9	52.7	52.0	55.0
运输业	**Transport**							
货运量结构	Cargo Structures							
铁路	Railway	32.8	41.3	17.0	10.5	6.4	5.0	4.1
公路	Highway	33.2	23.8	67.1	73.2	77.9	75.1	75.7
水运	Water Transport	30.3	34.8	15.9	16.3	15.7	19.9	21.2

1–5 续表 2 continued

指 标	Item	1978	2000	2005	2010	2014	2015
国内商业	**Domestic Trade**						
社会消费品零售总额结构	Total Retail Sales of Consumer Goods						
#批发零售贸易业	Wholesale and Retail Sale	85.1	61.9	81.5	85.3	85.3	86.8
住宿及餐饮业	Hotel and Catering	2.8	10.8	13.1	10.5	10.7	10.2
其他	Others	12.1	27.3	5.4	4.2	4.0	3.0
对外经济贸易和国际旅游	**Foreign Trade and Tourism**						
进出口总额	Total Imports and Exports						
#出口	Exports	8.1	39.8	51.1	55.7	61.9	64.1
进口	Imports	91.9	60.2	48.9	44.3	38.1	35.9
海外旅游人数结构	Structure of Tourists						
外国人	Foreigners	47.3	79.3	75.9	76.2	77.0	76.9
港澳台同胞	Compatriots from Hongkong, Macao and Taiwan	52.7	20.7	24.1	23.8	23.0	23.1
教育、科技、文化	**Education,Science and Culture**						
教 育	**Education**						
在校学生结构	Structure of Students Enrollment						
大学生	College and University Students	0.4	3.3	10.4	15.1	19.4	18.9
中学生	Secondary School Students	32.6	33.3	45.7	40.6	36.5	36.1
小学生	Primary School Students	67.0	63.4	43.9	44.3	43.9	45.0
专任教师结构	Full-Time Teacher by Type						
大学	College and Universities	2.9	11.9	17.5	18.2	16.3	16.4
中学	Secondary Schools	39.6	38.9	44.5	40.3	44.0	44.4
小学	Primary Schools	57.5	49.2	38.0	41.5	39.2	39.2
科 技	**Science and Technology**						
各类专业技术人员结构	Structure of Scientific and Technical Personel						
工程技术人员	Engineering Personel	34.2	18.5	11.1	10.5	9.7	
农业技术人员	Agriculture	5.5	3.4	3.2	2.2	2.2	
科学研究人员	Scientific Research	6.7	0.6	0.8	0.5	0.5	
卫生技术人员	Health Care	32.1	20.9	22.8	24.1	24.6	
教学人员	Teaching	21.5	56.6	62.2	62.6	63.0	
生活、环境	**People's Livelihood and Environment**						
生 活	**People's Livelihood**						
城镇居民消费结构	Consumption Structutre of Urban Residents						
食品	Food		38.3	39.0	38.7	32.1	32.0
衣着	Clothing		11.4	12.0	12.4	9.2	8.4
居住	Residence		14.1	10.2	10.4	21.7	20.8
其他	Others		36.2	38.8	38.5	37.1	38.8
农村居民消费结构	Consumption Structutre of Rural Residents						
食品	Food	70.8	53.2	49.1	43.1	34.7	30.1
衣着	Clothing	12.0	4.8	5.1	5.3	6.3	5.6
居住	Residence	8.9	11.5	12.8	20.0	24.8	21.9
其他	Others	8.3	30.5	33.0	31.6	34.2	42.9

1-6 湖北国民经济占全国的比重(2015)
PERCENTAGE OF HUBEI´S NATIONAL ECONOMY IN THE COUNTRY(2015)

指　　标	单位	Item	unit	全国 Country	湖北 Hubei	湖北占全国的比重(%) Percentage to the Country
土地面积	(万平方公里)	Ground space	(10 000 sq.km.)	960.00	18.59	1.94
年末常住人口	(万人)	Population	(Year-end)	137462	5852	4.26
地区生产总值	(亿元)	Local Gross Production	(100 million yuan)	676707.78	29550.19	4.37
第一产业		First Industry		60863.00	3309.84	5.44
第二产业		Second Industry		274277.83	13503.56	4.92
第三产业		Tertiary Industry		341566.95	12736.79	3.73
人均地区生产总值	(元)	Local Gross Production Per Capita	(yuan)	49351	50654	相当于全国102.64%
全社会固定资产投资	(亿元)	Total Investment in Fixed Assets	(100 million yuan)	561999.84	29191.06	5.19
#固定资产投资		Investment in Fixed Assets		551590.04	28250.48	5.12
#房地产开发		Development of Real Estate		95978.85	4249.23	4.43
地方公共财政收入	(亿元)	Local Public Financial Revenue		82982.70	3005.53	3.62
社会消费品零售总额	(亿元)	Total Retail Sales of Social Consumption	(100 million yuan)	300930.80	14003.24	4.65
进出口总额	(亿美元)	Total Imports and Exports	(100 million dollars)	39569.00	455.86	1.15
#出口		Exports		22749.50	292.14	1.28
实际外商直接投资	(亿美元)	Actual Foreign Direct Investment	(100 million dollars)	1262.67	89.48	7.09
普通高等学校本专科在校生	(万人)	Students Enrollment in Institutions of Higher Eductioan	(10 000 persons)	2625.30	140.87	5.37
医院卫生院床位数	(万张)	Number of Hospital Beds	(10 000 units)	701.52	34.38	4.90
卫生技术人员	(万人)	Number of Medical Technical Personnels	(10 000 persons)	800.75	36.76	4.59
#执业(助理)医师		Professional (assistant) Doctors		303.91	13.60	4.48
在岗职工平均工资	(元)	Average Wages of Employee		63241	47320	相当于全国74.82%
城镇居民人均可支配收入	(元)	Per Capita Disposable Income of Urban Residents	(yuan)	31195	27051	相当于全国86.72%
农村居民人均可支配收入	(元)	Per Capita Net Incomes of Rural Residents	(yuan)	11422	11844	相当于全国103.70%
工农业主要产品产量	(万吨)	Output of Major Products in Argriculture and Industry				
粮食		Grain		62143.92	2703.28	4.35
棉花		Cotton		560.34	29.83	5.32
油料		Oil-Bearing Crops		3536.98	339.60	9.60
粗钢		Crude steel		80382.50	2919.77	3.63
钢材		Steel		112349.60	3421.22	3.05
发电量	(亿千瓦小时)	Electricity	(100 million kWh)	58105.83	2301.40	3.96
原煤		Coal		374654.16	758.39	0.20
农用化肥(折100%)		Chemical Furtilizer		7431.99	1408.13	18.95
水泥		Cement		235939.55	11288.92	4.78
化学纤维		Chemical Fiber		4831.71	35.35	0.73
布	(亿米)	Cloth	(100 million meter)	892.58	79.85	8.95
汽车	(万辆)	Moter Vehicles	(10 000 units)	2450.35	196.85	8.03

1-7 全省人均国民经济主要指标

指 标	单位	Item	unit	1990
地区生产总值	(元)	Gross Domestic Product	(yuan)	1541.00
第一产业		First Industry		541.00
第二产业		Second Industry		586.00
第三产业		Tertiary Industry		414.00
地方公共财政预算收入	(元)	Government Revenue	(yuan)	145.54
地方财政支出	(元)	Government Expenditure	(yuan)	158.57
全社会固定资产投资额	(元)	TotaL Investment in Fixed Assets	(yuan)	270.00
社会消费品零售额	(元)	Total Retail Sales of Consumer Goods	(yuan)	610.00
进出口总额	(美元)	Total Imports and Exports	(US.dollars)	22.24
#出口		Exports	(US.dollars)	20.04
农村居民可支配收入	(元)	Net Income of Rural Residents	(yuan)	671.00
城镇居民可支配收入	(元)	Disposable Income of Urban Residents	(yuan)	1427.00
居民储蓄存款	(元)	Outstanding Amount of Saving Deposits of Urabn And Rural Residents	(yuan)	455.00
在校大学生数	(人/万人)	Number of Students Enrollment in Institutions of Higher Education	(person/10 000 persons)	24.38
医院病床数	(张/万人)	Hospital Beds	(bed/10000 persons)	24.50
卫生技术人员数	(人/万人)	Number of Medical Technical Personnels	(person/10000 persons)	39.11
#职业(助理)医师		Professional (assitant) Doctors		16.22
主要工农业产品产量	(千克)	Output of Major Industrial and Agricultural Products	(kg)	
粮 食		Grain		467.10
棉 花		Cotton		9.76
油 料		Oil-Bearing Crops		18.07
钢 材		Steel		100.60
原 煤		Coal		174.43
发电量	(千瓦小时)	Electricity	(kWh)	639.62

MAJOR PER CAPITA INDICATORS OF HUBEI'S

2000	2005	2010	2012	2013	2014	2015
6293.00	11554.00	27906.00	38572.33	42825.76	47144.59	50653.85
1164.00	1897.00	3766.67	4938.49	5234.53	5470.32	5673.61
2525.00	4926.00	13626.74	19403.83	20360.41	22130.69	23147.31
2540.00	4607.00	10619.95	14230.01	17230.82	19543.57	21832.94
376.61	658.36	1767.30	3160.35	3785.14	4419.97	5151.97
1647.93	1368.21	4371.64	6517.79	7551.65	8624.80	10446.47
2498.00	4970.00	18879.60	28610.85	35850.60	43050.83	50038.24
3144.00	5197.00	11743.40	16577.10	18804.46	21436.54	24003.84
56.40	159.40	452.77	554.03	628.61	741.52	781.42
33.93	78.02	252.40	336.33	394.51	458.82	500.78
2268.00	3099.00	5832.27	7851.71	8866.95	10849.06	11843.89
5524.00	8786.00	16058.37	20839.59	22906.40	24852.28	27051.47
3209.00	7929.00	17211.00	23589.00	27591.00	29698.80	33539.49
60.89	177.54	226.66	240.29	245.53	264.00	241.48
21.80	23.10	35.08	41.00	49.70	54.81	58.93
41.96	37.69	43.97	50.01	53.83	58.51	63.01
17.40	14.90	16.93	17.70	20.63	21.94	23.20
372.92	382.00	404.73	423.30	432.08	444.97	463.39
5.12	6.26	8.30	9.21	7.94	6.20	5.11
45.38	51.50	54.50	55.42	57.55	58.80	58.21
136.34	278.04	505.90	616.87	464.30	590.45	586.45
64.45	83.80	225.75	203.14	147.85	153.32	130.00
904.54	2204.00	3545.46	3768.87	3660.08	4037.56	3944.98

1-8 湖北的一天
ONE DAY IN HUBEI

指标	单位	Item	unit	2000	2005	2010	2013	2014	2015
每天创造的财富		**Daily Production**							
地区生产总值	(亿元)	Gross Domestic Products	(100 million yuan)	9.71	17.86	43.75	67.92	75.01	80.96
第一产业		First Industry		1.81	2.96	5.88	8.30	8.70	9.07
第二产业		Second Industry		3.94	7.70	21.28	32.29	35.21	37.00
第三产业		Tertiary Industry		3.96	7.20	16.58	27.33	31.10	34.90
地方公共财政预算收入	(亿元)	Government Revenue	(100 million yuan)	0.59	1.03	2.77	6.00	7.03	8.23
粮食	(万吨)	Grain	(10 000 tons)	6.08	5.97	6.34	6.85	7.08	7.41
肉类产量	(吨)	Meat	(tons)	7430.00	9387.00	10395.07	11783.01	12066.85	11833.70
水产品	(吨)	Aquatic Products	(tons)	6420.00	8718.00	9673.70	11259.45	11871.23	12487.67
粗钢	(万吨)	Steel	(10 000 tons)	2.45	4.31	6.85	7.36	8.37	8.00
成品钢材	(万吨)	Rolled-Steel	(10 000 tons)	2.22	4.34	7.93	9.27	9.39	9.37
发电量	(亿千瓦小时)	Electricity	(100 million kWh)	1.47	3.44	5.56	5.80	6.42	6.31
水泥	(万吨)	Cement	(10 000 tons)	6.74	12.36	24.61	30.65	31.97	30.93
布	(万米)	Cloth	(10 000 meters)	470.00	573.00	1270.69	2176.71	2257.53	2187.67
每天消费量		**Daily Consumption**							
最终消费	(亿元)	Final Consumption	(100 million yuan)	5.56	9.99	20.25	30.58	34.42	37.81
居民消费	(亿元)	Resident Consumption	(100 million yuan)	4.37	7.63	14.07	22.07	25.00	27.86
城镇居民每人消费性支出	(元)	Per Capita Living Expenditure of Urban Residents	(yuan)	12.72	18.46	31.37	42.01	45.70	49.84
#食品消费		Food Consumption		4.88	7.19	12.14	13.47	14.77	15.97
农村居民每人生活消费支出	(元)	Per Capita Living Expenditure of Rural Residents	(yuan)	4.26	6.66	11.21	21.51	23.78	26.86
#食品消费		Food Consumption		2.27	3.27	4.83	7.03	7.46	8.09
政府消费	(亿元)	Government Consumption Expenditure	(100 million yuan)	1.19	2.36	6.17	8.51	9.42	9.95
社会消费品零售总额	(亿元)	Total Retail Sales of Consumer Goods	(100 million yuan)	4.90	8.12	18.41	30.24	34.11	38.37
每天其他经济活动		**Other Daily Economic Acitivities**							
货物运输量	(万吨)	Freight Traffic	(10 000 tons)	25.60	136.78	265.77	382.85	423.93	439.43
旅客运输量	(万人)	Passenger Traffic	(10 000 persons)	86.56	195.61	288.81	392.06	284.03	292.42
竣工房屋面积	(万平方米)	Floor Space of Housing Completed	(10 000 sq.m)	8.63	18.90	35.11	62.39	68.13	73.49
出版报纸	(万份)	Newspapers Published	(10 000 pieces)	367.67	536.16	497.80	543.01	523.47	423.39
函件	(万件)	Letters Delivered	(10 000 pieces)	99.00	41.64	27.40	28.77	18.29	18.63
进出口总额	(万美元)	Total Imports and Exports	(10 000 USD)	879.45	2490.96	7097.81	9969.86	11798.36	12489.32
#出口		Exports		529.04	1219.18	3956.71	6256.99	7300.22	8003.84
实际外商直接投资	(万美元)	Actual Foreign Direct Investment	(10 000 USD)	258.63	598.63	1109.59	1887.12	2172.03	2451.51
每天人口变动和婚姻		**Daily Population Changes and Marriages**							
出生人数	(人)	Birth	(persons)	1582	1441	1625	1757	1887	1716
死亡人数	(人)	Death	(persons)	979	940	944	975	1107	932
结婚对数	(对)	Marriage	(couple)	969	1080	1564	1769	1704	1570
离婚对数	(对)	Divorce	(couple)	58	146	244	350	366	396

1-9 地区生产总值
GROSS DOMESTIC PRODUCT

本表按当年价格计算 (At current price)

年 份 Year	地区生产总值(亿元) Total Output (100 million yuan)	第一产业 Primary Industry	第二产业 Secondary Industry	工业 Industry	建筑业 Contruction	第三产业 Tertiary Industry	#金融业 Banking	#房地产业 Real Estate	人均地区生产总值(元) Per Capita GDP (yuan)	人均地区生产总值(美元) Per Capita GDP (USD)
1952	24.51	13.90	3.83	3.17	0.66	6.78			90.13	34.44
1955	34.05	18.14	7.45	6.25	1.20	8.46			117.88	47.88
1957	48.86	24.33	11.59	9.03	2.56	12.94			162.17	65.87
1962	52.13	29.30	10.63	9.10	1.53	12.20			161.47	65.59
1965	72.43	37.74	21.16	17.36	3.80	13.53			209.26	85.00
1970	88.15	44.41	26.90	21.79	5.11	16.84			221.78	90.09
1975	120.10	53.71	45.48	32.68	12.80	20.91			274.30	139.50
1978	151.00	61.11	63.71	52.17	11.54	26.18	4.54	1.42	332.03	210.53
1980	199.38	71.22	91.67	75.63	16.04	36.49	5.51	2.83	427.98	279.67
1982	241.55	101.73	94.97	82.69	12.28	44.85	6.50	3.10	506.33	267.53
1983	262.58	105.40	106.50	92.19	14.31	50.68	7.09	2.53	543.27	274.98
1984	328.22	126.36	136.50	120.32	16.18	65.36	9.04	3.89	670.97	288.34
1985	396.26	144.44	174.35	152.88	21.47	77.47	10.71	4.61	800.69	272.66
1986	442.04	163.61	187.96	164.93	23.03	90.47	13.68	5.97	881.61	255.33
1987	517.77	183.99	224.53	197.66	26.87	109.25	17.09	7.39	1018.42	273.61
1988	626.52	214.66	271.25	244.17	27.08	140.61	20.82	8.88	1215.93	326.68
1989	717.08	239.07	300.46	276.47	23.99	177.55	28.14	9.18	1373.22	364.72
1990	824.38	289.45	313.39	284.15	29.24	221.54	33.77	11.36	1541.17	322.20
1991	913.38	279.30	359.86	327.50	32.36	274.22	40.30	13.61	1668.03	313.34
1992	1088.39	303.00	444.61	402.59	42.02	340.78	48.07	17.22	1962.45	355.86
1993	1325.83	346.39	537.60	475.44	62.16	441.84	52.22	25.63	2360.53	409.67
1994	1700.92	501.44	657.63	580.80	76.83	541.85	56.83	37.85	2991.33	347.07
1995	2109.38	619.77	780.18	680.92	99.26	709.43	60.86	42.07	3671.41	439.64
1996	2499.77	716.34	923.68	805.53	118.15	859.75	65.37	62.23	4310.98	811.22
1997	2856.47	767.92	1071.86	929.91	141.95	1016.69	69.68	69.65	4883.80	589.13
1998	3114.02	778.22	1199.08	1041.20	157.88	1136.72	74.14	81.78	5287.03	638.60
1999	3229.29	653.99	1314.44	1139.52	174.92	1260.86	78.81	85.01	5452.46	658.65
2000	3545.39	662.30	1437.38	1243.24	194.14	1445.71	81.49	99.40	6293.41	760.22
2001	3880.53	692.17	1574.39	1360.10	214.29	1613.97	88.48	122.49	6866.99	829.65
2002	4212.82	707.00	1709.89	1473.00	236.89	1795.93	96.95	145.17	7436.58	898.46
2003	4757.45	798.35	1956.02	1682.16	273.86	2003.08	107.31	176.80	8378.01	1012.20
2004	5633.24	1020.09	2320.60	1987.50	333.10	2292.55	118.85	204.80	9897.64	1195.83
2005	6590.19	1082.13	2852.12	2478.66	373.46	2655.94	127.32	217.17	11554.00	1410.45
2006	7617.47	1140.41	3365.08	2929.19	435.89	3111.98	174.99	294.73	13360.00	1710.91
2007	9333.40	1378.00	4143.06	3588.00	555.06	3812.34	337.27	409.65	16386.00	2178.55
2008	11328.92	1780.00	5082.07	4391.23	690.84	4466.85	393.05	526.88	19858.00	2859.57
2009	12961.10	1795.90	6038.08	5183.68	854.40	5127.12	479.11	546.11	22677.00	3317.24
2010	15967.61	2147.00	7767.24	6726.53	1040.71	6053.37	561.27	564.41	27906.00	4122.31
2011	19632.26	2569.30	9815.94	8538.04	1277.90	7247.02	674.57	634.67	34197.27	5294.68
2012	22250.45	2848.77	11193.10	9735.15	1457.95	8208.58	870.36	692.82	38572.33	6110.47
2013	24791.83	3030.27	11786.64	10139.24	1705.95	9974.92	1179.55	972.40	42825.76	6914.96
2014	27379.22	3176.89	12852.40	10992.79	1925.09	11349.93	1372.61	1062.71	47144.60	7674.77
2015	29550.19	3309.84	13503.56	11532.37	2039.88	12736.79	1853.12	1136.72	50653.85	8132.72

注：从2013年起施行新的三次产业划分方法。
Note: The new classification of three industries has been implemented from 2013.

1-10 地区生产总值指数
INDICES OF GROSS DOMESTIC PRODUCT

按可比价计算，上年=100 (In comparable price, preceding year=100)

年 份 Year	地区生产总值(%) Total Output (%)	第一产业 Primary Industry	第二产业 Secondary Industry	工业 Industry	建筑业 Contruction	第三产业 Tertiary Industry	*金融业 Banking	*房地产业 Real Estate	人均地区生产总值(%) Per Capita GDP (%)
1953	114.0	107.4	129.4	141.0	93.3	122.7			111.6
1955	127.1	135.5	104.9	100.2	139.2	127.1			124.8
1957	107.4	106.4	115.3	109.5	146.0	102.6			104.8
1962	100.9	112.3	84.0	92.7	50.5	94.0			99.0
1965	118.1	111.5	132.5	124.5	196.4	114.9			115.4
1970	126.9	112.2	161.2	151.2	222.0	111.3			123.4
1975	111.4	94.5	139.0	135.2	152.5	116.0			110.0
1978	113.5	103.4	128.4	131.9	112.2	107.4			112.2
1980	106.4	86.9	123.5	126.7	107.0	111.0	96.3	160.6	105.1
1982	111.9	115.7	104.7	107.3	88.6	121.6	116.9	105.2	110.6
1983	105.9	99.6	109.9	109.2	115.9	111.5	107.5	80.3	104.6
1984	120.9	114.4	125.0	127.6	106.1	125.2	123.8	149.6	119.5
1985	116.2	108.3	124.7	124.7	124.3	112.4	112.4	112.3	114.8
1986	105.5	103.3	105.2	103.9	116.8	110.2	120.5	122.2	104.1
1987	108.4	103.1	111.3	112.9	99.0	110.7	114.5	113.4	106.9
1988	107.8	94.9	113.7	115.1	101.5	114.3	107.0	105.6	106.4
1989	104.5	105.2	102.1	104.2	81.3	109.3	121.8	93.2	103.1
1990	105.0	107.5	99.0	99.5	92.8	114.8	108.9	109.7	102.5
1991	106.6	95.1	111.1	111.6	106.1	115.4	114.4	114.7	104.2
1992	114.1	108.2	116.6	117.5	107.5	116.9	111.5	117.8	112.6
1993	113.0	105.8	116.7	116.1	123.3	115.2	112.0	119.4	111.6
1994	113.7	107.1	118.8	118.9	117.6	112.4	107.7	127.3	112.3
1995	113.2	108.9	116.1	115.9	118.5	112.5	107.3	121.0	112.0
1996	111.6	104.5	115.5	115.4	116.6	111.3	107.3	116.5	110.5
1997	111.9	106.9	113.4	113.5	112.3	113.5	103.4	110.3	110.9
1998	108.6	99.4	111.2	110.9	113.9	111.5	107.0	117.9	107.9
1999	107.8	101.9	108.2	108.2	107.5	111.0	103.7	106.1	107.2
2000	108.6	102.5	109.1	109.0	110.7	111.5	105.6	116.8	114.2
2001	108.9	102.5	109.9	110.1	108.5	110.8	107.4	122.1	108.5
2002	109.2	102.0	110.1	110.1	110.5	111.4	108.4	114.5	108.9
2003	109.7	105.8	110.2	110.2	110.6	110.8	110.1	119.0	109.5
2004	111.2	106.5	113.6	113.5	114.4	110.6	106.3	114.4	111.0
2005	112.1	104.0	115.2	116.0	109.9	111.8	104.4	103.5	111.8
2006	113.2	105.1	116.0	116.3	115.3	113.5	135.0	129.4	113.2
2007	114.6	104.7	116.7	115.7	123.3	115.9	167.3	132.0	114.7
2008	113.4	106.0	116.6	116.9	114.8	112.4	110.8	115.1	113.2
2009	113.5	105.2	116.8	115.7	123.7	112.3	122.8	111.1	113.3
2010	114.8	104.6	120.2	121.3	112.9	111.3	110.3	103.1	114.7
2011	113.8	104.4	117.9	119.1	110.1	112.0	112.8	104.4	113.5
2012	111.3	104.7	113.2	113.4	111.5	110.8	126.1	105.0	110.7
2013	110.1	104.5	111.3	111.2	111.9	110.1	115.6	110.2	109.7
2014	109.7	104.8	110.1	110.0	110.9	110.5	114.7	106.6	109.3
2015	108.9	104.5	108.3	108.5	106.9	110.7	130.7	106.5	108.4

1-11 地区生产总值指数
INDICES OF GROSS DOMESTIC PRODUCT

按可比价计算，1952=100 (In comparable price, 1952 = 100)

年 份 Year	地区生产总值(%) Total Output (%)	第一产业 Primary Industry	第二产业 Secondary Industry	工业 Industry	建筑业 Contruction	第三产业 Tertiary Industry	#金融业 Banking	#房地产业 Real Estate	人均地区生产总值(%) Per Capita GDP (%)
1953	114.0	107.4	129.4	141.0	93.3	122.7			111.6
1955	121.5	115.8	152.4	168.5	102.2	118.3			114.4
1957	169.6	143.9	280.1	295.3	233.2	172.1			153.0
1962	141.7	130.2	223.9	258.0	116.1	124.2			119.3
1965	205.6	161.5	490.4	538.5	338.9	161.1			161.5
1970	242.6	158.7	705.6	745.9	580.5	202.3			166.0
1975	320.2	185.3	1126.3	1165.1	995.9	259.1			198.9
1978	399.0	204.6	1616.5	1857.1	926.0	314.2			238.6
1980	490.8	211.4	2257.6	2637.6	1173.5	398.9	110.3	181.0	286.5
1982	585.4	277.2	2399.3	2950.6	905.2	508.6	135.1	206.0	333.7
1983	620.1	276.1	2637.8	3220.9	1048.9	567.0	145.2	165.4	348.9
1984	749.7	315.9	3297.0	4111.0	1113.2	709.9	179.8	247.5	416.8
1985	871.1	342.0	4111.1	5128.2	1383.1	797.9	202.1	277.9	478.7
1986	919.1	353.1	4326.3	5327.6	1615.8	879.3	243.5	339.6	498.5
1987	996.7	364.1	4816.5	6017.4	1599.1	973.3	278.8	385.1	533.1
1988	1074.3	345.4	5475.9	6925.0	1623.7	1112.1	298.3	406.7	567.0
1989	1122.7	363.3	5592.5	7218.5	1319.6	1215.1	363.4	379.1	584.7
1990	1178.9	390.6	5536.7	7181.9	1224.3	1394.6	395.7	415.8	599.3
1991	1257.2	371.2	6151.9	8018.2	1298.9	1609.6	452.7	477.0	624.3
1992	1434.3	401.6	7175.3	9419.0	1396.0	1881.8	504.7	561.8	703.3
1993	1621.2	424.7	8372.8	10939.2	1720.9	2166.9	565.3	670.8	784.9
1994	1843.3	454.7	9948.0	13008.9	2024.1	2435.8	608.7	854.0	881.6
1995	2086.5	495.2	11547.9	15073.3	2398.9	2740.9	653.4	1033.2	987.5
1996	2327.5	517.4	13342.9	17402.1	2796.6	3050.0	701.2	1204.1	1091.5
1997	2604.6	553.0	15131.7	19753.3	3139.6	3461.5	725.3	1328.7	1211.0
1998	2829.4	549.4	16822.5	21912.2	3576.3	3858.8	776.3	1566.2	1306.3
1999	3048.8	560.1	18195.4	23713.5	3845.1	4285.0	805.2	1661.6	1399.9
2000	3310.6	574.1	19858.1	25847.7	4254.6	4777.6	850.3	1941.2	1598.1
2001	3604.0	588.5	21828.1	28458.3	4618.0	5291.6	913.2	2370.0	1734.3
2002	3936.2	600.2	24038.5	31332.6	5104.3	5892.2	990.1	2713.0	1889.5
2003	4318.6	634.9	26494.8	34517.7	5643.2	6525.7	1090.1	3229.7	2068.1
2004	4802.5	676.2	30099.5	39171.3	6456.0	7218.6	1158.5	3696.0	2294.6
2005	5383.6	703.2	34674.7	45438.7	7095.2	8070.4	1209.5	3825.4	2565.4
2006	6094.2	739.1	40222.6	52845.2	8180.7	9159.9	1632.8	4948.5	2904.0
2007	6984.0	773.8	46939.8	61141.9	10086.8	10616.3	2731.6	6532.1	3330.9
2008	7919.8	820.3	54731.8	71474.9	11579.7	11932.8	3026.7	7518.4	3770.6
2009	8989.0	862.9	63926.7	82696.4	14324.1	13400.5	3716.7	8353.0	4272.1
2010	10319.4	902.6	76839.9	100310.7	16171.9	14914.8	4099.5	8611.9	4900.1
2011	11746.5	942.3	90571.2	119440.0	17810.1	16701.5	4623.8	8994.3	5561.6
2012	13073.9	986.6	102526.6	135444.9	19858.3	18505.3	5830.7	9444.0	6156.7
2013	14394.4	1031.0	114112.1	150614.7	22221.4	20542.7	6740.3	10407.3	6753.9
2014	15790.7	1080.5	125637.4	165676.2	24643.5	22699.7	7731.1	11094.2	7382.0
2015	17196.0	1129.1	136065.3	179758.6	26343.9	25128.6	10104.6	11815.3	8002.1

注：金融业、房地产业指数以1978年为100。
Note: The indices of banking and real estate are 1978=100

1-12 地区生产总值构成
COMPOSITION OF GROSS DOMESTIC PRODUCT

本表按当年价格计算 (At current prices)

年 份 Year	地区生产总值(%) Total Output (%)	第一产业 Primary Industry	第二产业 Secondary Industry	工业 Industry	建筑业 Contruction	第三产业 Tertiary Industry	#金融业 Banking	#房地产业 Real Estate
1952	100	56.7	15.6	12.9	2.7	27.7		
1955	100	53.3	21.9	18.4	3.5	24.8		
1957	100	49.8	23.7	18.5	5.2	26.5		
1962	100	56.2	20.4	17.5	2.9	23.4		
1965	100	52.1	29.2	24.0	5.2	18.7		
1970	100	50.4	30.5	24.7	5.8	19.1		
1975	100	44.7	37.9	27.2	10.7	17.4		
1978	100	40.5	42.2	34.5	7.6	17.3	3.0	0.9
1980	100	35.7	46.0	37.9	8.0	18.3	2.8	1.4
1982	100	42.1	39.3	34.2	5.1	18.6	2.7	1.3
1983	100	40.1	40.6	35.1	5.4	19.3	2.7	1.0
1984	100	38.5	41.6	36.7	4.9	19.9	2.8	1.2
1985	100	36.5	44.0	38.6	5.4	19.6	2.7	1.2
1986	100	37.0	42.5	37.3	5.2	20.5	3.1	1.4
1987	100	35.5	43.4	38.2	5.2	21.1	3.3	1.4
1988	100	34.3	43.3	39.0	4.3	22.4	3.3	1.4
1989	100	33.3	41.9	38.6	3.3	24.8	3.9	1.3
1990	100	35.1	38.0	34.5	3.5	26.9	4.1	1.4
1991	100	30.6	39.4	35.9	3.5	30.0	4.4	1.5
1992	100	27.8	40.9	37.0	3.9	31.3	4.4	1.6
1993	100	26.1	40.5	35.9	4.7	33.3	3.9	1.9
1994	100	29.5	38.7	34.1	4.5	31.9	3.3	2.2
1995	100	29.4	37.0	32.3	4.7	33.6	2.9	2.0
1996	100	28.7	37.0	32.2	4.7	34.4	2.6	2.5
1997	100	26.9	37.5	32.6	5.0	35.6	2.4	2.4
1998	100	25.0	38.5	33.4	5.1	36.5	2.4	2.6
1999	100	20.3	40.7	35.3	5.4	39.0	2.4	2.6
2000	100	18.7	40.5	35.1	5.5	40.8	2.3	2.8
2001	100	17.8	40.6	35.0	5.5	41.6	2.3	3.2
2002	100	16.8	40.6	35.0	5.6	42.6	2.3	3.4
2003	100	16.8	41.1	35.4	5.8	42.1	2.3	3.7
2004	100	18.1	41.2	35.3	5.9	40.7	2.1	3.6
2005	100	16.4	43.3	37.6	5.7	40.3	1.9	3.3
2006	100	15.0	44.2	38.5	5.7	40.8	2.3	3.9
2007	100	14.8	44.4	38.4	6.0	40.8	3.6	4.4
2008	100	15.7	44.9	38.8	6.1	39.4	3.5	4.7
2009	100	13.8	46.6	40.0	6.6	39.6	3.7	4.2
2010	100	13.5	48.6	42.1	6.5	37.9	3.5	3.5
2011	100	13.1	50.0	43.5	6.5	36.9	3.4	3.2
2012	100	12.8	50.3	43.8	6.5	36.9	3.9	3.1
2013	100	12.2	47.6	40.9	6.7	40.2	4.8	3.9
2014	100	11.6	46.9	40.2	6.7	41.5	5.0	3.9
2015	100	11.2	45.7	39.0	6.9	43.1	6.3	3.8

注:2013年产业结构根据三经普数据进行了调整。
Note:The data of 2013 has been adjusted basing on the files of the 3rd national economics census.

1-13 按支出法计算的地区生产总值
GROSS DOMESTIC PRODUCT BY EXPENDITURE APPROACH

本表按当年价格计算 (At current prices)

年份 Year	地区生产总值(亿元) Gross Domestic Product (100 million yuan)	最终消费 Final Consumption Expenditure	居民消费 Residents Consumption Expenditure	政府消费 Government Consumption Expenditure	资本形成总额 Gross Capital Formation	固定资本形成 Fixed Capital Formation	存货增加 Changes in Inventories	货物和服务净流出 Net Export of Goods and Services
1978	151.20	81.70	74.70	7.00	43.12	31.40	11.72	26.38
1980	200.19	107.79	93.51	14.28	40.10	33.19	6.91	52.30
1985	386.76	240.02	203.23	36.79	135.43	96.71	38.72	11.31
1989	718.07	478.66	398.09	80.57	201.39	115.50	85.89	38.02
1990	818.89	535.49	434.62	100.87	261.95	147.13	114.82	21.45
1991	913.22	597.42	475.85	121.57	281.92	176.32	105.60	33.88
1992	1089.68	689.93	546.61	143.32	355.46	235.63	119.83	44.29
1993	1423.92	876.16	694.49	181.67	512.31	377.95	134.36	35.45
1994	1858.89	1043.25	845.14	198.10	740.13	571.68	168.45	75.51
1995	2364.45	1305.21	1095.97	209.20	973.63	778.25	195.38	85.61
1996	2720.28	1599.74	1346.76	253.00	1191.75	985.03	206.72	-71.21
1997	3107.91	1720.23	1438.12	282.10	1466.81	1102.10	364.71	-79.13
1998	3344.45	1859.97	1518.92	341.10	1614.60	1238.90	375.70	-130.12
1999	3504.01	1887.86	1507.12	380.70	1754.79	1320.10	434.69	-138.64
2000	3760.48	2030.07	1594.08	436.00	1882.47	1451.85	430.62	-152.06
2001	4102.08	2262.67	1767.38	495.30	1884.57	1610.93	273.64	-45.16
2002	4416.88	2499.95	1951.54	548.41	1905.92	1699.78	206.14	11.01
2003	4910.53	2819.24	2188.05	631.20	2037.19	1875.78	161.41	54.10
2004	5633.30	3174.18	2452.62	721.56	2538.77	2325.87	212.90	-79.65
2005	6520.14	3645.71	2785.42	860.29	2943.58	2804.01	139.57	-69.15
2006	7972.33	4245.68	3124.37	1121.31	3634.13	3555.21	78.92	92.52
2007	9550.04	4999.66	3709.69	1289.97	4450.25	4371.14	79.11	100.13
2008	11728.64	5892.03	4225.38	1666.65	5716.36	5368.99	347.37	120.25
2009	13240.42	6325.15	4456.31	1868.84	6827.00	6612.85	214.15	88.27
2010	16182.27	7389.80	5136.78	2253.02	8511.17	8200.40	310.77	281.30
2011	20167.28	8931.48	6241.95	2689.53	11027.27	10597.82	429.45	208.53
2012	22659.38	9982.79	7085.46	2897.33	12554.67	12064.75	489.92	121.92
2013	25431.66	11161.21	8053.82	3107.39	14245.35	13701.86	543.49	25.10
2014	28728.18	12562.76	9124.48	3438.28	16109.59	15442.86	666.73	55.83
2015	31226.44	13799.70	10167.87	3631.83	17418.40	16757.35	661.05	8.34

1-14 按支出法计算的地区生产总值指数
INDICES OF GROSS DOMESTIC PRODUCT BY EXPENDITURE APPROACH

按可比价计算 1952=100 (In comparable price, 1952=100)

年 份 Year	地区生产总值(%) Gross Domestic Product(%)	最终消费 Final Consumption Expenditure	居民消费 Residents Consumption Expenditure	政府消费 Government Consumption Expenditure	资本形成总额 Gross Capital Formation	固定资本形成 Fixed Capital Formation	存货增加 Changes in Inventories
1952	100.0	100.0	100.0	100.0	100.0	100.0	100.0
1978	488.3	313.7	308.9	369.3	820.0	1396.6	388.5
1980	605.4	388.8	363.4	706.7	663.9	1270.1	209.7
1985	1007.5	736.7	674.8	1492.5	1962.9	3155.5	1067.1
1990	1337.5	1004.9	897.4	2307.0	2504.8	3460.7	1786.7
1991	1344.2	970.7	850.8	2403.9	2595.0	3955.5	1604.4
1992	1471.9	1023.1	870.3	2819.7	2979.1	4806.0	1670.2
1993	1764.8	1242.1	1045.3	3550.0	3598.7	6218.9	1747.0
1994	2075.4	1379.9	1174.9	3802.1	4530.8	8246.3	1920.0
1995	2339.0	1508.3	1302.9	3950.4	5432.4	9945.0	2261.8
1996	2619.7	1702.8	1467.1	4507.4	6475.4	12520.8	2257.2
1997	2902.6	1776.1	1541.9	4584.0	8120.2	14486.6	3634.1
1998	3140.6	1985.6	1697.7	5418.3	9257.0	16775.4	3961.2
1999	3357.3	2130.6	1765.6	6431.5	10099.4	17966.5	4543.5
2000	3629.3	2260.5	1852.1	7055.4	10927.6	19709.2	4738.9
2001	3930.5	2513.7	2042.9	8057.2	10807.4	21542.2	3028.2
2002	4276.4	2795.3	2281.9	8814.6	11099.2	23093.2	2313.5
2003	4618.5	3072.0	2494.1	9890.0	11443.2	24594.3	1753.6
2004	5052.7	3336.2	2683.6	11086.7	13422.9	28775.3	2121.9
2005	5709.6	3726.5	2976.1	12672.1	15288.7	34041.2	1398.3
2006	6531.8	4326.5	3318.4	16600.0	18315.8	42245.1	465.6
2007	7446.3	4785.1	3680.1	18226.8	21667.6	20102.7	450.2
2008	8399.4	5282.8	3952.4	21653.4	25026.1	22575.3	1848.5
2009	9356.9	5689.6	4177.7	24381.7	30606.9	28151.4	1144.2
2010	11014.0	6423.5	4658.1	28307.2	36758.9	33669.1	1660.3
2011	12886.4	7310.0	5319.6	31902.2	44662.1	40806.9	2148.4
2012	14162.2	7931.3	5862.2	33401.6	50021.5	45662.9	2440.6
2013	15706.9	8653.0	6507.0	34904.7	56574.3	51690.4	2723.7
2014	17513.2	9561.6	7235.8	37871.6	63476.4	57738.2	3391.0
2015	19001.8	10364.8	7959.4	39386.5	69125.8	63107.9	3455.4

1-15 三次产业贡献率
CONTRIBUTING RATE OF THE THREE INDUSTRIES

单位：% 本表按可比价格计算 (In comparable price) (%)

年 份 Year	地区生产总值 Gross Domestic Product	第一产业 Primary Industry	第二产业 Second Industry	#工 业 Industry	第三产业 Tertiary Industry
1990	100	42.68	-9.84	-4.64	67.16
1991	100	-25.9	65.6	62.7	60.3
1992	100	18.0	48.2	46.4	33.8
1993	100	13.0	53.5	47.7	33.5
1994	100	14.2	59.2	54.7	26.6
1995	100	17.5	54.9	49.8	27.6
1996	100	9.6	62.2	56.7	28.2
1997	100	13.5	53.9	49.8	32.6
1998	100	-1.6	62.8	56.4	38.8
1999	100	5.1	52.2	48.2	42.7
2000	100	5.6	53.0	47.9	41.3
2001	100	5.3	45.2	40.0	49.5
2002	100	3.8	45.1	38.9	51.1
2003	100	9.8	43.4	37.4	46.8
2004	100	9.2	50.4	43.2	40.5
2005	100	6.5	53.5	48.8	40.0
2006	100	6.3	52.4	46.6	41.3
2007	100	4.9	50.9	41.8	44.2
2008	100	6.2	56.0	49.2	37.8
2009	100	5.1	57.9	47.0	37.0
2010	100	3.7	66.1	60.3	30.2
2011	100	4.3	62.9	58.1	32.8
2012	100	5.1	59.1	52.6	35.8
2013	100	5.1	55.3	48.1	39.6
2014	100	5.3	52.1	45.1	42.6
2015	100	5.3	46.8	42.0	47.9

注：产业贡献率指各产业增加值增量与GDP增量之比。

Note: Contribution share of the three components to the increase of the GDP refers to the proportion of the increment of the each component of GDP expenditure approach to the increment of GDP.

1-16 三次产业拉动率

CONTRIBUTION OF THE THREE STRATA OF INDUSTRY TO GDP GROWTH

单位:百分点 本表按可比价格计算(In comparable price) (percentage point)

年 份 Year	地区生产总值 Gross Domestic Product	第一产业 Primary Industry	第二产业 Second Industry	#工 业 Industry	第三产业 Tertiary Industry
1990	5.00	2.1	−0.5	−0.2	3.4
1991	6.6	−1.7	4.3	4.1	4.0
1992	14.1	2.5	6.8	6.5	4.8
1993	13.0	1.7	7.0	6.2	4.4
1994	13.7	1.9	8.1	7.5	3.6
1995	13.2	2.3	7.3	6.6	3.6
1996	11.6	1.1	7.2	6.6	3.3
1997	11.9	1.6	6.4	5.9	3.9
1998	8.6	−0.1	5.4	4.8	3.3
1999	7.8	0.4	4.1	3.8	3.3
2000	8.6	0.5	4.6	4.1	3.6
2001	8.6	0.5	3.9	3.4	4.3
2002	9.2	0.4	4.1	3.6	4.7
2003	9.7	0.9	4.2	3.6	4.5
2004	11.2	1.0	5.6	4.8	4.5
2005	12.1	0.8	6.5	5.9	4.8
2006	13.2	0.8	6.9	6.1	5.5
2007	14.6	0.7	7.4	6.1	6.5
2008	13.4	0.8	7.5	6.6	5.1
2009	13.5	0.7	7.8	6.3	5.0
2010	14.8	0.5	9.8	8.9	4.5
2011	13.8	0.6	8.7	8.0	4.5
2012	11.3	0.6	6.7	5.9	4.0
2013	10.1	0.5	5.6	4.8	4.0
2014	9.7	0.5	5.1	4.4	4.1
2015	8.9	0.5	4.2	3.7	4.2

注:三次产业对生产总值增长的拉动指GDP增长速度与各产业贡献率之乘积。
Note:Contribution of the three components to GDP growth refers to the growth rate of GDP multiplied by the contribution share of the three components.

1-17 三大需求贡献率
CONTRIBUTING RATE OF THE THREE REQUIREMENTS

单位:% 本表按可比价格计算 (In comparable price) (%)

年 份 Year	地区生产总值 Gross Domestic Product	最终消费支出 Final Consumption Expenditure	资本形成总额 Gross Capital Formation	货物和服务净流出 Net Outflow of Goods and Services
1990	100.0	59.4	111.8	-71.3
1991	100.0	-464.2	238.4	325.8
1992	100.0	35.7	51.8	12.5
1993	100.0	65.2	36.3	-1.5
1994	100.0	38.8	51.3	10.0
1995	100.0	42.5	58.3	-0.8
1996	100.0	60.2	63.5	-23.7
1997	100.0	22.7	99.2	-21.8
1998	100.0	76.6	81.1	-57.6
1999	100.0	58.2	65.9	-24.1
2000	100.0	41.6	51.7	6.8
2001	100.0	72.3	-6.4	34.1
2002	100.0	70.3	13.9	15.8
2003	100.0	70.5	17.0	12.5
2004	100.0	52.6	76.1	-28.6
2005	100.0	50.7	49.0	0.3
2006	100.0	44.3	43.9	11.9
2007	100.0	40.8	58.7	0.5
2008	100.0	35.5	64.4	0.1
2009	100.0	27.4	74.0	-1.4
2010	100.0	27.8	61.6	10.6
2011	100.0	36.9	66.3	-3.2
2012	100.0	38.2	66.2	-4.4
2013	100.0	36.7	67.2	-3.9
2014	100.0	39.0	60.0	1.0
2015	100.0	42.0	60.0	-2.0

注:贡献率指三大需求增量与支出法地区生产总值增量之比。
Note:Contribution share of the three components to the increase of the GDP refers to the proportion of the increment of the each component of GDP expenditure approach to the increment of GDP.

1-18 三大需求拉动率
CONTRIBUTION OF THE THREE COMPONENTS OF GDP TO THE GROWTH OF GDP

单位:百分点　　本表按可比价格计算 (In comparable price)　　(percentage point)

年 份 Year	地区生产总值 Gross Domestic Product	最终消费支出 Final Consumption Expenditure	资本形成总额 Gross Capital Formation	货物和服务净流出 Net Outflow of Goods and Services
1990	5.0	3.0	5.6	-3.6
1991	6.6	-30.6	15.7	21.5
1992	14.1	5.0	7.3	1.8
1993	13.0	8.5	4.7	-0.2
1994	13.7	5.3	7.0	1.4
1995	13.2	5.6	7.7	-0.1
1996	11.6	7.0	7.4	-2.7
1997	11.9	2.7	11.8	-2.6
1998	8.6	6.6	7.0	-5.0
1999	7.8	4.5	5.1	-1.9
2000	8.6	3.6	4.4	0.6
2001	8.9	6.4	-0.6	3.0
2002	9.2	6.5	1.3	1.5
2003	9.7	6.8	1.6	1.2
2004	11.2	5.9	8.5	-3.2
2005	12.1	6.1	5.9	0.1
2006	13.2	5.8	5.8	1.6
2007	14.6	6.0	8.6	0.1
2008	13.4	4.8	8.6	
2009	13.5	3.7	10.0	-0.2
2010	14.8	4.1	9.1	1.6
2011	13.8	5.1	9.1	-0.4
2012	11.3	4.3	7.5	-0.5
2013	10.9	4.0	7.3	-0.4
2014	11.5	4.5	6.9	0.1
2015	8.5	3.6	5.1	-0.2

注:1.三大需求指支出法地区生产总值的三大构成项目,即最终消费支出、资本形成总额、货物和服务净流出。
2.三大需求对国内生产总值增长的拉动指地区生产总值增长速度与三大需求贡献率的乘积。

Notes: a)Three components of GDP by exoenditure approach are final consumption expenditure, gross capital formation and net exports of goods and services.
b)Contribution of the three components to GDP growth refers to the growth refers to the growth rate of GDP multiplied by the contribution share of the three components.

1-19 市、州生产总值(2015)
GROSS DOMESTIC PRODUCT OF CITIES AND PREFECTURES(2015)

单位:亿元 (100 million yuan)

地 区	Regions	地区生产总值 Gross Domestic Product	第一产业 Primary Industry	第二产业 Secondary Industry	第三产业 Tertiary Industry
武 汉	Wuhan	10905.60	359.81	4981.54	5564.25
黄 石	Huangshi	1228.11	108.56	679.88	439.67
十 堰	Shiyan	1300.12	157.48	636.11	506.53
宜 昌	Yichang	3384.80	361.40	1986.37	1037.03
襄 阳	Xiangyang	3382.12	402.14	1922.92	1057.06
鄂 州	Ezhou	730.01	84.66	422.44	222.91
荆 门	Jingmen	1388.46	200.86	729.66	457.94
孝 感	Xiaogan	1457.20	259.45	705.76	491.99
荆 州	Jingzhou	1590.50	353.01	695.12	542.37
黄 冈	Huanggang	1589.24	379.62	618.42	591.20
咸 宁	Xianning	1030.07	178.59	500.47	351.01
随 州	Suizhou	785.26	132.31	376.20	276.75
恩施州	Enshi	670.81	143.86	244.42	282.53
仙 桃	Xiantao	597.61	87.99	318.14	191.48
潜 江	Qianjiang	557.57	69.88	305.17	182.52
天 门	Tianmen	440.10	76.92	221.46	141.72
神农架	Shennongjia	20.95	1.96	7.74	11.25

1-20 市、州生产总值指数(2015)
INDICES OF GROSS DOMESTIC PRODUCT OF CITIES AND PREFECTURES(2015)

(上年=100,单位:%) (preceding year = 100,%)

地 区	Regions	地区生产总值 Gross Domestic Product	第一产业 Primary Industry	第二产业 Secondary Industry	第三产业 Tertiary Industry
武 汉	Wuhan	108.8	104.8	108.2	109.6
黄 石	Huangshi	105.3	105.1	102.2	111.2
十 堰	Shiyan	107.5	104.7	104.3	113.0
宜 昌	Yichang	108.9	105.0	108.8	110.2
襄 阳	Xiangyang	108.9	104.3	109.0	110.3
鄂 州	Ezhou	108.0	105.3	107.4	110.3
荆 门	Jingmen	109.2	105.1	110.0	109.7
孝 感	Xiaogan	108.9	105.2	109.0	110.6
荆 州	Jingzhou	108.5	105.2	107.4	112.0
黄 冈	Huanggang	108.9	104.8	108.1	112.4
咸 宁	Xianning	108.0	106.0	107.5	109.9
随 州	Suizhou	108.9	105.2	108.8	110.7
恩施州	Enshi	109.1	105.3	109.7	110.8
仙 桃	Xiantao	109.1	105.2	109.4	110.3
潜 江	Qianjiang	107.0	105.0	109.9	103.4
天 门	Tianmen	108.9	104.6	109.3	111.1
神农架	Shennongjia	106.6	103.6	99.2	113.0

1-21 市、州支出法生产总值(2015)
GROSS DOMESTIC PRODUCT BY EXPENDITURE APPROACH OF CITIES AND PREFECTURES(2015)

单位:亿元 (100 million yuan)

地　区	Regions	支出法地区生产总值 Total Gross Domestic Product by Expenditure	最终消费支出 Final Consumption Expenditure	资本形成总额 Gross Capital Formation	货物和服务净流出 Net Export of Goods and Services
武　汉	Wuhan	10907.17	4909.08	5889.03	109.06
黄　石	Huangshi	1228.13	482.55	735.36	10.22
十　堰	Shiyan	1944.38	550.72	1316.22	77.44
宜　昌	Yichang	3384.79	1459.56	1824.62	100.61
襄　阳	Xiangyang	3382.10	1559.50	1779.10	43.50
鄂　州	Ezhou	730.01	328.77	395.73	5.51
荆　门	Jingmen	1388.46	601.91	773.23	13.32
孝　感	Xiaogan	1464.88	626.65	823.81	14.42
荆　州	Jingzhou	1590.50	718.65	1333.71	-461.86
黄　冈	Huanggang	1589.24	812.43	776.81	0
咸　宁	Xianning	1195.24	400.37	779.35	15.52
随　州	Suizhou	784.20	344.25	428.09	11.86
恩施州	Enshi	670.81	580.31	569.18	-478.68
仙　桃	Xiantao	597.61	170.94	369.44	57.23
潜　江	Qianjiang	553.44	152.86	388.76	11.82
天　门	Tianmen	440.10	225.11	208.39	6.60
神农架	Shennongjia	20.95	10.92	11.40	-1.37

1-22 市、州民营经济增加值(2015)
VALUE ADDED OF PRIVATE ECONOMY(2015)

地　区	Regions	增加值(亿元) Value-Added (100 million yuan)		占GDP比重(%) Percentage(%)	
		2014	2015	2014	2015
全　省	Total	14905.74	16228.96	54.4	54.9
武　汉	Wuhan	3950.32	4620.40	39.2	42.4
黄　石	Huangshi	671.34	683.24	55.1	55.6
十　堰	Shiyan	538.39	600.93	44.8	46.2
宜　昌	Yichang	1883.08	2042.38	60.1	60.3
襄　阳	Xiangyang	1630.00	1764.84	52.1	52.2
鄂　州	Ezhou	436.34	461.34	63.5	63.2
荆　门	Jingmen	757.46	822.74	57.8	59.3
孝　感	Xiaogan	865.62	939.30	63.9	64.5
荆　州	Jingzhou	689.18	750.08	46.6	47.2
黄　冈	Huanggang	953.38	1057.13	64.5	66.5
咸　宁	Xianning	712.09	766.80	73.8	74.4
随　州	Suizhou	507.54	557.58	70.2	71.0
恩施州	Enshi	257.64	292.40	42.1	43.6
仙　桃	Xiantao	400.49	433.34	72.5	72.5
潜　江	Qianjiang	372.91	388.09	69.0	69.6
天　门	Tianmen	271.74	298.77	67.6	67.9
神农架	Shennongjia	8.21	8.41	40.6	40.1

主要统计指标解释

平均增长速度 计算平均增长速度有两种方法:一种是习惯上经常使用的“水平法”,又称几何平均法,是以间隔期最后一年的水平同基期水平对比来计算平均每年增长(或下降)速度;另一种是“累计法”,又称代数平均法或方程法,是以间隔期内各年水平的总和同基期水平对比来计算平均每年增长(或下降)速度。在一般正常情况下,两种方法计算的平均每年增长速度比较接近;但在经济发展不平衡、出现大起大落时,两种方法计算的结果差别较大。

国民经济行业分类 自2003年定期报表开始使用新的《国民经济行业分类》(GB/T4754-2002)该分类是由国家统计局组织修订,经国家质量监督检验检疫总局批准,于2002年5月10日发布实施。这次修订是在1994年分类标准的基础上,参照联合国《全部经济活动的国际标准产业分类》(ISIC/Rev.3)进行的。修订后的《国民经济行业分类》(GB/T4754-2002)共有门类20个,大类95个,中类396个,小类913个。新增门类4个,大类增加3个,中类增加28个,小类增加67个。

企业(单位)登记注册类型 是以在工商行政管理机关登记注册的各类企业为划分对象,以工商行政管理部门对企业登记注册的类型为依据,将企业登记注册类型分为内资企业、港澳台商投资企业和外商投资企业三大类。内资企业包括国有企业、集体企业、股份合作企业、联营企业、有限责任公司、股份有限公司、私营公司和其他企业;港澳台商投资企业和外商投资企业分别包括合资经营企业、合作经营企业、独资经营企业和股份有限公司。对不在工商行政管理部门进行登记注册的行政机关、事业单位和社会团体,主要按其经费来源和管理方式进行划分。

国有企业 指企业全部资产归国家所有,并按《中华人民共和国企业法人登记管理条例》规定登记注册的非公司制的经济组织。不包括有限责任公司中的国有独资公司。

集体企业 指企业资产归集体所有,并按《中华人民共和国企业法人登记管理条例》规定登记注册的经济组织。

股份合作企业 指以合作制为基础,由企业职工共同出资入股,吸收一定比例的社会资产投资组建,实行自主经营,自负盈亏,共同劳动,民主管理,按劳分配与按股分红相结合的一种集体经济组织。

联营企业 指两个及两个以上相同或不同所有制性质的企业法人或事业单位法人,按自愿、平等、互利的原则,共同投资组成的经济组织。联营企业包括国有联营企业、集体联营企业、国有与集体联营企业和其他联营企业。

有限责任公司 指根据《中华人民共和国公司登记管理条例》规定登记注册,由两个以上、五十个以下的股东共同出资,每个股东以其所认缴的出资额对公司承担有限责任,公司以其全部资产对其债务承担责任的经济组织。有限责任公司包括国有独资公司以及其他有限责任公司。

股份有限公司 指根据《中华人民共和国公司登记管理条例》规定登记注册,其全部注册资本由等额股份构成并通过发行股票筹集资本,股东以其认购的股份对公司承担有限责任,公司以其全部资产对其债务承担责任的经济组织。

私营企业 指由自然人投资设立或由自然人控股,以雇佣劳动为基础的营利性经济组织。包括按照《公司法》、《合伙企业法》、《私营企业暂行条例》规定登记注册的私营有限责任公司、私营股份有限公司、私营合伙企业和私营独资企业。

其他企业 指上述企业之外的其他内资经济组织。

与港澳台商合资经营企业 指港澳台地区投资者与内地企业依照《中华人民共和国中外合资经营企业法》及有关法律的规定,按合同规定的比例投资设立、分享利润和分担风险的企业。

与港澳台商合作经营企业 指港澳台地区投资者与内地企业依照《中华人民共和国中外合作经营企业法》及有关法律的规定,依照合作合同的约定进行投资或提供条件设立、分配利润和分担风险的企业。

港澳台商独资经营企业 指依照《中华人民共和国外资企业法》及有关法律的规定,在内地由港澳台地区投资者全额投资设立的企业。

港澳台商投资股份有限公司 指根据国家有关规定,经原外经贸部依法批准设立,其中港、澳、台商的股本占公司注册资本的比例达25%以上的股份有限公司。凡其中港、澳、台商的股本占公司注册资本的比例小于25%的，属于内资企业中的股份有限公司。

中外合资经营企业 指外国企业或外国人与中国内地企业依照《中华人民共和国中外合资经营企业法》及有关法律的规定，按合同规定的比例投资设立、分享利润和分担风险的企业。

中外合作经营企业 指外国企业或外国人与中国内地企业依照《中华人民共和国中外合作经营企业法》及有关法律的规定，依照合作合同的约定进行投资或提供条件设立、分配利润和分担风险的企业。

外资企业 指依照《中华人民共和国外资企业法》及有关法律的规定，在中国内地由外国投资者全额投资设立的企业。

外商投资股份有限公司 指根据国家有关规定，经原外经贸部依法批准设立，其中外资的股本占公司注册资本的比例达25%以上的股份有限公司。凡其中外资股本占公司注册资本的比例小于25%的，属于内资企业中的股份有限公司。

行政机关、事业单位和社会团体 参照企业登记注册类型，主要按其经费来源和管理方式划分。具体规定如下：

⑴行政机关：包括国家机关和政党机关，原则上均列为“国有”。但有特殊规定的，如供销社等，则列为“集体”。

⑵事业单位：包括经国家机构编制部门和有关业务主管部门批准成立的各类事业单位，不包括实行企业化管理的事业单位。事业单位的划分办法如下：

①由国家财政预算拨款或列入财政预算外资金管理以及经费主要来源于国有主管部门或国有上级单位的事业单位，列为“国有”。

②经费主要来源于集体单位的事业单位，列为“集体”。

③公民个人(或个人合伙)开办的事业单位，列为“私营”。

④上述以外的其他事业单位，如果其经费来源不明确，按管理方式进行归类。

⑶社会团体：包括经民政部门批准成立以及未纳入社会团体管理条例范围的工会、妇联等各类社会团体。社会团体的划分办法如下：

①未纳入民政部社会团体管理条例范围的工会、妇联、共青团、青联、工商联、科协、侨联等社会团体，国家拨款设立的基金会或基金管理组织以及经费主要来源于国有业务主管部门或国有上级单位的社会团体，列为“国有”。

②经费主要来源于集体单位的社会团体，列为“集体”。

③公民个人(或个人合伙)开办的社会团体，划为“私营”。

④上述以外的其他社会团体，如果其经费来源不明确，改按管理方式进行归类。

地区生产总值(GDP) 指按市场价格计算的一个地区所有常住单位在一定时期内生产活动的最终成果。地区生产总值有三种表现形态，即价值形态、收入形态和产品形态。从价值形态看，它是所有常住单位在一定时期内生产的全部货物和服务价值超过同期投入的全部非固定资产货物和服务价值的差额，即所有常住单位的增加值之和；从收入形态看，它是所有常住单位在一定时期内创造并分配给常住单位和非常住单位的初次收入之和；从产品形态看，它是所有常住单位在一定时期内最终使用的货物和服务价值减去货物和服务流进价值。在实际核算中，地区生产总值有三种计算方法，即生产法、收入法和支出法。三种方法分别从不同的方面反映地区生产总值及其构成。

国民总收入(GNI) 即国民生产总值，指一个国家(或地区)所有常住单位在一定时期内收入初次分配的最终结果。一国常住单位从事生产活动所创造的增加值在初次分配中主要分配给该国的常住单位，但也有一部分以生产税及进口税(扣除生产和进口补贴)、劳动者报酬和财产收入等形式分配给非常住单位；同时，国外生产所创造的增加值也有一部分以生产税及进口税(扣除生产和进口补贴)、劳动者报酬和财产收入等形式分配给该国的常住单位，从而产生了国民总收入的概念。它等于国内生产总值加上来自国外的净要素收入。与国内生产总值不同，国民总收入是个收入概念，而国内生产总值是个生产概念。

三次产业 三产业的划分是世界上较为常用的产业结构分类，但各国的划分不尽一致。我国的三次产业划分是：

第一产业是指农、林、牧、渔业。

第二产业是指采矿业，制造业，电力、煤气及水的生产和供应业，建筑业。

第三产业是指除第一、二产业以外的其他行业。

劳动者报酬 指劳动者因从事生产活动所获得的全部报酬。包括劳动者获得的各种形式的工资、奖金和津贴，既包括货币形式的，也包括实物形式的，还包括劳动者所享受的公费医疗和医药卫生费、上下班交通补贴、单位支付的社会保险费、住房公积金等。对于个体经济来说，其所有者所获得的劳动报酬和经营利润不易区分，这两部分统一作为劳动者报酬处理。

生产税净额 指生产税减生产补贴后的余额。生产税指政府对生产单位从事生产、销售和经营活动以及因从事生产活动使用某些生产要素(如固定资产、土地、劳动力)所征收的各种税、附加费和规费。生产补贴与生产税相反，指政府对生产单位的单方面转移支出，因此视为负生产税，包括政策亏损补贴、价格补贴等。

固定资产折旧 指一定时期内为弥补固定资产损耗按照规定的固定资产折旧率提取的固定资产折旧，或按国民经济核算统一规定的折旧率虚拟计算的固定资产折旧。它反映了固定资产在当期生产中的转移价值。各类企业和企业化管理的事业单位的固定资产折旧是指实际计提的折旧费；不计提折旧的政府机关、非企业化管理的事业单位和居民住房的固定资产折旧是按照统一规定的折旧率和固定资产原值计算的虚拟折旧。原则上，固定资产折旧应按固定资产当期的重置价值计算，但是目前我国尚不具备对全社会固定资产进行重估价的基础，所以暂时只能采用上述办法。

营业盈余 指常住单位创造的增加值扣除劳动者报酬、生产税净额和固定资产折旧后的余额。它相当于企业的营业利润加上生产补贴，但要扣除从利润中开支的工资和福利等。

支出法地区生产总值 是从最终使用的角度反映一个地区一定时期内生产活动最终成果的一种方法，包括最终消费支出、资本形成总额及货物和服务净流出三部分。计算公式为：

支出法国内生产总值=最终消费支出+资本形成总额+货物和服务净流出

最终消费支出 指常住单位为满足物质、文化和精神生活的需要，从本国经济领土和国外购买的货物和服务的支出。它不包括非常住单位在本国经济领土内的消费支出。最终消费支出分为居民消费支出和政府消费支出。

居民消费支出 指常住住户在一定时期内对于货物和服务的全部最终消费支出。居民消费支出除了直接以货币形式购买的货物和服务的消费支出外，还包括以其他方式获得的货物和服务的消费支出，即所谓的虚拟消费支出。居民虚拟消费支出包括如下几种类型：单位以实物报酬及实物转移的形式提供给劳动者的货物和服务；住户生产并由本住户消费了的货物和服务，其中的服务仅指住户的自有住房服务和付酬的家庭雇员提供的家庭和个人服务；金融机构提供的金融媒介服务；保险公司提供的保险服务。

政府消费支出 指政府部门为全社会提供的公共服务的消费支出和免费或以较低的价格向居民住户提供的货物和服务的净支出，前者等于政府服务的产出价值减去政府单位所获得的经营收入的价值，后者等于政府部门免费或以较低价格向居民住户提供的货物和服务的市场价值减去向住户收取的价值。

资本形成总额 指常住单位在一定时期内获得减去处置的固定资产和存货的净额，包括固定资本形成总额和存货增加两部分。

固定资本形成总额 指生产者在一定时期内获得的固定资产减处置的固定资产的价值总额。固定资产是通过生产活动生产出来的，且其使用年限在一年以上、单位价值在规定标准以上的资产，不包括自然资产。可分为有形固定资本形成总额和无形固定资本形成总额。有形固定资本形成总额包括一定时期内完成的建筑工程、安装工程和设备工器具购置(减处置)价值，以及土地改良、新增役、种、奶、毛、娱乐用牲畜和新增经济林木价值。无形固定资本形成总额包括矿藏的勘探、计算机软件等获得减处置。

存货增加 指常住单位在一定时期内存货实物量变动的市场价值，即期末价值减期初价值的差额，再扣除当期由于价格变动而产生的持有收益。存货增加可以是正值，也可以是负值，正值表示存货上升，负值表示存货下降。存货包括生产单位购进的原材料、燃料和储备物资等存货，以及生产单位生产的产成品、在制品和半成品等存货。

货物和服务净流出 指货物和服务流出减货物和服务流进的差额。流出包括常住单位向非常住单位出售或无偿转让的各种货物和服务的价值；流进包括常住单位从非常住单位购买或无偿得到的各种货物和服务的价值。由于服务活动的提供与使用同时发生，一般把常住单位从非常住单位得到的服务作为流进，非常住单位从常住单位得到的服务作为流出。

Explanatory Notes on Main Statistical Indicators

Average Annual Growth Rate Two methods for calculating average annual growth rate are applied, one is often called level approach, or the method of calculating geometric average, which is derived by comparing the level of the last year of the interval with that of the beginning year; the other is called accumulative approach or algebraic average or equation method, which is derived by the summation of the actual figure of each year in the interval divided by the figure in the base year. Usually the results calculated by the two methods are fairly close, but they differed sharply when uneven economic development occurred with striking fluctuations in growth.

Industrial Classification of the National Economy The new Industrial Classification of the National Economy (GB/T 4754–2002) is introduced starting from the compilation of 2003 annual statistics. The new revision was based on the 1994 classification and organized by the National Bureau of Statistics taking into consideration of the International Standards of the Industrial Classification of All Economic Activities (ISIC/Rev.3) of the United Nations, and the new Classification was promulgated by the National Administration of Quality Supervision, Inspection and Quarantine on May 10, 2002. The revised version of the Industrial Classification of the National Economy (GB/T 4754–2002) is composed of 20 major divisions, 95 divisions, 396 major groups and 913 groups, including 4 new major divisions, 3 new divisions, 28 major groups and 67 groups.

Registration Status of Enterprises Enterprises are classified into 3 categories, namely domestic–funded enterprises, enterprises with investment from Hong Kong, Macau and Taiwan, and enterprises with foreign investment, in the light of the registration status of an enterprise in industrial and commercial administration agencies. Domestic–funded enterprises include state–owned enterprises, collective–owned enterprises, cooperative enterprises, joint ownership enterprises, limited liability corporations, share–holding corporations Ltd., private enterprises and other enterprises. Included in the enterprises with investment from Hong Kong, Macau and Taiwan and enterprises with foreign investment are joint–venture enterprises, cooperative enterprises, sole investment enterprises and share–holding corporations Ltd. For government agencies, institutions and social organizations which are not requested to be registered in industrial and commercial administration agencies, they are classified mainly by their sources of funds and way of management.

State–owned Enterprises refer to non–corporation economic units where the entire assets are owned by the state and which have registered in accordance with the Regulation of the People's Republic of China on the Management of Registration of Corporate Enterprises. Excluded from this category are sole state–funded corporations in the limited liability corporations.

Collective–owned Enterprises refer to economic units where the assets are owned collectively and which have registered in accordance with the Regulation of the People's Republic of China on the Management of Registration of Corporate Enterprises.

Cooperative Enterprises refer to a form of collective economic units (enterprises) where capitals come mainly from employees as their shares, with certain proportion of capital from the outside, where production is organized on the basis of independent operation, independent accounting for profits and losses, joint work, democratic management, and a distribution system that integrates remuneration according to work with dividend according to capital share.

Joint Ownership Enterprises refer to economic units established by two or more corporate enterprises or corporate institutions of the same or different ownership, through joint investment on the basis of equality, voluntary participation and mutual benefits. They include state joint ownership enterprises, collective joint ownership enterprises, joint state–collective enterprises, other joint ownership enterprises.

Limited Liability Corporations refer to economic units established with investment from 2–50 investors and registered in accordance with the Regulation of the People's Republic of China on the Management of Registration of Corporations, each investor bearing limited liability to the corporation depending on its share of investment, and the corporation bearing liability to its debt to the maximum of its total assets. Limited liability corporations include exclusive state-funded limited liability corporations and other limited liability corporations.

Share-holding Corporations Ltd. refer to economic units registered in accordance with the Regulation of the People's Republic of China on the Management of Registration of Corporations, with total registered capitals divided into equal shares and raised through issuing stocks. Each investor bears limited liability to the corporation depending on the holding of shares, and the corporation bears liability to its debt to the maximum of its total assets.

Private Enterprises refer to profit-making economic units invested and established by natural persons, or controlled by natural persons using employed labour. Included in this category are private limited liability corporations, private share-holding corporations Ltd., private partnership enterprises and private-funded enterprises registered in accordance with the Corporation Law, Partnership Enterprises Law and Interim Regulations on Private Enterprises .

Other Domestic-funded Enterprises refer to domestic-funded economic units other than those mentioned above.

Cooperative Enterprises with Funds from Hong Kong Macau and Taiwan established by investors from Hong Kong, Macau and Taiwan with enterprises in the mainland of China in accordance with the Law of the People's Republic of China on Sino-foreign Cooperative Enterprises and other relevant laws, where the investment or provision of facilities, and the share of profits and risks is stipulated in the cooperative contract.

Enterprises with Sole (exclusive) Investment from Hong Kong, Macau and Taiwan refer to enterprises established in the mainland of China with exclusive investment from investors from Hong Kong, Macau and Taiwan in accordance with the Law of the People's Republic of China on Foreign-Funded Enterprises and other relevant laws.

Share-holding Corporations Ltd. with Investment from Hong Kong, Macau and Taiwan refer to share-holding corporations Ltd. established with the approval from the former Ministry of Foreign Trade and Economic Relations in line with relevant state regulations, where the share of investment from Hong Kong, Macau or Taiwan businessmen exceeds 25% of the total registered capital of the corporation. In case the share of investment from Hong Kong, Macau or Taiwan is less than 25% of the total registered capital, the enterprise is to be classified as domestic-funded share-holding corporation Ltd.

Joint-venture Enterprises with Foreign Investment refer to enterprises jointly established by foreign enterprises or foreigners with enterprises in the mainland of China in accordance with the Law of the People's Republic of China on Sino-foreign Joint Venture Enterprises and other relevant laws, where the share of investment, profits and risks is stipulated in the contract.

Cooperation Enterprises with Foreign Investment refer to enterprises jointly established by foreign enterprises or foreigners with enterprises in the mainland of China in accordance with the Law of the People's Republic of China on Sino-foreign Cooperative Enterprises and other relevant laws, where the investment or provision of facilities, and the share of profits and risks is stipulated in the cooperative contract.

Enterprises with Sole (exclusive) Foreign Investment refer to enterprises established in the mainland of China with exclusive investment from foreign investors in accordance with the Law of the People's Republic of China on Foreign-Funded Enterprises and other relevant laws.

Share-holding Corporations Ltd. with Foreign Investment refer to share-holding corporations Ltd. established with the approval from the Ministry of Foreign Trade and Economic Relations in line with relevant state regulations, where the share of investment from foreign investors exceeds 25% of the total registered capital of the corporation. In case the share of foreign investment is less than 25% of the total registered capital, the enterprise is to be classified as domestic-funded share-holding corporation Ltd.

Government Agencies, Institutions and Social Organizations are classified into following categories by source of funds and way of management taking reference of the registration status of enterprises:

(1) Government agencies: include state and party agencies, classified in principle as state-owned. There are exceptions, such as sup-

ply and marketing cooperatives which are classified as collective–owned.

(2) Institutions: include institutions of various types established with the approval by organization and staffing departments of the government, but exclude institutions where enterprise management system is introduced. Institutions are further classified as follows:

(a) Institutions whose main budget is listed in the government budget appropriations or extra–budget funds, or allocated from the budget of their competent government agencies. Such institutions are classified as state–owned.

(b) Institutions whose budget mainly comes from collective units. Such institutions are classified as collective–owned.

(c) Institutions other than those mentioned above whose source of budget is not clear. Such institutions are classified by way of management.

(3) Social organizations: include social organizations established with the approval from the Ministry of Civil Affairs, and organizations that are not covered by social organization management regulations such as trade unions, womens federations etc.. Social organizations are further classified as follows:

(a) Social organizations that are not covered by social organization management regulations of the Ministry of Civil Affairs such as trade unions, womens federations, communist youth leagues, youth associations, industrial and commerce associations, scientists associations, overseas Chinese associations, etc., foundations and fund management organizations established with funds from the state, and social organizations whose funds mainly come from the budget of their competent government agencies. Such institutions are classified as state–owned.

(b) Social organizations whose budget mainly comes from collective units. Such institutions are classified as collective–owned.

(c) Social organizations established by individual or a group of citizens, which are classified as private.

(d) Social organizations other than those mentioned above whose source of budget is not clear. Such organizations are classified by way of management.

Gross Domestic Product (GDP) refers to the final products at market prices produced by all resident units in a country (or a region) during a certain period of time. Gross domestic product is expressed in three different forms, i.e. value, income, and products respectively. GDP in its value form refers to the total value of all goods and services produced by all resident units during a certain period of time, minus the total value of input of goods and services of the nature of non–fixed assets; in other term, it is the sum of the value–added of all resident units. GDP in the form of income includes the income created by all resident units and distributed to resident and non–resident units. GDP in the form of products refers to the value of all goods and services for final consumption by all resident units minus the net exports of goods and services during a given period of time. In the practice of national accounting, gross domestic product is calculated with three approaches, i.e. production approach, income approach and expenditure approach, which reflect gross domestic product and its composition from different aspects.

Gross National Income (GNI) also known as gross national product, refers to the final result of the primary distribution of the income created by all the resident units of a country (or a region) during a certain period of time. The value–added created by the resident units of a country engaged in production activities is distributed, during the primary distribution, mainly to the resident units of that country, while part of it is distributed to the non–resident units in the form of production tax and import duties (minus subsidies to production and import), remuneration for the labourers and property income. At the meantime, a part of the value–added created abroad is distributed to the resident units of the country in the form of production tax and import duties (minus subsidies to production and import), remuneration for the labourers and property income. The concept of gross national income is thus developed, which equals to the gross domestic product plus the net factor income from abroad. Unlike the gross domestic product which is a concept of production, the gross national income is a concept of income.

Three Industries Classification of economic activities into three branches of industries is a common practice in the world, although the grouping varies to some extent form country to country. In China economic activities are categorized into following industries:

Primary industry: refers to agriculture, forestry, animal husbandry and fishery.

Secondary industry: refers to mining and quarrying, manufacturing, production and supply of electricity, water and gas, and construction.

Tertiary industry: refers to all other economic activities not included in primary or secondary industry.

Labourers Remuneration refers to the whole payment of various forms earned by the labourers from the productive activities they are engaged in. It includes wages, bonuses and allowances the labourers earned in monetary form and in kind. It also includes the free medical services provided to the labourers and the medicine expenses, traffic subsidies and social insurance, housing fund paid by the employers. As the individual economy is concerned, since the labourers remuneration is not easily distinguished from the operating profit, both are treated as labourers remuneration.

Net Taxes on Production refers to the difference of the taxes on production minus the subsidies on production. The taxes on production refers to the various taxes, extra charges and fees levied on the production units on their production, sale and business activities as well as on the use of some factors of production, such as fixed assets, land and labour force in the production activities they are engaged in. In contrast to the taxes on production, the subsidies on production refer to the unilateral government transfer to the production units and are therefore regarded as negative taxes on production. They include subsidies on the loss due to implementation of government policies, price subsidies, etc.

Depreciation of Fixed Assets refers to the depreciation of fixed assets of a given period, drawn in accordance with the stipulated depreciation rate for the purpose of compensating the wear loss of the fixed assets or the depreciation of fixed assets calculated in a fictitious way in accordance with the stipulated unified depreciation rate in the national economic accounting system. It reflects the value of transfer of the fixed assets in the production of the current period. The depreciation of fixed assets in various enterprises and institutions managed as enterprises refers to the depreciation expenses actually drawn. In government agencies and institutions not managed as enterprises which do not draw the depreciation expenses, as well as for the houses of residents, the depreciation of fixed assets is the imputed depreciation, which is calculated in accordance with the stipulated unified depreciation rate. In principle, the depreciation of fixed assets should be calculated on the basis of the re–purchased value of the fixed assets. However, there is no actual condition to re–evaluate all the fixed assets in China. Therefore, the above–mentioned methods are temporarily adopted at present.

Operating Surplus refers to the balance of the value added created by the resident units deducting the labourers remuneration, net taxes on production and the depreciation of fixed assets. It is equivalent to the business profit of the enterprises plus subsidies on production, but the wages and welfare expenses paid from the profits should be deducted.

GDP by Expenditure Approach refers to the method of measuring the final results of production activities of a country (region) during a given period from the perspective of final use. It includes final consumption expenditure, total capital formation and net export of goods and services, i.e.:

GDP by expenditure approach = final consumption expenditure + total capital formation + net export of goods and services

Final ConsumptionExpenditure refers to the total expenditure of resident units for purchases of goods and services from domestic economic territory and abroad to meet the requirements of material, cultural and spiritual life. It excludes the expenditure of non–resident units on consumption in the economic territory of the country. The final consumption expenditure is broken down into household consumption expenditure and government consumption expenditure.

Households ConsumptionExpenditure refers to the total expenditure of resident households on the final consumption of goods and services. In addition to the consumption of goods and services bought by the households directly with money, the households consumption expenditure also includes expenditure on goods and services obtained by the households in other ways, i.e. the so–called imputed consumption expenditure, which includes the following: (a) the goods and services provided to the households by the employer in the form of payment in kind and transfer in kind; (b) goods and services produced and consumed by the households themselves, in which the services refer only to the owner–occupied housing and domestic and individual services provided by the paid household workers; (c) financial intermediate services provided by financial institutions; (d) insurance services provided by insurance companies.

Government ConsumptionExpenditure refers to the expenditure on the consumption of the public services provided by the government to the whole society and the net expenditure on the goods and services provided by the government to the households free of charge or at low prices. The former equals to the output value of the government services minus the value of operating income obtained by the government departments. The latter equals to the market value of the goods and services provided by the government free of charge or at low prices to the households minus the value received by the government from the households.

Total Capital Formation refers to the fixed assets acquired minus those disposed of and the net value of inventory, including the total fixed capital formation and the increase in inventory.

Total Fixed Capital Formation refers to the value of fixed assets acquired minus those disposed of during a given period. Fixed assets are the assets produced through production activities with specified unit value which could be used for over one year, excluding natural assets. Total fixed capital formation can be categorized into total tangible capital formation and total intangible capital formation. The total tangible capital formation include the value of the construction projects, installation projects completed and the equipment, apparatus and instruments purchased as well as the value of land improved, the value of draught animals, breeding stock, animals for milk, wool and for recreational purpose, and the newly increased forest with economic value during a given period. The total intangible capital formation includes the prospecting of minerals, the acquisition of computer software minus the disposal of them.

Increase in Inventory refers to the market value of the change in inventory of resident units during a given period, i.e. the difference of value between the beginning and the end of the period minus the current gains due to the change in prices. The increase in inventory can be positive or negative. A positive value indicates the increase in inventory while a negative value indicates the decrease in stock. The inventory includes the raw materials, fuels and reserve materials purchased by the production units as well as the inventory of finished products, semi–finished products, work–in–progress, etc.

Outflow of Goods and Services refers to the difference of the exports of goods and services minus the imports of goods and services. The imports include the value of various goods and services sold or gratuitously transferred by the resident units to the non–resident units. The imports include the value of various goods and services purchased or gratuitously acquired by the resident units from the non–resident units. Because the provision of services and the use of them happen simultaneously, the acquisition of services by the resident units from abroad is usually treated as import while the acquisition of services by non–resident units in this country is usually treated as export. The export and import of goods are calculated at FOB.

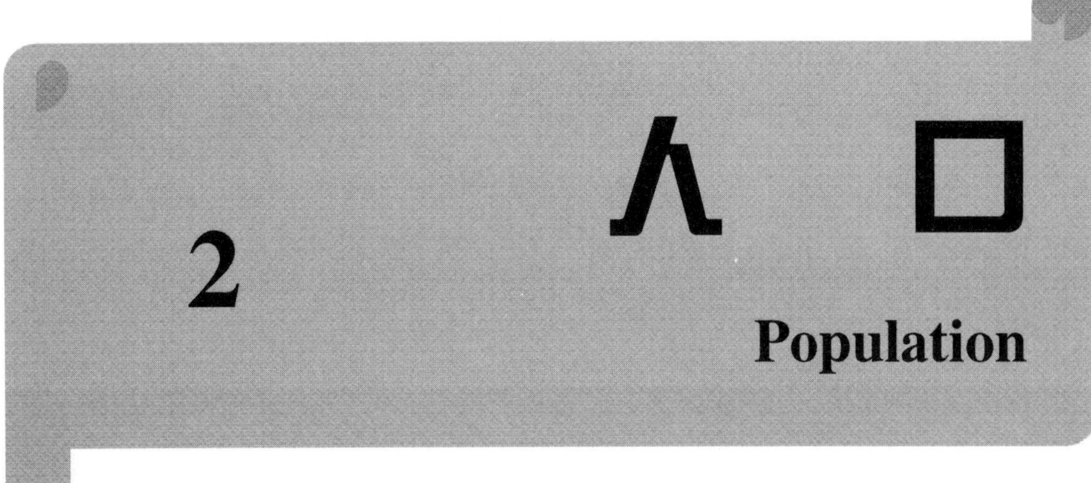

2 人口

Population

2-1 人 口 数
POPULATION

单位:万人 (年底数)(number at year-end) (10 000 persons)

年份	户籍人口			常住人口		
Year	Total Population	男 Male	女 Female	Total Population	男 Male	女 Female
1952	2745.0	1414.6	1330.4			
1957	3062.4	1579.7	1482.7			
1965	3504.5	1793.4	1711.2			
1975	4408.2	2261.6	2146.5			
1980	4684.5	2401.7	2282.7			
1982	4800.9	2464.3	2336.6	4780.8	2454.8	2326.0
1983	4835.3	2485.6	2349.8	4846.8	2491.8	2355.0
1984	4876.1	2510.9	2365.2	4913.8	2528.8	2384.0
1985	4931.0	2540.0	2391.0	4980.8	2565.8	2414.0
1986	4989.0	2573.4	2415.6	5047.8	2602.8	2444.1
1987	5058.1	2608.7	2449.4	5120.3	2639.8	2479.5
1988	5144.2	2652.1	2492.1	5184.9	2673.1	2511.8
1989	5223.9	2694.6	2529.3	5258.8	2712.6	2546.3
1990	5373.5	2771.5	2602.0	5439.3	2805.5	2633.8
1991	5446.8	2805.4	2641.4	5512.3	2839.2	2673.2
1992	5513.6	2841.3	2672.4	5579.9	2862.2	2717.6
1993	5590.5	2880.8	2709.6	5653.5	2913.3	2740.2
1994	5656.8	2915.6	2741.2	5718.8	2947.5	2771.3
1995	5727.1	2952.2	2775.0	5772.1	2959.6	2812.5
1996	5776.3	2979.6	2796.8	5825.1	3004.8	2820.3
1997	5838.8	3014.1	2824.8	5872.6	3016.6	2856.0
1998	5890.6	3039.9	2850.7	5907.2	3032.7	2874.6
1999	5942.5	3061.8	2880.7	5938.0	3031.9	2906.1
2000	5936.0	3066.1	2869.9	5646.0	2939.3	2706.7
2001	5956.6	3073.2	2883.4	5658.0	2919.1	2738.9
2002	5978.2	3086.2	2892.0	5672.0	2928.1	2743.9
2003	6000.5	3109.9	2890.6	5685.0	2946.3	2738.7
2004	6001.3	3107.8	2893.5	5698.0	2950.7	2747.3
2005	5984.1	3102.4	2881.7	5710.0	2960.2	2749.8
2006	6038.3	3129.7	2908.7	5693.0	2950.6	2742.4
2007	6084.9	3154.0	2930.9	5699.0	2953.9	2745.1
2008	6110.8	3167.5	2943.3	5711.0	2960.2	2750.8
2009	6141.9	3185.5	2956.4	5720.0	2966.6	2753.4
2010	6176.0	3202.0	2974.0	5723.8	2939.3	2784.5
2011	6164.1	3194.0	2970.1	5758.0	2956.1	2802.0
2012	6165.4	3193.9	2971.4	5779.0	2963.9	2815.1
2013	6170.6	3199.5	2971.1	5799.0	2972.0	2827.0
2014	6162.3	3198.1	2964.2	5816.0	2980.3	2835.7
2015	6138.9	3190.1	2948.8	5851.5	2984.5	2867.0

2-2 人口城乡构成
COMPOSITION OF URBAN AND RURAL POPULATION

单位:万人 (年底数)(number at year-end) (10 000 persons)

年份 Year	Total Population	城镇人口 Urban Population	乡村人口 Rural Population
1952	2745.00	271.41	2416.17
1957	3062.41	411.69	2650.72
1965	3504.54	485.06	3019.48
1975	4408.15	626.22	3781.93
1980	4684.45	786.49	3897.96
1982	4780.81	1026.72	3754.09
1983	4846.81	1069.23	3777.58
1984	4913.81	1078.22	3835.59
1985	4980.81	1464.65	3516.16
1986	5047.83	1187.23	3860.60
1987	5120.27	1288.61	3831.66
1988	5184.94	1389.99	3794.95
1989	5258.83	1491.37	3767.46
1990	5439.29	1551.51	3887.78
1991	5512.33	1433.06	4079.27
1992	5579.85	1637.68	3942.17
1993	5653.48	1731.66	3921.82
1994	5718.81	1604.13	4114.68
1995	5772.07	1800.89	3971.18
1996	5825.13	1965.40	3859.73
1997	5872.60	1834.60	4038.00
1998	5907.23	1884.41	4022.82
1999	5938.03	1990.17	3947.86
2000	5646.00	2285.11	3360.89
2001	5658.00	2308.50	3349.50
2002	5672.00	2348.20	3323.80
2003	5685.00	2387.70	3297.30
2004	5698.00	2427.30	2466.70
2005	5710.00	2466.70	3243.30
2006	5693.00	2493.50	3199.50
2007	5699.00	2524.70	3174.30
2008	5711.00	2581.40	3129.60
2009	5720.00	2631.20	3088.80
2010	5723.77	2844.51	2879.26
2011	5758.00	2984.32	2773.68
2012	5779.00	3091.77	2687.23
2013	5799.00	3161.03	2637.97
2014	5816.00	3237.80	2578.20
2015	5851.50	3326.58	2524.92

注:1981年及以前数据为户籍统计数;1982、1990、2000、2010年数据为当年人口普查时点数据;其余年份数据为年度人口抽样调查推算数据(下相关表同)。

2-3 人口自然变动
NATURAL CHANGE OF POLULATION

年 份	人口变动数(万人) Number of Population Changed (10 000 persons)			变动系数(‰) Growth Rates		
Year	出生数 Number of Birth	死亡数 Number of Death	自然增长数 Number of Nature Growth	出生率 Birth Rate	死亡率 Death Rate	自然增长率 Natural Growth Rate
1965	121.48	34.75	86.73	35.10	10.04	25.06
1975	90.80	34.52	56.28	20.74	7.88	12.86
1980	94.84	32.59	62.25	20.36	7.00	13.36
1985	97.83	37.37	60.46	19.95	7.62	12.33
1986	107.09	39.45	67.64	21.01	7.74	13.27
1987	108.56	36.12	72.44	21.43	7.13	14.30
1988	97.62	32.95	64.67	19.08	6.44	12.64
1989	110.13	36.24	73.89	21.09	6.94	14.15
1990	114.40	38.66	75.74	21.60	7.30	14.30
1991	113.34	40.30	73.04	20.70	7.36	13.34
1992	105.60	38.08	67.52	19.05	6.87	12.18
1993	112.55	38.92	73.63	20.04	6.93	13.11
1994	103.31	37.98	65.33	18.17	6.68	11.49
1995	92.96	39.70	53.26	16.18	6.91	9.27
1996	93.24	40.18	53.06	16.08	6.93	9.15
1997	86.62	39.13	47.49	14.81	6.69	8.12
1998	74.09	39.46	34.63	12.58	6.70	5.88
1999	68.52	37.73	30.79	11.57	6.37	5.20
2000	57.76	35.75	22.01	9.71	6.01	3.70
2001	50.84	36.27	14.57	8.51	6.07	2.44
2002	50.10	36.90	13.20	8.38	6.17	2.21
2003	49.50	35.60	13.90	8.26	5.94	2.32
2004	50.66	36.23	14.43	8.43	6.03	2.40
2005	52.60	34.30	18.30	8.74	5.69	3.05
2006	54.80	35.90	18.90	9.08	5.95	3.13
2007	55.69	36.12	19.57	9.19	5.96	3.23
2008	55.98	39.51	16.47	9.21	6.50	2.71
2009	57.80	36.58	21.22	9.48	6.00	3.48
2010	59.30	34.46	24.84	10.36	6.02	4.34
2011	59.67	34.52	25.15	10.39	6.01	4.38
2012	63.45	35.30	28.15	11.00	6.12	4.88
2013	64.14	35.60	28.54	11.08	6.15	4.93
2014	68.88	40.42	28.46	11.86	6.96	4.90
2015	62.65	34.01	28.64	10.74	5.83	4.91

2-4 分市、州、县年底人口数(2015)
POPULATION OF CITIES, TOWNS, AND COUNTIES OF HUBEI AT YEAR-END(2015)

单位: 万人 (10 000 persons)

地 区	Region	户籍人口(万人) Total Population	常住人口(万人) Population of Permnant Residents	地 区	Region	户籍人口(万人) Total Population	常住人口(万人) Population of Permnant Residents
全 省	**Province**	**6138.91**	**5851.50**	丹江口市	Danjiangkou	46.26	44.43
武汉市	**Wuhan**	**829.27**	**1060.77**	**宜昌市**	**Yichang**	**398.18**	**411.50**
江岸区	Jiang'an	71.95	95.43	西陵区	Xiling	43.60	53.94
江汉区	Jianghan	48.64	72.64	伍家岗区	Wujiagang	16.78	22.71
硚口区	Qiaokou	52.65	86.49	点军区	Dianjun	10.51	10.54
汉阳区	Hanyang	58.54	63.92	猇亭区	Xiaoting	5.06	6.43
武昌区	Wuchang	109.08	126.80	夷陵区	Yiling	52.34	52.41
青山区	Qingshan	43.37	52.35	远安县	Yuan'an	19.45	18.73
洪山区	Hongshan	91.41	156.51	兴山县	Xingshan	16.99	17.10
东西湖区	Dongxihu	28.85	52.70	秭归县	Zigui	38.02	36.17
汉南区	Hannan	11.32	13.10	长阳县	Changyang	39.89	38.64
蔡甸区	Caidian	45.66	70.35	五峰县	Wufeng	20.04	18.82
江夏区	Jiangxia	59.05	87.70	宜都市	Yidu	39.21	39.00
黄陂区	Huangpi	112.48	94.51	当阳市	Dangyang	47.66	46.86
新洲区	Xinzhou	96.26	88.27	枝江市	Zhijiang	48.66	50.15
黄石市	**Huangshi**	**267.97**	**245.80**	**襄阳市**	**Xiangyang**	**591.58**	**561.40**
黄石港区	Huangshigang	20.50	23.74	襄城区	Xiangcheng	45.90	49.26
西塞山区	Xisai mountainous	21.50	24.68	樊城区	Fancheng	78.84	89.10
下陆区	Xialu	15.41	18.26	襄州区	Xiangzhou	99.90	91.55
铁山区	Tieshan	5.18	5.83	南漳县	Nanzhang	58.06	54.05
大冶市	Daye	97.38	90.54	谷城县	Gucheng	59.92	52.35
阳新县	Yangxin	107.99	82.75	保康县	Baokang	26.92	25.30
十堰市		**345.94**	**338.30**	老河口市	Laohekou	52.22	48.53
茅箭区	Maojian	28.91	41.80	枣阳市	Zaoyang	113.56	99.10
张湾区	Zhangwan	26.16	38.39	宜城市	Yicheng	56.26	52.16
郧阳区	Yunyang	62.85	56.36	**鄂州市**	**Ezhou**	**110.29**	**105.95**
郧西县	Yunxi	51.72	45.21	梁子湖区	Liangzihu	18.87	14.43
竹山县	Zhushan	46.32	41.38	华容区	Huarong	26.25	24.01
竹溪县	Zhuxi	35.96	31.15	鄂城区	Ercheng	65.17	67.51
房 县	Fang	47.76	39.58				

2-4 续表 Continued

单位: 万人 (10 000 persons)

地 区	Regions	户籍人口 Total Population	常住人口 Permnant Population	地 区	Regions	户籍人口 Total Population	常住人口 Permnant Population
荆门市	**Jingmen**	**299.09**	**289.63**	蕲春县	Hanchun	101.27	77.66
东宝区	Dongbao	36.83	37.27	黄梅县	Huangmei	104.36	86.47
掇刀区	Zhuodao	32.64	30.64	麻城市	Macheng	116.66	87.95
京山县	Jingshan	64.41	62.73	武穴市	Wuxue	81.72	65.44
沙洋县	Shayang	59.31	57.44	**咸宁市**	**Xianning**	**300.41**	**250.70**
钟祥市	Zhongxiang	105.90	101.55	咸安区	Xian'an	61.49	52.41
孝感市	**Xiaogan**	**526.48**	**487.80**	嘉鱼县	Jiayu	37.00	31.40
孝南区	Xiaonan	97.34	92.20	通城县	Tongcheng	51.76	41.04
孝昌县	Xiaochang	67.13	59.63	崇阳县	Congyang	50.18	40.14
大悟县	Dawu	63.35	62.05	通山县	Tongshan	46.89	37.08
云梦县	Yunmeng	58.04	53.00	赤壁市	Chibi	53.08	48.63
应城市	Yingcheng	66.73	60.01	**随州市**	**Suizhou**	**250.97**	**219.08**
安陆市	Anlu	62.23	57.92	曾都区	Zengdu	64.98	62.98
汉川市	Hanchuan	111.66	102.99	随县	Sui	93.28	79.54
荆州市	**Jingzhou**	**643.19**	**570.59**	广水市	Guangshui	92.71	76.56
沙市区	Shashi	53.55	65.48	**恩施州**	**Enshi Prefecture**	**402.61**	**332.70**
荆州区	Jingzhou	54.74	57.47	恩施市	Enshi	80.55	76.87
公安县	Gong'an	101.16	88.01	利川市	Jianli	91.63	66.20
监利县	Jianli	154.91	106.99	建始县	Jianshi	51.38	41.64
江陵县	Jianglin	39.44	33.16	巴东县	Badong	49.26	42.50
石首市	Shishou	62.92	57.12	宣恩县	Xuan'en	36.04	30.26
洪湖市	Honghu	92.74	84.90	咸丰县	Xianfeng	38.57	30.48
松滋市	Songzi	83.74	77.46	来凤县	Laifeng	33.11	24.55
黄冈市	**Huanggang**	**744.42**	**629.10**	鹤峰县	Hefeng	22.08	20.20
黄州区	Huangzhou	34.82	37.68	**省直管单位**	**Jurisdictional**		
团风县	Tuanfeng	37.53	34.26	仙桃市	Xiantao	156.08	115.50
红安县	Hong'an	65.60	60.45	潜江市	Qianjiang	101.77	95.80
罗田县	Luotian	59.64	54.94	天门市	Tianmen	162.80	129.20
英山县	Yingshan	40.31	36.10	**神农架林区**	**Shennongjian**	**7.86**	**7.68**
浠水县	Xishui	102.50	88.15				

主要统计指标解释

人口数 指一定时点、一定地区范围内有生命的个人总和。

年度统计的年末人口数指每年12月31日24时的人口数。

城镇人口和乡村人口 城镇人口是指居住在城镇范围内的全部常住人口；乡村人口是除上述人口以外的全部人口。

出生率(又称粗出生率) 指在一定时期内(通常为一年)一定地区的出生人数与同期内平均人数(或期中人数)之比，用千分率表示。本资料中的出生率指年出生率，其计算公式为：

$$出生率=\frac{年出生人数}{年平均人数}\times 1000‰$$

式中：出生人数指活产婴儿，即胎儿脱离母体时(不管怀孕月数)，有过呼吸或其他生命现象。年平均人数指年初、年底人口数的平均数，也可用年中人口数代替。

死亡率(又称粗死亡率) 指在一定时期内(通常为一年)一定地区的死亡人数与同期内平均人数(或期中人数)之比，用千分率表示。本资料中的死亡率指年死亡率，其计算公式为：

$$死亡率=\frac{年死亡人数}{年平均人数}\times 1000‰$$

人口自然增长率 指在一定时期内(通常为一年)人口自然增加数(出生人数减死亡人数)与该时期内平均人数(或期中人数)之比，用千分率表示。计算公式为：

$$人口自然增长率=\frac{本年出生人数-本年死亡人数}{年平均人数}\times 1000‰$$
$$=人口出生率-人口死亡率$$

Explanatory Notes on Main Statistical Indicators

Total Population refers to the total number of people alive at a certain point of time within a given area.

The annual statistics on total population is taken at midnight, the 31st of December.

Urban Population and Rural Population Urban population refer to all people residing in cities and towns, while rural population refer to population other than urban population.

Birth Rate (or Crude Birth Rate) refers to the ratio of the number of births to the average population (or mid-period population) during a certain period of time (usually a year), expressed in ‰. Birth rate in the chapter refers to annual birth rate. The following formula is used:

Birth Rate = (Number of Births/Average Number of Population) × 1000‰

Number of births in the formula refers to live births, i.e. when a baby has breathed or showed any vital phenomena regardless of the length of pregnancy.

Annual average number of population is the average of the number of population at the beginning of the year and that at the end of the year. Sometimes it is substituted by the mid–year population.

Death Rate (or Crude Death Rate) refers to the ratio of the number of deaths to the average population (or mid–period population) during a certain period of time (usually a year), expressed in ‰. Death rate in the chapter refers to annual death rate. The following formula is used:

Death Rate= (Number of Deaths/Annual Average Number of Population) × 1000‰

Natural Growth Rate of Population refers to the ratio of natural increase in population (number of births minus number of deaths) in a certain period of time (usually a year) to the average population (or mid–period population) of the same period, expressed in ‰. The following formula is applied:

Natural Growth Rate of Population = [(Number of Births–Number of Deaths)/Average Number of Population] × 1000‰

Natural Growth Rate of Population = Birth Rate–Death Rate

3 就业人员和职工工资

Employment and Wages

3-1 全社会从业人员
NUMBER OF EMPLOYED PERSONS

单位：万人 (10 000 person)

年份 Year	合计 Total	按城乡分 Grouped by Areas		按产业分 Grouped by Industries		
		城镇 Urban	乡村 Rural	第一产业 Primary Industry	第二产业 Secondary Industry	第三产业 Tertiary Industry
1952	1020.30	141.60	878.70			
1965	1404.20	222.70	1181.60			
1970	1618.50	278.00	1340.80			
1975	1802.50	381.70	1420.80			
1978	1910.40	458.00	1452.30	1470.60	269.00	170.80
1980	1986.90	507.20	1479.70	1453.70	286.30	247.00
1985	2238.10	637.60	1600.50	1383.30	485.40	369.50
1990	3040.40	890.80	2149.60	1859.80	628.50	552.10
1991	3082.70	909.40	2173.30	1897.40	623.00	562.30
1992	3118.60	923.10	2195.50	1869.00	650.90	598.70
1993	3157.60	940.90	2216.70	1818.80	684.60	654.20
1994	3196.90	980.10	2216.80	1760.50	717.10	719.30
1995	3232.50	1015.00	2217.50	1697.00	743.50	792.00
1996	3275.50	1050.80	2224.70	1677.10	746.80	851.60
1997	3311.20	1070.50	2240.70	1663.20	752.00	896.00
1998	3328.20	1093.60	2234.60	1612.50	705.60	1010.10
1999	3358.10	1110.50	2247.60	1612.60	697.80	1047.70
2000	3384.90	1123.80	2261.10	1625.10	702.40	1057.40
2001	3414.50	1148.70	2265.80	1639.00	706.80	1068.70
2002	3443.00	1177.00	2266.00	1652.60	704.10	1086.30
2003	3476.00	1211.00	2265.00	1661.50	712.60	1101.90
2004	3507.00	1245.00	2262.00	1672.90	720.30	1113.80
2005	3537.00	1271.00	2266.00	1687.30	725.00	1124.70
2006	3564.00	1297.00	2267.00	1694.70	732.40	1136.90
2007	3584.00	1322.00	2262.00	1697.00	740.10	1146.90
2008	3607.00	1337.00	2270.00	1707.91	730.42	1168.67
2009	3622.00	1357.00	2265.00	1702.30	736.60	1183.10
2010	3645.00	1382.60	2262.40	1691.10	754.70	1199.20
2011	3672.00	1413.00	2259.00	1678.10	771.12	1222.78
2012	3687.00	1430.60	2256.40	1638.90	781.60	1266.50
2013	3692.00	1438.00	2254.00	1582.00	793.80	1316.20
2014	3687.50	1437.60	2249.90	1487.00	834.30	1366.20
2015	3658.00	1935.00	1723.00	1404.00	834.00	1420.00

注：因2015年开展全国1%人口抽样调查，根据调查结果对部分数据进行修正，使2015年全省全社会从业人员数据产生较大波动。

3-2 分行业城镇单位从业人员数(2015)
NUMBER OF EMPLOYEES IN URBAN UNITS BY SECTOR (2015)

单位：人 (person)

行业	Sector	城镇全部单位 All the Units In Urban Area	国有经济单位 State Owned Units	城镇集体单位 Urban Collective Owned Units	其他经济单位 Other Units	城镇私营单位 Urban Private Units
总计	**Total**	**10338541**	**2776395**	**138456**	**4208479**	**3215211**
农、林、牧、渔业	Farming,Forest,Herd, ishery	132795	89084	1039	1928	40744
采矿业	Mining and Quarrying	156775	10527	3805	56461	85982
制造业	Manufacturing	3354739	148894	22913	1722401	1460531
电力、燃气及水的生产和供应业	Power, Gas and water production and supply	180721	112670	1226	49155	17670
建筑业	Construction	2039136	79133	38192	1267710	654101
批发和零售业	Wholesale and Retail sale	825599	43022	18169	332408	432000
交通运输、仓储和邮政业	Transportation, storage and post	408142	191633	4529	147915	64065
住宿和餐饮业	Hotel and Catering	249272	8866	1318	89312	149776
信息传输、软件和信息技术服务业	Information Transmission, Software and Computer Services	146040	16954	221	97484	31381
金融业	Banking	200265	71359	12418	110909	5579
房地产业	Real Estate	212710	8780	1132	121324	81474
租赁和商务服务业	Leasing and Commerical Services	147322	31284	3646	54797	57595
科学研究、技术服务业	Scietific Research, polytechnical	181022	92637	2452	67715	18218
水利、环境和公共设施管理业	Water Conservance, Environment and Public Facilities Management	121745	93186	7409	12926	8224
居民服务、修理和其他服务业	Resident Service and Others	55333	4825	723	10030	39755
教育	Education	772038	701098	3715	33907	33318
卫生和社会工作	Health, Social Security and	427497	383067	14970	19999	9461
文化、体育和娱乐业	Culture, Sports and Entertainment	88393	50653	493	11910	25337
公共管理、社会保障和社会组织	Public management, social security and social organization	638997	638723	86	188	

注：城镇全部单位统计范围含城镇私营单位。(后表未经特别注明均同此口径)
Note: All Statistics of Units in Urban Areas of 2010 including all the private run unit.
(The following tables if without specific notes are considered the same standard with this one.)

3-3 分行业在岗职工人数(2015)
NUMBER OF STAFF AND WORKERS BY SECTOR(2015)

单位：人 (person)

行业	Sector	城镇全部单位 All the Units In Urban Area	国有经济单位 State Owned Units	城镇集体单位 Urban Collective Owned Units	其他经济单位 Other Units	城镇私营单位 Urban Private Units
总计	Total	9800097	2602666	126398	3855822	3215211
农、林、牧、渔业	Farming, Forest, Herd, Fishery	112916	69365	980	1827	40744
采矿业	Mining and Quarrying	151155	8193	3720	53260	85982
制造业	Manufacturing	3312131	142446	21939	1687215	1460531
电力、燃气及水的生产和供应业	Power, Gas and water production and supply	178242	111185	1221	48166	17670
建筑业	Construction	1782159	66882	34885	1026291	654101
批发和零售业	Wholesale and Retail sale	809608	41741	15540	320327	432000
交通运输、仓储和邮政业	Transportation, storage and post	395111	184897	4314	141835	64065
住宿和餐饮业	Hotel and Catering	246775	8530	1231	87238	149776
信息传输、软件和信息技术服务业	Information Transmission, Software and Computer Services	142131	16334	221	94195	31381
金融业	Banking	165235	65148	12215	82293	5579
房地产业	Real Estate	205758	7864	1003	115417	81474
租赁和商务服务业	Leasing and Commerical Services	143897	30733	3515	52054	57595
科学研究、技术服务业	Scietific Research, polytechnical	169122	87155	2286	61463	18218
水利、环境和公共设施 管理业	Water Conservance, Environment and Public Facilities Management	101006	75959	4301	12522	8224
居民服务、修理和其他服务业	Resident Service and Others	53735	4209	578	9193	39755
教育	Education	736949	668151	3521	31959	33318
卫生和社会工作	Health, Social Security and	407637	364385	14366	19425	9461
文化、体育和娱乐业	Culture, Sports and Entertainment	85503	48682	484	11000	25337
公共管理、社会保障和社会组织	Public management, social security and social organization	601027	600807	78	142	

3-4 分行业在岗女职工人数(2015)
NUMBER OF FEMALE STAFF AND WORKERS BY SECTOR(2015)

单位：人 (person)

行业	Sector	城镇全部单位(不含私营单位) All the Units In Urban Area	国有经济单位 State Owned Units	城镇集体单位 Urban Collective Owned Units	其他经济单位 Urban Private Units
总计	**Total**	**2436846**	**1035366**	**45373**	**1356107**
农、林、牧、渔业	Farming, Forest, Herd, Fishery	38006	37534	306	166
采矿业	Mining and Quarrying	14077	2828	248	11001
制造业	Manufacturing	733428	37565	8930	686933
电力、燃气及水的生产和供应业	Power, Gas and water production and supply	48384	32666	421	15297
建筑业	Construction	155863	12423	5507	137933
批发和零售业	Wholesale and Retail sale	212773	14029	10095	188649
交通运输、仓储和邮政业	Transportation, storage and post	96625	56293	1021	39311
住宿和餐饮业	Hotel and Catering	59746	5042	810	53894
信息传输、软件和信息技术服务业	Information Transmission, Software and Computer Services	42819	6107	97	36615
金融业	Banking	100096	35494	5321	59281
房地产业	Real Estate	48841	3153	444	45244
租赁和商务服务业	Leasing and Commerical Services	28591	9232	1055	18304
科学研究、技术服务业	Scietific Research, polytechnical	42194	25384	411	16399
水利、环境和公共设施管理业	Water Conservance, Environment and Public Facilities Management	43862	34867	3113	5882
居民服务、修理和其他服务业	Resident Service and Others	7357	1690	302	5365
教育	Education	312242	293781	1915	16546
卫生和社会工作	Health, Social Security and	243684	224992	5157	13535
文化、体育和娱乐业	Culture, Sports and Entertainment	26036	20168	204	5664
公共管理、社会保障和社会组织	Public Management、social security and Social Organization	182222	182118	16	88

3-5 城镇登记失业人数及失业率
NUMBER OF URBAN UNEMPLOYED PERSONS AND UNEMPLOYMENT RATE

单位：万人 (10 000 person)

年份 Year	年末城镇登记失业人数 The Number of Unemployeed in Urban Areas by the End of Year	年末城镇登记失业率(%) Year End Unemployment registered Rate %
1978	20.03	4.19
1980	15.54	2.97
1990	12.66	1.72
1991	14.20	1.88
1992	16.89	2.17
1993	17.96	2.20
1994	21.06	2.90
1995	24.45	3.10
1996	28.25	3.50
1997	29.83	3.50
1998	31.33	3.30
1999	33.10	3.30
2000	36.64	3.50
2001	42.15	4.00
2002	44.66	4.30
2003	49.34	4.30
2004	49.37	4.20
2005	52.60	4.33
2006	52.56	4.22
2007	46.72	4.21
2008	55.07	4.20
2009	55.25	4.21
2010	55.65	4.18
2011	55.11	4.10
2012	42.26	3.83
2013	40.26	3.49
2014	37.88	3.10
2015	33.43	2.64

3-6 职工平均工资及指数

年份	平均货币工资(元) Average Money Wages (yuan)					指数(上年=100) Indices(preceding year=100)	
Year	合计 Total	国有经济单位 State Owned Units	城镇集体经济单位 Urban Collective Owned	其他经济单位 Other Units	城镇私营单位 Urban private units	货币工资 Money Wages	国有经济单位 State Owned Units
1978	581	592	532			104.5	104.5
1980	719	744	619			116.0	115.9
1990	1903	2045	1467	2259		111.7	107.6
1992	2370	2532	1837	2575		113.9	114.4
1993	2933	3141	2183	3248		123.8	124.1
1994	4050	4348	2845	4352		138.1	138.4
1995	4685	4991	3308	5093		115.7	114.8
1996	5099	5411	3590	5754		108.8	108.4
1997	5401	5741	3731	5740		105.9	106.1
1998	6436	6783	4748	6166		108.7	109.1
1999	6991	7381	5001	6681		108.6	108.8
2000	7565	7989	5090	7327		108.2	108.2
2001	8619	9133	5677	8035		113.9	114.3
2002	9611	10403	6534	8180		111.5	113.9
2003	10692	11806	7137	8698		111.2	113.5
2004	11855	13096	7608	10270		110.9	110.9
2005	13330	14774	8663	11572		112.4	112.8
2006	15172	17078	9848	13098		113.8	115.6
2007	17397	21971	12921	16829		114.7	128.7
2008	19597	24756	14840	20293		112.6	112.7
2009	23709	30032	19181	23528	15615	121.0	121.3
2010	28092	35981	24429	28799	18626	118.5	119.8
2011	32050	40345	26988	34354	20788	114.1	112.1
2012	35179	43438	33551	38675	23037	109.8	107.7
2013	38720	46126	34181	43975	25898	110.1	106.2
2014	43217	55071	37599	48163	28534	111.6	119.4
2015	47320	60615	41152	52060	31051	109.5	110.1

注：1998年以后为在岗职工平均工资。2007年以后统计范围含城镇全部私营单位。

AVERAGE WAGES AND INDICES OF STAFF AND WORKERS

指数(上年=100) Indices(preceding year=100)							
城镇集体经济单位 Urban Collective Owned	其他经济单位 OtherUnits	城镇私营单位 Urban private units	实际工资 Real Wages	国有经济单位 State Owned Units	城镇集体经济单位 Urban Collective Owned	其他经济单位 OtherUnits	城镇私营单位 Urban private units
106.4			104.2	103.9	106.1		
116.4			108.6	108.5	109.0		
107.1	107.1		107.8	108.3	104.4	103.9	
110.5	109.0		103.1	103.5	100.0	98.7	
118.8	126.1		106.6	106.8	102.3	108.6	
130.3	134.0		108.7	109.0	102.6	105.5	
116.3	117.0		96.3	95.6	96.8	97.4	
108.5	113.0		95.1	94.0	95.3	99.9	
103.9	99.8		97.6	96.6	95.9	96.6	
109.2	99.1		110.2	110.2	110.8	100.5	
105.3	108.4		110.0	111.0	107.4	110.6	
101.8	109.7		109.3	109.3	102.7	110.8	
111.5	109.7		113.6	114.0	111.2	109.3	
115.1	101.8		112.0	114.4	115.6	102.2	
109.2	106.3		108.8	111.1	106.8	104.0	
106.6	118.1		105.7	105.7	101.6	112.6	
113.9	112.7		109.2	109.6	110.7	109.5	
113.7	113.2		112.0	113.8	111.9	111.4	
131.2	128.5		109.4	122.8	125.2	122.6	
114.9	120.6		106.0	106.0	108.0	113.4	
129.3	115.9		121.8	122.2	130.2	116.8	
127.4	122.4	119.3	115.1	116.4	123.8	119.0	115.9
110.5	119.3	111.6	107.8	106.0	104.4	112.8	105.5
124.3	112.6	110.8	106.7	104.6	120.8	109.4	107.7
101.9	113.7	112.4	107.1	103.3	99.1	110.6	109.4
110.0	109.5	110.2	109.4	117.1	107.8	107.4	108.0
109.4	108.1	108.8	107.9	108.4	107.8	106.5	107.2

Notes:Data after 1998 refers to average wages and indices of employed staff and workers.Statistics of 2007 involves all the private run units in urban areas.

3-7 分行业在岗职工平均工资(2015)
AVERAGE WAGES OF STAFF AND WORKER BY SECTOR(2015)

单位： 元 (yuan)

行业	Sector	城镇全部单位 All the Units In Urban Area	国有经济单位 State Owned Units	城镇集体单位 Urban Collective Owned Units	其他经济单位 Other Units	城镇私营单位 Urban Private Units
总计	**Total**	**47320**	**60615**	**41152**	**52060**	**31051**
农、林、牧、渔业	Farming, Forest, Herd, Fishery	28305	30845	30394	23645	24343
采矿业	Mining and Quarrying	41424	52131	51971	50727	34162
制造业	Manufacturing	41994	66993	37292	48845	31394
电力、燃气及水的生产和供应业	Power, Gas and water production and supply	74206	85316	42016	64979	30066
建筑业	Construction	44496	47292	35348	51854	33548
批发和零售业	Wholesale and Retail sale	35589	58228	30807	44294	26751
交通运输、仓储和邮政业	Transportation, storage and post	55404	69496	28068	51011	27931
住宿和餐饮业	Hotel and Catering	31328	34960	36762	36529	28032
信息传输、软件和信息技术服务业	Information Transmission, Software and Computer Services	65090	51814	30980	77871	36712
金融业	Banking	95489	94932	69386	103156	41546
房地产业	Real Estate	46811	47035	38177	53360	37788
租赁和商务服务业	Leasing and Commerical Services	38953	38889	42539	51392	27936
科学研究、技术服务业	Scietific Research, polytechnical	71767	61016	42203	99482	34501
水利、环境和公共设施管理业	Water Conservance, Environment and Public Facilities Management	41833	43197	36988	45755	26291
居民服务、修理和其他服务业	Resident Service and Others	31138	48534	45258	37365	27612
教育	Education	56397	58360	38757	44757	30269
卫生和社会工作	Health, Social Security and	62910	64966	52195	49405	28770
文化、体育和娱乐业	Culture, Sports and Entertainment	50336	58846	56218	64722	27778
公共管理、社会保障和社会组织	Public Management, social security and Social Organization	57162	57169	36295	39254	

主要统计指标解释

经济活动人口 指在16周岁及以上,有劳动能力,参加或要求参加社会经济活动的人口。包括就业人员和失业人员。

就业人员 指在16周岁及以上,从事一定社会劳动并取得劳动报酬或经营收入的人员。这一指标反映了一定时期内全部劳动力资源的实际利用情况,是研究我国基本国情国力的重要指标。

单位就业人员指报告期末最后一日24时在各类单位工作,并取得工资或其他形式劳动报酬的人员数。该指标为时点指标,不包括最后一日当天及以前已经与单位解除劳动合同关系的人员,是在岗职工、劳务派遣人员及其他从业人员之和。从业人员不包括:

1.离开本单位仍保留劳动关系,并定期领取生活费的人员;

2.利用课余时间打工的学生及在本单位实习的各类在校学生;

3.本单位因劳务外包而使用的人员。

在岗职工 指在本单位工作且与本单位签订劳动合同,并由单位支付各项工资和社会保险、住房公积金的人员,以及上述人员中由于学习、病伤、产假等原因暂未工作仍由单位支付工资的人员。在岗职工还包括:

1.应订立劳动合同而未订立劳动合同人员(如使用的农村户籍人员);

2.处于试用期人员;

3.编制外招用的人员,如临时人员;

4.派往外单位工作,但工资仍由本单位发放的人员(如挂职锻炼、外派工作等情况)。

在岗职工平均工资指单位在岗职工在一定时期内平均每人所得的货币工资。它表明一定时期在岗职工工资收入的高低程度,是反映在岗职工工资水平的主要指标。计算公式为:

$$平均工资=\frac{报告期实际支付的全部在岗职工工资总额}{报告期全部在岗职工平均人数}$$

平均工资指数 指报告期在岗职工平均工资与基期平均工资的比率,是反映不同时期在岗职工货币工资水平变动情况的相对数。计算公式为:

$$平均工资指数=\frac{报告期在岗职工平均工资}{基期在岗职工平均工资}\times 100\%$$

平均实际工资指数在岗职工平均实际工资指扣除物价变动因素后的在岗职工平均工资。在岗职工平均实际工资指数是反映实际工资变动情况的相对数,表明职工实际工资水平提高或降低的程度。计算公式为:

$$平均实际工资指数=\frac{报告期职工平均工资指数}{报告期城镇居民消费价格指数}\times 100\%$$

城镇登记失业人员 指有非农业户口,在一定的劳动年龄内(16周岁至退休年龄),有劳动能力,无业而要求就业,并在当地就业服务机构进行求职登记的人员。

城镇登记失业率 城镇登记失业人员与城镇单位就业人员(扣除使用的农村劳动力、聘用的离退休人员、港澳台及外方人员)、城镇单位中的不在岗职工、城镇私营业主、个体户主、城镇私营企业和个体就业人员、城镇登记失业人员之和的比。

$$城镇登记失业率=\frac{城镇登记失业人数}{(城镇单位就业人员-使用的农村劳动力-聘用的离退休人员-聘用的港澳台及外方人员)}\times 100\%$$

Explanatory Notes on Main Statistical Indicators

Economically Active Population refers to the population aged 16 and over who are capable to work, are participating in or willing to participate in economic activities, including employed persons and unemployed persons.

Employed Persons refer to the persons aged 16 and over who are engaged in social working and receive remuneration payment or earn business income. This indicator reflects the actual utilization of total labour force during a certain period of time and is often used for the research on China's economic situation and national power.

Persons Employed in Various Units refer to all the persons working in government agencies of various levels, political and party organizations, social organizations, enterprises and institutions, and receiving wages or other forms of payment. They include fully–employed staff and workers, re–employed retirees, teachers in schools run by the local people, foreigners and Chinese compatriots from Hong Kong, Macao, and Taiwan working in various units, part–time employees, employees of other units working temporarily at current posts, and employees holding the second job, but exclude staff and workers who have left their working units while keeping their labour contract (employment relation) unchanged. This indicator reflects the total number of laborers actually engaged in production or other operations in various units.

Persons Employed in Private Enterprises and Self–Employed Individuals in Urban Areas Persons employed in private enterprises refer to the persons employed in the private enterprises which have been registered at the departments of industrial and commercial administration and are situated at a county town (i.e. a town where the county government is located) for business operation or at urban areas with the level higher than a county town. The self–employed individuals in urban areas refer to persons who hold the certificates of residence in urban areas or have resided in the urban areas for a long time and have been registered at the departments of industrial and commercial administration and approved to be engaged in individual industrial or commercial business, including self–employed persons as well as helpers and hired labourers who work in the individual households engaged in industrial or commercial business.

Registered Urban Unemployed Persons refer to the persons with non–agricultural household registration at certain working ages (16–50 years for male and 16–45 years for females), who are capable of work, unemployed and willing to work, and have been registered at the local employment service agencies to apply for a job.

Registered Urban Unemployment Rate refers to the ratio of the number of the registered unemployed persons to the sum of the number of persons employed in various units (minus the rural labour force, retirees, and Hong Kong, Macao, Taiwan or foreign employees they employ) laid–off workers in urban units, owners and employees in urban private enterprises, urban self–employed individuals and the registered urban unemployed persons. The formula is as follows:

Registered urban unemployment rate = number of registered urban unemployed persons ÷ (number of persons employed in urban units – rural labour force employed retirees employed – Hong Kong, Macao, Taiwan or foreign employees employ + laid–off workers + owners and employees in urban private enterprises + self–employed individuals in urban areas + registered urban unemployed persons) × 100%.

Staff and Workers refer to persons working in, and receive payment from units of state ownership, collective ownership, joint ownership, share holding ownership, foreign ownership, and ownership by entrepreneurs from Hong Kong, Macao, and Taiwan, and other types of ownership and their affiliated units. They do not include 1) persons employed in township enterprises, 2) persons employed in private enterprises, 3) urban self–employed persons, 4) retirees, 5) re–employed retirees, 6) teachers in the schools run by the local people, 7) foreigners and persons from Hong Kong, Macao and Taiwan who work in urban units, and 8) other persons not to be included by relevant regulations. (Data of 1998 and afterward refer to fully employed staff and workers. Other related statistics such as total wage bill and average wage are adjusted since 1998 accordingly).

State-owned Units refer to economic units whose assets are owned by the state. Included are non-corporation units registered according to Regulation of the PeopleRepublic of China on the Registration of Enterprises and Corporations, state organs, institutions and social organizations at the central and local levels.

Collective-Owned Units refer to economic units registered according to Regulation of the People Republic of China on the Registration of Enterprises and Corporations where the means of production are collectively owned.

Units of Other Types of Ownership refer to units registered with other types of ownership, including cooperative units, joint ownership units, limited companies, share holding corporations, units invested by entrepreneurs from Hong Kong, Macao, and Taiwan, and foreign-invested units.

Fully Employed Staff and Workers refer to persons who work in, and receive wages from their working units, as well as persons who have their work posts, but are temporarily absent from work for reasons of study or on sick, injury or maternal leave and still receive wages from their working units.

Total Wages Bill refer to the total remuneration payment to staff and workers in various units during a certain period of time. The calculation of total wages is based on the total remuneration payment to the staff and workers. Therefore, all the wages and salaries and other payments to staff and workers are included in the total wages regardless of their sources, category, and forms (in kind or cash). (Total wages of staff and workers in this yearbook include only total wages of fully employed staff and workers, excluding the living allowances distributed to those who have left their working units while keeping their labour contract/employment relation unchanged).

Average Wage refers to the average wage in money terms per person during a certain period of time for staff and workers in enterprises, institutions, and government agencies, which reflects the general level of wage income during a certain period of time and is calculated as follows:

Average Wage = Total Wages of Staff and Workers at Reference Time /Average Number of Staff and Workers at Reference Time.

Average Wage Indices refers to the ratio of average wage of staff and workers in the report period to that in the base period, which reflects the change of wage of staff and workers at the different period. It is calculated as follows:

Average Wage Indices = Average Wage of Staff and Workers at Reference Time / Average Wage of Staff and Workers at Base Period x 100%

Average Real Wage Indices average real wage of staff and workers refers to the average wage of staff and workers after removing the effects of the price changes and average real wage indices of staff and workers refers to the change of real wage, which reflects the relative increasing or decreasing level of real wage of staff and workers, which is calculated as follows:

Average Real Wage Indices = Average Wage Indices of Staff and Workers at the Reference Time / Urban Consumer Price Indices at Reference Time × 100%

4 固定资产投资

Investment In Fixed Assets

固定资产投资
INVESTMENT IN FIXED ASSETS
2015

全社会固定资产投资完成额	Total Completed Investment in Fixed Assets	29191.06	亿元
固定资产投资	Urban Investment	28250.48	亿元
#房地产开发	Real Estate Development	4249.23	亿元
#国有经济	State-Owned	6983.99	亿元
集体经济	Collective-Owned	754.53	亿元
房屋施工面积	Floor Space of Building Under Construction	58095.72	万平方米
房屋竣工面积	Floor Space of Building Completed	22992.18	万平方米

全社会固定资产投资完成额(亿元)

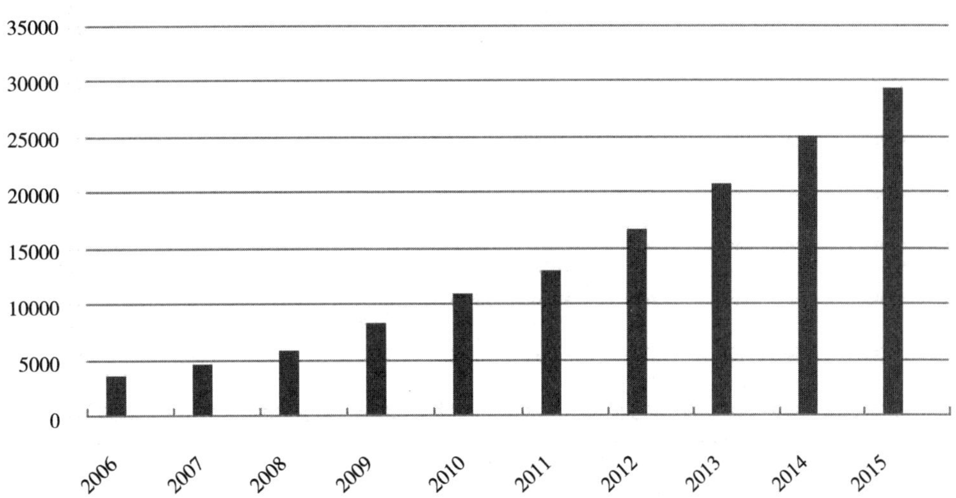

附:全社会固定资产投资完成额构成(%)

		2006	2007	2009	2010	2011	2012	2013	2014	2015
国有投资	State-Owned	41.2	39.9	38.1	34.9	29.1	25.8	24.4	23.3	23.9
集体投资	Collective-Owned	3.1	3.4	5.0	5.6	5.1	4.4	4.0	3.3	2.6
私营个体投资	Individuals	17.8	19.9	21.6	23.2	25.6	28.6	32.6	34.8	35.6
外商港澳台商投资	Foreign, HK, Macao and Taiwan	6.9	6.8	4.9	4.2	4.5	4.1	3.1	2.7	2.9
其他	Others	31.0	30.0	30.4	32.1	35.7	37.1	35.9	35.9	35.0

注:从2011年起固定资产投资统计口径调整为计划总投资500万元及以上项目,取消城镇农村公布口径,其他年份未做相应调整。
Note: Since 2011, the fixed assets investment accounts for investment over 5 million yuan, canceling town and countryside. Other years' statistics do not correspond to this adjustment.

4-1 全社会固定资产投资主要指标

指 标	Item	1990	2000	2005
投资总额(亿元)	**Total Investment (100 million yuan)**	**144.44**	**1421.55**	**2834.75**
按经济类型分	**Grouped by Ownership**			
国有经济	State-owned Units	100.35	857.01	1095.71
集体经济	Collective-owned Units	15.59	128.32	79.47
#农村	Rural Area	9.59	98.95	26.55
私营个体经济	Individuals	28.50	221.43	554.27
#农村	Rural Area	23.62	106.65	135.95
联营经济	Joint-ownership Economic Units		3.94	19.56
股份制经济	Share Holding Co.Ltd.		86.29	232.34
有限责任公司	Limited Liability Corporations		53.33	557.21
港澳台投资经济	Economic Units Funded by Hongkong, Macao and Taiwan		36.57	92.68
外商投资经济	Foreign Funded Enterprise Units		23.90	116.23
其他经济	Others		10.76	87.28
按资金来源分	**Grouped by Source of Finance**			
国家预算内资金	State Budgetary Apporpriations	11.38	141.48	255.76
国内贷款	Domestic Loans	22.22	243.90	474.21
利用外资	Foreign Investment	4.79	28.28	71.34
自筹资金	Fund Raising	92.96	781.50	1492.66
其他资金来源	Others	13.09	226.39	540.78
按构成分	**Grouped by Usage of Funds**			
建筑安装工程	Construction Installation	92.64	814.66	1696.80
设备工器具购置	Purchase of Equipments and Instruments	41.02	371.56	642.86
其他费用	Others	10.78	235.33	495.09
按产业分	**Grouped by Industry**			
#住宅	Residential Housing	39.61	290.24	510.04
第一产业	Primary Industry	12.16	103.05	92.88
第二产业	Second Industry	67.41	521.58	1086.34
第三产业	Tertiary Industry	64.87	796.92	1655.53
房屋建筑面积(万平方米)	**Floor Space of Building** (10000 sq.m)			
施工面积	Floor Space under Construction	5103.48	9920.42	12572.00
#住宅	Residential Housing	3507.53	6831.02	8401.20
竣工面积	Floor Space Completed	4169.12	7508.96	7863.85
#住宅	Residential Housing	3058.40	5417.38	5627.67
商品房销售面积(万平方米)	**Floor Space of Commercial House (sq.m)**	**130.53**	**612.05**	**1708.02**

注：2006年全社会投资(城镇投资)不含城镇工矿区私人建房投资(下同)。由于方法制度调整，按可比口径计算，2005年扣除城镇工矿区私人建房投资基数应为2788.92亿元；从2011年起固定资产投资统计口径调整为计划总投资500万元及以上项目，取消城镇农村公布口径，其他年份未做相应调整。从2012年起，三次产业采用新的划分标准。

MAJOR INDICATORS OF TOTAL INVESTMENT IN FIXED ASSETS

2008	2009	2010	2011	2012	2013	2014	2015
5798.56	**8211.85**	**10802.69**	**12935.02**	**16504.17**	**20753.91**	**25001.77**	**29191.06**
2273.83	3124.90	3768.95	3764.22	4265.95	5068.42	5829.79	6983.99
253.32	411.18	602.80	660.59	733.92	826.51	820.75	754.53
65.02	77.50	99.23	137.69	118.29	137.45	117.04	143.42
1201.53	1771.61	2510.61	3307.47	4712.60	6763.68	8708.83	10386.49
190.19	240.48	301.05	365.51	459.30	576.46	698.73	940.57
15.05	11.32	19.89	22.49	47.70	38.96	11.84	13.38
462.81	659.79	896.87	987.66	1319.31	1487.62	1238.81	1125.37
1109.43	1648.26	2221.99	3056.98	3805.18	4692.14	6026.42	6634.45
160.62	202.38	207.81	253.89	302.69	245.87	343.93	393.90
178.60	200.79	245.92	328.55	367.76	397.02	333.45	459.38
143.37	181.62	327.85	553.17	949.06	1233.69	1687.95	2439.57
570.17	711.98	868.46	663.18	784.27	886.58	1107.45	1339.03
894.57	1432.98	1768.79	1707.46	1964.14	2720.19	2874.92	2907.66
57.02	68.33	147.03	189.26	131.64	66.82	78.99	46.86
3677.00	4956.65	6703.61	8800.61	11812.15	14823.15	18732.35	22470.65
599.80	1041.91	1314.80	1574.51	1811.96	2257.17	2208.06	2426.86
3568.96	5025.62	6701.91	8056.53	11054.16	14312.25	18185.42	21826.03
1245.73	1753.28	2308.73	2812.91	3162.99	3856.68	4292.85	4845.70
983.87	1432.95	1792.05	2065.58	2287.02	2584.98	2523.50	2519.33
901.26	1127.28	1417.95	1750.16	2198.86	2907.29	3461.65	3853.52
231.25	321.59	393.00	440.91	525.45	590.61	799.35	997.94
2344.36	3097.68	4169.92	5526.40	7281.04	9187.25	10733.09	12146.51
3222.95	4792.58	6239.77	6967.71	8697.68	10976.04	13469.32	16046.61
16417.07	20142.81	25284.83	31388.88	40103.56	51939.51	58064.39	58095.72
9896.66	11762.06	14486.90	16337.96	19154.75	23443.19	27199.41	29006.34
7551.82	9772.28	11802.18	14585.68	16576.18	18828.87	21175.37	22992.18
4679.96	5556.71	6785.61	7375.38	7890.08	8006.06	8702.01	9381.09
1941.62	**2718.30**	**3508.61**	**4187.62**	**4037.85**	**5298.54**	**5601.98**	**6244.55**

Note: In 2006 the social investment (town investment) does not contain town private house industrial investment.(same below) Because of method adjustment, according to comparable caliber, 2005's investment base should be 278.892 billion yuan deducting industrial town private house. Since 2011, the fixed assets investment accounts for investment over 5 million yuan, canceling town and countryside. Other years' statistics do not correspond to this adjustment. Since 2012, the division of three industries emploies a new standard.

4-2 全社会固定资产投资额
TOTAL INVESTMENT IN FIXED ASSETS

单位：亿元　　(100 million yuan)

年 份 Year	投资额 Investment	#房地产开发 Real Estate Development	#国有经济 State Owned Units	#集体经济 Collective Owned Units	#私营个体 Individuals
"六五"时期 Period of the Six-Year Plan	**315.82**		**207.57**	**49.41**	**58.84**
1981	33.48		29.51	3.69	0.28
1982	48.83		34.46	8.45	5.92
1983	56.13		36.69	8.84	10.60
1984	74.47		45.25	10.99	18.23
1985	102.91		61.66	17.44	23.81
"七五"时期 Peroid of the Seven-Year Plan	**680.12**	**5.94**	**435.32**	**94.17**	**150.64**
1986	111.44		66.42	15.89	29.13
1987	140.08		85.32	22.31	32.46
1988	160.46		102.21	24.60	33.64
1989	123.70		81.02	15.78	26.91
1990	144.44	5.94	100.35	15.59	28.50
"八五"时期 Peroid of the Eight-Year Plan	**2211.67**	**253.77**	**1467.69**	**190.04**	**261.87**
1991	168.19	7.88	119.07	19.49	29.63
1992	240.73	12.55	182.86	22.52	35.35
1993	383.18	37.01	275.84	30.62	40.37
1994	593.07	76.20	401.16	44.83	56.62
1995	826.50	121.13	518.76	72.58	99.90
"九五"时期 Peroid of the Nine-Year Plan	**6022.80**	**334.60**	**3425.23**	**573.74**	**943.77**
1996	984.38	118.40	593.32	96.50	124.78
1997	1083.60	126.47	567.60	107.12	160.56
1998	1231.10	131.23	661.94	116.92	194.52
1999	1302.17	123.87	745.36	124.88	242.48
2000	1421.55	134.63	857.01	128.32	221.43
"十五"时期 Peroid of the Ten-Year Plan	**10321.69**	**1354.15**	**4817.55**	**541.41**	**1806.78**
2001	1551.75	151.24	918.21	126.41	249.59
2002	1695.22	178.64	963.18	121.42	263.00
2003	1883.59	239.04	888.72	109.05	303.90
2004	2356.38	337.28	951.73	105.06	436.02
2005	2834.75	447.95	1095.71	79.47	554.27
"十一五"时期 Peroid of the Eleven-Year Plan	**32919.93**	**4999.84**	**12449.99**	**1533.63**	**7020.48**
2006	3572.69	564.76	1473.70	110.67	636.25
2007	4534.14	723.73	1808.61	155.66	900.48
2008	5798.56	892.67	2273.83	253.32	1201.53
2009	8211.85	1200.44	3124.90	411.18	1771.61
2010	10802.69	1618.24	3768.95	602.80	2510.61
"十二五"时期 Peroid of the Twelve-Year Plan	**104385.93**	**16124.98**	**25912.37**	**3796.30**	**33879.07**
2011	12935.02	2066.48	3764.22	660.59	3307.47
2012	16504.17	2539.46	4265.95	733.92	4712.60
2013	20753.91	3286.02	5068.42	826.51	6763.68
2014	25001.77	3983.79	5829.79	820.75	8708.83
2015	29191.06	4249.23	6983.99	754.53	10386.49

注：房地产开发投资统计制度从1990年开始建立。从2011年起固定资产投资统计口径调整为计划总投资500万元及以上项目，取消城镇农村公布口径，其他年份未做相应调整。

Note: The statistical system of real estate development investment is established in 1990. Since 2011, the fixed assets investment accounts for investment over 5 million yuan, canceling town and countryside. Other years' statistics do not correspond to this adjustment.

4-3 按登记注册类型分全社会固定资产投资
TOTAL INVESTMENT IN FIXED ASSETS BY TYPE OF REGISTRATION

单位：亿元

指 标	Item	2012	2013	2014	2015
总 计	**Total**	**16504.17**	**20753.91**	**25001.77**	**29191.06**
内资企业	Domestic Funded Enterprises	15315.74	19497.88	23594.86	27369.80
国有企业	State-owned Enterprises	4117.99	4871.98	5548.96	6604.96
集体企业	Collective-owned Enterprises	651.70	677.53	707.76	655.99
股份合作企业	Share Holding Cooperative Enterprises	73.43	131.21	89.71	86.11
联营企业	Joint Owned Enterprise	68.75	78.13	44.09	56.73
国有联营	State Joint ownership	12.27	21.40	8.98	30.92
集体联营	Collective Joint Ownership	8.79	17.77	23.27	12.43
国有与集体联营	Joint State-Collective	12.16	21.23	4.50	7.61
其他联营企业	Other Joint Owned Enterprise	35.54	17.73	7.34	5.77
有限责任公司	Co. Ltd	3940.87	4867.18	6298.27	6982.56
国有独资公司	Solely State Funded Co.	135.69	175.04	271.85	348.11
其他有限责任公司	Other Co. Ltd	3805.18	4692.14	6026.42	6634.45
股份有限公司	Share Holding Co.Ltd.	1319.31	1487.62	1238.81	1125.37
私营企业	Private - owned enterprises	4194.63	6150.55	7979.30	9418.51
其他企业	Others	949.05	1233.69	1687.96	2439.57
港、澳、台商投资企业	Hongkong, Macao and Taiwan Funded	302.69	245.87	343.93	393.90
合资经营企业	Joint Funded Enterprises	121.23	63.81	102.28	108.68
合作经营企业	Cooperative Operation Enterprises	1.54	1.12	7.56	6.51
独资经营企业	Solely Funded Enterprises	147.23	142.00	187.34	257.15
股份有限公司	Share Holding Co.Ltd.	29.64	35.62	44.38	18.44
外商投资企业	Foreign Invested Enterprises	367.76	397.02	333.45	459.38
合资经营企业	Joint Funded Enterprises	195.14	227.87	104.57	215.16
合作经营企业	Cooperative Operation Enterprises	11.67	8.06	10.60	1.34
独资企业	Solely Funded Enterprises	124.48	116.11	154.10	167.97
股份有限公司	Share Holding Co.Ltd.	14.09	34.38	35.93	42.41
个体经营	Individual Investment	517.97	613.13	729.53	967.98
个体户	Individual Self-Employed	487.04	595.47	717.82	954.25
个人合伙	Individual Pattenership	30.94	17.66	11.71	13.73

注：从2011年起固定资产投资统计口径调整为计划总投资500万元及以上项目，取消城镇农村公布口径，其他年份未做相应调整。
Note: Since 2011, the fixed assets investment accounts for investment over 5 million yuan, canceling town and countryside. Other years' statistics do not correspond to this adjustment.

4-4 按构成分固定资产投资(不含农户) (2015)
URBAN INVESTMENT IN FIXED ASSETS BY USAGE OF FUNDS(2015)

单位：亿元 (100 million yuan)

行业	Sector	投资额 Investment	建筑工程 Construction	安装工程 Installation	设备工器具购置 Purchases of Equipments and Instruments	其他 Others
总计	**Total**	**28250.48**	**18655.37**	**2540.77**	**4535.02**	**2519.32**
农、林、牧、渔业	Farming, Forestry, Animal Husbandry and Fishery	927.95	609.55	86.21	142.89	89.32
农业	Farming	339.81	223.83	31.27	50.12	34.59
林业	Forestry	93.73	58.01	5.04	11.50	19.18
畜牧业	Animal Husbandry	177.02	107.02	20.10	35.18	14.73
渔业	Fishery	76.69	52.26	8.79	10.51	5.13
农、林、牧、渔服务业	Farming, Forestry, Animal Husbandry and Fishery Services	240.70	168.41	21.01	35.58	15.70
采矿业	Mining	453.25	267.62	46.09	116.63	22.91
制造业	Manufacturing	10783.16	6111.07	1119.51	2964.53	588.06
农副食品加工业	Food Processing	935.56	522.78	105.50	245.10	62.18
食品制造业	Food Production	297.41	161.87	43.85	73.31	18.38
酒、饮料和精制茶制造业	Beverage Production	299.60	187.41	28.32	67.18	16.69
烟草制品业	Tobacco Processing	33.93	29.96		3.50	0.48
纺织业	Textile Industry	439.59	224.53	62.14	129.76	23.16
纺织服装、服饰业	Textile Wearing Apparel and Accessaries	331.25	183.62	35.98	92.28	19.37
皮革、毛皮、羽毛及其制品和制鞋业	Leather, Fur, Feather and Related Products	87.72	45.40	5.43	31.92	4.97
木材加工和木、竹、藤、棕、草制品业	Timber Processing and Wood, Bamboo, Rattan, Palm and Straw Products	156.43	88.07	16.36	43.85	8.15
家具制造业	Furniture Manufacturing	151.36	93.21	14.43	36.09	7.63
造纸和纸制品业	Papermaking and Paper Products	199.53	105.31	11.84	71.36	11.02
印刷和记录媒介复制业	Printing and Record Processing	95.95	54.28	8.60	27.07	6.01
文教、工美、体育和娱乐用品制造业	Stationery, Education, Art, Sport and Entertainment Products	124.29	79.05	18.25	22.75	4.24
石油加工、炼焦和核燃料加工业	Petroleum Processing, Coking Products and Nuclear Fuel Processing	67.95	28.67	8.26	26.01	5.02
化学原料和化学制品制造业	Raw Chemical Material and Chemical Products	631.75	326.46	78.42	192.05	34.82
医药制造业	Medical and Pharmaceutical Products	420.98	247.13	45.08	105.11	23.66
化学纤维制造业	Chemical Fibres	14.50	5.13	1.78	6.61	0.98
橡胶和塑料制品业	Rubber Products and Plastic Products	344.45	186.62	32.56	108.99	16.28
非金属矿物制品业	Non-metal Material Products	1054.28	553.01	111.91	314.35	75.01
黑色金属冶炼和压延加工业	Smelting and Processing of Ferrous Metals	238.26	115.06	32.09	82.07	9.04
有色金属冶炼和压延加工业	Smelting and Processing of Non-ferrous Metals	125.32	65.46	15.02	39.19	5.66
金属制品业	Metal Products	417.73	240.36	43.88	114.73	18.75
通用设备制造业	General Machinery Manufacturing	566.23	321.72	58.55	154.28	31.68
专用设备制造业	Special Purpose Equipment Manufacturing	686.75	429.12	65.60	152.88	39.14
汽车制造业	Automobile Manufacturing	1399.79	854.48	103.75	379.87	61.69
铁路、船舶、航空航天和其他运输设备制造业	Realway, Ship, Aircraft and Other Transport Equipment Manufacturing	136.07	84.12	13.46	35.31	3.17
电气机械和器材制造业	Electric Machinery and Equipment	651.86	380.84	80.12	155.42	35.48
计算机、通信和其他电子设备制造业	Computers, Communication Equipment and Other Electronic Equipment Manufacturing	594.86	328.33	51.50	187.14	27.88
仪器仪表制造业	Measuring Instruments Manufacturing	115.90	61.17	11.76	34.46	8.52
其他制造业	Other Equipment	83.48	63.02	5.30	11.22	3.94
废弃资源综合利用业	Recycling and Disposal of Waste	65.67	36.91	8.37	16.28	4.11
金属制品、机械和设备修理业	Repairing of Metal and Mechanical Equipment	14.73	7.97	1.42	4.41	0.94
电力、热力、燃气及水生产和供应业	Electric Power, Gas and Water Production and Supply	769.17	381.47	104.31	229.89	53.49
电力、热力生产和供应业	Electric Power and and Heat Power Production and Supply	528.95	219.97	80.55	188.77	39.65
燃气生产和供应业	Gas Production and Supply	65.60	43.63	8.11	12.64	1.22
水的生产和供应业	Water Production and Supply	174.62	117.88	15.65	28.48	12.61

注：从2011年起固定资产投资统计口径调整为计划总投资500万元及以上项目，取消城镇农村公布口径，其他年份未做相应调整。从2012年起执行新的国民经济行业代码(GB/T4754-2011)

Note:Since 2011, the fixed assets investment accounts for investment over 5 million yuan, canceling town and countryside. Other years' statistics do not correspond to this adjustment.Since 2012,a new national economy industry code(GB/T4754-2011)is implemented.

4-4 续表 continued

单位：亿元 (100 million yuan)

行 业	Sector	投资额 Investment	建筑工程 Construction	安装工程 Installation	设备工器具购置 Purchases of Equipments and Instruments	其他 Others
建筑业	Construction	164.06	102.04	18.90	33.33	9.79
交通运输、仓储和邮政业	Transportation, Storage and Post	2574.55	1970.72	120.42	256.79	226.62
铁路运输业	Railway Transportation	83.02	58.41	2.94	9.41	12.26
道路运输业	Road Transportation	1793.83	1445.28	66.38	122.76	159.41
水上运输业	Waterway Transportation	170.77	110.47	8.34	33.99	17.98
航空运输业	Air Transportation	48.26	45.69	1.05	0.21	1.31
管道运输业	Pipeline Transportation	5.49	3.14	0.62	1.29	0.44
装卸搬运和运输代理业	Load, Unload, and Agency	105.15	56.18	10.36	31.48	7.13
仓储业	Transportation Storage	362.18	247.09	30.37	57.09	27.64
邮政业	Post	5.85	4.46	0.37	0.57	0.45
信息传输、软件和信息技术服务业	Information Transmission, Software and Information Technology Service	156.88	89.27	17.62	42.91	7.08
电信、广播电视和卫星传输服务	Telecom, Radio Tv and Satellite	96.75	56.07	13.64	24.37	2.66
互联网和相关服务	Internet and Related	20.99	4.83	0.73	14.38	1.05
软件和信息技术服务业	Software and Information Technology	39.14	28.37	3.25	4.16	3.37
批发和零售业	Wholesale and Retail	858.15	598.64	84.67	105.67	69.17
住宿和餐饮业	Hotel and Catering Service	353.51	247.34	36.56	38.99	30.61
金融业	Finance	60.82	44.13	5.05	7.47	4.18
货币金融服务	Monetary Financial Service	23.66	13.55	2.01	5.61	2.49
资本市场服务	Monetary Financial Service	32.01	26.95	2.38	1.40	1.28
保险业	Insurance	2.19	1.57	0.27	0.21	0.14
其他金融业	Other Financial Acitivities	2.96	2.04	0.40	0.25	0.27
房地产业	Real Estate	5873.57	4199.24	503.48	143.95	1026.90
租赁和商务服务业	Leasing and Commercial Service	700.14	508.64	75.49	69.82	46.21
租赁业	Leasing Service	22.23	12.14	1.59	7.59	0.90
商务服务业	Commercial Service	677.91	496.49	73.90	62.22	45.30
科学研究和技术服务业	Scientific Research and Technical Services	144.24	97.72	8.48	25.27	12.76
水利、环境和公共设施管理业	Water Conservancy, Environment and Public Facility Management	3061.06	2426.73	201.60	188.43	244.30
水利管理业	Water Conservancy Management	438.27	365.42	19.92	29.11	23.81
生态保护和环境治理业	Environment Management	156.74	121.14	8.05	9.50	18.05
公共设施管理业	Public Facility Management	2466.05	1940.17	173.62	149.82	202.44
居民服务、修理和其他服务业	Resident Service and Others	134.09	101.17	12.06	13.89	6.97
教育	Education	280.81	196.34	19.81	48.35	16.30
卫生和社会工作	Health Care and Social Work	227.11	149.60	20.58	41.22	15.70
卫生	Health Care	181.43	113.78	17.62	37.82	12.22
社会工作	Social Work	45.67	35.83	2.96	3.40	3.48
文化、体育和娱乐业	Culture, Sports and Recreation	314.06	248.38	18.62	25.76	21.31
新闻和出版业	News and Publication	3.02	2.68	0.18		0.16
广播、电视、电影和影视录音制作业	Radio, Television, Film and Recording	12.01	7.84	1.22	2.40	0.56
文化艺术业	Culture and Arts	131.88	99.73	10.38	12.95	8.83
体育	Sports	53.89	39.88	3.17	5.60	5.24
娱乐业	Receation	113.25	98.25	3.67	4.82	6.52
公共管理、社会保障和社会组织	Public Management and Social Organizations	413.92	305.71	41.32	39.23	27.66

4-5 按建设性质分固定资产投资(不含农户) (2015)
URBAN INVESTMENT IN FIXED ASSETS BY TYPE OF CONSTRUCTION(2015)

单位：亿元 (100 million yuan)

行业	Sector	投资额 Investment	#新建 New Construction	#扩建 Expension	#改建 Replacement
总计	**Total**	**28250.48**	**15971.89**	**2659.43**	**4810.99**
农、林、牧、渔业	Farming, Forestry, Animal Husbandry and Fishery	927.95	725.63	98.08	96.76
农业	Farming	339.81	281.21	35.57	21.54
林业	Forestry	93.73	80.34	8.63	3.80
畜牧业	Animal Husbandry	177.02	140.37	18.61	16.26
渔业	Fishery	76.69	55.13	6.81	14.75
农、林、牧、渔服务业	Farming, Forestry, Animal Husbandry and Fishery Services	240.70	168.58	28.47	40.40
采矿业	Mining and Qarrying	453.25	170.95	138.04	139.02
制造业	Manufacturing	10783.16	6323.81	836.62	3375.98
农副食品加工业	Food Processing	935.56	565.94	120.32	240.79
食品制造业	Food Production	297.41	171.53	20.26	100.50
酒、饮料和精制茶制造业	Beverage Production	299.60	156.73	23.83	112.92
烟草制品业	Tobacco Processing	33.93	23.04		10.89
纺织业	Textile Industry	439.59	186.18	25.28	218.42
纺织服装、服饰业	Textile Wearing Apparel and Accessaries	331.25	204.58	27.40	92.29
皮革、毛皮、羽毛及其制品和制鞋业	Leather, Fur, Feather and Related Products	87.72	40.45	13.23	32.71
木材加工和木、竹、藤、棕、草制品业	Timber Processing and Wood, Bamboo, Rattan, Palm and Sraw Works	156.43	94.87	15.12	45.23
家具制造业	Furniture Manufacturing	151.36	112.51	14.27	24.24
造纸和纸制品业	Papermaking and Paper Products	199.53	112.41	23.32	57.00
印刷和记录媒介复制业	Printing and Record Processing	95.95	62.19	8.97	21.23
文教、工美、体育和娱乐用品制造业	Stationery, Education, Art, Sport and Entertainment Products	124.29	100.83	3.08	20.38
石油加工、炼焦和核燃料加工业	Petroleum Processing,Coking products and Nuclear Fuel Processing	67.95	43.22	0.62	22.92
化学原料和化学制品制造业	Raw Chemical Material and Chemical Products	631.75	297.21	39.28	289.20
医药制造业	Medical and pharmaceutical Products	420.98	255.61	29.94	126.70
化学纤维制造业	Chemical Fibers	14.50	4.79	1.10	6.57
橡胶和塑料制品业	Rubber Products and Plastic Products	344.45	169.35	36.71	116.78
非金属矿物制品业	Nonmetal Material Products	1054.28	555.37	108.51	362.02
黑色金属冶炼和压延加工业	Smelting and Processing of ferrous Metals	238.26	104.75	29.18	103.36
有色金属冶炼和压延加工业	Smelting and Processing of Nonferrous Metals	125.32	44.70	22.72	42.44
金属制品业	Metal Products	417.73	250.70	46.79	110.48
通用设备制造业	Ordinaryly Machinery Manufacturing	566.23	361.85	25.78	155.53
专用设备制造业	Special Purpose Equipment Manufacturing	686.75	501.61	52.82	119.84
汽车制造业	Automobile Manufacturing	1399.79	805.94	70.88	492.41
铁路、船舶、航空航天和其他运输设备制造业	Realway, Ship, Aircraft and Other Transport Equipment Manufacturing	136.07	105.59	15.51	7.89
电气机械和器材制造业	Electric Machinery and Equipment	651.86	446.31	26.69	161.92
计算机、通信和其他电子设备制造业	Computers, Communication Equipment and Other Electronic Equipment Manufacturing	594.86	367.91	7.56	213.54
仪器仪表制造业	Measuring Instruments Manufacturing	115.90	73.26	13.75	27.16
其他制造业	Other Equipment	83.48	59.61	1.91	21.34
废弃资源综合利用业	Recycling and Disposal of Waste	65.67	36.17	10.91	17.76
金属制品、机械和设备修理业	Repairing of Metal and Mechanical Equipment	14.73	8.60	0.87	1.52
电力、热力、燃气及水生产和供应业	Electric Power, Gas and Water Production and Supply	769.17	454.62	55.27	250.48
电力、热力生产和供应业	Electric Power, Steam and Hot Water Production and Supply	528.95	296.81	22.31	205.74
燃气生产和供应业	Gas Production and Supply	65.60	48.38	6.67	9.90
水的生产和供应业	Tap Water Production and Supply	174.62	109.44	26.28	34.84

注：从2011年起固定资产投资统计口径调整为计划总投资500万元及以上项目，取消城镇农村公布口径，其他年份未做相应调整。从2012年起执行新的国民经济行业代码(GB/T4754-2011)

Note: Since 2011, the fixed assets investment accounts for investment over 5 million yuan, canceling town and countryside. Other years' statistics do not correspond to this adjustment.Since 2012,a new national econmy industry code(GB/T4754-2011) is implemanted.

4-5 续表 continued

单位：亿元 (100 million yuan)

行 业	Sector	投资额 Investment	#新 建 New Construction	#扩 建 Expension	#改 建 Replacement
建筑业	Construction	164.06	131.57	8.26	6.21
交通运输、仓储和邮政业	Transportation, storage and Post	2574.55	1766.79	549.80	220.60
铁路运输业	Railway Transportation	83.02	57.44	3.91	19.84
道路运输业	Road Transportation	1793.83	1135.63	454.03	183.16
水上运输业	Waterway Transportation	170.77	139.69	20.89	3.43
航空运输业	Air Transportation	48.26	35.44	12.61	
管道运输业	Pipeline Transportation	5.49	5.49		
装卸搬运和运输代理业	Load, Unload, and Agency	105.15	81.89	13.02	4.86
仓储业	Transportation Storage	362.18	307.13	44.93	7.96
邮政业	Post	5.85	4.09	0.41	1.35
信息传输、软件和信息技术服务业	Information Transmission, Software and Information Technology Service	156.88	81.77	5.88	56.33
电信、广播电视和卫星传输服务	Telecom, Radio Tv and Satellite	96.75	43.14	4.52	37.50
互联网和相关服务	Internet and Related	20.99	5.67	0.06	14.21
软件和信息技术服务业	Software and Information Technology	39.14	32.96	1.30	4.61
批发和零售业	Wholesale and Retail Trade	858.15	675.92	82.51	90.51
住宿和餐饮业	Hotel and Catering Services	353.51	300.04	23.07	28.55
金融业	Finance	60.82	47.26	4.76	6.59
货币金融服务	Monetary Financial Service	23.66	12.52	4.58	4.35
资本市场服务	Capital Markets Service	32.01	31.12	0.18	0.71
保险业	Insurance	2.19	1.92		0.27
其他金融业	Other Financial Acitivities	2.96	1.70		1.26
房地产业	Real Estate Trade	5873.57	5609.72	100.24	98.36
租赁和商务服务业	Leasing and Commercial Service	700.14	668.90	15.45	9.18
租赁业	Leasing Service	22.23	16.91		0.51
商务服务业	Commercial Service	677.91	652.00	15.45	8.67
科学研究和技术服务业	Scientific Research, Polytechnical Services	144.24	122.31	5.81	7.79
水利、环境和公共设施管理业	Water Conservancy, Environment and Public Facility Management	3061.06	2122.18	576.41	315.17
水利管理业	Water Conservancy Management	438.27	259.49	57.77	114.55
生态保护和环境治理业	Environment Management	156.74	92.61	45.25	12.84
公共设施管理业	Public Facility Management	2466.05	1770.08	473.38	187.79
居民服务、修理和其他服务业	Resident Service and Others	134.09	116.60	3.71	11.62
教育	Education	280.81	190.43	38.63	23.84
卫生和社会工作	Health Care and Social Work	227.11	153.69	23.97	21.72
卫生	Health Care	181.43	118.07	19.76	16.59
社会工作	Social Work	45.67	35.63	4.21	5.13
文化、体育和娱乐业	Culture, Sports and Recreation	314.06	263.56	22.38	18.04
新闻和出版业	News and Publication	3.02		2.29	0.73
广播、电视、电影和影视录音制作业	Radio, Television, Film and Recording	12.01	8.29	0.24	2.59
文化艺术业	Culture and Arts	131.88	108.07	10.43	5.05
体育	Sports	53.89	47.34	2.95	3.24
娱乐业	Receation	113.25	99.86	6.46	6.43
公共管理、社会保障和社会组织	Public Management and Social Organizations	413.92	295.36	70.54	34.26

4-6 按控股情况分固定资产投资(不含农户)(2015)
URBAN INVESTMENT IN FIXED ASSETS BY THE SITUATION OF CONTROLLING SHARE HOLDING(2015)

单位：亿元　　(100 million yuan)

行　业	Sector	投资额 Investment	国有控股 State Share Holding	集体控股 Collective Share Holding	私人控股 Private Share Holding	港澳台商控股 Hongkong, Macao and Taiwan Share Holding	外商控股 Foreign Sgare Holding
总　计	**Total**	**28250.48**	**7983.10**	**1176.04**	**14796.98**	**375.67**	**346.22**
农、林、牧、渔业	Farming, Forestry, Animal Husbandry and Fishery	927.95	130.36	42.64	626.61	1.81	2.08
农业	Farming	339.81	29.08	23.03	239.25	0.94	
林业	Forestry	93.73	18.99	2.70	63.54		
畜牧业	Animal Husbandry	177.02	7.24	3.07	139.90	0.88	2.08
渔业	Fishery	76.69	8.04	2.35	58.33		
农、林、牧、渔服务业	Farming, Forestry, Animal Husbandry and Fishery Services	240.70	67.02	11.50	125.59		
采矿业	Mining and Qarrying	453.25	110.69	20.76	284.32		
制造业	Manufacturing	10783.16	833.63	231.94	8063.90	101.22	224.23
农副食品加工业	Food Processing	935.56	21.78	27.29	789.19	4.01	8.15
食品制造业	Food Production	297.41	13.62	1.97	240.73	5.34	5.63
酒、饮料和精制茶制造业	Beverage Production	299.60	5.48	2.76	230.96	6.41	0.93
烟草制品业	Tobacco Processing	33.93	28.51	0.11	5.31		
纺织业	Textile Industry	439.59	13.50	4.86	375.22	8.55	1.50
纺织服装、服饰业	Textile Wearing Apparel and Accessaries	331.25	2.44	2.52	272.58	0.60	
皮革、毛皮、羽毛及其制品和制鞋业	Leather, Fur, Feather and Related Products	87.72		0.97	82.52	0.92	0.84
木材加工和木、竹、藤、棕、草制品业	Timber Processing and Wwood, Bamboo,Rattan, Palm and Sraw Works	156.43	1.15	0.54	128.77	0.57	
家具制造业	Furniture Manufacturing	151.36		3.56	122.84		
造纸和纸制品业	Papermaking and Paper Products	199.53	6.81		161.00	16.50	12.39
印刷和记录媒介复制业	Printing and Record Processing	95.95	6.22	2.46	74.10	0.19	
文教、工美、体育和娱乐用品制造业	Stationery, Education, Art, Sport and Entertainment Products	124.29	1.47	2.46	109.87	1.06	
石油加工、炼焦和核燃料加工业	Petroleum Processing, Coking Products and Nuclear Fuel Processing	67.95	12.94	0.20	52.04		
化学原料和化学制品制造业	Raw Chemical Material and Chemical Products	631.75	21.10	5.70	509.09	9.36	8.19
医药制造业	Medical and pharmaceutical Products	420.98	44.95	8.37	288.16	26.49	5.08
化学纤维制造业	Chemical Fibers	14.50			12.57		0.60
橡胶和塑料制品业	Rubber Products and Plastic Products	344.45	0.41	11.72	302.86		2.07
非金属矿物制品业	Nonmetal Material Products	1054.28	18.27	3.84	899.29	0.01	0.54
黑色金属冶炼和压延加工业	Smelting and Processing of ferrous Metals	238.26	34.52	0.28	153.59		5.31
有色金属冶炼和压延加工业	Smelting and Processing of Nonferrous Metals	125.32	0.92	0.83	94.09		
金属制品业	Metal Products	417.73	21.95	2.21	322.92	1.73	4.27
通用设备制造业	Ordinaryly Machinery Manufacturing	566.23	55.78	8.72	409.14		11.16
专用设备制造业	Special Purpose Equipment Manufacturing	686.75	46.13	27.42	493.63		3.76
汽车制造业	Automobile Manufacturing	1399.79	189.21	58.01	857.24	9.12	122.15
铁路、船舶、航空航天和其他运输设备制造业	Realway, Ship, Aircraft and Other Transport Equipment Manufacturing	136.07	38.47	1.05	73.56		0.67
电气机械和器材制造业	Electric Machinery and Equipment	651.86	30.33	10.80	502.52	1.86	17.54
计算机、通信和其他电子设备制造业	Computers, Communication Equipment and Other Electronic Equipment Manufacturing	594.86	186.59	28.68	294.32	8.40	13.46
仪器仪表制造业	Measuring Instruments Manufacturing	115.90	9.47	14.53	80.29		
其他制造业	Other Equipment	83.48	13.96		59.26		
废弃资源综合利用业	Recycling and Disposal of Waste	65.67	6.65		52.88		
金属制品、机械和设备修理业	Repairing of Metal and Mechanical Equipment	14.73	0.99	0.06	13.38	0.11	
电力、热力、燃气及水生产和供应业	Electric Power, Gas and Water Production and Supply	769.17	465.39	36.75	199.92	3.40	1.89
电力、热力生产和供应业	Electric Power, Steam and Hot Water Production and Supply	528.95	342.22	10.18	134.36	3.40	1.76
燃气生产和供应业	Gas Production and Supply	65.60	24.17	2.49	35.22		0.13
水的生产和供应业	Tap Water Production and Supply	174.62	99.00	24.08	30.34		

注：从2011年起固定资产投资统计口径调整为计划总投资500万元及以上项目，取消城镇农村公布口径，其他年份未做相应调整。从2012年起执行新的国民经济行业代码(GB/T4754−2011)

Note: Since 2011, the fixed assets investment accounts for investment over 5 million yuan, canceling town and countryside. Other years' statistics do not correspond to this adjustment.Since 2012,a new national econmy industry code(GB/T4754−2011) is implemanted.

4-6 续表 continued

单位：亿元 (100 million yuan)

行　　业	Sector	投资额 Investment	国有控股 State Share Holding	集体控股 Collective Share Holding	私人控股 Private Share Holding	港澳台商控股 Hongkong, Macao and Taiwan Share Holding	外商控股 Foreign Sgare Holding
建筑业	Construction	164.06	78.22	0.18	24.33		
交通运输、仓储和邮政业	Transportation, storage and Post	2574.55	1752.69	88.45	533.21	9.12	32.22
铁路运输业	Railway Transportation	83.02	77.22		3.07		
道路运输业	Road Transportation	1793.83	1475.33	70.48	133.86	1.91	19.39
水上运输业	Waterway Transportation	170.77	87.92	4.78	72.52		0.09
航空运输业	Air Transportation	48.26	40.97		0.82		
管道运输业	Pipeline Transportation	5.49	2.97		2.51		
装卸搬运和运输代理业	Load, Unload, and Agency	105.15	10.57	2.04	78.61		4.35
仓储业	Transportation Storage	362.18	54.08	10.86	241.29	7.20	8.40
邮政业	Post	5.85	3.64	0.29	0.51		
信息传输、软件和信息技术服务业	Information Transmission, Software and Information Technology Service	156.88	86.91	13.29	31.22	1.76	3.98
电信、广播电视和卫星传输服务	Telecom, Radio Tv and Satellite	96.75	62.69	12.43	0.84	1.76	3.98
互联网和相关服务	Internet and Related	20.99	16.13	0.86	3.05		
软件和信息技术服务业	Software and Information Technology	39.14	8.09		27.33		
批发和零售业	Wholesale and Retail Trade	858.15	69.39	36.46	617.48	0.05	3.72
住宿和餐饮业	Hotel and Catering Services	353.51	20.25	9.45	276.46	3.18	5.88
金融业	Finance	60.82	19.38	3.58	33.73		
货币金融服务	Monetary Financial Service	23.66	9.61	3.13	7.94		
资本市场服务	Capital Markets Service	32.01	9.25	0.02	22.56		
保险业	Insurance	2.19	0.52		1.66		
其他金融业	Other Financial Acitivities	2.96		0.42	1.57		
房地产业	Real Estate Trade	5873.57	1390.13	357.22	2690.98	236.88	67.98
租赁和商务服务业	Leasing and Commercial Service	700.14	127.50	33.01	448.06	5.99	1.49
租赁业	Leasing Service	22.23	1.21		12.17	3.87	
商务服务业	Commercial Service	677.91	126.29	33.01	435.89	2.13	1.49
科学研究和技术服务业	Scientific Research, Polytechnical Services	144.24	65.12	2.17	67.44		2.75
水利、环境和公共设施管理业	Water Conservancy, Environment and Public Facility Management	3061.06	2053.36	214.16	545.34	12.24	
水利管理业	Water Conservancy Management	438.27	368.06	23.36	16.11		
生态保护和环境治理业	Environment Management	156.74	101.74	12.19	28.61		
公共设施管理业	Public Facility Management	2466.05	1583.56	178.61	500.61	12.24	
居民服务、修理和其他服务业	Resident Service and Others	134.09	51.46	10.39	47.97		
教育	Education	280.81	199.68	8.09	54.86		
卫生和社会工作	Health Care and Social Work	227.11	148.91	15.88	53.41		
卫生	Health Care	181.43	119.69	12.52	42.43		
社会工作	Social Work	45.67	29.22	3.36	10.98		
文化、体育和娱乐业	Culture, Sports and Recreation	314.06	144.55	26.71	124.79		
新闻和出版业	News and Publication	3.02	2.29		0.73		
广播、电视、电影和	Radio, Television, Film and	12.01	6.49	1.43	3.36		
影视录音制作业	Recording		58.20	23.12	44.68		
文化艺术业	Culture and Arts	131.88	32.27	1.08	16.54		
体育	Sports	53.89	45.30	1.08	59.48		
娱乐业	Receation	113.25	235.49	24.93	72.98		
公共管理、社会保障和社会组织	Public Management and Social Organizations	413.92					

4-7 按行业分施工投产项目个数(2015)
NUMBER OF URBAN PROJECTS UNDER CONSTRUCTION AND PUT INTO PRODUCTION BY SECTOR(2015)

行业	Sector	施工项目(个) Number of Projects under Construction (unit)	#新开工 Newly Started	全部建成投产项目(个) Completion and Put into Production of All Projects (unit)	项目建成投产率(%) Rate of Completion and Put into Production (%)
总计	**Total**	**28130**	**19868**	**20397**	**72.5**
农、林、牧、渔业	Farming, Forestry, Animal Husbandry and Fishery	1897	1423	1430	75.4
农业	Farming	619	457	447	72.2
林业	Forestry	171	130	121	70.8
畜牧业	Animal Husbandry	403	291	324	80.4
渔业	Fishery	166	128	122	73.5
农、林、牧、渔服务业	Farming, Forestry, Animal Husbandry and Fishery Services	538	417	416	77.3
采矿业	Mining and Qarrying	521	377	401	77.0
制造业	Manufacturing	10944	7591	8177	74.7
农副食品加工业	Food Processing	1288	904	989	76.8
食品制造业	Food Production	368	246	278	75.5
酒、饮料和精制茶制造业	Beverage Production	348	225	235	67.5
烟草制品业	Tobacco Processing	9	5	8	88.9
纺织业	Textile Industry	501	318	413	82.4
纺织服装、服饰业	Textile Wearing Apparel and Accessaries	374	275	285	76.2
皮革、毛皮、羽毛及其制品和制鞋业	Leather, Fur, Feather and Related Products	112	82	76	67.9
木材加工和木、竹、藤、棕、草制品业	Timber Processing and Wwood, Bamboo, Rattan, Palm and Sraw Works	221	162	177	80.1
家具制造业	Furniture Manufacturing	189	132	125	66.1
造纸和纸制品业	Papermaking and Paper Products	171	120	128	74.9
印刷和记录媒介复制业	Printing and Record Processing	121	83	91	75.2
文教、工美、体育和娱乐用品制造业	Stationery, Education, Art, Sport and Entertainment Products	75	56	56	74.7
石油加工、炼焦和核燃料加工业	Petroleum Processing, Coking Products and Nuclear Fuel Processing	49	27	26	53.1
化学原料和化学制品制造业	Raw Chemical Material and Chemical Products	784	580	608	77.6
医药制造业	Medical and pharmaceutical Products	370	234	246	66.5
化学纤维制造业	Chemical Fibers	25	13	16	64.0
橡胶和塑料制品业	Rubber Products and Plastic Products	394	284	314	79.7
非金属矿物制品业	Nonmetal Material Products	1483	1088	1185	79.9
黑色金属冶炼和压延加工业	Smelting and Processing of ferrous Metals	183	127	140	76.5
有色金属冶炼和压延加工业	Smelting and Processing of Nonferrous Metals	97	69	68	70.1
金属制品业	Metal Products	429	296	335	78.1
通用设备制造业	Ordinaryly Machinery Manufacturing	635	471	484	76.2
专用设备制造业	Special Purpose Equipment Manufacturing	614	436	439	71.5
汽车制造业	Automobile Manufacturing	925	592	667	72.1
铁路、船舶、航空航天和其他运输设备制造业	Realway, Ship, Aircraft and Other Transport Equipment Manufacturing	86	42	61	70.9
电气机械和器材制造业	Electric Machinery and Equipment	502	358	346	68.9
计算机、通信和其他电子设备制造业	Computers, Communication Equipment and Other Electronic Equipment Manufacturing	317	188	189	59.6
仪器仪表制造业	Measuring Instruments Manufacturing	104	60	60	57.7
其他制造业	Other Equipment	77	57	61	79.2
废弃资源综合利用业	Recycling and Disposal of Waste	66	40	53	80.3
金属制品、机械和设备修理业	Repairing of Metal and Mechanical Equipment	27	21	18	66.7
电力、热力、燃气及水生产和供应业	Electric Power, Gas and Water Production and Supply	1051	780	731	69.6
电力、热力生产和供应业	Electric Power, Steam and Hot Water Production and Supply	556	414	372	66.9
燃气生产和供应业	Gas Production and Supply	133	92	98	73.7
水的生产和供应业	Tap Water Production and Supply	362	274	261	72.1

注:从2011年起固定资产投资统计口径调整为计划总投资500万元及以上项目,取消城镇农村公布口径,其他年份未做相应调整。从2012年起执行新的国民经济行业代码(GB/T4754-2011)

Note:Since 2011, the fixed assets investment accounts for investment over 5 million yuan, canceling town and countryside. Other years' statistics do not correspond to this adjustment.Since 2012,a new national econmy industry code(GB/T4754-2011) is implemanted.

4-7 续表 continued

行　业	Sector	施工项目(个) Number of Projects under Construction (unit)	#新开工 Newly Started	全部建成投产项目(个) Completion and Put into Production of All Projects (unit)	项目建成投产率(%) Rate of Completion and Put into Production (%)
建筑业	Construction	217	194	186	85.7
交通运输、仓储和邮政业	Transportation, storage and Post	2730	1893	1905	69.8
铁路运输业	Railway Transportation	66	38	29	43.9
道路运输业	Road Transportation	2153	1550	1533	71.2
水上运输业	Waterway Transportation	86	32	53	61.6
航空运输业	Air Transportation	7	3	2	28.6
管道运输业	Pipeline Transportation	7	5	4	57.1
装卸搬运和运输代理业	Load, Unload, and Agency	91	56	63	69.2
仓储业	Transportation Storage	303	194	206	68.0
邮政业	Post	17	15	15	88.2
信息传输、软件和信息技术服务业	Information Transmission, Software and Information Technology Service	178	140	131	73.6
电信、广播电视和卫星传输服务	Telecom, Radio Tv and Satellite	115	92	91	79.1
互联网和相关服务	Internet and Related	16	13	10	62.5
软件和信息技术服务业	Software and Information Technology	47	35	30	63.8
批发和零售业	Wholesale and Retail Trade	1080	745	797	73.8
住宿和餐饮业	Hotel and Catering Services	554	412	385	69.5
金融业	Finance	95	74	75	78.9
货币金融服务	Monetary Financial Service	68	52	55	80.9
资本市场服务	Capital Markets Service	15	11	11	73.3
保险业	Insurance	4	3	2	50.0
其他金融业	Other Financial Acitivities	8	8	7	87.5
房地产业	Real Estate Trade	1605	1006	1076	67.0
租赁和商务服务业	Leasing and Commercial Service	453	273	279	61.6
租赁业	Leasing Service	22	19	20	90.9
商务服务业	Commercial Service	431	254	259	60.1
科学研究和技术服务业	Scientific Research, Polytechnical Services	194	147	143	73.7
水利、环境和公共设施管理业	Water Conservancy, Environment and Public Facility Management	3759	2666	2591	68.9
水利管理业	Water Conservancy Management	1002	787	772	77.0
生态保护和环境治理业	Environment Management	200	146	124	62.0
公共设施管理业	Public Facility Management	2557	1733	1695	66.3
居民服务、修理和其他服务业	Resident Service and Others	286	235	223	78.0
教育	Education	777	622	586	75.4
卫生和社会工作	Health Care and Social Work	478	361	332	69.5
卫生	Health Care	325	234	226	69.5
社会工作	Social Work	153	127	106	69.3
文化、体育和娱乐业	Culture, Sports and Recreation	398	248	278	69.8
新闻和出版业	News and Publication	2		2	100.0
广播、电视、电影和影视录音制作业	Radio, Television, Film and Recording	23	22	17	73.9
文化艺术业	Culture and Arts	201	127	143	71.1
体育	Sports	77	44	52	67.5
娱乐业	Receation	95	55	64	67.4
公共管理、社会保障和社会组织	Public Management and Social Organizations	913	681	671	73.5

4-8 按资金来源和构成分全社会固定资产投资
TOTAL INVESTMENT IN FIXED ASSETS BY SOURCE OF FUNDS AND USE OF FUNDS

年份	按资金来源分 Grouped by Source of Finance					按构成分 Grouped by Use of Funds		
Year	国家预算内资金 State Budgetary Appropriations	国内贷款 Domestic Loans	利用外资 Foreign Investment	自筹资金 Fund Raising	其他资金来源 Others	建筑安装工程 Construction Installation	设备工器具购置 Purchases of Equipment and Instruments	其他费用 Others
投资额(亿元) Investment(100 million yuan)								
1990	11.38	22.22	4.79	92.96	13.09	92.64	41.02	10.78
1995	58.40	173.47	88.71	422.92	83.00	454.40	248.51	123.59
1997	68.08	172.05	51.24	651.08	141.15	600.04	264.16	219.40
1998	85.18	225.95	33.86	703.44	182.66	695.55	323.47	212.08
1999	108.18	207.61	36.57	730.92	218.89	771.24	329.26	201.67
2000	141.48	243.90	28.28	781.50	226.39	814.66	371.56	235.33
2001	174.03	241.96	29.89	874.60	231.27	890.60	419.20	241.95
2002	200.95	280.11	63.22	717.24	433.69	974.73	418.55	301.94
2003	150.20	291.60	57.41	786.40	597.98	1059.98	463.23	360.38
2004	197.03	383.78	64.74	1182.36	528.47	1409.25	537.25	409.88
2005	255.76	474.21	71.34	1492.66	540.78	1696.80	642.86	495.09
2006	378.79	708.39	79.32	1902.71	503.48	2252.72	717.10	602.87
2007	472.98	790.84	88.37	2470.28	711.66	2857.31	896.36	780.47
2008	570.17	894.57	57.02	3677.00	599.80	3568.96	1245.73	983.87
2009	711.93	1432.89	68.32	4956.88	1041.83	5025.62	1753.28	1432.95
2010	868.46	1768.79	147.03	6703.61	1314.80	6701.91	2308.73	1792.05
2011	663.18	1707.46	189.26	8800.61	1574.51	8056.52	2812.91	2065.59
2012	784.27	1964.14	131.64	11812.15	1811.96	11054.16	3162.99	2287.02
2013	886.58	2720.19	66.82	14823.15	2257.17	14312.25	3856.68	2584.98
2014	1107.45	2874.92	78.99	18732.35	2208.06	18185.42	4292.85	2523.50
2015	1339.03	2907.66	46.86	22470.65	2426.86	21826.03	4845.70	2519.33
构成(%) Composition (%)								
1990	7.9	15.4	3.3	64.4	9.0	64.1	28.4	7.5
1995	7.1	21.0	10.7	51.2	10.0	58.6	30.3	11.1
1997	6.3	15.9	4.7	60.1	13.0	67.7	22.1	10.2
1998	6.9	18.4	2.8	57.1	14.8	70.2	18.4	11.4
1999	8.3	15.9	2.8	56.1	16.9	63.4	26.5	10.1
2000	10.0	17.2	2.0	55.0	15.8	64.3	23.9	11.8
2001	11.2	15.6	1.9	56.4	14.9	64.8	24.3	10.9
2002	11.9	16.5	3.7	42.3	25.6	64.4	23.6	12.1
2003	8.0	15.5	3.0	41.8	31.7	60.9	23.4	15.7
2004	8.4	16.3	2.7	50.2	22.4	63.9	20.8	15.3
2005	9.0	16.7	2.5	52.7	19.1	59.9	22.7	17.4
2006	10.6	19.8	2.2	53.3	14.1	63.1	20.1	16.8
2007	12.6	19.7	1.3	81.1	13.2	78.7	27.5	21.7
2008	9.8	15.4	1.0	63.4	10.4	61.5	21.5	17.0
2009	8.7	17.4	0.8	60.4	12.7	61.2	21.4	17.4
2010	8.1	16.4	1.4	62.1	12.0	62.0	21.4	16.6
2011	5.1	13.2	1.5	68.0	12.2	62.3	21.7	16.0
2012	4.8	11.9	0.8	71.6	11.0	67.0	19.2	13.9
2013	4.3	13.1	0.3	71.4	10.9	69.0	18.6	12.4
2014	4.4	11.5	0.3	74.9	8.9	72.7	17.2	10.1
2015	4.6	10.0	0.2	77.0	8.3	74.8	16.6	8.6

注：从2011年起固定资产投资统计口径调整为计划总投资500万元及以上项目，取消城镇农村公布口径，其他年份未做相应调整。

Note: Since 2011,the fixed assets investment statistical adjustment plan for a total investment of 5 million yuan RMB and the above project, cancel the town and countryside,other years did not do corresponding adjustment.

4-9 国有单位固定资产投资
INVESTMENT IN FIXED ASSETS BY STATE OWNED UNITS

指标	Item	2013		2014		2015	
		合计 Total	*房地产开发 Real Estate Development	合计 Total	*房地产开发 Real Estate Development	合计 Total	*房地产开发 Real Estate Development
建设项目	**Number of Construction Projects**						
施工项目(个)	Projects under Construction (unit)	8861		8747		8910	
全部建成投产项目(个)	Total Projects Completed Put into Operation	5663		5461		5905	
建成项目投产率(%)	Rate of Projects Completed Put into Operation %	63.9		62.4		66.3	
建设周期(年)	Construction Cycle (year)	1.56		1.60		1.51	
资金来源(亿元)	**Tatal Financial Allocation and Loans(100 million yuan)**	**5248.89**	**467.81**	**5961.19**	**162.88**	**6904.50**	**201.15**
国家预算内资金	State Appropriation	782.29		959.15		1159.51	
国内贷款	Domestic Loans	855.37	111.51	810.50	48.90	782.99	52.69
利用外资	Foreign Investment	16.47		25.57		7.51	
自筹资金	Fund Raising	3082.45	123.30	3882.26	66.29	4636.95	95.79
其他资金	Others	512.32	233.00	283.71	47.69	306.54	52.67
投资总额(亿元)	**Total Value of Investment (100 million yuan)**	**5068.42**	**243.23**	**5829.79**	**126.28**	**6983.99**	**174.68**
按构成分	Grouped by Use of Funds						
*建筑工程	Construction Projects	3481.50	164.77	4312.42	89.15	5330.32	120.17
安装工程	Installation Projects	318.10	15.15	349.58	16.22	423.67	14.66
设备工具器具购置	Purchase of Equipment, Tools and Instruments	606.81	8.41	655.97	3.57	702.53	1.54
按产业分	Grouped by Industry						
第一产业	Primary Industry	41.40		40.73		62.76	
第二产业	Second Industry	1083.13		1117.12		1177.53	
第三产业	Tertiary Industry	3943.88	243.23	4671.94	126.28	5743.70	174.68
*住宅	Residential Housing	266.36	171.32	188.42	82.92	244.67	149.50
按建设性质分	Grouped by Type of Construction						
*新建	New Construction	3168.09	243.23	3836.47	126.28	4367.02	174.68
扩建	Expension	613.32		851.17		1285.59	
改建	Replacement	862.82		808.71		964.64	
房屋建筑面积(万平方米)	**Floor Space of Building (10000 sq.m)**						
施工面积	Floor Space Under Construction	6695.15	1485.48	5872.98	1107.98	4793.87	1302.81
*住宅	Residential Buildings	2457.39	1231.75	2199.38	875.67	1935.21	1061.57
竣工面积	Floor Spaace Completed	2344.15	276.69	2045.37	165.04	1924.06	132.57
*住宅	Residential Buildings	757.20	246.64	546.44	146.85	511.83	108.92

注：建设周期按项目个数计算；本表资金来源均为资金到位数。从2012年起，三次产业采用新的划分标准。

Note: The constructive period is counted by the numbers of project.The sources of capital in this table are the number of achieved funds.Since 2012, the division of three industries emploies a new standard.

4-10 房地产开发投资主要指标

指　标	Item	1990	1995	2000
企业个数(个)	**Number of Enterprises (unit)**	**129**	**571**	**1052**
内资	Inner Funded	129	404	848
#国有	State - owned	129	292	380
集体	Collective-owned		51	105
港澳台投资	Funded by Enterprises from Hongkong, Macao and Taiwan		68	149
外商投资	Foreign Funded		99	55
投资完成额(亿元)	**Investment Completed This Year**	**5.94**	**121.13**	**134.63**
按构成分	Grouped by Use of Funds			
#建筑安装工程	Construction Projects	5.45	89.56	99.59
设备工器具购置	Installation Projects		4.47	2.83
按工程用途分	Grouped by Use of Projects			
#住宅	Residential Houses	4.70	61.78	93.15
#经济适用房屋	Economical Houses		7.44	23.53
资金来源	Grouped by Source of Finance	5.94	138.88	117.88
国内贷款	Domestic Loans	1.21	39.01	18.08
利用外资	Foreign Investments		16.35	1.15
自筹投资	Fund Raising	3.72	41.26	47.27
其他投资	Others	1.01	42.26	51.38
房屋建筑面积(万平方米)	**Floor Space of Building (10000 sq.m)**			
施工面积	Floor Space Under Construction	390.11	2049.30	2102.86
#住宅	Residential Buildings	325.82	1299.03	1673.84
竣工面积	Floor Spaace Completed	183.91	518.88	843.55
#住宅	Residential Buildings	156.77	427.19	733.27
土地开发及购置(万平方米)	**Land Development and Purchase** (10000sq.m)			
本年土地开发面积	Area of Land development This Year		903.00	469.28
本年土地购置面积	Area of Land Purchased This Year		719.00	838.12
商品房销售情况	**Selling of Commercial Houses**			
房屋销售面积(万平方米)	Floor Psace of Selling Houses (10000sq.m)	130.53	240.00	612.05
#住宅	Residential Buildings	112.67	211.00	571.04
#经济适用房	Economic Houses		40.00	172.99
商品房销售额(亿元)	Sales Value of Commercial House	6.93	31.00	83.74
#住宅				

注：本表资金来源均为资金到位数；从2010年起本年土地开发面积指标取消；从2011年起经济适用房分组指标取消。

MAJOR INDICATORS OF INVESTMENT IN REAL ESTATE DEVELOPMENT

2005	2010	2011	2012	2013	2014	2015
1990	**3556**	**3648**	**3785**	**4267**	**4214**	**4212**
1782	3395	3505	3654	4140	4101	4107
228	187	189	184	194	140	134
74	66	66	59	57	19	14
129	106	96	90	87	81	78
79	55	47	41	40	32	27
447.95	**1618.24**	**2066.48**	**2539.46**	**3286.02**	**3983.79**	**4249.23**
315.15	1059.26	1407.17	1902.65	2426.17	3092.49	3243.50
4.68	29.07	36.29	56.16	75.79	67.78	68.09
317.65	1040.25	1334.42	1698.38	2251.56	2755.42	3020.54
13.49	40.33					
513.44	2219.50	2864.05	3363.83	4224.48	4322.24	4880.42
100.41	415.43	462.25	512.05	796.57	737.54	777.89
1.82	97.29	39.03	1.27		19.63	0.90
186.95	784.39	1195.28	1425.31	1735.33	1971.63	2357.67
224.26	922.40	1167.49	1425.20	1692.58	1593.44	1743.96
4804.35	11589.44	13922.07	16819.71	21865.81	26321.99	28296.28
4012.13	9172.43	11013.30	13013.01	16640.27	19610.09	20906.65
1627.03	2541.21	3221.05	3273.71	3040.84	3431.18	2785.17
1411.67	2129.33	2728.39	2795.21	2547.39	2812.35	2193.44
941.26						
1530.64	1422.06	1582.27	1303.19	1894.68	1244.99	729.91
1708.02	3508.61	4187.62	4037.85	5298.54	5601.98	6244.55
1549.19	3236.88	3788.68	3620.10	4765.68	5002.60	5647.72
111.31	99.48					
386.57	1313.20	1878.73	2036.20	2790.32	3088.31	3661.37
335.19	1134.94	1569.32	1689.86	2310.04	2543.76	3198.53

Note: The source of capital in this table are the number of achieved funds; From 2010 the land development indicators of this year had been canceled. From 2011 the group index of affordable housing had been canceled.

4-11 按登记注册类型分房地产开发投资(2015)

单位：亿元

项 目	Item	总计 Total	内资 Inner Funded	国有 State-owned	集体 Collective-owned	股份合作 Share Holding Cooperation	联营 Joint-Owned	国有独资公司 Solely co.	其他有限责任公司 Responsibility Co. Ltd
企业个数(个)	**Number of Enterprises (unit)**	**4212**	**4107**	**75**	**14**			**59**	**1835**
*亏损企业个数	Loss- Making Enterprises	2021	1968	29	4			20	907
本年完成投资	**Investment Completed This Year**	**4249.23**	**3947.58**	**50.27**	**12.58**	**6.74**		**124.41**	**2256.00**
按构成分	Grouped by Use of Funds								
建筑工程	Construction Projects	2868.69	2639.66	42.19	9.89	2.92		77.98	1484.00
安装工程	Installation Projects	374.81	367.22	3.25	0.57	0.02		11.41	161.32
设备工器具购置	Purchase of Equipment, Tools and Instruments	68.09	64.27	0.03	0.59	0.02		1.52	23.53
其他费用	Other Funds	937.64	876.43	4.81	1.52	3.77		33.50	587.15
*土地购置费	Purchase of Land	665.36	626.52	2.93	0.80	3.48		32.29	415.40
按构成用途分	Grouped by Use of Projects								
住宅	Residential Buildings	3020.54	2825.58	44.14	10.22	3.97		105.36	1592.41
*经济适用房	Economical Houses								
别墅、高档公寓	Villa, Top Grade Flat	68.98	60.80					0.02	39.82
办公楼	Office Building	215.70	194.02	2.23	0.12			5.48	107.68
商业营业用房	Business Buildings	593.85	560.02	2.32	0.25	0.22		8.47	306.71
其他	Others	419.13	367.96	1.59	1.99	2.54		5.09	249.20
本年新增固定资产	**Newly Increased Fixed Assets This Year**	**1182.38**	**1121.19**	**18.54**	**3.05**			**21.58**	**595.28**
资金来源	**Finance Sources**	**4880.42**	**4601.59**	**48.41**	**12.99**	**7.69**		**152.74**	**2675.54**
国内贷款	Domestic Loans	777.89	746.33	9.92	1.20	0.90		42.77	497.75
利用外资	Foreign Investments	0.90	0.40						0.20
自筹资金	Fund Raising	2357.67	2225.74	22.39	4.44	5.96		73.40	1266.84
*自有资金	Self Owned	940.95	848.09	12.17	1.04	2.92		47.67	473.50
其他资金来源	Others	1743.96	1629.13	16.09	7.35	0.83		36.57	910.75
*定金及预收款	Funds Ordered and Pre-received	898.92	832.36	8.79	4.21	0.44		22.54	455.40
土地开发(万平方米)	**Land Development (10000 sq.m)**								
待开发土地面积	Area of Land to be Developed	1198.60	1049.60	1.36				58.78	561.07
本年购置土地面积	Area of Land Purchased This Year	729.91	712.18	2.99	3.38				398.38
本年土地成交价款	Value of Land Transaction	238.74	233.44	3.45	1.65				145.19

注：本表资金来源均为资金到位数，从2010年起土地开发投资额和本年土地开发面积指标取消。

INVESTMENT IN REAL ESTATE DEVELOPMENT BY TYPE OF REGISTRATION(2015)

(100 million yuan)

股份有限公司 Share Holding Co.Ltd.	私营 Private	其他 Others	港澳台商投资 Hongkong, Macao and Taiwan Funded	合资经营 Joint Venture Corperation	合作经营 Cooperative Corperation	独资 Solely Funded	股份有限公司 Share Holding Co.Ltd.	外商投资 Foreign nvestment	合资经营 Joint Venture Corperation	合作经营 Cooperative Corperation	独资 Solely Funded	股份有限公司 Share Holding Co.Ltd.
193	**1926**	**5**	**78**	**34**	**3**	**38**	**2**	**27**	**14**		**10**	**1**
70	935	3	38	19	2	16		15	7		6	
251.05	**1240.47**	**6.06**	**241.36**	**61.85**	**4.60**	**174.25**	**0.01**	**60.29**	**14.84**		**22.88**	**0.29**
171.46	848.48	2.73	185.67	56.77	1.79	126.66		43.36	6.23		20.40	0.29
44.43	146.08	0.14	6.13	2.30	0.11	3.70	0.01	1.47	0.96		0.42	
13.76	24.83		3.75	0.23		3.52		0.06				
21.41	221.08	3.19	45.81	2.54	2.69	40.37		15.41	7.65		2.06	
12.20	156.84	2.59	25.13	2.38		22.63		13.71	6.51		1.50	
157.24	911.63	0.61	155.63	58.43	0.11	96.46	0.01	39.33	10.31		14.83	0.29
1.24	19.72		8.11	5.95		2.16		0.06	0.06			
33.90	44.06	0.55	18.81	1.70		17.11		2.88	0.56		1.88	
43.53	195.41	3.11	27.14	1.70	0.06	25.34		6.70	2.46		3.80	
16.39	89.38	1.78	39.79	0.02	4.43	35.34		11.38	1.51		2.37	
39.11	**442.55**	**1.09**	**61.19**	**49.17**	**0.97**	**11.06**						
295.42	**1402.74**	**6.05**	**226.67**	**64.19**	**3.01**	**158.69**	**0.06**	**52.16**	**14.68**		**19.57**	**0.74**
21.31	172.48		25.59	0.02	0.20	25.37		5.98	4.10		1.88	
	0.20		0.50			0.50						
92.03	754.82	5.85	125.46	32.55		92.19		6.47	2.54		3.50	
14.01	296.24	0.54	86.82	5.92		80.90		6.04	2.54		3.50	
182.09	475.24	0.20	75.12	31.62	2.81	40.63	0.06	39.71	8.04		14.19	0.74
99.27	241.71		46.86	15.18	2.45	29.23		19.71	2.06		0.52	0.39
14.91	413.49		139.67	0.32	41.63	97.72		9.33	9.33			
12.97	294.45		3.16	0.32		2.84		14.57	4.57			
4.08	79.08		0.37	0.15		0.22		4.92	1.92			

Note: The sources of capital in this table are the number of achieved funds.From 2010,the indicators of investment and area of land development had been canceled.

4-12 市、州全社会固定资产投资
TOTAL INVESTMENT IN FIXED ASSETS IN CITIES AND PREFECTURES

单位：亿元 (100 million yuan)

市、州	Cities and Prefectures	2007	2008	2009	2010	2011	2012	2013	2014	2015
全省	**Total**	**4534.14**	**5798.56**	**8211.85**	**10802.694**	**12935.02**	**16504.17**	**20753.91**	**25001.77**	**29191.06**
武汉市	Wuhan Municipality	1732.79	2222.91	3001.10	3752.92	4263.24	5031.25	6001.96	7002.85	7725.26
黄石市	Huangshi Municipality	179.85	232.90	343.05	474.06	597.45	750.95	963.50	1168.46	1380.02
十堰市	Shiyan Municipality	141.66	185.44	278.35	406.31	522.37	702.72	904.32	1101.51	1307.25
宜昌市	Yichang Municipality	390.36	523.46	750.27	949.51	1189.92	1620.98	2106.96	2570.41	3085.35
襄阳市	Xiangyang Municipality	265.80	373.77	574.79	835.32	1134.74	1600.09	2086.64	2553.46	3071.94
鄂州市	Ezhou Municipality	105.01	150.01	220.60	298.64	336.85	450.01	571.69	698.04	823.69
荆门市	Jingmen Municipality	153.25	210.08	317.18	448.62	590.63	794.40	1014.64	1232.55	1456.93
孝感市	Xiaogan Municipality	195.93	270.83	397.26	570.70	729.24	980.82	1260.82	1536.96	1824.92
荆州市	Jingzhou Municipality	210.75	291.46	435.16	600.93	771.42	1042.89	1355.60	1651.63	1950.49
黄冈市	Huanggang Municipality	258.50	370.85	553.29	736.06	823.71	1102.94	1416.02	1717.39	2027.25
咸宁市	Xianning Municipality	138.38	200.83	301.58	436.29	563.08	756.45	971.84	1170.85	1372.52
随州市	Suizhou Municipality	101.92	147.07	208.70	291.18	384.48	514.73	654.60	799.33	959.66
恩施自治州	Enshi Prefecture	116.09	139.37	182.21	244.38	314.27	406.19	510.40	613.95	726.10
仙桃市	Xiantao Municipality	64.29	85.24	120.05	167.46	178.11	241.33	314.99	384.55	461.60
潜江市	Qianjiang Municipality	72.37	88.32	123.96	172.92	175.54	237.06	305.88	372.25	438.90
天门市	Tianmen Municipality	67.28	86.07	116.51	153.62	156.07	210.99	272.18	330.65	392.11
神农架林区	Shennongjia Forest Zone	5.63	7.50	10.65	14.15	15.77	20.02	25.56	31.06	36.38
不分地区	Azoanl	334.29	212.43	277.14	249.61	188.13	40.34	16.30	65.86	39.37

注：2006年全社会投资(城镇投资)不含城镇工矿区私人建房投资(下同)。由于方法制度调整,按可比口径计算,2005年扣除城镇工矿区私人建房投资基数应为2788.92亿元,各市、州全社会投资未做调整。
从2011年起固定资产投资统计口径调整为计划总投资500万元及以上项目,取消城镇农村公布口径,其他年份未做相应调整。
Note: in 2006 the social investment (town investment) does not contain town private house industrial investment (the same below). Because method system adjustment, the comparable caliber calculation, 2005 deduct industrial town private house should be 278.892 billion yuan investment base; Since 2011,the fixed assets investment statistical adjustment plan for a total investment of 5 million yuan RMB and the above project, cancel the town and countryside,other years did not corresponding adjustment.

4-13 市、州国有单位固定资产投资
INVESTMENT IN FIXED ASSETS BY STATE OWNED UNITS IN CITIES AND PREFECTURES

单位：亿元 (100 million yuan)

市、州	Cities and Prefectures	2007	2008	2009	2010	2011	2012	2013	2014	2015
全省	**Total**	**1808.61**	**2273.83**	**3124.16**	**3768.95**	**3764.22**	**4265.95**	**5068.42**	**5829.79**	**6983.99**
武汉市	Wuhan	748.71	1072.32	1312.11	1655.04	1703.62	1676.10	1717.62	1883.46	2126.13
黄石市	Huangshi	45.70	57.71	106.17	166.26	126.63	166.27	220.15	227.18	304.88
十堰市	Shiyan	71.51	76.53	136.88	176.18	226.42	344.22	454.68	479.50	610.17
宜昌市	Yichang	163.69	200.93	281.88	279.98	246.92	368.67	474.67	546.80	702.34
襄阳市	Xiangyang	63.70	96.61	111.61	144.10	202.59	300.18	323.20	368.97	523.17
鄂州市	Ezhou	36.40	62.67	112.80	107.33	63.70	102.35	76.26	154.37	177.88
荆门市	Jingmen	37.70	37.64	69.84	113.69	121.27	166.31	203.16	227.23	241.68
孝感市	Xiaogan	54.81	74.62	111.71	119.95	136.08	121.02	214.72	281.76	340.04
荆州市	Jingzhou	59.14	67.44	130.57	144.46	164.24	191.88	291.50	339.64	430.71
黄冈市	Huanggang	79.98	116.76	199.84	236.10	194.99	271.21	399.09	450.68	521.45
咸宁市	Xianning	44.53	59.27	103.42	129.30	155.54	184.16	238.80	291.23	313.67
随州市	Suizhou	25.71	37.99	70.68	77.94	77.30	73.57	124.28	140.37	158.34
恩施自治州	Enshi	45.29	57.47	88.85	111.07	110.16	149.84	193.99	233.63	319.55
仙桃市	Xiantao	9.47	6.54	26.99	12.79	14.48	16.52	25.56	35.45	34.51
潜江市	Qianjiang	38.88	38.82	53.64	68.65	51.62	63.30	60.47	85.85	106.91
天门市	Tianmen	15.78	28.47	30.47	46.30	25.51	15.31	30.16	17.78	15.16
神农架林区	Shennongjia	3.18	4.89	8.69	10.20	13.36	14.79	17.69	18.36	19.09
不分地区	Azoanl	264.43	177.16	168.00	169.60	129.79	40.24	2.40	47.53	38.31

4-14 市、州按经济类型分的全社会固定资产投资(2015)
TOTAL INVESTMENT IN FIXED ASSETS BY OWNERSHIP IN CITIES AND PREFECTURES(2015)

单位：亿元 (100 million yuan)

市、州	Cities and Prefectures	合 计 Total	国有经济单位 State Owned Units	集体经济单位 Collective Owned Units	城乡私人 Private Owned Units	其他经济单位 Others
全省	**Total**	**29191.06**	**6983.99**	**754.53**	**10386.49**	**11066.05**
武汉市	Wuhan	7725.26	2126.13	218.04	1129.31	4251.78
黄石市	Huangshi	1380.02	304.88	19.82	595.42	459.89
十堰市	Shiyan	1307.25	610.17	8.08	524.47	164.53
宜昌市	Yichang	3085.35	702.34	38.77	1063.75	1280.49
襄阳市	Xiangyang	3071.94	523.17	46.28	1184.54	1317.94
鄂州市	Ezhou	823.69	177.88	53.65	393.46	198.70
荆门市	Jingmen	1456.93	241.68	58.43	947.22	209.60
孝感市	Xiaogan	1824.92	340.04	82.80	893.07	509.01
荆州市	Jingzhou	1950.49	430.71	48.35	682.62	788.81
黄冈市	Huanggang	2027.25	521.45	108.28	886.20	511.32
咸宁市	Xianning	1372.52	313.67	33.12	598.44	427.28
随州市	Suizhou	959.66	158.34	29.26	410.61	361.46
恩施自治州	Enshi	726.10	319.55	1.40	283.68	121.47
仙桃市	Xiantao	461.60	34.51		350.61	76.48
潜江市	Qianjiang	438.90	106.91	7.98	174.15	149.86
天门市	Tianmen	392.11	15.16		260.77	116.18
神农架林区	Shennongjia	36.38	19.09	0.25	8.17	8.87
不分地区	Azoanl	39.37	38.31			1.06

4-15 市、州基本建设投资
INVESTMENT IN INFRASTRUCTION CONSTRUCTION IN CITIES AND PREFECTURES

单位：亿元 (100 million yuan)

市、州	Cities and Prefectures	2007	2008	2009	2010	2011	2012	2013	2014	2015
全省	**Total**	**2623.06**	**3393.06**	**4955.85**	**6504.20**	**8037.32**	**10715.01**	**13511.09**	**16140.94**	**18842.05**
武汉市	Wuhan	846.72	1132.30	1511.96	1873.82	2312.36	2851.17	3438.78	3676.30	4032.80
黄石市	Huangshi	107.58	135.11	214.79	295.51	368.95	550.46	718.40	822.00	1016.18
十堰市	Shiyan	78.47	99.94	165.87	266.99	335.23	468.50	641.53	808.56	968.72
宜昌市	Yichang	275.39	371.91	547.86	680.30	854.05	1092.25	1527.28	2028.62	2447.93
襄阳市	Xiangyang	133.85	210.13	310.74	428.23	651.27	980.84	1287.08	1707.23	2205.65
鄂州市	Ezhou	66.35	84.44	125.34	200.98	266.48	369.63	484.67	608.46	715.97
荆门市	Jingmen	75.34	122.10	207.60	278.03	336.03	519.00	578.07	683.41	858.27
孝感市	Xiaogan	119.52	149.33	226.40	338.58	425.55	619.60	824.23	985.19	1156.36
荆州市	Jingzhou	121.12	173.44	290.16	390.92	534.24	750.55	947.60	1181.00	1418.68
黄冈市	Huanggang	151.82	245.58	413.73	547.27	567.38	787.85	976.36	1172.58	1337.48
咸宁市	Xianning	72.63	117.42	175.98	287.62	395.79	526.46	601.17	718.79	852.52
随州市	Suizhou	65.07	96.23	152.87	206.41	257.42	406.04	466.65	571.49	638.12
恩施自治州	Enshi	76.86	90.74	122.32	158.37	214.65	292.50	365.62	435.87	523.94
仙桃市	Xiantao	39.62	52.62	89.47	135.29	145.69	159.09	238.72	172.70	89.31
潜江市	Qianjiang	26.34	39.40	36.41	66.68	97.11	150.18	167.45	216.79	194.22
天门市	Tianmen	43.09	56.79	75.96	101.33	80.24	130.98	210.89	279.01	326.66
神农架林区	Shennongjia	5.47	7.25	10.40	13.80	15.37	19.56	22.71	27.92	32.19
不分地区	Azoanl	317.81	208.32	277.99	234.06	179.52	40.34	13.90	45.04	27.06

4-16 市、州技术改造投资
INVESTMENT IN TECHNOLOGY TRANFER IN CITES AND PREFECTURES

单位：亿元 (100 million yuan)

市、州	Cities and Prefectures	2007	2008	2009	2010	2011	2012	2013	2014	2015
全省	**Total**	**807.56**	**1033.28**	**1301.07**	**1609.33**	**1696.12**	**2032.15**	**2333.72**	**3344.93**	**4245.94**
武汉市	Wuhan	316.90	406.15	410.32	419.75	374.97	331.50	249.30	569.55	705.43
黄石市	Huangshi	38.75	48.91	64.46	83.45	128.33	93.12	119.49	194.68	198.26
十堰市	Shiyan	27.66	31.67	46.87	54.38	35.19	62.66	84.19	123.08	146.74
宜昌市	Yichang	47.67	65.62	86.65	105.96	114.68	257.85	235.32	233.95	224.80
襄阳市	Xiangyang	57.34	70.35	137.43	205.46	229.29	258.40	275.00	313.97	323.38
鄂州市	Ezhou	22.88	38.90	64.77	65.08	31.83	44.37	58.08	58.08	66.29
荆门市	Jingmen	46.26	52.92	60.57	100.51	159.65	165.63	221.70	269.47	272.33
孝感市	Xiaogan	31.16	55.47	79.35	105.82	158.31	190.66	255.04	329.83	403.50
荆州市	Jingzhou	42.15	61.98	75.23	121.84	113.04	131.57	129.36	213.49	257.78
黄冈市	Huanggang	53.16	56.74	61.45	68.45	96.79	142.12	213.75	279.96	388.97
咸宁市	Xianning	25.65	38.68	61.43	62.46	61.96	113.14	177.29	275.99	414.31
随州市	Suizhou	10.87	11.45	12.02	28.86	54.64	45.95	117.72	135.14	225.14
恩施自治州	Enshi	11.33	17.30	21.62	31.96	29.72	37.42	35.71	33.11	30.36
仙桃市	Xiantao	7.99	8.82	4.75	9.10	4.80	54.92	28.60	166.67	328.05
潜江市	Qianjiang	34.02	43.17	81.01	94.07	59.74	73.14	107.68	120.32	223.57
天门市	Tianmen	17.26	21.00	29.68	36.60	34.57	29.69	22.96	5.55	21.55
神农架林区	Shennongjia	0.04	0.05	0.02	0.05			2.35	2.03	3.16
不分地区		16.48	4.11	3.43	15.56	8.60		0.18	20.08	12.31

4-17 市、州房地产开发投资
INVESTMENT IN REAL ESTATE DEVELOPMENT IN CITIES AND PREFECTURES

单位：亿元 (100 million yuan)

市、州	Cities and Prefectures	2007	2008	2009	2010	2011	2012	2013	2014	2015
全省	**Total**	**723.73**	**892.67**	**1200.44**	**1618.24**	**2066.48**	**2539.46**	**3286.02**	**3983.79**	**4249.23**
武汉市	Wuhan	459.75	560.36	778.59	1017.40	1282.25	1574.86	1905.60	2353.63	2581.79
黄石市	Huangshi	19.66	21.53	25.30	38.36	42.51	56.04	84.68	115.77	130.14
十堰市	Shiyan	26.05	28.99	35.73	41.08	52.00	76.64	101.11	90.80	83.01
宜昌市	Yichang	48.71	56.68	79.33	105.78	135.97	176.59	203.18	194.60	241.89
襄阳市	Xiangyang	36.87	46.21	55.39	106.52	144.97	186.19	301.94	330.94	334.58
鄂州市	Ezhou	9.39	10.79	8.11	11.49	18.82	11.65	22.78	20.39	21.09
荆门市	Jingmen	11.38	16.84	27.19	38.83	55.65	64.31	87.79	123.98	118.11
孝感市	Xiaogan	19.16	28.57	32.40	49.60	56.40	74.95	111.13	136.35	171.58
荆州市	Jingzhou	22.20	26.59	32.87	35.53	55.80	54.89	76.79	134.17	113.33
黄冈市	Huanggang	23.33	27.38	37.33	43.84	62.15	78.57	132.73	174.27	200.05
咸宁市	Xianning	14.60	25.35	39.55	59.57	65.46	84.96	112.06	109.14	59.94
随州市	Suizhou	9.11	15.96	17.05	21.66	24.68	19.79	29.23	33.98	28.77
恩施自治州	Enshi	16.22	16.48	16.97	25.65	35.47	40.28	57.06	91.54	100.99
仙桃市	Xiantao	2.95	3.92	4.79	7.75	16.34	15.66	26.62	24.80	22.66
潜江市	Qianjiang	1.44	2.76	3.57	6.39	5.75	9.15	18.11	22.58	15.60
天门市	Tianmen	2.92	4.27	6.27	8.77	12.26	14.93	15.24	26.84	25.68
神农架林区	Shennongjia									

4-18 按国民经济行业分的基本建设投资
ACCORDING TO THE NATIONAL ECONOMIC CONSTRUCTION OF BASIC INDUSTRY INVESTMENT

单位：亿元 (100 million yuan)

行业	sector	全省		#地方	
		2014	2015	2014	2015
总 计	**Total**	**16140.94**	**18842.05**	**15760.07**	**18449.16**
农、林、牧、渔业	Farming, Forestry, Animal Husbandry and Fishery	621.01	829.39	620.73	829.39
农业	Farming	205.36	318.27	205.08	318.27
林业	Forestry	71.10	89.92	71.10	89.92
畜牧业	Animal Husbandry	177.65	160.03	177.65	160.03
渔业	Fishery	47.95	61.94	47.95	61.94
农、林、牧、渔服务业	Farming, Forestry, Animal Husbandry and Fishery Services	118.94	199.22	118.94	199.22
采矿业	Mining and Qarrying	274.33	309.87	208.84	233.97
制造业	Manufacturing	6812.02	7192.19	6741.83	7109.09
农副食品加工业	Food Processing	570.65	686.26	570.65	686.26
食品制造业	Food Production	216.91	192.49	216.91	192.49
酒、饮料和精制茶制造业	Beverage Production	195.42	183.80	194.92	183.80
烟草制品业	Tobacco Processing	19.86	23.04	19.86	23.04
纺织业	Textile Industry	229.40	211.97	229.40	211.97
纺织服装、服饰业	Textile Wearing Apparel and Accessaries	191.75	232.20	191.75	232.20
皮革、毛皮、羽毛及其制品和制鞋业	Leather, Fur, Feather and Related Products	51.45	54.01	51.45	54.01
木材加工和木、竹、藤、棕、草制品业	Timber Processing and Wwood, Bamboo,Rattan, Palm and Sraw Works	101.82	110.59	101.17	110.59
家具制造业	Furniture Manufacturing	115.81	126.88	115.81	126.88
造纸和纸制品业	Papermaking and Paper Products	136.41	135.73	136.41	135.73
印刷和记录媒介复制业	Printing and Record Processing	111.89	71.43	111.89	71.43
文教、工美、体育和娱乐用品制造业	Stationery, Education, Art, Sport and Entertainment Products	89.67	103.91	89.67	103.91
石油加工、炼焦和核燃料加工业	Petroleum Processing, Coking Products and Nuclear Fuel Processing	19.79	44.00	19.79	41.35
化学原料和化学制品制造业	Raw Chemical Material and Chemical Products	362.24	336.98	362.24	336.98
医药制造业	Medical and pharmaceutical Products	267.45	287.20	263.34	287.20
化学纤维制造业	Chemical Fibers	10.07	5.89	10.07	5.89
橡胶和塑料制品业	Rubber Products and Plastic Products	180.02	209.45	180.02	209.04
非金属矿物制品业	Nonmetal Material Products	636.61	674.14	636.61	674.14
黑色金属冶炼和压延加工业	Smelting and Processing of ferrous Metals	132.96	133.93	131.99	131.59
有色金属冶炼和压延加工业	Smelting and Processing of Nonferrous Metals	75.80	67.68	75.80	67.68
金属制品业	Metal Products	336.42	297.79	335.77	295.14
通用设备制造业	Ordinaryly Machinery Manufacturing	364.95	388.86	346.50	375.32
专用设备制造业	Special Purpose Equipment Manufacturing	475.38	555.10	456.92	537.66
汽车制造业	Automobile Manufacturing	751.75	879.06	737.33	855.97
铁路、船舶、航空航天和其他运输设备制造业	Realway, Ship, Aircraft and Other Transport Equipment Manufacturing	95.46	121.09	94.74	112.84
电气机械和器材制造业	Electric Machinery and Equipment	426.83	476.83	426.83	476.83
计算机、通信和其他电子设备制造业	Computers, Communication Equipment and Other Electronic Equipment Manufacturing	424.98	375.47	417.22	368.70
仪器仪表制造业	Measuring Instruments Manufacturing	72.95	87.01	70.75	82.03
其他制造业	Other Equipment	74.66	61.52	73.35	61.52
废弃资源综合利用业	Recycling and Disposal of Waste	58.54	47.08	58.54	47.08
金属制品、机械和设备修理业	Repairing of Metal and Mechanical Equipment	14.15	10.78	14.15	9.79
电力、热力、燃气及水生产和供应业	Electric Power, Gas and Water Production and Supply	380.41	514.61	342.36	490.71
电力、热力生产和供应业	Electric Power, Steam and Hot Water Production and Supply	221.71	320.03	186.76	299.50
燃气生产和供应业	Gas Production and Supply	62.25	55.10	59.15	53.22
水的生产和供应业	Tap Water Production and Supply	96.44	139.48	96.44	137.99

注：从2012年起执行新的国民经济行业代码(GB/T4754-2011)
Note: Since 2012,a new national economy industry code(GB/T4754-2011)is implemented.

4-18 续表 continued

单位：亿元 (100 million yuan)

行业	sector	全省		#地方	
		2014	2015	2014	2015
建筑业	Construction	104.15	141.13	102.79	139.49
交通运输、仓储和邮政业	Transportation, storage and Post	1871.58	2328.42	1804.02	2276.96
铁路运输业	Railway Transportation	69.91	61.35	15.26	29.45
道路运输业	Road Transportation	1267.18	1600.69	1256.46	1585.35
水上运输业	Waterway Transportation	117.66	160.71	117.66	160.71
航空运输业	Air Transportation	48.23	48.05	48.23	48.05
管道运输业	Pipeline Transportation	3.95	5.49	3.95	5.49
装卸搬运和运输代理业	Load, Unload, and Agency	73.06	94.91	73.06	94.91
仓储业	Transportation Storage	285.83	352.72	283.64	348.50
邮政业	Post	5.76	4.50	5.76	4.50
信息传输、软件和信息技术服务业	Information Transmission, Software and Information Technology Service	60.45	88.48	57.00	77.67
电信、广播电视和卫星传输服务	Telecom, Radio Tv and Satellite	30.76	48.49	27.31	37.84
互联网和相关服务	Internet and Related	6.77	5.73	6.77	5.73
软件和信息技术服务业	Software and Information Technology	22.92	34.26	22.92	34.10
批发和零售业	Wholesale and Retail Trade	639.70	761.26	635.85	758.16
住宿和餐饮业	Hotel and Catering Services	298.90	324.96	298.90	324.96
金融业	Finance	64.12	52.02	62.27	50.98
货币金融服务	Monetary Financial Service	30.43	17.10	28.59	16.06
资本市场服务	Capital Markets Service	30.60	31.30	30.60	31.30
保险业	Insurance	0.38	1.92	0.38	1.92
其他金融业	Other Financial Acitivities	2.71	1.70	2.71	1.70
房地产业	Real Estate Trade	1255.75	1524.60	1252.23	1519.97
租赁和商务服务业	Leasing and Commercial Service	464.88	685.32	464.88	681.40
租赁业	Leasing Service	12.11	16.91	12.11	16.91
商务服务业	Commercial Service	452.78	668.42	452.78	664.50
科学研究和技术服务业	Scientific Research, Polytechnical Services	102.76	129.46	95.76	112.11
水利、环境和公共设施管理业	Water Conservancy, Environment and Public Facility Management	1956.30	2740.50	1905.89	2677.19
水利管理业	Water Conservancy Management	224.21	323.44	204.22	298.92
生态保护和环境治理业	Environment Management	99.29	142.99	99.29	131.86
公共设施管理业	Public Facility Management	1632.80	2274.08	1602.38	2246.41
居民服务、修理和其他服务业	Resident Service and Others	173.25	121.76	173.25	121.47
教育	Education	223.98	241.75	190.90	217.26
卫生和社会工作	Health Care and Social Work	174.73	188.10	163.30	181.71
卫生	Health Care	127.00	147.96	115.57	141.57
社会工作	Social Work	47.73	40.14	47.73	40.14
文化、体育和娱乐业	Culture, Sports and Recreation	261.18	294.82	248.56	277.60
新闻和出版业	News and Publication	0.45	2.29	0.45	2.29
广播、电视、电影和影视录音制作业	Radio, Television, Film and Recording	4.85	8.53	4.85	8.53
文化艺术业	Culture and Arts	100.15	126.71	98.63	126.16
体育	Sports	56.84	50.65	48.37	49.87
娱乐业	Receation	98.88	106.64	96.26	90.75
公共管理、社会保障和社会组织	Public Management and Social Organizations	401.46	373.40	390.67	369.08

4-19 按国民经济行业分的技术改造投资
ACCORDING TO THE NATIONAL ECONOMIC

单位：亿元 (100 million yuan)

行业	sector	全省 2014	全省 2015	#地方 2014	#地方 2015
总 计	**Total**	**3344.93**	**4245.94**	**3206.66**	**4149.02**
农、林、牧、渔业	Farming, Forestry, Animal Husbandry and Fishery	48.89	74.07	48.89	74.07
农业	Farming	15.44	19.38	15.44	19.38
林业	Forestry		2.95		2.95
畜牧业	Animal Husbandry	5.27	9.90	5.27	9.90
渔业	Fishery	5.13	12.87	5.13	12.87
农、林、牧、渔服务业	Farming, Forestry, Animal Husbandry and Fishery Services	23.06	28.96	23.06	28.96
采矿业	Mining and Qarrying	118.61	137.60	118.61	137.60
制造业	Manufacturing	2501.14	3257.19	2450.69	3198.05
农副食品加工业	Food Processing	201.00	231.41	201.00	231.41
食品制造业	Food Production	96.99	100.00	96.99	100.00
酒、饮料和精制茶制造业	Beverage Production	94.58	104.59	94.58	104.59
烟草制品业	Tobacco Processing	9.07	10.89	9.07	10.89
纺织业	Textile Industry	161.62	210.39	159.47	206.16
纺织服装、服饰业	Textile Wearing Apparel and Accessaries	55.51	89.50	55.51	89.50
皮革、毛皮、羽毛及其制品和制鞋业	Leather, Fur, Feather and Related Products	22.11	31.87	22.11	31.87
木材加工和木、竹、藤、棕、草制品业	Timber Processing and Wwood, Bamboo,Rattan, Palm and Sraw Works	32.22	45.23	32.22	45.23
家具制造业	Furniture Manufacturing	20.30	24.24	20.30	24.24
造纸和纸制品业	Papermaking and Paper Products	42.96	56.82	42.96	56.82
印刷和记录媒介复制业	Printing and Record Processing	15.95	20.94	15.95	20.94
文教、工美、体育和娱乐用品制造业	Stationery, Education, Art, Sport and Entertainment Products	14.32	20.38	14.32	20.38
石油加工、炼焦和核燃料加工业	Petroleum Processing, Coking Products and Nuclear Fuel Processing	42.87	22.36	18.95	12.16
化学原料和化学制品制造业	Raw Chemical Material and Chemical Products	253.53	277.15	253.03	276.86
医药制造业	Medical and pharmaceutical Products	83.42	122.41	82.96	122.41
化学纤维制造业	Chemical Fibers	12.08	6.57	12.08	6.57
橡胶和塑料制品业	Rubber Products and Plastic Products	85.13	115.19	85.13	115.19
非金属矿物制品业	Nonmetal Material Products	276.67	341.37	275.37	341.37
黑色金属冶炼和压延加工业	Smelting and Processing of ferrous Metals	76.65	101.71	74.65	81.75
有色金属冶炼和压延加工业	Smelting and Processing of Nonferrous Metals	60.74	42.44	60.74	42.44
金属制品业	Metal Products	89.45	107.27	89.45	107.27
通用设备制造业	Ordinaryly Machinery Manufacturing	114.05	150.69	114.05	150.48
专用设备制造业	Special Purpose Equipment Manufacturing	117.12	116.68	117.11	116.68
汽车制造业	Automobile Manufacturing	241.83	464.43	232.10	446.12
铁路、船舶、航空航天和其他运输设备制造业	Realway, Ship, Aircraft and Other Transport Equipment Manufacturing	24.76	7.60	15.75	4.86
电气机械和器材制造业	Electric Machinery and Equipment	99.27	160.11	99.27	160.11
计算机、通信和其他电子设备制造业	Computers, Communication Equipment and Other Electronic Equipment Manufacturing	107.09	210.47	105.76	208.63
仪器仪表制造业	Measuring Instruments Manufacturing	18.40	25.10	18.39	25.10
其他制造业	Other Equipment	10.17	20.10	10.17	20.10
废弃资源综合利用业	Recycling and Disposal of Waste	18.95	17.76	18.95	16.40
金属制品、机械和设备修理业	Repairing of Metal and Mechanical Equipment	2.32	1.52	2.32	1.52
电力、热力、燃气及水生产和供应业	Electric Power, Gas and Water Production and Supply	199.47	220.38	144.86	202.84
电力、热力生产和供应业	Electric Power, Steam and Hot Water Production and Supply	155.21	181.88	101.07	164.35
燃气生产和供应业	Gas Production and Supply	4.11	8.05	4.11	8.05
水的生产和供应业	Tap Water Production and Supply	40.15	30.46	39.67	30.44

4-19 续表 continued

单位：亿元 (100 million yuan)

行业	sector	全省 2014	全省 2015	#地方 2014	#地方 2015
建筑业	Construction	2.96	2.37	2.96	2.37
交通运输、仓储和邮政业	Transportation, storage and Post	157.52	138.69	133.34	120.34
铁路运输业	Railway Transportation	24.93	19.14	1.00	0.80
道路运输业	Road Transportation	119.35	104.75	119.35	104.75
水上运输业	Waterway Transportation	4.47	3.15	4.47	3.15
航空运输业	Air Transportation				
管道运输业	Pipeline Transportation				
装卸搬运和运输代理业	Load, Unload, and Agency	1.11	3.77	1.11	3.77
仓储业	Transportation Storage	7.49	6.59	7.24	6.59
邮政业	Post	0.18	1.28	0.18	1.28
信息传输、软件和信息技术服务业	Information Transmission, Software and Information Technology Service	14.59	33.04	9.02	32.66
电信、广播电视和卫星传输服务	Telecom, Radio Tv and Satellite	10.97	17.56	5.41	17.18
互联网和相关服务	Internet and Related	3.38	13.41	3.38	13.41
软件和信息技术服务业	Software and Information Technology	0.23	2.07	0.23	2.07
批发和零售业	Wholesale and Retail Trade	37.99	70.80	37.34	70.80
住宿和餐饮业	Hotel and Catering Services	15.04	13.55	15.04	13.55
金融业	Finance	3.62	2.29	2.83	1.82
货币金融服务	Monetary Financial Service	3.62	1.29	2.83	0.82
资本市场服务	Monetary Financial Service		0.71		0.71
保险业	Insurance				
其他金融业	Other Financial Acitivities		0.29		0.29
房地产业	Real Estate Trade	20.16	33.50	20.16	33.10
租赁和商务服务业	Leasing and Commercial Service	5.77	7.02	5.77	7.02
租赁业	Leasing Service	0.28		0.28	
商务服务业	Commercial Service	5.50	7.02	5.50	7.02
科学研究和技术服务业	Scientific Research, Polytechnical Services	4.46	6.23	4.46	6.23
水利、环境和公共设施管理业	Water Conservancy, Environment and Public Facility Management	142.45	175.34	141.49	174.91
水利管理业	Water Conservancy Management	45.03	72.34	45.03	72.34
生态保护和环境治理业	Environment Management	10.40	9.32	10.40	9.32
公共设施管理业	Public Facility Management	87.02	93.68	86.07	93.25
居民服务、修理和其他服务业	Resident Service and Others	9.23	8.13	9.23	8.13
教育	Education	12.03	18.07	12.03	18.07
卫生和社会工作	Health Care and Social Work	16.10	11.48	15.25	11.48
卫生	Health Care	15.06	10.39	14.21	10.39
社会工作	Social Work	1.04	1.09	1.04	1.09
文化、体育和娱乐业	Culture, Sports and Recreation	13.01	10.59	12.81	10.59
新闻和出版业	News and Publication	0.47	0.73	0.47	0.73
广播、电视、电影和影视录音制作业	Radio, Television, Film and Recording	1.47	0.40	1.47	0.40
文化艺术业	Culture and Arts	1.58	1.21	1.38	1.21
体育	Sports	2.23	2.25	2.23	2.25
娱乐业	Receation	7.26	6.00	7.26	6.00
公共管理、社会保障和社会组织	Public Management and Social Organizations	21.88	25.61	21.88	25.41

4-20 全社会按构成分的投资额
ACCORDING TO THE COMPOSITION OF SOCIAL CAPITAL

单位: 亿元 (100 million yuan)

年份 In copies	全省 建筑安装工程 Building installation	全省 设备工器具购置 Equipment tools, equipment purchase	全省 其他费用 Other expenses	*地方 建筑安装工程 Building installation	*地方 设备工器具购置 Equipment tools, equipment purchase	*地方 其他费用 expenses Other
1978	20.30	9.98	3.30	9.89	4.51	0.48
1980	23.85	9.76	1.89	14.01	4.55	0.97
"六五"时期	**216.19**	**83.11**	**16.52**	**155.63**	**59.71**	**7.43**
1985	67.53	28.67	6.71	54.64	23.00	3.39
"七五"时期	**434.43**	**195.59**	**50.10**	**352.24**	**152.75**	**32.96**
1986	72.40	31.24	7.84	60.18	23.91	4.81
1987	86.83	40.54	12.71	71.79	32.83	7.83
1988	100.58	49.28	10.60	82.40	41.51	7.35
1989	81.98	33.51	8.21	64.30	25.19	5.86
1990	92.64	41.02	10.78	73.58	29.31	7.11
"八五"时期	**1300.95**	**606.68**	**304.04**	**972.09**	**429.78**	**178.69**
1991	108.07	45.11	15.01	86.74	33.68	10.64
1992	149.34	68.03	23.36	119.61	51.46	15.94
1993	227.25	98.91	57.02	174.02	74.17	39.83
1994	361.89	146.12	85.06	261.27	99.72	49.60
1995	454.40	248.51	123.59	330.45	170.75	62.68
"九五"时期	**3392.01**	**1596.34**	**1034.45**	**2593.68**	**1108.81**	**598.32**
1996	510.52	307.89	165.97	392.06	218.14	82.28
1997	600.04	264.16	219.40	405.69	171.97	201.38
1998	695.55	323.47	212.08	556.36	230.59	101.48
1999	771.24	329.26	201.67	594.41	248.78	94.54
2000	814.66	371.56	235.33	645.16	239.33	118.64
"十五"时期	**6031.36**	**2481.09**	**1809.24**	**5317.08**	**1883.69**	**1216.75**
2001	890.60	419.20	241.95	739.97	276.93	124.89
2002	974.73	418.55	301.94	829.11	303.57	155.49
2003	1059.98	463.23	360.38	945.58	363.78	243.47
2004	1409.25	537.25	409.88	1282.71	416.98	307.87
2005	1696.80	642.86	495.09	1519.71	522.43	385.03
"十一五"时期	**20406.53**	**6921.20**	**5592.20**	**18649.08**	**5890.61**	**4859.93**
2006	2252.72	717.10	602.87	1918.63	601.90	477.07
2007	2857.31	896.36	780.47	2492.24	756.58	660.27
2008	3568.97	1245.73	983.86	3226.13	971.37	819.50
2009	5025.62	1753.28	1432.95	4683.30	1472.52	1243.52
2010	6701.91	2308.73	1792.05	6328.78	2088.24	1659.57
"十二五"时期	**73434.38**	**18971.13**	**11980.42**	**71272.16**	**18040.47**	**11545.96**
2011	8056.52	2812.91	2065.59	7626.28	2520.40	1950.61
2012	11054.16	3162.99	2287.02	10609.45	2942.10	2192.00
2013	14312.25	3856.68	2584.98	13934.73	3702.30	2508.97
2014	18185.42	4292.85	2523.50	17765.47	4160.35	2425.92
2015	21826.03	4845.70	2519.33	21336.23	4715.32	2468.46

4-21 全社会按国民经济行业分的固定资产投资
ACCORDING TO THE NATIONAL ECONOMY SOCIETY OF FIXED ASSETS INVESTMENT

单位：亿元 (100 million yuan)

行业	sector	全省		#地方	
		2014	2015	2014	2015
总 计	**Total**	**25001.77**	**29191.06**	**24351.75**	**28520.01**
农、林、牧、渔业	Farming, Forestry, Animal Husbandry and Fishery	951.70	1238.63	951.42	1238.63
农业	Farming	485.12	650.49	484.85	650.49
林业	Forestry	71.57	93.73	71.57	93.73
畜牧业	Animal Husbandry	188.86	177.02	188.86	177.02
渔业	Fishery	53.79	76.69	53.79	76.69
农、林、牧、渔服务业	Farming, Forestry, Animal Husbandry and Fishery Services	152.35	240.70	152.35	240.70
采矿业	Mining and Qarrying	404.80	453.25	339.31	377.35
制造业	Manufacturing	9633.97	10783.16	9505.59	10634.87
农副食品加工业	Food Processing	794.99	935.56	794.99	935.56
食品制造业	Food Production	322.51	297.41	322.51	297.41
酒、饮料和精制茶制造业	Beverage Production	305.83	299.60	305.33	299.60
烟草制品业	Tobacco Processing	28.93	33.93	28.93	33.93
纺织业	Textile Industry	406.90	439.59	404.74	435.35
纺织服装、服饰业	Textile Wearing Apparel and Accessaries	253.76	331.25	253.76	331.25
皮革、毛皮、羽毛及其制品和制鞋业	Leather, Fur, Feather and Related Products	76.70	87.72	76.70	87.72
木材加工和木、竹、藤、棕、草制品业	Timber Processing and Wwood, Bamboo,Rattan, Palm and Sraw Works	138.08	156.43	137.43	156.43
家具制造业	Furniture Manufacturing	137.11	151.36	137.11	151.36
造纸和纸制品业	Papermaking and Paper Products	186.73	199.53	186.73	199.53
印刷和记录媒介复制业	Printing and Record Processing	131.93	95.95	131.93	95.95
文教、工美、体育和娱乐用品制造业	Stationery, Education, Art, Sport and Entertainment Products	104.82	124.29	104.82	124.29
石油加工、炼焦和核燃料加工业	Petroleum Processing, Coking Products and Nuclear Fuel Processing	67.64	67.95	41.00	55.12
化学原料和化学制品制造业	Raw Chemical Material and Chemical Products	635.40	631.75	634.90	631.46
医药制造业	Medical and pharmaceutical Products	362.42	420.98	357.84	420.98
化学纤维制造业	Chemical Fibers	22.56	14.50	22.56	14.50
橡胶和塑料制品业	Rubber Products and Plastic Products	271.24	344.45	271.24	344.04
非金属矿物制品业	Nonmetal Material Products	949.41	1054.28	948.11	1054.28
黑色金属冶炼和压延加工业	Smelting and Processing of ferrous Metals	213.67	238.26	210.64	215.95
有色金属冶炼和压延加工业	Smelting and Processing of Nonferrous Metals	142.70	125.32	142.70	125.32
金属制品业	Metal Products	447.01	417.73	446.36	415.08
通用设备制造业	Ordinaryly Machinery Manufacturing	493.65	566.23	474.78	551.44
专用设备制造业	Special Purpose Equipment Manufacturing	617.43	686.75	598.76	669.30
汽车制造业	Automobile Manufacturing	1036.29	1399.79	1012.14	1354.10
铁路、船舶、航空航天和其他运输设备制造业	Realway, Ship, Aircraft and Other Transport Equipment Manufacturing	125.69	136.07	112.58	124.78
电气机械和器材制造业	Electric Machinery and Equipment	540.69	651.86	540.69	651.86
计算机、通信和其他电子设备制造业	Computers, Communication Equipment and Other Electronic Equipment Manufacturing	538.08	594.86	528.02	586.13
仪器仪表制造业	Measuring Instruments Manufacturing	94.73	115.90	92.52	110.63
其他制造业	Other Equipment	87.48	83.48	86.17	83.48
废弃资源综合利用业	Recycling and Disposal of Waste	77.56	65.67	77.56	64.30
金属制品、机械和设备修理业	Repairing of Metal and Mechanical Equipment	22.04	14.73	22.04	13.75
电力、热力、燃气及水生产和供应业	Electric Power, Gas and Water Production and Supply	604.47	769.17	508.74	726.80
电力、热力生产和供应业	Electric Power, Steam and Hot Water Production and Supply	384.17	528.95	293.17	490.26
燃气生产和供应业	Gas Production and Supply	72.17	65.60	69.07	63.71
水的生产和供应业	Tap Water Production and Supply	148.13	174.62	146.51	172.83

注：从2012年起执行新的国民经济行业代码（GB/T4754-2011）

4–21 续表 continued

单位：亿元 (100 million yuan)

行业	sector	全省 2014	全省 2015	#地方 2014	#地方 2015
建筑业	Construction	120.51	164.06	109.01	151.96
交通运输、仓储和邮政业	Transportation, storage and Post	2157.93	2574.55	2063.15	2503.19
铁路运输业	Railway Transportation	96.59	83.02	16.26	32.08
道路运输业	Road Transportation	1497.30	1793.83	1486.58	1778.49
水上运输业	Waterway Transportation	126.22	170.77	124.93	169.91
航空运输业	Air Transportation	55.57	48.26	55.57	48.26
管道运输业	Pipeline Transportation	3.95	5.49	3.95	5.49
装卸搬运和运输代理业	Load, Unload, and Agency	75.92	105.15	75.92	105.15
仓储业	Transportation Storage	296.23	362.18	293.78	357.97
邮政业	Post	6.14	5.85	6.14	5.85
信息传输、软件和信息技术服务业	Information Transmission, Software and Information Technology Service	104.72	156.88	95.10	142.19
电信、广播电视和卫星传输服务	Telecom, Radio Tv and Satellite	68.64	96.75	59.31	82.21
互联网和相关服务	Internet and Related	10.55	20.99	10.55	20.99
软件和信息技术服务业	Software and Information Technology	25.53	39.14	25.25	38.99
批发和零售业	Wholesale and Retail Trade	695.08	858.15	690.59	854.81
住宿和餐饮业	Hotel and Catering Services	320.85	353.51	320.85	353.51
金融业	Finance	89.11	60.82	85.21	59.31
货币金融服务	Monetary Financial Service	52.34	23.66	48.44	22.15
资本市场服务	Monetary Financial Service	30.87	32.01	30.87	32.01
保险业	Insurance	3.20	2.19	3.20	2.19
其他金融业	Other Financial Acitivities	2.71	2.96	2.71	2.96
房地产业	Real Estate Trade	5723.24	6503.46	5627.90	6358.54
租赁和商务服务业	Leasing and Commercial Service	496.70	700.14	496.70	696.22
租赁业	Leasing Service	14.92	22.23	14.92	22.23
商务服务业	Commercial Service	481.78	677.91	481.78	673.99
科学研究和技术服务业	Scientific Research, Polytechnical Services	108.24	144.24	101.24	122.78
水利、环境和公共设施管理业	Water Conservancy, Environment and Public Facility Management	2212.19	3061.06	2158.90	2994.38
水利管理业	Water Conservancy Management	297.63	438.27	275.73	413.76
生态保护和环境治理业	Environment Management	117.67	156.74	117.67	145.61
公共设施管理业	Public Facility Management	1796.89	2466.05	1765.51	2435.01
居民服务、修理和其他服务业	Resident Service and Others	187.72	134.09	187.72	133.80
教育	Education	253.54	280.81	210.49	245.50
卫生和社会工作	Health Care and Social Work	215.48	227.11	202.12	220.07
卫生	Health Care	165.84	181.43	152.48	174.40
社会工作	Social Work	49.64	45.67	49.64	45.67
文化、体育和娱乐业	Culture, Sports and Recreation	280.95	314.06	268.14	296.84
新闻和出版业	News and Publication	0.92	3.02	0.92	3.02
广播、电视、电影和影视录音制作业	Radio, Television, Film and Recording	9.04	12.01	9.04	12.01
文化艺术业	Culture and Arts	102.90	131.88	101.18	131.33
体育	Sports	59.49	53.89	51.02	53.11
娱乐业	Receation	108.60	113.25	105.98	97.37
公共管理、社会保障和社会组织	Public Management and Social Organizations	440.56	413.92	429.55	409.24

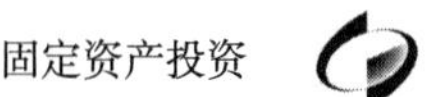

4-22 全社会按三次产业划分的投资额
ACCORDING TO THE THREE INDUSTRIES OF WHOLE SOCIETY OF INVESTMENT

单位：亿元 (100 million yuan)

年 份 In copies	全省			地方		
	第一产业 The first industry	第二产业 The second industry	第三产业 The third industry	第一产业 The first industry	第二产业 The second industry	第三产业 The third industry
1978	2.24	25.28	6.06	2.24	8.80	3.85
1980	2.11	22.75	10.64	2.03	9.98	7.52
"六五"时期	**24.77**	**155.02**	**136.03**	**24.05**	**83.83**	**114.89**
1985	8.37	47.42	47.12	8.09	31.48	41.46
"七五"时期	**49.76**	**335.53**	**294.83**	**47.24**	**245.00**	**245.71**
1986	7.89	50.33	53.22	7.40	34.88	46.62
1987	9.52	70.17	60.39	9.07	52.40	50.98
1988	11.11	85.76	63.59	10.53	67.14	53.59
1989	9.08	61.86	52.76	8.63	44.28	42.43
1990	12.16	67.41	64.87	11.61	46.30	52.09
"八五"时期	**78.98**	**1074.06**	**1058.63**	**73.97**	**674.84**	**831.75**
1991	12.48	77.95	77.76	12.12	55.25	63.69
1992	12.42	121.00	107.31	11.04	87.18	88.79
1993	11.89	170.93	200.36	10.10	114.05	163.87
1994	14.97	302.49	275.61	14.38	173.32	222.89
1995	27.22	401.69	397.59	26.11	220.95	316.82
"九五"时期	**272.08**	**2298.38**	**3452.34**	**271.69**	**1265.99**	**2763.13**
1996	29.76	451.28	503.34	29.73	272.79	389.96
1997	41.02	436.04	606.54	41.02	269.87	468.15
1998	59.48	450.16	721.46	59.48	234.94	594.01
1999	71.22	439.32	791.63	71.22	227.20	639.31
2000	70.60	521.58	829.37	70.24	261.19	671.70
"十五"时期	**416.79**	**3952.90**	**5969.82**	**414.74**	**2724.92**	**5277.86**
2001	77.48	590.01	902.08	77.33	323.55	740.91
2002	80.08	648.81	966.33	79.02	375.77	833.38
2003	88.80	714.81	1079.98	88.35	489.49	974.99
2004	77.55	912.93	1365.90	77.16	684.54	1245.86
2005	92.88	1086.34	1655.53	92.88	851.57	1482.72
"十一五"时期	**1202.88**	**12641.78**	**19075.27**	**1197.58**	**10748.83**	**17471.71**
2006	107.64	1317.12	2147.93	107.56	1044.17	1845.87
2007	149.40	1710.74	2674.00	148.72	1395.28	2365.09
2008	231.25	2346.32	3220.99	230.95	1859.42	2926.62
2009	321.59	3097.68	4792.58	319.58	2656.02	4442.25
2010	393.00	4169.92	6239.77	390.77	3793.94	5891.88
"十二五"时期	**3354.26**	**44874.29**	**56157.36**	**3351.93**	**43109.22**	**54397.45**
2011	440.91	5526.40	6967.71	440.51	5032.88	6623.90
2012	525.45	7281.04	8697.68	525.13	6891.67	8326.75
2013	590.61	9187.25	10976.04	589.28	8883.83	10672.89
2014	799.35	10733.09	13469.32	799.07	10432.00	13120.68
2015	997.94	12146.51	16046.61	997.94	11868.84	15653.23

注：从2012年起，三次产业采用新的划分标准。

4–23 全社会竣工房屋建筑面积及竣工率
THE FLOOR SPACE OF BUILDINGS COMPLETED ALL SOCIAL AND COMPLETION RATE

年 份 In copies	施工面积(万平方米) Construction area (million square meters)	#住宅 # residential	竣工面积(万平方米) Completion of (million square meters)	#住宅 # residential	竣工率(%) Completion rate (%)	#住宅 # residential
1978	1343.27	513.20	666.76	280.16	49.6	54.6
1980	1951.16	1004.17	1024.51	586.27	52.5	58.4
"六五"时期			**25700.97**	**19626.87**		
1985	8079.90	5965.71	6899.59	5434.20	85.4	91.1
"七五"时期			**29202.17**	**22387.23**		
1986	8760.15	6686.78	7754.53	6308.96	88.5	94.3
1987	7922.23	5684.88	6803.61	5233.59	85.9	92.1
1988	7225.98	4892.04	6060.44	4484.69	83.9	91.7
1989	5250.24	3590.22	4414.47	3301.59	84.1	92.0
1990	5103.48	3507.53	4169.12	3058.40	81.7	87.2
"八五"时期			**23403.26**	**16559.28**		
1991	5300.98	3652.67	4211.39	3157.13	79.4	86.4
1992	5954.84	4066.51	4621.87	3383.72	77.6	83.2
1993	5807.24	3540.57	4050.56	2798.42	69.8	79.0
1994	7158.68	4476.46	4916.24	3482.20	68.7	77.8
1995	8294.84	5304.79	5603.20	3737.81	67.6	70.5
"九五"时期			**35861.86**	**26378.48**		
1996	8749.65	5581.32	6073.43	4485.82	69.4	80.4
1997	8963.28	5976.86	6430.48	4790.34	71.7	80.1
1998	10485.86	7179.25	7897.96	5792.97	75.3	80.7
1999	10228.93	7219.06	7951.03	5891.97	77.7	81.6
2000	9920.42	6831.02	7508.96	5417.38	75.7	79.3
"十五"时期			**40164.49**	**29588.06**		
2001	10040.11	7273.21	7716.37	5850.27	76.9	80.4
2002	10301.00	7019.76	7796.76	5583.27	75.7	79.5
2003	10667.78	7276.62	7469.17	5457.42	70.0	75.0
2004	13152.08	9285.64	9318.34	7069.45	70.6	75.9
2005	12572.00	8401.20	7863.85	5627.67	62.6	67.0
"十一五"时期			**43810.54**	**26870.86**		
2006	12346.48	8039.75	7126.64	4812.39	57.7	59.9
2007	13686.34	8910.75	7557.62	5036.19	55.2	56.5
2008	16417.07	9896.66	7551.82	4679.96	46.0	47.3
2009	20142.81	11762.06	9772.28	5556.71	48.5	47.2
2010	25284.83	14486.90	11802.18	6785.61	46.7	46.8
"十二五"时期			**94158.28**	**41354.62**		
2011	31388.88	16337.96	14585.68	7375.38	46.5	45.1
2012	40103.56	19154.75	16576.18	7890.08	41.3	41.2
2013	51939.51	23443.19	18828.87	8006.06	36.3	34.2
2014	58064.39	27199.41	21175.37	8702.01	36.5	32.0
2015	58095.72	29006.34	22992.18	9381.09	39.6	32.3

主要统计指标解释

全社会固定资产投资 是以货币形式表现的在一定时期内全社会建造和购置固定资产的工作量以及与此有关的费用的总称。该指标是反映固定资产投资规模、结构和发展速度的综合性指标,又是观察工程进度和考核投资效果的重要依据。全社会固定资产投资按登记注册类型可分为国有、集体、个体、联营、股份制、外商、港澳台商、其他等。

固定资产投资 指各种登记注册类型的企业、事业、行政单位及个体户进行的计划总投资500万元及500万元以上的建设项目投资、房地产开发投资、城镇和工矿区私人建房投资。

房地产开发投资 指各种登记注册类型的房地产开发公司、商品房建设公司及其他房地产开发法人单位和附属于其他法人单位实际从事房地产开发或经营活动的单位统一开发的包括统代建、拆迁还建的住宅、厂房、仓库、饭店、宾馆、度假村、写字楼、办公楼等房屋建筑物和配套的服务设施,土地开发工程(如道路、给水、排水、供电、供热、通讯、平整场地等基础设施工程)的投资;不包括单纯的土地交易活动。

城镇和工矿区私人建房投资 包括市、县城、城关镇、工矿区所辖范围内的全部私人建房,不论其房主是否系本地的常住户口均应包括。

农村投资 包括在农村区域范围内进行固定资产投资活动的企业、事业、行政单位及农村个人投资。

固定资产投资的资金来源 根据固定资产投资的资金来源不同,分为国家预算内资金、国内贷款、利用外资、自筹资金和其他资金。

(1)国家预算内资金:分为财政拨款和财政安排的贷款两部分。包括中央财政的基本建设基金(分经营性基金和非经营性基金两部分)、专项支出(如煤代油专项等)、收回再贷、贴息资金,财政安排的挖潜改造和新产品试制支出、城建支出、商业部门简易建筑支出、不发达地区发展基金等资金中用于固定资产投资的资金;地方财政中由国家统筹安排的资金等。

(2)国内贷款:指报告期固定资产投资单位向银行及非银行金融机构借入的用于固定资产投资的各种国内借款,包括银行利用自有资金及吸收的存款发放的贷款、上级主管部门拨入的国内贷款、国家专项贷款(包括煤代油贷款、劳改煤矿专项贷款等)、地方财政专项资金安排的贷款、国内储备贷款、周转贷款等。

(3)利用外资:指报告期收到的用于固定资产建造和购置的国外资金(包括设备、材料、技术在内)。包括对外借款(外国政府、国际金融组织贷款、出口信贷、外国银行商业贷款、对外发行债券和股票)、外商直接投资及外商其他投资。不包括我国自有外汇资金(国家外汇、地方外汇、留成外汇、调剂外汇和中国银行自有资金发行的外汇贷款等)。计算利用外资时,需要折算成人民币,折算中所使用的外汇汇率按现汇计算,即按使用外汇时的汇率计算。

(4)自筹资金:指固定资产投资单位报告期收到的,由各地区、各部门及企、事业单位筹集用于固定资产投资的预算外资金,包括中央各部门、各级地方和企、事业单位的自筹资金。

(5)其他资金:指在报告期收到的除以上各种资金之外其他用于固定资产投资的资金,包括企业或金融机构通过发行各种债券筹集到的资金、群众集资、个人资金、无偿捐赠的资金及其他单位拨入的资金等。

固定资产投资按国民经济行业分 根据建设项目建成投产后的主要产品或主要用途及社会经济活动性质来确定国民经济行业。一般情况下,一个建设项目或一个企业、事业单位只能属于一种国民经济行业。

固定资产投资按隶属关系分 是按建设单位或企业、事业、行政单位的主管上级机关确定的。

(1)中央:是指中共中央、人大常委会和国务院各部、委、局、总公司以及直属机构直接领导的建设项目和企业、事业、行政单位。这些单位的固定资产投资计划由国务院各部门直接编制和下达,建设中所需物资、主要设备以及建设中的问题都由中央有关部门安排和解决。

(2)地方:是由省(自治区、直辖市)、地区(州、盟、省辖市)、县(旗、县级市)三级政府及业务主管部门直接领导和管理的建设项目、企业、事业、行政单位。地方项目还包括不隶属以上各级政府及主管部门的建设项目和企业、事业单位,如外商投资企业和无主管部门的企业等。

固定资产投资按建设性质分 根据整个建设项目情况来确定。建设项目的性质一般分为新建、扩建、改建和技术改造、迁建、恢复。房地产开发单位、农村投资、城镇工矿区私人建房投资不划分建设性质。

(1)新建:一般指从无到有“平地起家”开始建设的企业、事业和行政单位或建设项目。现有企业、事业、行政单位一般不属于新建。但如有的单位原有基础很小,经过建设后新增的固定资产价值超过该企、事业、行政单位原有固定资产价值(原值)三倍以上的也应作为新建。

(2)扩建:指在厂内或其他地点,为扩大原有产品的生产能力(或效益)或增加新的产品生产能力,而增建主要的生产车间(或主要工程)、分厂、独立的生产线。行政、事业单位在原单位增建业务用房(如学校增建教学用房、医院增建门诊部、病房等)也作为扩建。

现有企、事业单位为扩大原有主要产品生产能力或增加新的产品生产能力,增建一个或几个主要生产车间(或主要工程)、分厂,同时进行一些更新改造工程的,也应作为扩建。

(3)改建和技术改造:指现有企业、事业单位,对原有设施进行技术改造或更新(包括相应配套的辅助性生产、生活福利设施)的建设项目。现有企业、事业单位为适应市场变化的需要,而改变企业的主要产品种类(如军工企业转产民用品等) 的建设项目,应作为改建。原有产品生产作业线由于各工序(车间)之间能力不平衡,为填平补齐充分发挥原有生产能力而增建不增加本企业主要产品设计能力的车间,也应作为改建。技术改造是指企业、事业单位在现有基础上,用先进的技术代替落后的技术,用先进的工艺和装备代替落后的工艺和装备,以改变企业落后的技术经济面貌,实现以内涵为主的扩大再生产,达到提高产品质量、促进产品更新换代、节约能源、降低消耗、扩大生产规模、全面提高社会经济效益的目的。技术改造具体包括以下内容:机器设备和工具的更新改造;生产工艺改革、节约能源和原材料的改造;厂房建筑和公共设施的改造;劳动条件和生产环境的改造等。

固定资产投资按构成分 固定资产投资活动按其工作内容和实现方式分为建筑安装工程,设备、工具、器具购置,其他费用三个部分。

(1)建筑安装工程(建筑安装工作量):指各种房屋、建筑物的建造工程和各种设备、装置的安装工程。包括各种房屋建造工程;各种用途设备基础和各种工业窑炉的砌筑工程及金属结构工程;为施工而进行的各种准备工作和临时工程以及完工后的清理工作等;铁路、道路的铺设,矿井的开凿及石油管道的架设等;水利工程;防空地下建筑等特殊工程;列入房屋工程预算内的暖气、卫生、通风、照明、煤气等设备的价值及装设油饰工程;列入建筑工程预算内的各种管道(蒸汽、压缩空气、石油、给排水等管道)、电力、电讯电缆导线等的敷设工程;以及各种机械设备的安装工程;为测定安装工程质量,对设备进行的试运工作;房地产开发单位进行的商品房屋开发建设工程、土地开发工程。

在安装工程中,不包括被安装设备本身的价值。

(2)设备、工具、器具购置:指建设单位或企、事业单位购置或自制的,达到固定资产标准的设备、工具、器具的价值。新建单位及扩建单位的新建车间,按照设计或计划要求购置或自制的全部设备、工具、器具,不论是否达到固定资产标准均计入“设备、工具、器具购置”中。

(3)其他费用:指在固定资产建造和购置过程中发生的,除上述几项内容以外的各种应分摊计入固定资产的费用。

施工项目 指报告期内进行过建筑或安装施工活动的项目。凡是报告期内施过工的建设项目,不论施工时间长短,均作为施工项目统计。施工项目个数可以反映一定时期固定资产投资的实际规模,与同期全部建成投产项目个数相比,可以从建设速度的角度反映固定资产投资的效果。根据建设项目施工活动的不同性质,施工项目又分为:本年正式施工项目、本年收尾项目和以前年度全部停缓建项目。

全部建成投产项目 工业项目指设计文件规定形成生产能力的主体工程及其相应配套的辅助设施全部建成,经负荷试运转,证明具备生产设计规定合格产品的条件,并经过验收鉴定合格或达到竣工验收标准,与生产性工程配套的生活福利设施可以满足近期正常生产的需要,正式移交生产的建设项目。非工业项目指设计文件规定的主体工程和相应的配套工程全部建成,能够发挥设计规定的全部效益,经验收鉴定合格或达到竣工验收标准,正式移交使用的建设项目。

新增生产能力(或工程效益) 指通过固定资产投资活动而增加的设计能力(或工程效益),该指标是以实物形态表现的反映固定资产投资成果的指标,也是考核投资经济效果的重要依据之一。

房屋建筑面积 指房屋建筑物勒脚以上外墙外围的水平截面面积,包括房屋建筑物的有效面积和结构面积。该指标是从实物形态上反映建设规模和建设成果的重要指标之一,也是检查工程形象进度、计算工程造价、分析投资效果、研究施工任务和建筑材料之间平衡情况的重要依据。

住宅建筑面积 指施工和竣工房屋建筑面积中供居住用的房屋建筑面积。

施工面积 指报告期内施工的全部房屋建筑面积。包括本期新开工的面积和上期开工跨入本期继续施工的房屋面积,以及上期已停建在本期恢复施工的房屋面积。本期竣工和本期施工后又停缓建的房屋，其建筑面积仍计入本期房屋施工面积中。

竣工面积 指在报告期内房屋建筑按照设计要求已经全部完工，达到住人和使用条件，经验收鉴定合格(或达到竣工验收标准)，正式移交使用单位的各栋房屋建筑面积的总和。

房屋建筑面积竣工率 指一定时期内房屋竣工面积占同期房屋施工面积的比率。是从房屋建筑施工速度的角度反映投资效果的指标。

新增固定资产 指报告期内已经完成建造和购置过程，并已交付生产或使用单位的固定资产价值。该指标是表示固定资产投资成果的价值指标，也是反映建设进度，计算固定资产投资效果的重要指标。

项目建设投产率 指一定时期内全部建成投产项目个数与同期施工项目个数的比率。该指标是从建设单位建设速度的角度反映投资效果的指标。

固定资产交付使用率 指一定时期新增固定资产与同期完成投资额的比率。该指标是反映固定资产动用速度，衡量建设过程中宏观投资效果的综合指标。由于新增固定资产是较长时期内形成的结果，而投资额则是当年完成的，因此，该指标一般适宜于反映较长时期内固定资产的动用情况。

商品房销售面积 指报告期内出售商品房屋的合同总面积(即双方签署的正式买卖合同中所确定的建筑面积)。由现房销售建筑面积和期房销售建筑面积两部分组成。

商品房销售额 指报告期内出售商品房屋的合同总价款(即双方签署的正式买卖合同中所确定的合同总价)。该指标与商品房销售面积同口径，由现房销售额和期房销售额两部分组成。

经济适用房 指根据地方经济适用房计划安排建设的政策性住宅。经济是指房屋建筑造价和销售价格低于一般商品住宅；适用是指适合中低收入家庭购买使用。经济适用房主要是由国家统一下达投资计划，房地产公司开发，对外销售；用地一般采用行政划拨或招标投标方式，免收土地出让金；对各种经批准的收费减半征收，开发利润不超过3%；销售价格实行政府指导价。该指标可以分析房地产投资结构，反映中低收入家庭商品住宅的供求平衡情况。

Explanatory Notes on Main Statistical Indicators

Total Investment in Fixed Assets in the Whole Country refers to the volume of activities in construction and purchases of fixed assets and related fees, expressed in monetary terms. It is a comprehensive indicator which shows the size, structure and growth of the investment in fixed assets, providing basis for observing the progress of construction projects and evaluating results of investment. Total investment in fixed assets in the whole country includes, by type of ownership, the investment by the state-owned units, collective units, individuals, joint ownership units, share-holding units, as well as investment by businessmen from foreign countries and from Hong Kong, Macao and Taiwan, and by other units.

Investment in Fixed Assets refers to construction projects involving a total planned investment of 500,000 yuan and over by enterprises and institutions of various types of ownership, by administrative units and by individuals, investment in real estate development, and housing investment by individuals in urban areas and in industrial and mining areas.

Investment in Real Estate Development refers to the investment by the real estate development companies, commercial buildings construction companies and other real estate development units of various types of ownership in the construction of house buildings, such as residential buildings, factory buildings, warehouses, hotels, guesthouses, holiday villages, office buildings, and the complementary service facilities and land development projects, such as roads, water supply, water drainage, power supply, heating, telecommunications, land leveling and other projects of infrastructure. It excludes the activities in pure land transactions.

Investment in Housing Construction in Urban Areas and in Industrial and Mining Areas refers to all private housing construction under the jurisdiction of cities, county towns and industrial and mining areas, no matter whether the owner of the house is registered as the permanent resident in the locality or not.

Investment in Rural Areas refers to investment in fixed assets by enterprises, institutions and individuals in rural areas.

Sources of Funds for Investment in Fixed Assets include fund from state budget, domestic loans, foreign investment, self-raised funds, and others depending on the source of investment.

(1) Fund from state budget consists of budgetary appropriation and loans from state budget. More specifically, it includes, from the budget of the central government, capital construction fund (operation fund and non–operational fund), special expenses (e.g. expenses on substituting petroleum with coal), loans from repayment, discount fund, expenses on innovation and trial production of new products, expenses on urban construction, expenses on temporary construction by trade departments, development fund for less developed areas, as well as local budgetary fund transferred from the central budget.

(2) Domestic loans refer to loans of various forms borrowed by investing units from banks and non–bank financial institutions during the reference period for the purpose of investment in fixed assets, including loans issued by banks from their self–owned funds and deposit, loans appropriated by higher responsible authorities, special loans by government (including loan for substituting petroleum with coal, special loan for reform–through–labour coal mines), loans arranged by local government from special funds, domestic reserve loan, and working loan, etc..

(3) Foreign Investment refers to foreign funds received during the reference period for the construction and purchase of investment in fixed assets (covering equipment, materials and technology), including foreign borrowings (loans from foreign governments and international financial institutions, export credit, commercial loans from foreign banks, issue of bonds and stocks overseas), foreign direct investment and other foreign investment. Excluded in this category are capitals in foreign exchanges owned by China (foreign exchanges owned by the central and local governments, foreign exchanges retained by enterprises, foreign exchanges by enterprises through regulating mechanism, loans in foreign exchanges issued by the Bank of China with its own fund, etc.). In calculating the utilization of foreign capitals, foreign currencies are converted into Chinese Renminbi applying the current exchange rate when the foreign capitals are actually used.

(4) Self–raised funds refer to extra–budgetary funds for investment in fixed assets received by investing units from central government ministries, local governments, enterprises and institutions, including their self–raised funds.

(5) Others refer to funds for investment in fixed assets received from the sources other than those listed above, including capitals raised through issuing bonds by enterprises or financial institutions, funds raised from individuals and through donations, and funds transferred from other units.

Investment in Fixed Assets by Sector The classification of construction projects by sector is determined by the major products or the purpose of the projects when they are put into production or use, and by the nature of their social economic activities. In general, one project or one enterprise or institution can only be classified into one sector.

Investment in Fixed Assets by Jurisdiction of Management refers to the classification of investment by the competent authorities under which investment is made by construction units, enterprises, institutions or administrative units.

(1) Central investment refers to the investment in projects or by enterprises, institutions or administrative units which are under the direct leadership and management of the CPC Central Committee, the NPC Standing Committee, the State Council and of the national commissions, ministries, agencies and state–owned large corporations. Various ministries and departments of the State Council prepare and implement plans for investment in fixed assets by those departments, and arrange and ensure the supply of materials and key equipment required for the projects.

(2) Local investment refers to the investment in projects or by enterprises, institutions or administrative units which are under the direct leadership and management of departments under the provincial, prefecture and county governments. Also included are projects by foreign–invested enterprises and enterprises without competent managing authorities.

Investment in Fixed Assets by Type of Construction The construction projects in general can be classified, by the type of construction, into new construction, expansion, reconstruction and technical transformation, moving and restoration. However, investment by type of construction is not applied to investment by real–estate development units, investment in rural areas and investment in housing by urban individuals.

(1) New construction in general refers to newly constructed enterprises, institutions, administrative agencies or independent projects from scratch. Construction in the existing enterprises, institutions or agencies is not considered as new construction. In case the assets of the existing unit is quite small, and the value of newly added fixed assets exceeds the original value of assets by three times, the expansion will be considered as new construction.

(2) Expansion refers to construction of new major production workshop, branch factory or independent production line within a facto–

ry or in other locations, for the purpose of increasing the production capacity (or improving efficiency) of the original products. Newly constructed houses for the operation of institutions and administrative organizations (such as the newly constructed buildings for teaching in schools, buildings for clinics or wards in hospitals, etc.) are also classified as expansion.

Also included in the expansion are investments by existing enterprises or institutions in building major production line(s) or branch factory(ies) along with some work on innovation, for the purpose of expending the production capacity of original products or producing new products.

(3) Reconstruction refers to construction projects by existing enterprises or institutions in innovation or technical transformation of the old facilities (including auxiliary production equipment and welfare facilities). Also considered as reconstruction is the construction of new workshops by the existing enterprises or institutions to change the variety of products to meet the market demand (such as the production of civil products by defence industries), or to bring the designed production capacity into full play through a more balanced production process on production lines. Technical transformation refers to replacement of old technology or equipment by new technology or equipment, in order to expand the reproduction through improvement of technology contents in production, to improve product quality, to promote new products, to save energy and reduce consumption and to improve overall social-economic efficiency. Contents of technical transformation include: updating of machinery, equipment and tools; reforming production process by using energy or materials saving technology; construction of factory workshops and transformation of public facilities; improvement of working conditions and environment, etc.

Investment in Fixed Assets by Structure By their contents, investment activities are classified into 3 categories, i.e. construction and installation, purchase of equipment and instrument, and other expenses.

(1) Construction and installation (work volume of construction and installation) refers to the construction of various houses and buildings and installation of various kinds of equipment and instruments. They include construction of various houses; equipment foundations, industrial kilns and stoves, and metal structure work; preparation works for project construction, and clearing up works post project construction; pavement of railways and roads, drilling of mines and putting up of oil pipes; construction of projects of water conservancy; construction of underground air-raid shelters and construction of other special projects; value of equipment for heating, sanitation, ventilation, lighting, gas, painting, etc. that are covered by the budget of housing projects; laying out of various pipelines (for steam, compressed air, petroleum, tap water and sewage) and lines for electric power and for communications; installation of various machinery equipment, testing operation for pre-testing the quality of installation projects, and land and other development work conducted by real estate developers for commercial housing. The value of equipment installed is not included in the value of installation projects.

(2) Purchase of equipment and instruments refers to the total value of equipment, tools, and instruments purchased or self-produced which come up to standards for fixed assets by the construction units or investing enterprises or institutions. Equipment, tools and instruments purchased or self-produced for new workshops by newly established or expanded units are categorized as "purchase of equipment and instruments" no matter whether they come up to the standards for fixed assets.

(3) Other expenses refer to expenses occurring during the construction or purchase of fixed assets other than those mentioned above.

Projects under Construction refer to projects with construction and installation activities undertaken in the reference period. All projects that have construction activities undertaken during the reference period are reported as projects under construction irrespective of the length of construction work. The number of projects under construction can reflect the actual size of investment in fixed assets during a given period, and when compared with the number of projects completed and put into use during the same period, it demonstrates the results of investment in fixed assets. Depending on the nature of construction activities, projects under construction can also be classified into projects under construction in current year, winding-up projects in current year and stopped or suspended projects in previous years (with preservation work in current year).

Projects Completed and Put into Use Industrial projects refer to the major projects and accessory facilities completed which result in forming production capacity and have been checked and accepted while the living and welfare facilities have been completed and can ensure normal production and formally put into production. Non-industrial projects refer to the major projects and accessory facilities completed which possess the designed capacity and have been checked, accepted and formally put into production.

Newly Increased Production Capacity(or Project Efficiency) refers to the increase of designed capacity (or project efficiency) through investment in fixed assets, which reflects the accomplishment of investment in fixed assets in kind and serves as important basis for evaluating the economic efficiency of investment.

Floor Space of Buildings under Construction refers to total floor space of the horizontal section of outer walls above the plinth of the building, including the effective area and the area occupied by the structure. This indicator is one of the important indicators in physical terms to reflect the scale and accomplishment of the construction industry, and important basis for monitoring the progress, calculating the cost, analyzing the efficiency and studying the supply of building materials in relation with the construction projects.

Floor Space of Residential Buildings refers to the floor space of the residential buildings among the total space of buildings under construction or completed.

Floor Space under Construction refers to total floor space of all buildings under construction during the reference period, including floor space of newly started buildings during the reference period, floor space of construction extended from the previous period to the current period, and floor space of construction suspended during the previous period and resumed in the current period. Floor space of construction completed in the current period, and floor space of construction started and then suspended in the current period are also included in the floor space under construction of the current year.

Floor Space of Buildings Completed refers to the floor space of all buildings completed in the reference period, which have been appraised and accepted (or come up to the designed standards) and have been transferred to the owners for use.

Completion Rate of Floor Space of Buildings refers to the ratio of the floor space of buildings completed in certain period of time to the floor space of buildings under construction in the same period. This indicator reflects the investment result from the perspective of the speed of construction.

Newly Increased Fixed Assets refer to the newly increased value of fixed assets, constructed or purchased, that have been transferred to the investors. This is an indicator that demonstrates the results of investment in fixed assets in monetary terms, and an important indicator to reflect the speed of construction and to calculate the efficiency of investment.

Rate of Construction Projects Completed and Put into Use refers to the ratio of the number of construction projects completed and put into use in certain period of time to the number of projects under construction in the same period. This reflects the investment efficiency from the perspective of the speed of projects construction.

Rate of Projects of Fixed Assets Completed and Put into Operation refers to the ratio of the newly increased fixed assets to the total investment made in the same period. This is a comprehensive indicator reflecting the speed of the employment of fixed assets and the investment efficiency at the macro-level. As the newly increase fixed assets is the result of a long period while the investment is completed in the current year, this indicator is expected to be used to reflect the employment of fixed assets over a long period of time.

Area of Commercial Housing Sold refers to total contracted area of commercial housing (i.e. area of floor space as designated in the formal contracts signed by both sides) during the reference time. It constitutes floor space of completed housing and floor space of future housing.

Value of Commercial Housing Sold refer to total value of contracts (i.e. value of sales/purchase for selling/purchase of commercial housing as designated in the contracts signed by both sides) during the reference time. It has the same coverage as the area of commercial housing sold, constituting completed housing and floor space of future housing

Economically Affordable Housing refers to housing constructed according to the state plan for economically affordable housing. Houses of this category featured in low cost in construction and low prices, and therefore are affordable to mid-income or low income households. Economically affordable housing projects are developed by real estate companies under the state investment plan, with the land provided through government allocation or tendering procedures. Developers are exempted from land utilization fees and enjoy another 50% exemption of all other legitimate fees, while their profits are limited to less than 3%, and the completed houses are sold under the government-guided prices. This indicator helps to analyze the investment structure of the real estate industry and the demand and supply of housing for mid or low income households.

5 对外经济贸易和旅游

Foreign Economic, Trade and Tourism

5-1 对外经济主要指标
MAJOR INDICATORS OF FOREIGN TRADE AND ECONOMIC COOPERATION

单位:万美元 (USD 10 000)

指 标	Item	1995	2000	2005	2010	2011	2012	2013	2014	2015
进出口总额	**Total Imports and Exports**	**340920**	**320249**	**905475**	**2593211**	**3358693**	**3196409**	**3638928**	**4306401**	**4558578**
进口总额	Total Imports	142484	127369	462607	1149031	1405233	1256525	1355160	1641821	1637232
出口总额	Total Exports	198435	192880	442868	1444180	1953460	1939884	2283768	2664580	2921346
合同外商直接投资项目(个)	**Contracted Projets of Foreign Direct Investment (uint)**	**881**	**331**	**520**	**306**	**339**	**271**	**297**	**301**	**274**
合同外商直接投资	**Contracted Value of Foreign Direct Investment**	**108847**	**106583**	**211023**	**278627**	**497130**	**363927**	**485467**	**629624**	**416112**
实际外商直接投资	**Actual Value of Foreign Direct Investment**	**62253**	**94368**	**218475**	**405015**	**465503**	**566591**	**688847**	**792792**	**894801**
对外经济合作	**Economic and Technical Cooperation with Foreign** Countries									
合同金额	Contracted Value	7300	36706	35953	776945	639273	737945	1033540		
#对外承包工程	#Contracted Projects			27952	765547	631308	726900	1015084	1269954	1145362
对外劳务合作	Labor Services			5568	11398	7965	11045	12286		
完成营业额	Value of Business Fulfilled	4100	15815	31843	327164	415002	465863	538927		
#对外承包工程	#Contracted Projects			28852	319979	406741	456194	520733	579636	523369
对外劳务合作	Labor Services			2601	7186	8261	9669	18194		

5-2 对外贸易进出口总额
TOTAL IMPORTS AND EXPORTS

单位:万美元 (USD 10 000)

年 份 Year	合 计 Total	进 口 Imports	出 口 Exports
1992	174533	58696	115837
1993	222912	100170	122743
1994	274880	103035	171845
1995	340920	142484	198435
1996	286287	133684	152603
1997	320668	128583	192084
1998	283189	112478	170711
1999	268107	116729	151378
2000	320249	127369	192880
2001	357720	178041	179679
2002	395314	185488	209826
2003	510930	245393	265537
2004	676581	338361	338219
2005	905475	462607	442868
2006	1176219	550157	626063
2007	1489647	669593	820054
2008	2070567	899676	1170891
2009	1725102	727222	997880
2010	2593211	1149031	1444180
2011	3358693	1405233	1953460
2012	3196409	1256525	1939884
2013	3638928	1355160	2283768
2014	4306401	1641821	2664580
2015	4558578	1637232	2921346

注:根据海关统计有关文件规定2008年年终数据部分调整。

Note:According to the provisions of the relevant documents to customs statistics data portion of the 2008 year-end adjustments.

5-3 按贸易方式和经济类型分的进出口总额

单位:万美元

项 目	Item	2000 进口 Imports	2000 出口 Exports	2005 进口 Imports	2005 出口 Exports
总 计	**Total**	**127369**	**192880**	**462607**	**442868**
按贸易方式分	**Grouped by Type of Trade**				
一般贸易	General Trade	91576	138907	340768	350354
来料加工装配贸易	Processing and Assembling Trade	20136	13265	15428	22381
进料加工贸易	Raw Material Input Processing Trade	32803	14154	54328	71920
来料加工装配进口的设备	Processing and Assembling Import Equipment Provided With Material	6		18	
外商作为投资进口的设备	Goods as Invested for Import Equipments	8602		45087	
租赁贸易	Leasing Trade			114	
出料加工贸易	Raw Material Output Processing Trade				
易货贸易	Repalce Goods with Goods				
保税仓库进出境货物	Import and Export Goods of Protcetive Tariff Storage	105		8028	33
按经济类型分	**Grouped by Ownership**				
#国有企业	#State-Owned Enterprises	64805	140826	221963	213955
集体企业	Collective-Owned Enterprises	1255	9124	5719	20033
外商投资企业	Foreign-funded Enterprises	61691	42901	190170	130579
民营企业	Private-Owned Enterprises	111	240	45839	80397

TOTAL IMPORTS AND EXPORTS VOLUME BY TYPE OF TRADE AND OWNERSHIP

(USD 10 000)

2010		2012		2013		2014		2015	
进口 Imports	出口 Exports	进口 Imports	出口 Exports	进口 Imports	出口 Exports	进口 Imports	出口 Exports	进口 Imports	出口 Exports
1149031	**1444180**	**1256525**	**1939884**	**1355160**	**2283768**	**1641821**	**2664580**	**1637232**	**2921346**
841306	829994	947733	1152839	1000601	1520152	1164862	1845637	1088411	1961768
28304	32269	21218	39039	18128	38854	14331	54818	11584	798372
210483	518911	208043	622969	281413	593316	430709	704313	487467	53984
348				230		38		29	
43809		24772		13487		12775		8312	
5	144	7	92	5	150	96	70		10
320	212	187	322	729	532	822	729	913	607
20511	16794	50275	41619	32427	38794	9389	17789	1630	16982
513134	472230	500014	540497	452200	527257	481941	545399	401246	574791
4021	16161	3802	18511	2427	19933	1746	19684	1398	18099
534565	569501	618044	762022	665555	732420	682190	772107	556216	674909
93032	386177	130133	618934	190004	1002635	455332	1326652	679603	1653454

5-4 进出口商品主要国别和地区
IMPORTS AND EXPORTS VALUE BY COUNTRIES AND REGIONS

单位:万美元 (USD 10 000)

国家(地区)	Countries (Regions)	2014			2015		
		进出口 Imports and Exports	进口 Imports	出口 Exports	进出口 Imports and Exports	进口 Imports	出口 Exports
亚 洲	**Asia**	**2230534**	**838644**	**1391889**	**2687717**	**956719**	**1730999**
#香港	#Hongkong	430030	92164	337866	723497	78844	644653
印度	India	126569	11965	114604	179956	8760	171196
日本	Japan	291864	187856	104008	304607	205522	99085
新加坡	Singapore	105161	25775	79385	85489	28734	56755
韩国	Korea, Rep.	182928	95983	86945	209909	124842	85067
台湾省	Taiwan Province	184491	134034	50457	175970	122480	53490
非 洲	**Afria**	**208550**	**82662**	**125888**	**198382**	**74157**	**124225**
#南非	#South Africa				59448	45158	14290
欧 洲	**European**	**826684**	**290948**	**535737**	**705112**	**233314**	**471798**
#比利时	#Belgium						
英国	United Kingdom						
德国	Germany	138948	74270	64678	136453	68803	67650
法国	France	132127	109297	22830	101523	78865	22658
意大利	Italy						
荷兰	Netherland						
西班牙	Spanish						
芬兰	Finland						
拉丁美洲	**Latin America**	**326200**	**102367**	**223833**	**325830**	**124259**	**201571**
#巴西	#Brazil	65939	28862	37077	82284	47393	34891
智利	Chile						
北美洲	**North America**	**489994**	**154774**	**335219**	**469525**	**142621**	**326905**
#加拿大	#Canada	76071	57561	18509			
美国	United States of America	413902	97213	316690	425177	118461	306716
大洋洲	**Occeania**	**224404**	**177526**	**52014**	**173929**	**107386**	**66543**
#澳大利亚	#Australia	214661	172128	42533	150332	107185	43147
附:东南亚国家联盟	**Association of Southeast-Asia Nations**	**598448**	**177526**	**420922**	**637841**	**268060**	**369781**
欧洲联盟	**European Union**	**70972**	**275711**	**434002**	**612001**	**220188**	**391813**
亚太经济合作组织	**Asia-Pacific Economic Cooperation**	**2715725**	**1146844**	**1568881**	**2883838**	**1098367**	**1785470**

5-5 合同外商直接投资项目
NUMBER OF CONTRACTED PROJECTS OF FOREIGN DIRECT INVESTMENT

单位:个 (unit)

指 标	Item	1990	1995	2000	2005	2010	2011	2012	2013	2014	2015
合 计	**Total**	**99**	**881**	**331**	**520**	**306**	**339**	**271**	**297**	**301**	**274**
合资经营企业	Joint Venture	17	577	156	203	108	138	102	116	127	101
合作经营企业	Cooperative Operation	75	44	16	29	5	8	5	8	3	4
独资经营企业	Foreign Solely Funded Enterprises	7	260	158	285	193	193	164	173	169	168
外商投资股份制企业	Share Holding Enterprises With Foreign Investment			1	3					2	1

5-6 合同外商直接投资金额
VALUE OF CONTRACTED PROJECTS OF FOREIGN DIRECT INVESTMENT

单位:万美元 (USD 10 000)

指 标	Item	1990	1995	2000	2005	2010	2011	2012	2013	2014	2015
合 计	**Total**	**3947**	**108847**	**106583**	**211023**	**278627**	**497130**	**363927**	**485467**	**629624**	**416112**
合资经营企业	Joint Venture	1364	68923	27936	51010	132679	253542	93573	135618	262121	78912
合作经营企业	Cooperative Operation	2464	7899	48711	24480	3319	11217	7315	15924	13424	11078
独资经营企业	Foreign Solely Funded	119	32025	29936	132897	235498	224344	252964	334151	345271	313337
外商投资股份制企业	Share Holding Enterprises With Foreign Investment				2636	33519	8027	10075	-226	8808	12785

5-7 实际外商直接投资金额
ACTUAL VALUE OF FOREIGN DIRECT INVESTMENT

单位:万美元 (USD 10 000)

指 标	Item	1990	1995	2000	2003	2004	2005
合 计	**Total**	**2900**	**62253**	**94368**	**155702**	**207126**	**218475**
合资经营企业	Joint Venture	2492	40259	59879	104622	130048	65472
合作经营企业	Cooperative Operation	85	5012	2789	5513	11741	5089
独资经营企业	Foreign Solely Funded	323	16982	31700	45139	62155	75305
外商投资股份制企业	Share Holding With Foreign Investment						2739

5-7 续表 continued

单位:万美元

指 标	Item	2010	2011	2012	2013	2014	2015
合 计	**Total**	**405015**	**465503**	**566591**	**688847**	**792792**	**894801**
合资经营企业	Joint Venture	132679	202268	257765	223950	300982	329123
合作经营企业	Cooperative Operation	3319	2992	647	3758	759	4261
独资经营企业	Foreign Solely Funded	235498	231847	298393	442107	440949	548452
外商投资股份制企业	Share Holding Enterprises With Foreign Investment	33519	28396	9786	19032	35969	9325

5-8 按行业分外商直接投资(2015)
FOREIGN DIRECT INVESTMENT GROUPED BY SECTOR (2015)

行 业	Item	项目(个) Number of Projects (unit)	合同外资 (万美元) Contracted Foreign Capital (USD 10 000)	实际投资 (万美元) Actual Foreign Investment (USD 10 000)
总 计	**Total**	**274**	**416112**	**894801**
农、林、牧、渔业	Farming, Forestry, Animal Husbandry and Fishery	17	-259	16593
采矿业	Mining and Quarrying	2	9580	962
制造业	Manufactruring	88	118841	391977
电力、燃气及水的生产和供应业	Power, Gas and Water Production and Supply	10	23135	39287
建筑业	Construction	3	16559	
交通运输、仓储和邮政业	Transportation, Storage and Post	7	39101	30256
信息传输、计算机服务和软件业	Information Transmmision, Computer Service and software	12	1345	3282
批发和零售业	Wholesale and Retail sale	44	15050	46476
住宿和餐饮业	Hotel and Catering	12	-439	4628
金融业	Finance			4086
房地产业	Real Estate	7	108013	298829
租赁和商务服务业	Leasing and Commerical Service	42	24924	16135
科学研究、技术服务和地质勘查业	Scietific research, Polytechnical Service and Geological Prospecting	18	31983	13550
水利、环境和公共设施管理业	Water Conservancy, Environment and Public Facility Management	5	22294	25490
居民服务和其他服务业	Resident Service and Others	2	1474	3176
教育	Education			
卫生、社会保障和社会福利业	Health Care, Social Security and Social Welfare	4	2876	
文化、体育和娱乐业	Culture, Sports and Recreation	1	1635	74

5-9 年末登记外商投资企业行业分布情况(2015)
SECTOR DISTRIBUTION REGISTERED OF FOREIGN-FUNDED ENTERPRISES AT THE YEAR-END(2015)

单位:个 (unit)

行 业	Item	企业数 Number of Enterprises
总 计	**Total**	**274**
农、林、牧、渔业	Farming, Forestry, Animal Husbandry and Fishery	17
采矿业	Mining and Quarrying	2
制造业	Manufactruring	88
电力、燃气及水的生产和供应业	Power, Gas and Water Production and Supply	10
建筑业	Construction	3
交通运输、仓储和邮政业	Transportation, Storage and Post	7
信息传输、计算机服务和软件业	Information Transmmision, Computer Service and software	12
批发和零售业	Wholesale and Retail sale	44
住宿和餐饮业	Hotel and Catering	12
金融业	Finance	
房地产业	Real Estate	7
租赁和商务服务业	Leasing and Commerical Service	42
科学研究、技术服务和地质勘查业	Scietific research, Polytechnical Service and Geological Prospecting	18
水利、环境和公共设施管理业	Water Conservancy, Environment and Public Facility Management	5
居民服务和其他服务业	Resident Service and Others	2
教育	Education	
卫生、社会保障和社会福利业	Health Care, Social Security and Social Welfare	4
文化、体育和娱乐业	Culture, Sports and Recreation	1

5-10 对外承包工程和劳务合作
CONTRACTED PROJECTS AND LABOR SERVICES CO-OPERATION WITH FOREIGN COUNTRIES

年份 Year		合同金额 (万美元) Contracted Value (USD 10 000)	实际完成营业额 (万美元) Value of Business Fulfilled (USD 10 000)	年末在外人数(人) Number of Persons Working Abroad at Year-end (person)
对外承包工程	**Contracted Projects**			
2003		17900	28552	1759
2004		28027	25334	2199
2005		27952	28852	2365
2006		56930	36266	2671
2007		183749	54416	5950
2008		318872	142456	9145
2009		526671	256368	10546
2010		765547	319978	17655
2011		631308	406741	13961
2012		726900	456194	16404
2013		1021254	520733	20801
2014		1269954	579636	31957
2015		1145362	523369	16406
对外劳务合作	**Labor Cooperation**			
2003		823	1783	3136
2004		1565	1597	3583
2005		5568	2601	5143
2006		6331	4379	7602
2007		6520	5340	8704
2008		6016	6856	6239
2009		6208	6988	4602
2010		11398	7186	4717
2011		7965	8261	3425
2012		11045	9669	8258
2013		12286	18194	8296
2014				
2015				
对外设计咨询	**Design Consulting**			
2002		541	267	42
2003		507	650	28
2004		475	1517	72
2005		390	2433	91
2006		983	452	90
2007		5423	2511	461
2008		6531	2804	22

注: 2009年起"对外设计咨询"指标数并入"对外承包工程"中;"年末在外人数(人)"修订为"劳务外派人数(人)"

Note:From 2009, "design and consultation," index number into the "International Contractors" in; "at the end of outer (person)" to "manning (person)".

5-11 湖北旅游主要指标
MAJOR INDICATORS OF HUBEI TOURISM

年份 Year	旅游总收入 (亿元) Total Earnings of Tourism (100 million yuan)	国内旅游收入 (亿元) Earnings from Domestic Tourism (100 million yuan)	国内旅游人数 (万人次) Number of Domestic Tourists (10 000 persons-time)	外汇收入 (万美元) Foreign Exchange Earnings (USD 10 000)	入境旅游人数 (万人次) Number of Tourists Received (10 000 persons-time)
1982				299.60	2.00
1983				355.30	2.40
1984				731.30	5.40
1985				1008.60	8.50
1986	3.47	2.50	1262	1166.00	10.50
1987	3.67	2.40	1184	1545.00	12.20
1988	3.56	2.40	1208	1411.80	11.30
1989	3.99	3.10	1034	1085.50	8.20
1990	4.56	2.70	890	2263.20	15.60
1991	5.83	3.90	984	2350.00	17.00
1992	9.03	5.40	1071	4432.20	26.30
1993	13.26	9.50	1350	4588.90	23.10
1994	18.09	13.00	1500	6211.40	24.70
1995	24.00	18.00	1700	7316.90	27.10
1996	163.28	153.00	3152	12545.60	36.90
1997	193.92	180.00	3600	16977.50	58.00
1998	217.24	210.00	4044	8831.40	29.60
1999	247.11	238.50	4659	10498.50	30.50
2000	282.26	270.30	5478	14572.10	45.10
2001	353.66	337.20	6064	20075.20	66.80
2002	407.48	384.20	6670	28390.90	102.40
2003	342.77	331.60	5684	13626.90	40.50
2004	410.00	394.20	6849	19240.40	61.20
2005	473.15	450.80	7630	27636.30	82.60
2006	539.74	514.24	8459.78	32000.38	105.57
2007	640.87	609.40	10135.00	41264.00	131.81
2008	744.19	713.43	11678.00	44255.31	118.75
2009	1004.48	969.63	15065.18	51020.22	133.46
2010	1460.53	1409.48	20946.00	75116.49	181.74
2011	1992.89	1931.80	27154.87	94018.00	213.52
2012	2629.54	2553.55	34230.00	120296.72	264.72
2013	3205.61	3130.13	40621.04	121892.18	267.96
2014	3752.11	3675.98	46900.00	123851.30	277.07
2015	4308.76	4206.02	50668.24	167190.01	311.76

5-12 接待入境旅游人数
NUMBER OF ENTRANCE TOURISTS

单位:人次 (person-times)

年份 Year	总计 Total	外国人 Foreigners	港澳台同胞 Compatroits from Hongkong, Maco and Taiwan	#港澳同胞 #Compatroits from Hongkong, Macao	#台湾同胞 #Compatroits from Taiwan
1982	19775	15126	4649		
1983	24200	18903	5297		
1984	53800	40496	13304		
1985	84598	68103	16495		
1986	105300	83570	21730		
1987	122390	82029	40361		
1988	113051	78206	34845	19725	15120
1989	81781	49511	32270	13908	18362
1990	155734	36374	119360	11560	107800
1991	170121	53055	117066	12645	104421
1992	263401	72691	190323	14054	176269
1993	230883	84552	146331	28460	117871
1994	247212	133343	113869	56417	57452
1995	270890	172869	98021	42785	55236
1996	368877	243595	125282	58949	66333
1997	580223	359700	220523	64466	156057
1998	295643	209402	86241	30337	55904
1999	305408	224748	80660	30935	49725
2000	450805	357352	93453	42928	53162
2001	667818	542737	125081	48417	76664
2002	1024312	755718	268594	49113	219481
2003	405214	323151	82063	40294	41769
2004	611859	501873	109986	57086	52900
2005	825700	626805	198895	107141	91754
2006	1055752	857028	198724	110246	88478
2007	1318179	1077189	240990	140384	100606
2008	1187549	926625	260924	152631	108293
2009	1334634	1017620	317014	182616	134398
2010	1817416	1385457	431959	241430	190529
2011	2135247	1601129	534118	291487	242631
2012	2647163	1929571	717592	410921	306671
2013	2679623	2047316	632307	365184	267123
2014	2770689	2132562	638127	363810	274317
2015	3117592	2397892	719700	377115	342585

5-13 入境旅游外汇收入
FOREIGN EXCHANGE REVENUE OF ENTRANCE TOURISTS

年份 Year	外汇收入(万美元) Foreign Exchange Earnings (USD 10 000)	发展指数(1978年为100) Development Index (year1978=100)	同比 Comparision Percentage (±%)	人均天花费(美元) Expenditures Per Capita (USD)
1982	299.64	129.85	82.00	
1983	355.30	153.98	18.58	
1984	731.30	316.92	105.83	
1985	1008.58	327.69	37.92	
1986	1166.00	505.31	15.61	
1987	1545.00	669.56	32.50	
1988	1411.75	611.81	-8.62	
1989	1085.45	470.40	-23.11	
1990	2263.18	980.79	108.50	
1991	2350.00	1018.42	3.84	
1992	4432.16	1920.76	88.60	
1993	4588.88	1988.68	3.54	
1994	6211.42	2691.84	35.36	125.10
1995	7316.86	3170.90	17.80	155.70
1996	12545.60	5436.88	71.46	167.04
1997	16977.51	7357.53	35.33	168.52
1998	8831.43	3827.27	-47.98	162.87
1999	10498.49	4549.72	18.88	166.31
2000	14572.13	6315.12	38.80	166.58
2001	20075.16	8699.96	37.76	164.25
2002	28390.95	12303.77	41.42	160.57
2003	13626.93	5905.50	-52.00	160.57
2004	19240.41	8338.21	51.00	169.92
2005	27636.30	11976.73	43.64	170.14
2006	32000.38	13867.99	15.79	177.16
2007	41264.00	17882.56	28.95	181.68
2008	44255.31	19178.90	7.25	197.56
2009	51020.22	22110.60	15.29	193.43
2010	75116.49	32553.20	47.23	192.84
2011	94018.00	40744.53	25.16	195.36
2012	120296.72	52132.92	27.95	193.04
2013	121892.18	52824.35	1.33	194.44
2014	123851.30	53675.70	1.61	194.40
2015	167190.01	72458.19	34.99	230.65

5-14 接待入境旅游者天数

NUMBER OF DAYS THE ENTRANCE TOURISTS STAYED IN HUBEI

单位:人天 (person/day)

年份 Year	总计 Total	外国人 Foreigners	港澳台同胞 Compatroits from Hongkong, Maco and Taiwan	#港澳同胞 #Compatroits from Hongkong, Macao	#台湾同胞 #Compatroits from Taiwan
1981	22946	15282	7664		
1982	29016	24188	4828		
1983	29830	25298	4532		
1984	107600	37806	69794		
1985	143815	115774	28041		
1986	186379	139677	46702		
1987	167035	115219	51816		
1988	190486	132301	58185	35505	22680
1989	127891	79217	48674	20862	27812
1990	178737	49487	129250	11960	117290
1991	235595	74913	160682	17450	143232
1992	351591	101878	249713	18973	230740
1993	324350	142240	182110	49959	132151
1994	472467	231716	240751	117889	122862
1995	501038	317246	183792	86910	96882
1996	729968	477152	252816	131993	120823
1997	949661	591127	358534	111291	247243
1998	513569	366348	147221	61491	85730
1999	622037	478486	143551	57765	85786
2000	852455	676130	176325	81432	94893
2001	1208938	891787	317151	93376	223775
2002	1712230	1232818	479412	86427	392985
2003	799824	603001	196823	98230	98593
2004	1069442	849071	220371	118234	102137
2005	1513678	1135995	377683	194122	183561
2006	1824387	1502277	322110	176901	145209
2007	2342786	1926484	416302	233946	182356
2008	2217172	1734211	482961	243638	239323
2009	2640362	2025972	614390	338898	275492
2010	3750746	2868024	882722	481484	401238
2011	4596252	3494098	1102154	581193	520961
2012	5934359	4424239	1510060	822210	687850
2013	6009111	4581165	1427946	802642	625304
2014	6370867	4926991	1443876	805502	638374
2015	7248536	5634388	1614448	833216	781232

注：2000年国家不再设“华侨”指标，“华侨”人数含在“外国人”中。
Note:The item of "overseas Chinese" is cancled by state since 2000, The number of "Overseas Chinese" is included in the number of "Foreigner".

5-15 湖北国内旅游接待人数及收入
TOATL NUMBER OF DOMESTIC TOURISTS AND EARNINGS FORM DOMESTIC TORUISM

年份 Year	接待人数(万人次) Number of Tourists Received (10 000person-times)	同比(±%) Comparision Percentage (±%)	旅游收入(亿元) Earnings (100 million yuan)	同比(±%) Comparision Percentage (±%)	人均天花费(元) Expenditures Per Capita a day (yuan) 全国 The Whole Nation	湖北 Hubei
1987	1184	-6.18	2.37	-6.0		
1988	1208	2.03	2.42	2.1		
1989	1034	-14.40	3.10	28.1		
1990	890	-13.92	2.67	-13.9		
1991	984	10.56	3.93	47.2		
1992	1071	8.84	5.36	36.4		
1993	1350	26.05	9.50	77.2		
1994	1500	11.11	13.00	36.8		
1995	1700	13.33	18.00	38.5		
1996	3152	85.41	152.95		256	485
1997	3600	14.21	180.00	17.7	328	500
1998	4044	12.33	210.03	16.7	344	519
1999	4659	15.21	238.50	13.6	394	511
2000	5478	17.58	270.31	13.3	427	493
2001	6064	10.70	337.18	24.7	450	556
2002	6670	9.99	384.24	14.0	441	576
2003	5684	-14.78	331.60	-13.7	395	583
2004	6849	20.50	394.22	18.9	550	576
2005	7630	11.40	450.76	14.3	436	591
2006	8460	10.88	514.24	14.1	447	607
2007	10135	19.80	609.40	18.5	482	601
2008	11678	15.2	713.43	17.1	511	610
2009	15065	29.0	969.63	35.9	535	644
2010	20946	39.0	1409.48	45.4	598	673
2011	27155	29.6	1931.80	37.1	731	711
2012	34230	26.1	2553.55	32.2	766	746
2013	40621	18.6	3130.13	22.6	806	771
2014	46900	15.5	3752.11	17.1	839	782
2015	50668	12.7	4206.02	14.3	857	830

注：表中所列是人均花费(元)。
Note: The table is a list of per capita spending ($).

5-16 湖北旅游总收入
THE TOTAL EARNINGS OF HUBEI TOURISM

年份 Year	旅游总收入 Total Earnings of Tourism	
	绝对额(亿元) (100 million yuan)	同比(±%) Comparision Percentage (±%)
1997	193.92	18.8
1998	217.27	12.0
1999	247.11	13.7
2000	282.26	14.2
2001	353.64	24.9
2002	407.52	15.2
2003	342.77	-15.9
2004	410.00	19.6
2005	473.15	15.5
2006	539.74	14.1
2007	640.87	18.7
2008	744.19	16.1
2009	1004.48	35.0
2010	1460.53	45.4
2011	1992.89	36.5
2012	2629.54	32.0
2013	3205.61	21.9
2014	3752.11	17.1
2015	4308.76	14.8

主要统计指标解释

进出口总额 指实际进出我国国境的货物总金额。包括对外贸易实际进出口货物,来料加工装配进出口货物,国家间、联合国及国际组织无偿援助物资和赠送品,华侨、港澳台同胞和外籍华人捐赠品,租赁期满归承租人所有的租赁货物,进料加工进出口货物,边境地方贸易及边境地区小额贸易进出口货物(边民互市贸易除外),中外合资企业、中外合作经营企业、外商独资经营企业进出口货物和公用物品,到、离岸价格在规定限额以上的进出口货样和广告品(无商业价值、无使用价值和免费提供出口的除外),从保税仓库提取在中国境内销售的进口货物,以及其他进出口货物。该指标可以观察一个国家在对外贸易方面的总规模。我国规定出口货物按离岸价格统计,进口货物按到岸价格统计。

商品经营单位所在地进、出口额 指所在地海关注册登记的有进出口经营权的企业实际进、出口额。

商品目的地进口额和商品货源地出口额 目的地进口额指进口货物的消费、使用或最终抵运地的实际进口额;货源地出口额指出口货物的产地或原始发货地的实际出口额。

利用外资 指我国各级政府、部门、企业和其他经济组织通过对外借款、吸收外商直接投资以及用其他方式筹措的境外现汇、设备、技术等。

对外借款 指通过对外正式签订借款协议,从境外筹措的资金,包括外国政府贷款、国际金融组织贷款、外国银行商业贷款、出口信贷以及对外发行债券等。1996年及以前还包括对外发行股票。该指标是我国利用外资的重要部分。

外商直接投资 指外国企业和经济组织或个人(包括华侨、港澳台胞以及我国在境外注册的企业)按我国有关政策、法规,用现汇、实物、技术等在我国境内开办外商独资企业、与我国境内的企业或经济组织共同举办中外合资经营企业、合作经营企业或合作开发资源的投资(包括外商投资收益的再投资),以及经政府有关部门批准的项目投资总额内企业从境外借入的资金。

外商其他投资 指除对外借款和外商直接投资以外的各种利用外资的形式。包括企业在境内外股票市场公开发行的以外币计价的股票(目前主要是在香港证券市场发行的H股和在境内证券市场发行的B股)发行价总额,国际租赁进口设备的应付款,补偿贸易中外商提供的进口设备、技术、物料的价款,加工装配贸易中外商提供的进口设备、物料的价款。

对外直接投资 指我国国内投资者以现金、实物、无形资产等方式在国外及港澳台地区设立、购买国(境)外企业,并以控制该企业的经营管理权为核心的经济活动。

对外承包工程 指各对外承包公司以招标议标承包方式承揽的下列业务:(1)承包国外工程建设项目;(2)承包我国对外经援项目;(3)承包我国驻外机构的工程建设项目;(4)承包我国境内利用外资进行建设的工程项目;(5)与外国承包公司合营或联合承包工程项目时我国公司分包部分;(6)对外承包兼营的房屋开发业务。对外承包工程的营业额是以货币表现的本期内完成的对外承包工程的工作量,包括以前年度签订的合同和本年度新签订的合同在报告期内完成的工作量。

对外劳务合作 指以收取工资的形式向业主或承包商提供技术和劳动服务的活动。我国对外承包公司在境外开办的合营企业,中国公司同时又提供劳务的,其劳务部分也纳入劳务合作统计。劳务合作营业额按报告期内向雇主提交的结算数(包括工资、加班费和奖金等)统计。

对外设计咨询 指以服务成果向业主收费的技术服务项目。包括承担地形地貌测绘,地质资源勘探与普查,建设区域规划,提供设计文件、图纸、生产工艺技术资料和工程技术经济咨询,工程项目的可行性考察、研究和评估,进行技术指导和培训人员等;也包括承担国(境)内利用外资建设工程项目中的设计咨询项目内收取外币部分。

旅游者人数

(1)入境国际旅游者人数:指来中国参观、访问、旅行、探亲、访友、休养、考察、参加会议和从事经济、科技、文化、教育、宗教等活动的外国人、华侨、港澳同胞和台湾同胞的人数。不包括外国在我国的常驻机构,如使领馆、通讯社、企业办事处的工作人员;来我国常住的外国专家、留学生以及在岸逗留不过夜人员。

(2)出境居民人数:指大陆居民因公务活动或私人事务短期出境的人数。公务活动出境居民人数包括在国际交通工具上的中国服务员工,因私出境居民人数不包括在国际交通工具上的中国服务员工。

(3)国内旅游者人数:指我国大陆居民和在我国常住1年以上的外国人、华侨、港澳台同胞离开常住地在境内其他地方的旅游设施内至少停留一夜,最长不超过6个月的人数。

国际旅游(外汇)收入 指入境旅游的外国人、华侨、港澳同胞和台湾同胞在中国大陆旅游过程中发生的一切旅游支出，其对于国家来说就是国际旅游(外汇)收入。

国际旅行社 指经营对外招徕并接待外国人、华侨、港澳同胞和台湾同胞来中国、归国或回内地旅游业务的旅行社。

国内旅行社 指负责经营招徕、组团、接待国内旅客的旅游业务，以及不对外招徕，负责经营接待国际旅行社或其它涉外部门组织的外国人、华侨、港澳同胞和台湾同胞来中国、归国或回内地的旅游业务的旅行社。

星级饭店 指已评定星级的饭店。

Explanatory Notes on Main Statistical Indicators

Total Imports and Exports at Customs refer to the real value of commodities imported into and exported from the boundary of China. They include the actual imports and exports through foreign trade, imported and exported goods under the processing and assembling trades and materials, supplies and gifts as aid given gratis between governments and by the United Nations and other international organizations, and contributions donated by overseas Chinese, compatriots in Hong Kong and Macao and Chinese with foreign citizenship, leasing commodities owned by tenant at the expiration of leasing period, the imported and exported commodities processed with imported materials, commodities trading in border areas (excluding mutual exchange goods), the imported and exported commodities and articles for public use of the Sino-foreign joint ventures, cooperative enterprises and ventures exclusively with foreign own investment. Also included are import or export of samples and advertising goods for whose CIF or FOB value are beyond the permitted ceiling (excluding goods of no trading or use value and free commodities for export), imported goods sold in China from bonded warehouses and other imported or exported goods. The indicator of the total imports and exports at customs can be used to observe the total size of external trade in a country. In accordance with the stipulation of the Chinese government, imports are calculated at CIF, while exports are calculated at FOB.

Import Export Value by Location of China's Foreign Trade Managing Units refers to actual value of imports and exports carried out by corporations which have been registered by the local customhouse and are vested with right to run import export business.

Import Value of Commodities by the Places of their Destination and Export Value of Commodities by the Places of their Origin in China The former indicator refers to the value of import commodities of the places of their consumption, utilization or the places of their final destination. The latter indicator refers to the value of export commodities of the places of their origin or the places of the commodities dispatched.

Utilization of Foreign Capitals refers to remittance, equipment and technology financed from abroad, by loans, foreign direct investment and other forms undertaken by the Chinese governments at all levels, by various departments, enterprises and other economic units.

Foreign Borrowings refer to funds borrowed from abroad through formal signing of borrowing agreements with foreign institutions, including loans of foreign governments, loans of international financial institutions, commercial loans of foreign banks, export credit, and funds raised by Chinese bonds (and shares before 1996) issued abroad. It is an important part of China's utilization of foreign capitals.

Foreign Direct Investment refers to the investments inside China by foreign enterprises and economic organizations or individuals (including overseas Chinese, compatriots from Hong Kong, Macao and Taiwan, and Chinese enterprises registered abroad), following the relevant policies and laws of China, for the establishment of ventures exclusively with foreign own investment, Sino-foreign joint ventures and cooperative enterprises or for co-operative exploration of resources with enterprises or economic organizations in China. It includes the re investment of the foreign entrepreneurs with the profits gained from the investment and the funds that enterprises borrow from abroad in the total investment of projects which are approved by the relevant department of the government.

Overseas Direct Investment refers to enterprises set up or bought by domestic investors in foreign countries and in Hong Kong, Macao and Taiwan, and the economic activities centering on operation and management of those enterprises are under the control of domestic investors. The statistical scope covers various corporation type enterprises and non-corporation type enterprises receiving direct investment from domestic investment entities.

Other Investment by Foreign Entrepreneurs refers to all forms of utilization of foreign capitals other than foreign borrowings and foreign direct investment. It includes the total value of stock shares in foreign currencies issued by enterprises at domestic or foreign stock exchanges (now mainly consisting of H shares issued at Hong Kong Security Market and B shares issued at domestic security markets), rent payable for the imported equipment through international leasing arrangement, cost of imported equipment, technology and materials provided by foreign counterparts in compensation trade and processing and assembly trade.

Contracted Projects with Foreign Count riesrefer to projects undertaken by Chinese contractors (project contracting companies) through bidding process. They include: (1) overseas civil engineering construction projects financed by foreign investors; (2) overseas projects financed by the Chinese government through its foreign aid programs; (3) construction projects of Chinese diplomatic missions, trade offices and other institutions stationed abroad; (4) construction projects in China financed by foreign investment; (5) sub-contracted projects to be taken by Chinese contractors through a joint umbrella project with foreign contractor(s); (6) housing development projects. The business income from international contracted projects is the work volume of contracted projects completed during the reference period, expressed in monetary terms, including completed work on projects signed in previous years.

Service Cooperation with Foreign Countries refers to the activities of providing technology and labor services to employers or contractors in the forms of receiving salaries and wages. Labor services providing by contractual joint ventures of Chinese international contracting corporations should be included in the statistics of service co-operation with foreign countries. The business income of labor service cooperation is the income in the form of wages and salaries, overtime pay, bonuses and other remuneration received from the employers during the reference period.

Overseas Design and Consultation Service refers to projects with charges for technical services from overseas operators. It includes geographic and topographic mapping, geological resource prospecting and survey, planning of construction areas, provision of design documents, blueprints, materials on production process and techniques, as well as engineering, technical and economic consultation, and feasibility study, research and evaluation of projects. Also included under this category are the above-mentioned services of foreign-financed projects in China that are paid in foreign currencies.

Number of Tourists

(1) International tourists refer to foreigners, overseas Chinese, Chinese compatriots from Hong Kong, Macao and Taiwan coming to China for sight-seeing, visits, tours, family reunions, vacations, study tours, conferences and other activities of a business, scientific and technological, cultural, educational and religious nature. It does not include representatives and employees of resident institutions of foreign countries in China such as embassies, consulates, news agencies and offices of foreign companies and organizations, nor does it include long-term foreign experts or students residing in China, or persons in transition without spending a night in China.

(2) Chinese residents going abroad refer to Chinese residents going abroad for short terms for either public business or private purposes. Chinese employees working on international transport carriers are included in those going abroad for public business purpose, not in those for private purpose.

(3) Domestic tourists refer to residents of the mainland of China who stay for one night at least but no more than 6 months at tourist facilities in other places than their permanent residence within the territory of the mainland China, including foreigners, overseas Chinese and Chinese compatriots from Hong Kong, Macao and Taiwan who have resided in China for over one year.

Foreign Exchange Earnings from International Tourism refer to the total expenditures of foreigners, overseas Chinese, Chinese compatriots from Hong Kong, Macao and Taiwan during their stay in the mainland of China, which are earnings of foreign exchange from international tourism from the point of view from China.

International Travel Agencies refer to travel agencies engaged in the promotion, solicitation, organization and reception of tours to the mainland of China by foreigners, overseas Chinese, Chinese compatriots from Hong Kong, Macao and Taiwan.

Domestic Travel Agencies refer to travel agencies engaged in the promotion, solicitation, organization and reception of domestic tourists, and in the reception of foreigners, overseas Chinese, Chinese compatriots from Hong Kong, Macao and Taiwan organized by international travel agencies or other departments concerned, without their own promotion and solicitation programmes.

Star-Hotels refer to hotels rated with stars.

6 能　源

Energy

6-1 工业能源生产量
OUTPUT OF ENERGY PRODUCTION OF INDUSTRY

产品	单位	Item	Unit	2012	2013	2014	2015
一次能源生产量	（万吨标煤）	Primary Energy Output	(10 000 tons standardized coal)	5582.98	5165.45	5708.76	5256.27
原煤	（万吨）	Coal	(10 000 ton)	887.44	885.42	890.40	758.39
原油	（万吨）	Crude Oil	(10 000 ton)	78.90	80.08	79.00	71.00
天然气	（亿立方米）	Natural Gas	(100 million cu.m)	1.65	3.09	1.45	1.35
水电	（亿千瓦时）	Water and Electricity	(100 million KW/h)	1379.59	1175.95	1375.80	1289.96

说明：1.一次能源生产量为全部工业一次能源生产量；原煤、原油、天然气以及水电产量为规模以上工业生产量。
2.按照国家统计局统一部署和要求，2013年、2014年数据为根据第三次全国经济普查资料进行调整后的数据（下同）。
Note: 1.Primary energy production is the entire industrial primary energy production, raw coal, crude oil, natural gas and hydropower output are the above scale industrial production.
2.According to the requirements of the NBS, the data in 2013 and 2014 have been adjusted basing on the files of the third national economic census.

6-2 规模以上工业能源消费量
ENERGY CONSUMPTION OF INDUSTRY ABOVE DESIGNATED SIZE

产品	计量单位	Item	Unit	2012	2013	2014	2015
能源消费量合计	（万吨标煤）	Total	（10000 tons standardized coal）	12083.97	13310.45	13766.37	13827.77
原煤	（万吨）	Coal	（10000 ton）	7674.12	8270.13	7984.97	7724.61
洗精煤	（万吨）	Cleaned Coal	（10000 ton）	1340.05	1382.42	1346.53	1320.69
其他洗煤	（万吨）	Other Washed Coal	（10000 ton）	10.72	13.04	11.16	7.78
煤制品	（万吨）	Moulded Coal	（10000 ton）	8.69	11.35	10.92	10.48
焦炭	（万吨）	Coke	（10000 ton）	1113.90	1114.39	1124.40	1030.01
其他焦化产品	（万吨）	Other Coked Products	（10000 ton）	3.96	1.34	1.93	4.05
焦炉煤气	（亿立方米）	Coke-oven Gas	（100 million cu.m）	39.18	38.59	38.23	37.80
高炉煤气	（亿立方米）	Bblast Furnace Gas	（100 million cu.m）	344.72	345.87	342.73	315.53
其他煤气	（亿立方米）	Other Gases	（100 million cu.m）	22.80	24.04	21.07	20.81
天然气	（亿立方米）	Natural Gas	（100 million cu.m）	13.56	18.10	17.42	23.20
原油	（万吨）	Crude Oil	（10000 ton）	946.99	1176.30	1290.47	1299.01
汽油	（万吨）	Gasoline	（10000 ton）	14.62	13.48	12.09	11.11
煤油	（万吨）	Kerasene	（10000 ton）	0.93	1.08	1.34	1.00
柴油	（万吨）	Diesel Oil	（10000 ton）	48.30	49.72	58.52	54.59
燃料油	（万吨）	Fuel Oil	（10000 ton）	8.55	6.74	6.87	6.05
液化石油气	（万吨）	LPG	（10000 ton）	2.47	8.95	31.30	39.14
炼厂干气	（万吨）	Dry Gas	（10000 ton）	29.62	34.68	38.47	38.32
其他石油制品	（万吨）	Other Petroleum Products	（10000 ton）	110.13	176.62	280.52	385.07
热力	（万百万千焦）	Heat	（10 billion kilo-joule）	7916.47	7744.13	7626.11	8313.48
电力	（亿千瓦时）	Electricity	（100 million kW/h）	1215.06	1281.29	1317.88	1311.13
其他燃料	（万吨标准煤）	Other Fuels	（10000 tons standardized coal）	18.20	22.97	24.69	25.77

注：能源消费量包括加工转换投入量，且为当量值。
Note: The conversion of energy consumption, including processing input, and when the money is.

6-3 规模以上工业分行业能源消费量(2015)
ENERGY CONSUMPTION OF INDUSTRY ABOVE DESGINATED SIZE(2015)

行业	Item	原煤消费量(万吨) Coal Consumption (10000 tons)	汽油消费量(万吨) Gasoline Consumption (10000tons)	柴油消费量(万吨) Diesel Consumption (10000tons)	电力消费量(亿千瓦小时) Electricity Consumption (100million kw/h)
总消费量	**Total Consumption**	**7724.61**	**11.11**	**54.59**	**1311.13**
采矿业	**Mining**	**157.15**	**0.75**	**15.94**	**37.51**
煤炭开采和洗选业	Mining and Washing of Coal	80.23	0.07	0.21	2.72
石油和天然气开采业	Extraction of Petroleum and Natural Gas	11.18	0.18	0.88	8.47
黑色金属矿采选业	Mining and Processing of Ferrous Metal Ores	7.04	0.07	0.96	9.85
有色金属矿采选业	Mining and Processing of Non-Ferrous Metal Ores	1.18	0.01	0.09	2.77
非金属矿采选业	Mining and Processing of Non-metal Ores	45.78	0.25	5.01	12.32
开采辅助活动	Mining Auxiliary	11.74	0.16	8.79	1.35
其他采矿业	Mining of Other Ores				0.03
制造业	**Manufacturing**	**3906.96**	**10.13**	**37.54**	**1104.23**
农副食品加工业	Processing of Food from Agricultural Products	107.59	0.51	2.83	47.25
食品制造业	Manufacture of Foods	95.59	0.29	0.41	18.18
酒、饮料和精制茶制造业	Manufacture of Wine, Beverages and Tea	58.91	0.28	0.43	15.04
烟草制品业	Manufacture of Tobacco	1.26	0.00	0.01	1.27
纺织业	Manufacture of Textile	32.30	0.22	0.40	71.57
纺织服装、服饰业	Manufacture of Textile Wearing Apparel	5.62	0.28	0.64	7.95
皮革、毛皮、羽毛及其制品和制鞋业	Manufacture of Leather, Fur, Feather and Related and Footware	1.07	0.04	0.03	3.55
木材加工和木、竹、藤、棕、草制品业	Processing of Timber, Manufacture of Wood, Bamboo, Rattan, Palm, and Straw Products	5.00	0.06	0.39	11.62
家具制造业	Manufacture of Furniture	0.77	0.04	0.24	1.76
造纸和纸制品业	Manufacture of Paper and Paper Products	62.64	0.05	0.89	18.07
印刷和记录媒介复制业	Printing and Reproduction of Recording Media	2.17	0.18	0.12	4.59
文教、工美、体育和娱乐用品制造业	Manufacture of Articles for Culture, Education, Art, Sport and Entertainment	3.00	0.01	0.02	2.70
石油加工、炼焦和核燃料加工业	Processing of Petroleum, Coking and Nuclear Fuel	7.67	0.08	0.06	12.37
化学原料和化学制品制造业	Manufacture of Raw Chemical Materials and Chemical Products	1607.19	0.61	2.59	258.86
医药制造业	Manufacture of Medicines	103.75	0.58	2.54	23.07
化学纤维制造业	Manufacture of Chemical Fibres	22.67	0.01	0.06	3.47
橡胶和塑料制品业	Manufacture of Rubber and Plastics	11.19	0.70	1.31	28.52
非金属矿物制品业	Manufacture of Non-metal Mineral Products	1054.77	0.69	8.82	150.13
黑色金属冶炼和压延加工业	Smelting an Processing of Ferrous Metals	519.33	0.25	2.38	190.78
有色金属冶炼和压延加工业	Smelting an Processing of Non-ferrous Metals	49.14	0.08	0.79	37.12
金属制品业	Manufacture of Metal Products	9.77	0.44	1.23	26.01
通用设备制造业	Manufacture of General Purpose Machinery	8.01	0.83	3.55	17.82
专用设备制造业	Manufacture of Special Purpose Machinery	4.56	0.50	2.27	15.80
汽车制造业	Manufacture of Automobile	123.61	2.28	3.61	84.10
铁路、船舶、航空航天和其他运输设备制造业	Manufacture of Realway, Ship, Aircraft and Other Transport Equipment	2.42	0.14	0.34	4.06
电气机械和器材制造业	Manufacture of Electrical Machinery and Equipment	3.26	0.41	0.31	28.88
计算机、通信和其他电子设备制造业	Manufacture of Computers, Communication Equipment and Other Electronic Equipment	1.37	0.16	0.05	14.08
仪器仪表制造业	Manufacture of Measuring Instruments	0.17	0.23	0.05	1.73
其他制造业	Manufacture of Other Products	1.29	0.01	0.04	2.62
废弃资源综合利用业	Recycling and Disposal of Waste	0.88	0.03	0.25	1.03
金属制品、机械和设备修理业	Repairing of Metal Products and Mechanical Equipment		0.12	0.89	0.25
电力、燃气及水生产和供应业	**Electric Power, Gas and Water Production and Supply**	**3660.50**	**0.23**	**1.10**	**169.39**
电力、热力生产和供应业	Production and Supply of Electric Power and Heat Power	3660.47	0.08	1.02	157.85
燃气生产和供应业	Production and Supply of Gas		0.06	0.03	4.00
水的生产和供应业	Production and Supply of Water	0.03	0.09	0.04	7.54

6-4 全社会综合能源平衡表(等价值)
BALANCE SHEET OF DOMESTIC ENERGY (EQIVALENCE PRICE)

单位:万吨标准煤 (10000 tons standardized coal)

项 目	Item	2014	2015
一、可供量	**Quantity Available**	**16320**	**16404**
一次能源生产量	Primary Energy Production	5709	5256
外省(区、市)调入量	Engery moblized from other Province	13606	13468
进口量	Import Volume		
我轮、机在外国加油量	Volume of Fuel Charged Abroad		
本省(区、市)调出量(-)	Engery moblized to other Province	2892	2542
出口量(-)	Output Volume		
外轮、机在我国加油量(-)	Volume of Fuel Charged at Home		
年初年末库存差额	Storage Balance Difference between the Beginning and the End of the Year	-102	222
年初库存量	Storage Volume at the Beginning of the Year	624	749
年末库存量(-)	Storage Volume by the End of the Year	726	527
二、消费量	**Consumption**	**16320**	**16404**
消费量分组一	Consumption Group 1.	16320	16404
1.农.林.牧.渔业	Agriculture, Forestry, Animal Husbandary, Fishing	507	485
2.工业	Industry	10570	10404
3.建筑业	Construction	417	428
4.交通运输.仓储和邮政业	Transport communication, Storage, Post Service	1552	1600
5.批发、零售业和住宿、餐饮业	Wholesale,Retail Sale, Hotel and Catering Industry	749	786
6.其他	Others	683	759
7.生活消费	Living Consumption	1843	1942
消费量分组二	Consumption Group 2.	16320	16404
1. 终端消费	Terminal Consumption	16172	16234
#工业	Industry	10422	10234
2. 加工转换损失	Loss in Processing	-179	-126
火力发电损失	Loss in Thermal Power Generation		
供热损失	Loss in Heating	234	241
洗选煤损失	Loss in Coal Seperation	1	3
炼焦损失	Loss in Coke Making	33	29
炼油及煤制油损失	Loss in Oil Refining	2	17
制气损失	Loss in Gas Drying		
天然气液化损失	Loss in Natural gas liquefaction	1	8
煤制品加工损失	Loss in Coal Products Processing	1	
回收能	Recuperated Energy	-449	-424
3. 损失量	Loss in Processing	327	296
三、平衡差额	**Balance**		

6-5 全社会煤炭平衡表
BALANCE SHEET OF DOMESTIC COAL CONSUMPTION

单位: 万吨 (10 000 tons)

项 目	Item	2014	2015
一、可供量	**Quantity Available**	**11888**	**11766**
生产量	Production Capacity	1057	860
外省(区、市)调入量	Engery moblized from other Province	10968	10605
进口量	Import Volume		
本省(区、市)调出量(-)	Engery moblized to other Province		
出口量(-)	Output Volume		
年初年末库存差额	Storage Balance Difference between the Beginning and the End of the Year	-137	301
年初库存量	Storage Volume at the Beginning of the Year	724	877
年末库存量(-)	Storage Volume by the End of the Year	861	576
二、消费量	**Consumption**	**11888**	**11766**
消费量分组一	Consumption Group 1.	11888	11766
1.农.林.牧.渔业	Agriculture, Forestry, Animal Husbandary, Fishing	232	217
2.工 业	Industry	10381	10284
3.建 筑 业	Construction	129	125
4.交通运输.仓储和邮政业	Transport communication, Storage, Post Service	67	68
5.批发、零售业和住宿、餐饮业	Wholesale,Retail Sale, Hotel and Catering Industry	263	264
6.其 他	Others	235	234
7.生活消费	Living Consumption	582	575
消费量分组二	Consumption Group 2.	11888	11766
1. 终端消费	Terminal Consumption	6466	6348
*工业	Industry	4959	4866
2. 用于加工转换	Coal Used for Processing	5422	5418
火力发电	Thermal Power Generation	3646	3638
供 热	Heating	447	465
洗煤损耗	Loss in Washing Coal	13	18
炼 焦	Coke Making	1316	1297
炼油及煤制油	Oil Refining and Coal Preparation		
制 气	Air Drying		
型煤加工损耗	Loss in Standardlized Coal Processing	0.03	0.01
3. 损 失 量	Loss		
三、平衡差额	**Balance**		

6-6 全社会石油平衡表
BALANCE SHEET OF DOMESTIC PETROLEUM

单位: 万吨 (10 000 tons)

项 目	Item	2014	2015
一、可供量	**Quantity Available**	**2505**	**2551**
生产量	Production Capacity	79	71
外省(区、市)调入量	Engery moblized from other Province	2457	2524
进 口 量	Import Volume		
我轮、机在外国加油量	Volume of Fuel Charged Abroad		
本省(区、市)调出量(－)	Engery moblized to other Province	25	43
出 口 量(-)	Output Volume		
外轮、机在我国加油量(-)	Volume of Fuel Charged at Home		
年初年末库存差额	Storage Balance Difference between the Beginning and the End of the Year	-5	
年初库存量	Storage Volume at the Beginning of the Year	35	41
年末库存量(-)	Storage Volume by the End of the Year	40	41
二、消费量	**Consumption**	**2505**	**2551**
消费量分组一	Consumption Group 1.	2505	2551
1.农.林.牧.渔业	Agriculture, Forestry, Animal Husbandary, Fishing	162	168
2.工 业	Industry	740	713
3.建 筑 业	Construction	168	175
4.交通运输.仓储和邮政业	Transport communication, Storage, Post Service	882	901
5.批发、零售业和住宿、餐饮业	Wholesale,Retail Sale, Hotel and Catering Industry	157	168
6.其他	Others	96	107
7.生活消费	Living Consumption	299	319
消费量分组二	Consumption Group 2.	2505	2551
1. 终端消费	Terminal Consumption	2541	2545
*工业	Industry	776	707
2. 加工转换损失	Coal Used for Processing	-36	6
火力发电	Thermal Power Generation	2	2
供 热	Heating	3	3
炼油损耗	Loss in Oil Refining	-40	1
制 气	Gas Making		
3. 损 失 量	Loss		
三、平衡差额	**Balance**		

6-7 全社会电力平衡表
BALANCE SHEET OF DOMESTIC ELECTRICITY

单位: 亿千瓦时 (100 million kw/h)

项 目	Item	2014	2015
一、可供量	**Quantity Available**	**1854**	**1862**
生产量	Production Capacity	2383	2302
火力发电	Thermal Power Generation	962	994
水力发电、核发电、其它发电	Hydroelectricity Generation, Nuclearpower Generation, and others	1421	1308
外省(区、市)调入量	Engery moblized from other Province	383	336
进口量	Import Volume		
本省(区、市)调出量(-)	Engery moblized to other Province	913	775
出口量(-)	Output Volume		
二、消费量	**Consumption**	**1854**	**1862**
消费量分组一	Consumption Group 1.	1854	1862
1.农.林.牧.渔业	Agriculture, Forestry, Animal Husbandary, Fishing	30	22
2.工　业	Industry	1318	1291
3.建筑业	Construction	25	26
4.交通运输.仓储和邮政业	Transport communication, Storage, Post Service	38	42
5.批发、零售业和住宿、餐饮业	Wholesale,Retail Sale, Hotel and Catering Industry	80	86
6.其他	Others	101	116
7.生活消费	Living Consumption	262	279
消费量分组二	Consumption Group 2.	1854	1862
1. 终端消费	Terminal Consumption	1749	1767
#工业	Industry	1213	1196
2. 输配电损失量	Distribution Loss	104	95
三、平衡差额	**Balance**		

6-8 分市州单位GDP能耗降低率
UNIT GDP ENERGY CONSUMPTION OF SUB-CITY

地 区	Regions	2010年单位GDP能耗比2005年降低(±%)	2014年单位GDP能耗比2013年降低(±%)	2015年单位GDP能耗比2014年降低(±%)
		2010year Unit GDP energy consumption lower than in 2005	2014year Unit GDP energy consumption lower than in 2013	2015year Unit GDP energy consumption lower than in 2014
全 省	**Total**	**-21.67**	**-5.24**	**-7.66**
武汉市	Wuhan	-21.85	-2.88	-5.95
黄石市	Huangshi	-21.71	-6.83	-10.84
十堰市	Shiyan	-20.13	-9.91	-8.86
宜昌市	Yichang	-20.87	-5.78	-8.96
襄阳市	Xiangyang	-21.40	-3.53	-7.84
鄂州市	Ezhou	-22.83	-3.91	-8.51
荆门市	Jingmen	-21.15	-6.48	-8.35
孝感市	Xiaogan	-22.55	-5.98	-5.48
荆州市	Jingzhou	-21.93	-3.91	-5.31
黄冈市	Huanggang	-22.02	-6.98	-5.80
咸宁市	Xianning	-22.10	-4.72	-5.11
随州市	Suizhou	-20.04	-3.12	-6.90
恩施州	Enshi	-20.20	-3.66	-4.88
仙桃市	Xiantao	-20.03	-5.25	-4.92
潜江市	Qianjiang	-20.91	-3.60	-8.43
天门市	Tianmen	-20.99	-3.86	-4.03
神农架	Shennon-gjia	-19.35	-2.42	-2.99

主要统计指标解释

一次能源生产量　指一定时期内，一次能源生产量的总和。该指标是观察能源生产水平、规模、构成和发展速度的总量指标。一次能源生产量包括原煤、原油、天然气、水电、核能及其他动力能(如风能、地热能等)发电量，不包括低热值燃料生产量、生物质能、太阳能等的利用和由一次能源加工转换而成的二次能源产量。

能源消费总量　指一定区域内(国家或地区)国民经济各行业和居民家庭在一定时期消费的各种能源的总和。能源消费总量分为三部分，即终端能源消费量、能源加工转换损失量和能源损失量。

(1)终端能源消费量：指一定时期内地区各行业和居民生活消费的各种能源在扣除了用于加工转换二次能源消费量和损失量以后的数量。

(2)能源加工转换损失量：指一定时期内地区投入加工转换的各种能源数量之和与产出各种能源产品之和的差额。该指标是观察能源在加工转换过程中损失量变化的指标。

(3)能源损失量：指一定时期内，能源在输送、分配、储存过程中发生的损失和由客观原因造成的各种损失量，不包括各种气体能源放空、放散量。

单位国内生产总值能耗　指一定时期内，一个国家或地区每生产一个单位的国内生产总值所消耗的能源。计算公式为：

$$\text{单位国内生产总值能耗}=\frac{\text{能源消费总量}}{\text{国内生产总值}}$$

Explanatory Notes on Main Statistical Indicators

Primary Energy Production　refers to the total production of primary energy by all energy producing enterprises in a given period of time. It is a comprehensive indicator to show the capacity, scale, composition and development of energy production. The production of primary energy includes that of coal, crude oil, natural gas, hydro–power and electricity generated by nuclear energy and other means such as wind power and geothermal power. However, it excludes the production of fuels of low calorific value, bio–energy, solar energy and the secondary energy converted from the primary energy.

Total Domestic Energy Consumption　refers to the total consumption of energy of various kinds by material production sectors, non material production sectors and households in a given period of time. It is a comprehensive indicator to show the scale, composition and development of energy consumption. The total energy consumption includes that of coal, crude oil and their products, natural gas and electricity, However, it excludes the consumption of fuel of low calorific value, bio–energy and solar energy. Total domestic energy consumption can be divided into three parts: final energy consumption, loss during the process of energy conversion, and energy loss.

(1)Final Energy Consumption: It refers to the total energy consumption by material production sectors, non material production sectors and households in a given period of time, but excludes the consumption in conversion of the primary energy into the secondary energy and the loss in the process of energy conversion.

(2)Loss During the Process of Energy Conversion: It refers to the total input of various kinds of energy for conversion, minus the total output of various kinds of energy in a given period of time. It is an indicator to show the loss that occurs during the process of energy conversion.

(3)Energy Loss: It refers to the total of the loss of energy during the course of energy transport, distribution and storage and the loss caused by any objective reason in a given period of time. The loss of various kinds of gas due to gas discharges and stocktaking is excluded.

Energy Consumption per Unit of GDP refers to the energy consumption per unit of gross domestic production in a country or the gross region production in a region in the same reference period. The formula is:

Energy Consumption per Unit of GDP = Total Energy Consumption / Gross Domestic Production

7 财政、金融、保险

Government Finance, Banking and Insurance

财政、金融、保险

GOVERNMENT FINANCE, BANKING AND INSURANCE

2015

地方一般公共预算收入	Local Public Financial Revenue(100 million yuan)	3005.53	(亿元)
地方一般公共预算支出	Local Public Financial Expenditure(100 million yuan)	6132.84	(亿元)
金融机构(含外资)人民币存款年末余额	Balance of RMB Deposits of Financial Organizations (including Foreign Funded Enterprises) By the End of the year(100 million yuan)	40896.5	(亿元)
#住户存款	Household Deposit	19566.1	(亿元)
金融机构(含外资)人民币贷款年末余额	Balance of RMB Loans of Financial Organizations (including Foreign Funded Enterprises) By the End of the year(100 million yuan)	28338.9	(亿元)

一般公共预算收入与一般公共预算支出(亿元)

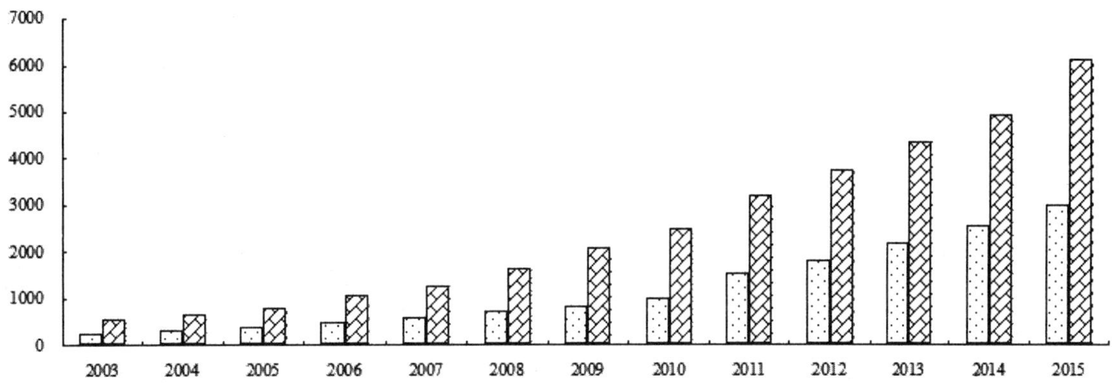

一般公共预算收入与一般公共预算支出(亿元)

Local Budgetary Revenue and Expenditure(100 million yuan)

年份(Year)	2003	2004	2005	2006	2007	2008	2009	2010	2011	2012	2013	2014	2015
一般公共预算收入 (Local Public Financial Revenue)	260	311	376	476	590	711	815	1011	1527	1823	2191	2567	3006
一般公共预算支出 (Local Public Financial Expenditure)	540	646	779	1047	1274	1650	2091	2501	3215	3760	4372	4934	6133

7-1 历年地方财政收支额及指数
AMOVNT AND INDICES OF FINANCIAL REVENUE AND EXPENDITURE OVER THE YEARS

单位: 亿元 (100 million yuan)

年份 Year	财政总收入 Total fiscal revenue	地方一般公共预算收入 Local Public Financial Revenue	地方一般公共预算支出 Local Public Financial Expenditure	指数(上年=100) Index (previous year=100)	
				收入 Revenue	支出 Expenditure
1952	3.81	3.81	1.96	100.0	100.0
1957	6.27	6.27	3.55	109.8	96.7
1965	11.26	11.26	6.85	97.4	105.2
1970	15.20	15.20	15.73	170.6	158.1
1975	24.05	24.05	17.52	139.5	103.9
1978	31.38	31.38	29.98	149.0	148.6
1980	34.01	34.01	26.53	107.6	94.5
1985	50.26	50.26	43.60	119.3	137.5
1990	77.85	77.85	84.82	100.8	106.1
1993	115.07	115.07	114.58	122.2	115.8
1994	149.64	77.46	137.20		119.7
1995	180.57	99.69	162.43	128.7	118.4
1996	216.68	124.51	197.44	124.9	121.6
1997	246.35	139.89	223.70	112.4	113.3
1998	284.44	168.95	280.12	120.8	125.2
1999	314.91	194.44	336.46	115.1	120.1
2000	343.98	214.35	368.77	110.2	109.6
2001	374.15	231.94	484.40	108.2	131.4
2002	435.50	243.44	511.39	105.0	105.6
2003	483.90	259.76	540.44	106.7	105.7
2004	589.65	310.45	646.29	119.5	119.6
2005	727.61	375.52	778.72	121.0	120.5
2006	901.17	476.08	1047.00	126.8	134.5
2007	1115.47	590.36	1274.27	124.0	121.7
2008	1338.75	710.85	1650.28	120.4	129.5
2009	1541.55	814.87	2090.92	114.6	126.7
2010	1918.94	1011.23	2501.40	124.1	119.7
2011	2639.81	1526.91	3214.74	151.0	128.5
2012	3115.63	1823.05	3759.79	119.4	117.0
2013	3566.89	2191.22	4371.65	120.2	116.3
2014	4096.00	2566.90	4934.15	117.1	112.9
2015	4705.00	3005.53	6132.84	117.1	124.3

7-2 财政收支
FINANCIAL REVENUE AND EXPENDITURE

单位：亿元 (100 million yuan)

指标	Item	2012	2013	2014	2015
地方一般公共预算收入	Local Public Financial Revenue	1823.05	2191.22	2566.90	3005.53
#税收收入	Revenue	1324.44	1604.85	1856.53	2086.50
#增值税	#Taxes on Value Added	162.39	225.68	254.92	285.48
营业税	Run Taxes	472.36	526.43	593.27	678.30
企业所得税	Enterprise Income Taxes	196.87	215.23	250.45	276.78
个人所得税	Individual Income Taxes	48.55	57.74	64.50	78.53
城市维护建设税	Taxes on City Maintenance and Construction	92.50	109.04	121.34	138.62
房产税	Real Estate Taxews	29.28	34.70	42.28	53.14
耕地占用税	Taxes on Use of Cultivated Land	69.29	80.39	99.66	116.42
地方一般公共预算支出	Local Public Financial Expenditure	3759.79	4371.65	4934.15	6132.84
1.一般公共服务	General Public Service	466.51	546.49	598.45	618.14
2.外交	Foreign Affairs				
3.国防	National Defence	2.99	4.12	4.18	4.25
4.公共安全	Public Security	204.53	227.04	259.05	295.24
5.教育	Education	732.37	690.63	773.35	913.05
6.科学技术	Science and Technology	54.39	77.21	134.46	157.36
7.文化体育与传媒	Culture, Sports and Media	62.47	72.44	76.65	84.03
8.社会保障和就业	Social Security and Employment	501.13	605.70	717.63	858.70
9.医疗卫生与计划生育	Medical Care and family planning	267.99	322.08	410.31	515.25
10.节能环保	Environmental Protecction	95.63	109.72	103.78	145.84
11.城乡社区	Community Service in Urban and Rural Community	201.73	320.36	364.31	545.16
12.农林水	Water Affairs of Agriculture and Forestry	419.02	465.34	483.80	616.57
13.交通运输	Transportation	212.68	308.82	396.04	452.05
14.其他支出	Others	538.35	621.70	612.14	927.20

7-3 财政收入占地区生产总值的比重
FINANCIAL REVENUE AS PERCENTAGE TO GROSS DOMESTIC PRODUCT

年 份 Year	地方一般公共预算收入(亿元) Local Public Financial Revenue (100 million yuan)	地区生产总值(亿元) Gross Domestic Product (100 million yuan)	一般公共预算收入占地区生产总值的比重(%) Percentage of Local Financial Revenue to GDP (%)
1980	26.53	199.38	13.31
1981	23.60	219.75	10.74
1982	25.47	241.55	10.54
1983	28.32	262.58	10.79
1984	31.72	328.22	9.66
1985	43.50	396.26	10.98
1986	58.04	442.04	13.13
1987	60.98	517.77	11.78
1988	68.66	626.52	10.96
1989	79.07	717.08	11.03
1990	84.82	824.38	10.29
1991	95.09	913.38	10.41
1992	94.14	1088.39	8.65
1993	115.07	1325.83	8.68
1994	77.46	1700.92	4.55
1995	99.69	2109.38	4.73
1996	124.51	2499.77	4.98
1997	139.89	2856.47	4.90
1998	168.95	3114.02	5.43
1999	194.44	3229.29	6.02
2000	214.35	3545.39	6.05
2001	231.94	3880.53	5.98
2002	243.44	4212.82	5.78
2003	259.76	4757.45	5.46
2004	310.45	5633.24	5.51
2005	375.52	6590.19	5.70
2006	476.08	7617.47	6.25
2007	590.36	9333.40	6.33
2008	710.85	11328.92	6.27
2009	814.87	12961.10	6.29
2010	1011.23	15967.61	6.33
2011	1526.91	19632.26	7.78
2012	1823.05	22250.45	8.19
2013	2191.22	24668.49	8.88
2014	2566.90	27379.22	9.38
2015	3005.53	29550.19	10.17

7-4 市州一般公共预算收入
FINANCIAL REVENUE OF CITIES AND PREFECTURES

单位：亿元 (100 million yuan)

市州	Municipalities	2005	2006	2007	2008	2009	2010	2011	2012	2013	2014	2015
全 省	**The Total**	**375.52**	**476.08**	**590.36**	**710.85**	**814.87**	**1011.23**	**1526.91**	**1823.05**	**2191.22**	**2566.90**	**3005.53**
省 级	Provinial	94.59	131.60	161.83	174.37	184.06	206.78	188.67	130.07	126.27	133.16	155.96
武汉市	Wuhan	138.82	178.60	221.68	277.32	316.07	390.19	673.26	828.58	978.52	1101.02	1245.63
黄石市	Huangshi	11.96	15.33	19.71	24.09	26.03	34.10	53.84	65.64	78.36	89.38	100.53
十堰市	Shiyan	11.37	13.20	15.59	19.89	25.76	43.77	66.71	76.93	73.53	85.77	93.38
荆州市	Jingzhou	12.05	12.86	15.24	18.71	22.36	27.60	44.33	56.76	71.95	88.17	103.95
宜昌市	Yichang	22.53	27.37	35.57	44.27	54.94	70.24	113.98	153.25	206.31	271.51	339.10
襄阳市	Xiangyang	18.40	20.62	24.02	30.06	37.02	51.01	97.41	139.85	191.53	249.24	339.10
鄂州市	Ezhou	4.93	6.46	8.51	10.70	13.02	15.66	26.31	33.02	38.43	42.74	47.17
荆门市	Jingmen	9.34	10.17	12.06	14.92	18.14	23.25	39.39	50.69	59.84	69.82	80.43
孝感市	Xiaogan	10.78	12.73	16.63	21.46	26.97	34.20	51.58	69.50	89.05	107.22	122.77
黄冈市	Huanggang	13.14	15.35	19.93	26.21	32.17	38.98	51.61	62.92	79.98	96.04	112.82
咸宁市	Xianning	7.43	8.71	11.10	14.33	18.14	23.34	35.56	45.82	58.71	70.76	80.12
恩施自治州	Enshi	8.35	10.03	13.05	15.40	18.28	22.16	31.89	40.43	50.05	57.82	67.23
随州市	Suizhou	4.25	4.76	5.47	6.68	7.60	9.53	17.07	22.99	29.67	36.68	43.34
仙桃市	Xiantao	2.81	2.80	3.31	4.21	5.05	7.35	13.13	17.14	21.00	24.16	27.69
天门市	Tianmen	1.37	1.67	2.18	2.80	3.53	4.71	7.90	11.00	15.02	17.35	19.59
潜江市	Qianjiang	3.02	3.29	3.85	4.71	4.86	7.25	12.50	16.02	20.00	22.69	22.85
神农架林区	Shennongjia	0.42	0.50	0.60	0.73	0.87	1.10	1.77	2.44	3.00	3.37	3.86

7-5 市州一般公共预算支出
FINANCIAL EXPENDITURE OF CITIES AND PREFECTURES

单位：亿元 (100 million yuan)

市州	Municipalities	2005	2006	2007	2008	2009	2010	2011	2012	2013	2014	2015
全 省	**The Total**	**778.7**	**1047.00**	**1274.27**	**1650.28**	**2090.92**	**2501.40**	**3214.74**	**3759.79**	**4371.65**	**4934.15**	**6132.84**
省 级	Provinial	205.75	284.30	312.94	388.90	258.00	273.40	378.50	449.69	484.45	661.60	893.13
武汉市	Wuhan	176.88	257.81	307.23	377.88	503.64	583.55	765.04	885.55	1122.88	1175.10	1338.05
黄石市	Huangshi	23.47	31.43	40.90	53.06	80.85	102.56	128.69	140.43	150.79	152.97	225.94
十堰市	Shiyan	33.42	42.83	54.24	73.97	118.50	146.98	185.09	207.75	231.42	258.87	307.65
荆州市	Jingzhou	39.51	52.57	65.80	90.41	130.35	163.15	197.18	226.83	255.92	276.29	346.48
宜昌市	Yichang	47.63	62.76	79.78	105.86	156.50	196.51	241.13	297.45	364.44	439.92	537.53
襄阳市	Xiangyang	49.19	56.78	71.52	96.64	148.16	184.92	248.14	313.97	364.87	437.93	584.50
鄂州市	Ezhou	10.38	13.55	17.85	23.97	35.67	43.01	56.66	62.69	70.87	75.65	86.80
荆门市	Jingmen	24.58	29.33	38.65	49.18	81.66	95.46	125.34	142.20	158.79	178.96	225.90
孝感市	Xiaogan	32.50	41.89	54.60	74.64	109.79	133.58	172.61	201.79	227.90	253.18	290.38
黄冈市	Huanggang	44.40	57.13	76.23	104.47	155.09	188.13	225.54	278.92	305.16	344.66	401.03
咸宁市	Xianning	21.41	27.72	37.87	56.50	84.97	100.02	127.07	143.03	158.14	176.97	190.85
恩施自治州	Enshi	32.12	41.92	54.89	71.04	102.25	129.79	160.14	179.69	216.69	216.32	332.59
随州市	Suizhou	14.11	18.08	23.10	31.73	46.11	57.23	72.32	85.55	100.04	103.70	153.10
仙桃市	Xiantao	8.29	9.81	13.30	17.03	26.25	32.91	42.34	47.71	50.08	59.56	69.30
天门市	Tianmen	6.22	8.11	10.79	15.14	23.44	28.27	38.51	41.84	46.53	54.36	64.73
潜江市	Qianjiang	6.99	8.62	11.43	15.36	23.03	28.60	37.68	42.01	46.80	51.27	64.11
神农架林区	Shennongjia	1.86	2.37	3.13	4.26	6.66	13.33	12.76	12.69	15.88	16.84	20.78

7-6 金融机构(含外资)人民币存款年末余额
BALANCE OF RMB DEPOSITS IN FINANCIAL ORGANIZATIONS (INCLUDING FOREIGN FUNDED ENTERPRISES) BY THE END

单位：亿元

指 标	Item	2015
各项存款	Deposits	40896.52
(一)境外存款	Domestic Deposits	40871.93
1.住户存款	Household Deposits	19566.11
(1)活期存款	Demand Deposits	7095.16
(2)定期及其他存款	Regular and Other Deposits	12470.95
2.非金融企业存款	Non Financial Enterprise Deposits	12079.57
(1)活期存款	Demand Deposits	6114.09
(2)定期及其他存款	Regular and Other Deposits	5965.47
3.广义政府存款	General Government Deposits	7894.00
(1)财政性存款	Public Financial Deposits	1305.30
(2)机关团体存款	Bank Deposits	6588.71
4.非银行业金融机构存款	Non Banking Financial Institutions Deposits	1332.25
(二)境外存款	Offshore Deposits	24.59

注：本表采用数据为新口径数据。
Note: Data from this table are based on the new standard.

7-7 金融机构(含外资)人民币贷款年末余额
BALANCE OF RMB LOANS OF FINANCIAL ORGANIZTIONS (INCLUDING FOREIGN FUNDED ENTERPISES) BY THE END

单位：亿元 (100 million yuan)

指 标	Item	2015
各项贷款	Loans	28338.90
(一)境内贷款	Domestil Loans	28336.23
1.住户贷款	Household Loans	7363.50
(1)短期贷款	Short-term Loans	1606.55
消费贷款	Consumer Loans	435.17
经营贷款	Operating Loans	1171.39
(2)中长期贷款	Medium-term and Long-term Loans	5756.95
消费贷款	Consumer Loans	4693.04
经营贷款	Operating Loans	1063.91
2.非金融企业及机关团体贷款	Non Financial Enterprise and Institution Loans	20972.59
(1)短期贷款	Short-term Loans	7121.55
(2)中长期贷款	Medium and Long Term Loans	12397.47
(3)票据融资	Bill Financing	954.94
(4)融资租赁	Loans for Accomodation and Rent	424.30
(5)各项垫款	Money Advanced Payment for Others	74.33
3.非银行业金融机构贷款	Non Banking Financial Institution Loans	0.13
(二)境外贷款	Foreign Loans	2.67

注：本表采用数据为新口径数据。
Note: Data from this table are based on the new standard.

7-8 保险业务主要指标
MAJOR INDICATORS OF INSURANCE BUSINESS

项　目		Item		2012	2013	2014	2015
一、保险密度	(元/人)	Density of Insurance	(yuan/person)	922.84	1012.94	1204.00	1441.73
二、保险深度	(%)	Depth of Insurance	(%)	2.40	2.38	2.56	2.85
三、保费收入	(亿元)	Premium	(100 million yuan)	533.31	587.40	700.23	843.63
(一)财产保险		Property Insurnce		135.26	169.35	204.55	238.24
1.财产险		Property Insurnce		10.13	11.04	12.29	12.44
2.机动车辆保险		Machine Driving Cars Insurnce		103.31	128.98	161.27	193.35
3.责任险		Responsibility Insurance		5.46	6.63	7.84	9.47
4.信用保证险		Credit Guarantee Insurance		4.60	8.40	9.05	8.03
5.其它		Others		11.76	14.29	14.10	14.95
(二)人身保险		Life Insurance		398.05	418.07	495.67	605.38
1.人身意外伤害保险		Accident Insurance		13.06	15.79	18.52	22.01
团体保险		Group Insurance		6.74	8.06	9.35	10.36
个人保险		Individual Insurance		6.32	7.73	9.17	11.65
2.健康险		Healthy Insurance		27.70	39.47	55.64	87.97
团体保险		Group Insurance		6.82	14.69	21.24	25.80
个人保险		Individual Insurance		20.88	24.78	34.40	62.17
3.寿险		Personal Insurance		357.29	362.81	421.51	495.40
团体保险		Group Insurance		3.99	1.80	2.77	1.15
个人保险		Individual Insurance		353.30	361.01	418.74	494.25
四、各项赔款和给付	(亿元)	Claim and Payment	(100 million yuan)	128.55	187.61	230.59	283.34
(一)财产保险		Property Insurnce		68.34	86.32	100.90	114.42
1.财产险		Property Insurnce		3.53	4.01	4.51	4.30
2.机动车辆保险		Machine Driving Cars Insurnce		56.10	71.60	83.82	97.27
3.责任险		Responsibility Insurance		2.42	3.00	3.69	4.13
4.信用保证险		Credit Guarantee Insurance		0.46	0.50	1.17	2.15
5.其它		Others		5.83	7.21	7.71	6.57
(二)人身保险		Life Insurance		60.21	101.28	129.69	168.92
1.人身意外伤害保险		Accident Insurance		3.42	3.93	4.67	5.97
团体保险		Group Insurance		1.43	1.61	2.03	3.01
个人保险		Individual Insurance		1.99	2.32	2.64	2.96
2.健康险		Healthy Insurance		10.29	14.43	26.73	32.33
团体保险		Group Insurance		4.47	7.49	18.54	22.00
个人保险		Individual Insurance		5.82	6.94	8.19	10.33
3.寿险		Personal Insurance		46.50	82.92	98.29	130.62
团体保险		Group Insurance		7.57	7.69	8.10	8.10
个人保险		Individual Insurance		38.93	75.23	90.19	122.52

注：本表采用数据均为保险业新口径数据。
Note: Data from this table are based on the new standard.

主要统计指标解释

财政总收入 指地方一般预算收入与上划中央税收收入之和。

公共财政收入 是指各级政府为履行职能，按照国家法律、法规规定收取的纳入一般预算管理的各项税收及非税收入总和。主要包括：

(1)各项税收：包括国内增值税、国内消费税、进口货物增值税和消费税、出口货物退增值税和消费税、营业税、企业所得税、个人所得税、资源税、城市维护建设税、房产税、印花税、城镇土地使用税、土地增值税、车船税、船舶吨税、车辆购置税、关税、耕地占用税、契税、烟叶税等。

(2)非税收入：包括专项收入、行政事业性收费、罚没收入和其他收入。

公共财政支出 国家财政将筹集起来的资金进行分配使用，以满足经济建设和各项事业的需要。主要包括：

(1)一般公共服务：指政府提供基本公共管理与服务的支出，包括人大事务、政协事务、政府办公厅(室)及相关机构事务、发展与改革事务、统计信息事务、财政事务、税收事务、审计事务、海关事务、人力资源事务、纪检监察事务、人口与计划生育事务、商贸事务、知识产权事务、工商行政管理事务、国土资源事务、海洋管理事务、测绘事务、地震事务、气象事务、民族事务、宗教事务、港澳台侨事务、档案事务、共产党事务、民主党派事务及工商联事务、群众团体事务、彩票事务等。

(2)外交：指政府外交事务支出，包括外交行政管理、驻外机构、对外援助、国际组织、对外合作与交流、边界勘界联检等方面的支出。

(3)国防：指政府用于国防方面的支出，包括用于现役部队、预备役部队、民兵、国防科研事业、专项工程、国防动员等方面的支出。

(4)公共安全：指政府维护社会公共安全方面的支出，包括武装警察、公安、国家安全、检察、法院、司法行政、监狱、劳教、国家保密、缉私警察等。

(5)教育：指政府教育事务支出，包括教育行政管理、学前教育、小学教育、初中教育、普通高中教育、普通高等教育、初等职业教育、中专教育、技校教育、职业高中教育、高等职业教育、广播电视教育、留学生教育、特殊教育、干部继续教育、教育机关服务等。

(6)科学技术：指用于科学技术方面的支出，包括科学技术管理事务、基础研究、应用研究、技术研究与开发、科技条件与服务、社会科学、科学技术普及、科技交流与合作等。

(7)文化教育与传媒：指政府在文化、文物、体育、广播影视、新闻出版等方面的支出。

(8)社会保障和就业：指政府在社会保障与就业方面的支出，包括社会保障和就业管理事务、民政管理事务、财政对社会保险基金的补助、补充全国社会保障基金、行政事业单位离退休、企业改革补助、就业补助、抚恤、退役安置、社会福利、残疾人事业、城市居民最低生活保障、其他城镇社会救济、农村社会救济、自然灾害生活救助、红十字事务等。

(9)医疗卫生：指政府医疗卫生方面的支出，包括医疗卫生管理事务支出、医疗服务支出、医疗保障支出、疾病预防控制支出、卫生监督支出、妇幼保健支出、农村卫生支出等。

(10)节能环保：指政府环境保护支出，包括环境保护管理事务支出、环境监测与监察支出、污染治理支出、自然生态保护支出、天然林保护工程支出、退耕还林支出、风沙荒漠治理支出、退牧还草支出、已垦草原退耕还草、能源节约利用、污染减排、可再生能源和资源综合利用等支出。

(11)城乡社区事务：指政府城乡社区事务支出，包括城乡社区管理事务支出、城乡社区规划与管理支出、城乡社区公共设施支出、城乡社区住宅支出、城乡社区环境卫生支出、建设市场管理与监督支出等。

(12)农林水事务：指政府农林水事务支出，包括农业支出、林业支出、水利支出、扶贫支出、农业综合开发支出等。

(13)交通运输:指政府交通运输和邮政业方面的支出,包括公路运输支出、水路运输支出、铁路运输支出、民用航空运输支出、邮政业支出等。

信贷资金 指金融机构以信用方式积聚和分配的货币资金。金融机构信贷资金的来源有各项存款、金融债券发行、应付及暂收款、对国际金融机构负债、流通中货币、各项准备、所有者权益和其他项目等;信贷资金的运用有各项贷款、有价证券及投资、应收及预付款、委托投资、金银占款、外汇占款、库存现金、财政借款及在国际金融机构中的资产等。

存款 指企业、机关、团体或居民根据资金必须收回的原则,把货币资金存入银行或其他信贷机构保管并取得一定利息的一种信用活动形式。根据存款对象或性质的不同可划分为企业存款、财政存款、机关团体存款、基本建设存款、储蓄存款、农村存款、委托存款、其他存款等科目。它是银行信贷资金的主要来源。

贷款 指银行或其他信贷机构根据资金必须归还的原则,按一定利率,为企业、个人等提供资金的一种信用活动形式。我国银行贷款分为短期贷款、中期流动资金贷款、中长期贷款、信托贷款、融资租赁、委托贷款、票据融资、各项垫款等。

保险公司 在中国境内的、经过保险监督管理部门批准设立,并依法登记注册的各类商业保险公司。

保险金额 指保险人承担赔偿或者给付保险金责任的最高限额。

保费 指投保人为取得保险人在约定范围内所承担赔偿责任而支付给保险人的费用。

赔款 指保险人根据保险合同的规定,向被保险人支付的赔偿保险责任损失的金额。

给付 包括死伤医疗给付和满期给付。死伤医疗给付是指保险人根据人寿保险及长期健康保险合同的规定,因被保险人在保险期内发生保险责任范围内的保险事故支付给被保险人(或受益人)的金额。满期给付是指被保险人生存期满,保险人按人寿保险合同规定支付给被保险人的满期保险金额。

Explanatory Notes on Main Statistical Indicators

Total income refers to the local fiscal revenue and the general budget tax revenue and central planning.Public Financial revenue is to perform its functions in accordance with national laws and regulations collected into the general budget of the revenue management and non-tax revenues combined. Public FinancialExpenditure refers to the distribution and use of the funds the government finances has risen, so as to meet the needs of economic construction and various causes. It includes the following main items:

(1) Expenditure for general public services: It refers to the spending on the basic public management and services which provided by governments, including the expense on affairs of People's Congress, affairs of People's Political Consultative Conference, affairs of government general office and relative institutions, affairs of development and reform, affairs of statistics, affairs of finance, affairs of taxation, affairs of audit, affairs of customs, affairs of human resources and social security, affairs of discipline inspection and supervision, affairs of population and family planning, affairs of commerce and trade, affairs of intellectual property, affairs of administration for industry and commerce, affairs of land and resources, affairs of oceanic administration, affairs of surveying and mapping, affairs of earthquake, ethnic affairs, religious affairs, affairs of Hong Kong, Macao, Taiwan, and Overseas Chinese, affairs of archives administration, affairs of Chinese Communist Party, affairs of democratic parties and federation of industry and commerce, affairs of mass organization, and affairs of lottery, etc.

(2) Expenditure for foreign affairs: It refers to the spending of government on foreign affairs, including the expense on administration of foreign affairs, missions overseas, external assistance, international organizations, foreign cooperation and communication, surveying and joint inspection on borderline, etc.

(3) Expenditure for national defence: It refers to the spending of government on national defence, including the expense on active force, reserve force, militia, scientific research on national defence, special projects, mobilization of national defence, etc.

(4) Expenditure for public security: It refers to the spending of government on maintaining social and public security, including the

expense on armed police force, public security, state security, prosecution, courts, justice, prison, labour education and rehabilitation, protection of state secrecy, anti-smuggling police, etc.

(5) Expenditure for education: It refers to the spending of government on education, including the expense on the administration of education, pre-primary education, primary education, secondary education, high school education, regular higher education, primary vocational education, secondary vocational education, technical school education, vocational high school education and higher vocational education, radio and television education, student abroad education, special education, on the job training of cadres, education authorities services, etc.

(6) Expenditure for science and technology: It refers to the spending of government on science and technology (S&T), including the expense on the administration of S&T, basic research, applied research, research and development, conditions and services of S&T, popularization of social science, science and technology, exchanges and cooperation of S&T, etc.

(7) Expenditure for culture, sport and media: It refers to the spending of government on culture, cultural heritage, sports, radio, film, television, press and publication, etc.

(8) Expenditure for social safety net and employment effort: It refers to the spending of government on social safety net and employment, including the expense on administration of social safety net and employment, civil affairs, budgetary subsidy on the social insurance funds, subsidy on National Social Security Fund, retirees of administrative units and institutions, subsidy on enterprise reform, subsidy on employment effort, pension, placement of ex-serviceman, social welfare, the handicapped undertakings, the system of cost of living allowances for urban residents, other urban social relief, rural social relief, living relief of natural disasters, affairs of Red Cross Society, etc.

(9) Expenditure for medical and health care: It refers to the spending of government on medical and health care, including the expense on administration of medical and health care, medical services, health care, disease prevention and control, health inspection and supervision, women and children's health, rural health care, etc.

(10) Expenditure for environment protection: It refers to the spending of government on environment protection, including the expense on administration of environment protection, environment monitoring and supervision, pollution control, natural ecology protection, project of virgin forests protection, reforesting farmland, controlling the sources of dust storms, returning pastureland to grassland, returning pastureland to grassland, returning cultivated land to grassland, energy conservation, emissions reduction, comprehensive utilization of renewable energy and resources, etc.

(11) Expenditure for urban and rural community affairs: It refers to the spending of government on urban and rural community affairs, including the expense on administration of urban and rural community, planning and management of urban and rural community, public facilities of urban and rural community, housing of urban and rural community, sanitation of urban and rural community, management and supervision on the construction market, etc.

(12) Expenditure for agriculture, forestry and water conservancy: It refers to the spending of government on agriculture, forestry and water conservancy, including the expense on agriculture, forestry, water conservancy, poverty alleviation, comprehensive agricultural development, etc.

(13) Expenditure for transportation: It refers to the spending of government on transportation and postal services, including the expense on road transportation, waterway transportation, railway transportation, civil aviation transportation, and postal services.

Credit Funds refer to the funds issued as loans by banking institutions. The sources of credit funds of the banking institutions included deposits, issue of financial bonds, account-payable and temporary gathering, liabilities to international financial institutions, currency in circulation, various reserves, owners' rights and interests and other items. The credit funds can be used in forms of loans, securities and investment, account receivable and advance payment, entrusted investment, gold, foreign exchange, cash on hand, government debt and assets in the international financial institutions.

Deposit is a form of credit by which enterprises, institutions, organizations or households can put money into banks and other credit institutions for safekeeping and interest earning under the principle of free withdrawal. According to different depositors, deposits are divided into enterprise deposits, treasury deposits, deposits of government agencies and organizations, capital construction deposits, savings deposits, rural saving deposits, entrusted deposits and other deposits. Deposits are major sources of the credit funds of banks.

Loan is a form of credit by which banks and other credit institutions provide funds at certain interest rate to enterprises and individuals in the light of the principle of unconditional repayment. Loans from Chinese banks include circulating capital loans, fixed assets loans, loans to urban and rural individuals engaged in industrial and commercial business and agricultural loans.

Insurance Companies refer to commercial insurance companies of various forms registered by law and established in China with the approval of insurance regulatory agencies.

Amount Insured refers to the maximum that the insurant will get for the claim of the case insured.

Premium is the fee paid by the insurant to the insurer to obtain the obligation of compensation from the insurance within the agreed terms.

Settled Claim is the compensation paid by the insurer to the insurant in accordance with the insurance contract.

Payment includes payment for death, injury or medical treatment and mature payment. Payment for death, injury or medical treatment refers to the money paid to the insurant (or the beneficiary) in accordance with the life or health insurance contract when the insurant encounters accidents within the insured period covered in the contract. Mature payment refers to the mature payment to the insurant in accordance with the life insurance contract at the end of the insured period.

8 价　格

Price

8-1 物价总指数(2015)
GENERAL PRICE INDICES(2015)

基 期	Base Period	商品零售价格总指数 General Rtail Price Index	居民消费价格总指数 General Consumption Price Index
以1950年价格为100	The Price of 1950 Equals 100	658.7	1030.1
以1952年价格为100	The Price of 1952 Equals 100	584.1	906.2
以1957年价格为100	The Price of 1957 Equals 100	528.8	803.3
以1965年价格为100	The Price of 1965 Equals 100	473.9	706.7
以1970年价格为100	The Price of 1970 Equals 100	477.6	709.4
以1975年价格为100	The Price of 1975 Equals 100	478.3	702.5
以1978年价格为100	The Price of 1978 Equals 100	474.5	699.8
以1980年价格为100	The Price of 1980 Equals 100	447.3	639.0
以1985年价格为100	The Price of 1985 Equals 100	389.9	537.2
以1990年价格为100	The Price of 1990 Equals 100	241.9	338.8
以1995年价格为100	The Price of 1995 Equals 100	129.6	159.4
以2000年价格为100	The Price of 2000 Equals 100	132.0	148.3
以2005年价格为100	The Price of 2005 Equals 100	127.2	134.4
以2010年价格为100	The Price of 2010 Equals 100	111.8	115.9
以上年价格为100	The Price of Last Year Equals 100	100.5	101.5

8-2 各市、县物价指数(2015)
GENERAL PRICE INDICES(2015)

(上年=100) (preceding year = 100)

地 区	Region	居民消费价格指数 Consumer Price Index	商品零售价格指数 Retail Price Index	农业生产资料价格指数 Agricultural Production Material Price Index
湖北省	**Hubei**	**101.5**	**100.5**	**100.4**
武汉市	Wuhan	101.4	100.0	
黄石市	Huangshi	101.6	100.4	
十堰市	Shiyan	101.4	100.3	
竹山县	zhushan	101.3	101.1	100.4
宜昌市	Yichang	101.5	100.6	
宜都市	Yidu	102.3	101.1	105.2
襄阳市	Xiangyang	102.0	101.5	
老河口市	Laohekou	101.4	100.6	101.3
鄂州市	Ezhou	101.4	100.4	
荆门市	Jingmen	101.6	100.9	
孝感市	Xiaogan	101.3	100.3	
大悟县	Dawu	101.7	101.1	98.3
荆州市	Jingzhou	101.5	100.7	
洪湖市	Honghu	101.0	100.5	99.3
黄冈市	Huanggang	101.4	100.0	
浠水县	Xishui	101.6	100.2	100.9
麻城市	Macheng	102.8	101.4	102.2
咸宁市	Xianning	101.4	100.4	98.8
崇阳县	Chongyang	102.0	101.1	99.7
恩施市	Enshi	102.5	100.8	99.9
随州市	Suizhou	101.3	100.1	
天门市	Tianmen	101.3	100.4	100.1

8-3 全省居民消费、商品零售价格分类指数(2015)
RETAIL PRICE INDICES BY CATEGORY OF COMMODITIES(2015)

(上年=100) (preceding year=100)

类别	Item	全省 Provincial Indices	城市 Urban Indices	农村 Rural Indices
居民消费价格总指数	**General Consumer Price Index**	101.5	101.4	101.7
*服务项目价格指数	Service Price Index	101.9	101.6	102.5
一、食品	Foods	102.2	102.0	102.6
二、烟酒及用品	Tobacco,Liquor and Articles	102.6	102.4	102.9
三、衣着	Clothing	102.7	103.3	101.3
四、家庭设备用品及维修服务	Household Facilities and Articles	100.6	100.7	100.4
五、医疗保健和个人用品	Medicine and Medical Articles	101.7	101.6	102.0
六、交通和通讯	Transportation and Communication	100.2	100.5	99.5
七、娱乐教育文化用品及服务	Receation, Education and Culture Articles and Services	101.3	100.8	102.2
八、居住	Housing Condition	100.6	100.4	101.0
商品零售价格总指数	**General Price Index**	100.5	100.4	100.7
一、食品	Foods	102.3	102.1	102.6
二、饮料、烟酒	Beverage, Tobacco and Liquor	102.1	102.0	102.3
三、服装、鞋帽	Garments, Shoes and Hats	102.4	103.3	101.1
四、纺织品	Texiles	101.0	101.5	100.4
五、家用电器及音像器材	Household Electric Appliance and Stereo	97.9	97.0	99.0
六、文化办公用品	Stationery and Business Articles	99.9	99.5	100.4
七、日用品	Daily Use Articles	100.5	100.9	100.1
八、体育娱乐用品	Sports and Receation Articles	100.2	100.1	100.3
九、交通、通信用品	Transportation and Communication Articles	97.6	97.2	98.2
十、家具	Furniture	99.9	99.7	100.2
十一、化妆品	Cosmetics	100.0	99.8	100.4
十二、金银珠宝	Gold, Silver and Pearls Jewelery	92.5	90.3	94.8
十三、中西药品及医疗保健用品	Chinese Traditional Medicine, Western Medicines and Health Care Appliances	103.3	103.2	103.3
十四、书报杂志及电子出版物	Books, Newspaper, Magzines and Electronic Publications	101.4	100.8	102.3
十五、燃料类	Fuels	89.9	89.9	89.9
十六、建筑材料及五金电料	Building and Decoration Materials	99.7	99.7	99.6
农业生产资料价格指数	**General Price Index of Means of Agricultural Production**	100.4		100.4

8-4 工业生产者出厂价格指数
EX-FACTORY PRICE INDICES OF INDUSTRIAL PRODUCTS

分 类	Group Name	上年=100 preceding year=100	1990年=100 1990=100	
		2015	2014	2015
总指数	General Indices	96.7	276.46	267.25
一、按轻重工业分	Grouped by Light Industry and Heavy Industry			
1.轻工业	Light Industry	99.3	225.34	223.81
以农产品为原料	Using Farm Products as Raw Material	99.3	257.73	256.00
以非农产品为原料	Using Non-Farm Products as Raw Material	99.3	147.93	146.89
2.重工业	Heavy Industry	95.7	326.56	312.56
采 掘	Mining and Quarrying	84.5	713.10	602.35
原 料	Raw Material	93.0	480.96	447.47
加 工	Processing	97.9	192.75	188.71
二、按两大部类分	Grouped by Two Sectors			
1.生产资料	Means of Production	95.2	317.93	302.54
采 掘	Mining and Quarrying	84.5	712.52	601.86
原 料	Raw Material	92.7	395.66	366.96
加 工	Processing	97.2	202.51	196.78
2.生活资料	Consumer Goods	100.5	204.19	205.24
食 品	Foods	100.4	276.41	277.38
衣 着	Clothing	100.5	227.67	228.82
一般日用品	Daily Use Articles	100.4	192.79	193.53
耐用消费品	Durable Consumer Goods	100.9	62.53	63.06

8-5 原材料、燃料、动力购进价格指数
RAW MATERIAL, FUEL, POWER PURCHASE PRICE INDICES

分 类	Group Name	上年=100 preceding year=100	1990年=100 1990=100	
		2015	2014	2015
总指数	**General Index**	**92.80**	**414.90**	**385.03**
燃料、动力类	Fuel Powers	88.10	676.65	596.13
黑色金属材料类	Ferrous Metal	90.70	305.20	276.82
有色金属材料类	Non-ferrous Metal	92.80	317.31	294.46
化工原材料类	Chemical Materials	97.30	218.90	212.99
木材及纸浆类	Timber and Pulp	100.20	183.49	183.86
建筑材料及非金属矿类	Construction Materials and Non-Metal Mining Industry	97.00	316.72	307.22
其它工业原材料及半成品类	Other Industrial Raw Materials and Semi-Finished Products	96.90	190.97	185.05
农副产品类	Farm and Sideline Products	99.80	430.85	429.99
纺织原料类	Textile Raw Materials	91.30	211.78	193.36

8-6 固定资产投资价格指数
PRICE INDICES OF INVESTMENT IN FIXED ASSETS

分类	Name of Group	上年=100 preceding year=100	1990年=100 1990=100
		2015	2015
总指数	Total Indices	99.4	291.6
建筑安装工程	Construction and Installation	99.1	329.0
设备、工器具	Equipment and Devices	99.5	177.0
其他费用	Others	101.2	373.1

主要统计指标解释

居民消费价格指数 是反映一定时期内城乡居民所购买的生活消费品价格和服务项目价格变动趋势和程度的相对数，是对城市居民消费价格指数和农村居民消费价格指数进行综合汇总计算的结果。该指数可以观察和分析消费品的零售价格和服务价格变动对城乡居民实际生活费支出的影响程度。

城市居民消费价格指数 是反映一定时期内城市居民家庭所购买的生活消费品价格和服务项目价格变动趋势和程度的相对数。该指数可以观察和分析消费品的零售价格和服务项目价格变动对城镇职工货币工资的影响，作为研究职工生活和确定工资政策的依据。

农村居民消费价格指数 是反映一定时期内农村居民家庭所购买的生活消费品价格和服务项目价格变动趋势和程度的相对数。该指数可以观察农村消费品的零售价格和服务项目价格变动对农村居民生活消费支出的影响，直接反映农民生活水平的实际变化情况，为分析和研究农村居民生活问题提供依据。

商品零售价格指数 是反映一定时期内城乡商品零售价格变动趋势和程度的相对数。商品零售价格的变动直接影响到城乡居民的生活支出和国家的财政收入，影响居民购买力和市场供需的平衡，影响到消费与积累的比例关系。因此，该指数可以从一个侧面对上述经济活动进行观察和分析。

农业生产资料价格指数 指反映一定时期内农业生产资料价格变动趋势和程度的相对数。农业生产资料价格指数分为小农具、饲料、产品畜、役畜、半机械化农具、机械化农具、化学肥料、农药及农药械、农机用油、其他农业生产资料十大类。其编制目的是了解农业生产中物质资料投入价格的变动状况，服务于国民经济核算。1994年以前，农业生产资料价格指数仅仅是商品零售价格指数的一个类别，此后，从商品零售价格指数中分离出来，单独编制。

农产品生产价格指数 是反映一定时期内，农产品生产者出售农产品价格水平变动趋势及幅度的相对数。该指数可以客观反映全国农产品生产价格水平和结构变动情况，满足农业与国民经济核算需要。其中某代表品生产价格指数是通过对全部有出售该产品行为的调查单位的个体指数进行几何平均求得的，类价格指数是通过对其所属的类(或代表品)的价格指数进行加权平均求得的。季度累计价格指数的计算方法与分季指数的计算方法相同。

工业生产者出厂价格指数 是反映一定时期内全部工业产品出厂价格总水平的变动趋势和程度的相对数，包括工业企业售给本企业以外所有单位的各种产品和直接售给居民用于生活消费的产品。该指数可以观察出厂价格变动对工业总产值及增加值的影响。

工业生产者购进价格指数 是反映工业企业作为生产投入，而从物资交易市场和能源、原材料生产企业购买原材料、燃料和动力产品时，所支付的价格水平变动趋势和程度的统计指标，是扣除工业企业物质消耗成本中的价格变动影响的重要依据。

目前，我国编制的原材料、燃料和动力购进价格指数所调查的产品包括燃料动力、黑色金属、有色金属、化工、建材等九大类的近1800种产品。

固定资产投资价格指数 是反映一定时期内固定资产投资品及项目的价格变动趋势和程度的相对数。固定资产投资额是由建筑安装工程投资完成额、设备工器具购置投资完成额和其他费用投资完成额三部分组成的。编制固定资产投资价格指数应首先分别编制上述三部分投资的价格指数，然后采用加权算术平均法求出固定资产投资价格总指数。

该指数可以准确地反映固定资产投资中涉及的各类投资品和取费项目价格变动趋势和变动幅度，消除按现价计算的固定资产投资指标中的价格变动因素，真实地反映固定资产投资的规模、速度、结构和效益，为国家科学地制定、检查固定资产投资计划并提高宏观调控水平，为完善国民经济核算体系提供科学的、可靠的依据。

房地产价格指数 是反映一定时期内房地产价格变动趋势和程度的相对数，包括房屋销售价格指数、房屋租赁价格指数、土地交易价格指数和物业管理价格指数。这四套指数的计算方法相似，均采用由下到上逐级汇总的方法。

Explanatory Notes on Main Statistical Indicators

Urban Consumer Price Indices reflect the trend and degree of changes in prices of consumer goods and services purchased by urban households during a given period. It can be used to observe and analyze the impact of price changes in consumer goods and services on wages (in monetary terms) of urban staff and workers, and provide basis for policy–making concerning the living cost and wages of staff and workers.

Rural Consumer Price Indices reflect the trend and degree of changes in prices of consumer goods and services purchased by rural households during a given period. It can be used to observe the impact of change in retail prices of consumer goods and service prices in rural areas on living expenditure of rural households, and to show the changes in the living standard of peasants. It provides basis for analysis and research on condition of life in rural areas.

Retail Price Indices reflect the trend and degree of change in retail prices of commodities during a given period. The change in retail prices of commodities directly affect the living expenditure of urban and rural residents, government revenue, purchasing power of residents and the equilibrium of market supply and demand, and the ratio of consumption to accumulation. Therefore, the retail price indices are useful to analyze the changes of the above economic activities.

Price Indices of Means of Agricultural Production reflect the trend and degree of changes in prices of means of agricultural production during a given period. Price indices of means of agricultural production are composed of 10 categories including small farm tools, feeds, domestic animals for meat, draught domestic animals, semi–mechanized farm machinery, mechanized farm machinery, chemical fertilizers, pesticides and spraying machinery, fuels for farm machinery and other means of agricultural production. Compilation of these indices helps to understand the changes in prices of input into agricultural production and facilitate the compilation of national account statistics. Before 1994, price indices of means of agricultural production was a sub–category in the in the retail price indices of commodities, and it has been compiled separately since 1994.

Indices of Producers' Prices for Farm Products reflect the trend and degree of changes in producers' prices received by farmers when they sell farm products during a given period. These indices depict the change in the level and structure of producers' prices of farm products of the country and meet the needs of agriculture statistics and national account statistics. The producers' price index of a given product is calculated through geometrical mean of individual indices of all surveyed units who sell such product, and the indices of a product category is obtained through weighted mean of price indices of all products in the category. Method for calculating accumulative quarterly indices is the same as for calculating the distinctive quarterly indices.

Ex–factory Price Indices of Industrial Products reflect the trend and degree of changes in general ex–factory prices of all industrial products during a given period, including sales of industrial products by an industrial enterprise to all units outside the enterprise, as well as sales of consumer goods to residents. It can be used to analyze the impact of ex–factory prices on gross output value and value–added of the industrial sector.

Indices of Purchasing Prices of Raw Materials, Fuels and Power reflect changes in the level and degree of prices paid by industrial enterprises when they purchase production input such as raw materials, fuels and power from the market or from other energy or raw materials producing enterprises. These indices provide important basis for measuring the material consumption of industrial enterprises after removing influence of price changes.

At present, close to 1,800 products in 9 categories, including fuels and power, ferrous metals, non–ferrous metals, chemicals, building materials, are covered in China for the survey to produce indices of purchasing prices of raw materials, fuels and power.

Price Indices of Investment in Fixed Assets reflect the trend and degree of changes in prices of investment goods and projects in fixed assets during a given period. The investment in fixed assets consists of three components, namely the investment in construction and installation, the investment in purchases of equipment and instrument, and the investment in other items. Price indices of investment in fixed assets are calculated as the weighted arithmetic mean of the price indices of the three components of investment in fixed assets.

Removing the factor of price change in the aggregates of investment at current prices, this indicator shows the changes in the prices of commodities and fees involved in the investment of fixed assets, and can be used to observe the actual size, growth, structure, and efficiency of investment in fixed assets and provides reliable and scientific data for government planning, management, decision–making, and further improving the current national accounting system.

Price Indices for Real Estate reflect the trend and degree of changes in prices of real estate during a given period, including price indices for selling houses and buildings, price indices for leasing houses and buildings and price indices for land transaction. The methods for the compilation of the three sets of indices are similar in that they all use bottom–up approach under which data are reported from lower level to higher level.

9 居民生活

People's Livelihood

9-1 居民生活水平情况
PEOPLE'S LIVING STANDARD

项　目	Item	单位	unit	2005	2010	2013	2014	2015
一、城乡就业	Employment							
每一农村劳动力负担人数	Average Person Supported by a Rural Laborer	人	person	1.34	1.27	1.31	1.41	1.41
每一城镇就业者负担人数	Average Person Supported by a Urban Laborer	人	person	1.96	2.01	1.81	1.79	1.86
城镇登记失业率	The Rate of Registered Unemployment	%	percentage	4.33	4.18	3.49	3.10	2.64
二、城乡居民收入	Revenue							
农村居民人均可支配收入	Net Income of Rural Residents Per Capita	元	yuan	3099.00	5832.00	8866.95	10849.06	11843.89
农村居民人均可支配收入指数(1990=100)	Indices of Net Income of Rural Residents Per Capita (1990=100)	%	percentage	461.80	869.24	1321.48	1617.33	1765.63
城镇居民人均可支配收入	Annual Disposable Income of Urban Residents	元	yuan	8786.00	16058.00	22906.40	24852.28	27051.47
城镇居民人均可支配收入指数(1990=100)	Indices of Net Annual Disposable Income of Urban Residents (1990=100)	%	percentage	615.80	1125.45	1604.71	1741.33	1895.42
国有职工平均工资	Average Wages of Staff and Workers in State-Owned Units	元	yuan	14774	35981	46126	55071	60615
三、城乡居民人平消费水平	Consumption Level							
农村居民	Rural Residents	元	yuan	2503	4758	7755	8608	9542
城镇居民	Urban Residents	元	yuan	8051	13576	19156	21854	23561
四、储蓄	Savings							
城乡居民人平储蓄存款余额	Balance of Saving Deposits of Rural and Urban Residents Per Capita	元	yuan	7929	17216	27591	30686	33539
五、平均每人居住面积	Floor Area of Housing Per Capita							
城市(大、中)	Municipalities (Large and Medium-sized)	平方米	sq.m	29.90	33.20	38.82	41.90	43.18
农村	Rural Areas	平方米	sq.m	36.05	40.99	41.84	54.78	55.61
六、交通	Transportations							
城镇每百户拥有汽车	Cars Ouned Per 100	辆	set		5.53	13.28	13.65	17.68
七、文化	Culture							
每百人每天有报纸	Newspaper Owned Per 100 Persons Every Day	份	unit	8.89	8.70	9.36	9.01	7.23
每人每年有图书、杂志	Books and Magazines Owned Per Capita Anuually	册	unit	8.99	9.90	9.87	9.52	8.82
八、教育	Education							
学龄儿童入学率	Emrollment Ratio of School-Age Children	%	percentsge	99.65	99.96	99.98	99.99	99.99
每万人口有大学生数	Number of University Students Per 10000 Persons	人	person	167.91	226.58	245.12	244.10	241.49
九、卫生	Health Care							
每千人有医院病床数	Number of Hospital-Beds Owned By Per 1000 Person	张	unit	2.31	3.26	4.97	5.47	5.87
每千人有医生	Number of Doctors Owned By Per 1000 Persons	人	person	1.49	1.62	2.06	2.19	2.32

注：平均每人居住面积中，城市(大、中)从2002年起为建筑面积，以前年份为居住面积。
Notes: Of Average Housing Areas, it refers to Construction Area of Municipalities (large and medium-sized)areas.since 2002, before2002, it refers to living areas.

9-2 居民消费水平
PEOPLE'S CONSUMPTION LEVEL

年份 year	居民消费 (亿元) People's Censurption (100 million yuan)	农村居民 rural residernts	城镇居民 wrban residernts	居民消费水平 (元) level of consumption	农村居民 rural residernts	城镇居民 wrban residernts
1982	126.75	90.67	36.08	266	227	462
1983	141.49	101.17	40.32	293	251	502
1984	172.19	120.41	51.78	352	300	592
1985	203.23	129.78	73.45	411	328	738
1986	247.13	158.31	88.82	493	402	825
1987	271.22	172.47	98.75	533	434	891
1988	328.82	204.21	124.61	638	509	1092
1989	398.09	255.09	143.00	762	630	1218
1990	434.62	273.27	161.35	813	659	1341
1991	475.85	286.08	189.77	869	674	1541
1992	546.61	301.60	245.01	986	706	1926
1993	694.49	357.10	337.35	1236	831	2554
1994	845.14	413.40	431.75	1486	964	3086
1995	1095.97	504.10	591.85	1908	1183	3989
1996	1346.76	594.80	751.99	2323	1396	4892
1997	1438.12	614.90	823.26	2459	1441	5208
1998	1518.92	610.20	908.68	2579	1427	5632
1999	1507.12	558.40	948.69	2545	1302	5802
2000	1594.08	559.10	1034.96	2680	1302	6250
2001	1767.38	585.40	1181.96	2962	1365	7042
2002	1951.54	606.80	1344.70	3263	1418	7899
2003	2188.05	637.70	1550.36	3853	1926	6547
2004	2452.62	700.80	1751.85	4309	2134	7277
2005	2785.42	815.32	1970.10	4883	2503	8051
2006	3124.37	906.15	2218.22	5480	2813	8944
2007	3709.69	1051.82	2657.87	6513	3300	10593
2008	4225.38	1217.95	3007.43	7406	3864	11780
2009	4456.31	1277.72	3178.59	7791	4137	12080
2010	5136.78	1419.65	3717.13	8977	4758	13576
2011	6241.95	1597.69	4644.26	10873	5653	15935
2012	7085.46	1830.83	5254.63	12283	6705	17296
2013	8053.82	2064.74	5989.08	13912	7755	19156
2014	9124.48	2292.06	6832.42	15762	8608	21854
2015	10167.87	2434.73	7733.14	17429	9542	23561

9-3 居民消费水平指数
INDICES OF PEOPLE'S CONSUMPTION LEVEL

(1978年=100)

年份 year	居民消费 (%) People's Censurption (%)	农村居民 rural residernts	城镇居民 wrban residernts	居民消费水平 (%) level of consumption(%)	农村居民 rural residernts	城镇居民 wrban residernts
1982	156.2	169.2	132.3	149.0	164.2	111.5
1983	172.2	186.6	145.4	162.1	179.7	119.0
1984	196.6	205.4	181.4	183.3	198.7	136.6
1985	218.4	212.2	233.3	201.1	208.2	154.2
1986	253.2	247.7	267.4	229.7	244.3	163.5
1987	263.0	255.1	282.4	235.4	249.4	167.4
1988	268.8	257.1	295.6	237.8	248.6	170.4
1989	278.8	273.6	292.7	243.0	262.6	163.9
1990	290.5	281.2	312.9	247.6	263.3	170.8
1991	275.4	257.6	314.1	229.3	235.7	167.6
1992	281.7	254.0	339.6	231.8	230.5	175.3
1993	338.3	276.9	460.8	274.7	250.1	229.1
1994	380.3	292.4	553.4	304.9	264.6	259.6
1995	421.7	303.5	653.0	334.8	276.3	288.9
1996	474.9	340.2	737.9	373.6	310.0	315.2
1997	499.1	342.9	802.9	389.3	311.8	333.1
1998	549.5	354.6	927.3	425.5	321.8	377.1
1999	571.5	356.0	989.4	440.0	322.1	397.1
2000	599.5	361.0	1062.6	459.8	326.0	420.9
2001	661.3	377.2	1206.1	505.8	341.3	471.0
2002	738.6	391.9	1394.3	564.0	355.3	537.0
2003	807.3	393.9	1578.3	614.7	359.2	595.0
2004	868.7	405.3	1726.7	659.6	372.5	640.2
2005	963.4	458.4	1899.3	729.5	425.0	692.7
2006	1074.2	502.9	2132.9	826.5	480.7	777.9
2007	1191.3	557.2	2365.4	917.4	538.4	853.4
2008	1279.5	599.5	2540.4	984.4	585.8	900.3
2009	1352.4	631.3	2690.3	1038.5	625.0	935.4
2010	1507.9	676.1	3045.4	1156.9	693.1	1017.7
2011	1722.0	710.6	3584.4	1316.6	768.6	1125.6
2012	1897.6	785.9	3946.4	1444.3	880.0	1188.6
2013	2106.3	863.7	4396.3	1597.4	991.8	1286.1
2014	2342.2	941.4	4919.5	1769.9	1107.8	1399.3
2015	2576.4	985.6	5500.0	1932.7	1209.7	1490.3

注：2003年以前数据根据2004年第一次经济普查资料修订。
Notes: Data before 2003 is Gmended accordity to ecorymic survey 2004.

9-4 城镇居民家庭基本情况

年份 Year	调查户数 (户) Number of Households Surveyed (household)	平均每户家庭人口 (人) Average Number of people Per Household (person)	平均每户就业人口 (人) Number of Employees Per Household (person)	每一就业者负担人数 (人) Average Persons Supported by a Labor (person)
1963	240	5.30	1.63	3.25
1964	299	5.36	1.61	3.33
1965	370	5.22	1.60	3.26
1980	571	4.20	2.32	1.81
1985	1658	3.84	2.15	1.79
1987	1900	3.73	2.12	1.76
1988	1950	3.61	2.07	1.74
1989	1990	3.52	2.05	1.72
1990	1990	3.47	2.04	1.70
1991	1990	3.45	2.04	1.69
1992	1940	3.36	2.02	1.66
1993	1890	3.29	1.98	1.66
1994	1330	3.23	1.95	1.66
1995	1330	3.22	1.92	1.68
1996	1390	3.24	1.95	1.66
1997	1790	3.23	1.89	1.71
1998	1640	3.19	1.90	1.68
1999	1540	3.15	1.86	1.69
2000	1540	3.14	1.81	1.73
2001	1540	3.10	1.77	1.75
2002	1600	3.07	1.64	1.87
2003	1600	3.06	1.68	1.82
2004	1700	3.03	1.65	1.83
2005	1800	2.98	1.52	1.96
2006	1800	2.96	1.55	1.91
2007	1850	2.95	1.59	1.86
2008	1900	2.96	1.50	1.97
2009	1900	2.94	1.48	1.99
2010	1900	2.93	1.46	2.01
2011	1900	2.90	1.47	1.97
2012	1900	2.89	1.48	1.95
2013	1718	2.77	1.53	1.81
2014	3060	2.85	1.59	1.79
2015	3073	2.85	1.53	1.86

注：①2002年方法制度重新修订,部分指标有所变化:原"平均每人居住面积"改为"平均每人建筑总面积";原"平均每人实际收入"改为"平均每人总收入";原"平均每人实际支出"改为"平均每人总支出"。
②2014年起使用城乡一体化住户收支与生活状况调查数据,与之前的分城镇和农村住户调查的范围、方法、指标口径有所不同(此后相关表同)。
③2014年起为城镇常住居民人均可支配收入,与2014年以前不同。

BASIC CONDITIONS OF URBAN HOUSEHOLDS

平均每户就业面 (%) Percentage of Employed Persons Per Household (%)	平均每人 Per Capita		平均每人 Per Capita			平均每人建筑面积 (平方米) Average Living Floor Space Per Cappita (sq.m)
	总收入 (元) Actual Income (yuan)	*可支配收入 (元) Disposable Income (yuan)	总支出 (元) Actual Expenditures (yuan)	消费性支出 Living Expenditures	*食品 Food	
30.75	238.1	238.1	237.2	218.4	133.9	
30.04	232.9	232.9	228.3	211.7	122.7	
30.65	224.3	224.3	218.8	204.4	118.0	3.3
55.24	413.7	413.7	394.2	369.3	210.6	5.1
55.99	713.3	704.2	693.1	644.2	324.5	7.9
56.84	960.6	951.8	919.1	836.1	443.2	8.4
57.34	1136.4	1128.1	1153.1	1058.8	538.9	8.9
58.24	1271.6	1262.6	1250.0	1130.7	607.0	9.1
58.79	1437.1	1427.2	1349.4	1220.3	652.4	9.8
59.13	1603.7	1592.9	1538.2	1380.2	717.4	9.6
60.12	1886.4	1874.2	1799.9	1577.7	799.0	9.9
60.18	2453.5	2438.7	2358.1	2097.6	941.5	10.5
60.37	3360.0	3346.0	3588.6	2733.1	1307.1	11.1
59.63	4031.9	4016.7	3977.3	3433.8	1680.6	11.9
60.19	4367.0	4350.2	4290.6	3713.5	1731.4	11.8
58.51	4693.8	4673.2	4549.7	3855.6	1773.6	12.8
59.56	4849.4	4826.4	4903.1	4074.4	1787.7	12.7
59.04	5234.5	5212.8	5333.8	4340.6	1783.4	13.2
57.64	5542.6	5524.5	5643.6	4644.5	1779.4	13.9
57.10	5888.7	5856.0	5774.8	4804.8	1799.4	15.2
53.42	7142.2	6789.0	7159.7	5608.9	2087.8	26.2
54.90	7745.8	7322.0	7551.1	5963.3	2279.6	26.3
54.46	8522.1	8022.8	8076.1	6398.5	2516.2	27.3
51.01	9395.1	8786.0	8582.8	6737.0	2625.4	29.9
52.36	10533.3	9803.0	9839.7	7397.0	2868.4	31.0
53.90	12421.8	11485.0	11476.7	8701.0	3456.0	32.3
50.68	14174.3	13153.0	12471.0	9478.0	3996.0	32.0
50.34	15698.0	14367.0	13868.0	10294.0	4160.5	32.8
49.83	17572.8	16058.4	15612.3	11451.0	4429.3	33.2
50.69	20193.3	18373.9	18123.4	13163.8	5363.7	35.5
51.21	22903.9	20839.6	20107.1	14496.0	5837.9	35.8
55.23	25180.5	22906.4	20419.5	15749.5	6259.2	38.8
55.73	27538.9	24852.3	23175.1	16681.4	3688.3	41.9
53.69	30057.4	27051.5	24798.4	18192.3	3897.6	43.2

Note: ①" Per Capita Living Space (sq.m)" in the above table was changed into "Per Capita Living Floor Space(sq.m)";"Per Capita Actual Income(yuan)"into; "Per Capita Actual Expenditures(yuan)" into "Per Capita Total Expenditures(yuan)';owing to the changes of items in the reversion of 2002 mearurement system.

② The integrated household income and expenditure survey has been used since 2014, including both urban and rural households. The coverage ,methodology and definitions used in the survey are different from those used for the separate urban and rural household survey prior to 2014(···).

③ The concept is Per Capita Disposable Income of Rural Permanent Residents since 2014 ,different from that before 2014.

9-5 城镇居民家庭收支情况(2015)

单位：元

项　　目	Item	总　计 Total
调查户数(户)	Households Surveyed	3073.42
比　重(%)	Ratio	100.00
平均每户家庭人口(人)	Average Number of Residents Per Household	2.85
平均每户离退休人口(人)	Average Number of Retirees Per Household	0.44
平均每一就业者负担人数(人)	Average Persons supported by a Urban Labor	1.86
平均每户就业面(%)	Average Employment Rate Per Household	53.69
平均每人总收入	Per Capita Total Income	30057.39
#可支配收入	Disposable Income	27051.47
平均每人借贷收入	Income of Loans Per Capita	856.29
#提取储蓄存款	Savings Withdrawn	558.84
平均每人借贷支出	Expenditures of Loans Per Capita	835.71
#存入储蓄款	Money Saved	288.59
平均每人总支出	Total Expenditure Per Capita	24798.38
#消费性支出	Consumption Expenditure	18192.28
一、食品烟酒	Food Cigarettes and Wine	5828.55
食品	Food	3897.62
谷物	Grain	567.02
薯类	Patato	28.74
豆类	Bean	71.59
食用油	Edible Oil	194.31
蔬菜和食用菌	Vegetable and Edible Fungi	652.32
肉类	Meat	855.22
禽类	Poultry	157.41
水产品	Aquatic Products	302.32
蛋类	Egg	115.01
奶类	Milk	206.88
干鲜瓜果类	Fruits and Processed Products	379.13
糖果糕点类	Sweet	127.36
其他食品	Others	240.32
烟酒	Cigarettes and Wine	623.38
饮料	Drink	93.46
饮食服务	Food Service	1214.09
二、衣　　着	Clothing	1523.08
衣类	Clothing	1205.67
鞋类	Shoes	317.42
三、居　　住	Residence	3742.72
租赁房房租	Rent	158.51
住房维修及管理	Management	425.34
水电燃料及其他	Water and Power	753.84
自有住房折算租金	Converted Rent of Zts Own	2405.03
四、生活用品及服务	Household Facilities Articles and Services	1099.31
家具及室内装饰品	Furniture	139.59
家用器具	Appliances	301.76
家用纺织品	Drygoods	88.63
家庭日用杂品	Commodity	341.05
个人用品	Personal Helongings	186.57
家庭服务	Households Service	41.72
五、交通通信	Transport and Communication	2155.38
交通	Transport	1413.55
通信	Communication	741.83
六、教育文化娱乐	Education Culture and Recreation	1972.20
教　　育	Education	1148.33
文化娱乐用品	Cultural Recreation Articals	251.86
文化娱乐服务	Cultural Recreation Services	572.01
七、医疗保健	Medicine and Medical Service	1482.05
医疗器具及药品	medical apparatus and instruments	447.60
医疗服务	Medical Service	1034.45
八、其他用品和服务	Miscellaneous Goods and Services	388.98
其他用品	Goods	214.26
其他服务	Services	174.72

注：2014年起城镇居民消费居住支出中自有住房折算租金指现住房为自有住房的住户为自身消费提供住房服务的折算价值，属于实物消费，不包括在现金消费支出中。

PER CAPITA INCOME AND EXPENDITURE OF URBAN HOUSEHOLDS(2015)

(yuan)

低收入户 Low Income Households	中低收入户 Lower Middle Income Households	中等收入户 Middle Income Households	中高收入户 Upper Middle Income Households	高收入户 High Income Households
613.33	619.25	616.17	614.67	610.00
19.96	20.15	20.05	20.00	19.85
3.27	3.19	2.89	2.66	2.24
0.19	0.33	0.49	0.67	0.50
2.10	1.82	1.86	1.87	1.64
47.67	54.83	53.75	53.48	61.02
13586.09	21859.04	28374.24	38732.03	58250.44
10621.75	19427.94	26341.77	34969.59	53979.02
619.71	782.49	770.41	1175.83	1052.41
369.38	546.78	603.21	538.06	822.65
412.43	464.64	868.98	944.92	1822.59
143.97	182.79	268.46	245.97	728.86
16330.36	18674.65	23327.11	31770.84	39899.35
11336.06	13402.67	17687.48	23353.38	29851.85
3857.87	4768.23	5718.33	7384.48	8598.19
2890.96	3285.52	3867.97	4883.79	5157.40
437.21	428.92	512.60	663.16	915.40
25.14	22.65	25.47	38.04	36.24
59.60	63.03	70.62	90.11	81.39
169.37	184.03	196.95	224.49	207.53
514.74	567.31	649.00	807.97	801.35
653.84	736.33	875.40	1071.81	1046.06
115.59	141.10	157.59	200.53	192.37
207.73	255.60	306.24	386.59	406.28
92.58	104.40	113.47	144.37	131.34
143.90	170.89	200.85	276.03	279.13
226.24	312.84	390.37	499.25	546.26
68.23	96.94	124.60	183.45	196.85
176.78	201.48	244.82	297.99	317.22
372.05	562.95	595.96	767.07	950.15
60.77	83.79	83.93	116.89	140.75
534.08	835.97	1170.47	1616.73	2349.88
803.21	1047.20	1444.79	2035.76	2775.10
616.26	806.19	1129.11	1611.36	2277.21
186.95	241.02	315.68	424.40	497.90
2292.67	2825.19	3608.67	4685.65	6279.24
167.89	95.81	168.34	155.28	225.44
289.84	425.97	346.13	437.56	712.69
544.18	630.61	704.73	904.03	1129.42
1290.76	1672.79	2389.48	3188.77	4211.68
596.14	775.01	1177.29	1411.18	1844.99
68.50	112.66	194.03	116.22	239.84
156.71	190.02	356.40	393.92	498.68
44.32	59.00	80.44	132.75	156.01
221.78	269.84	323.38	447.93	518.23
82.67	113.78	193.89	273.07	334.66
22.16	29.70	29.16	47.30	97.57
1217.85	1483.49	2111.22	2993.54	3588.65
758.88	892.25	1398.48	2074.12	2381.54
458.97	591.24	712.74	919.42	1207.11
1578.08	1386.35	1741.40	2540.77	3032.77
1209.79	951.47	1043.39	1435.34	1142.71
173.95	185.36	257.20	336.16	357.68
194.35	249.52	440.82	769.28	1532.38
783.62	858.30	1532.23	1840.13	2927.05
248.87	307.59	474.82	592.06	739.16
534.75	550.71	1057.41	1248.07	2187.89
206.63	258.90	353.54	461.87	805.85
130.84	147.38	202.33	247.64	409.96
75.80	111.52	151.21	214.23	395.89

Note : Home ownership conversion in urban household residence consumption expenditure Since 2014,refers to a resident who lives on a self-owned house now, provides housing service the conversion value for their own consumption. It belongs to material consumption, not included in cash consumption expenditure.

9-6 城镇居民家庭平均每百户年末耐用品拥有量(2015)

品　名		Item		总平均 Total Average	低收入户 Low Income Households
摩托车	(辆)	Motorcycles	unit	30.41	44.49
助力车	(辆)	Auxiliary Drving Bikes	unit	24.25	26.93
家用汽车	(辆)	Cars for Household Use	unit	17.68	10.44
洗衣机	(台)	Washing Machins	unit	91.02	85.91
电冰箱	(台)	Refrigerators	unit	95.21	92.09
彩色电视机	(台)	Color TV Sets	unit	116.90	113.47
家用电脑	(台)	Computers	unit	74.05	54.01
组合音响	(套)	Hi-Fi Stereo Systems	unit	8.29	5.67
摄像机	(台)	TV Cameras	unit	5.09	0.99
照相机	(架)	Cameras	unit	25.44	9.17
中高档乐器	(件)	Medium and High-Grade Musical Instruments	unit	3.23	0.86
微波炉	(台)	Microwave Stove	unit	47.61	28.04
空调器	(台)	Air Conditioners	unit	128.43	87.66
热水器	(台)	Showers	unit	87.40	76.98
消毒碗柜	(台)	Disinfection cabinet	unit	9.77	4.93
洗碗机	(台)	Dishwasher	unit	1.83	0.35
健身器材	(件)	Health Care Instruments	unit	3.82	1.29
固定电话	(部)	Fixed telephone	set	33.91	30.28
移动电话	(部)	Mobile Phones	set	223.13	227.05

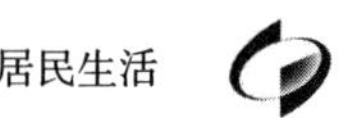

NUMBER OF DURABLE CONSUMER GOODS OWNED PER 100 URBAN HOUSEHOLDS AT THE YEAR-END BY INCOME LEVEL(2015)

中低收入户 Lower Middle Income Households	中等收入户 Middle Income Households	中高收入户 Upper Middle Income Households	高收入户 High Income Households
40.79	30.93	19.42	16.44
29.81	25.44	21.83	17.25
12.49	17.45	21.27	26.77
90.53	93.53	92.95	92.20
96.29	96.03	98.15	93.51
116.80	122.90	117.39	113.92
69.17	74.17	78.93	93.88
5.25	6.88	10.58	13.06
2.91	4.24	7.53	9.75
17.85	24.57	35.35	40.22
1.74	3.99	5.26	4.31
36.55	45.45	64.48	63.52
115.73	130.93	148.98	158.78
84.17	90.08	93.20	92.56
5.46	7.06	15.56	15.85
1.23	1.40	3.67	2.51
1.93	3.60	5.79	6.49
34.40	33.28	36.05	35.54
231.72	228.32	222.28	206.32

9-7 城镇居民家庭房屋居住分布情况
URABN HOUSEHOLDS HOUSING CONDITIONS

分　组	Group	各组户数占总户数比重(%) Percentage of Household in Each Group of the Total Households				
		2011	2012	2013	2014	2015
总　计	Total	1900	1900	1718	3060	3073
一、房屋产权	Building Property Right					
租赁公房	Leased Pubilc Houses	6.0	5.5	3.6	5.3	4.6
租赁私房	Leased Private Houses	1.9	1.9	7.5	7.7	6.4
原有私房	Original Private Houses	15.2	14.1	24.4	28.9	28.9
房改私房	Private Houses	44.5	44.1	28.3	24.5	23.5
商品房	Commercial Houses	30.1	32.4	32.8	26.1	28.9
借用房	Borrowed			1.4	1.1	0.9
其他	Others	2.4	1.0	1.9	6.3	6.8
二、住宅样式	Housing Pattens					
单栋住宅	Sole-Unit Houses	10.9	10.5	23.1	35.7	34.3
四居室	Four-Room Houses	4.6	4.9	3.8	3.2	3.7
三居室	Three-Room Houses	28.1	28.7	25.3	25.5	26.5
二居室	Two-Room Houses	42.9	43.6	35.2	27.0	26.7
一居室	One-Room Houses	3.9	4.2	5.8	6.3	6.4
普通楼房	Ordinary Houses	7.7	6.4	2.1	-	-
平房及其他	Bungalow and Others	1.9	1.7	4.6	2.2	2.5
三、用水情况	Waters					
独用自来水	Private Tap Water	99.8	99.8	97.8	94.7	95.0
公用自来水	Public Tap Water	0.2	0.2		-	-
井、河水	Water from Rivers and Wells			1.5	3.9	4.1
其他	Others			0.7	1.4	0.9
四、卫生设备	Sanitary Faciities					
无卫生设备	Have not	0.9	0.7	3.5	3.0	2.6
独立卫生设备	Independent Health Facilities	97.8	98.3	93.8	89.2	90.7
公用卫生设备	Public Health Facilities	1.3	1.0	2.6	7.8	6.7
五、取暖设备	Warming Facilities					
无取暖设备	Have not	24.7	22.5	29.5	33.8	37.3
空调设备	Air Conditioner	65.9	66.7		-	-
暖　气	Heater	4.0	5.2		-	-
其　他	Others	5.4	5.6	70.4	66.2	62.7
六、燃料使用情况	Fuel Material Usage Conditions					
煤	Coal	5.9	5.1	2.3	2.1	2.2
罐装液化石油气	LPG cylinders	43.4	43.0	47.5	30.6	30.5
管道液化石油气	LPG Pipeline	2.0	1.6	2.6	1.3	1.6
管道煤气	Piped Coal Gas	5.2	4.0	6.9	2.3	1.6
管道天然气	Gas pipeline	42.7	45.5	31.1	18.6	22.4
其　他	Others	0.9	0.8	9.2	45.1	41.8
七、通信设备使用情况	Telecommunication Facilities Usage Conditions					
1.每百户固定电话	Per 100 fixed telephone	61.2	59.3	39.2	41.7	33.91
2.每百户移动电话	Mobile Phones Per 100 Households	193.8	204.4	207.6	212.3	223.13

注：2014年起住宅样式为四居室的数据包含四居室及以上单元房的占比。
Note: The data refers to four bedroom and above for four bedroom units Since 2014.

9-8 农民家庭基本情况
BASIC CONDITIONS OF RURAL HOUSEHOLDS

年份	调查户数 Number of Households Surveyed	常住人口(人) Permanent Residents (person)	平均每户常住人口(人) Average Permanent Residents Per Households (person)	平均每户整半劳动力(人) Average Full-Time and Part-Time Labors Per Household (person)	平均每个劳动力负担人口(人) Average Person Supported by Each Labor (person)
1982	948	5364	5.66	2.73	2.08
1983	1470	8267	5.62	2.99	1.88
1984	1510	8317	5.51	3.02	1.83
1985	3300	16473	5.07	2.98	1.71
1986	3300	16432	4.98	2.96	1.68
1987	3300	16195	4.91	2.94	1.67
1988	3300	15966	4.84	2.93	1.65
1989	3300	15567	4.72	2.86	1.65
1990	3300	15411	4.67	2.84	1.65
1991	3300	15094	4.57	2.66	1.72
1992	3300	14900	4.52	2.63	1.71
1993	3300	14651	4.44	2.65	1.67
1994	3300	14466	4.38	2.72	1.61
1995	3300	14447	4.38	2.77	1.58
1996	3300	14053	4.26	2.75	1.55
1997	3200	13453	4.20	2.64	1.60
1998	3200	13239	4.14	2.62	1.58
1999	3200	13082	4.09	2.63	1.55
2000	3300	13557	4.11	2.76	1.49
2001	3300	13490	4.09	2.75	1.49
2002	3300	13420	4.07	2.78	1.46
2003	3300	13385	4.06	2.86	1.42
2004	3300	13356	4.05	2.92	1.39
2005	3300	13228	4.01	2.99	1.34
2006	3300	13259	4.02	3.03	1.34
2007	3300	13186	4.00	3.06	1.30
2008	3300	13163	3.99	3.08	1.29
2009	3300	13151	3.99	3.12	1.28
2010	3300	13123	3.98	3.14	1.27
2011	3300	13120	3.98	3.12	1.27
2012	3300	13140	3.98	3.12	1.28
2013	2096	7921	3.78	2.88	1.31
2014	2522	7233	2.87	2.03	1.41
2015	2540	7309	2.88	2.04	1.41

注:①2014年起使用城乡一体化住户收支与生活状况调查数据,与之前的分城镇和农村住户调查的范围、方法、指标口径有所不同(此后相关表同)。②2014年起农民人均纯收入改为农村常住居民人均可支配收入。

Note: ①The integrated household income and expenditure survey has been used since 2014 , including both urban and rural households. The coverage , methodology and definitions used in the survey are different from those used for the separate urban and rural household survey prior to 2014.(Related tables the same ever since).
② Per Capita Income of Rural Households has been changed into Per Capita Disposable Income of Rural Permanent Residents since 2014.

9-8 续表 1 continued

年 份 year	平均每户经营耕地面积(亩) Space of Cultivation land Per Household (mu)	平均每户年末拥有生产性固定资产原值(元) Value of Production Fixed Assets Per Household (yuan)	平均每户年内新建购房屋面积(平方米) Floor Space of Rooms Newly Built Per Household (sq.m)	平均每人年末使用房屋面积(平方米) Lving Space Per Capita (sq.m)
1982	0.57	159.20	5.36	16.45
1983	8.95	389.97	5.65	18.04
1984	8.66	530.20	6.70	19.03
1985	7.60	557.86	8.24	21.18
1986	7.48	610.47	8.45	22.63
1987	7.31	672.87	7.79	23.50
1988	7.04	759.61	4.90	24.15
1989	6.95	819.53	5.50	25.10
1990	6.79	861.91	6.20	25.73
1991	6.58	1068.45	4.56	27.33
1992	6.47	1146.94	4.07	27.94
1993	6.36	1281.66	3.75	25.80
1994	6.69	1542.58	3.91	25.22
1995	6.73	1775.57	4.66	25.92
1996	6.82	2291.60	4.25	26.58
1997	6.56	2688.67	4.98	27.99
1998	6.08	2604.21	4.74	28.38
1999	6.08	2543.61	4.19	29.87
2000	5.93	2482.02	3.48	30.11
2001	5.94	2773.52	2.98	31.19
2002	6.01	2953.37	4.65	31.55
2003	6.03	2989.82	4.01	32.44
2004	6.15	3046.47	2.82	33.68
2005	6.15	4121.20	3.88	36.05
2006	6.12	4297.19	4.22	36.77
2007	6.41	4996.00	3.36	37.96
2008	6.36	5434.99	5.90	39.04
2009	6.51	6368.83	4.40	40.11
2010	6.73	7078.46	5.05	40.99
2011	6.44	9636.11	7.88	44.24
2012	6.80	10813.13	5.46	44.98
2013	7.08	13839.73	6.06	41.84
2014	6.97	12048.41	5.81	54.78
2015	7.90	12226.49	4.08	55.61

9-8 续表 2 continued

年 份	平均每户年末使用房屋价值(元) Value of Per Households Living Space (yuan)	平均每人总收入(元) Total Income Per Capita (yuan)	平均每人纯收入(元) Net Income Per Capita (yuan)	平均每人生活消费支出(元) Living Expenditures Per Capita (yuan)
1982	1261.51	311.51	286.07	226.96
1983	1688.93	405.14	299.24	252.47
1984	1786.54	525.86	392.29	305.03
1985	2068.78	569.74	421.24	334.63
1986	2319.44	605.67	445.13	373.53
1987	2514.22	638.64	460.66	408.69
1988	2751.40	710.47	497.84	450.62
1989	3095.15	820.70	571.84	540.13
1990	3545.50	957.01	670.80	607.58
1991	4661.58	936.57	626.92	615.40
1992	4885.77	1015.62	677.82	611.84
1993	5004.02	1135.77	783.18	722.09
1994	5887.81	1690.49	1170.06	1012.95
1995	6729.46	2184.20	1511.22	1245.10
1996	10050.26	2642.45	1863.62	1630.41
1997	11432.61	2913.16	2102.20	1660.13
1998	12966.45	2917.66	2172.24	1699.43
1999	13654.80	2871.62	2217.08	1572.90
2000	13717.28	3008.13	2268.50	1555.61
2001	16007.50	3124.10	2352.16	1649.18
2002	16581.94	3239.81	2444.06	1745.63
2003	19010.48	3378.80	2566.76	1801.63
2004	20254.50	3826.27	2890.01	2088.98
2005	24815.99	4221.81	3099.20	2430.19
2006	27772.00	4580.79	3419.35	2732.46
2007	31696.83	5365.78	3997.48	3090.00
2008	36250.27	6266.27	4656.38	3652.57
2009	41493.01	6663.13	5035.26	3725.40
2010	47606.56	7699.27	5832.27	4090.78
2011	61870.37	9387.20	6897.92	5010.74
2012	77338.15	10525.66	7851.71	5726.73
2013	101314.51	11896.06	8866.95	6279.52
2014	110492.00	14836.14	10849.06	8680.93
2015	125534.00	15819.16	11843.89	9803.15

9-9 农民家庭年人均纯收入(可支配收入)及构成
PER CAPITA DISPOSABLE INCOME OF RURAL HOUSEHOLDS PER CAPITA AND COMPOSITION

单位：元 (yuan)

指标	Item	2005	2006	2007	2008	2009	2010	2011	2012	2013	2014	2015
全年总收入	Total Revenue	4221.81	4580.79	5365.78	6266.27	6663.13	7699.27	9387.20	10525.66	11896.06	14836.14	15819.16
全年纯收入	Annual Net Income	3099.20	3419.35	3997.48	4656.38	5035.26	5832.27	6897.92	7851.71	8866.95	10849.06	11843.89
工资性收入	Money Wage	941.64	1199.16	1454.50	1742.33	1900.54	2186.11	2703.05	3189.84	3648.20	3298.61	3682.91
家庭经营纯收入	House Business Revenue	2049.04	2095.15	2379.82	2690.83	2828.53	3234.94	3731.34	4123.49	4616.55	5009.34	5281.41
转移性收入	Transfer Income	91.71	99.13	125.46	182.40	247.81	304.30	379.08	472.51	518.07	2415.66	2718.79
财产性收入	Property Income	16.81	25.91	37.70	40.82	58.37	106.92	84.45	65.87	84.13	125.44	160.78
比重(纯收入=100)	Ratio (net income = 100)											
工资性收入	Money Wage	30.38	35.07	36.39	37.42	37.74	37.48	39.19	40.63	41.14	30.40	31.10
家庭经营纯收入	House Business Revenue	66.12	61.27	59.53	57.79	56.17	55.47	54.09	52.52	52.06	46.17	44.59
转移性收入	Transfer Income	2.96	2.90	3.14	3.92	4.92	5.22	5.50	6.02	5.84	22.27	22.96
财产性收入	Property Income	0.54	0.76	0.94	0.88	1.16	1.83	1.22	0.84	0.95	1.16	1.35

注：2014年起为农村常住居民人均可支配收入、工资性收入、家庭经营净收入、财产净收入、转移净收入。
Note: It has been Per Capita Disposable Income of Rural Permanent Residents, Money Wage, House Business Revenue. Property Income, Transfer Income since 2014.

9-10 农民家庭年人均纯收入(可支配收入)分组
RURAL HOUSEHOLDS GROUPED BY PER CAPITA DISPOSABLE INCOME

单位：户 (household)

指标	Item	2004	2005	2006	2007	2008	2009	2010	2011	2012	2013	2014	2015
调查户总计	Total Households Surveyed	3300	3300	3300	3300	3300	3300	3300	3300	3300	2096	2522	2540
2000元以下	Below 2000 yuan	935	888	710	508	414	411	257	233	155	48	70	69
2000–3000元	2000–3000 yuan	1034	840	787	659	519	478	365	295	197	83	57	51
3000–4000元	3000–4000 yuan	611	702	684	660	559	492	419	313	289	127	118	85
4000–5000元	4000–5000 yuan	339	413	479	510	510	460	469	373	286	170	139	147
5000元以上	5000 yuan and Over	381	457	640	969	1298	1459	1790	2086	2373	1668		
5000–10000元	5000–10000 yuan											814	796
10000–15000元	10000–15000 yuan											661	612
15000–20000元	15000–20000 yuan											353	349
20000元以上	20000 yuan and Over											311	431

注：2014年起为农村常住居民人均可支配收入分组。
Note: It has been Rural Permanent Grouped by Per Capita Disposable Income since 2014.

9-11 农民家庭年人均经营总收入
ANNUAL TOTAL INCME OF RURAL HOUSEHOLDS PER CAPITA

单位：元 (yuan)

指标	Item	2008	2009	2010	2011	2012	2013	2014	2015
家庭经营总收入	Total Income of Family Business	4287.96	4435.68	5077.04	6134.62	6718.36	7022.00	8699.22	8928.74
农业收入	Farming	2546.31	2638.00	3115.06	3682.89	4056.77	4049.41	4663.10	4927.80
林业收入	Forestry	61.54	59.33	65.63	79.26	88.49	140.80	272.35	292.41
牧业收入	Animal Husbandry	946.28	863.14	869.13	1013.07	1044.46	1077.50	1610.39	1235.80
渔业收入	Fishery	271.92	311.80	329.55	389.88	423.50	403.93	476.41	696.02
工业收入	Industry	53.95	58.65	69.15	135.22	144.59	60.66	204.82	160.40
建筑业收入	Construction	99.12	133.29	154.25	167.18	177.49	307.83	188.27	110.67
交通运输邮电业收入	Transportation, Post Services	116.66	127.96	155.76	277.54	322.49	328.76	353.50	461.56
批零贸易餐饮业收入	Wholesales, Retail Sales and Catering	133.06	164.99	220.55	273.17	317.95	401.46	572.30	646.44
社会服务和文教卫生业收入	Social Services and Public Health Services	44.70	63.47	78.53	91.43	113.54	177.96	211.73	189.00
农林牧渔服务业收入	Agriculture and forestry services							133.44	171.08
其他家庭经营收入	Other Family Revenue	13.23	14.14	18.79	23.55	26.87	10.54	12.93	37.56

9-12 农民家庭年人均生产支出
ANNUAL PRODUCTION EXPENDITURES OF RURAL HOUSEHOLDS PER CAPITA

单位：元 (yuan)

指标	Item	2008	2009	2010	2011	2012	2013	2014	2015
一、家庭经营费用支出	Expenditures of Family Business	1493.00	1489.40	1713.15	2199.08	2402.73	2408.72	3413.49	3366.25
农业生产支出	Agricultural Expenditures	759.00	746.68	866.74	1029.67	1076.28	1049.49	1329.35	1566.04
林业生产支出	Forestry Expenditures	6.14	6.69	7.74	16.65	16.33	19.52	27.68	23.91
牧业生产支出	Animal Husbandary Expenditures	493.71	463.78	470.43	593.09	693.65	753.88	1279.08	923.32
渔业生产支出	Fishery Expenditures	86.30	104.37	125.68	216.01	230.50	174.04	217.63	366.77
工业生产支出	Industrial Expenditures	14.56	16.37	18.89	54.66	84.17	28.31	78.83	57.14
建筑业支出	Construction Expenditures	37.45	45.15	54.95	61.78	54.28	120.30	158.47	43.86
交通运输邮电业支出	Expenditures of Transportation and Post Services	35.09	38.14	60.29	107.32	120.00	81.99	74.77	136.61
批零贸易餐饮业支出	Expenditures of Wholesales, Retail Sales and Catering	46.38	51.96	88.76	90.88	100.13	82.03	166.42	175.88
社会服务和文教卫生业支出	Expenditures of Social Services and Public Health Services	10.76	13.73	14.89	19.82	20.52	69.33	39.98	18.10
农林牧渔服务业支出	Agriculture and forestry services							36.77	44.08
其他家庭经营支出	Other Family Expenditures	3.60	2.53	4.78	9.22	6.85	2.19	4.51	10.54
二、购置住房、生产性固定资产支出	Purchase of Housing, the Productive Expenditure of Fixed Assets	99.92	148.69	142.67	231.28	240.00	315.23	876.97	1244.33
三、税费支出	Expenditures of Taxation	13.30	11.21	10.28	9.28	11.09			

9-13　农民家庭年人均生活消费支出
LIVING EXPENDITURES OF RURAL HOUSEHOLDS PER CAPITA

单位：元　　(yuan)

指标	Item	2008	2009	2010	2011	2012	2013	2014	2015
全年总支出	Total Annual Expenditures	5402.06	5537.59	6131.23	7971.52	8923.73	9477.33	16775.27	18257.83
生活消费支出	Living Expenditures	3652.57	3725.40	4090.78	5010.74	5726.73	6279.52	8680.93	9803.15
一、食品消费	Food Consumption	1711.34	1668.35	1763.05	1954.62	2154.01	2308.45	2724.10	2952.69
主 食	Grain	323.50	320.19	329.34	334.56	350.86	334.10	440.21	446.36
副 食	Non-Staple Food	771.94	695.66	744.85	859.31	969.20	1037.53	1401.57	1539.65
其他食品	Others	369.51	392.37	413.46	480.38	542.32	514.98	691.15	744.25
在外饮食	Travelling Catering Service	237.24	249.14	264.06	273.91	282.94	393.63	191.17	222.44
二、衣着消费	Clothing Consumption	187.07	195.45	217.61	272.12	316.41	347.67	495.73	549.14
三、居住消费	Residence Consumption	651.50	702.62	816.42	1086.86	1206.16	1415.73	1944.56	2150.27
住 房	Housing	508.63	572.69	655.39	918.61	973.60	1013.20	1523.05	1693.72
电 费	Electricity Fees	58.77	70.08	80.50	85.04	112.57	138.37	209.40	230.15
燃 料	Fuel	63.96	39.16	50.14	55.28	91.16	197.33	115.15	116.80
四、家庭设备用品及服务	Familty facilities and Services	234.92	229.32	262.26	359.57	397.86	425.00	574.31	599.92
耐用消费品	Durable Consumer Goods	117.85	133.42	158.37	230.49	238.55	249.85	298.95	298.90
日用杂品	Daily Necessities	110.17	88.20	94.33	116.88	142.41	164.10	260.06	286.12
五、交通通讯消费	Transportation and Telecommunication Fees	290.44	307.22	331.35	414.36	496.10	605.95	816.43	1218.42
交通工具	Transportation	97.88	108.82	124.59	186.09	235.85	324.51	378.07	743.70
通讯工具	Telecommunication	26.17	23.71	34.86	33.04	39.84	45.85	76.43	89.87
交通、邮电服务费	Transport, Postal Services	166.38	174.70	171.90	195.23	220.41	235.48	361.94	384.85
六、教育文化娱乐	Culture, Education and Receation	267.13	281.68	288.12	341.87	394.63	407.42	1010.19	1118.15
文教娱乐用品	Cultural, Educational and Receational Articles	53.40	61.71	62.30	94.96	107.87	104.20	122.61	156.33
学杂费	School Fees	156.51	146.81	102.61	139.02	136.21	159.18	98.51	90.58
技术培训费	Technical Training	5.23	5.44	7.19	10.43	12.85	28.88	20.89	36.57
一揽子教育服务费	Education Service Charge							661.05	712.83
文体休闲娱乐费	Sports Recreation Fee	11.03	9.92	13.81	17.44	23.05	35.58	62.47	78.67
七、医疗保健消费	Medicine and Medical Services Fees	210.36	236.31	295.24	438.20	591.87	624.40	907.33	985.09
医疗保健用品	Health Care Supplies	64.34	71.18	71.61	102.19	117.28	127.71	200.10	225.14
医疗保健服务费	Health Care Service Fees	146.02	165.13	223.63	336.01	474.59	496.69	707.22	759.94
八、其他商品和服务	Other Commdities and Services	99.80	104.29	116.73	143.14	169.68	144.90	208.28	229.48

9-14 农民家庭年人均现金收支

ANNUAL CASH REVENUE AND EXPENDITURE OF RURAL HOUSEHOLDS PER CAPITA

单位：元 (yuan)

指 标	Item	2008	2009	2010	2011	2012	2013	2014	2015
期内现金收入合计	Total Cash Income at Year-End	5256.32	5718.37	6664.44	8232.92	9337.04	10819.88	13243.58	13958.40
一、工资性现金收入	Cash Income By Wages	1742.25	1898.93	2185.60	2696.32	3186.99	3858.97	3282.57	3663.96
二、家庭经营现金收入	Cash Income By Family Business	3289.11	3509.20	4063.37	5011.97	5546.68	5959.60	7328.03	7336.22
农业	Farm Products	1782.47	1924.84	2306.34	2807.96	3096.78	3179.27	3614.71	3658.73
林业	Forestry Products	55.94	55.54	60.38	80.14	88.34	142.91	163.40	172.04
牧业	Animal husbandary Products	722.03	658.16	675.22	773.47	837.81	891.19	1404.35	1039.15
渔业	Fishery Products	266.99	307.25	323.77	380.89	418.62	395.83	468.59	689.58
工业	Industry Products	53.95	58.65	69.15	135.22	144.59	60.66	204.82	160.40
建筑业	Building Industry	98.93	133.29	154.25	167.18	177.49	307.83	188.27	110.67
交通运输邮电业	Transportation and Post Service	116.66	127.96	155.76	277.54	322.49	328.76	353.50	461.56
批零贸易餐饮业	Retail Sales and Catering	133.06	164.99	220.55	273.17	317.95	401.46	572.30	646.44
社会服务和文教卫生业	Social services and educational sector	44.70	63.47	78.53	91.43	113.54	177.96	211.73	189.00
农林牧渔服务业	Agriculture and forestry services							133.44	171.08
其他家庭经营收入	Cash Income of Other	14.38	14.14	19.42	23.55	26.87	10.54	12.93	37.56
三、转移性现金收入	Transfer Cash Income	194.68	264.72	328.92	460.73	544.46	902.05	2497.66	2791.31
四、财产性现金收入	Property Cash Income	30.29	45.52	86.55	63.91	58.91	99.26	135.33	166.91
期内现金支出合计	Total Cash Expenditures at Year-End	4496.87	4723.52	5294.37	7194.75	8149.22	8563.81	14688.88	15923.32
一、家庭经营费用现金支出	Cash Expenditures By Family Business	1383.60	1368.00	1562.32	2051.67	2285.75	2243.66	3249.87	3222.08
购买化肥	Fertilizers Purchases	340.71	313.95	320.80	377.07	374.44	396.06	456.72	515.12
购买农药	Purchases of Farm Chemical	94.78	87.72	94.03	125.52	129.82	112.80	140.48	142.26
购买农用薄膜	Purchase of Agricultural Film	5.42	3.40	5.07	6.80	6.31	4.80	7.94	8.01
二、购买住房、生产性固定资产支出	Purchase of Housing, the Productive Expenditure	99.92	148.38	142.17	231.28	240.00	315.23	876.97	1244.33
三、税费现金支出	Cash Expenditures of Taxations	13.29	11.20	10.28	9.28	10.85			
四、生活消费现金支出	Cash Expenditures of Living Consumption	2857.78	3033.37	3406.12	4382.95	5070.68	5531.07	6738.17	7612.82
五、转移性现金支出	Transfer Cash Expenditures	133.30	153.91	162.25	511.12	530.85	471.72	287.31	321.74
六、财产性现金支出	Property Cash Expenditures	8.97	8.33	10.74	8.45	11.10	2.13	8.67	6.12

9-15 农民家庭年人均出售主要农副产品情况
ANNUAL SELLING OF FARM AND SIDELINE PRODUCTS OF RURL HOUSEHOLDS PER CAPITA

单位: 千克

品　名	Item	2005	2006	2007	2008	2009	2010	2011	2012	2013	2014	2015
粮食	Grain	383.48	391.24	386.98	390.60	422.65	447.78	451.98	489.22	591.56	770.96	888.88
小麦	Wheat	54.25	77.67	94.39	76.73	62.01	75.44	86.70	91.93	79.55	111.05	129.72
稻谷	Paddy	302.70	288.86	268.94	292.78	320.27	331.71	302.69	329.15	432.85	528.86	588.64
棉花	Cotton	55.95	69.22	81.48	70.09	76.43	55.03	88.30	93.94	72.29	48.98	30.33
油料	Oil Producer	77.73	62.04	61.27	65.14	77.04	72.15	60.91	58.57	73.99	77.34	52.15
糖料	Sugar	5.47	6.28	9.16	4.31	4.48	6.43	0.16	0.17	2.16	2.08	2.21
烟草	Tobacco	2.34	2.07	1.55	2.11	2.92	2.77	2.97	3.82	7.89	7.07	14.35
蔬菜	Vegetable	135.09	133.11	138.89	136.45	133.11	139.41	137.62	143.53	99.54	134.68	163.39
瓜类	Melon	14.21	26.56	16.20	14.80	19.07	19.69	17.40	17.60	40.74	33.63	10.12
水果	Fruits	69.54	76.41	82.72	90.38	99.70	78.09	66.13	109.87	62.86	111.30	97.70
茶叶	Tea	1.24	1.25	1.56	1.56	1.29	1.95	4.17	8.08	5.02	5.01	7.55
猪肉	Pork	29.70	30.80	26.03	26.38	28.70	30.92	22.91	25.68	28.51	58.86	41.76
家禽	Poultry	4.47	5.19	4.44	7.16	7.29	8.38	2.28	2.80	1.65	8.63	4.26
蛋类	Eggs	11.98	10.69	8.99	8.25	10.94	11.19	10.33	13.01	16.54	29.12	14.59
水产品	Aquatic Products	28.59	33.06	35.66	37.26	42.12	38.70	43.09	43.25	39.61	40.65	68.30

9-16 农民家庭主要生活用品购买量
ANNUAL PURCHASES OF ARTICLES FOR BAILY USE OF RURAL HOUSEHOLDS PER CAPITA

品 名		Item		2006	2007	2008	2009	2010	2011	2012	2013	2014	2015
粮 食	(千克/人)	Grain	(Kg/person)	26.28	25.72	26.56	27.45	29.46	42.35	44.45	38.34	44.06	47.43
植物油	(千克/人)	Edible Vegetable Oil	(Kg/person)	2.85	3.21	3.55	3.35	3.61	5.20	5.70	5.11	7.41	8.07
动物油	(千克/人)	Edible Animal Oil	(Kg/person)	0.63	0.50	0.47	0.38	0.33	0.43	0.39	0.27	0.47	0.49
蔬菜	(千克/人)	Vegetables	(Kg/person)	16.33	16.44	17.85	16.21	17.73	19.40	18.27	16.51	25.95	27.28
猪肉	(千克/人)	Pork	(Kg/person)	7.46	6.27	6.22	7.04	7.43	8.38	8.71	8.76	13.13	14.32
牛羊肉	(千克/人)	Beef and Mutton	(Kg/person)	0.42	0.49	0.41	0.41	0.51	0.56	0.47	0.54	0.85	1.04
家禽	(千克/人)	Poultry	(Kg/person)	0.79	1.08	1.21	1.16	1.17	1.26	1.24	0.97	2.40	2.46
鲜蛋	(千克/人)	Fresh Eggs	(Kg/person)	0.97	0.97	1.33	1.55	1.30	1.85	2.20		2.83	4.32
鲜活鱼类	(千克/人)	Fresh Fish	(Kg/person)	7.07	7.69	7.29	6.97	6.99	7.11	7.06		9.58	10.13
卷烟	(盒/人)	Tobacco	(pack/person)	30.98	29.06	28.88	27.51	27.50	31.12	31.42	26.93	41.00	40.03
酒	(千克/人)	Wine	(Kg/person)	11.90	12.30	11.70	11.35	10.72	11.37	11.06	10.06	14.24	12.76
水 果	(千克/人)	Fruits	(Kg/person)	6.34	6.87	6.80	6.72	6.22	6.87	8.27		17.63	19.69
服 装	(件/人)	Clothing	(piece/person)	1.82	1.82	1.99	2.94	1.95	2.46	2.52			
鞋 类	(双/人)	Footwear	(Two/person)	1.45	1.35	1.43	1.28	1.36	1.39	1.80		2.10	2.37
水 泥	(千克/人)	Cement	(Kg/person)	108.80	85.93	134.97	137.25	150.72	236.88	149.81			
钢材	(千克/人)	Steel	(Kg/person)	6.66	5.84	10.45	10.11	10.21	13.85	9.72			
生活用煤	(千克/人)	Coal	(Kg/person)	52.65	49.44	32.82	20.22	19.70	14.77	13.18		14.84	15.18
电视机	(台/百户)	TV Sets	(set/100 households)	6.79	5.79	4.95	3.97	3.70	6.67	6.48	5.76	5.31	7.17
洗衣机	(台/百户)	Washing Machine	(set/100 households)	1.79	1.92	2.73	2.67	3.21	6.09	5.09	4.44	4.93	4.35
电风扇	(台/百户)	Electric Fans	(set/100 households)	9.73	8.85	9.73	11.45	10.52	10.79	13.67			
电冰箱	(台/百户)	Refrigerators	(set/100 households)	2.67	4.18	5.64	7.06	7.00	8.30	7.12	6.16	6.03	6.61
自行车(含电动)	(辆/百户)	Bycicle	(set/100 households)	5.26	5.40	6.80	7.04	4.67	7.18	7.30	6.54	6.99	6.27
摩托车	(辆/百户)	Motocycle	(set/100 households)	5.00	5.28	4.73	4.26	3.88	6.09	5.30	3.91	3.65	3.51
热水器	(台/百户)	Shower	(set/100 households)	1.67	2.06	3.11	3.79	4.36	6.18	5.70	3.58	2.75	3.20
电话机	(部/百户)	Telephone Sets	(set/100 households)	6.15	4.52	4.33	4.37	3.36	3.41	2.76	1.86	1.03	1.37
手 机	(部/百户)	Mobile Phones	(set/100 households)	8.30	12.97	13.82	14.42	18.92	25.39	28.00	33.40	39.75	39.44

9-17 农民家庭年人均主要食品消费量
RURAL HOUSEHOLD ANNUAL CONSUMPTION ON MAJOR FOOD PER CAPITA

单位：千克 (Kg)

品　名		2006	2007	2008	2009	2010	2011	2012	2013	2014	2015
一、粮食	Grain	213.71	208.29	193.60	192.22	178.37	162.86	151.06	125.59	153.08	152.05
小麦	Wheat	23.11	21.80	22.02	19.87	17.60	17.41	15.55	10.17	16.74	17.90
稻谷	Paddy	170.17	168.61	155.37	155.18	146.13	135.87	126.67	104.27	121.21	118.83
豆类	Bean	3.65	3.82	3.30	3.27	3.22	2.53	1.97	3.85	7.25	7.86
二、蔬菜及菜制品	Fresh Vegetables and	143.75	143.57	132.58	137.04	137.51	131.68	119.33	88.16	118.03	123.06
鲜菜	Fresh Vegetables	138.12	140.57	130.05	134.69	136.22	130.67	118.25	86.56	116.30	121.40
三、油脂类	Oil and Fats	3.56	3.77	4.11	3.85	5.49	8.17	10.39	11.05	29.71	16.04
植物油	Edible Vegetable Oil	2.89	3.23	3.58	3.39	5.13	7.71	9.93	10.61	29.02	15.24
动物油	Edible Animal Oil	0.67	0.53	0.53	0.47	0.36	0.46	0.47	0.43	0.70	0.79
四、肉禽及其制品	Meat and Processed Products	25.27	22.70	22.21	22.99	22.79	22.90	22.80	22.91	29.82	31.20
猪肉	Pork	20.91	17.83	17.51	18.14	17.98	17.40	17.63	18.11	23.12	24.12
牛羊肉	Beef and Mutton	0.53	0.52	0.50	0.48	0.57	0.65	0.53	0.63	0.93	1.14
家禽	Poultry	2.91	3.30	3.23	3.22	2.91	3.23	2.94	2.87	4.19	4.27
五、蛋类及蛋制品	Eggs and Processed Products	4.15	4.17	4.69	4.93	4.47	5.03	5.02	4.68	6.65	8.31
六、奶及奶制品	Milk and Dariy Products	0.33	0.50	0.81	1.11	1.22	1.55	1.67	2.11	3.53	3.58
七、水产品	Aquatic Products	8.51	9.38	8.71	8.34	8.33	8.38	8.54	7.93	11.10	11.75
鱼类	Fish	8.18	9.03	8.40	7.97	7.93	8.03	8.09	7.58	10.55	10.97
八、干鲜瓜果	Fresh and Dry	19.75	18.66	16.01	16.84	15.70	16.38	16.83	13.33	20.74	22.42
九、酒类	Liquor and Drinks	11.93	12.35	11.76	11.41	10.77	11.40	11.12	10.08	14.25	12.78
白酒	Wine Spirit	4.06	3.87	3.85	3.94	3.70	3.69	3.52	3.65	5.82	5.51
啤酒	Beer	7.83	8.42	7.84	7.40	7.01	7.67	7.53	6.41	8.41	7.24

9-18 农民家庭每百户主要耐用消费品拥有量
POSSESSTION OF URABLE CONSUMER GOODS PER 100 RURAL HOUSEHOLDS

品名		Item		2006	2007	2008	2009	2010	2011	2012	2013	2014	2015
彩电	(台)	Color TV Set	(unit)	92.12	98.82	102.24	105.42	109.18	114.36	116.24	114.35	116.50	118.46
照相机	(架)	Camera	(unit)	1.76	1.82	2.06	2.58	2.64	3.55	3.64	5.24	4.89	3.84
洗衣机	(台)	Washing Machine	(unit)	30.12	34.68	37.12	41.70	47.97	57.09	62.42	53.79	57.94	65.02
电冰箱	(台)	Refrigerator	(unit)	19.18	26.18	30.52	41.36	51.48	73.73	80.18	75.82	79.53	84.75
摩托车	(辆)	Motocycle	(unit)	45.00	51.45	55.52	59.76	64.12	72.33	74.76	68.84	76.52	77.87
摄像机	(台)	Videorecorder	(unit)	0.76	1.06	0.91	0.52	0.70	1.42	1.52	0.62	0.50	0.44
抽油烟机	(台)	Ventilator	(unit)	3.72	5.03	6.10	7.70	10.03	13.70	15.82	10.94	13.59	14.89
空调机	(台)	Air Conditioner	(unit)	5.39	7.61	9.91	12.45	18.36	28.58	33.15	33.05	37.79	43.49
热水器	(台)	Shower	(unit)	8.79	12.21	16.03	22.73	32.00	48.24	55.91	52.16	58.01	61.71
电话机	(部)	Telephone Set	(set)	57.20	58.36	59.33	55.61	55.70	41.94	40.06	31.44	37.15	27.43
移动电话	(部)	Moblile Phone	(set)	90.10	104.67	117.88	134.21	152.27	204.82	215.06	211.52	223.46	232.18
家用计算机	(台)	PC	(unit)	2.33	2.00	3.00	5.15	7.39	15.58	19.73	22.14	25.72	26.23

9-19 市、州农民年人均纯收入(可支配收入)
ANAUAL NET INCOME OF RURAL HOUCEHOLD PER CAPITA IN CITIES AND PREFERCTURES

单位：元 (yuan)

地 区	Item	农村居民人均纯收入								农村常住居民人均可支配收入		
		2006	2007	2008	2009	2010	2011	2012	2013	2013	2014	2015
全 省	**Province**	**3419**	**3997**	**4656**	**5035**	**5832**	**6898**	**7852**	**8867**	**9692**	**10849**	**11844**
武汉市	Wuhan	4748	5371	6349	7161	8295	9814	11190	12713	14390	16160	17722
黄石市	Huangshi	3182	3742	4374	4811	5524	6487	7477	8492	9781	10957	12004
十堰市	Shiyan	2191	2490	2841	3110	3499	4044	4566	5226	6212	7046	7779
宜昌市	Yichang	3433	4022	4686	5186	5980	7055	8046	9121	10458	11837	12990
襄阳市	Xiangyang	3519	4114	4880	5440	6365	7549	8684	9785	11176	12534	13650
鄂州市	Ezhou	3799	4393	5096	5718	6645	7909	9072	10210	11309	12692	13812
荆门市	Jingmen	4059	4652	5332	5956	6951	8248	9387	10615	12082	13481	14716
孝感市	Xiaogan	3336	3915	4636	5131	5943	7029	7988	9023	10360	11597	12655
荆州市	Jingzhou	3502	4140	4889	5464	6453	7664	8710	9909	11280	12625	13728
黄冈市	Huanggang	2861	3295	3744	4130	4634	5438	6142	6966	8385	9388	10252
咸宁市	Xianning	3213	3737	4411	4873	5606	6588	7505	8480	9709	10891	11940
随州市	Suizhou	3581	4177	4967	5457	6279	7427	8419	9490	10702	11984	13022
恩施自治州	Enshi	1848	2143	2519	2810	3255	3939	4571	5235	6364	7194	7969
仙桃市	Xiantao	4190	4695	5248	5856	6807	8006	9076	10365	11809	13193	14422
天门市	Tianmen	3658	4207	4761	5326	6207	7407	8507	9608	10809	12086	13178
潜江市	Qianjiang	3813	4378	4929	5531	6486	7684	8785	10017	11448	12862	14076
神农架林区	Shennongjia	2394	2850	3330	3707	4083	4640	5110	5677	6305	6920	7578

注：2013年前分城镇和农村开展住户调查，指标为农民人均纯收入。2014年起使用城乡一体化住户收支与生活状况调查数据，指标改为农村常住居民人均可支配收入。

Note：Urban and rural household surveys are separate prior to 2013,the concept is Per Capita Net Income of Rural Households, The data from an integrated household income and expenditure survey has been used since 2014 , the concept was changed into Per Capita Disposable Income of Rural Permanent Residents.

主要统计指标解释

一、城镇住户调查(到2012年)

城镇家庭人口 指居住在一起,经济上合在一起共同生活的家庭成员。凡计算为家庭人口的成员其全部收支都包括在本家庭中。

城镇就业面 指就业人口占家庭人口的百分比。

城镇就业者负担人数 指家庭人口与就业人口之比。

城镇家庭总收入 指家庭成员得到的工资性收入、经营净收入、财产性收入、转移性收入之和,不包括出售财物收入和借贷收入。

城镇居民家庭可支配收入 指家庭成员得到可用于最终消费支出和其它非义务性支出以及储蓄的总和,即居民家庭可以用来自由支配的收入。它是家庭总收入扣除交纳的个人所得税、个人交纳的社会保障支出以及记账补贴后的收入。计算公式为:

城镇居民家庭可支配收入=家庭总收入-交纳所得税-个人交纳的社会保障支出-记帐补贴

城镇家庭总支出 指家庭除借贷支出以外的全部实际支出。包括现金消费支出、财产性支出、转移性支出、社会保障支出、购房与建房支出。

城镇家庭现金消费支出 指家庭用于日常生活的全部现金支出,包括食品、衣着、家庭设备及用品、交通通信、文教娱乐、医疗保健、其他等八大类支出。

城镇家庭服务性消费支出 指家庭用于支付社会提供的各种文化和生活方面的非商品性服务费用。

城镇家庭收入分组方法 是将所有调查户依户人均可支配收入由低到高排队,按10%,10%,20%,20%,20%,10%,10%的比例依次分成:最低收入户、较低收入户、中等偏下收入户、中等收入户、中等偏上收入户、高收入户、最高收入户等七组。总体中最低5%的户为困难户。

恩格尔系数 指食品支出在现金消费支出中所占的比例。计算公式为:

$$\text{恩格尔系数}=\frac{\text{食品支出}}{\text{现金消费支出}}\times 100\%$$

二、农村住户调查(到2012年)

农村住户 指农村常住户。农村常住户指长期(一年以上)居住在乡镇(不包括城关镇)行政管理区域内的住户,以及长期居住在城关镇所辖行政村范围内的农村住户。户口不在本地而在本地居住一年及以上的住户也包括在本地农村常住户范围内;有本地户口,但举家外出谋生一年以上的住户,无论是否保留承包耕地都不包括在本地农村住户范围内。

常住人口 指全年经常在家或在家居住6个月以上,而且经济和生活与本户连成一体的人口。外出从业人员在外居住时间虽然在6个月以上,但收入主要带回家中,经济与本户连为一体,仍视为家庭常住人口;在家居住,生活和本户连成一体的国家职工、退休人员也为家庭常住人口。但是现役军人、中专及以上(走读生除外)的在校学生、以及常年在外(不包括探亲、看病等)且已有稳定的职业与居住场所的外出从业人员,不算家庭常住人口。家庭常住人口主要作为计算农村住户平均每人收入、消费和积累水平及分析家庭人口状况的依据。

整、半劳动力 整劳动力指男子18周岁到50周岁,女子18周岁到45周岁;半劳动力指男子16周岁到17周岁,51周岁到60周岁;女子16周岁到17周岁,46周岁到55周岁,同时具有劳动能力的人。虽然在劳动年龄之内,但已丧失劳动能力的人,不应算为劳动力;超过劳动年龄,但能经常参加劳动,计入半劳动力数内。常住人口中的职工,若这些职工为劳动力,就包括在本户的整半劳动力中。

总收入 指调查期内农村住户和住户成员从各种来源渠道得到的收入总和。按收入的性质划分为工资性收入、家庭经营收入、财产性收入和转移性收入。

工资性收入 指农村住户成员受雇于单位或个人,靠出卖劳动而获得的收入。

家庭经营收入 指农村住户以家庭为生产经营单位进行生产筹划和管理而获得的收入。农村住户家庭经营活动按行业划分为农业、林业、牧业、渔业、工业、建筑业、交通运输业邮电业、批发和零售贸易餐饮业、社会服务业、文教卫生业和其他家庭经营。

财产性收入 指金融资产或有形非生产性资产的所有者向其他机构单位提供资金或将有形非生产性资产供其支配,作为回报而从中获得的收入。

转移性收入 指农村住户和住户成员无须付出任何对应物而获得的货物、服务、资金或资产所有权等,不包括无偿提供的用于固定资本形成的资金。一般情况下,是指农村住户在二次分配中的所有收入。

现金收入 指农村住户和住户成员在调查期内得到以现金形态表现的收入。按来源分成工资性收入、家庭经营现金收入、财产性收入、转移性收入。

农村居民家庭纯收入 指农村住户当年从各个来源得到的总收入相应地扣除所发生的费用后的收入总和。计算方法:

农村居民家庭纯收入=总收入-家庭经营费用支出-税费支出-生产性固定资产折旧-赠送农村内部亲支

纯收入主要用于再生产投入和当年生活消费支出,也可用于储蓄和各种非义务性支出。"农民人均纯收入"按人口平均的纯收入水平,反映的是一个地区农村居民的平均收入水平。

总支出 指农村住户用于生产、生活和再分配的全部支出。包括家庭经营费用支出、购置生产性固定资产支出、税费支出、消费支出、财产性支出和转移性支出。

三、一体化住户调查

从2012年四季度起,国家统计局对分别进行的城乡住户调查实施了一体化改革,统一了城乡居民收入指标名称、分类和统计标准,建立了城乡统一的一体化住户调查《住户收支与生活状况调查》,并据此获得全国居民有关数据。

居民可支配收入 居民可支配收入指居民可用于最终消费支出和储蓄的总和,即居民可用于自由支配的收入。既包括现金收入、也包括实物收入。按照收入的来源,可支配收入包含四项,分别为:工资性收入、经营性净收入、转移性净收入和财产性净收入。

居民消费支出 居民消费支出是指居民用于满足家庭日常生活消费需要的全部支出,既包括现金消费支出,也包括实物消费支出。消费支出可划分为食品烟酒、衣着、居住、生活用品及服务、交通和通信、教育文化和娱乐、医疗保健以及其他用品及服务八大类。

Explanatory Notes on Main Statistical Indicators

Ⅰ.Urban Households(to the year of 2012)

Population of Urban Households refer to members of the household living and sharing economically together. All income and expenditure of the population of the household are included in the income and expenditure of the household.

Proportion of Urban Employment referto the proportion of employed population to the population of urban households.

Number of Dependents per Urban Employee refers to the ratio between number of persons in urban households and the number of dependents.

Total Income of Urban Households refers to the sum of wage and salary, net business income, income from properties, and in-come from transfers of members of the households, excluding income from selling of properties and income from borrowings.

Disposable Income of Urban Households refers to the actual income at the disposal of members of the households which can be used for final consumption, other non–compulsory expenditure and savings. This equals to total income minus income tax, personal contribution to social security and sample household subsidy for keeping diaries. Following formula is used:

Disposable income = total household income – income tax – personal contribution to social security – sample household subsidy for keeping diaries

Total Expenditure of Urban Households refer to all expenditure of the households except expenditure on leading. It includes expenditure on consumption, on purchasing or building houses, on transfers, on properties and on social security.

Consumption Expenditure of Urban Households refers to total expenditure of the sample households for consumption in daily life, including expenditure on eight categories such as food, clothing, household appliances and services, health care and medical services, transport and communications, recreation, education and cultural services, housing, miscellaneous goods and services.

Expenditure of Urban Households on Consumption of Services refers to expenditure of households on services of various kinds provided by the society.

Urban Households by Income Group All households in the sample are grouped, by per capita disposable income of the household, into groups of lowest income, low income, lower middle income, middle income, upper middle income, high income and highest income, each group consisting of 10%, 10%, 20%, 20%, 20%, 10% and 10% of all households respectively. The lowest 5% of households are also referred to as poor households.

Engel Coefficient refers to the percentage of expenditure on food in the total consumption expenditure, using the following formula:

Engel Coefficient = (expenditure on food / total living consumption expenditure) x 100%

Ⅱ. Rural Households(to the year of 2012)

Rural Households refer to resident households in rural areas. Resident households in rural areas are the households residing for more than one year in the areas under the jurisdiction of administration of township governments (excluding county towns), and in the areas under the jurisdiction of administration of villages in county towns. Migrated households residing in the current addresses for over one year with their household registration in other places are included in the resident households of their current addresses. For households with their household registration in one place but all members of the households moving away for living in another place for over one year, they will not be included in the rural households of the area where they are registered, irrespective of whether they still keep their contracted land.

Resident Population refers to population staying at home permanently or for over 6 months during a year and sharing life economically with the household. Members of the household staying away from the household for over 6 months but keeping a close economic relation with the household by sending the majority of income to the household are regarded as resident population of the household. Government staff and workers or retirees living as close members of the household are also considered as resident population. However, servicemen, students of secondary technical schools or schools of higher education and persons with stable jobs and residence outside the household (excluding those visiting relatives or seeking medical service) are not included as resident population of the household. Resident population is used in calculating income, consumption, accumulation on per capita basis of rural households and in analyzing composition of rural households.

Full/Semi Labor Force Full labor force refers to persons capable of work, aged 18–50 for males and 18–45 for females. Semi labor force refers to persons capable of work, aged 16–17 and 51–60 for males and 16–17 and 46–55 for females. Persons at their working ages but not capable of work are not to be included as labor force. Persons not at working ages but participating regularly in work are included in semi labor force. For staff and workers as resident population of the household, they are included as full or semi labor force of the household if they are in the labor force.

Total Income refers to the sum of income earned from various sources by the rural households and their members during the reference period, and is classified as income from wages and salaries, income from household operations, income from properties and income from transfers.

Income from Wages and Salaries refers to income from labor earned by the members of rural households employed by other units or individuals.

Income from Household Operations refers to income by the rural households as units of production and operations. Operations by rural households are classified by economic activities as agriculture, forestry, animal husbandry, fishery, manufacturing, construction, transportation, post and telecommunications, wholesale, retail and catering, social service, culture, education, health, and other household operations.

Income from Properties refers to the income received as returns by owners of financial assets or tangible non-productive assets by providing capitals or tangible non-productive assets to other institutional units.

Income from Transfers refers to the receipt by rural households and their members of goods, services, capitals or rights of assets without giving or repaying accordingly, excluding capitals provided to them for the formation of fixed assets. In general, it refers to all income received by rural households through redistribution.

Cash Income refers to income received by rural households and their members in the form of cash during the reference period. It is classified, by source of income, into income from wages and salaries, cash income from household operations, income from properties and income from transfers.

Net Income refers to the total income of rural households from all sources minus all corresponding expenses. The formula for calculation is as follows:

Net income = total income – taxes and fees paid – household operation expenses – taxes and fees depreciation of fixed assets for production – subsidy for participating in household survey – gifts to non-rural relatives

Net income is mainly used as input for reproduction and as consumption expenditure of the year, and also used for savings and non-compulsory expenses of various forms. "Per capital net income of farmers" is the level of net income averaged by population which reflects the average income level of rural households in a given area.

Total Expenditure refers to total expenses of rural households on production, consumption and redistribution, including expenditure on household operations, on purchase of productive fixed assets, depreciation of productive fixed assets, taxes and fees, expenses on household consumption, expenses on properties and expenses on transfers.

Ⅲ. Integrated Household Survey

In the fourth quarter of 2012, the NBS launched its reform on the household survey programin order to produceaggregates with the same concepts and definitions for urban and rural population. This new survey program is an integrated one whereas there had existed two separate household surveys for the urban and rural households. The reform took a number of measures, including the integration of concepts, classifications and standards, which provided a basis for producing data covering all households. The new survey includes the following indicators:

Disposable Income of Households has a national coverage comparable between urban and rural households, and refers to the kind ofincome that households call have at them disposal. It includes income both in cash and in kind from four categories: income from wages and salaries, cash income from household operations, income from properties and income from transfers.

Consumption Expenditure of Households has anational coverage comparable between urban and rural households, and refers to the all the expenditures of households for consumption in daily life. It includes expenditure in cash and in kind on eight categories: food; clothing; housing; household appliances and services; transport and communications; education, cultural and recreational activities; and medical care. The expenditure on housing also includes rents, water, electricity, fuels and imputed rents Of owner—occupied dwellings.

10 城市概况

City Overview

10-1 主要城市土地面积、人口情况(2015)
LAND AREA AND PULATION OF MAJOR MUNICIPALITIES (2015)

城市	Municipalities	土地面积(平方公里) Land Area (sq.km)	常住人口(万人) Resident Population (10 000 persons)	当年出生人口(人) Births (persons)	当年死亡人口(人) Deaths (persons)	人口密度(人/平方公里) Population Desity (person/sq.km)
武汉	Wuhan Municipality	8494	1060.77	105169	47637	1248.85
黄石	Huangshi Municipality	4586	245.80	47993	13089	535.98
十堰	Shiyan Municipality	23680	338.30	65963	17866	142.86
宜昌	Yichang Municipality	21084	411.50	36524	31540	195.17
襄阳	Xiangyang Municipality	19724	561.40	84630	28892	284.63
鄂州	Ezhou Municipality	1596	105.95	21498	3944	663.85
荆门	Jingmen Municipality	12404	289.63	29693	13066	233.50
孝感	Xiaogan Municipality	8910	487.80	73151	25834	547.47
荆州	Jingzhou Municipality	14067	570.59	105357	39755	405.62
黄冈	Huanggang Municipality	17457	629.10	149571	25838	360.37
咸宁	Xianning Municipality	10049	250.70	74550	8948	249.48
随州	Suizhou Municipality	9636	219.08	39578	8062	227.36

10-2 主要城市就业情况(2015)
EMPLOYMENT OF MAJOR MUNICIPALITIES (2015)

单位：人 (persons)

城市	Municipalities	年末单位从业人数 Employment (year-end)	从业人员按三次产业分(城镇) Employment Grouped by Type of Industry			城镇私营和个体人数 Employment in Private Enterprises and Self-employed Individuals of Urban Areas
			第一产业 Primary Industry	第二产业 Secondary Industry	第三产业 Tertiary Industry	
武汉	Wuhan Municipality	2072768	3577	1046760	1022431	2372521
黄石	Huangshi Municipality	320758	1279	196322	123157	362700
十堰	Shiyan Municipality	640976	7125	314013	319838	656535
宜昌	Yichang Municipality	934399	3830	515474	415095	1689300
襄阳	Xiangyang Municipality	992278	19321	503445	469512	344695
鄂州	Ezhou Municipality	215512	100	143301	72111	108535
荆门	Jingmen Municipality	386916	6918	211153	168845	372529
孝感	Xiaogan Municipality	815130	7647	462423	345060	702916
荆州	Jingzhou Municipality	427800	14900	190300	222600	420395
黄冈	Huanggang Municipality	637671	21356	372553	243762	176850
咸宁	Xianning Municipality	232957	442	94850	137665	251000
随州	Suizhou Municipality	139893	609	66643	72641	543671

10-3 主要城市地区生产总值(2015)
GROSS DOMESTIC PRODUCTS OF MAJOR MUNICIPALITIES (2015)

城市	Municipalities	地区生产总值(亿元) Gross Domestic Product (100 million yuan)	(当年价格) 第一产业 Primary Industry	第二产业 Secondary Industry	第三产业 Tertiary Industry	人均地区生产总值(元) Per Capita GDP(yuan)
武汉	Wuhan Municipality	10905.60	359.81	4981.54	5564.25	104132
黄石	Huangshi Municipality	1228.11	108.56	679.88	439.67	50053
十堰	Shiyan Municipality	1300.12	157.48	636.11	506.53	38490
宜昌	Yichang Municipality	3384.80	361.40	1986.37	1037.03	82360
襄阳	Xiangyang Municipality	3382.12	402.14	1922.92	1057.06	60319
鄂州	Ezhou Municipality	730.01	84.66	422.44	222.91	68924
荆门	Jingmen Municipality	1388.46	200.86	729.66	457.94	47999
孝感	Xiaogan Municipality	1457.20	259.45	705.76	491.99	29924
荆州	Jingzhou Municipality	1590.50	353.01	695.12	542.37	27781
黄冈	Huanggang Municipality	1589.24	379.62	618.42	591.20	25319
咸宁	Xianning Municipality	1030.07	178.59	500.47	351.01	41234
随州	Suizhou Municipality	785.26	132.31	376.20	276.75	35901

10-4 主要城市固定资产投资(2015)
INVESTMENT IN FIXED ASSETS OF MAJOR MUNICIPALITIES (2015)

单位：亿元 (100 million yuan)

城市	Municipalities	固定资产投资 Investment in Fixed Assets	房地产开发投资 Investment in Real Estate	#住宅 #Residential Buildings	新增固定资产 Newly Increased Fixed Assets	商品房屋销售面积(万平方米) Construction Floor Space of Commercial House Sold (10 000 sq.km)	#住宅 #Residential Buildings
武汉	Wuhan Municipality	7680.89	2581.79	1777.93	2821.06	2627.19	2413.70
黄石	Huangshi Municipality	1351.93	130.14	95.82	957.84	212.97	206.18
十堰	Shiyan Municipality	1225.51	83.01	63.34	706.57	149.46	142.47
宜昌	Yichang Municipality	2921.38	241.89	190.77	2433.67	559.12	477.72
襄阳	Xiangyang Municipality	2921.78	334.58	230.89	1958.65	603.06	513.25
鄂州	Ezhou Municipality	806.21	21.09	17.91	487.23	61.75	56.06
荆门	Jingmen Municipality	1404.58	118.11	80.91	1184.66	235.58	217.74
孝感	Xiaogan Municipality	1762.35	171.58	139.65	1347.88	260.58	241.35
荆州	Jingzhou Municipality	1853.59	113.33	86.96	1176.36	183.33	172.47
黄冈	Huanggang Municipality	1958.41	200.05	153.81	1424.79	465.61	423.65
咸宁	Xianning Municipality	1349.62	59.94	46.82	902.38	292.73	261.27
随州	Suizhou Municipality	907.68	28.77	21.33	766.89	65.87	60.90

10-5 主要城市规上工业基本情况(2015)
BASIC STATISTICS ON INDUSTRY OF MAJOR MUNICIPALITIES (2015)

单位: 亿元 (100 million yuan)

城市	Municipalities	工业企业单位数(个) Number of Industrial Enterprises (unit)	主营业务收入 Major Business Income	利润总额 Total Profits
武汉	Wuhan Municipality	2558	11771.72	481.75
黄石	Huangshi Municipality	761	2505.68	61.13
十堰	Shiyan Municipality	976	1677.70	159.83
宜昌	Yichang Municipality	1543	5403.72	408.05
襄阳	Xiangyang Municipality	1826	5389.08	431.59
鄂州	Ezhou Municipality	489	1189.38	31.07
荆门	Jingmen Municipality	1132	2965.75	149.86
孝感	Xiaogan Municipality	1306	2536.15	126.30
荆州	Jingzhou Municipality	1258	2185.88	129.84
黄冈	Huanggang Municipality	1493	1640.25	85.70
咸宁	Xianning Municipality	867	1560.83	131.17
随州	Suizhou Municipality	688	1207.48	106.94

10-6 主要城市规上工业总产值(2015)
GROSS OUTPUT VALUE OF INDUSTRY OF MAJOR MUNICIPALITIES (2015)

单位: 亿元 (100 million yuan)

城市	Municipalities	工业总产值(当年价) Total Value of Industry	内资企业 Inner Funded Enterprises	#国有企业	外商港澳台投资企业
武汉	Wuhan Municipality	12862.95	9119.99	2318.79	3742.96
黄石	Huangshi Municipality	2005.91	1621.58	2.82	384.33
十堰	Shiyan Municipality	1822.54	1425.45	26.98	397.09
宜昌	Yichang Municipality	5714.37	5322.16	206.43	392.21
襄阳	Xiangyang Municipality	5879.06	5347.04	87.89	532.02
鄂州	Ezhou Municipality	1286.41	1185.29	6.48	101.12
荆门	Jingmen Municipality	3089.60	2919.94	2.30	169.66
孝感	Xiaogan Municipality	2671.40	2463.63	54.78	207.77
荆州	Jingzhou Municipality	2368.55	2224.12	32.07	144.44
黄冈	Huanggang Municipality	1853.61	1734.26	10.14	119.35
咸宁	Xianning Municipality	1734.86	1591.47	4.26	143.39
随州	Suizhou Municipality	1268.89	1214.23	2.72	54.66

10-7 主要城市财政收支(2015) GOVERNMENT REVENUE AND EXPENDITURES OF MAJOR MUNICIPALITIES (2015)

单位：亿元 (100 million yuan)

城市	Municipalities	公共财政收入 The public finance income	*各项税收 *Taxes	公共财政支出 The public finance expenditures	*社会保障和就业支出 *Subsides Expenditures for Social Security	*城乡社区事务支出 *Expenditures for City Maintenance
武汉	Wuhan Municipality	1245.63	1015.91	1338.05	204.09	235.24
黄石	Huangshi Municipality	100.53	68.29	225.94	35.87	23.60
十堰	Shiyan Municipality	93.38	66.30	307.65	48.63	10.39
宜昌	Yichang Municipality	339.10	200.00	537.53	56.16	79.67
襄阳	Xiangyang Municipality	339.10	210.67	584.50	72.86	88.46
鄂州	Ezhou Municipality	47.17	29.83	86.80	12.62	11.55
荆门	Jingmen Municipality	80.43	56.47	225.90	33.64	17.63
孝感	Xiaogan Municipality	122.77	79.04	290.38	46.92	15.58
荆州	Jingzhou Municipality	103.95	74.95	346.48	63.37	18.82
黄冈	Huanggang Municipality	112.82	75.35	401.03	70.40	10.12
咸宁	Xianning Municipality	80.12	50.29	190.85	27.43	5.94
随州	Suizhou Municipality	43.34	29.25	153.10	24.54	9.35

10-8 主要城市金融机构存贷款余额(2015) DEPOSITS AND LOANS BALANCE OF BANKING INSTITUTIONS OF MAJOR MUNICIPALITIES (2015)

单位：亿元 (100 million yuan)

城市	Municipalities	年末金融机构人民币各项存款余额 Deposit Balance	*居民储蓄存款 *Savings Deposits from Residents	年末金融机构人民币各项贷款余额 Loans Balance
武汉	Wuhan Municipality	19057	6059	16018
黄石	Huangshi Municipality	1342	732	927
十堰	Shiyan Municipality	1832	1010	1031
宜昌	Yichang Municipality	2822	1474	2133
襄阳	Xiangyang Municipality	2695	1739	1684
鄂州	Ezhou Municipality	508	299	329
荆门	Jingmen Municipality	1431	960	794
孝感	Xiaogan Municipality	1857	1238	915
荆州	Jingzhou Municipality	2234	1538	1071
黄冈	Huanggang Municipality	2321	1611	991
咸宁	Xianning Municipality	1035	593	629
随州	Suizhou Municipality	968	675	454

10-9 主要城市贸易、外经情况(2015)
DOMESTIC TRADE AND FOREIGN ECONOMY OF MAJOR MUNICIPALITIES (2015)

城市	Municipalities	社会消费品零售总额(亿元) Total Retail Sales of consumer Goods (100 million yuan)	进出口总额(亿美元) Total Import and Export (USD 100 million)	进口 Imports	出口 Exports	当年实际使用外资金额(亿美元) ActualForeign Direct Investment (USD 100 million)
武汉	Wuhan Municipality	5102.24	280.72	129.19	151.53	59.91
黄石	Huangshi Municipality	582.36	30.33	13.48	16.85	1.25
十堰	Shiyan Municipality	639.41	6.60	0.21	6.39	2.38
宜昌	Yichang Municipality	1089.47	30.86	3.95	26.91	3.40
襄阳	Xiangyang Municipality	1165.10	24.12	2.55	21.58	7.28
鄂州	Ezhou Municipality	261.95	5.44	3.15	2.30	2.45
荆门	Jingmen Municipality	541.43	11.75	2.94	8.81	3.40
孝感	Xiaogan Municipality	797.14	11.87	2.14	9.73	3.45
荆州	Jingzhou Municipality	946.14	12.08	1.47	10.61	1.33
黄冈	Huanggang Municipality	880.91	6.50	0.74	5.76	1.04
咸宁	Xianning Municipality	401.04	4.84	0.62	4.22	0.65
随州	Suizhou Municipality	399.57	14.06	2.28	11.78	1.14

10-10 主要城市邮电、电力情况(2015)
POST SERVICE AND POWER IN MAJOR MUNICIPALITIES(2015)

城市	Municipalities	邮电业务收入(全市)(亿元) Revenue from Posts and Telecommunication Services(100 million yuan)	固定电话用户(万户) Telephones (10 000 Subscribers)	移动电话用户(万户) Mobile Telephones (10 000 Subscribers)	国际互联网用户(万户) Internet Service (10 000 Subscribers)	全社会用电量(亿千瓦小时) Power Consumption (100 million kWh)	#城乡居民生活用电 #Urban and Rural Residents Power Consumption
武汉	Wuhan Municipality	193.67	249.03	1584.5	463.49	464.28	70.72
黄石	Huangshi Municipality	23.84	39.16	226.83	43.58	112.25	12.42
十堰	Shiyan Municipality	27.11	214.00	263.00	58.00	83.67	13.61
宜昌	Yichang Municipality	31.41	60.69	365.01	78.52	205.66	19.06
襄阳	Xiangyang Municipality	37.88	63.14	450.82	83.93	124.26	22.98
鄂州	Ezhou Municipality	10.21	19.05	95.98	17.70	62.65	5.41
荆门	Jingmen Municipality	19.30	32.65	211.86	39.53	84.07	11.38
孝感	Xiaogan Municipality	26.98	56.41	318.64	49.01	105.89	19.66
荆州	Jingzhou Municipality	36.83	60.48	391.10	112.19	100.43	24.05
黄冈	Huanggang Municipality	33.20	78.67	383.05	77.90	95.78	22.75
咸宁	Xianning Municipality	15.26	41.31	248.20	43.37	58.47	12.55
随州	Suizhou Municipality	12.80	49.81	174.23	33.74	31.29	8.33

10-11 主要城市环境保护(2015)
ENVIRONMENTAL PROTECTION OF MAJOR MUNICIPALITIES(2015)

城市	Municipalities	工业废水排放量(万吨) Industrial Waste Water Discharged (10,000 tons)	工业二氧化硫排放量(万吨) Industrial Sulphur Dioxide Emission (100 million tons)	工业固体废物综合利用率(%) Ratio of Industrial Solid Wastes Vtilized (%)	污水处理厂集中处理率(%) Ratio of Central Sewage Treatment (%)	生活垃圾无害化处理率(%) Ratio of Consumption Treated
武汉	Wuhan Municipality	15452.00	7.50	98.0	95.0	100.0
黄石	Huangshi Municipality	5313.20	6.30	92.0	91.7	100.0
十堰	Shiyan Municipality	2104.93	1.60	52.8	88.7	83.5
宜昌	Yichang Municipality	18129.81	7.28	26.3	91.7	93.6
襄阳	Xiangyang Municipality	8183.99	3.36	92.2	89.6	70.7
鄂州	Ezhou Municipality	1734.00	3.88	98.2	82.1	100.0
荆门	Jingmen Municipality	3567.59	3.46	94.0	84.4	83.7
孝感	Xiaogan Municipality	4539.83	3.41	66.4	85.0	100.0
荆州	Jingzhou Municipality	10897.06	3.97	30.9	88.5	42.3
黄冈	Huanggang Municipality	2988.59	1.67	90.4	65.3	62.7
咸宁	Xianning Municipality	1876.42	2.24	49.3	91.0	100.0
随州	Suizhou Municipality	1606.30	0.28		90.0	96.0

10-12 主要城市居民收支情况(2015)
INCOME AND EXPENDITURE OF MAJOR URBAN HOUSEHOLDS (2015)

单位：元 (yuan)

城市	Municipalities	城镇常住居民人均可支配收入 Per Capita Disposable Income of Urban Residents	城镇常住居民人均消费性支出 Per Capita Living Expenditure of Urban Residents	人均住房建筑面积(平方米) Per Capita Utility Floor Space of Residential Buildings (sq.m)
武汉	Wuhan Municipality	36436	23943	37.3
黄石	Huangshi Municipality	27536	17241	33.0
十堰	Shiyan Municipality	24057	14000	36.0
宜昌	Yichang Municipality	27275	16959	50.9
襄阳	Xiangyang Municipality	26282	15822	54.0
鄂州	Ezhou Municipality	24774	15565	50.6
荆门	Jingmen Municipality	26731	18245	28.1
孝感	Xiaogan Municipality	25753	16985	44.7
荆州	Jingzhou Municipality	25382	15685	48.8
黄冈	Huanggang Municipality	22620	16184	38.2
咸宁	Xianning Municipality	23505	15234	45.1
随州	Suizhou Municipality	22791	14531	43.0

10-13 主要城市居民消费支出、价格(2015)
LIVING EXPENDITURES AND PRICE OF MAJOR URBAN HOUSEHOLDS (2015)

单位：元 (yuan)

城市	Municipalities	城镇常住居民人均消费性支出 Per Capita Living Expenditures for Consumption of Urban Residents				市辖区居民消费价格指数(上年=100) Consumer Price Index (preceding year=100)
		#医疗保健 #Medicine and Medicine and Medical Service	#交通和通讯 #Transport and Telecom-munication	#娱乐、教育、文化服务 #Recreation,Education and Cultural Services	#居住 #Residence	
武汉	Wuhan Municipality	1492	2639	2372	6171	101.4
黄石	Huangshi Municipality	1229	2086	2090	2750	101.6
十堰	Shiyan Municipality	1040	1926	1552	2317	101.4
宜昌	Yichang Municipality	1513	1923	1762	3889	101.5
襄阳	Xiangyang Municipality	1146	1599	1560	3294	102.0
鄂州	Ezhou Municipality	1327	1279	1543	2453	101.4
荆门	Jingmen Municipality	1741	1695	2270	3248	101.6
孝感	Xiaogan Municipality	1070	1532	1899	1735	101.3
荆州	Jingzhou Municipality	1123	1610	1800	2806	101.5
黄冈	Huanggang Municipality	1866	1131	1444	1744	101.4
咸宁	Xianning Municipality	1369	1440	2010	3272	101.4
随州	Suizhou Municipality	958	1300	1664	2557	101.3

10-14 主要城市文教、科技、卫生情况(2015)
CULTURE, EDUCATION, SCIENCE AND TECHNOLOGY AND PUBLIC HEALTH OF MAJOR MUNICIPALITIES (2015)

城市	Municipalities	普通高等学校在校学生数(万人) Number of Students Enrolled in Institutions of Higher Education (10 000 persons)	从事科技活动人员数(人) Number of Scientific and technical Personel (person)	公共图书馆图书总藏量(万册) Total Volume of Collection of Public Libraries (10 000 volumes)	医院、卫生院数(个) Number of Health Care Institutions (unit)	医院、卫生院数床位数(万张) Number of Beds In Health Care Intitutions (10 000 units)	执业(助理)医师(万人) Practioner Doctors (Assitant) (10 000 persons)
武汉	Wuhan Municipality	95.68		1445.44	372	7.18	3.29
黄石	Huangshi Municipality	4.31	13383	131.10	72	1.32	0.52
十堰	Shiyan Municipality	5.13	13058	122.41	176	2.66	0.92
宜昌	Yichang Municipality	5.81	25653	207.21	174	2.40	1.01
襄阳	Xiangyang Municipality	5.10	30315	186.53	220	3.15	1.28
鄂州	Ezhou Municipality	1.53	3142	41.00	479	0.53	0.24
荆门	Jingmen Municipality	1.41	8567	87.84	113	1.56	0.68
孝感	Xiaogan Municipality	4.38	72065	99.20	160	1.81	0.82
荆州	Jingzhou Municipality	9.75	9650	119.93	177	2.45	1.10
黄冈	Huanggang Municipality	4.08	9478	206.30	285	2.97	1.27
咸宁	Xianning Municipality	4.02	19180	92.84	95	1.16	0.65
随州	Suizhou Municipality	0.60	5818	22.43	103	1.00	0.40

主要统计指标解释

供水综合生产能力 指按供水设施取水、净化、送水、出厂输水干管等环节设计能力计算的综合生产能力。包括在原设计能力的基础上,经挖、革、改增加的生产能力。计算时,以四个环节中最薄弱的环节为主确定能力。

年末供水管道长度 指从送水泵至用户水表之间所有管道的长度。不包括新安装尚未使用的管道。

全年供水总量 指报告期供水企业(单位)供出的全部水量。包括有效供水量和漏损水量。

生活用水量 包括公共服务用水和居民家庭用水。公共服务用水指为城市社会公共生活服务的用水。包括行政事业单位、部队营区和公共设施服务、社会服务业、批发零售贸易业、旅馆饮食业以及其他公共服务业等单位的用水。居民家庭用水指城市范围内所有居民家庭的日常生活用水。包括城市居民、农民家庭、公共供水站用水。

用水普及率 指城市用水人口数与城市人口总数的比率。计算公式:

$$用水普及率=\frac{城市用水人口数}{城市人口总数}\times 100\%$$

供气管道长度 指报告期末从气源厂压缩机的出口或门站出口至各类用户引入管之间的全部已经通气投入使用的管道长度。不包括煤气生产厂、输配站、液化气储存站、灌瓶站、储配站、气化站、混气站、供应站等厂(站)内的管道。

全年供气总量 指全年燃气企业(单位)向用户供应的燃气数量。包括销售量和损失量。

用气普及率 指报告期末使用燃气的城市人口数与城市人口总数的比率。计算公式为:

$$用气普及率=\frac{城市用气人口数}{城市人口总数}\times 100\%$$

城市供热能力 指供热企业(单位)向城市热用户输送热能的设计能力。

城市供热总量 指在报告期供热企业(单位)向城市热用户输送全部蒸汽和热水的总热量。

城市供热管道长度 指从各类热源到热用户建筑物接入口之间的全部蒸汽和热水的管道长度。不包括各类热源厂内部的管道长度。

年末道路长度 指年末道路长度和与道路相通的广场、桥梁、隧道的长度,按车行道中心线计算。在统计时只统计路面宽度在3.5米(含3.5米)以上的各种铺装道路,包括开放型工业区和住宅区道路在内。

城市桥梁 指为跨越天然或人工障碍物而修建的构筑物。包括跨河桥、立交桥、人行天桥以及人行地下通道等。包括永久性桥和半永久性桥。

城市排水管道长度 指所有排水总管、干管、支管、检查井及连接井进出口等长度之和。

城市污水日处理能力 指污水处理厂(或处理装置)每昼夜处理污水量的设计能力。

年末运营车数 指年末公交企业(单位)用于运营业务的全部车辆数。以企业(单位)固定资产台帐中已投入运营的车辆数为准。

城市园林绿地面积 指报告期末用作园林和绿化的各种绿地面积。包括公共绿地、居住区绿地、单位附属绿地、防护绿地、生产绿地、道路绿地和风景林地面积。不包括:

1.屋顶绿化、垂直绿化、阳台绿化和室内绿化。

2.以物质生产为主的林地、耕地、牧草地、果园和竹园等。

3.城市总体规划中不列入绿地的水域。

公共绿地 指向公众开放的市级、区级、居住区级各类公园、街旁游园,包括其范围内的水域。其中居住区级公园应不小于

1万平方米，街旁游园的宽度不小于8米，面积不小于400平方米。

Explanatory Notes on Main Statistical Indicators

Production Capacity of Water Supply refers to the designed comprehensive production capacity of water facilities, covering the 4 links of water collection, purification, conveyance, and outflow through trunk pipelines. Increase capacity through transformation and innovation projects are included as well. The capacity is determined mainly on the weakest of the above–mentioned 4 links.

Length of Water Supply Pipelines at the Year–end refers to the total length of all the pipelines between the water pumps and the user担 water meters, excluding pipelines newly installed but not used yet.

Annual Volume of Water Supply refers to the total volume of water supplied by water–works (units) during the reference period, including both the effective water supply and loss during the water supply.

Consumption of Water for Residential Use refers to the water consumption of households for daily life and the water consumption of public service facilities. The latter refers to water consumption for urban public services, including the consumption of government agencies and public institutions, military barracks, public facilities, wholesale and retail outlets, restaurants, hotels, and other units providing public services. Household water consumption refers to consumption of water for daily life of all households in the boundary of cities, including households of urban residents and farmers, and public water supply stations.

Percentage of Urban Population with Access to Tap Water refers to the ratio of the urban population with access to tap water to the total urban population. The formula is:

Percentage of population with access to tap water= (Urban population with access to tap water) / (Urban population) × 100%

Length of Gas Pipelines refers to the total length of pipelines in use between the outlet of the compressor of gas–work or outlet of gas stations and the leading pipe of users, excluding pipelines within gasworks, delivery stations, LPG storage stations, refilling stations, gas–mixing stations and supply stations.

Volume of Gas Supply refers to the total volume of gas provided to users by gas–producing enterprises (units) in a year, including the volume sold and the volume lost.

Percentage of Urban Population with Access to Gas refers to the ratio of the urban population with access to gas to the total urban population at the end of the reference period. The formula is:

Percentage of population with access to gas = (Urban population with access to gas / Urban population) x 100%

Heating Capacity in Urban Area refers to the designed capacity of heating enterprises (units) in supplying heating energy to urban users during the reference period.

Quantity of Heat Supplied in Urban Area refers to the total quantity of heat from steam and hot water supplied to urban users by heating enterprises (units) during the reference period.

Length of Heating Pipelines refers to the total length of steam or hot water pipelines for sources of heat to the leading pipelines of the buildings of the users, excluding internal pipelines in heat generating enterprises.

Length of Paved Roads at the Year–end refers to the length of roads with paved surface including squares bridges and tunnels connected with roads by the end of the year. Length of the roads is measured by the central lines for vehicles for paved roads with a width of 3.5 meters and over, including roads in open–ended factory compounds and residential quarters.

Urban Bridges refer to bridges built to cross over natural or man–made barriers, including bridges over rivers, overpasses for traffic and for pedestrian, underpasses for pedestrian, etc. Both permanent and semi–permanent bridges are included.

Length of Urban Sewage Pipes refers to the total length of general drainage, trunks. branch and inspection wells, connection wells, inlets and outlets, etc.

Daily Disposal Capacity of Urban Sewage refers to the designed 24 hour capacity of sewage disposal by the sewage treatment works or facilities.

Number of Vehicles under Operation at the Year–end refers to the total number of vehicles under operation by public transport enterprises (units) at the end of the year, based on the records of operational vehicles by the enterprises (units).

Area of Urban Gardens and Green Areas refers to the total area occupied for green projects at the end of the reference period, including public green land, green land in residential quarters, green land attached to institutions, protection green land, production green land, roadside green land and forest in scenic spots. It does not include the following:

(1) Greenery and plants on roofs, balconies, indoors and vertical green areas;

(2) Forest, cultivated land, grassland, orchards and bamboo grooves that are for production purpose; and

(3) Water areas that are not included in urban master plan as green land.

Public Green Area refers to green areas open to the public such as municipal, community and neighborhood parks and roadside parks, including waters within parks. Neighborhood parks should occupy an area larger than 10,000 square meters, and the width of road–side parks should occupy an area larger than 400 square meters, with a width of more that 8 meters.

11 资源和环境

Resources and Environment

11-1 “三废”排放和处理综合利用情况
"THREE WASTES" DISCHARGE AND TREATMENT UTILIZATION SITUATION

分　　类	Item	2012	2013	2014	2015
一、废水排放总量　(万吨)	Total Volume of Waste Water Discharged　(10 000 ton)	290200	294054	301703	313785
工业废水排放总量	Total Volume of Industrial Waste Water Discharged	91609	84993	81657	80817
二、废气排放总量　(亿标立方米)	Total Volume of Waste Gas Discharged　(100 million cu.m)	19512	19986	21702	23643
三、废气中污染物排放量　(万吨)	Pollutants Discharged in Waste Gas　(10 000 ton)				
二氧化硫	Sulfur Dioxide	62.24	59.94	58.38	55.14
#工业二氧化硫	#Industrial Sulfur Dioxide	54.86	52.40	50.62	47.07
烟粉尘	Soot and Dust	34.97	35.95	50.40	44.69
四、工业固体废物产生量　(万吨)	Volume of Industrial Solid Wastes Producced　(10 000 ton)	7611	8181	8006	7750
已处置的	Teated	1561	1646	1701	2078
已综合利用的	Utilized In a Comprehensive Way	5737	6196	6139	5253
已贮存的	Stored	377	412	221	488
工业固体废物排放量	Volume of Industrial Solid Wastes Emission	1.06	0.80	0.46	0.50
五、锅炉总数　(台)	Total Number of Boiler　(unit)	2451	2413	2617	3107
锅炉蒸吨数　(蒸吨)	Steam Tons of Boiler　(steam ton)	72444	75469	87176	83972
六、工业炉窑　(座)	Number of Industrial Kiln Stove　(unit)	2475	2298	2262	2157

11-2 工业污染治理情况

项　　目		Item	Unit	1990	1995	2000
一、汇总工业企业单位数	(个)	Total Number of Industrial Enterprises	(unit)	991	613	583
二、污染治理项目本年投资来源合计	(万元)	Total Resource of Investment in Pollutant Treatment Projects	(10 000 yuan)	18051	27433	85238
国家预算内资金		State Budgetary Funds		5568	3540	962
环境保护补助资金		Environmental Protection Subsidy Funds		2531	5430	1282
环保贷款		Environmental Protection Loans		2149	3143	7579
其　他		Others		1372	7966	61881
三、污染治理项目本年完成投资合计	(万元)	Total Investment in Pollutant Treatment Projects	(10 000 yuan)			85238
治理废水		Waste Water		5637	12042	45653
治理废气		Waste Gas		9891	9164	26668
治理固体废物		Solid Waste		1371	5293	6072
治理噪声		Noise Abatement		534	583	644
其　他		Others		618	351	6201
四、本年施工项目数	(个)	Projects Carried Out in This Year	(unit)	1545	939	851
治理废水		Waste Water		450	305	384
治理废气		Waste Gas		758	367	361
治理固体废物		Solid Waste		119	121	27
治理噪声		Noise Abatement		139	109	31
其　他		Others		79	37	48
五、本年竣工项目	(个)	Projects Completed in This Year	(unit)	1312	832	692
治理废水		Waste Water		353	256	316
治理废气		Waste Gas		662	339	286
治理固体废物		Solid Waste		99	96	22
治理噪声		Noise Abatement		126	106	26
其　他		Others		72	35	42

STATISTICS ON TREATMENT OF INDUSTRIAL POLLUTION

2005	2007	2008	2009	2010	2011	2012	2013	2014	2015
336	342	307	225	159	232	171	147	152	161
148097	169405	161453	281332	277416	153812	154496	251745	262884	157944
7591	4434	4244	5602	3892	7216	4128	3667	1890	1035
7385	5543	3713	4092	1894	1290	676	210	2177	992
		3487			2950				
133121	159428	153497	271638	271631	145306	149693	247868	258817	155917
148097	169405	161453	281332	277416	153812	154496	251745	262884	157944
48068	78246	82635	54002	35627	84573	35868	15873	18409	26067
40008	74455	60834	213918	197293	47920	80510	216673	230712	120301
11408	2004	3960	5970	9580	10505	3565	1720	2762	1375
440	1411	1041	675	867	1081	1114	52	104	275
48173	13288	12983	6768	34050	9734	33439	17427	10896	9927
473	504	406	318	226	364	136	113	127	199
191	224	178	126	98	158	43	28	38	63
176	188	139	132	74	122	56	59	78	96
15	21	23	11	13	17	7	3	2	7
20	21	15	11	12	18	8	1	4	5
71	50	51	38	29	49	22	22	5	28
428	442	345	273	195	331	117	148	134	146
174	197	152	108	84	143	42	42	37	41
160	168	115	111	64	112	49	83	88	73
11	18	19	10	10	16	7	3	1	4
18	20	14	9	10	18	6		3	5
65	39	45	35	27	42	13	20	5	23

11-3 排污费征收、使用和污染赔(罚)款情况
STATISTICS ON COLLECTION, REPARATIONS AND FINES ON POLLUTION DSICHARGES

项 目	Item	1990	1995	2000	2009	2010	2011	2012	2013	2014	2015
交纳排污费单位 (个)	Number of Enterprises Charged (unit)	4072	9409	32581	15584	12017	10581	10895	7269	7566	8763
本年征收排污费数 (万元)	Amount of Pollutant Fees (10 000 yuan)	7823	13870	20092	38176	40300	44975	50587	60161	65626	62645

11-4 工业企业废水处理设施情况
STATISTICS ON INDUSTRIAL WASTE WATER TREATMENT FACILITES

项 目	Item	2000	2005	2010	2011	2012	2013	2014	2015
汇总企业单位数 (个)	Total Number of Enterprises (unit)	2172	2313	2643	3911	3699	3590	3911	4555
治理设施数量 (套)	Number of Treatment Facilities	2120	2163	2093	5296	2110	2084	2238	2562
处理能力 (万吨/日)	Treatment Capacity(10 000 ton/day)		912	1037	1322	1023	1029	1043	1052
运行费用 (万元)	Operation Fees (10 000 yuan)	46651	77931	137920	344256	176058	168277	232869	224053

11-5 全省当年建成投产的建设项目“三同时”执行情况

STATISTICS ON IMPLEMENTATION OF "THREE MEANWHILE" OF CONSTRUCTION PROJECTS IN HUBEI PROVINCE

项 目	Item	1990	1995	2000	2005	2009	2010	2011	2012	2013	2014	2015
一、建设项目 (个)	Numberof Construction Projects (unit)	306	245	359	1437	2150	2107	3078	4912	3267	3250	3014
二、建设项目投资总额(亿元)	Total investmentin Construction Projects (100 million yuan)	12.72	33.60	69.61	1603.13	2085.81	624.86	1099.26	3913.09	1180.10	1889.70	2641.21
#环保工程投资(亿元)	#Investment in Environmental Protection Projects (100 million yuan)	0.32	1.5	2.37	11.22	51.89	29.16	53.06	117.40	73.00	71.40	85.12
三、“三同时”执行情况	Implementation of "Three Meanwhile"											
实际执行项目数(个)	Number of Projects Actually Being Implemented (unit)	221	227	356	1336	2148	2107	3078	2076	3267	3250	3014
执行项目中合格的(个)	Qualified (unit)	217	211	356	1191	2135	2087	2977	2032	3138	3154	2607

主要统计指标解释

工业废水排放量 指经过企业厂区所有排放口排到企业外部的工业废水量。包括生产废水、外排的直接冷却水、超标排放的矿井地下水和与工业废水混排的厂区生活污水，不包括外排的间接冷却水(清污不分流的间接冷却水应计算在内)。

工业废气排放量 指报告期内企业厂区内燃料燃烧和生产工艺过程中产生的各种排入大气的含有污染物的气体的总量，以标准状态(273K，101325Pa)计算。

工业固体废物产生量 指报告期内企业在生产过程中产生的固体状、半固体状和高浓度液体状废弃物的总量，包括危险废物、冶炼废渣、粉煤灰、炉渣、煤矸石、尾矿、放射性废物和其他废物等；不包括矿山开采的剥离废石和掘进废石(煤矸石和呈酸性或碱性的废石除外)。酸性或碱性废石指采掘的废石其流经水、雨淋水的pH值小于4或pH值大于10.5者。

工业固体废物综合利用量 指报告期内企业通过回收、加工、循环、交换等方式，从固体废物中提取或者使其转化为可以利用的资源、能源和其他原材料的固体废物量(包括当年利用往年的工业固体废物贮存量)，如用作农业肥料、生产建筑材料、筑路等。综合利用量由原产生固体废物的单位统计。

Explanatory Notes on Main Statistical Indicators

Waste Water Discharged by Industry refers to the volume of waste water discharged by industrial enterprises through all their outlets, including waste water from production process, directly cooled water, groundwater from mining wells which does not meet discharge standards and sewage from households mixed with waste water produced by industrial activities, but excluding indirectly cooled water discharged (It should be included if the discharge is not separated with waste water).

Industrial Waste Air Emission refers to discharge into atmosphere of waste air containing pollutants generated from fuel burning and production process in enterprises within a given period of time.

Industrial Solid Wastes Produced refers to total volume of solid, semi-solid and high concentration liquid residues produced by industrial enterprises from production process in a given period of time, including hazardous wastes, slag, coal ash, gangue, tailings, radioactive residues and other wastes, but excluding stones stripped or dug out in mining (gangue and acid or alkaline stones not included). A stone is acid or alkaline depending on the pH value of the water below 4 or above 10.5 when the stone is in, or soaked by, the water.

Industrial Solid Wastes Utilized refers to volume of solid wastes from which useful materials can be extracted or which can be converted into usable resources, energy or other materials by means of reclamation, processing, recycling and exchange (including utilizing in the year the stocks of industrial solid wastes of the previous year). Examples of such utilizations include fertilizers, building materials and road materials. The information shall be collected by the producing units of the wastes.

12 农业

Agriculture

12-1 农村基层组织和农业基本情况
BASIC CONDITIONS OF RURAL GRASSROOTS UNITS AND AGRICULTURE

指 标	Item	2000	2005	2010	2012	2013	2014	2015
农村组织情况 (个)	**Rural Units (unit)**							
乡个数	Township	476	217	201	188	175	170	168
镇个数	Town Governments	853	737	742	746	757	761	761
村委会个数	Village Committees	32400	26678	26018	25991	25452	25606	25343
村民小组个数	Villager Group	259250	212587	209598	210432	210108	208966	208546
乡村户数、人口	**Rural Households,Population**							
乡村户数 (万户)	Rural Households (10 000 units)	983.94	1015.72	1062.14	1084.79	1088.01	1094.98	1091.08
乡村人口 (万人)	Rural Population (10 000 persons)	3947.26	3991.47	4031.73	4089.38	4092.19	4110.29	4093.90
乡村从业人员 (万人)	**Rural Employment (10 000 persons)**	**1781.70**	**1931.15**	**2154.44**	**2259.91**	**2280.14**	**2308.72**	**2300.88**
按性别分	Grouped by Sex							
男	Male	937.67	1026.48	1154.45	1208.63	1217.97	1238.01	1330.47
女	Female	844.03	904.67	999.99	1051.28	1062.17	1070.71	1177.15
按行业分	Grouped by Sector							
农林牧渔业	Farming, Forestry, Animal husbandary and Fishery	1159.13	1101.29	900.14	863.49	869.79	865.21	869.32
国营农林牧渔场从业人员	Employees in State-run Agriculture, forestry,animal husbandry, fishery Farm	54.94	55.73	54.31	50.89	47.38	51.69	51.23
农业从业人员	Agriculture Employees	34.08	35.27	31.56	30.04	27.93	28.96	28.65
非农业从业人员	Non-agriculture Employees	20.86	20.46	22.37	20.85	19.45	22.73	22.58
年末实有耕地面积 (千公顷)	**Cultivated Areas (Year-End) (1 000 hectares)**	**3282.96**	**3161.17**	**3323.92**	**3390.00**	**3409.91**	**3420.51**	**3436.24**
农业机械总动力(万千瓦)	Total Agricultural Machinery Power (10 000 kW)	1414.00	2057.37	2796.99	3842.00	4081.05	4292.90	4465.51
化肥施用量 (万吨)	Consumption of Chemical Fertilizers (10 000 tons)	247.08	285.83	350.77	357.66	351.93	348.27	333.87
农村用电量 (亿千瓦小时)	Electricity Consumed in Rural Areas (100 million kWh)	60.86	70.09	109.78	121.23	130.14	142.23	149.10
农作物总播种面积(千公顷)	Total Sown Area (1 000 hectares)	7584.07	7391.30	7997.57	8105.69	8106.19	8112.26	7952.36
#粮食	Grain Crops	4156.20	4068.15	4068.37	4180.05	4258.40	4370.34	4466.03
主要农产品产量(万吨)	**Volume of Major Agricultural Products (10 000 tons)**							
粮食	Grain Crops	2218.49	2177.38	2315.80	2442.00	2501.30	2584.16	2703.28
棉花	Cotton Crops	30.43	37.50	47.18	53.15	45.97	35.95	29.83
油料	Oil-Bearing Crops	269.98	293.90	311.80	319.70	333.17	341.73	339.60
肉类产量	Output of Meat	271.19	342.63	379.42	412.30	430.08	440.44	431.93
水产品产量	Output of Aquatic Products	234.34	318.21	353.09	388.90	410.37	433.30	455.80

注：主要生产品产量2006、2007年数据按农业普查数据进行衔接、调整。
Note:Statistics of output of major farm products of 2006,2007 is adusted according to Second Agriculture Survey.

12-2 耕地面积
AREAS UNDER CULTIVATION

单位:千公顷 (1 000 hectares)

年 份 Year	年末实有耕地面积 Cultivated Areas (Year-End)	水 田 Paddy Fields	旱 地 Dry Fields	年内减少 Dereased in Cultivated Areas in This Year	#国家基建占地 Capital Construction	人均占有耕地(公顷) Per Capita Cultivated Area (sq.m) 按乡村人口计算 By Rural Population	按农林牧渔业劳动力计算 By Farming, Forestry, Animal husbandry and Fishery Laborers
1949	2742.58	1765.11	1977.47			0.12	0.29
1952	4015.90	1876.62	2139.28			0.16	0.39
1957	4172.31	1945.05	2227.26			0.16	0.37
1962	4271.33	1847.19	2424.56			0.15	0.39
1965	4239.93	1966.38	2273.55			0.14	0.37
1970	3964.01	1982.20	1981.81			0.11	0.31
1975	3823.00	1996.10	1826.77	54.10		0.10	0.28
1978	3768.07	1959.63	1808.43	30.77	7.75	0.10	0.28
1979	3754.51	1940.27	1814.24	29.13	5.50	0.10	0.27
1980	3738.51	1929.50	1809.01	35.82	4.69	0.10	0.27
1982	3718.20	1916.53	1801.67	22.53	2.68	0.09	0.26
1983	3698.74	1907.51	1791.23	28.83	4.93	0.09	0.25
1984	3643.68	1892.89	1750.79	65.23	8.18	0.09	0.25
1985	3584.61	1864.15	1720.46	71.70	8.56	0.09	0.27
1986	3545.00	1847.63	1697.37	49.30	7.30	0.09	0.27
1987	3517.99	1845.17	1672.82	36.16	7.13	0.09	0.26
1988	3498.47	1838.37	1660.10	25.98	4.55	0.09	0.25
1989	3486.57	1858.25	1628.33	17.47	1.83	0.09	0.25
1990	3476.77	1871.77	1605.00	15.60	2.73	0.08	0.24
1991	3458.46	1869.19	1589.27	24.11	4.03	0.08	0.24
1992	3421.57	1845.31	1576.26	41.67	4.95	0.08	0.24
1993	3392.74	1815.75	1576.99	32.84	6.11	0.08	0.24
1994	3375.60	1805.42	1570.18	21.21	3.77	0.08	0.24
1995	3358.01	1780.40	1577.61	21.36	4.23	0.08	0.25
1996	3349.25	1800.00	1549.25	13.80	2.85	0.08	0.26
1997	3342.45	1796.07	1546.38	12.24	2.43	0.08	0.26
1998	3327.16	1788.95	1538.21	19.95	3.83	0.08	0.27
1999	3310.40	1786.34	1524.06	23.08	5.13	0.08	0.27
2000	3282.96	1757.63	1525.33	34.15	5.18	0.08	0.28
2001	3242.85	1742.69	1500.16	46.26	7.76	0.08	0.27
2002	3094.03	1708.58	1385.45	110.10	12.04	0.08	0.27
2003	3033.45	1665.49	1367.96	181.18	7.51	0.08	0.27
2004	3091.75	1789.10	1302.65	39.81	5.36	0.08	0.28
2005	3131.17	1856.17	1305.00	40.70	4.93	0.08	0.28
2006	3201.66	1881.74	1319.92	20.65	5.49	0.08	0.29
2007	3226.62	1890.04	1336.58	21.08	5.67	0.08	0.31
2008	3289.33	1914.07	1375.26	10.68	4.29	0.08	0.33
2009	3308.35	1928.67	1379.68	15.06	5.61	0.08	0.34
2010	3323.92	1932.05	1391.87	14.90	9.44	0.08	0.37
2011	3361.86	1954.61	1407.25	14.09	5.15	0.08	0.38
2012	3390.06	1963.13	1426.93	14.82	6.93	0.08	0.39
2013	3409.91	1976.12	1433.79	16.33	6.75	0.08	0.39
2014	3420.51	1986.01	1434.50	12.69	4.69	0.08	0.40
2015	3436.24	2010.40	1425.84	13.76	4.62	0.08	0.40

注：1996年及以后为农业普查接轨数(下同)。
Notes:Since 1996,the relative targers were in line with the data of agricultural gereral survey (the same as the following tables).

12-3 农林牧渔业总产值
GROSS OUTPUT VALUE OF FARMING, FORESTRY, ANIMAL HUSBANDRY AND FISHERY

单位:亿元　　当年价格　　(At current price, 100 million yuan)

年 份 Year	农林牧渔业总产值 Gross Output Value of FFAF	农业 Farming	林业 Foresty	畜牧业 Animal Husbandry	渔业 Fishery	农林牧渔服务业 Service Industry for Farming, Forestry, Animal husbandry and Fishery
1949	10.72	7.22	0.69	0.97	0.10	
1952	16.59	12.08	0.79	1.48	0.18	
1957	28.59	20.55	1.46	3.81	0.46	
1962	33.66	26.52	1.71	3.61	0.46	
1965	47.48	37.44	1.98	6.02	0.51	
1970	51.27	40.62	2.07	6.41	0.92	
1975	74.68					
1978	84.46					
1979	109.85					
1980	94.95	64.70	7.28	17.29	1.46	
1981	111.68	82.78	6.47	14.88	1.61	
1982	128.35	95.32	7.24	17.97	2.12	
1983	134.09	97.53	7.29	20.05	2.96	
1984	169.20	123.09	7.54	26.51	4.79	
1985	192.32	129.61	8.15	39.08	8.18	
1986	219.10	146.79	8.75	43.86	10.77	
1987	249.68	160.13	9.97	54.86	14.19	
1988	297.51	175.12	10.98	80.80	18.83	
1989	335.04	198.56	11.75	91.47	20.66	
1990	402.23	252.92	14.15	98.04	23.88	
1991	405.04	247.01	16.81	102.19	25.06	
1992	435.42	265.53	17.36	110.37	27.59	
1993	501.17	301.99	22.39	134.02	42.77	
1994	786.84	481.82	26.47	219.53	59.01	
1995	988.53	612.12	28.33	268.09	79.98	
1996	1140.76	670.27	33.62	337.02	99.86	
1997	1243.68	711.91	37.33	381.40	113.04	
1998	1222.58	688.06	41.29	371.37	121.86	
1999	1126.10	645.98	40.86	311.43	127.83	
2000	1125.64	615.74	40.24	338.77	130.89	
2001	1172.82	658.26	27.11	352.63	134.82	
2002	1203.30	671.20	28.33	354.84	148.93	
2003	1342.09	733.36	34.78	383.71	170.43	
2004	1695.44	921.59	31.78	514.52	205.68	21.87
2005	1775.58	932.15	37.30	545.40	236.49	24.24
2006	1842.20	995.46	40.50	487.09	221.42	97.73
2008	2940.47	1395.76	49.69	1008.65	372.98	113.39
2009	2985.19	1511.49	57.67	881.78	413.14	121.11
2010	3501.99	1921.67	65.37	925.04	458.58	131.33
2011	4252.90	2299.30	86.10	1205.80	508.80	152.90
2012	4732.10	2488.10	100.10	1334.00	626.20	183.70
2013	5161.00	2678.10	122.00	1395.40	748.40	216.70
2014	5452.80	2761.70	157.00	1427.60	844.20	262.30
2015	5728.56	2780.37	180.60	1503.34	922.77	341.48

12-4 农、林、牧、渔业总产值指数
INDICES OF GROSS OUTPUT VALUE OF FARMING, FORESTRY, ANIMAL HUSBANDRY AND FISHERY

单位:% 上年=100 (preceding year=100)

年份 Year	合计 Total	农业 Farming	林业 Forestry	畜牧业 Animal Husbandry	渔业 Fishery	农林牧渔服务业 Service Industry for Farming, Forestry, Animal husbandry and Fishery
1978	104.00	103.10	104.90	107.60	94.20	
1980	88.80	83.70	102.80	108.10	111.30	
1985	106.30	101.70	103.00	127.80	133.30	
1986	103.40	100.60	98.50	107.30	129.80	
1987	102.70	101.20	104.50	101.00	120.10	
1988	97.20	93.90	90.60	105.40	105.60	
1989	105.00	104.50	101.60	105.20	108.30	
1990	107.10	108.40	106.00	104.90	106.70	
1991	100.70	97.66	118.80	104.23	104.94	
1992	107.50	107.50	103.27	108.00	110.10	
1993	115.10	113.73	128.97	121.43	155.02	
1994	157.00	159.55	118.27	163.80	137.93	
1995	125.63	127.04	106.99	122.12	135.54	
1996	115.40	109.50	118.67	125.71	124.87	
1997	109.02	106.21	111.04	113.17	113.20	
1998	98.30	96.65	110.61	97.37	107.80	
1999	92.11	93.88	98.95	83.86	104.90	
2000	99.96	95.32	98.48	108.78	102.39	
2001	104.19	106.91	67.37	104.09	103.00	
2002	102.60	101.97	104.50	100.63	110.47	
2003	111.53	109.26	122.77	108.14	114.44	
2004	126.33	125.67	91.37	134.09	120.68	
2005	104.73	101.15	117.37	106.00	114.98	110.84
2006	105.37	109.29	108.58	96.04	109.87	116.05
2007	124.68	115.73	103.36	140.88	140.38	108.33
2008	128.02	121.15	118.17	146.99	119.99	107.10
2009	101.52	108.29	116.10	87.42	110.77	106.81
2010	109.95	121.28	113.35	94.12	106.86	100.16
2011	121.40	119.70	137.70	130.40	110.90	116.40
2012	111.30	108.20	116.30	110.60	123.10	120.10
2013	109.06	107.64	121.88	104.60	119.51	117.96
2014	105.70	103.10	128.70	102.30	112.80	121.00
2015	105.70	104.70	129.40	100.30	105.70	130.90

注: 2009年畜牧业数据变动原因为与农普数衔接。
Note: 2009 data changes due to livestock and agricultural census data convergence.

12-5 农、林、牧、渔业总产值指数
INDICES OF GROSS OUTPUT VALUE OF FARMING, FORESTRY, ANIMAL HUSBANDRY AND FISHERY

单位:% 1978年=100 (year 1978 =100)

年份 Year	合计 Total	农业 Farming	林业 Forestry	牧业 Animal Husbandry	渔业 Fishery
1980	97.3	91.4	104.7	127.9	121.5
1981	108.2	102.4	95.4	138.2	134.1
1982	122.6	116.5	104.1	135.6	156.8
1983	122.7	115.9	105.3	160.5	181.2
1984	148.4	140.0	110.6	164.7	254.0
1985	157.7	142.4	114.0	206.2	338.6
1987	167.5	145.0	117.3	282.7	527.8
1988	162.9	136.1	106.3	285.5	557.3
1989	171.0	142.3	108.0	301.0	603.6
1990	183.1	154.2	114.5	315.7	644.0
1991	181.7	147.7	125.9	334.0	631.8
1992	194.4	158.7	120.1	360.7	689.3
1993	207.4	168.0	129.5	410.9	936.1
1994	227.8	175.0	152.0	461.7	1203.0
1995	259.9	195.3	156.0	535.1	1530.2
1996	277.6	198.0	168.5	611.1	1732.0
1997	304.0	213.4	179.3	671.6	2007.4
1998	307.3	209.1	204.6	682.3	2164.0
1999	309.5	220.2	196.7	627.9	2270.0
2000	318.1	226.3	194.2	650.4	2324.5
2001	327.6	238.7	141.6	669.6	2382.4
2002	334.2	233.1	145.9	700.2	2677.3
2003	351.8	237.2	167.2	730.8	2824.4
2004	374.7	257.9	153.9	760.8	2979.6
2005	392.4	260.9	180.6	806.4	3425.9
2006	171.8	137.9	58.7	502.2	2214.2
2007	214.3	159.6	60.7	707.4	3108.3
2008	274.3	193.3	72.0	1039.8	3729.8
2009	278.5	209.3	83.6	909.1	4131.4
2010	326.7	266.2	94.7	953.6	4585.8
2011	396.7	318.5	124.8	1243.1	5088.0
2012	441.4	344.6	145.1	1375.3	6262.0
2013	481.4	370.9	176.8	1438.6	7484.0
2014	508.6	382.5	227.6	1471.8	8442.0
2015	534.4	400.5	294.5	1476.2	8923.2

12-6 农、林、牧、渔业增加值(2015)
VALUE ADDED OF FARMING, FORESTRY, ANIMAL HUSBANDRY AND FISHERY(2015)

单位:亿元 (100 million yuan)

项 目	Item	合计 Total	农业 Farming	林业 Forestry	牧业 Animal Husbandry	渔业 Fishery	农林牧渔服务业 Service Industry for Farming, Forestry,Animal husbandry and Fishery
一、总产值(现价)	Gross Output Value(current price)	5728.56	2180.37	180.60	1503.33	922.77	341.48
二、中间消耗	Intermedium-Consumption	2311.23	1083.54	88.01	628.3	376.11	234.00
三、增加值	Value-Added	3417.32	1795.56	92.58	875.03	546.66	107.48

12-7 农作物播种面积

单位:千公顷

年 份 Year	总播种面积 Total Sown Areas	粮食作物 Grain Crops	小麦 Wheat	稻谷 Rice	薯类 Tubers	玉米 Corn	大豆 Soybean	经济作物 Economic Crops
1978	7931.05	5544.78	1122.28	2894.63	427.23	403.14	173.43	971.53
1980	7477.06	5352.04	1292.29	2708.22	387.46	406.91	138.94	977.58
1985	7331.71	5108.25	1331.42	2538.57	354.01	374.17	134.64	1280.89
1990	7361.14	5200.01	1352.10	2636.47	391.90	386.11	164.65	1343.23
1991	7423.92	5194.50	1347.53	2622.79	402.38	395.19	150.61	1414.37
1992	7183.83	4955.35	1287.91	2537.49	392.59	376.18	140.23	1405.87
1993	7125.47	4812.05	1271.23	2377.82	384.33	365.96	181.69	1381.64
1994	7181.43	4797.95	1225.60	2373.26	203.39	373.02	201.52	1456.00
1995	7431.71	4776.65	1179.93	2408.66	397.65	393.77	188.01	1683.56
1996	7579.01	4880.28	1230.14	2448.58	419.53	405.07	174.71	1676.71
1997	7739.21	4944.66	1276.52	2467.51	415.74	400.30	182.51	1689.03
1998	7695.98	4737.15	1212.08	2244.74	431.02	442.84	201.32	1703.80
1999	7788.66	4673.11	1074.43	2284.98	448.72	460.82	207.01	1739.07
2000	7584.07	4156.20	845.10	1995.29	467.61	424.10	224.75	1984.76
2001	7488.99	4015.73	735.85	1953.77	237.75	401.11	218.01	1972.36
2002	7281.61	3816.08	679.02	1888.75	430.61	384.04	217.82	1981.04
2003	7153.24	3572.74	603.43	1808.75	208.56	349.81	196.47	2083.26
2004	7225.13	3817.89	605.08	2084.02	403.79	357.49	186.05	2079.51
2005	7391.30	4068.05	730.61	2162.39	397.75	428.79	179.79	1974.56
2006	7100.59	3902.27	1016.93	1975.07	218.67	431.93	118.40	1825.40
2007	7130.01	3981.43	1096.25	1978.82	219.19	436.34	114.75	1787.79
2008	7272.33	3906.69	1000.57	1978.94	216.09	470.37	206.79	1973.85
2009	7527.50	4012.53	993.36	2045.08	237.93	507.28	195.76	2018.78
2010	7997.57	4068.37	1000.11	2038.17	274.29	531.38	104.76	2116.92
2011	8009.57	4122.07	1013.61	2036.17	303.64	549.66	152.97	2127.49
2012	8105.69	4180.05	1065.50	2017.88	299.65	593.34	95.31	2204.36
2013	8106.19	4258.40	1094.80	2101.15	303.27	573.47	86.67	2159.12
2014	8112.26	4370.34	1074.33	2143.95	308.81	642.38	98.90	2102.34
2015	7952.36	4466.03	1093.43	2188.46	317.61	687.85	147.78	2172.36

注:2006、2007年度农业普查衔接数据。

TOTAL SOWN AREAS OF FARM CROPS

(1 000 hectares)

棉花 Cotton	油菜籽 Rape-Seed	花生 Peanuts	芝麻 Sesame	黄红麻 Jute and Ambary	甘蔗 Sugar-cane	甜菜 Beet-Roots	烤烟 Flue-Cured Tobacco	其他作物 Others
593.19	165.27	34.14	102.71	8.39	2.31	0.13	24.75	1414.73
591.67	175.75	40.76	113.51	12.17	1.49	0.12	9.69	1147.44
464.97	361.42	65.94	173.31	94.17	7.85	0.08	37.67	942.56
455.92	744.31	63.75	126.85	27.33	8.07	0.01	46.35	817.90
461.55	610.10	61.59	128.17	20.42	8.47	0.02	56.83	815.05
507.19	534.41	64.73	126.32	18.15	10.64	0.02	72.76	822.61
486.06	522.14	79.70	127.24	22.41	15.00	0.03	64.32	931.78
497.58	615.87	86.97	114.77	11.70	15.73		38.69	927.48
502.03	838.82	91.91	110.04	10.83	15.97	0.03	41.16	953.50
474.38	855.26	90.82	107.72	8.59	16.59		51.92	1022.02
480.56	829.80	95.20	107.35	10.10	18.00		70.99	1105.52
431.58	887.01	121.48	113.62	7.94	19.97		48.47	1255.03
310.70	1003.64	143.87	127.14	4.30	23.34		48.32	1376.48
318.07	1158.94	193.42	143.82	3.14	22.17		48.10	1443.11
346.65	1118.06	210.06	129.93	2.65	18.88		40.43	1500.90
286.37	1155.25	206.04	138.88	5.13	19.18		42.90	1484.49
355.02	1174.63	201.11	124.00	2.97	17.24		39.45	1497.24
408.30	1186.10	173.03	111.20	1.36	10.01		39.94	1327.73
360.95	1178.65	171.71	102.52	0.98	9.95		43.68	1348.69
496.40	1001.20	140.10	97.24	0.69	3.70		32.13	1372.92
514.22	927.10	137.80	94.67	0.59	3.60		32.70	1360.79
542.96	1089.61	142.26	92.18	0.50	6.62		46.78	1391.79
460.08	1165.88	183.73	99.64	0.35	10.35		55.87	1496.19
480.05	1159.88	189.26	92.46	0.11	8.05		40.76	1812.28
488.66	1141.38	192.17	89.16	0.10	7.80		47.65	1760.01
472.87	1167.33	239.80	88.19	0.09	7.75	0.03	52.06	1721.28
415.59	1226.30	200.35	84.37	0.08	7.50	0.02	49.64	1688.67
344.81	1248.70	198.52	89.88	0.05	7.56	0.02	39.17	1639.58
264.74	1232.13	199.12	86.35	0.06	8.46	0.02	42.84	1459.14

Note:Statistics of 2006 and 2007 are linkage data of Second Agricluture Survey.

12-8 主要农作物播种面积和产量(2015)
TOTAL SOWN AREAS AND OUTPUT OF FARM CROPS(2015)

指 标	Item	播种面积(千公顷) Sown Areas (1 000 hectares)	总产量(万吨) Total Output(10000 ton)
农作物总播种面积	**Total Sown Areas of Farm Crops**	**7952.36**	
粮食作物总计	**Total Grain**	**4466.03**	**2703.28**
夏粮	Summer Grain	1389.92	504.45
小麦	Wheat	1093.43	420.93
大麦	Barley	28.78	9.76
蚕豌豆	Broad and Dea Bean	64.21	14.42
秋粮	Autumn Grain	3076.11	2198.83
稻谷	Rice	2188.46	1810.69
#中稻	#Semilate Rice	1283.04	1228.9
双季晚稻	Late Double- crop Rice	482.42	329.50
秋薯	Tubers	86.90	32.13
玉米	Corn	687.85	332.90
高粱	Sorghum	2.92	1.22
大豆	Soybeans	100.25	21.20
绿豆	#Green Beans	9.21	1.20
经济作物(全口径)	**Economic Crops**	**3486.33**	
棉花	Cotton	264.74	29.83
油料	Oil-Bearing Crops	1524.19	339.60
#花生	#Peanuts	199.12	67.91
油菜籽	Rapeseed	1232.13	255.19
芝麻	Sesame	86.35	14.51
麻类	Hemp Crops	8.84	2.19
#黄麻	#Jute	0.06	0.01
苎麻	Ramie	8.78	2.17
糖类	Sugar Crops	8.5	32.03
#甘蔗	#Sugarcane	8.46	31.99
烟叶	Tobacco Crops	47.62	8.68
药材	Crude Drugs	173.3	0.35
#蔬菜及食用菌面积	#Vegetable	1212.94	3851.96
瓜果类	Melon and Fruits	101.03	350.42
花卉种植面积	Flower Gardening	43.33	
其他农作物	Others	145.17	

12-9 主要农产品产量
OUTPUT OF MAJOR FARM CROPS

单位:万吨 (10 000 ton)

年 份 Year	粮 食 Grain	夏 粮 Summer Grain	秋 粮 Autumn Grain	棉 花 Cotton	油 料 Oil Bearing Crops	#花 生 Peanuts	#油菜籽 Rapeseed
1949	578.13	101.85	476.28	5.74	13.37	3.17	4.12
1952	747.54	148.81	598.73	12.17	22.34	4.56	7.09
1957	986.08	180.87	805.21	21.02	25.26	11.23	4.86
1962	960.41	246.34	714.07	14.22	18.30	3.81	4.29
1965	1241.34	255.01	986.33	38.29	22.32	5.15	6.76
1970	1268.67	187.06	1081.62	29.64	14.93	4.82	3.94
1975	1561.51	230.10	1331.41	40.61	21.44	5.12	10.65
1978	1725.60	315.04	1410.56	36.67	23.71	4.90	10.72
1980	1536.43	341.32	1195.11	31.63	20.58	5.85	11.59
1985	2216.13	429.58	1786.56	49.22	72.98	13.52	41.14
1990	2475.03	474.96	2000.07	51.73	95.75	12.79	70.90
1991	2244.10	476.20	1767.90	49.11	106.29	11.44	83.75
1992	2426.60	450.90	2022.83	60.99	99.74	15.72	70.86
1993	2325.70	471.87	1853.85	42.50	111.74	20.68	78.35
1994	2422.10	472.70	1949.40	45.00	137.77	24.81	98.07
1995	2463.84	447.20	2016.64	58.60	189.44	27.28	146.24
1996	2484.40	465.24	2019.16	43.01	181.82	30.77	134.88
1997	2634.40	542.60	2091.80	58.09	195.47	31.24	147.53
1998	2475.79	501.69	1974.10	32.50	216.69	42.87	154.76
1999	2451.88	392.71	2059.17	28.15	228.27	48.15	159.97
2000	2218.49	322.39	1896.10	30.43	269.98	53.46	192.40
2001	2138.49	319.14	1819.35	37.35	279.45	63.99	194.79
2002	2047.00	232.27	1841.73	32.26	245.29	72.25	151.40
2003	1921.02	255.65	1665.37	32.50	272.72	68.37	187.10
2004	2100.12	271.24	1828.96	39.54	314.38	63.19	235.12
2005	2177.38	302.49	1874.89	37.50	293.90	60.19	219.15
2006	2099.10	369.08	1730.02	55.20	254.45	48.40	191.83
2007	2185.44	406.44	1779.00	55.73	254.75	48.60	193.30
2008	2227.23	386.24	1840.99	51.30	283.56	49.41	214.89
2009	2309.10	398.45	1910.65	48.05	314.05	62.62	236.51
2010	2315.80	420.60	1895.18	47.18	311.80	64.45	232.57
2011	2388.53	425.83	1962.70	52.58	304.72	68.74	220.39
2012	2441.81	447.44	1994.37	53.15	319.66	74.34	230.03
2013	2501.30	501.00	2000.30	45.97	333.17	68.11	250.47
2014	2584.16	505.60	2078.56	35.95	341.73	69.06	257.16
2015	2703.28	504.45	2198.83	29.83	339.60	67.91	255.19

注：2006、2007年为农业普查衔接数据。
Note:Statistics 2006 and 2007 are linkage data of Second Agriculture Survey.

12-10 人均占有主要农产品产量
PER CAPITA OUTPUT OF MAJOR FARM PRODUCTS

单位:千克/人 (kg/person)

年 份 Year	粮 食 Grain	棉 花 Cotton	油 料 Oil Bearing Crops	猪、牛、羊肉 Output of Pork, Beef and Mutton	水产品 Output of Aquatic Products
1952	275	4.5	8.2		2.9
1957	327	7.0	8.4		4.0
1962	302	4.4	5.8		2.3
1965	359	11.1	6.4		3.3
1970	319	7.5	3.8		2.8
1975	357	9.3	4.9		2.6
1978	379	8.1	5.2		2.4
1980	330	6.8	4.4	11.9	2.9
1985	452	10.0	14.9	20.7	7.6
1990	467	9.8	18.1	27.7	13.4
1991	415	8.9	19.6	29.0	12.9
1992	443	11.1	18.2	31.9	14.9
1993	416	7.6	20.0	35.3	18.1
1994	431	8.0	24.5	41.8	23.0
1995	429	10.2	33.0	48.6	26.3
1996	428	7.4	31.4	40.4	30.1
1997	450	9.9	33.4	44.4	34.6
1998	419	5.5	36.7	44.2	37.0
1999	413	5.0	38.4	44.8	38.6
2000	372	5.1	45.3	45.5	39.3
2001	358	6.3	46.8	48.3	40.5
2002	342	5.4	41.0	49.4	45.4
2003	316	6.5	45.5	51.4	47.8
2004	349	6.6	52.3	54.1	50.2
2005	361	6.2	48.7	56.8	52.8
2006	365	7.4	46.2	42.0	46.7
2007	360	9.2	42.0	42.5	49.1
2008	390	9.0	49.7	49.8	54.9
2009	404	8.4	54.9	53.5	59.1
2010	405	8.2	54.5	54.6	61.7
2011	416	9.2	53.1	55.2	62.1
2012	423	9.2	55.4	59.7	67.4
2013	431	7.9	57.5	61.9	70.8
2014	445	6.2	58.8	63.7	74.6
2015	462	5.1	58.0	77.1	77.9

注:按全省常住人口计算的人均占有量。
Notes:The data is caculated by resident population.

12-11 蚕、茶、果生产情况
STATISTICS ON SILKWORM COCOONS, TEA AND FRUITS

指 标	Item	1995	2000	2005	2010	2012	2013	2014	2015
蚕茧产量 (万吨)	Silkworm Cocoons (10 000 tons)	2.24	1.22	1.07	0.71	0.82	0.77	0.64	0.67
茶叶产量 (万吨)	Tea (10 000 tons)	3.90	6.37	8.50	16.57	20.70	22.20	25.03	26.88
红茶	Red Tea	0.12		0.65	1.54	2.17	2.38	2.75	3.09
绿茶	Green Tea	3.05	5.15	6.72	13.71	16.50	17.04	18.65	19.45
其他茶	Others			0.18	0.33	0.46	0.44	0.39	0.31
园林水果产量 (万吨)	Garden fruit production (10 000 tons)	114.70	215.68	260.79	437.13	541.72	569.42	614.25	615.84
#苹果	#Apples	3.21	3.02	1.24	0.97	1.06	1.02	0.99	1.31
柑桔	Citrus	58.14	94.62	146.26	301.04	385.31	400.39	437.12	426.66
梨	Pears	26.02		46.80	48.05	53.64	56.31	54.63	50.92
葡萄	Grapes			4.97	13.12	20.49	23.68	27.15	27.07
桃子	Peaches	14.59	30.87	46.88	60.75	67.42	72.49	77.81	93.16
猕猴桃	Kiwi fruit			0.85	1.06	1.95	2.10	2.32	2.65
红枣	Dates			2.02	2.91	3.21	3.39	3.62	4.00
柿子	Persimmons			4.77	5.05	5.83	6.61	6.78	6.64
茶园面积 (千公顷)	Area of Tea Plantations (1 000 hectares)	113.39	121.02	138.43	214.61	260.13	291.77	303.80	324.11
#当年采摘面积	#Pick Area	7.42		101.62	155.92	189.36	205.39	218.90	231.27
果园 (千公顷)	Area of Orchards (1 000 hectares)	199.80	233.93	265.05	376.77	400.75	403.55	423.26	413.41
#苹果园	#Apples	13.66	8.98	3.30	0.17	2.01	1.63	1.33	1.23
柑桔园	Citrus	98.39	99.13	143.15	229.19	243.59	239.66	245.58	239.97
梨园	Pears	35.42	33.49	35.90	36.60	37.35	39.35	41.75	38.81
葡萄园	Grapes			4.77	5.57	10.21	10.01	12.65	11.90

12-12 林业生产情况
STATISTICS ON FORESTRY

单位:公顷 (hectare)

指标名称	Item	2013	2014	2015
造林面积	Build Forestry Areas	246858	243799	246911
用材林	Material Forests	83439	85622	95377
经济林	Economic Forests	58163	51338	49235
防护林	Windbreak Forests	103083	105254	99746
薪炭林	Firewood Forests	112	13	327
特种用途林	Forests for Soecial Puppse	2061	1572	2226
更新造林	Updateing Areas	2952	3589	3918
四旁(零星)植树	Planting	12014	13786	14449
育苗面积	Raise Seedlings Areas	39353	39658	50269
本年新增	The Nw Seedlings	8181	9938	
主要林产品产量(吨)	Output of Forestry Products (ton)			
生漆	Lacquer	6897	6298	4092
油桐籽	Tung-Oil Seeds	25290	24895	24081
乌桕籽	Tea-oil Seeds	18344	18503	14136
油茶籽	Tallow Seeds	87483	127419	141857
五倍子	Gallnut	3710	3241	2937
棕片	palm pieces	3656	3714	2183
松脂	Turpentine	39867	44994	46174
竹笋干	Bamboo Shoots	8428	12299	18237
核桃	Walnut	93987	94241	94357
板栗	Chestnut	410983	414049	412402
花椒	Pepper	3324	3475	3693
八角	Star anise	18	23	29
香菇	Mushroom(吨)	95996	105849	125828
黑木耳	Jew's-ear (吨)	23784	25624	26715
木材采伐量(万立方米)	Output of Timber Cut(10 000 cu.m)	388.98	333	398.5
竹材采伐量(万根)	Output of Bamboo Cut (10 000 cu.m)	3297.30	3414	3123.7

12-13 畜牧业生产情况
STATISTICS ON LIVESTOCK

指 标	Item	2000	2005	2010	2012	2013	2014	2015
牲畜年末存栏头数 (万头)	(10 000 heads)							
大牲畜	Large Animals	431.50	384.32	327.54	334.90	345.29	353.19	362.23
牛	Cattles and Buffalloes	428.38	382.14	326.00	333.60	344.07	352.25	361.33
马	Horses	1.83	1.58	0.92	0.75	0.61	0.59	0.54
驴	Donkeys	0.98	0.44	0.46	0.36	0.41	0.26	0.29
骡	Mules	0.30	0.16	0.16	0.11	0.18	0.07	0.58
猪	Hogs	2132.79	2289.05	2476.10	2543.20	2566.07	2550.67	2497.14
羊 (万只)	Sheep (10 000 heads)	224.80	337.66	401.70	435.10	462.91	469.89	465.70
山羊	Goats	223.55	336.97	401.23	434.50	462.75	469.73	465.60
绵羊	Sheep	1.25	0.69	0.47	0.60	0.15	0.16	0.20
畜产品产量	**Livestock Products**							
猪牛羊出栏头数 (万头)	Hogs, Sheep and Goats (10 000heads)	3023.96	3841.82	4459.80	4823.50	5011.74	5169.09	5073.70
当年肉猪出栏头数	Hogs	2714.44	3345.18	3827.40	4180.80	4356.43	4475.11	4363.23
当年出售和自宰的肉用牛	Ox by Sold and Killed	104.26	115.49	123.10	131.70	140.28	152.11	159.87
当年出售和自宰的肉用羊(万只)	Sheep by Slod and Killed (10 000heads)	205.26	381.15	509.30	511.00	515.03	541.87	550.60
肉类产量 (万吨)	Output of Meat (10 000 tons)	271.19	342.63	379.42	412.30	430.08	440.44	431.93
猪肉	Pork	215.84	271.23	287.00	317.30	330.60	339.60	331.50
牛肉	Beef	13.80	16.91	17.70	18.90	20.17	21.87	23.00
羊肉	Mutton	3.04	6.00	8.10	8.20	8.22	8.61	8.80
禽肉	Poultry	38.51	48.49	65.80	67.00	70.11	69.20	68.60
其他禽产品产量 (吨)	Others (tons)							
牛奶产量	Milk Cow	56400	122223	140000	153000	154048	161000	168500
绵羊毛产量	Sheep's Wool	34.57	4.00		3.30	3.56	4.00	7.00
山羊毛产量	Goats' Wool	52.17	16.00	13.73	74.90	73.82	74.00	104.00
蜂蜜	Cashmere	9187	7890	10182	20071	23288.8	26504	27430.00
禽蛋 (万吨)	Poultry Eggs (10 000 tons)	102.56	121.25	132.60	139.40	145.05	155.06	165.29

12-14 水产品产量
OUTPUT OF AQUATIC PRODUCTS

指 标	Item	2000	2005	2010	2012	2013	2014	2015
水产品产量 (万吨)	**Output of Aquatic Products (10 000 tons)**	**234.34**	**318.03**	**353.00**	**388.94**	**410.37**	**433.30**	**455.80**
鱼类产量	Fish	219.88	277.82	308.42	331.46	349.18	359.68	377.88
虾蟹产量	Shrimp, Prawn and Crab	7.51	7.71	35.93	46.25	51.00	56.83	69.66
贝类产量	Shell Fish	5.38	1.13	4.32	5.91	5.47	4.08	3.68
其它类产量	Others	1.58		3.66	5.32	4.72	5.62	4.66
养殖产量	Artificially Cultivated	194.84	274.45	321.56	350.23	371.06	399.64	436.79
捕捞产量	Captured	39.50	43.58	31.44	38.71	39.32	33.66	19.10
养殖按水面分类产量(万吨)	Grouped by waters (10 000 tons)	193.92	274.45	321.56	350.23	371.06	399.64	436.79
湖 泊	Lakes	20.84	28.44	33.03	33.17	32.96	33.77	32.70
水 库	Reservoir	8.15	12.52	19.96	19.58	19.56	20.66	19.94
塘 堰	Pools	33.05	38.87	26.61	31.03	32.60	35.07	33.35
精 养 池	Fine Cultivated Pools	122.96	177.54	224.86	264.23	283.98	297.99	322.29
河 沟	Rivers	2.90	6.03	2.03	1.84	1.78	1.71	1.50
其 它	Others	6.02	8.03	1.33	1.26	1.32	1.31	1.36
鱼苗产量 (亿尾)	Young Fry (100 million tons)	444.01	521.39	750.00	773.00	901.00	1050	1159
鱼种产量 (万吨)	Advanced Fry (10 000 tons)	38.79	54.04	82.03	94.30	100.26	110.37	116.01
投放鱼种量 (万吨)	Volume of Advanced Fry (10 000 tons)	40.16	57.08	80.74	92.31	97.54	104.38	110.35
水产养殖面积 (千公顷)	**Aquatic Raised Areas (1 000 hectares)**							
湖 泊	Lakes	196.46	175.34	196.17	212.73	207.66	190.07	187.32
水 库	Reservoir	166.07	102.18	110.77	140.35	150.53	106.64	103.77
塘 堰	Pools	134.79	119.20	87.44	92.36	97.36	99.66	97.66
精 养 池	Fine Cultivated Pools	156.33	220.37	252.96	275.13	275.15	284.75	292.94
河 沟	Rivers	20.86	21.89	5.71	23.56	22.91	22.40	4.52
其 它	Others	32.92	34.56	3.67	25.40	28.91	21.68	2.46

注：2008年为国家核定数据。

Note:Data for 2008 approved a number of countries.

12-15 农业现代化情况
STATISTICS ON AGRICULTURAL MODERNIZATION

单位：千公顷

指 标	Item	2000	2005	2010	2012	2013	2014	2015
农业机械化情况	**Statistics on Agricultural Machinery**							
机耕面积	Areas Ploughed by Tractors	1969.55	2015.93	4517.14	5118.70	5459.02	5847.00	6036.19
机播面积	Seeded Areas by Tractors	255.69	233.66	815.61	1419.31	1821.53	2091.28	2335.23
机械植保面积	Plant Protection Area by Tractors	2426.95	2848.66	4074.38	4430.36	4611.68	4792.82	4850.88
机械收获面积	Harvest Area by Tractors	643.65	1407.62	2780.52	3461.33	3746.95	4179.37	4233.67
农村电气化情况	**Electrification of Rural Area**							
农村用电量 (亿千瓦小时)	Electricity Consumed in Rural Area (100 million kWh)	60.86	70.09	109.78	121.23	130.14	142.23	149.10
农用物资使用情况	**Used Agricultural Product Material**							
化肥施用量(折纯量) (万吨)	Consumption of Chemical Fertilizers (10 000 tons)	247.08	285.83	350.77	357.66	351.93	348.27	333.87
每亩耕地施用化肥(折纯量)(千克)	Per Mu Consumption of Chemical Fertilizers (kg)	50.17	60.28	70.35	70.34	68.81	67.88	64.77
农用塑料薄膜使用量 (万吨)	Used Plastic Film (10 000 tons)		5.46	6.38	6.98	6.63	6.92	7.13
农用柴油使用量 (万吨)	Used Diesel Oil (10 000 tons)	107.81	41.31	58.29	66.48	65.73	67.33	65.61
农药使用量 (万吨)	Used Agricultural Chemical Insecticides (10 000 tons)	11.54	11.02	14.00	13.59	12.72	12.61	12.07
农田水利情况	**Irrigation and Water Conservancy**							
有效灌溉面积	Effective Irrigation Area	2072.53	2064.59	2187.17	2252.91	2291.17	2325.84	2359.60
#机电排灌面积	#Electrical Well		1236.11	1320.53	1339.66	1357.19	1416.82	1436.61
占有效灌溉面积的比重(%)	Rate in Effective Irrigation Area (%)		59.9	60.4	59.5	59.2	60.9	60.9

12-16 主要农业机械和农产品加工机械拥有量

年 份 Year	农业机械总动力 (万千瓦) Total Power of Agricultural Machinery(1000 kW)	农用大中型拖拉机 (万台) Large and Medium Agricultural Tractors(10 000 units)	农用小型及手扶拖拉机(万台) Mini and Walking Agricultural Tractors (10 000 units)	农用排灌动力机械 (万千瓦) Machinery for Machinery for Agricultural Drainage and Irrigation (1000 kW)	农用水泵 (万台) Agricultual Water Pump(10 000 units)
1978	616.07	2.80	7.75		21.22
1980	772.53	3.60	10.90		23.70
1985	910.94	5.72	14.62	55.22	21.06
1990	1099.62	8.60	17.70	99.28	24.30
1991	1120.92	8.60	18.30	362.88	24.10
1992	1120.90	8.45	17.92	368.46	23.98
1993	1108.99	7.89	16.99	360.75	23.95
1994	1136.13	7.38	15.72	368.55	24.37
1995	1174.34	7.12	15.47	384.48	26.56
1996	1222.20	7.03	16.47	401.49	27.62
1997	1276.04	7.11	18.50	408.09	28.76
1998	1325.90	7.13	20.60	410.77	29.59
1999	1363.70	7.03	22.67	419.83	32.57
2000	1414.00	6.82	23.63	434.49	35.47
2001	1469.24	6.58	24.88	450.40	40.46
2002	1557.40	6.64	26.68	461.86	43.89
2003	1661.70	6.59	28.23	469.45	45.63
2004	1768.60	6.83	32.09	484.71	50.82
2005	2057.37	7.66	48.39	518.49	55.92
2006	2263.15	8.50	55.69	531.33	71.42
2007	2551.08	9.30	74.12	541.33	82.70
2008	2796.99	10.42	85.23	559.24	87.73
2009	3057.24	11.85	90.84	594.17	87.70
2010	3371.00	12.71	99.10	663.92	85.40
2011	3571.23	13.08	106.48	673.50	89.48
2012	3842.16	13.84	111.56	668.19	103.30
2013	4081.05	14.94	114.12	714.05	105.63
2014	4292.90	15.85	112.98	732.89	110.60
2015	4468.12	16.84	113.81	749.75	110.13

NUMBER OF AGRICULTURAL MACHINERY AND MACHINERY FOR PROCESSING FARM PRODUCTS OWNED AT YEAR-END

喷灌机械 (万套) Machinery for Sprinkling (10 000 units)	联合收割机 (台) Combine Hearvesters (unit)	机动脱粒机 (万台) Motorized Huller (10 000 units)	机动喷雾(粉)器 (万部) Motorized Duster (10 000 units)	饲料粉碎机 (万台) Fodder Grinder (10 000 units)	大中型拖拉机配套农具 (万部) Large and Medium Tractors Towing Farm Machinery (10 000 units)	小型拖拉机配套农具 (万部) Mini Tractors Towing Farm Machinery (10 000 units)
0.30	425	15.00	0.78	7.78	4.66	4.92
1.08	602	17.40	1.00	8.20	4.99	7.20
0.73	479	15.22	0.60	5.90	2.39	4.95
0.31	2335	12.60	3.70	5.60	2.70	10.14
0.34	455	12.50	4.60	5.55	3.00	11.87
0.60	390	12.35	4.70	5.32	3.86	12.30
0.48	345	11.97	4.77	5.12	3.05	11.64
0.47	346	11.39	5.29	5.50	2.91	12.38
0.72	312	11.25	6.44	5.32	2.85	15.48
0.72	553	12.33	6.74	8.70	3.05	23.02
7.75	1521	11.11	7.36	8.79	3.63	29.46
0.80	2338	11.56	8.27	9.65	4.33	37.75
0.71	2559	11.56	8.00	10.48	4.80	42.84
0.85	2704	12.25	8.70	10.73	4.81	37.48
1.01	3363	12.79	9.07	12.60	5.22	41.12
1.08	5722	12.81	9.72	9.59	5.97	46.44
1.17	6708	12.62	10.26	12.33	6.21	49.03
1.20	10585	12.88	11.86	15.01	7.45	59.31
1.55	16085	14.33	15.98	23.88	9.36	96.69
1.75	22407	12.54	25.44	26.37	11.18	111.02
1.81	29803	13.14	30.58	27.04	12.96	149.08
2.23	34983	12.99	35.41	29.94	15.49	169.69
2.21	41904	15.37	38.40	33.46	20.37	178.55
2.52	50509	18.09	43.56	35.50	21.49	204.66
2.88	58398	23.33	48.73	36.23	24.01	211.97
4.77	66860	24.28	55.07	32.30	25.74	214.51
10.73	73808	26.43	60.41	32.87	28.00	215.42
11.04	81410	32.03	72.26	33.09	31.80	223.01
	88704	35.21	73.02		37.13	222.44

12-17 市、州乡村从业人员
RURAL EMPLOYMENT IN CITIES AND PREFECTURES

单位：万人

市、州	Municipalities and Prefecrures	2014	农林牧渔业从业人员 Employment in Farming, Forestry, Animal Husbandry and Fishery	2015	农林牧渔业从业人员 Employment in Farming, Forestry, Animal Husbandry and Fishery
全　省	**Province**	**2308.72**	**865.21**	**2300.88**	**869.32**
武汉市	Wuhan	145.83	49.91	136.42	44.52
黄石市	Huangshi	92.74	20.82	97.49	27.20
十堰市	Shiyan	137.78	52.83	138.73	53.21
荆州市	Jingzhou	240.36	100.68	242.89	99.79
宜昌市	Yichang	164.89	69.30	164.99	68.31
襄阳市	Xiangyang	221.32	77.58	220.84	77.13
鄂州市	Ezhou	39.96	18.56	39.97	18.57
荆门市	Jingmen	108.46	36.64	109.66	36.06
孝感市	Xiaogan	244.87	79.72	245.35	78.40
黄冈市	Huanggang	328.67	127.65	331.35	132.49
咸宁市	Xianning	111.84	41.11	113.19	44.10
随州市	Suizhou	107.17	40.66	106.87	38.58
恩施自治州	Enshi	195.23	91.16	183.44	87.46
仙桃市	Xiantao	66.88	24.26	67.28	29.35
天门市	Tianmen	60.67	17.50	60.58	17.33
潜江市	Qianjiang	39.35	14.14	39.32	15.32
神农架林区	Shennongjia	2.70	2.69	2.51	1.50

12-18 市、州耕地面积
CULTIVATED AREA OF CITIES AND PREFECTURES

市、州	Municipalities and Prefecrures	2000		2010		2014		2015	
		年末耕地面积(千公顷) Cultivated Area at Year-end(1 000 hectares)	人平耕地(亩) Cultivated Area Per Capita(Mu)	年末耕地面积(千公顷) Cultivated Area at Year-end(1000 hectares)	人平耕地(亩) Cultivated Area Per Capita(Mu)	年末耕地面积(千公顷) Cultivated Area at Year-end(1000 hectares)	人平耕地(亩) Cultivated Area Per Capita(Mu)	年末耕地面积(千公顷) Cultivated Area at Year-end(1000 hectares)	人平耕地(亩) Cultivated Area Per Capita(Mu)
全 省	**Province**	**3282.96**	**0.83**	**3323.92**	**0.87**	**3420.51**	**0.88**	**3436.24**	**0.88**
武汉市	Wuhan	217.84	0.40	204.79	0.31	197.25	0.29	196.46	0.28
黄石市	Huangshi	79.32	0.48	89.80	0.55	89.24	0.55	89.41	0.55
十堰市	Shiyan	181.54	0.79	169.91	0.76	175.54	0.78	174.92	0.78
宜昌市	Yichang	257.71	0.94	230.14	0.85	267.80	0.98	269.39	0.98
襄阳市	Xiangyang	412.96	1.09	436.91	1.19	451.58	1.21	453.87	1.21
鄂州市	Ezhou	40.28	0.59	41.05	0.59	40.40	0.57	46.27	0.66
荆门市	Jingmen	256.53	1.29	255.69	1.33	266.92	1.39	268.66	1.39
孝感市	Xiaogan	247.10	0.74	261.27	0.81	267.88	0.83	267.91	0.82
荆州市	Jingzhou	432.58	1.03	464.80	1.22	469.39	1.23	470.17	1.24
黄冈市	Huanggang	312.36	0.65	337.52	0.82	344.21	0.83	351.00	0.84
咸宁市	Xianning	145.94	0.81	155.85	0.95	167.90	1.01	167.37	1.00
随州市	Suizhou	136.58	0.85	144.94	1.00	143.39	0.99	143.39	0.98
恩施州	Enshi	280.59	1.11	255.89	1.17	261.33	1.18	260.37	1.17
仙桃市	Xiantao	98.68	1.01	90.59	1.16	90.54	1.16	90.33	1.17
潜江市	Qianjiang	66.99	1.01	70.22	1.11	72.18	1.14	72.19	1.13
天门市	Tianmen	107.62	1.00	108.36	1.15	110.16	1.28	109.93	1.28
神农架	Shennongjia	8.35	1.54	6.19	1.22	4.80	0.94	4.60	0.90

12-19 市、州农、林、牧、渔业总产值及指数
GROSS OUTPUT VALUE AND ITS INDICES OF FARMING, FORESTRY, ANIMAL HUSBANDRY AND FISHERY OF CITIES AND PREFECTURES

市、州	Municipalities and Prefecrures	绝对数(亿元) Absolute Number (100 milion yuan)					指数(%) Indices (%)				
		2000	2010	2013	2014	2015	2000	2010	2013	2014	2015
全　省	**Province**	**1125.64**	**3501.99**	**5161.00**	**5452.80**	**5728.56**	**102.8**	**110.0**	**109.1**	**105.7**	**105.7**
武汉市	Wuhan	126.94	281.09	530.27	559.44	620.28	105.3	111.6	129.1	105.5	104.9
黄石市	Huangshi	27.63	83.91	133.76	147.01	158.75	104.2	115.3	108.9	109.9	105.3
十堰市	Shiyan	44.65	133.19	250.15	273.11	286.78	111.1	119.0	117.7	109.2	105.2
荆州市	Jingzhou	147.69	423.79	578.34	616.16	631.45	91.0	110.1	108.1	106.5	105.2
宜昌市	Yichang	97.19	294.05	555.63	581.45	617.68	102.6	117.4	110.5	104.6	105.4
襄阳市	Xiangyang	158.15	409.04	678.91	704.46	725.55	93.5	111.8	108.7	103.8	105.2
鄂州市	Ezhou	13.92	92.82	138.50	143.13	149.83	106.7	115.8	109.3	103.3	105.6
荆门市	Jingmen	100.13	253.14	337.93	351.67	365.84	103.0	109.2	106.7	104.1	105.4
孝感市	Xiaogan	111.63	306.61	452.40	470.53	476.88	90.7	117.7	108.3	104.0	105.2
黄冈市	Huanggang	127.48	374.79	532.22	559.63	593.01	102.4	115.0	105.2	105.2	105.6
咸宁市	Xianning	52.87	168.52	264.70	280.29	301.15	104.5	120.2	111.4	105.9	105.4
随州市	Suizhou	58.06	150.29	216.72	225.93	244.36	141.5	113.9	111.0	104.2	105.3
恩施州	Enshi	76.78	174.25	227.22	237.01	247.39	102.3	114.3	108.6	104.3	105.3
仙桃市	Xiaotao	39.01	94.41	136.29	142.59	147.49	102.2	113.2	106.6	104.6	105.4
天门市	Tianmen	33.15	80.94	108.58	113.73	129.98	100.4	111.6	107.3	104.7	105.1
潜江市	Qianjiang	30.58	85.55	109.28	114.24	119.24	101.9	122.2	107.8	104.5	105.2
神农架	Shennongjia	0.99	2.59	3.56	3.77	4.07	87.1	112.6	112.4	106.1	104.6

注：本表产值按当年价格计算，指数按不变价格计算；全省合计数为调整数，故市、州相加不等于合计数。
Notes:The data of in this table is caculated at current prices of output valul,and the data of indices is calulaled at constort prices therefore,the total of provice is an adiusted number,and that of municipalities and prefecture if added are not egual to the total number.

12-20 市、州农、林、牧、渔业产值(现价)(2015)

GROSS OUTPUT VALUE OF FARMING, FORESTRY, ANIMAL HUSBANDRY AND FISHERY OF CITIES AND PREFECTURES (AT CURRENT PRICES)(2015)

单位:亿元 (100 million yuan)

市、州	Municipalities and Prefecrures	合计 Total	农业 Farming	林业 Forestry	牧业 Animal Husbandry	渔业 Fishery	农林牧渔服务业 Service Industry for Farming, Forestry, Animal Husbandry and Fishery
全省	**Province**	**5728.56**	**2780.37**	**180.6**	**1503.34**	**922.77**	**341.48**
武汉市	Wuhan	620.28	359.16	9.95	135.27	91.81	24.09
黄石市	Huangshi	158.75	61.71	3.14	45.52	45.91	2.47
十堰市	Shiyan	286.78	164.49	12.79	91.68	16.40	1.42
荆州市	Jingzhou	631.45	257.99	7.77	134.58	209.40	21.71
宜昌市	Yichang	617.68	318.37	7.43	231.07	44.40	16.40
襄阳市	Xiangyang	725.55	334.90	7.80	318.46	31.28	33.12
鄂州市	Ezhou	149.83	41.37	2.55	36.88	68.61	0.42
荆门市	Jingmen	365.84	155.72	6.00	123.46	70.97	9.69
孝感市	Xiaogan	476.88	201.18	10.81	171.41	84.19	9.29
黄冈市	Huanggang	593.01	284.47	10.33	213.48	71.37	13.37
咸宁市	Xianning	301.15	154.11	15.89	71.35	57.63	2.17
随州市	Suizhou	244.36	131.15	5.37	88.79	11.63	7.42
恩施州	Enshi	247.39	139.19	10.07	94.88	1.23	2.02
仙桃市	Xiaotao	147.49	53.31	1.35	32.72	57.43	2.68
天门市	Tianmen	129.98	60.40	0.65	29.86	32.17	6.90
潜江市	Qianjiang	119.24	46.29	4.41	33.91	32.25	2.38
神农架	Shennongjia	4.07	2.48	0.46	1.05	0.03	0.05

12-21 市、州农、林、牧、渔业中间消耗(2015)
INTERMEDIATE-CONSUMPTION OF OF FARMING, FORESTRY, ANIMAL HUSBANDRY AND FISHERY OF CITIES AND PREFECTURES(2015)

单位：亿元 (100 million yuan)

市、州	Municipalities and Prefecrures	合计 Total	农业 Farming	林业 Forestry	牧业 Animal Husbandry	渔业 Fishery	农林牧渔服务业 Service Industry for Farming, Forestry, Animal Husbandry and Fishery
全省	**Province**	**2311.23**	**984.84**	**88.01**	**628.30**	**376.11**	**233.97**
武汉市	Wuhan	250.25	136.62	4.70	65.05	35.80	8.08
黄石市	Huangshi	48.42	17.59	0.80	16.46	12.87	0.70
十堰市	Shiyan	128.61	70.13	6.57	44.83	6.45	0.62
荆州市	Jingzhou	267.05	96.99	2.03	61.56	96.14	10.32
宜昌市	Yichang	247.36	124.77	3.19	93.79	18.13	7.49
襄阳市	Xiangyang	305.42	134.59	2.76	139.16	13.78	15.13
鄂州市	Ezhou	64.84	21.50	1.88	13.44	27.75	0.26
荆门市	Jingmen	158.92	59.34	2.12	62.84	30.99	3.64
孝感市	Xiaogan	212.68	83.52	4.80	78.22	41.61	4.53
黄冈市	Huanggang	203.93	94.74	5.89	79.33	20.07	3.90
咸宁市	Xianning	121.10	63.46	5.94	29.95	21.04	0.71
随州市	Suizhou	106.48	61.66	2.01	37.19	3.75	1.86
恩施州	Enshi	102.28	57.68	4.55	38.93	0.34	0.77
仙桃市	Xiaotao	59.50	17.92	1.05	14.57	24.95	1.00
天门市	Tianmen	48.53	25.54	0.25	10.56	9.81	2.37
潜江市	Qianjiang	48.11	16.24	0.77	22.87	7.11	1.12
神农架	Shennongjia	1.99	1.24	0.18	0.52	0.02	0.02

注：全省中间消耗为省级核算数，故市、州相加不等于合计数。

Note: The statistics of Intermedium Consumption is checked by Provincial Statistical Burea,thus the total of municipalities and prefecture do not equal to the total of the whole province.

12-22 市、州农、林、牧、渔业增加值(2015)
VALUE ADDED OF FARMING, FORESTRY, ANIMAL HUSBANDRY AND FISHERY OF CITIES AND PREFECTURES(2015)

单位：亿元 (100 million yuan)

市、州	Municipalities and Prefecrures	合计 Total	农业 Farming	林业 Forestry	牧业 Animal Husbandry	渔业 Fishery	农林牧渔服务业 Service Industry for Farming, Forestry, Animal Husbandry and Fishery
全省	**Province**	**3417.32**	**1795.53**	**92.58**	**875.04**	**546.66**	**107.51**
武汉市	Wuhan	370.04	222.54	5.25	70.22	56.01	16.02
黄石市	Huangshi	110.33	44.12	2.34	29.07	33.04	1.77
十堰市	Shiyan	158.18	94.36	6.22	46.85	9.95	0.80
荆州市	Jingzhou	364.40	161.00	5.74	73.02	113.26	11.39
宜昌市	Yichang	370.31	193.60	4.25	137.29	26.27	8.91
襄阳市	Xiangyang	420.13	200.31	5.04	179.29	17.50	17.99
鄂州市	Ezhou	84.99	19.88	0.66	23.44	40.86	0.16
荆门市	Jingmen	206.92	96.38	3.89	60.62	39.98	6.05
孝感市	Xiaogan	264.21	117.65	6.02	93.19	42.58	4.76
黄冈市	Huanggang	389.08	189.72	4.44	134.15	51.31	9.46
咸宁市	Xianning	180.05	90.65	9.95	41.40	36.58	1.47
随州市	Suizhou	137.88	69.49	3.36	51.60	7.87	5.56
恩施州	Enshi	145.11	81.50	5.51	55.95	0.89	1.25
仙桃市	Xiaotao	87.99	35.39	0.29	18.15	32.47	1.68
天门市	Tianmen	81.45	34.87	0.40	19.30	22.35	4.53
潜江市	Qianjiang	71.14	30.05	3.63	11.05	25.14	1.26
神农架	Shennongjia	2.07	1.24	0.28	0.53	0.01	0.02

注：全省数为省级核算数，故分市州汇总不等于全省。

Note: The statistics of the whole province is checked by Provincial Statistical Burea, thus the total of municipalities and prefecture do not equal to the total of the whole province.

12-23 市、州主要农作物产量(2015)

单位：万吨

市、州	Municipalities and Prefecrures	粮食 Grain	稻谷 Rice	小麦 Wheat	玉米 Corn	薯类 Tubers	大豆 Soybean	棉花 Cotton
全省	**Province**	**2703.28**	**1839.76**	**420.93**	**332.90**	**99.47**	**100.25**	**29.83**
武汉市	Wuhan	127.00	102.83	5.80	10.48	3.84	2.14	1.65
黄石市	Huangshi	65.94	50.53	3.77	4.84	4.91	0.85	0.41
十堰市	Shiyan	117.64	25.90	24.17	37.82	22.20	4.88	0.01
荆州市	Jingzhou	410.74	340.35	40.13	16.48	4.84	5.88	7.71
宜昌市	Yichang	170.79	71.55	15.13	53.43	26.10	2.26	1.62
襄阳市	Xiangyang	505.32	186.70	215.54	79.17	19.23	1.52	2.58
鄂州市	Ezhou	36.74	31.28	1.07	0.28	2.58	0.63	0.39
荆门市	Jingmen	278.18	192.94	48.02	23.41	7.52	5.02	2.14
孝感市	Xiaogan	231.02	183.51	31.53	4.33	7.51	2.12	2.35
黄冈市	Huanggang	331.99	273.08	17.83	6.41	29.72	2.61	3.75
咸宁市	Xianning	109.43	87.36	2.55	9.11	7.64	1.35	0.28
随州市	Suizhou	163.42	102.35	43.10	6.11	8.96	0.78	0.80
恩施州	Enshi	167.41	38.58	1.33	69.27	51.62	4.17	0.00
仙桃市	Xiaotao	83.71	65.15	8.01	6.86	0.84	1.90	1.76
天门市	Tianmen	75.30	51.06	13.72	3.07	2.48	4.44	2.34
潜江市	Qianjiang	53.49	36.53	9.92	4.23	0.89	1.85	1.40
神农架	Shennongjia	2.26	0.05	0.10	0.96	1.03	0.06	

OUTPUT OF MAJOR FARM CROPS OF CITIES AND PREFECTURES(2015)

(10 000tons)

油料 Oil Bearing Crops	花生 Peanuts	油菜籽 Rapeseed	芝麻 Sesame	麻类 Hemp Crops	苎麻 Ramie	糖类 Sugar Crops	甘蔗 Crane	烟叶 Tobacoo Crops	烤烟 Tobacco
339.60	**67.91**	**255.19**	**14.51**	**2.19**	**2.17**	**32.03**	**31.99**	**8.68**	**7.68**
18.33	4.56	11.88	1.88	0.02	0.02	4.28	4.28		
9.47	1.03	7.10	1.34	0.84	0.84	0.16	0.16		
13.35	4.23	7.36	1.60			1.64	1.63	1.60	1.56
59.93	0.70	57.73	1.49	0.01		6.21	6.21		
24.19	3.59	19.96	0.52			0.23	0.23	0.86	0.54
24.08	12.50	10.44	1.05			0.70	0.70	0.89	0.89
6.22	0.43	5.20	0.59	0.03	0.03	0.86	0.86		
40.04	8.26	30.50	1.10			3.06	3.06		
23.92	7.74	15.32	0.86	0.01	0.01	2.35	2.35		
55.70	14.33	39.56	1.59	0.55	0.55	3.35	3.35		
10.64	1.73	8.23	0.67	0.73	0.73	5.67	5.67		
6.98	3.50	2.70	0.78			0.52	0.52		
10.50	2.19	7.51	0.06			0.01	0.01	5.33	4.68
14.26	0.27	12.94	0.59			2.46	2.46		
11.73	2.30	9.23	0.20			0.27	0.27		
10.22	0.54	9.49	0.20			0.24	0.24		
0.04		0.03						0.01	0.01

12-24 市、州大牲畜、羊、猪年末存栏、出栏、肉产量(2015)

市、州	Municipalities and Prefecrures	牛存栏(万只) Cattles and Bufflaoes	羊存栏 (万只) Sheep in Stock (10 000 heads)	山羊 Goats	年末生猪存栏 (万头) Hogs in Stock at Year-end(10 000 heads)
全省	**Province**	**361.33**	**465.7**	**465.6**	**2497.14**
武汉市	Wuhan	18.73	5.38	5.34	206.04
黄石市	Huangshi	9.00	7.30	7.30	89.36
十堰市	Shiyan	45.45	120.01	120.01	190.61
荆州市	Jingzhou	8.52	14.57	14.57	342.94
宜昌市	Yichang	17.95	148.64	148.63	485.00
襄阳市	Xiangyang	105.27	140.49	139.22	504.29
鄂州市	Ezhou	3.92	2.32	2.32	73.41
荆门市	Jingmen	24.33	47.47	47.39	273.33
孝感市	Xiaogan	49.39	28.89	28.89	289.78
黄冈市	Huanggang	107.64	102.40	100.48	433.49
咸宁市	Xianning	16.82	18.43	18.36	197.04
随州市	Suizhou	28.06	50.43	50.43	155.70
恩施州	Enshi	44.49	94.82	94.82	418.03
仙桃市	Xiaotao	0.91	0.41	0.23	63.3
天门市	Tianmen	7.96	1.69	1.69	70.77
潜江市	Qianjiang	3.34	1.95	1.93	56.82
神农架	Shennongjia	0.61	3.03	3.03	3.95

STATISTICS ON LIVE ANIMALS, SHEEP, HOGS IN STOCK AND OUT OF STOCK AT YEAR-END AND OUTPUT OF MEAT OF CITIES AND PREFECTURES(2015)

年内出栏肉猪 (万头) Hogs out of Stock at Year-end(10 000 heads)	年内出栏羊 (万只) Sheep out of Stock at Year-end(10 000 heads)	出笼禽 (万只) Poultry out of Stock at Year-end(10 000 heads)	猪肉产量 (万吨) Output of pork Meat (10 000 tons)	牛肉产量 beef	羊 肉 muttom	禽蛋产量 (万吨) Output of Eggs (10 000 tons)
4363.23	**550.60**	**51222.71**	**331.50**	**23.00**	**8.80**	**165.29**
304.04	5.11	5247.40	22.49	0.87	0.10	22.92
119.40	5.60	2866.00	8.94	0.31	0.12	4.52
199.55	111.59	3126.00	14.86	1.99	1.67	5.61
492.60	18.54	7720.00	37.68	0.85	0.24	20.42
608.64	166.54	3560.00	49.88	1.42	3.49	6.95
620.44	177.56	8317.04	49.86	11.17	4.31	28.07
119.00	2.21	1463.00	9.60	0.03	0.04	5.90
408.91	62.26	4752.00	30.75	2.89	1.47	17.23
395.26	26.51	11634.00	30.60	2.41	0.57	40.47
501.22	80.62	5652.00	38.73	7.95	2.01	62.03
281.23	20.96	3749.45	21.06	0.42	0.52	3.29
240.10	61.62	8443.00	18.26	2.20	1.00	8.58
491.55	90.07	1253.00	40.63	2.37	1.76	3.28
107.35	0.75	871.00	8.28	0.25	0.01	4.96
100.56	1.28	1144.00	7.54	0.47	0.02	5.27
106.40	2.56	1676.00	8.14	0.51	0.04	4.71
5.06	1.81	31.28	0.50	0.02	0.04	0.03

12-25 市、州主要土特产品产量(2015)
OUTPUT OF LOCAL SPECIALITY OF CITIES AND PREFECTURES(2015)

市、州	Municipalities and Prefecrures	茶叶 (万吨) Tea (10 000 tons)	蚕茧 (吨) Silkworm Coccons (ton)	桑蚕茧 Mulbeery Silkworm Coccons	园林水果 (万吨) Fruits (10,000 tons)	桃子 Peaches	柑橘 Citrus	苹果 Apples	黑木耳 (吨) Jew's Ear (ton)
全省	**Province**	**26.88**	**6711**	**6565**	**615.84**	**93.16**	**426.66**	**1.31**	**26716**
武汉市	Wuhan	0.30			11.50	3.13	4.50		160
黄石市	Huangshi	0.05	43	43	4.74	0.24	3.71	0.01	41
十堰市	Shiyan	1.49	814	814	31.98	0.89	28.63	0.06	2531
荆州市	Jingzhou	0.03	6	6	48.76	0.84	31.84		353
宜昌市	Yichang	6.51	1402	1402	308.22	3.37	300.70	0.04	795
襄阳市	Xiangyang	1.38	962	959	73.56	53.02	5.17	0.36	5064
鄂州市	Ezhou	0.01			4.50	0.41	3.38		
荆门市	Jingmen	0.02			37.39	4.22	13.34	0.03	1208
孝感市	Xiaogan	1.02	2	2	18.73	9.23	2.56	0.06	901
黄冈市	Huanggang	3.60	3211	3211	13.03	3.62	6.26	0.10	640
咸宁市	Xianning	3.84	92	17	7.10	0.74	3.77	0.10	251
随州市	Suizhou	0.28	126		15.98	9.59	0.85	0.17	14702
恩施州	Enshi	8.33	128	128	31.55	2.19	20.13	0.39	6
仙桃市	Xiaotao				2.89	0.44	1.11		
天门市	Tianmen				1.82	0.13	0.39		
潜江市	Qianjiang				4.06	1.10	0.32		12
神农架	Shennongjia	0.01			0.02				52

12-26 市、州人平粮、棉、油、肉、水产品生产水平(2015)
PER CAPITA PRODUCTION LEVEL OF GRAIN,COTTON,OIL,MEAT AND AQUATIC PRODUCTS OF CITIES AND PREFECTURES(2015)

单位: 千克 (kg)

市、州	Municipalities and Prefecrures	粮食 Grain	棉花 Cotton	油料 Oil Bearing Crops	猪肉 Pork	水产品 Aquatic Products	禽蛋 Eggs
按常住人口平均	**Average of Total Population**						
全省	**Province**	**461.98**	**5.10**	**58.04**	**56.65**	**77.91**	**28.25**
武汉市	Wuhan	119.73	1.55	17.28	21.20	49.31	21.61
黄石市	Huangshi	268.28	1.68	38.53	36.37	92.40	18.41
十堰市	Shiyan	347.74	0.03	39.47	43.93	22.64	16.59
宜昌市	Yichang	415.04	3.93	58.79	121.22	52.77	16.88
襄阳市	Xiangyang	900.11	4.60	42.89	88.81	85.08	50.01
鄂州市	Ezhou	346.77	3.68	58.73	90.61	519.88	55.69
荆门市	Jingmen	960.47	7.40	138.23	106.17	160.34	59.48
孝感市	Xiaogan	473.60	4.82	49.03	62.73	278.82	82.97
荆州市	Jingzhou	719.85	13.52	105.02	66.04	36.33	35.80
黄冈市	Huanggang	527.72	5.97	88.55	61.56	84.73	98.60
咸宁市	Xianning	436.51	1.11	42.44	84.00	105.29	13.10
随州市	Suizhou	745.94	3.63	31.87	83.35	43.34	39.18
恩施州	Enshi	503.18	0.00	31.56	122.12	2.36	9.85
仙桃市	Xiaotao	724.80	15.24	123.48	71.69	294.74	42.97
潜江市	Qianjiang	786.06	14.63	106.71	84.97	143.64	49.21
天门市	Tianmen	414.01	18.11	90.76	58.36	96.97	40.78
神农架	Shennongjia	293.82		5.00	65.10	3.70	3.88
按乡村人口平均	**Average of Country Population**						
全省	**Province**	**660.32**	**7.29**	**82.95**	**80.97**	**111.36**	**40.37**
武汉市	Wuhan	516.12	6.70	74.51	91.40	212.55	93.16
黄石市	Huangshi	355.88	2.23	51.11	48.25	122.57	24.42
十堰市	Shiyan	478.16	0.04	54.27	60.40	31.13	22.81
宜昌市	Yichang	628.85	5.95	89.07	183.66	79.95	25.57
襄阳市	Xiangyang	1352.17	6.90	64.44	133.42	127.81	75.12
鄂州市	Ezhou	476.65	5.06	80.73	124.55	714.60	76.55
荆门市	Jingmen	1443.89	11.13	207.80	159.61	241.04	89.41
孝感市	Xiaogan	553.49	5.63	57.30	73.31	325.85	96.96
荆州市	Jingzhou	930.48	17.47	135.75	85.36	46.96	46.27
黄冈市	Huanggang	567.73	6.42	95.26	66.23	91.15	106.08
咸宁市	Xianning	502.13	1.28	48.82	96.63	121.12	15.07
随州市	Suizhou	826.32	4.02	35.30	92.33	48.01	43.40
恩施州	Enshi	522.12	0.00	32.75	126.72	2.45	10.22
仙桃市	Xiaotao	709.86	14.92	120.94	70.21	288.66	42.09
潜江市	Qianjiang	1049.54	19.54	142.48	113.45	191.79	65.71
天门市	Tianmen	419.96	18.37	92.06	59.20	98.36	41.37
神农架	Shennongjia	503.68		8.57	111.61	6.34	6.65

12-27 市、州农业机械、用电、化肥、水利情况(2015)

AGRICULTURAL MACHINERY, ELECTRICITY CONSUMPTION, CHEMICAL FERTILIZERS AND IRRAGATION IN CITIES AND PREFECTURES(2015)

市、州	Municipalities and Prefecrures	农业机械总动力 (万千瓦特) Total Power of Agricultural Machinery (10 000kW)	当年实际机耕面积 (千公顷) Actual Sown Areas (1 000 hectares)	农村用电量 (万千瓦小时) Rural Electricity Consumption (1 000kW/h)	化肥施用量 (折纯量)(万吨) Consumption of Chemical Fertilizers (pure) (10 000tons)	有效灌溉面积 (千公顷) Effective Irrigation Area (1 000 hectares)
全省	**Province**	**4468.12**	**6004.05**	**1490991.56**	**333.87**	**2359.60**
武汉市	Wuhan	284.20	293.81	158531.00	12.89	150.27
黄石市	Huangshi	105.95	155.94	125186.00	5.44	55.56
十堰市	Shiyan	216.20	232.06	57003.70	13.37	36.86
荆州市	Jingzhou	615.18	809.23	164582.00	34.18	422.96
宜昌市	Yichang	318.23	392.19	114864.00	36.58	121.92
襄阳市	Xiangyang	626.52	873.46	102075.72	57.83	281.89
鄂州市	Ezhou	65.40	80.49	47920.00	8.75	27.73
荆门市	Jingmen	460.56	563.97	101042.00	30.40	215.28
孝感市	Xiaogan	260.71	409.12	127945.67	20.89	242.56
黄冈市	Huanggang	371.58	782.43	241327.59	34.08	259.05
咸宁市	Xianning	202.66	258.99	52267.27	12.64	93.35
随州市	Suizhou	212.12	264.44	48294.00	17.64	125.92
恩施州	Enshi	264.26	290.64	48181.25	28.40	71.61
仙桃市	Xiaotao	145.87	199.90	55883.00	6.43	82.32
天门市	Tianmen	178.25	227.89	31209.42	7.27	109.93
潜江市	Qianjiang	129.28	166.90	14678.80	6.90	62.24
神农架	Shennongjia	11.17	2.60	0.14	0.67	0.15

主要统计指标解释

农林牧渔业总产值 指以货币表现的农、林、牧、渔业全部产品和对农林牧渔业生产活动进行的各种支持性服务活动的价值总量,它反映一定时期内农林牧渔业生产总规模和总成果。1957年以前的农林牧渔业总产值中包括了厩肥和农民自给性手工业(如农民自制衣服、鞋、袜,自己从事粮食初步加工等)。1958年及以后,林业中增加了村及村以下竹木采伐产值;牧业中取消了厩肥产值;副业中取消了农民自给性手工业产值,增加了村及村以下办的工业产值;渔业中增加了海洋捕捞水产品产值。1980年及以后,在副业中增加了农民家庭兼营工业商品部分的产值。从1984年起村及村以下工业产值划归工业。从1993年起取消副业,将野生动物的捕猎划入牧业,野生植物采集和农民家庭兼营商品性工业划归农业。从2003年起,执行新的国民经济行业分类标准,农林牧渔业总产值中包括了农林牧渔服务业产值。林业中增加了森林采运业产值。农业中取消了家庭兼营商品性工业产值,将野生林产品的采集划归林业。第一次农业普查以后,由于畜牧业产品年报数据与普查数据之间存在一定的差距,国家统计局农调总队对畜牧业年报数据与普查数据进行衔接,对畜牧业产值进行相应调整。

农林牧渔业总产值的计算方法通常是按农、林、牧、渔业产品及其副产品的产量分别乘以各自单位产品价格求得;少数生产周期较长,当年没有产品或产品产量不易统计的,则采用间接方法匡算其产值;然后将四业产品产值相加即为农林牧渔业总产值。

粮食产量 指全社会的产量。包括国有经济经营的、集体统一经营的和农民家庭经营的粮食产量,还包括工矿企业办的农场和其他生产单位的产量。粮食除包括稻谷、小麦、玉米、高粱、谷子及其他杂粮外,还包括薯类和豆类。其产量计算方法,豆类按去豆荚后的干豆计算;薯类(包括甘薯和马铃薯,不包括芋头和木薯)1963年以前按每4公斤鲜薯折1公斤粮食计算,从1964年开始改为按5公斤鲜薯折1公斤粮食计算。城市郊区作为蔬菜的薯类(如马铃薯等)按鲜品计算,并且不作粮食统计。其他粮食一律按脱粒后的原粮计算。1989年以前全国粮食产量数据主要靠全面报表取得,1989年开始使用抽样调查数据。

棉花产量 指全社会的产量。包括春播棉和夏播棉。产量按皮棉计算。不包括木棉。

油料产量 指全部油料作物的生产量。包括花生、油菜籽、芝麻、向日葵籽、胡麻籽(亚麻籽)和其他油料。不包括大豆、木本油料和野生油料。花生以带壳干花生计算。

水产品产量 指人工养殖的水产品和天然生长的水产品的捕捞量。包括海水的鱼类、虾蟹类、贝类和藻类以及内陆水域的鱼类、虾蟹类和贝类,不包括淡水生植物。水产品产量是通过各级水产和统计部门逐级上报取得数据。1995年及以前,贝类中牡蛎按鲜肉计算;蚶、蛤、蛏按5斤鲜品折1斤计算。1996年以后则统一按鲜品计算。

猪、牛、羊肉产量指当年出栏并已屠宰、除去头蹄下水后带骨肉(即胴体重)的重量。包括全社会范围内的产量。1996年前为各级逐级上报数据。1996年第一次农业普查以后,由于畜牧业产品年报数据与普查数据之间存在一定的差距,国家统计局农调总队对畜牧业年报数据与普查数据进行衔接。1999年以后,国家统计局开展了猪、牛、羊、禽等主要畜禽品种的抽样调查,并用抽样数据作为国家定案数据使用。未开展抽样调查的品种,仍使用各级统计部门逐级上报数据。

期初(末)畜禽存栏头(只)数 指报告期初(末)农村各种合作经济组织和国营农场、农民个人、机关、团体、学校、工矿企业、部队等单位以及城镇居民饲养的大牲畜、猪、羊、家禽等畜禽的存栏数。数据上报方式及数据调整情况同猪、牛、羊肉产量。

常用耕地 是指耕地总资源中专门种植农作物并经常进行耕种、能够正常收获的土地。包括当年实际耕种的熟地;弃耕、休闲不满三年,随时可以复耕的地;开荒利用三年以上的土地。在统计口径上包括南方小于1米、北方小于2米宽的沟、渠、路和田埂。不包括临时种植农作物的坡度在25度以上的陡坡地;在河套、湖畔、库区临时开发的成片或零星土地;也不包括已列为国家和省(区、市)退耕计划但临时耕种的土地。常用耕地是国家需要重点保护的耕地,是反映我国农业综合生产能力的一个重要指标。

农作物播种面积 指实际播种或移植有农作物的面积。凡是实际种植有农作物的面积,不论种植在耕地上还是种植在非耕地上，均包括在农作物播种面积中。在播种季节基本结束后，因遭灾而重新改种和补种的农作物面积，也包括在内。它是反映我国耕地面积利用情况的一个重要指标。目前，农作物播种面积主要包括粮食、棉花、油料、糖料、麻类、烟叶、蔬菜和瓜类、药材和其他农作物九大类。

有效灌溉面积 指具有一定的水源，地块比较平整，灌溉工程或设备已经配套，在一般年景下，当年能够进行正常灌溉的耕地面积。在一般情况下，有效灌溉面积应等于灌溉工程或设备已经配备，能够进行正常灌溉的水田和水浇地面积之和。它是反映我国耕地抗旱能力的一个重要指标。

农用化肥施用量 指本年内实际用于农业生产的化肥数量，包括氮肥、磷肥、钾肥和复合肥。化肥施用量要求按折纯量计算数量。折纯量是指把氮肥、磷肥、钾肥分别按含氮、含五氧化二磷、含氧化钾的百分之百成份进行折算后的数量。复合肥按其所含主要成分折算。公式为：

折纯量=实物量×某种化肥有效成份含量的百分比

农业机械总动力 指主要用于农、林、牧、渔业的各种动力机械的动力总和。包括耕作机械、排灌机械、收获机械、农用运输机械、植物保护机械、牧业机械、林业机械、渔业机械和其他农业机械〔内燃机按引擎马力折成瓦(特)计算、电动机按功率折成瓦(特)计算〕。不包括专门用于乡、镇、村、组办工业、基本建设、非农业运输、科学试验和教学等非农业生产方面用的动力机械与作业机械。这个指标的统计数据主要来源于农机部门。

乡村从业人员 指乡村人口中劳动年龄在16周岁以上实际参加生产经营活动并取得实物或货币收入的人员，包括劳动年龄内经常参加劳动的人员，也包括超过劳动年龄但经常参加劳动的人员，但不包括户口在家的在外学生、现役军人和丧失劳动能力的人，也不包括待业人员和家务劳动者。从业人员按从事主业时间最长(时间相同按收入)分为农林牧渔业从业人员、工业从业人员、建筑业从业人员、交通运输业、仓储及邮电通信业从业人员、批零贸易业、餐饮业从业人员、其他非农行业从业人员。

Explanatory Notes on Main Statistical Indicators

Gross Output Value of Farming, Forestry, Animal Husbandry and Fishery refers to the total value of products of farming, forestry, animal husbandry and fishery, and total value of services rendered to support farming, forestry, animal husbandry and fishery activities. It reflects the total scale and results of agricultural production during a given period. Prior to 1957, Chinas gross agricultural output value included barnyard manure and handicraft products for self-consumption (clothes, shoes, stockings, and initial grain processing undertaken by peasants). Since 1958, cutting and felling of bamboo and trees by villages and other cooperative organizations under villages have been included in forestry; value of barnyard manure has been excluded from animal husbandry; self consumed handicrafts has been excluded from sideline occupations, while the output value of industries run by villages and cooperative organizations under village had been included in sideline occupations and the output value of fish catches by motor fishing boats has been added to fishery. Since 1980, the value of handicraft products made for sale by individuals in households had been added to sideline occupations. Since 1984, industries run by villages and under villages have been included in the sector of industry. Since 1993, the subdivision of sideline occupations has been canceled, and the hunting of wild animals has been classified into animal husbandry, and the gathering of wild plants and commodity industry run by rural household have been included in farming. A new industrial classification of economic activities was introduced in 2003. Under the new classification, value of services to farming, forestry, animal husbandry and fishery is included in the gross output value of agriculture, value of wood felling and transport is included in forestry, value of industrial output by rural households is not included in agriculture, and the collection of wild forest products is taken from agriculture and included in the forestry. The first agriculture census of China revealed some discrepancy between the production of animal products from the annual reports and that from the census. Efforts were made by the Rural Socio-economic Survey Organization of NBS to adjust the output value of animal husbandry to make the figures from the annual reports consistent with the census data.

Gross output value of agriculture is obtained by first multiplying the output of each product or by product by its price, resulting in the output value of each single item. For a small number of products, annual output of which is not available or difficult to get due to the long production (growing) process involved, the output value is estimated through an indirect approach. The sum of output value of all products of farming, forestry, animal husbandry and fishery is then equal to the gross output value of agriculture.

Grain Output refers to the total output in the whole country including grains produced by state farms, collective units, rural households, as well as by farms affiliated to industrial and mining enterprises and other production units. Grain includes rice, wheat, corn, sorghum, millet and other miscellaneous grains as well as tubers and bean. Output of beans refers to dry beans without pods. The output of tubers (sweet potatoes and potatoes, not including taros and cassava) was converted into that of grain at the ratio 4:1, i.e. 4 kilograms of fresh tubers was equivalent to 1 kilogram of grain up to 1963. Since 1964 the ratio for conversion has been 5:1. Tubers supplied as vegetables (such as potatoes) in cities and suburbs are calculated as fresh vegetables and their output is not included in the output of grain. Output of all other grains refers to husked grain. Data on grain production before 1989 were obtained through Comprehensive Statistical Reporting System. Since 1989, data from sample surveys are used.

Cotton Output refers to the cotton production in the whole country including cotton sown in spring and in autumn. Output is measured as the weight of ginned cotton. Ceiba is not included.

Output of Oil–bearing Crops refers to the total production of oil–bearing crops of various kinds, including peanuts, (dry, in shell) rapeseeds, sesame, sunflower seeds, flax seeds, and other oil–bearing crops. Soybeans, oil–bearing woody plants, and wild oil–bearing crops are not included.

Output of Aquatic Products refers to catches of both artificially cultured and naturally grown aquatic products, including fish, shrimps, crabs and shellfish in sea and inland water as well as seaweed. Freshwater plants are not included. Data on output of aquatic products are reported by aquatic product and statistical agencies level by level. Before 1995, among the shellfish, the oyster was counted as fresh meat; 5 kilograms of ark shell, clams and frogs are equivalent to 1 kilogram of fresh aquatic products; they are all counted as fresh aquatic products since 1996.

Output of Pork, Beef, and Mutton refers to the meat of slaughtered hogs, cattle, sheep and goats with head, feet, and offal taken away. Data refers to the production of the whole country. The first agriculture census of China in 1996 revealed some discrepancy between the production of animal products from the annual reports and that from the census. Efforts were made by the Rural Socio–economic Survey Organization of NBS to adjust the output value of animal husbandry to make the figures from the annual reports consistent with the census data. Since 1999, NBS conducted sample survey for the major animal husbandry products, such as hogs, cattle, sheep and goats and fowls, and the data from sample surveys are used as national finalized data. Those products, which are not covered by the sample survey, are still reported by statistical agencies level by level.

Number of Livestock or Poultry in Stock at Beginning (or End) refers to the total number of large animals, pigs, sheep, fowls, etc. raised by rural cooperative organizations, state farms, rural individuals, government agencies, schools, industrial and mining enterprises, army, and urban residents at the beginning (or end) of the reference period. Data reporting system and data adjustment are the same as that in the output of pork, beef and mutton.

Regularly Cultivated Land refers to farmland among the total land resources, which is exclusively used for farming and is under regular cultivation with harvest in normal years. Included are currently cultivated land, land that has been abandoned or put in idle for less than 3 years and could be re–used for cultivation at any time, and new–claimed land that has been put into cultivation for more than 3 years. According to statistical coverage, it includes the gouges, dykes, roads and ridges of field with 1 meter wide in Southern areas and 2 meters wide in Northern areas. Excluded under this category are steep slope land over 25 degrees under temporary cultivation, land (large or small plots) that is claimed along river bends, lake sides or banks of reservoirs, as well as land that has been designated under the "Green for Grain" programme of the state and provincial governments but is still temporarily under cultivation. The regularly cultivated land is the key protection land of the nation, an important indicator reflecting the comprehensive productivity of agriculture of China.

Sown Area of Crops refers to area of land sown or transplanted with crops regardless of being in cultivated area or non–cultivated area. Area of land re–sown due to natural disasters is also included. This is an important indicator that can reflect the utilization condition of the cultivated land in China. At present, the sown area of crops mainly include the following 9 categories of crops: grain, cotton, oil–bearing crops, sugar crops, fiber crops, Tobacco, Vegetables and melons, medicinal materials and other farm crops.

Irrigated Area refers to areas that are effectively irrigated, i.e. level land, which has water source and complete sets of irrigation facilities to lift and move adequate water for irrigation purpose under normal conditions. Under normal conditions, irrigated area is the sum of watered fields and irrigated fields where irrigation systems or equipment have been installed for regular irrigation purpose. This important indicator reflects drought resistance capacity of the cultivated land in China.

Consumption of Chemical Fertilizers in Agriculture refers to the quantity of chemical fertilizers applied in agriculture in the year, including nitrogenous fertilizer, phosphate fertilizer, potash fertilizer, and compound fertilizer. The consumption of chemical fertilizers is required in calculation to convert the gross weight into weight containing 100% effective component (e.g. 100% nitrogen content in nitrogenous fertilizer, 100% phosphorous pent oxide contents in phosphate fertilizer, 100% potassium oxide contents in potash fertilizer). Compound fertilizer is converted with its major component. The formula is :

Volume of effective component= physical quantity x effective component of certain chemical fertilizer (%)

Total Power of Farm Machinery refers to total mechanical power of machinery used in farming, forestry, animal husbandry, and fishery, including ploughing, irrigation and drainage, harvesting, transport, plant protection, stock breeding, forestry and fishery. The power of internal combustion engines is required to convert horsepower into watts and the power of electric motors is required to be converted into watts. Machinery employed for non–agricultural purposes, such as the machines used in township run and village–run industry, construction, non–agricultural transport, scientific experiments and teaching, is excluded. Data are mainly from agricultural machinery agencies.

Rural Employed Persons refer to rural labor forces aged over 16 years old who are engaged in real production and management activities and receive payment in kind or wages, including those covered within the age frame and regularly participating in production activities, and those who are out of the range of age frame and also participating in production activities regularly. Excluding students studying in other places with their permanent residence registered in local areas, servicemen and persons incapable of working; also excluding those who are waiting for jobs and those engaged in household work. Persons employed are classified as persons engaged in agriculture, forestry, animal husbandry or fishery activities; persons engaged in industrial activities; persons engaged in construction activities; persons engaged in transport, storage and telecommunications activities; persons engaged in whole sales and retail sales trade and catering activities; and persons engaged in other non–agriculture activities, depending upon the longest period of employment in major activities (or using income indicator when period of employment is the same).

13 工业

Industry

工 业
INDUSTRY
2015

规模以上工业企业	Industrial Enterprises Above Designated Size		
工业总产值(现价)	Total Output Value (at current price)	45809.57	(亿元)
*轻工业	Light Industry	16810.65	(亿元)
重工业	Heavy Industry	28998.91	(亿元)
*大型企业	Large Scale Enterprises	16072.70	(亿元)
中型企业	Medium Scale Enterprises	10191.48	(亿元)
资产总计	Total Assets	35399.12	(亿元)
负债合计	Total Liability	19459.99	(亿元)
主营业务收入	Income from Major Business	43179.21	(亿元)
利税总额	Total Revenue	4599.15	(亿元)
从业人员年平均人数	Annually Average number of Employment	352.64	(万人)

规模以上工业总产值构成(%)
Composition of Industry above desginated size

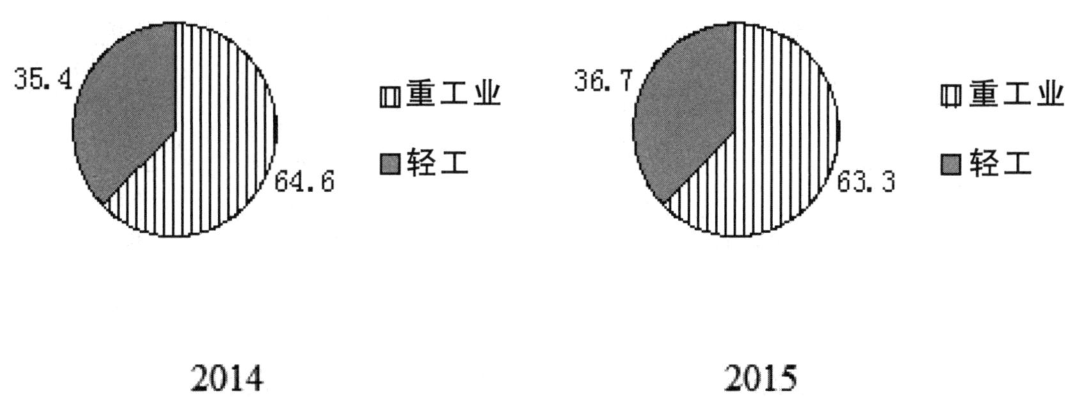

规模以上工业增加值指数(上年 = 100)

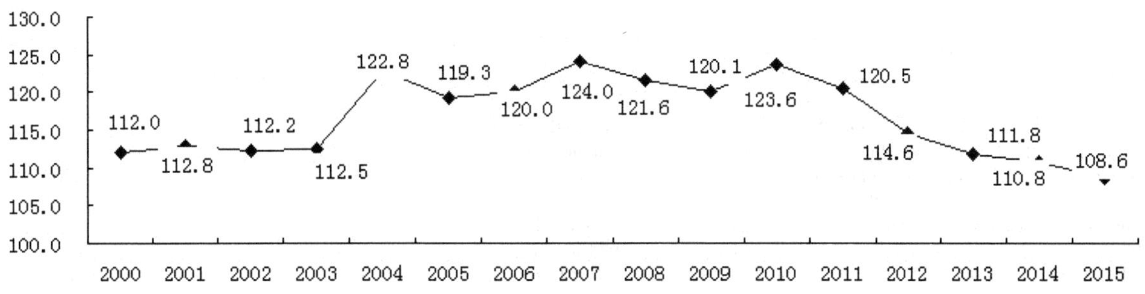

13-1 工业发展基本情况
THE BASIC SITUATION OF INDUSTRIAL DEVELOPMENT

年份 Year	工业企业单位数(个) Number of Industrial Enterprises (unit)	轻工业 Light industry	重工业 Heavy industry	工业总产值(当年价) (亿元) Total Output Value (currentprice) (100 million yuan)	轻工业 Light industry	重工业 Heavy industry
1979	16073	10100	5973	220.82	93.45	107.37
1982	18066	11960	6106	272.08	137.66	134.42
1983	18926	12325	6637	319.21	157.33	161.88
1984	22713	14664	8049	371.93	182.57	189.36
1985	25011	15309	9702	467.22	216.47	250.75
1986	27697	16890	10807	538.28	256.06	282.22
1987	26294	15528	10766	659.19	315.49	343.70
1988	26016	15279	10737	834.84	405.13	429.71
1989	25999	15035	10964	976.93	463.35	513.58
1990	25913	14885	11028	1008.20	476.76	531.44
1991	25204	14317	10887	1136.02	531.26	604.76
1992	23985	13428	10557	1373.66	605.11	768.55
1993	22600	11958	10642	1992.31	770.20	1222.11
1994	23275	12096	11179	3024.72	1360.78	1663.94
1995	27815	14827	12988	3697.91	1870.12	1827.79
1996	25986	13618	12368	4836.33	2470.90	2365.43
1997	24498	12723	11775	5977.00	3158.47	2818.53
1998	7399	3581	3818	6731.31	3534.67	3196.64
1999	6874	3308	3566	2831.70	1109.92	1721.78
2000	6282	3026	3256	3064.43	1177.24	1887.18
2001	6197	2981	3216	3239.51	1194.90	2044.61
2002	6183	2947	3236	3589.26	1184.78	2404.48
2003	6271	2789	3482	3631.29	1192.46	2438.82
2004	6232	2632	3600	4960.25	1180.07	3780.17
2005	6813	2953	3860	6066.96	1503.00	4563.95
2006	7546	3272	4274	7454.07	1898.34	5555.73
2007	8996	3808	5188	9601.52	2492.88	7108.64
2008	12067	4806	7261	13454.94	3344.80	10110.14
2009	14027	5515	8512	15567.02	4234.52	11332.50
2010	16106	6326	9780	21623.12	5935.78	15687.33
2011	10633	4347	6286	28072.73	8370.27	19702.45
2012	12441	5012	7429	33450.66	10941.70	22508.95
2013	14650	5855	8795	39208.98	13405.24	25803.74
2014	15957	6453	9504	43393.87	15378.14	28015.73
2015	16413	6646	9767	45809.57	16810.65	28998.91

注：1.本表规模以上工业1997年及以前统计范围为乡及乡以上工业。1998-2006年为全部国有工业及年销售收入500万元以上非国有工业企业;2007年-2010年为主营业务收入500万元以上工业企业。2011年起为主营业务收入2000万元及以上的工业法人企业。(下表同)

2."国有及国有控股经济"一栏,1998年以前统计范围为国有工业。

3.2011年行业小类码按照《国民经济行业分类》(GB/T4754-2011)填写。(下表同)

Note: 1.The scopes of industrial statistics are all township and above town industrial enterprises before 1998.The scopes are all state-owned industrial enterprises and non-state-owned industrial enterprise with revenue from principal business over 5 million yuan from 1998 to 2006.For 2007 to 2010,the scopes are all industrial enterprices with revenue from principal business over 5 million yuan.From 2011,the scopes are all industrial enterprises with revenue from principal business over 20 millon yuan.The same applies to the talbe following.

2."State-owned and state-controlled economy"a column,prior to 1998 statistics the range of state-owned industries.

3.Accordring to GB/T4754-2011,the small classes code of industries are filled in the table from 2011.The same applies to the talbe following.

13-1 续表 continued

单位: 亿元 (100 million yuan)

年份 Year	主营业务收入(亿元) Main business income (100 million yuan)	利润总额(亿元) Total profit (100 million yuan)	利税总额(亿元) Total profits and taxes (100 million yuan)	职工人数(万人) Number of employees (1000 persons)
1979	163.52	20.70	34.19	161.98
1982	239.64	27.50	47.82	197.62
1983	268.98	31.77	53.46	202.80
1984	308.66	37.33	62.38	292.49
1985	381.43	43.64	80.82	306.83
1986	438.95	40.22	82.14	333.63
1987	526.95	48.54	96.16	343.43
1988	654.72	58.85	117.28	356.43
1989	706.99	50.99	112.12	360.88
1990	705.97	26.73	88.40	358.65
1991	800.01	31.79	103.46	367.41
1992	1041.66	43.19	127.15	357.74
1993	1500.71	67.00	167.92	357.97
1994	1690.94	74.06	190.29	381.45
1995	2066.38	52.26	181.57	379.84
1996	2305.57	43.93	181.41	369.80
1997	2681.36	57.71	221.53	362.50
1998	2433.92	44.71	195.96	274.43
1999	2602.26	68.82	232.24	250.07
2000	2870.36	106.47	29.36	230.36
2001	3043.82	134.49	335.36	212.48
2002	3378.31	175.60	404.23	205.82
2003	3993.99	194.40	444.96	198.60
2004	4832.43	270.98	559.28	176.70
2005	5962.54	371.84	727.48	188.30
2006	7314.81	454.00	897.19	190.85
2007	9390.43	647.85	1229.16	200.35
2008	13081.90	909.03	1761.47	235.90
2009	15331.62	1092.47	1987.88	272.39
2010	21151.56	1668.55	2950.08	294.97
2011	27072.02	1864.46	3093.57	279.59
2012	32325.95	2046.28	3528.80	311.13
2013	38183.39	2475.07	4451.87	346.29
2014	41401.49	2402.63	4465.72	359.45
2015	43179.21	2456.00	4599.15	352.64

13-2 规模以上工业企业单位数和产销总值 (2015)

单位: 亿元

项 目	Item	企业单位数(个) Number of Enterprises (unit)
总 计	**Total**	**16413**
一、按登记注册类型分组:	**Grouped by Type of Registration**	
内资企业	Inner Funded Enterprises	15579
国有企业	State Owned Enterprises	152
中央企业	Central Enterprises	46
地方企业	Local Enterprises	106
集体企业	Collective-owned Enterprise	98
股份合作企业	Share Holding Cooperative Enterprises	17
联营企业	Joint Owned Enterprise	4
国有联营企业	State Joint Ownership	
集体联营企业	Collective Joint Ownership	1
国有与集体联营企业	Joint State- Collective Ownership	1
其他联营企业	Other Joint Owned Enterprise	2
有限责任公司	Responsibility Co. Ltd	5739
国有独资公司	State Solely Funded Co.	113
其他有限责任公司	Others	5626
股份有限公司	Share Holding Co.Ltd.	656
私营企业	Private - owned enterprises	8833
私营独资企业	Solely Private - owned enterprises	286
私营合伙企业	Private Joint Venture	49
私营有限责任公司	Private Responsibility Co. Ltd	8024
私营股份有限公司	Private Share Holding Co.Ltd.	474
其他企业	Others	80
港、澳、台商投资企业	Hongkong, Macao and Taiwan Funded Enterprises	365
合资经营企业(港或澳、台资)	Joint Venture with Hongkong, Macao and Taiwan	157
合作经营企业(港或澳、台资)	Cooperate with Hongkong, Macao and Taiwan Funded	4
港澳台商独资经营企业	Enterprises Solely Funded by Hongkong, Macao and Taiwan Businessmen	192
港澳台商投资股份有限公司	Share Holding Co.Ltd. With Hongkong, Macao and Taiwan Investment	11
外商投资企业	Foreign Funded Enterprises	469
中外合资经营企业	Sino - Foreign Joint Funded Enterprises	254
中外合作经营企业	Sino - Foreign Cooperative Funded Enterprises	7
外资企业	Foreign Solely Funded Enterprises	191
外商投资股份有限公司	Foreign Funded Share Holding Co.Ltd.	15
二、在总计中:亏损企业	**Of the Total: enterprises running under deficit**	**1441**
在总计中:国有控股企业	Of the Total: State-Owned Share Holding Enterprises	759
在总计中:农村工业	Of the Total: Rural Industry	112
在总计中:轻工业	Of the Total: Light Industry	6646
重工业	Heavy Industry	9767
在总计中:大型企业	Of the Total: Large Scale Enterprises	349
中型企业	Medium Scale Enterprises	1853
小型企业	Small Enterprises	14211

THE NUMBER OF UNITS OF INDUSTRIAL ENTERPRISES ABOVE

工业总产值 （当年价格） Total Output Value (current price)	工业销售产值 (当年价格) Output Value of Industrial Products Sales (current price)	出口交货值 Delivery Value for Export
45809.57	**44113.44**	**1688.02**
39108.01	37819.51	1248.99
2788.62	2752.54	117.10
2608.64	2579.13	102.41
179.99	173.41	14.69
124.87	121.80	
20.08	19.09	0.02
7.68	7.51	
2.85	2.75	
0.64	0.58	
4.19	4.19	
15109.73	14533.26	521.68
1829.70	1737.37	39.99
13280.03	12795.88	481.68
4850.64	4696.47	178.79
16053.39	15538.20	428.96
412.27	404.46	3.77
67.57	66.24	
14372.69	13912.03	403.70
1200.86	1155.48	21.49
152.99	150.64	2.44
2073.46	1858.95	258.82
1220.41	1042.71	94.04
10.35	9.76	
803.37	767.95	163.87
38.21	37.41	0.90
4628.10	4434.98	180.20
3549.44	3381.24	74.64
48.31	47.62	1.38
820.18	794.64	91.03
209.14	210.57	12.83
4417.28	**4288.04**	**156.37**
11042.16	10658.49	335.17
185.30	176.43	
16810.65	16132.56	726.52
28998.91	27980.88	961.49
16072.70	15460.32	823.76
10191.48	9821.25	433.93
19545.39	18831.87	430.33

13-2 续表 continued

单位: 亿元

项 目	Item	企业单位数(个) Number of Enterprises(unit)
按行业分	Grouped by sector	
采矿业	Mining and Qarrying	724
煤炭开采和洗选业	Coal Mining and Processing	127
石油和天然气开采业	Petroleum and Natural Gas Extraction	1
黑色金属矿采选业	Ferrous Metals Mining and Processing	114
有色金属矿采选业	Non-ferrous Metals Mining and Processing	41
非金属矿采选业	Non-metal Minerals Mining and Processing	435
开采辅助活动	Mining Auxiliary Activities	4
其他采矿业	Other Minerals Mining and Processing	2
制造业	Manufacturing	15364
农副食品加工业	Food Processing	1789
食品制造业	Food Production	422
酒、饮料和精制茶制造业	Wine,Beverage and Refined Tea Production	468
烟草制品业	Tobacco Processing	7
纺织业	Textile Industry	1017
纺织服装、服饰业	Textile,Garments, and Fashion Industry	564
皮革、毛皮、羽毛及其制品和制鞋业	Leather, Furs,Down and Related Products	166
木材加工和木、竹、藤、棕、草制品业	Timber Processing, Wood, Bamboo, Cane, Palm and Sraw Products	284
家具制造业	Furniture Manufacturing	162
造纸和纸制品业	Papermaking and Paper Products	284
印刷和记录媒介复制业	Printing and Record Processing	219
文教、工美、体育和娱乐用品制造业	Stationery, Education and Sports Goods	120
石油加工、炼焦和核燃料加工业	Petroleum Processing, Coking Products and Nuclear Fuel Processing	47
化学原料和化学制品制造业	Raw Chemical Material and Chemical Products	1120
医药制造业	Medical and pharmaceutical Products	409
化学纤维制造业	Chemical Fibers	24
橡胶和塑料制品业	Rubber and plastic products	648
非金属矿物制品业	Nonmetal Material Products	1989
黑色金属冶炼和压延加工业	Smelting and Pressing of Ferrous Metals	321
有色金属冶炼和压延加工业	Smelting and Pressing of Nonferrous Metals	166
金属制品业	Metal Products	802
通用设备制造业	Ordinary Machinery Manufacturing	724
专用设备制造业	Special Purpose Equipment Manufacturing	653
汽车制造业	Motor manufacturing	1481
铁路、船舶、航空航天和其他运输设备制造业	Railway,Watercraft,Aviation and other Transporlation Equipment manufacturing	165
电气机械和器材制造业	Electric Machinery and Equipment	662
计算机、通信和其他电子设备制造业	Telecommunication Computer,Equipment and Other Electronic Equipment Manufacturing	347
仪器仪表制造业	Instruments and Meters, Manufacturing	138
其他制造业	Other Manufacturing	82
废弃资源综合利用业	Waste Comprehensive Vtilization of Resources Industry	61
金属制品、机械和设备修理业	Metal products,Machinery and Equipment Repairing	23
电力、燃气及水的生产和供应业	Electric Power, Gas and Water Production and Supply	325
电力、热力生产和供应业	Electric Power, Steam and Hot Water Production and Supply	170
燃气生产和供应业	Gas Production and Supply	66
水的生产和供应业	Tap Water Production and Supply	89

(100 million Yuan)

工业总产值 (当年价格) Total Output Value(current price)	工业销售产值 (当年价格) Output Value of Industrial Products Sales(current price)	出口交货值 Delivery Value for Export
1244.14	1209.93	0.53
106.09	104.67	0.04
40.31	40.08	0.46
334.56	326.66	
53.73	52.67	
643.69	621.25	0.01
64.37	63.21	0.01
1.39	1.39	
42770.51	41134.69	1687.49
4879.01	4705.89	147.78
1216.24	1172.91	58.63
1740.57	1685.20	5.25
678.51	610.48	0.80
2279.44	2211.36	129.80
992.67	966.06	137.50
222.76	217.78	54.49
456.17	440.40	2.82
192.92	184.46	1.79
572.52	545.34	1.01
380.80	362.21	3.27
276.86	270.60	21.66
754.50	744.47	
4220.90	4091.64	155.41
1126.86	1068.16	90.30
76.61	74.84	4.18
1222.03	1171.84	5.27
3219.03	3138.38	25.19
2093.75	2054.82	54.21
859.82	837.39	11.23
1486.98	1439.85	30.56
1360.91	1303.16	34.53
1139.58	1094.62	24.81
5974.92	5797.40	70.45
706.34	684.46	53.33
1901.55	1813.06	88.35
2172.86	1917.46	457.27
194.48	184.84	6.20
180.46	163.72	6.18
140.53	134.20	5.23
49.92	47.68	
1794.91	1768.82	
1572.14	1559.07	
155.12	145.97	
67.66	63.78	

13-3 规模以上工业企业主要经济指标 (2015)

单位: 亿元

项 目	Item	企业单位数(个) Number of Enterprises (unit)
总　计	**Total**	**16413**
一、按登记注册类型分组:	**Grouped by Type of Registration**	
内资企业	Inner Funded Enterprises	15579
国有企业	State Owned Enterprises	152
中央企业	Central Enterprises	46
地方企业	Local Enterprises	106
集体企业	Collective-owned Enterprise	98
股份合作企业	Share Holding Cooperative Enterprises	17
联营企业	Joint Owned Enterprise	4
国有联营企业	State Joint Ownership	
集体联营企业	Collective Joint Ownership	1
国有与集体联营企业	Joint State- Collective Ownership	1
其他联营企业	Other Joint Owned Enterprise	2
有限责任公司	Responsibility Co. Ltd	5739
国有独资公司	State Solely Funded Co.	113
其他有限责任公司	Others	5626
股份有限公司	Share Holding Co.Ltd.	656
私营企业	Private - owned enterprises	8833
私营独资企业	Solely Private - owned enterprises	286
私营合伙企业	Private Joint Venture	49
私营有限责任公司	Private Responsibility Co. Ltd	8024
私营股份有限公司	Private Share Holding Co.Ltd.	474
其他企业	Others	80
港、澳、台商投资企业	Hongkong, Macao and Taiwan Funded Enterprises	365
合资经营企业(港或澳、台资)	Joint Venture with Hongkong, Macao and Taiwan	157
合作经营企业(港或澳、台资)	Cooperate with Hongkong, Macao and Taiwan Funded	4
港澳台商独资经营企业	Enterprises Solely Funded by Hongkong, Macao and Taiwan Businessmen	192
港澳台商投资股份有限公司	Share Holding Co.Ltd. With Hongkong, Macao and Taiwan Investment	11
外商投资企业	Foreign Funded Enterprises	469
中外合资经营企业	Sino - Foreign Joint Funded Enterprises	254
中外合作经营企业	Sino - Foreign Cooperative Funded Enterprises	7
外资企业	Foreign Solely Funded Enterprises	191
外商投资股份有限公司	Foreign Funded Share Holding Co.Ltd.	15
二、在总计中:亏损企业	**Of the Total: enterprises running under deficit**	**1441**
在总计中:国有控股企业	Of the Total: State-Owned Share Holding Enterprises	759
在总计中:农村工业	Of the Total: Rural Industry	112
在总计中:轻工业	Of the Total: Light Industry	6646
重工业	Heavy Industry	9767
在总计中:大型企业	Of the Total: Large Scale Enterprises	349
中型企业	Medium Scale Enterprises	1853
小型企业	Small Enterprises	14211

MAJOR ECONOMIC INDICATORS OF INDUSTRIAL

(100 million Yuan)

资产总计 Total Assets	流动资产合计 Circulating Funds	应收帐款净额 Net Value of Account Received	固定资产合计 Total Fixed Assets
35399.12	**15976.10**	**4056.46**	**13328.90**
30229.07	13475.38	3437.34	11351.51
4599.57	1510.64	273.06	2056.64
4331.12	1368.86	255.37	1961.29
268.45	141.79	17.68	95.35
53.27	28.67	10.54	16.79
12.55	8.08	3.38	1.96
3.67	1.83	0.72	1.80
2.55	1.06	0.31	1.49
0.83	0.66	0.39	0.17
0.29	0.11	0.02	0.14
11687.65	5876.63	1612.53	4126.55
2064.86	1012.51	172.33	711.50
9622.79	4864.13	1440.20	3415.05
6830.30	2744.73	598.56	2508.73
6989.18	3280.58	932.86	2617.86
106.56	45.71	11.78	46.37
20.24	9.20	2.16	7.69
6373.45	3015.18	868.70	2378.31
488.93	210.50	50.22	185.49
52.90	24.21	5.70	21.19
1425.67	625.74	179.16	604.34
817.19	381.53	95.41	325.29
12.22	5.64	0.85	2.50
546.63	214.57	74.26	263.31
46.13	22.45	8.00	11.69
3744.39	1874.98	439.96	1373.04
2665.70	1350.40	270.71	965.19
26.42	4.79	2.03	20.48
732.34	438.15	149.52	219.54
318.65	81.03	17.50	167.46
6719.60	**2824.94**	**557.76**	**2554.61**
15743.77	6111.10	1185.02	6579.06
88.32	46.04	13.29	24.16
8621.32	4429.61	970.71	2840.92
26777.81	11546.49	3085.75	10487.98
17866.20	7479.63	1536.61	6911.15
6630.87	3351.72	927.24	2411.28
10902.06	5144.74	1592.61	4006.47

13-3 续表 1 continued

单位: 亿元

项 目	Item	企业单位数(个) Number of Enterprises(unit)
按行业分	**Grouped by sector**	
采矿业	**Mining and Qarrying**	**724**
煤炭开采和洗选业	Coal Mining and Processing	127
石油和天然气开采业	Petroleum and Natural Gas Extraction	1
黑色金属矿采选业	Ferrous Metals Mining and Processing	114
有色金属矿采选业	Non-ferrous Metals Mining and Processing	41
非金属矿采选业	Non-metal Minerals Mining and Processing	435
开采辅助活动	Mining Auxiliary Activities	4
其他采矿业	Other Minerals Mining and Processing	2
制造业	Manufacturing	15364
农副食品加工业	Food Processing	1789
食品制造业	Food Production	422
酒、饮料和精制茶制造业	Wine,Beverage and Refined Tea Production	468
烟草制品业	Tobacco Processing	7
纺织业	Textile Industry	1017
纺织服装、服饰业	Textile,Garments, and Fashion Industry	564
皮革、毛皮、羽毛及其制品和制鞋业	Leather, Furs,Down and Related Products	166
木材加工和木、竹、藤、棕、草制品业	Timber Processing, Wood, Bamboo, Cane, Palm and Sraw Products	284
家具制造业	Furniture Manufacturing	162
造纸和纸制品业	Papermaking and Paper Products	284
印刷和记录媒介复制业	Printing and Record Processing	219
文教、工美、体育和娱乐用品制造业	Stationery, Education and Sports Goods	120
石油加工、炼焦和核燃料加工业	Petroleum Processing, Coking Products and Nuclear Fuel Processing	47
化学原料和化学制品制造业	Raw Chemical Material and Chemical Products	1120
医药制造业	Medical and pharmaceutical Products	409
化学纤维制造业	Chemical Fibers	24
橡胶和塑料制品业	Rubber and Plastic Products	648
非金属矿物制品业	Nonmetal Material Products	1989
黑色金属冶炼和压延加工业	Smelting and Pressing of Ferrous Metals	321
有色金属冶炼和压延加工业	Smelting and Pressing of Nonferrous Metals	166
金属制品业	Metal Products	802
通用设备制造业	Ordinary Machinery Manufacturing	724
专用设备制造业	Special Purpose Equipment Manufacturing	653
汽车制造业	Motor manufacturing	1481
铁路、船舶、航空航天和其他运输设备制造业	Railway,Watercraft,Aviation and other Transporlation Equipment manufacturing	165
电气机械和器材制造业	Electric Machinery and Equipment	662
计算机、通信和其他电子设备制造业	Telecommunication Computer,Equipment and Other Electronic Equipment Manufacturing	347
仪器仪表制造业	Instruments and Meters, Manufacturing	138
其他制造业	Other Manufacturing	82
废弃资源综合利用业	Waste Comprehensive Vtilization of Resources Industry	61
金属制品、机械和设备修理业	Metal products,Machinery and Equipment Repairing	23
电力、燃气及水的生产和供应业	**Electric Power, Gas and Water Production and Supply**	**325**
电力、热力生产和供应业	Electric Power, Steam and Hot Water Production and Supply	170
燃气生产和供应业	Gas Production and Supply	66
水的生产和供应业	Tap Water Production and Supply	89

(100 million Yuan)

资产总计 Total Assets	流动资产合计 Circulating Funds	应收帐款净额 Net Value of Account Received	固定资产合计 Total Fixed Assets
1052.05	**383.90**	**109.15**	**433.35**
60.13	20.64	2.66	27.14
149.26	39.08	0.95	96.94
133.71	52.78	13.91	64.55
54.75	18.47	3.64	15.53
537.54	186.00	49.30	187.59
115.72	66.36	38.68	41.42
0.96	0.57	0.01	0.16
29915.36	15122.60	3844.98	9563.76
1711.59	782.55	150.09	696.46
550.76	244.39	52.05	198.07
1129.17	685.41	67.71	291.73
422.51	331.75	19.88	30.83
900.06	408.38	80.41	380.42
427.94	231.75	44.98	138.77
90.79	47.51	15.54	34.77
242.91	97.06	17.03	95.88
120.47	45.76	8.76	39.06
336.97	174.08	44.58	118.63
213.85	117.46	37.95	71.79
184.32	142.49	99.68	20.10
228.11	88.44	15.87	127.58
2978.76	1179.78	204.90	1335.74
979.15	460.26	116.37	314.35
62.56	23.83	4.66	17.02
588.03	304.85	81.15	194.76
1912.18	733.83	219.87	840.69
2705.68	838.34	143.75	1251.68
597.92	315.88	41.19	164.51
958.88	546.04	151.27	286.01
1386.09	752.68	225.35	305.56
1032.23	664.11	180.60	262.66
5697.43	2989.31	721.35	1348.04
847.73	510.61	157.67	208.00
1283.99	778.91	304.56	356.13
1875.95	1376.79	555.58	289.41
201.63	123.62	40.80	61.60
124.98	64.32	18.72	49.50
97.06	44.93	14.31	28.05
25.65	17.50	8.34	5.96
4431.71	**469.59**	**102.33**	**3331.79**
3895.48	290.48	81.22	3134.04
199.96	61.68	7.32	95.78
336.28	117.43	13.78	101.98

13-3 续表 2 continued

单位: 亿元

项 目	Item	资产总计 Total Assets 固定资产原价 Original Price of Fixed Assets
总 计	**Total**	**24361.81**
一、按登记注册类型分组:	**Grouped by Type of Registration**	
内资企业	Inner Funded Enterprises	21180.81
国有企业	State Owned Enterprises	3934.14
中央企业	Central Enterprises	3792.47
地方企业	Local Enterprises	141.67
集体企业	Collective-owned Enterprise	31.68
股份合作企业	Share Holding Cooperative Enterprises	2.82
联营企业	Joint Owned Enterprise	3.09
国有联营企业	State Joint Ownership	
集体联营企业	Collective Joint Ownership	2.52
国有与集体联营企业	Joint State- Collective Ownership	0.39
其他联营企业	Other Joint Owned Enterprise	0.18
有限责任公司	Responsibility Co. Ltd	6612.38
国有独资公司	State Solely Funded Co.	1135.91
其他有限责任公司	Others	5476.47
股份有限公司	Share Holding Co.Ltd.	4059.04
私营企业	Private - owned enterprises	6505.76
私营独资企业	Solely Private - owned enterprises	83.72
私营合伙企业	Private Joint Venture	10.57
私营有限责任公司	Private Responsibility Co. Ltd	6061.98
私营股份有限公司	Private Share Holding Co.Ltd.	349.49
其他企业	Others	31.90
港、澳、台商投资企业	Hongkong, Macao and Taiwan Funded Enterprises	1021.24
合资经营企业(港或澳、台资)	Joint Venture with Hongkong, Macao and Taiwan	576.63
合作经营企业(港或澳、台资)	Cooperate with Hongkong, Macao and Taiwan Funded	5.52
港澳台商独资经营企业	Enterprises Solely Funded by Hongkong, Macao and Taiwan Business-men	419.10
港澳台商投资股份有限公司	Share Holding Co.Ltd. With Hongkong, Macao and Taiwan Investment	18.44
外商投资企业	Foreign Funded Enterprises	2159.76
中外合资经营企业	Sino - Foreign Joint Funded Enterprises	1489.56
中外合作经营企业	Sino - Foreign Cooperative Funded Enterprises	39.20
外资企业	Foreign Solely Funded Enterprises	357.78
外商投资股份有限公司	Foreign Funded Share Holding Co.Ltd.	272.73
二、在总计中:亏损企业	**Of the Total: enterprises running under deficit**	**4430.26**
在总计中:国有控股企业	Of the Total: State-Owned Share Holding Enterprises	11019.03
在总计中:农村工业	Of the Total: Rural Industry	77.40
在总计中:轻工业	Of the Total: Light Industry	6685.71
重工业	Heavy Industry	17676.10
在总计中:大型企业	Of the Total: Large Scale Enterprises	12308.40
中型企业	Medium Scale Enterprises	5105.98
小型企业	Small Enterprises	6947.43

(100 million Yuan)

累计折旧 Accumulated Depreciation	负债合计 Total Liability	流动负债合计 Total Circulating Liability	应付账款 Account Payable
11860.43	**19459.99**	**14914.59**	**4363.48**
10527.45	16385.26	12444.11	3395.15
1903.83	3106.23	2498.03	622.48
1844.86	2934.38	2383.63	601.52
58.97	171.85	114.41	20.95
17.16	32.18	24.35	8.63
1.32	8.50	7.87	1.90
1.41	1.62	1.62	0.58
1.11	0.97	0.97	0.30
0.26	0.54	0.54	0.28
0.04	0.11	0.11	0.01
2761.95	6863.77	5250.92	1521.87
470.29	1248.45	953.10	311.18
2291.66	5615.32	4297.81	1210.69
1736.71	3111.12	2214.33	455.82
4093.64	3241.14	2429.81	780.72
39.68	38.38	26.05	5.72
3.58	10.18	5.69	2.43
3870.24	2976.80	2232.93	736.04
180.15	215.78	165.14	36.53
11.44	20.71	17.19	3.15
437.66	725.14	532.70	198.88
258.82	451.36	342.68	137.03
3.61	5.14	1.72	0.92
167.61	247.76	169.20	55.80
7.63	19.41	17.88	4.55
895.31	2349.59	1937.78	769.46
623.01	1710.30	1466.77	603.95
20.37	13.38	6.86	1.07
146.42	423.56	340.59	125.05
105.38	201.81	123.01	39.30
1997.54	**4936.69**	**3858.86**	**853.76**
4670.40	9327.69	7198.52	2004.94
57.32	45.11	34.21	7.96
4163.16	4079.70	3107.43	796.11
7697.27	15380.29	11807.16	3567.37
5742.50	10502.12	8231.50	2260.08
2863.81	3571.64	2772.54	874.77
3254.12	5386.23	3910.54	1228.63

13-3 续表 3 continued

单位: 亿元

项 目	Item	资产总计 Total Assets 固定资产原价 Original Price of Fixed Assets
按行业分	**Grouped by sector**	
采矿业	**Mining and Qarrying**	**793.99**
煤炭开采和洗选业	Coal Mining and Processing	32.62
石油和天然气开采业	Petroleum and Natural Gas Extraction	311.92
黑色金属矿采选业	Ferrous Metals Mining and Processing	101.54
有色金属矿采选业	Non-ferrous Metals Mining and Processing	28.83
非金属矿采选业	Non-metal Minerals Mining and Processing	255.45
开采辅助活动	Mining Auxiliary Activities	63.38
其他采矿业	Other Minerals Mining and Processing	0.25
制造业	**Manufacturing**	**18289.82**
农副食品加工业	Food Processing	2247.34
食品制造业	Food Production	720.87
酒、饮料和精制茶制造业	Wine,Beverage and Refined Tea Production	495.75
烟草制品业	Tobacco Processing	90.72
纺织业	Textile Industry	854.68
纺织服装、服饰业	Textile,Garments, and Fashion Industry	270.64
皮革、毛皮、羽毛及其制品和制鞋业	Leather, Furs,Down and Related Products	74.51
木材加工和木、竹、藤、棕、草制品业	Timber Processing, Wood, Bamboo, Cane, Palm and Sraw Products	167.02
家具制造业	Furniture Manufacturing	69.68
造纸和纸制品业	Papermaking and Paper Products	353.60
印刷和记录媒介复制业	Printing and Record Processing	154.75
文教、工美、体育和娱乐用品制造业	Stationery, Education and Sports Goods	60.85
石油加工、炼焦和核燃料加工业	Petroleum Processing, Coking Products and Nuclear Fuel Processing	204.71
化学原料和化学制品制造业	Raw Chemical Material and Chemical Products	2288.56
医药制造业	Medical and pharmaceutical Products	450.54
化学纤维制造业	Chemical Fibers	37.18
橡胶和塑料制品业	Rubber and Plastic Products	407.24
非金属矿物制品业	Nonmetal Material Products	1407.53
黑色金属冶炼和压延加工业	Smelting and Pressing of Ferrous Metals	2386.26
有色金属冶炼和压延加工业	Smelting and Pressing of Nonferrous Metals	244.60
金属制品业	Metal Products	525.60
通用设备制造业	Ordinary Machinery Manufacturing	537.96
专用设备制造业	Special Purpose Equipment Manufacturing	531.32
汽车制造业	Motor manufacturing	2078.55
铁路、船舶、航空航天和其他运输设备制造业	Railway,Watercraft,Aviation and other Transporlation Equipment manufacturing	279.67
电气机械和器材制造业	Electric Machinery and Equipment	542.87
计算机、通信和其他电子设备制造业	Telecommunication Computer,Equipment and Other Electronic Equipment Manufacturing	577.33
仪器仪表制造业	Instruments and Meters, Manufacturing	82.68
其他制造业	Other Manufacturing	100.02
废弃资源综合利用业	Waste Comprehensive Vtilization of Resources Industry	36.54
金属制品、机械和设备修理业	Metal products,Machinery and Equipment Repairing	10.26
电力、燃气及水的生产和供应业	**Electric Power, Gas and Water Production and Supply**	**5278.00**
电力、热力生产和供应业	Electric Power, Steam and Hot Water Production and Supply	5001.81
燃气生产和供应业	Gas Production and Supply	116.45
水的生产和供应业	Tap Water Production and Supply	159.75

(100 million Yuan)

累计折旧 Accumulated Depreciation	负债合计 Total Liability	流动负债合计 Total Circulating Liability	应付账款 Account Payable
387.49	**601.08**	**497.64**	**150.29**
7.89	26.40	18.83	3.40
214.97	113.17	101.41	-3.58
41.73	71.14	55.80	17.71
15.03	26.61	21.55	2.57
83.17	275.33	212.32	104.32
24.61	87.84	87.72	25.87
0.09	0.60		
9482.22	**16466.69**	**13084.54**	**3928.43**
1691.09	692.44	530.68	110.07
535.29	223.77	181.13	38.52
249.88	673.02	515.96	90.68
60.14	136.67	136.40	59.78
506.59	415.98	316.92	66.08
139.23	193.85	144.02	33.44
43.24	47.20	31.65	8.48
83.74	112.78	75.53	13.30
32.88	47.58	30.58	6.07
242.09	182.72	145.19	34.39
85.87	94.62	74.46	22.27
43.00	142.09	122.98	96.14
100.50	120.71	108.53	24.72
1011.87	1763.67	1221.35	283.93
153.70	459.72	335.67	66.39
21.02	26.43	22.28	4.82
228.65	258.00	201.15	52.73
605.91	866.33	616.84	183.06
1149.94	1933.12	1564.81	274.83
86.98	406.70	333.05	36.26
258.15	549.14	451.57	158.65
272.69	869.94	616.17	117.07
285.65	619.56	493.14	162.01
876.18	2952.16	2561.73	1081.63
94.46	612.49	490.29	213.76
211.72	697.08	572.59	212.11
305.46	1115.34	1007.20	426.44
35.78	101.48	84.12	29.28
54.30	76.68	33.37	9.28
11.77	62.56	55.74	6.63
4.43	12.85	9.46	5.62
1990.72	**2392.22**	**1332.41**	**284.76**
1892.68	2078.52	1124.02	245.97
24.69	132.64	108.37	28.54
73.36	181.06	100.03	10.25

13-3 续表 4 continued

单位: 亿元

项 目	Item	非流动负债合计 Total Non-current Liabilities	所有者权益合计 Total Rights of Owners
总 计	**Total**	**3211.43**	**15875.33**
一、按登记注册类型分组:	**Grouped by Type of Registration**		
内资企业	Inner Funded Enterprises	2762.61	13783.18
国有企业	State Owned Enterprises	600.05	1493.34
中央企业	Central Enterprises	550.67	1396.74
地方企业	Local Enterprises	49.38	96.60
集体企业	Collective-owned Enterprise	5.22	20.97
股份合作企业	Share Holding Cooperative Enterprises	0.09	4.05
联营企业	Joint Owned Enterprise		2.05
国有联营企业	State Joint Ownership		
集体联营企业	Collective Joint Ownership		1.57
国有与集体联营企业	Joint State- Collective Ownership		0.29
其他联营企业	Other Joint Owned Enterprise		0.18
有限责任公司	Responsibility Co. Ltd	1022.45	4784.40
国有独资公司	State Solely Funded Co.	250.03	816.41
其他有限责任公司	Others	772.43	3968.00
股份有限公司	Share Holding Co.Ltd.	801.27	3718.20
私营企业	Private - owned enterprises	332.10	3728.57
私营独资企业	Solely Private - owned enterprises	3.92	67.85
私营合伙企业	Private Joint Venture	3.62	10.07
私营有限责任公司	Private Responsibility Co. Ltd	300.48	3378.95
私营股份有限公司	Private Share Holding Co.Ltd.	24.08	271.70
其他企业	Others	1.42	31.60
港、澳、台商投资企业	Hongkong, Macao and Taiwan Funded Enterprises	160.26	699.12
合资经营企业(港或澳、台资)	Joint Venture with Hongkong, Macao and Taiwan	95.59	365.80
合作经营企业(港或澳、台资)	Cooperate with Hongkong, Macao and Taiwan Funded	2.94	7.08
港澳台商独资经营企业	Enterprises Solely Funded by Hongkong, Macao and Taiwan Businessmen	60.33	297.50
港澳台商投资股份有限公司	Share Holding Co.Ltd. With Hongkong, Macao and Taiwan Investment	1.15	26.71
外商投资企业	Foreign Funded Enterprises	288.56	1393.02
中外合资经营企业	Sino - Foreign Joint Funded Enterprises	168.14	955.41
中外合作经营企业	Sino - Foreign Cooperative Funded Enterprises	6.49	13.04
外资企业	Foreign Solely Funded Enterprises	35.20	307.00
外商投资股份有限公司	Foreign Funded Share Holding Co.Ltd.	78.74	116.84
二、在总计中:亏损企业	**Of the Total: enterprises running under deficit**	**782.72**	**1780.94**
在总计中:国有控股企业	Of the Total: State-Owned Share Holding Enterprises	1897.84	6401.45
在总计中:农村工业	Of the Total: Rural Industry	6.41	43.04
在总计中:轻工业	Of the Total: Light Industry	539.98	4523.20
重工业	Heavy Industry	2671.45	11352.12
在总计中:大型企业	Of the Total: Large Scale Enterprises	1957.25	7364.08
中型企业	Medium Scale Enterprises	546.53	3059.10
小型企业	Small Enterprises	707.65	5452.15

(100 million Yuan)

实收资本 Assets Recevied	国家资本 National Assets	所有者权益合计 Total Rights of Owners			
		集体资本 Collective Assets	法人资本 Corperative Assets	个人资本 Individual Assets	港澳台资本 Assets from Hongkong, Maco and Taiwan Funded Enterprises
7132.11	**2132.71**	**119.39**	**2527.84**	**1738.62**	**155.11**
6009.31	1902.92	111.81	2265.25	1701.24	8.50
555.35	528.93	1.53	16.47	6.13	
516.53	502.42	0.48	13.32	0.32	
38.82	26.51	1.05	3.15	5.81	
9.49	1.16	3.39	2.88	2.05	
2.15		0.53	1.42	0.20	
0.21		0.08	0.05	0.08	
0.02				0.02	
0.14		0.08	0.05		
0.05				0.05	
2312.79	622.07	68.74	1084.55	522.41	6.20
315.50	219.46		95.30	0.73	
1997.29	402.60	68.74	989.25	521.68	6.20
841.06	342.48	16.03	201.99	274.87	1.29
2278.46	407.84	21.51	955.49	888.54	1.01
34.01			9.54	24.24	
5.55			2.57	2.98	
2125.31	406.03	20.14	901.34	792.94	1.01
113.58	1.81	1.37	42.03	68.38	
9.81	0.45		2.39	6.97	
336.59	12.50	2.45	103.92	13.43	112.21
177.32	6.20	2.43	69.96	5.33	52.12
5.35			3.75	0.20	0.15
140.42	6.10	0.02	23.03	6.63	58.97
11.42	0.21		7.18	1.27	0.98
786.21	217.29	5.13	158.67	23.95	34.40
562.11	214.06	4.81	116.73	22.14	14.19
10.96		0.20	5.14	0.10	
179.53	0.86	0.12	21.63	1.26	15.23
33.12	2.37		14.68	0.45	4.98
1288.62	**621.69**	**18.72**	**349.71**	**164.82**	**28.68**
2451.28	1653.61	12.68	574.06	98.61	2.61
14.27	0.23	3.43	4.81	5.67	0.12
1668.79	120.56	27.80	617.93	709.63	65.13
5463.32	2012.15	91.59	1909.92	1028.99	89.97
2280.24	1296.37	13.89	478.12	254.00	54.08
1395.07	231.69	31.81	607.06	334.18	39.70
3456.80	604.65	73.68	1442.67	1150.44	61.33

13-3 续表 5 continued

单位: 亿元

项 目	Item	非流动负债合计 Total Non-current Liabilities	所有者权益合计 Total Rights of Owners
按行业分	**Grouped by sector**		
采矿业	**Mining and Qarrying**	**58.35**	**447.89**
煤炭开采和洗选业	Coal Mining and Processing	1.51	31.92
石油和天然气开采业	Petroleum and Natural Gas Extraction	11.75	36.09
黑色金属矿采选业	Ferrous Metals Mining and Processing	10.82	62.13
有色金属矿采选业	Non-ferrous Metals Mining and Processing	3.60	27.38
非金属矿采选业	Non-metal Minerals Mining and Processing	30.55	262.14
开采辅助活动	Mining Auxiliary Activities	0.12	27.87
其他采矿业	Other Minerals Mining and Processing		0.35
制造业	Manufacturing	2157.85	13388.15
农副食品加工业	Food Processing	75.42	1018.74
食品制造业	Food Production	23.80	325.94
酒、饮料和精制茶制造业	Wine,Beverage and Refined Tea Production	53.70	453.40
烟草制品业	Tobacco Processing	0.27	285.85
纺织业	Textile Industry	55.69	482.43
纺织服装、服饰业	Textile,Garments, and Fashion Industry	24.19	233.23
皮革、毛皮、羽毛及其制品和制鞋业	Leather, Furs,Down and Related Products	6.76	43.21
木材加工和木、竹、藤、棕、草制品业	Timber Processing, Wood, Bamboo, Cane, Palm and Sraw Products	26.12	129.23
家具制造业	Furniture Manufacturing	11.14	71.92
造纸和纸制品业	Papermaking and Paper Products	31.11	154.23
印刷和记录媒介复制业	Printing and Record Processing	14.63	119.08
文教、工美、体育和娱乐用品制造业	Stationery, Education and Sports Goods	13.40	42.23
石油加工、炼焦和核燃料加工业	Petroleum Processing, Coking Products and Nuclear Fuel Processing	8.89	108.85
化学原料和化学制品制造业	Raw Chemical Material and Chemical Products	344.43	1214.07
医药制造业	Medical and pharmaceutical Products	101.07	514.02
化学纤维制造业	Chemical Fibers	2.56	36.13
橡胶和塑料制品业	Rubber and plastic products	25.57	327.49
非金属矿物制品业	Nonmetal Material Products	158.03	1038.37
黑色金属冶炼和压延加工业	Smelting and Pressing of Ferrous Metals	322.46	762.93
有色金属冶炼和压延加工业	Smelting and Pressing of Nonferrous Metals	59.91	188.47
金属制品业	Metal Products	56.47	408.34
通用设备制造业	Ordinary Machinery Manufacturing	209.11	515.69
专用设备制造业	Special Purpose Equipment Manufacturing	26.33	414.56
汽车制造业	Motor manufacturing	225.13	2722.08
铁路、船舶、航空航天和其他运输设备制造业	Railway,Watercraft,Aviation and other Transporlation Equipment manufacturing	107.95	235.24
电气机械和器材制造业	Electric Machinery and Equipment	79.07	586.89
计算机、通信和其他电子设备制造业	Telecommunication Computer,Equipment and Other Electronic Equipment Manufacturing	71.00	759.80
仪器仪表制造业	Instruments and Meters, Manufacturing	10.81	100.14
其他制造业	Other Manufacturing	6.77	48.29
废弃资源综合利用业	Waste Comprehensive Vtilization of Resources Industry	3.30	34.51
金属制品、机械和设备修理业	Metal products,Machinery and Equipment Repairing	2.77	12.80
电力、燃气及水的生产和供应业	**Electric Power, Gas and Water Production and Supply**	**995.23**	**2039.28**
电力、热力生产和供应业	Electric Power, Steam and Hot Water Production and Supply	916.70	1816.75
燃气生产和供应业	Gas Production and Supply	14.44	67.31
水的生产和供应业	Tap Water Production and Supply	64.09	155.22

(100 million Yuan)

实收资本 Assets Recevied	国家资本 National Assets	所有者权益合计 Total Rights of Owners			
		集体资本 Collective Assets	法人资本 Corperative Assets	个人资本 Individual Assets	港澳台资本 Assets from Hongkong, Maco and Taiwan Funded Enterprises
170.06	**34.84**	**10.06**	**64.55**	**60.61**	
15.84	1.35	1.89	5.36	7.25	
35.14	13.11	2.78	10.67	8.57	
8.87	4.47	0.01	1.59	2.81	
94.61	0.77	5.12	46.93	41.78	
15.20	15.09			0.11	
0.40	0.04	0.26		0.10	
6168.56	1557.74	101.62	2312.44	1624.71	136.01
350.47	7.29	7.81	128.87	182.77	6.16
137.88	8.63	0.77	59.28	47.90	4.52
178.82	5.56	1.61	43.45	83.74	16.53
31.53	12.09	1.05	18.39		
193.95	6.02	4.28	72.68	99.51	3.24
111.57	0.55	0.51	59.03	44.55	5.14
23.97			6.35	7.79	5.64
44.47	3.71	1.11	10.45	28.98	0.07
22.18	0.01	0.04	10.40	11.42	0.16
76.27	0.86	0.86	29.37	35.54	1.15
42.56	5.90	0.40	16.37	18.34	1.19
24.28	1.36	0.61	8.16	7.40	6.25
58.25	40.90	0.30	2.68	4.46	
954.62	489.55	8.66	271.11	133.15	6.77
189.56	17.82	6.13	82.16	65.77	12.13
20.49	4.35		5.60	2.28	
130.26	3.19	2.87	50.54	70.00	1.98
682.86	25.24	14.68	414.76	188.50	9.11
369.04	220.15	1.35	52.07	45.37	2.13
121.08	77.62	0.91	9.02	33.39	0.07
211.89	34.72	4.79	84.94	76.45	5.75
194.96	44.40	3.70	54.95	78.83	3.90
188.60	31.35	3.04	96.52	47.34	0.79
964.67	329.98	15.96	355.67	126.83	4.79
163.22	100.09	0.48	45.85	15.49	0.65
267.91	22.83	16.15	85.30	94.35	13.80
337.18	50.93	1.45	204.01	49.81	22.51
35.87	4.64	0.27	18.09	11.78	0.65
13.04	5.72	0.21	2.15	4.95	
20.41	1.28	0.74	10.28	7.17	0.93
6.69	1.01	0.88	3.93	0.87	
793.48	**540.14**	**7.71**	**150.86**	**53.30**	**19.09**
703.60	503.31	3.71	128.22	41.89	16.98
33.66	4.96	3.10	16.62	2.35	2.11
56.22	31.87	0.90	6.01	9.06	

13-3 续表 6 continued

单位: 亿元

项 目	Item	所有者权益合计 Total owner 外商资本 Total Rights of the Owners Foreign Assets
总　计	**Total**	458.44
一、按登记注册类型分组:	**Grouped by Type of Registration**	
内资企业	Inner Funded Enterprises	19.59
国有企业	State Owned Enterprises	2.30
中央企业	Central Enterprises	
地方企业	Local Enterprises	2.30
集体企业	Collective-owned Enterprise	
股份合作企业	Share Holding Cooperative Enterprises	
联营企业	Joint Owned Enterprise	
国有联营企业	State Joint Ownership	
集体联营企业	Collective Joint Ownership	
国有与集体联营企业	Joint State- Collective Ownership	
其他联营企业	Other Joint Owned Enterprise	
有限责任公司	Responsibility Co. Ltd	8.82
国有独资公司	State Solely Funded Co.	
其他有限责任公司	Others	8.82
股份有限公司	Share Holding Co.Ltd.	4.39
私营企业	Private - owned enterprises	4.08
私营独资企业	Solely Private - owned enterprises	0.23
私营合伙企业	Private Joint Venture	
私营有限责任公司	Private Responsibility Co. Ltd	3.85
私营股份有限公司	Private Share Holding Co.Ltd.	
其他企业	Others	
港、澳、台商投资企业	Hongkong, Macao and Taiwan Funded Enterprises	92.07
合资经营企业(港或澳、台资)	Joint Venture with Hongkong, Macao and Taiwan	41.28
合作经营企业(港或澳、台资)	Cooperate with Hongkong, Macao and Taiwan Funded	1.25
港澳台商独资经营企业	Enterprises Solely Funded by Hongkong, Macao and Taiwan Businessmen	45.67
港澳台商投资股份有限公司	Share Holding Co.Ltd. With Hongkong, Macao and Taiwan Investment	1.77
外商投资企业	Foreign Funded Enterprises	346.78
中外合资经营企业	Sino - Foreign Joint Funded Enterprises	190.18
中外合作经营企业	Sino - Foreign Cooperative Funded Enterprises	5.52
外资企业	Foreign Solely Funded Enterprises	140.42
外商投资股份有限公司	Foreign Funded Share Holding Co.Ltd.	10.65
二、在总计中:亏损企业	**Of the Total: enterprises running under deficit**	105.01
在总计中:国有控股企业	Of the Total: State-Owned Share Holding Enterprises	109.72
在总计中:农村工业	Of the Total: Rural Industry	
在总计中:轻工业	Of the Total: Light Industry	127.74
重工业	Heavy Industry	330.70
在总计中:大型企业	Of the Total: Large Scale Enterprises	183.78
中型企业	Medium Scale Enterprises	150.64
小型企业	Small Enterprises	124.02

(100 million Yuan)

营业收入 Proceeds Of Business	主营业务收入 Revenue of Major Business	营业成本 Operating Costs	主营业务成本 Cost of Major Business	营业税金及附加 Tax of Major Business	主营业务税金及附加 Tax of Major Business	其他业务收入 Revenue of Other Business	其他业务利润 Profit from Other Business	销售费用 Selling Expenses
43936.03	43179.21	37226.89	36564.31	905.35	898.35	756.81	37.64	1281.28
37633.46	37093.58	32006.09	31535.32	787.41	780.92	539.88	24.73	1060.50
2813.04	2772.16	2605.30	2564.76	11.40	10.91	40.88	2.26	43.85
2630.11	2604.40	2450.45	2423.78	10.52	10.06	25.72	1.50	38.96
182.93	167.76	154.84	140.98	0.88	0.85	15.16	0.76	4.89
120.67	119.31	105.61	104.68	1.37	1.36	1.36	0.36	2.68
17.20	17.15	14.84	14.39	0.09	0.09	0.05		0.68
7.64	7.50	6.66	6.66	0.10	0.10	0.14	0.14	0.13
2.87	2.73	2.30	2.30	0.06	0.06	0.14	0.14	0.02
0.58	0.58	0.55	0.55					0.01
4.19	4.19	3.81	3.81	0.04	0.04			0.11
15205.57	14919.39	12754.91	12514.60	543.94	541.07	286.18	13.71	408.04
1954.75	1822.03	1286.03	1160.83	447.75	447.73	132.72	1.79	25.38
13250.82	13097.36	11468.88	11353.77	96.19	93.34	153.46	11.92	382.66
4463.70	4396.77	3580.72	3541.45	101.91	100.66	66.93	5.53	198.88
14859.24	14714.91	12806.35	12657.15	127.83	125.96	144.34	2.73	403.92
394.39	393.76	342.07	341.68	4.14	3.85	0.62	0.06	10.92
64.65	64.65	53.86	53.86	0.80	0.80			2.28
13352.05	13219.43	11528.33	11390.33	114.26	112.88	132.61	2.06	357.83
1048.16	1037.07	882.10	871.28	8.62	8.43	11.10	0.62	32.88
146.41	146.41	131.69	131.62	0.77	0.77			2.32
1830.33	1744.52	1548.99	1472.06	6.81	6.74	85.81	4.02	64.74
1057.82	996.82	898.25	842.84	3.63	3.61	61.00	2.12	33.44
9.71	9.70	8.68	8.67	0.05	0.05	0.01		0.47
721.43	697.67	608.00	587.24	2.70	2.68	23.76	1.64	29.82
40.25	39.21	33.07	32.33	0.43	0.41	1.04	0.27	0.95
4472.23	4341.11	3671.82	3556.93	111.13	110.69	131.13	8.89	156.04
3396.64	3284.83	2800.09	2700.40	102.52	102.14	111.81	6.67	105.57
47.97	47.48	37.36	36.92	0.33	0.33	0.49	0.05	0.69
817.98	800.86	665.74	652.18	5.94	5.89	17.12	1.84	36.06
208.73	207.03	168.26	167.06	2.32	2.32	1.70	0.32	13.71
4949.01	4811.16	4653.59	4529.17	94.88	94.26	137.86	5.28	120.65
11722.90	11360.87	9662.10	9355.14	639.89	638.34	362.03	20.46	276.96
171.96	171.82	149.75	149.71	1.49	1.48	0.14	0.11	4.67
15706.50	15439.10	12957.98	12714.54	489.24	486.71	267.40	7.35	581.32
28229.53	27740.11	24268.91	23849.77	416.11	411.64	489.42	30.30	699.96
16297.62	15881.60	13659.54	13316.35	681.65	679.53	416.02	21.98	469.45
9574.24	9427.55	8041.14	7910.31	77.46	75.44	146.69	7.39	287.17
18064.17	17870.07	15526.21	15337.65	146.24	143.38	194.10	8.28	524.65

13-3 续表 7 continued

单位:亿元

项 目	Item	所有者权益合计 Total owner 外商资本 Total Rights of the Owners Foreign Assets
按行业分	Grouped by sector	
采矿业	Mining and Qarrying	0.01
煤炭开采和洗选业	Coal Mining and Processing	
石油和天然气开采业	Petroleum and Natural Gas Extraction	
黑色金属矿采选业	Ferrous Metals Mining and Processing	
有色金属矿采选业	Non-ferrous Metals Mining and Processing	
非金属矿采选业	Non-metal Minerals Mining and Processing	0.01
开采辅助活动	Mining Auxiliary Activities	
其他采矿业	Other Minerals Mining and Processing	
制造业	Manufacturing	436.05
农副食品加工业	Food Processing	17.57
食品制造业	Food Production	16.78
酒、饮料和精制茶制造业	Wine,Beverage and Refined Tea Production	27.94
烟草制品业	Tobacco Processing	
纺织业	Textile Industry	8.22
纺织服装、服饰业	Textile,Garments, and Fashion Industry	1.79
皮革、毛皮、羽毛及其制品和制鞋业	Leather, Furs,Down and Related Products	4.20
木材加工和木、竹、藤、棕、草制品业	Timber Processing, Wood, Bamboo, Cane, Palm and Sraw Products	0.14
家具制造业	Furniture Manufacturing	0.16
造纸和纸制品业	Papermaking and Paper Products	8.50
印刷和记录媒介复制业	Printing and Record Processing	0.35
文教、工美、体育和娱乐用品制造业	Stationery, Education and Sports Goods	0.50
石油加工、炼焦和核燃料加工业	Petroleum Processing, Coking Products and Nuclear Fuel Processing	9.91
化学原料和化学制品制造业	Raw Chemical Material and Chemical Products	45.38
医药制造业	Medical and pharmaceutical Products	5.54
化学纤维制造业	Chemical Fibers	8.26
橡胶和塑料制品业	Rubber and plastic products	1.68
非金属矿物制品业	Nonmetal Material Products	30.57
黑色金属冶炼和压延加工业	Smelting and Pressing of Ferrous Metals	47.97
有色金属冶炼和压延加工业	Smelting and Pressing of Nonferrous Metals	0.08
金属制品业	Metal Products	5.26
通用设备制造业	Ordinary Machinery Manufacturing	9.18
专用设备制造业	Special Purpose Equipment Manufacturing	9.56
汽车制造业	Motor manufacturing	131.45
铁路、船舶、航空航天和其他运输设备制造业	Railway,Watercraft,Aviation and other Transporlation Equipment manufacturing	0.66
电气机械和器材制造业	Electric Machinery and Equipment	35.48
计算机、通信和其他电子设备制造业	Telecommunication Computer,Equipment and Other Electronic Equipment Manufacturing	8.46
仪器仪表制造业	Instruments and Meters, Manufacturing	0.44
其他制造业	Other Manufacturing	0.01
废弃资源综合利用业	Waste Comprehensive Vtilization of Resources Industry	
金属制品、机械和设备修理业	Metal products,Machinery and Equipment Repairing	
电力、燃气及水的生产和供应业	Electric Power, Gas and Water Production and Supply	22.38
电力、热力生产和供应业	Electric Power, Steam and Hot Water Production and Supply	9.48
燃气生产和供应业	Gas Production and Supply	4.51
水的生产和供应业	Tap Water Production and Supply	8.39

(100 million Yuan)

营业收入 Proceeds Of Business	主营业务收入 Revenue of Major Business	营业成本 Operating Costs	主营业务成本 Cost of Major Business	营业税金及附加 Tax of Major Business	主营业务税金及附加 Tax of Major Business	其他业务收入 Revenue of Other Business	其他业务利润 Profit from Other Business	销售费用 Selling Expenses
1157.92	1134.96	961.99	943.09	21.26	21.07	22.96	1.12	35.55
102.60	102.20	83.93	83.66	1.88	1.88	0.40		2.31
48.46	40.09	48.60	42.86	2.34	2.28	8.37		0.86
315.77	315.65	276.05	275.99	2.87	2.86	0.13	0.02	10.96
45.30	44.42	32.16	31.98	0.72	0.72	0.87		0.65
576.37	563.80	463.21	450.92	12.89	12.79	12.57	1.10	20.73
68.77	68.16	57.51	57.15	0.56	0.54	0.61		0.03
0.65	0.65	0.53	0.53					0.02
40981.88	40287.07	34851.38	34231.05	869.24	862.74	694.81	32.28	1235.15
4527.58	4513.03	3993.07	3979.87	19.83	19.60	14.56	0.67	103.84
1163.57	1153.13	966.59	957.84	7.63	7.35	10.44	0.34	59.15
1660.55	1634.74	1316.80	1311.18	34.39	34.23	25.81	0.46	121.17
657.97	592.38	183.77	117.97	369.73	369.73	65.58	-0.24	7.34
2158.84	2153.37	1877.86	1873.55	18.87	18.61	5.47	0.27	52.84
925.90	921.73	799.33	790.92	7.18	6.98	4.17	0.31	28.79
207.92	207.77	185.56	185.16	1.09	1.08	0.15	0.09	3.76
419.56	418.04	361.77	360.75	4.65	4.58	1.52		11.25
166.90	166.75	141.32	141.14	1.29	1.29	0.16	0.04	7.06
524.58	521.03	458.79	455.72	2.89	2.87	3.55	0.39	16.89
339.00	338.04	277.89	276.53	3.05	3.01	0.96	0.07	10.78
264.30	169.37	239.35	145.12	1.29	1.29	94.93	0.74	4.92
784.88	765.49	617.58	598.51	146.50	146.50	19.38	0.23	3.88
4072.12	4033.29	3558.01	3524.66	27.43	27.10	38.84	3.26	110.29
1075.29	1067.38	815.00	801.90	6.76	5.78	7.91	0.32	89.62
77.28	73.62	66.18	64.85	0.45	0.45	3.66	0.09	1.38
1120.29	1113.81	949.82	943.73	8.76	8.70	6.48	0.42	31.66
2949.72	2944.03	2471.33	2465.62	31.60	30.97	5.70	0.97	103.32
2150.10	2046.69	2030.65	1931.46	10.57	10.35	103.41	0.82	36.32
1515.27	1502.29	1451.68	1439.03	2.00	1.91	12.97	0.50	7.08
1369.23	1331.21	1167.48	1126.67	10.18	10.03	38.03	0.21	47.10
1212.43	1208.35	1027.22	1022.75	8.40	8.25	4.08	0.63	37.47
1029.36	1020.52	876.97	868.18	7.36	6.24	8.85	0.36	29.32
5749.14	5594.32	4805.90	4680.04	113.31	112.66	154.82	14.97	172.37
635.29	624.30	562.63	557.87	3.76	3.56	10.99	0.84	9.01
1732.63	1700.57	1473.10	1448.94	10.13	9.62	32.06	3.47	49.92
1980.52	1962.16	1747.85	1734.71	6.36	6.28	18.36	2.01	63.94
182.89	181.95	144.59	144.07	1.19	1.14	0.95	0.14	7.61
163.27	162.79	137.50	136.93	1.66	1.66	0.47	-0.12	4.64
125.35	124.90	112.10	111.70	0.54	0.54	0.45	0.01	1.56
40.12	40.00	33.71	33.67	0.39	0.38	0.13	0.01	0.88
1796.23	1757.18	1413.52	1390.16	14.85	14.53	39.05	4.25	10.58
1571.36	1546.58	1237.10	1221.28	13.20	13.03	24.79	2.23	1.19
154.35	145.49	121.63	117.49	1.03	0.96	8.86	0.85	5.15
70.51	65.11	54.80	51.40	0.62	0.54	5.40	1.17	4.24

13-3 续表 8 continued

单位: 亿元

项 目	Item	管理费用 Management Expense
总 计	**Total**	1811.39
一、按登记注册类型分组:	**Grouped by Type of Registration**	
内资企业	Inner Funded Enterprises	1527.75
国有企业	State Owned Enterprises	132.80
中央企业	Central Enterprises	120.24
地方企业	Local Enterprises	12.55
集体企业	Collective-owned Enterprise	5.07
股份合作企业	Share Holding Cooperative Enterprises	0.63
联营企业	Joint Owned Enterprise	0.25
国有联营企业	State Joint Ownership	
集体联营企业	Collective Joint Ownership	0.06
国有与集体联营企业	Joint State- Collective Ownership	0.05
其他联营企业	Other Joint Owned Enterprise	0.14
有限责任公司	Responsibility Co. Ltd	588.62
国有独资公司	State Solely Funded Co.	78.00
其他有限责任公司	Others	510.62
股份有限公司	Share Holding Co.Ltd.	256.10
私营企业	Private - owned enterprises	541.03
私营独资企业	Solely Private - owned enterprises	10.31
私营合伙企业	Private Joint Venture	3.08
私营有限责任公司	Private Responsibility Co. Ltd	486.74
私营股份有限公司	Private Share Holding Co.Ltd.	40.89
其他企业	Others	3.25
港、澳、台商投资企业	Hongkong, Macao and Taiwan Funded Enterprises	96.58
合资经营企业(港或澳、台资)	Joint Venture with Hongkong, Macao and Taiwan	66.10
合作经营企业(港或澳、台资)	Cooperate with Hongkong, Macao and Taiwan Funded	0.38
港澳台商独资经营企业	Enterprises Solely Funded by Hongkong, Macao and Taiwan Businessmen	27.71
港澳台商投资股份有限公司	Share Holding Co.Ltd. With Hongkong,	2.32
外商投资企业	Foreign Funded Enterprises	187.05
中外合资经营企业	Sino - Foreign Joint Funded Enterprises	129.07
中外合作经营企业	Sino - Foreign Cooperative Funded Enterprises	0.44
外资企业	Foreign Solely Funded Enterprises	45.27
外商投资股份有限公司	Foreign Funded Share Holding Co.Ltd.	12.17
二、在总计中:亏损企业	**Of the Total: enterprises running under deficit**	236.19
在总计中:国有控股企业	Of the Total: State-Owned Share Holding Enterprises	540.82
在总计中:农村工业	Of the Total: Rural Industry	6.65
在总计中:轻工业	Of the Total: Light Industry	636.01
重工业	Heavy Industry	1175.38
在总计中:大型企业	Of the Total: Large Scale Enterprises	664.72
中型企业	Medium Scale Enterprises	446.48
小型企业	Small Enterprises	700.19

(100 million Yuan)

税金 Tax	财务费用 Financial Expense	利息收入 Interest Income	利息支出 Interest Expense
105.33	516.99	28.34	442.62
92.67	476.58	32.76	403.26
8.19	72.59	7.69	65.14
7.49	70.92	7.36	63.46
0.70	1.68	0.33	1.69
0.20	0.65	0.01	0.47
0.01	0.12	0.01	0.08
	0.12		0.01
	0.04		
	0.01		0.01
	0.07		
29.72	175.80	12.49	157.16
2.59	24.35	2.29	25.00
27.13	151.44	10.20	132.16
17.65	69.38	9.96	76.76
36.66	157.19	2.59	103.08
0.68	4.61	0.02	2.56
0.06	0.94		0.50
32.91	141.34	2.28	92.87
3.02	10.30	0.29	7.15
0.24	0.72	0.01	0.55
4.35	15.34	0.70	15.58
2.48	7.04	0.41	8.65
0.03	0.24		0.13
1.72	7.09	0.27	6.35
0.13	0.97	0.02	0.45
8.31	25.07	-5.12	23.78
4.65	10.43	-1.86	18.23
0.01	0.46	0.03	0.44
2.72	5.86	-3.54	3.76
0.91	8.32	0.25	1.35
13.55	118.09	11.30	101.81
22.22	189.41	23.88	201.93
0.22	2.08	0.02	1.55
53.26	143.48	6.72	112.63
52.07	373.51	21.63	329.99
39.07	209.73	20.03	211.63
26.26	106.38	8.13	92.33
40.00	200.88	0.18	138.66

13-3 续表 9 continued

单位: 亿元

项 目	Item	管理费用 Management Expense
按行业分	Grouped by sector	
采矿业	Mining and Qarrying	60.02
煤炭开采和洗选业	Coal Mining and Processing	4.99
石油和天然气开采业	Petroleum and Natural Gas Extraction	8.28
黑色金属矿采选业	Ferrous Metals Mining and Processing	10.02
有色金属矿采选业	Non-ferrous Metals Mining and Processing	4.81
非金属矿采选业	Non-metal Minerals Mining and Processing	26.97
开采辅助活动	Mining Auxiliary Activities	4.89
其他采矿业	Other Minerals Mining and Processing	0.06
制造业	Manufacturing	1713.57
农副食品加工业	Food Processing	138.10
食品制造业	Food Production	54.38
酒、饮料和精制茶制造业	Wine,Beverage and Refined Tea Production	71.92
烟草制品业	Tobacco Processing	19.24
纺织业	Textile Industry	77.23
纺织服装、服饰业	Textile,Garments, and Fashion Industry	37.65
皮革、毛皮、羽毛及其制品和制鞋业	Leather, Furs,Down and Related Products	8.80
木材加工和木、竹、藤、棕、草制品业	Timber Processing, Wood, Bamboo, Cane, Palm and Sraw Products	12.32
家具制造业	Furniture Manufacturing	6.62
造纸和纸制品业	Papermaking and Paper Products	16.96
印刷和记录媒介复制业	Printing and Record Processing	20.95
文教、工美、体育和娱乐用品制造业	Stationery, Education and Sports Goods	7.54
石油加工、炼焦和核燃料加工业	Petroleum Processing, Coking Products and Nuclear Fuel Processing	12.95
化学原料和化学制品制造业	Raw Chemical Material and Chemical Products	134.44
医药制造业	Medical and pharmaceutical Products	70.54
化学纤维制造业	Chemical Fibers	4.30
橡胶和塑料制品业	Rubber and plastic products	41.83
非金属矿物制品业	Nonmetal Material Products	118.28
黑色金属冶炼和压延加工业	Smelting and Pressing of Ferrous Metals	89.96
有色金属冶炼和压延加工业	Smelting and Pressing of Nonferrous Metals	30.36
金属制品业	Metal Products	63.98
通用设备制造业	Ordinary Machinery Manufacturing	66.38
专用设备制造业	Special Purpose Equipment Manufacturing	56.09
汽车制造业	Motor manufacturing	283.88
铁路、船舶、航空航天和其他运输设备制造业	Railway,Watercraft,Aviation and other Transporlation Equipment manufacturing	33.66
电气机械和器材制造业	Electric Machinery and Equipment	90.48
计算机、通信和其他电子设备制造业	Telecommunication Computer,Equipment and Other Electronic Equipment Manufacturing	111.13
仪器仪表制造业	Instruments and Meters, Manufacturing	14.37
其他制造业	Other Manufacturing	7.65
废弃资源综合利用业	Waste Comprehensive Vtilization of Resources Industry	8.92
金属制品、机械和设备修理业	Metal products,Machinery and Equipment Repairing	2.67
电力、燃气及水的生产和供应业	Electric Power, Gas and Water Production and Supply	37.80
电力、热力生产和供应业	Electric Power, Steam and Hot Water Production and Supply	22.90
燃气生产和供应业	Gas Production and Supply	7.61
水的生产和供应业	Tap Water Production and Supply	7.29

(100 million Yuan)

税金 Tax	财务费用 Financial Expense	利息收入 Interest Income	利息支出 Interest Expense
2.38	15.52	0.41	10.58
0.18	0.56	0.09	0.45
0.54	0.98	0.09	1.05
0.56	3.62	0.03	2.34
0.14	0.36	0.04	0.29
0.92	9.11	0.10	5.95
0.04	0.88	0.07	0.51
	0.01		
100.48	420.04	25.90	352.71
11.33	38.97	1.19	30.54
5.09	9.10	0.93	7.96
9.67	14.37	1.22	12.79
0.42	-0.60	-0.11	0.12
7.53	28.65	0.43	19.17
3.43	8.75	0.25	6.94
0.65	1.88	0.04	1.18
0.94	5.19	0.05	3.60
0.28	1.68	0.02	1.34
0.93	5.37	1.84	5.97
2.08	2.74	0.27	1.83
0.39	2.78	-0.03	1.21
0.25	1.06	1.37	2.37
8.41	58.60	1.93	52.81
5.61	12.66	0.63	8.90
0.11	1.09	0.05	0.77
2.28	13.27	0.14	9.63
6.68	41.22	1.44	24.38
6.70	71.36	4.80	58.36
1.27	9.79	4.21	9.40
2.40	16.31	0.86	12.59
2.73	17.57	1.32	14.30
1.61	12.14	1.21	8.52
12.15	15.44	7.00	31.30
0.84	4.83	0.38	4.70
3.57	14.11	-0.17	9.77
2.06	6.94	-5.68	8.74
0.41	1.76	0.08	1.57
0.45	1.39	0.07	0.69
0.17	1.12	0.01	0.66
0.03	0.52	0.14	0.59
2.47	81.42	2.04	79.33
1.69	77.67	1.96	75.83
0.24	1.52	0.03	1.39
0.54	2.24	0.05	2.11

13-3 续表 10 continued

单位: 亿元

项 目	Item	营业利润 Operating Profit
总　　计	**Total**	**2313.30**
一、按登记注册类型分组:	**Grouped by Type of Registration**	
内资企业	Inner Funded Enterprises	1895.94
国有企业	State Owned Enterprises	-52.19
中央企业	Central Enterprises	-60.27
地方企业	Local Enterprises	8.08
集体企业	Collective-owned Enterprise	5.17
股份合作企业	Share Holding Cooperative Enterprises	0.81
联营企业	Joint Owned Enterprise	0.37
国有联营企业	State Joint Ownership	
集体联营企业	Collective Joint Ownership	0.39
国有与集体联营企业	Joint State- Collective Ownership	-0.04
其他联营企业	Other Joint Owned Enterprise	0.02
有限责任公司	Responsibility Co. Ltd	710.78
国有独资公司	State Solely Funded Co.	81.13
其他有限责任公司	Others	629.65
股份有限公司	Share Holding Co.Ltd.	401.55
私营企业	Private - owned enterprises	822.33
私营独资企业	Solely Private - owned enterprises	22.26
私营合伙企业	Private Joint Venture	3.68
私营有限责任公司	Private Responsibility Co. Ltd	722.74
私营股份有限公司	Private Share Holding Co.Ltd.	73.65
其他企业	Others	7.11
港、澳、台商投资企业	Hongkong, Macao and Taiwan Funded Enterprises	96.03
合资经营企业(港或澳、台资)	Joint Venture with Hongkong, Macao and Taiwan	47.50
合作经营企业(港或澳、台资)	Cooperate with Hongkong, Macao and Taiwan Funded	0.03
港澳台商独资经营企业	Enterprises Solely Funded by Hongkong, Macao and Taiwan Businessmen	46.43
港澳台商投资股份有限公司	Share Holding Co.Ltd. With Hongkong, Macao and Taiwan Investment	2.07
外商投资企业	Foreign Funded Enterprises	321.33
中外合资经营企业	Sino - Foreign Joint Funded Enterprises	250.34
中外合作经营企业	Sino - Foreign Cooperative Funded Enterprises	8.59
外资企业	Foreign Solely Funded Enterprises	59.00
外商投资股份有限公司	Foreign Funded Share Holding Co.Ltd.	2.98
二、在总计中:亏损企业	**Of the Total: enterprises running under deficit**	**-330.35**
在总计中:国有控股企业	Of the Total: State-Owned Share Holding Enterprises	527.36
在总计中:农村工业	Of the Total: Rural Industry	7.32
在总计中:轻工业	Of the Total: Light Industry	909.71
重工业	Heavy Industry	1403.59
在总计中:大型企业	Of the Total: Large Scale Enterprises	741.61
中型企业	Medium Scale Enterprises	617.70
小型企业	Small Enterprises	953.99

(100 million Yuan)

补贴收入 Income from subsidy	营业外收入 Non-operating Income	营业外支出 Non-operating Expense	利润总额 Total Profit	应交所得税 Income Tax	亏损企业 亏损总额 Total Loss of Enterprises Running under Deficit
94.38	**207.09**	**63.62**	**2456.00**	**317.47**	**310.78**
74.44	174.04	54.74	2014.48	237.45	273.75
8.04	26.95	6.35	-31.59	6.51	117.91
7.97	24.08	3.83	-40.02	5.55	116.56
0.06	2.87	2.52	8.43	0.96	1.34
0.10	0.18	0.08	5.28	0.24	0.45
	0.01	0.04	0.79	0.02	
0.04	0.05		0.42		
			0.39		
0.04	0.05		0.01		
			0.02		
32.10	67.63	20.65	756.99	106.87	87.40
5.25	11.55	3.55	89.13	23.49	27.77
26.85	56.08	17.10	667.87	83.38	59.63
27.50	55.93	8.24	449.24	65.27	43.50
6.64	22.67	19.35	825.66	57.84	24.24
	0.06	0.33	21.99	1.01	0.29
	0.02	0.13	3.56	0.09	0.08
5.93	19.98	17.59	725.14	53.37	21.83
0.71	2.61	1.30	74.97	3.38	2.04
0.03	0.60	0.03	7.68	0.69	0.25
2.41	7.68	1.91	101.81	16.35	7.63
1.46	5.10	0.64	51.96	7.79	2.63
	0.02	0.26	-0.21	-0.13	0.38
0.73	2.32	1.00	47.76	8.33	3.26
0.21	0.22	0.01	2.29	0.34	1.36
17.53	25.37	6.98	339.72	63.68	29.40
14.17	19.21	4.09	265.46	47.96	19.01
0.02	0.04	0.04	8.59	2.08	
1.58	3.86	2.45	60.41	11.72	9.26
1.77	2.25	0.39	4.84	1.90	1.14
9.43	**28.71**	**9.14**	**-310.78**	**-8.42**	**310.78**
62.23	110.69	23.10	614.18	128.78	223.48
0.03	0.09	0.10	7.32	0.72	0.26
15.63	46.21	25.27	930.65	105.12	32.57
78.75	160.88	38.35	1525.35	212.35	278.21
59.13	114.13	23.13	831.85	155.98	207.10
17.73	45.42	12.33	650.79	84.76	42.17
17.52	47.53	28.16	973.37	76.73	61.51

13-3 续表 11 continued

单位: 亿元

项 目	Item	营业利润 Operating Profit
按行业分	**Grouped by sector**	
采矿业	**Mining and Qarrying**	**55.16**
煤炭开采和洗选业	Coal Mining and Processing	8.92
石油和天然气开采业	Petroleum and Natural Gas Extraction	-19.42
黑色金属矿采选业	Ferrous Metals Mining and Processing	11.31
有色金属矿采选业	Non-ferrous Metals Mining and Processing	6.54
非金属矿采选业	Non-metal Minerals Mining and Processing	42.99
开采辅助活动	Mining Auxiliary Activities	4.79
其他采矿业	Other Minerals Mining and Processing	0.02
制造业	**Manufacturing**	**1993.95**
农副食品加工业	Food Processing	233.29
食品制造业	Food Production	70.23
酒、饮料和精制茶制造业	Wine,Beverage and Refined Tea Production	112.52
烟草制品业	Tobacco Processing	74.86
纺织业	Textile Industry	103.40
纺织服装、服饰业	Textile,Garments, and Fashion Industry	44.32
皮革、毛皮、羽毛及其制品和制鞋业	Leather, Furs,Down and Related Products	6.83
木材加工和木、竹、藤、棕、草制品业	Timber Processing, Wood, Bamboo, Cane, Palm and Sraw Products	23.78
家具制造业	Furniture Manufacturing	8.95
造纸和纸制品业	Papermaking and Paper Products	23.84
印刷和记录媒介复制业	Printing and Record Processing	22.81
文教、工美、体育和娱乐用品制造业	Stationery, Education and Sports Goods	8.44
石油加工、炼焦和核燃料加工业	Petroleum Processing, Coking Products and Nuclear Fuel Processing	1.90
化学原料和化学制品制造业	Raw Chemical Material and Chemical Products	190.79
医药制造业	Medical and pharmaceutical Products	80.53
化学纤维制造业	Chemical Fibers	5.55
橡胶和塑料制品业	Rubber and plastic products	75.66
非金属矿物制品业	Nonmetal Material Products	183.23
黑色金属冶炼和压延加工业	Smelting and Pressing of Ferrous Metals	-96.95
有色金属冶炼和压延加工业	Smelting and Pressing of Nonferrous Metals	1.83
金属制品业	Metal Products	63.39
通用设备制造业	Ordinary Machinery Manufacturing	50.91
专用设备制造业	Special Purpose Equipment Manufacturing	46.53
汽车制造业	Motor manufacturing	479.66
铁路、船舶、航空航天和其他运输设备制造业	Railway,Watercraft,Aviation and other Transporlation Equipment manufacturing	14.48
电气机械和器材制造业	Electric Machinery and Equipment	95.24
计算机、通信和其他电子设备制造业	Telecommunication Computer,Equipment and Other Electronic Equipment Manufacturing	43.07
仪器仪表制造业	Instruments and Meters, Manufacturing	13.87
其他制造业	Other Manufacturing	8.44
废弃资源综合利用业	Waste Comprehensive Vtilization of Resources Industry	0.59
金属制品、机械和设备修理业	Metal products,Machinery and Equipment Repairing	1.95
电力、燃气及水的生产和供应业	**Electric Power, Gas and Water Production and Supply**	**264.19**
电力、热力生产和供应业	Electric Power, Steam and Hot Water Production and Supply	242.44
燃气生产和供应业	Gas Production and Supply	18.07
水的生产和供应业	Tap Water Production and Supply	3.67

(100 million Yuan)

补贴收入 Income from subsidy	营业外收入 Non-operating Income	营业外支出 Non-operating Expense	利润总额 Total Profit	应交所得税 Income Tax	亏损企业亏损总额 Total Loss of Enterprises Running
1.86	**2.44**	**2.38**	**55.23**	**5.40**	**23.85**
0.01	0.12	0.07	8.97	0.58	0.45
0.68	0.72	0.92	-19.62	-0.27	19.62
0.03	0.08	0.31	11.09	1.20	1.49
	0.07	0.17	6.44	1.30	0.70
0.70	0.97	0.87	43.09	2.24	1.38
0.44	0.48	0.03	5.24	0.36	0.21
			0.02		
65.43	**170.83**	**57.64**	**2106.38**	**246.62**	**278.95**
3.10	8.63	7.92	234.01	16.88	5.46
1.31	2.73	1.87	71.10	6.84	1.65
1.75	6.39	4.84	114.08	20.48	3.40
0.09	0.85	1.88	73.83	17.15	0.03
1.06	2.33	2.24	103.48	8.29	4.76
0.28	0.54	1.17	43.69	3.77	2.35
0.01	0.17	0.08	6.92	0.34	0.53
0.90	1.38	0.14	25.02	1.32	0.35
0.02	0.05	0.04	8.96	1.32	0.69
0.98	1.46	0.56	24.74	3.13	2.65
0.43	1.05	0.79	23.07	3.04	2.12
0.35	0.53	0.15	8.81	0.82	0.87
0.10	0.69	0.01	2.58	0.32	2.19
4.63	9.87	4.26	196.40	31.44	15.13
2.43	10.84	1.67	89.71	9.33	1.90
0.06	0.22	0.03	5.74	0.60	0.16
0.82	1.72	1.12	76.26	7.16	0.86
6.85	16.81	8.63	191.41	15.52	7.55
1.90	9.68	1.32	-88.59	-3.22	127.43
1.00	2.55	0.50	3.87	0.40	13.14
1.09	7.04	0.86	69.58	7.47	6.58
3.93	8.18	0.97	58.12	4.94	10.67
1.86	3.88	0.73	49.69	5.45	3.63
18.13	35.82	10.69	504.79	59.00	29.70
1.84	3.66	0.27	17.87	3.53	9.31
2.46	9.63	2.68	102.20	10.61	7.93
5.75	20.37	1.99	60.68	8.97	15.25
0.58	1.43	0.15	15.16	1.09	0.98
0.36	0.41	0.05	8.79	0.29	0.34
1.36	1.69	0.04	2.24	0.20	1.21
0.01	0.21	0.01	2.16	0.12	0.14
27.09	**33.81**	**3.60**	**294.40**	**65.45**	**7.98**
26.40	31.43	2.89	270.99	61.85	6.87
0.17	0.95	0.49	18.53	3.27	0.11
0.52	1.43	0.22	4.89	0.33	1.01

13-3 续表 12 continued

单位: 亿元 (100 million Yuan)

项 目	Item	利税总额 Total Profit	本年应付职工薪酬 Wages Welfarism payable This Year
总 计	**Total**	**4599.15**	**2255.65**
一、按登记注册类型分组:	**Grouped by Type of Registration**		
内资企业	Inner Funded Enterprises	3737.94	1940.92
国有企业	State Owned Enterprises	45.34	297.17
中央企业	Central Enterprises	32.61	275.69
地方企业	Local Enterprises	12.73	21.48
集体企业	Collective-owned Enterprise	10.22	8.75
股份合作企业	Share Holding Cooperative Enterprises	1.09	0.74
联营企业	Joint Owned Enterprise	0.75	0.22
国有联营企业	State Joint Ownership		
集体联营企业	Collective Joint Ownership	0.64	0.07
国有与集体联营企业	Joint State- Collective Ownership	0.05	0.03
其他联营企业	Other Joint Owned Enterprise	0.06	0.11
有限责任公司	Responsibility Co. Ltd	1713.88	804.31
国有独资公司	State Solely Funded Co.	659.07	92.94
其他有限责任公司	Others	1054.81	711.37
股份有限公司	Share Holding Co.Ltd.	692.61	278.32
私营企业	Private - owned enterprises	1263.11	547.69
私营独资企业	Solely Private - owned enterprises	33.29	14.98
私营合伙企业	Private Joint Venture	5.46	1.55
私营有限责任公司	Private Responsibility Co. Ltd	1116.50	487.53
私营股份有限公司	Private Share Holding Co.Ltd.	107.86	43.63
其他企业	Others	10.92	3.73
港、澳、台商投资企业	Hongkong, Macao and Taiwan Funded Enterprises	155.85	89.79
合资经营企业(港或澳、台资)	Joint Venture with Hongkong, Macao and Taiwan	79.88	53.01
合作经营企业(港或澳、台资)	Cooperate with Hongkong, Macao and Taiwan Funded	0.05	0.52
港澳台商独资经营企业	Enterprises Solely Funded by Hongkong, Macao and Taiwan Businessmen	72.26	34.15
港澳台商投资股份有限公司	Share Holding Co.Ltd. With Hongkong, Macao and Taiwan Investment	3.80	2.09
外商投资企业	Foreign Funded Enterprises	705.36	224.94
中外合资经营企业	Sino - Foreign Joint Funded Enterprises	588.26	156.40
中外合作经营企业	Sino - Foreign Cooperative Funded Enterprises	12.07	1.60
外资企业	Foreign Solely Funded Enterprises	88.48	48.12
外商投资股份有限公司	Foreign Funded Share Holding Co.Ltd.	16.13	18.75
二、在总计中:亏损企业	**Of the Total: enterprises running under deficit**	**-134.89**	**366.22**
在总计中:国有控股企业	Of the Total: State-Owned Share Holding Enterprises	1778.62	885.77
在总计中:农村工业	Of the Total: Rural Industry	11.73	6.60
在总计中:轻工业	Of the Total: Light Industry	1831.12	707.62
重工业	Heavy Industry	2768.04	1548.03
在总计中:大型企业	Of the Total: Large Scale Enterprises	2114.84	998.68
中型企业	Medium Scale Enterprises	984.86	538.24
小型企业	Small Enterprises	1499.46	718.73

13-3 续表 13 continued

单位: 亿元

项 目	Item	利税总额 Total Profit	本年应付职工薪酬 Wages Welfarism Payable this year
按行业分	**Grouped by sector**		
采矿业	**Mining and Qarrying**	**121.04**	**74.77**
煤炭开采和洗选业	Coal Mining and Processing	15.37	11.30
石油和天然气开采业	Petroleum and Natural Gas Extraction	-12.76	18.66
黑色金属矿采选业	Ferrous Metals Mining and Processing	20.85	8.75
有色金属矿采选业	Non-ferrous Metals Mining and Processing	9.89	3.80
非金属矿采选业	Non-metal Minerals Mining and Processing	73.92	21.92
开采辅助活动	Mining Auxiliary Activities	13.73	10.17
其他采矿业	Other Minerals Mining and Processing	0.04	0.16
制造业	Manufacturing	4051.72	2019.89
农副食品加工业	Food Processing	314.73	119.11
食品制造业	Food Production	112.20	48.39
酒、饮料和精制茶制造业	Wine,Beverage and Refined Tea Production	189.70	64.73
烟草制品业	Tobacco Processing	526.09	19.83
纺织业	Textile Industry	172.55	129.34
纺织服装、服饰业	Textile,Garments, and Fashion Industry	70.34	83.34
皮革、毛皮、羽毛及其制品和制鞋业	Leather, Furs,Down and Related Products	12.14	13.67
木材加工和木、竹、藤、棕、草制品业	Timber Processing, Wood, Bamboo, Cane, Palm and Sraw Products	38.63	17.84
家具制造业	Furniture Manufacturing	13.77	10.39
造纸和纸制品业	Papermaking and Paper Products	38.66	26.97
印刷和记录媒介复制业	Printing and Record Processing	36.03	16.24
文教、工美、体育和娱乐用品制造业	Stationery, Education and Sports Goods	13.11	8.02
石油加工、炼焦和核燃料加工业	Petroleum Processing, Coking Products and Nuclear Fuel Processing	179.02	9.48
化学原料和化学制品制造业	Raw Chemical Material and Chemical Products	302.41	128.40
医药制造业	Medical and pharmaceutical Products	138.51	64.65
化学纤维制造业	Chemical Fibers	8.00	4.65
橡胶和塑料制品业	Rubber and plastic products	117.33	50.18
非金属矿物制品业	Nonmetal Material Products	302.18	135.80
黑色金属冶炼和压延加工业	Smelting and Pressing of Ferrous Metals	-40.02	151.82
有色金属冶炼和压延加工业	Smelting and Pressing of Nonferrous Metals	15.55	41.14
金属制品业	Metal Products	108.52	64.20
通用设备制造业	Ordinary Machinery Manufacturing	93.73	60.66
专用设备制造业	Special Purpose Equipment Manufacturing	79.73	63.49
汽车制造业	Motor manufacturing	888.61	401.74
铁路、船舶、航空航天和其他运输设备制造业	Railway,Watercraft,Aviation and other Transporlation Equipment manufacturing	33.24	47.25
电气机械和器材制造业	Electric Machinery and Equipment	151.68	79.62
计算机、通信和其他电子设备制造业	Telecommunication Computer,Equipment and Other Electronic Equipment Manufacturing	92.91	126.84
仪器仪表制造业	Instruments and Meters, Manufacturing	20.84	17.47
其他制造业	Other Manufacturing	13.23	6.45
废弃资源综合利用业	Waste Comprehensive Vtilization of Resources Industry	4.50	4.01
金属制品、机械和设备修理业	Metal products,Machinery and Equipment Repairing	3.79	4.18
电力、燃气及水的生产和供应业	**Electric Power, Gas and Water Production and Supply**	**426.40**	**160.99**
电力、热力生产和供应业	Electric Power, Steam and Hot Water Production and Supply	396.11	141.73
燃气生产和供应业	Gas Production and Supply	23.00	7.02
水的生产和供应业	Tap Water Production and Supply	7.29	12.24

13-3 续表 14 continued

单位: 亿元 (100 million Yuan)

项 目	Item	应交税金及附加 Tax and Extra Charges	本年应交增值税 Value Added Payable of the Current Year	全部从业人员年平均人数(万人) Average Number of Empolyment of the Current Year (10000 persons)
总 计	**Total**	**2565.95**	**1237.80**	**352.64**
一、按登记注册类型分组:	**Grouped by Type of Registration**			
内资企业	Inner Funded Enterprises	2053.58	936.05	308.15
国有企业	State Owned Enterprises	91.63	65.53	27.11
中央企业	Central Enterprises	85.67	62.11	24.25
地方企业	Local Enterprises	5.96	3.42	2.86
集体企业	Collective-owned Enterprise	5.39	3.58	1.91
股份合作企业	Share Holding Cooperative Enterprises	0.34	0.22	0.17
联营企业	Joint Owned Enterprise	0.33	0.23	0.09
国有联营企业	State Joint Ownership			
集体联营企业	Collective Joint Ownership	0.25	0.19	0.03
国有与集体联营企业	Joint State- Collective Ownership	0.04	0.03	0.04
其他联营企业	Other Joint Owned Enterprise	0.04		0.02
有限责任公司	Responsibility Co. Ltd	1093.48	412.95	121.04
国有独资公司	State Solely Funded Co.	596.03	122.20	10.61
其他有限责任公司	Others	497.45	290.75	110.42
股份有限公司	Share Holding Co.Ltd.	326.29	141.46	37.89
私营企业	Private - owned enterprises	531.95	309.63	118.93
私营独资企业	Solely Private - owned enterprises	12.99	7.16	3.21
私营合伙企业	Private Joint Venture	2.03	1.09	0.42
私营有限责任公司	Private Responsibility Co. Ltd	477.64	277.10	106.60
私营股份有限公司	Private Share Holding Co.Ltd.	39.29	24.27	8.71
其他企业	Others	4.17	2.47	1.01
港、澳、台商投资企业	Hongkong, Macao and Taiwan Funded Enterprises	74.75	47.24	17.03
合资经营企业(港或澳、台资)	Joint Venture with Hongkong, Macao and Taiwan	38.19	24.29	8.92
合作经营企业(港或澳、台资)	Cooperate with Hongkong, Macao and Taiwan Funded	0.16	0.22	0.09
港澳台商独资经营企业	Enterprises Solely Funded by Hongkong, Macao and Taiwan Businessmen	34.55	21.80	7.69
港澳台商投资股份有限公司	Share Holding Co.Ltd. With Hongkong, Macao and Taiwan Investment	1.98	1.09	0.32
外商投资企业	Foreign Funded Enterprises	437.62	254.51	27.47
中外合资经营企业	Sino - Foreign Joint Funded Enterprises	375.42	220.28	17.27
中外合作经营企业	Sino - Foreign Cooperative Funded Enterprises	5.57	3.15	0.18
外资企业	Foreign Solely Funded Enterprises	42.51	22.13	7.93
外商投资股份有限公司	Foreign Funded Share Holding Co.Ltd.	14.11	8.98	2.07
二、在总计中:亏损企业	**Of the Total: enterprises running under deficit**	**181.02**	**81.01**	**50.16**
在总计中:国有控股企业	Of the Total: State-Owned Share Holding Enterprises	1315.44	524.54	81.05
在总计中:农村工业	Of the Total: Rural Industry	5.36	2.92	1.61
在总计中:轻工业	Of the Total: Light Industry	1058.84	411.22	139.45
重工业	Heavy Industry	1507.10	826.58	213.20
在总计中:大型企业	Of the Total: Large Scale Enterprises	1478.04	601.34	118.79
中型企业	Medium Scale Enterprises	445.10	256.61	95.95
小型企业	Small Enterprises	642.81	379.85	137.91

13-3 续表 15 continued

单位: 亿元 (100 million Yuan)

项 目	Item	应交税金及附加 Tax and Extra Charges	本年应交增值税 Value Added Payable of the Current Year	全部从业人员年平均人数(万人) Average Number of Empolyment of the Current Year (10000 persons)
按行业分	Grouped by sector			
采矿业	Mining and Qarrying	73.58	44.54	13.60
煤炭开采和洗选业	Coal Mining and Processing	7.16	4.52	2.20
石油和天然气开采业	Petroleum and Natural Gas Extraction	7.12	4.51	1.76
黑色金属矿采选业	Ferrous Metals Mining and Processing	11.52	6.89	2.39
有色金属矿采选业	Non-ferrous Metals Mining and Processing	4.89	2.73	0.67
非金属矿采选业	Non-metal Minerals Mining and Processing	33.99	17.94	4.81
开采辅助活动	Mining Auxiliary Activities	8.89	7.93	1.73
其他采矿业	Other Minerals Mining and Processing	0.01	0.01	0.04
制造业	Manufacturing	2292.44	1076.10	323.82
农副食品加工业	Food Processing	108.94	60.89	23.58
食品制造业	Food Production	53.04	33.48	9.93
酒、饮料和精制茶制造业	Wine,Beverage and Refined Tea Production	105.77	41.23	11.59
烟草制品业	Tobacco Processing	469.84	82.54	0.82
纺织业	Textile Industry	84.89	50.20	27.47
纺织服装、服饰业	Textile,Garments, and Fashion Industry	33.85	19.47	17.24
皮革、毛皮、羽毛及其制品和制鞋业	Leather, Furs,Down and Related Products	6.21	4.13	3.90
木材加工和木、竹、藤、棕、草制品业	Timber Processing, Wood, Bamboo, Cane, Palm and Sraw Products	15.87	8.96	4.08
家具制造业	Furniture Manufacturing	6.41	3.52	1.98
造纸和纸制品业	Papermaking and Paper Products	17.98	11.03	4.63
印刷和记录媒介复制业	Printing and Record Processing	18.07	9.91	3.36
文教、工美、体育和娱乐用品制造业	Stationery, Education and Sports Goods	5.50	3.01	2.16
石油加工、炼焦和核燃料加工业	Petroleum Processing, Coking Products and Nuclear Fuel Processing	177.01	29.94	1.13
化学原料和化学制品制造业	Raw Chemical Material and Chemical Products	145.87	78.58	22.38
医药制造业	Medical and pharmaceutical Products	63.75	42.05	11.40
化学纤维制造业	Chemical Fibers	2.98	1.81	0.83
橡胶和塑料制品业	Rubber and plastic products	50.52	32.31	10.63
非金属矿物制品业	Nonmetal Material Products	132.98	79.17	25.83
黑色金属冶炼和压延加工业	Smelting and Pressing of Ferrous Metals	52.04	37.99	14.70
有色金属冶炼和压延加工业	Smelting and Pressing of Nonferrous Metals	13.35	9.68	4.64
金属制品业	Metal Products	48.81	28.76	11.99
通用设备制造业	Ordinary Machinery Manufacturing	43.28	27.20	12.00
专用设备制造业	Special Purpose Equipment Manufacturing	37.10	22.68	10.81
汽车制造业	Motor manufacturing	454.96	270.51	41.60
铁路、船舶、航空航天和其他运输设备制造业	Railway,Watercraft,Aviation and other Transporlation Equipment manufacturing	19.74	11.61	7.73
电气机械和器材制造业	Electric Machinery and Equipment	63.66	39.35	15.44
计算机、通信和其他电子设备制造业	Telecommunication Computer,Equipment and Other Electronic Equipment Manufacturing	43.26	25.87	15.89
仪器仪表制造业	Instruments and Meters, Manufacturing	7.18	4.49	2.78
其他制造业	Other Manufacturing	5.18	2.78	1.61
废弃资源综合利用业	Waste Comprehensive Vtilization of Resources Industry	2.63	1.72	0.85
金属制品、机械和设备修理业	Metal products,Machinery and Equipment Repairing	1.78	1.24	0.86
电力、燃气及水的生产和供应业	Electric Power, Gas and Water Production and Supply	199.92	117.16	15.22
电力、热力生产和供应业	Electric Power, Steam and Hot Water Production and Supply	188.67	111.93	12.18
燃气生产和供应业	Gas Production and Supply	7.98	3.44	0.90
水的生产和供应业	Tap Water Production and Supply	3.28	1.78	2.15

13-4 国有控股工业企业单位数和主要经济指标 (2015)

单位: 亿元

项 目	Item	企业单位数(个) Number of Enterprises(unit)	工业总产值(当年价格) Total Output Value (current price)
总　　计	**Total**	**759**	**11042.16**
在总计中:	Of the Total		
亏损企业	Enterprises running under Deficit	181	2762.97
在总计中:	Of the Total:		
中央企业	Central Enterprises	46	2608.64
地方企业	Local Enterprises	106	179.99
在总计中:	Of the Total:		
轻工业	Light Industry	216	1403.51
重工业	Heavy Industry	543	9638.65
在总计中:	Of the Total:		
大型企业	Large Scale Enterprises	113	9078.41
中型企业	Medium Scale Enterprises	199	1186.46
小型企业	Small Enterprises	447	777.29
按行业分	Grouped by sector		
采矿业	**Mining and Qarrying**	**28**	**166.72**
煤炭开采和洗选业	Coal Mining and Processing	6	6.18
石油和天然气开采业	Petroleum and Natural Gas Extraction	1	40.31
黑色金属矿采选业	Ferrous Metals Mining and Processing	3	34.92
有色金属矿采选业	Non-ferrous Metals Mining and Processing	4	12.23
非金属矿采选业	Non-metal Minerals Mining and Processing	11	9.08
开采辅助活动	Mining Auxiliary Activities	3	64.01
其他采矿业	Other Minerals Mining and Processing		
制造业	**Manufacturing**	**585**	**9358.08**
农副食品加工业	Food Processing	50	190.95
食品制造业	Food Production	10	36.97
酒、饮料和精制茶制造业	Wine,Beverage and Refined Tea Production	10	22.67
烟草制品业	Tobacco Processing	6	677.85
纺织业	Textile Industry	19	69.20
纺织服装、服饰业	Textile,Garments, and Fashion Industry	8	17.59
皮革、毛皮、羽毛及其制品和制鞋业	Leather, Furs,Down and Related Products	1	3.04
木材加工和木、竹、藤、棕、草制品业	Timber Processing, Wood, Bamboo, Cane, Palm and Sraw Products	6	16.50
家具制造业	Furniture Manufacturing		
造纸和纸制品业	Papermaking and Paper Products	3	12.23
印刷和记录媒介复制业	Printing and Record Processing	14	36.03
文教、工美、体育和娱乐用品制造业	Stationery, Education and Sports Goods	3	0.89
石油加工、炼焦和核燃料加工业	Petroleum Processing, Coking Products and Nuclear Fuel Processing	6	561.58
化学原料和化学制品制造业	Raw Chemical Material and Chemical Products	51	1102.88
医药制造业	Medical and pharmaceutical Products	18	67.48
化学纤维制造业	Chemical Fibers	1	0.12
橡胶和塑料制品业	Rubber and plastic products	8	35.75
非金属矿物制品业	Nonmetal Material Products	50	121.68
黑色金属冶炼和压延加工业	Smelting and Pressing of Ferrous Metals	18	1118.86
有色金属冶炼和压延加工业	Smelting and Pressing of Nonferrous Metals	4	346.42
金属制品业	Metal Products	33	176.78
通用设备制造业	Ordinary Machinery Manufacturing	36	137.24
专用设备制造业	Special Purpose Equipment Manufacturing	30	169.46
汽车制造业	Motor manufacturing	85	2952.06
铁路、船舶、航空航天和其他运输设备制造业	Railway,Watercraft,Aviation and other Transporlation Equipment manufacturing	30	470.32
电气机械和器材制造业	Electric Machinery and Equipment	27	285.51
计算机、通信和其他电子设备制造业	Telecommunication Computer,Equipment and Other Electronic Equipment Manufacturing	32	650.52
仪器仪表制造业	Instruments and Meters, Manufacturing	14	29.65
其他制造业	Other Manufacturing	6	38.74
废弃资源综合利用业	Waste Comprehensive Vtilization of Resources Industry	3	4.42
金属制品、机械和设备修理业	Metal products,Machinery and Equipment Repairing	3	4.69
电力、燃气及水的生产和供应业	**Electric Power, Gas and Water Production and Supply**	**146**	**1517.36**
电力、热力生产和供应业	Electric Power, Steam and Hot Water Production and Supply	87	1401.60
燃气生产和供应业	Gas Production and Supply	10	71.86
水的生产和供应业	Tap Water Production and Supply	49	43.90

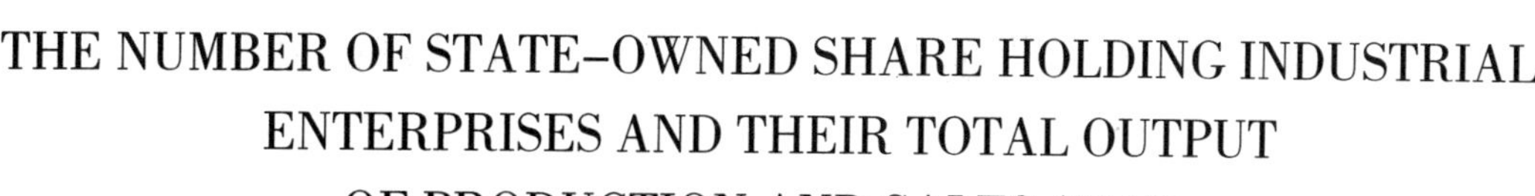

THE NUMBER OF STATE-OWNED SHARE HOLDING INDUSTRIAL ENTERPRISES AND THEIR TOTAL OUTPUT OF PRODUCTION AND SALES (2015)

(100 million yuan)

工业销售产值(当年价格) Output Value of Industrial Products Sales (current price)	出口交货值 Delivery Value for Export	资产总计 Total Assets				主营业务收入 Revenue of Major Business	全部从业人员年平均人数(万人) Average Number of Empolyment of the Curreat Year (10 000 Bersons)
			流动资产合计 Circulating Funds	固定资产合计 Total Fined Assets	固定资产原价 Original Value of Fixed Assets		
10658.49	**335.17**	**15743.77**	**6111.10**	**6579.06**	**11019.03**	**11360.87**	**81.05**
2730.27	107.36	4694.00	1824.57	1884.97	3498.65	3410.46	26.73
2579.13	102.41	4331.12	1368.86	1961.29	3792.47	2604.40	24.25
173.41	14.69	268.45	141.79	95.35	141.67	167.76	2.86
1312.45	25.27	1316.73	757.25	290.53	523.42	1290.26	10.01
9346.04	309.90	14427.04	5353.86	6288.53	10495.62	10070.61	71.04
8772.43	309.92	12878.27	4896.24	5322.98	9166.08	9487.40	62.08
1149.71	19.52	1683.42	781.72	631.18	989.95	1132.25	12.67
736.35	5.72	1182.08	433.15	624.90	863.01	741.22	6.30
164.85	**0.47**	**344.84**	**134.99**	**167.25**	**427.10**	**168.63**	**4.51**
6.06		5.82	3.41	2.06	3.21	5.31	0.27
40.08	0.46	149.26	39.08	96.94	311.92	40.09	1.76
34.86		23.63	4.52	14.83	32.17	35.53	0.33
11.93		19.56	4.18	4.68	11.62	11.16	0.25
9.07		31.05	17.59	7.37	4.85	8.71	0.17
62.85	0.01	115.53	66.22	41.37	63.33	67.83	1.73
8994.23	**334.69**	**11503.24**	**5648.66**	**3382.03**	**5756.08**	**9689.55**	**63.09**
187.45	0.21	49.94	28.81	15.30	40.20	185.94	0.52
35.64	6.00	66.72	32.36	14.42	28.87	51.00	0.55
21.75		24.10	11.65	8.78	16.87	16.73	0.63
609.81	0.50	419.97	330.81	30.37	89.86	591.76	0.80
64.12	1.21	46.07	26.77	14.75	34.20	67.14	0.98
16.21	3.68	29.76	19.10	4.82	10.37	14.43	0.87
2.74		0.11	0.05	0.01	0.02	2.99	0.01
16.30		13.02	6.31	4.64	6.56	16.14	0.14
11.55		33.58	20.50	10.59	15.66	11.66	0.08
36.09		42.37	25.51	14.83	26.81	34.74	0.39
0.82		0.98	0.74	0.11	0.17	0.85	0.02
550.82		153.41	58.16	95.17	159.42	563.66	0.67
1074.08	80.62	1403.04	441.58	733.83	1002.35	1132.69	5.34
64.24	5.63	112.61	51.16	32.55	47.68	80.14	1.01
0.12		6.15	3.38	0.55	1.57	0.12	0.01
33.91	1.63	30.95	17.05	8.49	14.49	25.28	0.48
112.00	2.02	175.35	57.25	70.70	97.60	117.31	1.18
1110.55	30.10	2191.73	611.61	1031.73	1992.77	1167.42	9.02
331.12	7.77	346.85	196.76	85.27	137.53	1019.32	1.75
173.31	5.71	297.81	199.97	52.94	81.58	168.58	2.02
130.81	6.34	267.49	173.01	63.26	90.36	124.31	2.32
152.55	8.42	214.26	149.34	44.84	70.25	122.48	2.15
2826.07	28.03	3466.98	1779.16	606.45	1065.46	2810.33	16.91
458.48	51.97	728.67	447.31	167.65	220.98	412.41	5.45
285.88	11.81	327.09	200.35	78.72	116.15	294.18	2.40
616.22	80.80	944.12	705.09	142.34	331.44	587.26	6.05
29.08	1.04	57.29	25.53	29.06	31.56	28.20	0.59
33.43	1.20	44.82	24.99	17.15	21.95	33.46	0.57
4.42		5.93	2.86	2.18	2.40	4.35	0.05
4.69		2.09	1.48	0.55	0.95	4.66	0.11
1499.41		**3895.69**	**327.46**	**3029.78**	**4835.86**	**1502.69**	**13.45**
1391.45		3516.02	206.22	2891.79	4642.82	1390.61	11.35
66.96		95.76	19.73	57.35	69.58	68.90	0.37
40.99		283.91	101.51	80.64	123.46	43.18	1.73

13-5 集体工业企业单位数和主要经济指标 (2015)

单位: 亿元

项 目	Item	企业单位数(个) Number of Enterprises (unit)	工业总产值(当年价格) Total Output Value (current price)
总　计	**Total**	**98**	**124.87**
在总计中:	Of the Total:		
亏损企业	Enterprises running under Deficit	10	6.40
在总计中:	Of the Total:		
农村工业	Rural Industry	13	12.39
在总计中:	Of the Total:		
轻工业	Light Industry	18	19.29
重工业	Heavy Industry	80	105.58
在总计中:	Of the Total:		
大型企业	Large Scale Enterprises		
中型企业	Medium Scale Enterprises	15	29.08
小型企业	Small Enterprises	83	95.79
按行业分	Grouped by sector		
采矿业	**Mining and Qarrying**	**20**	**42.84**
煤炭开采和洗选业	Coal Mining and Processing	2	4.07
石油和天然气开采业	Petroleum and Natural Gas Extraction		
黑色金属矿采选业	Ferrous Metals Mining and Processing	5	18.17
有色金属矿采选业	Non-ferrous Metals Mining and Processing		
非金属矿采选业	Non-metal Minerals Mining and Processing	13	20.6
开采辅助活动	Mining Auxiliary Activities		
其他采矿业	Other Minerals Mining and Processing		
制造业	**Manufacturing**	**73**	**78.59**
农副食品加工业	Food Processing		
食品制造业	Food Production	1	3.38
酒、饮料和精制茶制造业	Wine,Beverage and Refined Tea Production	2	1.29
烟草制品业	Tobacco Processing		
纺织业	Textile Industry	1	0.19
纺织服装、服饰业	Textile,Garments, and Fashion Industry	3	1.94
皮革、毛皮、羽毛及其制品和制鞋业	Leather, Furs,Down and Related Products		
木材加工和木、竹、藤、棕、草制品业	Timber Processing, Wood, Bamboo, Cane, Palm and Sraw Products		
家具制造业	Furniture Manufacturing		
造纸和纸制品业	Papermaking and Paper Products	1	0.46
印刷和记录媒介复制业	Printing and Record Processing	2	2.34
文教、工美、体育和娱乐用品制造业	Stationery, Education and Sports Goods		
石油加工、炼焦和核燃料加工业	Petroleum Processing, Coking Products and Nuclear Fuel Processing		
化学原料和化学制品制造业	Raw Chemical Material and Chemical Products	6	9.77
医药制造业	Medical and pharmaceutical Products	2	2.12
化学纤维制造业	Chemical Fibers		
橡胶和塑料制品业	Rubber and plastic products	6	5.99
非金属矿物制品业	Nonmetal Material Products	13	21.31
黑色金属冶炼和压延加工业	Smelting and Pressing of Ferrous Metals	5	6.29
有色金属冶炼和压延加工业	Smelting and Pressing of Nonferrous Metals	4	2.81
金属制品业	Metal Products	5	2.56
通用设备制造业	Ordinary Machinery Manufacturing	4	1.45
专用设备制造业	Special Purpose Equipment Manufacturing		
汽车制造业	Motor manufacturing	9	10.84
铁路、船舶、航空航天和其他运输设备制造业	Railway,Watercraft,Aviation and other Transporlation Equipment manufacturing	3	3.1
电气机械和器材制造业	Electric Machinery and Equipment		
计算机、通信和其他电子设备制造业	Telecommunication Computer,Equipment and Other Electronic Equipment Manufacturing		
仪器仪表制造业	Instruments and Meters, Manufacturing	1	0.23
其他制造业	Other Manufacturing		
废弃资源综合利用业	Waste Comprehensive Vtilization of Resources Industry	3	1.83
金属制品、机械和设备修理业	Metal products,Machinery and Equipment Repairing	2	0.68
电力、燃气及水的生产和供应业	**Electric Power, Gas and Water Production and Supply**	**5**	**3.44**
电力、热力生产和供应业	Electric Power, Steam and Hot Water Production and Supply		
燃气生产和供应业	Gas Production and Supply		
水的生产和供应业	Tap Water Production and Supply	5	3.44

THE NUMBER OF COLLECTIVE-OWNED INDUSTRIAL ENTERPRISES(2015)

(100 million yuan)

工业销售产值(当年价格) Output Value of Industrial Products Sales (current price)	出口交货值 Delivery Value for Export	资产总计 Total Assets	流动资产合计 Circulating Funds	固定资产合计 Total Fined Assets	固定资产原价 Original Value of Fixed Assets	主营业务收入 Revenue of Major Business	全部从业人员年平均人数(万人) Average Number of Empolyment of the Curreat Year (10 000 Bersons)
121.80		**53.27**	**28.67**	**16.79**	**31.68**	**119.31**	**1.91**
6.04		6.97	4.41	1.82	1.91	9.27	0.34
12.00		4.87	1.66	1.44	1.95	10.68	0.23
18.78		6.20	2.18	2.55	3.47	18.41	0.23
103.02		47.07	26.48	14.24	28.22	100.90	1.68
28.50		16.67	7.86	6.23	14.39	32.63	0.84
93.30		36.60	20.81	10.55	17.30	86.68	1.07
42.1		**15.19**	**6.36**	**7.11**	**10.39**	**38.58**	**0.45**
4.06		1.28	0.5	0.72	0.8	4.06	0.07
17.77		5.46	2.68	2.67	4.43	15.46	0.15
20.28		8.44	3.18	3.72	5.15	19.07	0.24
76.44		**36.14**	**22.07**	**8.45**	**19.66**	**77.53**	**1.43**
3.24		0.39	0.27	0.12	0.27	3.24	0.02
1.29		0.26	0.08	0.04	0.04	1.29	0.03
0.19		0.63	0.08	0.05	0.14	0.19	0.04
1.93		0.7	0.47	0.08	0.15	1.94	0.05
0.45		0.09	0.07	0.01	0.05	0.45	0.01
2.34		0.52	0.23	0.1	0.15	2.34	0.02
9.54		1.81	1.15	0.66	1.08	8.85	0.11
2.09		1.19	0.46	0.73	0.77	2.09	0.03
5.83		2.1	1.44	0.42	0.7	5.49	0.09
21.12		5.42	3.71	1.6	2.64	21.86	0.25
5.98		4.26	1.28	1.36	8.22	6.03	0.11
2.86		2.01	1.63	0.2	0.54	2.98	0.09
2.33		2.82	2.07	0.31	0.64	2.79	0.11
1.43		0.76	0.38	0.33	0.34	1.37	0.02
10.47		5.96	4.21	0.78	2.4	7.28	0.13
2.72		1.43	1.15	0.16	0.27	3.05	0.08
0.23		0.23	0.23	0.01	0.03	0.23	0.02
1.79		3.91	2.18	1.38	1.04	5.46	0.16
0.62		1.66	0.98	0.11	0.2	0.61	0.09
3.25		**1.94**	**0.24**	**1.22**	**1.64**	**3.19**	**0.03**
3.25		1.94	0.24	1.22	1.64	3.19	0.03

13-6 外商投资和港澳台商投资工业企业单位数和主要经济指标 (2015)

单位: 亿元

项 目	Item	企业单位数(个) Number of Enterprises (unit)
总计	**Total**	**834**
在总计中:	Of the Total:	
亏损企业	Enterprises running under Deficit	153
在总计中:	Of the Total:	
港、澳、台商投资企业	Hongkong, Macao and Taiwan Funded Enterprises	365
合资经营企业(港或澳、台资)	Joint Venture with Hongkong, Macao and Taiwan	157
合作经营企业(港或澳、台资)	Cooperate with Hongkong, Macao and Taiwan Funded	4
港澳台商独资经营企业	Enterprises Solely Funded by Hongkong, Macao and Taiwan Businessmen	192
港澳台商投资股份有限公司	Share Holding Co.Ltd.With Hongkong,Macao and Taiwan Businessmen	11
其他港澳台投资	Othes	1
外商投资企业	Foreign Funded Enterprises	469
中外合资经营企业	Sino – Foreign Joint Funded Enterprises	254
中外合作经营企业	Sino – Foreign Cooperative Funded Enterprises	7
外资企业	Foreign Solely Funded Enterprises	191
外商投资股份有限公司	Foreign Funded Share Holding Co.Ltd.	15
其他外商投资	Othes	2
在总计中:	Of the Total:	
国有控股企业	State–Owned Share Holding Enterprises	45
在总计中:	Of the Total:	
农村工业	Rural Industry	2
在总计中:	Of the Total:	
轻工业	Light Industry	362
重工业	Heavy Industry	472
在总计中:	Of the Total:	
大型企业	Large Scale Enterprises	69
中型企业	Medium Scale Enterprises	234
小型企业	Small Enterprises	531
按行业分	Grouped by sector	
采矿业	**Mining and Qarrying**	**6**
煤炭开采和洗选业	Coal Mining and Processing	1
石油和天然气开采业	Petroleum and Natural Gas Extraction	
黑色金属矿采选业	Ferrous Metals Mining and Processing	1
有色金属矿采选业	Non–ferrous Metals Mining and Processing	1
非金属矿采选业	Non–metal Minerals Mining and Processing	3
开采辅助活动	Mining Auxiliary Activities	
其他采矿业	Other Minerals Mining and Processing	
制造业	**Manufacturing**	**782**
农副食品加工业	Food Processing	41
食品制造业	Food Production	33
酒、饮料和精制茶制造业	Wine,Beverage and Refined Tea Production	32
烟草制品业	Tobacco Processing	
纺织业	Textile Industry	55
纺织服装、服饰业	Textile,Garments, and Fashion Industry	42
皮革、毛皮、羽毛及其制品和制鞋业	Leather, Furs,Down and Related Products	14
木材加工和木、竹、藤、棕、草制品业	Timber Processing, Wood, Bamboo, Cane, Palm and Sraw Products	4
家具制造业	Furniture Manufacturing	4
造纸和纸制品业	Papermaking and Paper Products	25
印刷和记录媒介复制业	Printing and Record Processing	9
文教、工美、体育和娱乐用品制造业	Stationery, Education and Sports Goods	10
石油加工、炼焦和核燃料加工业	Petroleum Processing, Coking Products and Nuclear Fuel Processing	2
化学原料和化学制品制造业	Raw Chemical Material and Chemical Products	50
医药制造业	Medical and pharmaceutical Products	40
化学纤维制造业	Chemical Fibers	3
橡胶和塑料制品业	Rubber and plastic products	22
非金属矿物制品业	Nonmetal Material Products	41
黑色金属冶炼和压延加工业	Smelting and Pressing of Ferrous Metals	10
有色金属冶炼和压延加工业	Smelting and Pressing of Nonferrous Metals	3
金属制品业	Metal Products	28
通用设备制造业	Ordinary Machinery Manufacturing	30
专用设备制造业	Special Purpose Equipment Manufacturing	20
汽车制造业	Motor manufacturing	166
铁路、船舶、航空航天和其他运输设备制造业	Railway,Watercraft,Aviation and other Transporlation Equipment manufacturing	6
电气机械和器材制造业	Electric Machinery and Equipment	46
计算机、通信和其他电子设备制造业	Telecommunication Computer,Equipment and Other Electronic Equipment Manufacturing	34
仪器仪表制造业	Instruments and Meters, Manufacturing	8
其他制造业	Other Manufacturing	1
废弃资源综合利用业	Waste Comprehensive Vtilization of Resources Industry	3
金属制品、机械和设备修理业	Metal products,Machinery and Equipment Repairing	
电力、燃气及水的生产和供应业	**Electric Power, Gas and Water Production and Supply**	**46**
电力、热力生产和供应业	Electric Power, Steam and Hot Water Production and Supply	18
燃气生产和供应业	Gas Production and Supply	23
水的生产和供应业	Tap Water Production and Supply	5

THE NUMBER OF FOREIGN FUNDED AND HONGKONG MACO AND TAIWAN FUNDED INDUSTRIAL ENTERPRISES AND THEIR TOTAL OUTPUT OF PRODUCTION AND SALES (2015)

(100 million yuan)

工业总产值(当年价格) Total Output Value (current price)	工业销售产值(当年价格) Output Value of Industrial Products Sales (current price)	出口交货值 Delivery Value for Export	资产总计 Total Assets	流动资产合计 Circulating Funds	固定资产合计 Total Fined Assets	固定资产原价 Original Value of Fixed Assets	主营业务收入 Revenue of Major Business	全部从业人员年平均人数(万人) Average Number of Empolyment of the curreat Year (10 000 Bersons)
6701.56	**6293.93**	**439.02**	**5170.05**	**2500.72**	**1977.38**	**3181.00**	**6085.63**	**44.49**
656.32	646.90	44.35	929.21	469.00	304.77	440.87	642.74	9.41
2073.46	1858.95	258.82	1425.67	625.74	604.34	1021.24	1744.52	17.03
1220.41	1042.71	94.04	817.19	381.53	325.29	576.63	996.82	8.92
10.35	9.76		12.22	5.64	2.50	5.52	9.70	0.09
803.37	767.95	163.87	546.63	214.57	263.31	419.10	697.67	7.69
38.21	37.41	0.90	46.13	22.45	11.69	18.44	39.21	0.32
1.12	1.12		3.50	1.55	1.54	1.54	1.12	0.02
4628.10	4434.98	180.20	3744.39	1874.98	1373.04	2159.76	4341.11	27.47
3549.44	3381.24	74.64	2665.70	1350.40	965.19	1489.56	3284.83	17.27
48.31	47.62	1.38	26.42	4.79	20.48	39.20	47.48	0.18
820.18	794.64	91.03	732.34	438.15	219.54	357.78	800.86	7.93
209.14	210.57	12.83	318.65	81.03	167.46	272.73	207.03	2.07
1.03	0.91	0.33	1.27	0.60	0.37	0.49	0.90	0.02
2283.40	2179.34	25.14	1841.02	930.82	658.88	1034.77	2168.15	9.40
7.00	5.75		3.97	3.56	0.31	0.86	6.46	0.04
1794.60	1691.04	140.86	1103.94	571.23	378.91	687.99	1590.46	17.16
4906.96	4602.89	298.16	4066.11	1929.49	1598.47	2493.01	4495.17	27.33
4000.18	3709.92	264.52	2885.66	1346.67	1115.30	1795.86	3593.71	24.59
1716.19	1626.07	96.98	1372.81	733.53	486.12	799.19	1562.84	13.36
985.19	957.94	77.52	911.58	420.52	375.96	585.95	929.08	6.54
25.93	**25.14**		**7.02**	**3.18**	**1.44**	**1.71**	**16.72**	**0.12**
0.18	0.18		0.81	0.42	0.1	0.14	0.18	0.03
16.01	15.24		0.97	0.09	0.05	0.05	12.7	0.02
8.53	8.53		4.26	2.05	1.16	1.47	2.94	0.05
1.21	1.19		0.98	0.62	0.13	0.05	0.89	0.01
6471.49	**6071.13**	**439.02**	**4748.7**	**2400.29**	**1709.97**	**2808.47**	**5863.87**	**43.42**
291.84	254.91	13.67	125.45	66.37	39.87	65.51	235.09	1.07
212.76	203.35	3.84	92.94	35.9	41.57	113.25	197.91	1.54
305.65	289.23	0.05	224.19	123.28	75.2	125.74	280.19	1.87
201.08	195.5	36.88	85.28	38.03	39.97	77.97	191.39	2.76
100.24	97.98	25.98	57.83	37.68	8.41	17.97	93.32	2.01
31.57	30.77	11.08	19.52	7.2	10.77	11.92	26.12	1.69
5.63	5.36		3.29	1.26	1.61	2.32	4.13	0.12
8.85	5.98	1.26	4.72	3.16	0.98	1.76	4.58	0.14
116.04	105.6	0.78	129.09	70.98	39.77	90.39	110.96	0.78
19.73	18.06		19.63	14.07	4.46	12.43	17.41	0.22
22.31	20.93	2.24	23.79	12.42	3.83	9.66	21.23	0.46
29.56	27.68		21.02	5.14	13.77	19.45	8.28	0.06
384.79	377.01	32.17	323.61	80.05	190.4	261.68	389.44	1.46
225.87	217.43	25.81	182.09	82.13	67.76	89.63	209.53	2.52
14.74	13.5	2.33	12.55	4.13	6.85	11.54	12.16	0.09
31.67	31.37	0.15	34.05	19.59	8.49	14.18	28.83	0.29
227.65	231.07	5.63	374.98	92.41	210.52	336.66	220.4	2.24
146.44	147.62	21.11	180.14	55.18	105.07	163.58	141.66	0.86
59.26	58.78	0.18	9.2	4.06	2.44	3.36	59.08	0.09
120.74	115.62	2.98	76.37	30.71	39.91	64.74	112.19	0.56
64.79	63.21	16.41	81.83	53.61	21.35	28.17	60.97	0.82
53.35	49.45	13.15	65.91	38.12	16.51	21.34	57.64	0.96
2834.14	2723.65	32.76	2101.67	1211.55	626.17	1033.21	2655.07	14.22
7.48	7.2	1.26	10.27	8.49	1.23	2.17	7.03	0.12
411.62	401.93	50.08	284.15	169.13	88.73	162.56	370	2.82
523.96	359.79	135.37	192.78	126.85	42.21	64.79	328.56	3.2
11.73	10.18	3.85	6.72	4.15	1.54	2.08	12.76	0.43
0.36	0.32		0.14	0.13	0.01	0.06	0.32	0.01
7.64	7.63		5.51	4.52	0.55	0.4	7.62	0.02
204.14	**197.67**		**414.34**	**97.25**	**265.98**	**370.82**	**205.04**	**0.95**
126.11	124.52		285.18	52.75	204.5	292.32	121.18	0.25
73.36	69.23		100.76	34.48	49.54	61.86	79.76	0.53
4.66	3.91		28.4	10.03	11.94	16.64	4.1	0.18

13-7 私营工业企业单位数和主要经济指标 (2015)

单位: 亿元

项 目	Item	企业单位数(个) Number of Enterprises (unit)	工业总产值(当年价格) Total Output Value (current price)
总计	**Total**	**8833**	**16053.39**
在总计中:	Of the Total:		
亏损企业	Enterprises running under Deficit	493	488.97
在总计中:	Of the Total:		
轻工业	Light Industry	3807	7674.15
重工业	Heavy Industry	5026	8379.25
在总计中:	Of the Total:		
大型企业	Large Scale Enterprises	59	1435.33
中型企业	Medium Scale Enterprises	710	3686.90
小型企业	Small Enterprises	8064	10931.16
按行业分	Grouped by Sector		
采矿业	**Mining and Qarrying**	**441**	**555.31**
煤炭开采和洗选业	Coal Mining and Processing	78	59.22
石油和天然气开采业	Petroleum and Natural Gas Extraction		
黑色金属矿采选业	Ferrous Metals Mining and Processing	61	104.81
有色金属矿采选业	Non-ferrous Metals Mining and Processing	24	24.69
非金属矿采选业	Non-metal Minerals Mining and Processing	277	365.58
开采辅助活动	Mining Auxiliary Activities		
其他采矿业	Other Minerals Mining and Processing	1	1.01
制造业	**Manufacturing**	**8333**	**15431.51**
农副食品加工业	Food Processing	1173	2926.9
食品制造业	Food Production	210	544.57
酒、饮料和精制茶制造业	Wine,Beverage and Refined Tea Production	265	396.5
烟草制品业	Tobacco Processing		
纺织业	Textile Industry	616	1347.5
纺织服装、服饰业	Textile,Garments, and Fashion Industry	319	517.45
皮革、毛皮、羽毛及其制品和制鞋业	Leather, Furs,Down and Related Products	123	135
木材加工和木、竹、藤、棕、草制品业	Timber Processing, Wood, Bamboo, Cane, Palm and Sraw Products	174	268.81
家具制造业	Furniture Manufacturing	95	113.52
造纸和纸制品业	Papermaking and Paper Products	145	232.5
印刷和记录媒介复制业	Printing and Record Processing	99	149.37
文教、工美、体育和娱乐用品制造业	Stationery, Education and Sports Goods	67	165.92
石油加工、炼焦和核燃料加工业	Petroleum Processing, Coking Products and Nuclear Fuel Processing	22	26.48
化学原料和化学制品制造业	Raw Chemical Material and Chemical Products	613	1520.61
医药制造业	Medical and pharmaceutical Products	168	293.5
化学纤维制造业	Chemical Fibers	15	49.92
橡胶和塑料制品业	Rubber and plastic products	368	659.55
非金属矿物制品业	Nonmetal Material Products	1240	1884.17
黑色金属冶炼和压延加工业	Smelting and Pressing of Ferrous Metals	146	365.39
有色金属冶炼和压延加工业	Smelting and Pressing of Nonferrous Metals	92	233.12
金属制品业	Metal Products	411	630.61
通用设备制造业	Ordinary Machinery Manufacturing	351	556.97
专用设备制造业	Special Purpose Equipment Manufacturing	314	494
汽车制造业	Motor manufacturing	697	853.17
铁路、船舶、航空航天和其他运输设备制造业	Railway,Watercraft,Aviation and other Transporlation Equipment manufacturing	69	148.06
电气机械和器材制造业	Electric Machinery and Equipment	273	379.32
计算机、通信和其他电子设备制造业	Telecommunication Computer,Equipment and Other Electronic Equipment Manufacturing	137	309.92
仪器仪表制造业	Instruments and Meters, Manufacturing	47	68.37
其他制造业	Other Manufacturing	52	75.63
废弃资源综合利用业	Waste Comprehensive Vtilization of Resources Industry	27	79.73
金属制品、机械和设备修理业	Metal products,Machinery and Equipment Repairing	5	4.96
电力、燃气及水的生产和供应业	**Electric Power, Gas and Water Production and Supply**	**59**	**66.57**
电力、热力生产和供应业	Electric Power, Steam and Hot Water Production and Supply	30	38.47
燃气生产和供应业	Gas Production and Supply	12	17.79
水的生产和供应业	Tap Water Production and Supply	17	10.32

THE NUMBER OF PRIVATE-OWNED INDUSTRIAL ENTERPRISES AND THEIR MAJOR ECONOMIC INDICATORS (2015)

(100 million yuan)

工业销售产值(当年价格) Output Value of Industrial Products Sales(current price)	出口交货值 Delivery Value for Export	资产总计 Total Assets	流动资产合计 Circulating Funds	固定资产合计 Total Fined Assets	固定资产原价 Original Value of Fixed Assets	主营业务收入 Revenue of Major Business	全部从业人员年平均人数(万人) Average Number of Empolyment of the Curreat Year (10 000 Bersons)
15538.20	**428.96**	**6989.18**	**3280.58**	**2617.86**	**6505.76**	**14714.91**	**118.93**
469.27	3.23	581.22	293.19	184.74	243.56	401.31	6.44
7414.54	313.33	2839.38	1340.19	1068.18	3517.16	7029.44	59.08
8123.66	115.63	4149.80	1940.39	1549.69	2988.60	7685.47	59.85
1397.03	79.05	625.97	318.29	235.45	763.62	1311.33	10.25
3575.35	173.63	1535.00	730.83	622.01	2097.46	3433.30	33.81
10565.82	176.28	4828.21	2231.47	1760.40	3644.69	9970.27	74.87
539.05	**0.05**	**422.95**	**112.56**	**182.89**	**238**	**529.74**	**4.49**
57.62	0.04	32.48	9.72	15.25	18.33	56.7	1.14
102.5		49.91	16.55	23.94	29.09	100.88	0.58
24.01		15.82	7.72	6.68	11.01	22.86	0.24
353.91	0.01	324.48	78.51	137.02	179.56	348.95	2.51
1.01		0.27	0.05	0.01	0.02	0.35	0.02
14933.57	**428.91**	**6482.26**	**3143.84**	**2387.57**	**6180.9**	**14125.64**	**113.95**
2842.58	90.97	935.07	454.07	346.21	1559.66	2717.43	13.52
521.46	8.43	201.21	89.64	67.82	444.56	492.24	3.66
380.29	3.57	179.96	78.68	67.01	102.46	360.56	3.08
1312.59	66.3	448.02	189.41	205.47	556.74	1268.22	14.85
507.13	51.5	194.41	91.15	77.87	175.99	486.84	8.17
132.38	40.9	45.74	24.45	16.75	49.31	130.36	1.29
258.31	2.82	127.91	47.86	44.31	92.62	245.25	2.12
110.47	0.25	76.22	23.97	24.43	52.72	98.17	1.09
225.98		95.89	46.38	35.89	85.89	213.47	1.84
144.78		62.09	26.94	26.29	67.76	138.87	1.32
163.52	9.26	118.47	106.71	8.22	40.86	67.67	1.07
25.76		13.39	5.74	5.62	5.5	25.77	0.18
1467.6	11.6	672.85	298.71	276.06	666.98	1376.27	7.51
274.07	19.08	151.99	66.3	53.83	84.84	262.53	2.23
49.24		19.64	9.73	5.65	13.06	49.27	0.36
634.35	1.43	259.42	120.2	99.75	247.94	604.15	4.83
1846.77	6.75	796.11	330.53	339.26	599.78	1715.44	13.81
358.9		153.78	82.64	58.19	115	345.23	2.05
228.76	1.57	93.87	45.31	38.44	55.68	216.35	1.34
608.21	3.67	251.79	130.86	88.18	210.73	582.51	4.85
529.9	6.84	254.76	132.39	89.29	214.81	520.65	4.37
482.87	1.85	343.33	202.78	112.95	234.24	451.3	3.62
815.35	5.49	481.48	253.68	154.65	223.36	747.29	7.77
141.02	0.05	52.98	24.34	20.35	30.74	133.05	1.24
362.67	7.97	196.42	107.71	62.13	99.03	345.8	3.3
288.86	82.96	153.54	104.41	30.85	67.18	326.46	2.47
64.4	0.68	41.68	22.55	16.25	27.99	60.84	0.91
71.76	4.97	19.7	9.56	7.51	42.2	71.9	0.76
78.65		38.79	15.99	8.21	13.02	67.26	0.19
4.95		1.74	1.14	0.12	0.25	4.49	0.13
65.58		**83.97**	**24.18**	**47.4**	**86.85**	**59.52**	**0.5**
38.02		62.89	16.27	36.2	71.98	32.57	0.26
17.63		11.91	4.84	5.73	7.66	17.35	0.09
9.93		9.17	3.07	5.48	7.21	9.6	0.15

13-8 大中型工业企业单位数和产销总值(2015)

单位: 亿元

项目	Item	企业单位数(个) Number of Enterprises (unit)
总　计	**Total**	**2202**
一、按登记注册类型分组:	Grouped by Type of Registration	
内资企业	Inner Funded Enterprises	1899
国有企业	State Owned Enterprises	59
中央企业	Central Enterprises	31
地方企业	Local Enterprises	28
集体企业	Collective-owned Enterprise	15
股份合作企业	Share Holding Cooperative Enterprises	
联营企业	Joint Owned Enterprise	1
国有联营企业	State Joint Ownership	
集体联营企业	Collective Joint Ownership	
国有与集体联营企业	Joint State- Collective Ownership	1
其他联营企业	Other Joint Owned Enterprise	
有限责任公司	Responsibility Co. Ltd	836
国有独资公司	State Solely Funded Co.	53
其他有限责任公司	Others	783
股份有限公司	Share Holding Co.Ltd.	214
私营企业	Private - owned enterprises	769
私营独资企业	Solely Private - owned enterprises	14
私营合作企业	Private Joint Venture	1
私营有限责任公司	Private Responsibility Co. Ltd	679
私营股份有限公司	Private Share Holding Co.Ltd.	75
其他企业	Others	5
港、澳、台商投资企业	Hongkong, Macao and Taiwan Funded Enterprises	133
合资经营企业(港或澳、台资)	Joint Venture with Hongkong, Macao and Taiwan	63
合作经营企业(港或澳、台资)	Cooperate with Hongkong, Macao and Taiwan Funded	1
港澳台商独资经营企业	Enterprises Solely Funded by Hongkong, Macao and Taiwan Businessmen	64
港澳台商投资股份有限公司	Share Holding Co.Ltd. With Hongkong, Macao and Taiwan Investment	5
其他港澳台投资	Others	
外商投资企业	Foreign Funded Enterprises	170
中外合资经营企业	Sino - Foreign Joint Funded Enterprises	92
中外合作经营企业	Sino - Foreign Cooperative Funded Enterprises	2
外资企业	Foreign Solely Funded Enterprises	66
外商投资股份有限公司	Foreign Funded Share Holding Co.Ltd.	10
其他外商投资	Others	
二、在总计中:亏损企业	**Of the Total: enterprises running under deficit**	**254**
在总计中:国有控股企业	Of the Total: State-Owned Share Holding Enterprises	312
在总计中:农村工业	Of the Total: Rural Industry	11
在总计中:轻工业	Of the Total: Light Industry	1062
重工业	Heavy Industry	1140
在总计中:大型企业	Of the Total: Large Scale Enterprises	349
中型企业	Medium Scale Enterprises	1853
按行业分	Grouped by Sector	
采矿业	**Mining and Qarrying**	**57**

NUMBER OF LARGE AND MEDIUM SCALE INDUSTRIAL ENTERPRISES AND THEIR TOTAL VALUE OF PRODUCTION AND SALES (2015)

(100 million yuan)

工业总产值(当年价格) Total Output Value (current price)	工业销售产值(当年价格) Output Value of Industrial Products Sales (current price)	出口交货值 Delivery Value for Export
26264.18	**25281.57**	**1257.69**
20547.81	19945.58	896.19
2674.31	2640.48	115.48
2572.84	2543.42	100.79
101.47	97.05	14.69
29.08	28.50	
0.64	0.58	
0.64	0.58	
8606.25	8305.08	370.55
1728.01	1642.41	39.98
6878.24	6662.67	330.57
4080.74	3964.19	157.47
5122.23	4972.38	252.68
49.85	49.30	3.76
1.06	1.01	
4488.73	4362.19	240.10
582.59	559.88	8.83
34.57	34.37	
1650.35	1453.38	235.34
1004.00	833.34	79.28
4.20	4.16	
620.38	594.27	155.16
21.77	21.61	0.90
4066.01	3882.61	126.16
3242.56	3080.42	49.30
31.74	31.20	
598.16	574.52	65.23
193.55	196.47	11.63
3459.56	**3384.13**	**135.70**
10264.87	9922.14	329.44
96.34	90.22	
8833.85	8448.78	489.73
17430.32	16832.79	767.96
16072.70	15460.32	823.76
10191.48	9821.25	433.93
389.51	**381.28**	**0.47**

13-8 续表1 continued

单位: 亿元

项 目	Item	企业单位数(个) Number of Enterprises(unit)
煤炭开采和洗选业	Coal Mining and Processing	12
石油和天然气开采业	Petroleum and Natural Gas Extraction	1
黑色金属矿采选业	Ferrous Metals Mining and Processing	13
有色金属矿采选业	Non-ferrous Metals Mining and Processing	5
非金属矿采选业	Non-metal Minerals Mining and Processing	23
开采辅助活动	Mining Auxiliary Activities	3
其他采矿业	Other Minerals Mining and Processing	
制造业	**Manufacturing**	**2094**
农副食品加工业	Food Processing	154
食品制造业	Food Production	84
酒、饮料和精制茶制造业	Wine,Beverage and Refined Tea Production	59
烟草制品业	Tobacco Processing	2
纺织业	Textile Industry	269
纺织服装、服饰业	Textile,Garments, and Fashion Industry	155
皮革、毛皮、羽毛及其制品和制鞋业	Leather, Furs,Down and Related Products	16
木材加工和木、竹、藤、棕、草制品业	Timber Processing, Wood, Bamboo, Cane, Palm and Sraw Products	23
家具制造业	Furniture Manufacturing	10
造纸和纸制品业	Papermaking and Paper Products	40
印刷和记录媒介复制业	Printing and Record Processing	31
文教、工美、体育和娱乐用品制造业	Stationery, Education and Sports Goods	17
石油加工、炼焦和核燃料加工业	Petroleum Processing, Coking Products and Nuclear Fuel Processing	5
化学原料和化学制品制造业	Raw Chemical Material and Chemical Products	135
医药制造业	Medical and pharmaceutical Products	74
化学纤维制造业	Chemical Fibers	6
橡胶和塑料制品业	Rubber and plastic products	75
非金属矿物制品业	Nonmetal Material Products	161
黑色金属冶炼和压延加工业	Smelting and Pressing of Ferrous Metals	44
有色金属冶炼和压延加工业	Smelting and Pressing of Nonferrous Metals	34
金属制品业	Metal Products	72
通用设备制造业	Ordinary Machinery Manufacturing	74
专用设备制造业	Special Purpose Equipment Manufacturing	65
汽车制造业	Motor manufacturing	232
铁路、船舶、航空航天和其他运输设备制造业	Railway,Watercraft,Aviation and other Transporlation Equipment manufacturing	36
电气机械和器材制造业	Electric Machinery and Equipment	98
计算机、通信和其他电子设备制造业	Telecommunication Computer,Equipment and Other Electronic Equipment Manufacturing	78
仪器仪表制造业	Instruments and Meters, Manufacturing	19
其他制造业	Other Manufacturing	12
废弃资源综合利用业	Waste Comprehensive Vtilization of Resources Industry	6
金属制品、机械和设备修理业	Metal products,Machinery and Equipment Repairing	8
电力、燃气及水的生产和供应业	**Electric Power, Gas and Water Production and Supply**	**51**
电力、热力生产和供应业	Electric Power, Steam and Hot Water Production and Supply	29
燃气生产和供应业	Gas Production and Supply	6
水的生产和供应业	Tap Water Production and Supply	16

(100 million yuan)

工业总产值(当年价格) Total Output Value	工业销售产值(当年价格) Output Value of Industrial Products Sales (current price)	出口交货值 Delivery Value for Export
27.34	27.25	
40.31	40.08	0.46
127.88	125.91	
21.01	21.08	
108.96	104.11	
64.01	62.85	0.01
24446.12	**23482.83**	**1257.22**
1867.76	1785.43	77.60
698.44	671.27	48.06
1264.71	1231.63	0.14
664.39	596.75	0.50
1307.98	1270.00	102.17
564.73	551.30	116.56
61.07	59.50	10.76
128.80	125.62	
58.29	54.34	
290.61	274.77	0.37
159.38	148.18	3.27
55.36	53.88	7.15
682.66	683.89	
2504.28	2447.85	137.01
607.38	574.59	73.46
35.02	33.35	2.02
515.31	505.26	3.87
935.59	917.98	9.87
1680.08	1658.73	53.41
651.88	634.09	9.48
556.25	544.61	14.73
512.73	490.96	24.15
517.16	492.77	19.84
4467.06	4346.17	49.36
546.43	533.21	51.46
1149.33	1092.63	69.57
1723.66	1485.13	360.31
70.57	66.83	4.74
111.55	98.40	2.15
27.45	24.83	5.22
30.17	28.89	
1428.55	**1417.46**	
1350.33	1340.76	
53.03	53.04	
25.19	23.66	

13-8 续表2 continued

单位: 亿元

项 目	Item	资产总计 Total Assets
总 计	**Total**	**24497.06**
一、按登记注册类型分组:	Grouped by Type of Registration	
内资企业	Inner Funded Enterprises	20238.60
国有企业	State Owned Enterprises	4430.44
中央企业	Central Enterprises	4246.31
地方企业	Local Enterprises	184.14
集体企业	Collective-owned Enterprise	16.67
股份合作企业	Share Holding Cooperative Enterprises	
联营企业	Joint Owned Enterprise	0.83
国有联营企业	State Joint Ownership	
集体联营企业	Collective Joint Ownership	
国有与集体联营企业	Joint State- Collective Ownership	0.83
其他联营企业	Other Joint Owned Enterprise	
有限责任公司	Responsibility Co. Ltd	7378.18
国有独资公司	State Solely Funded Co.	1927.05
其他有限责任公司	Others	5451.13
股份有限公司	Share Holding Co.Ltd.	6238.44
私营企业	Private – owned enterprises	2160.97
私营独资企业	Solely Private – owned enterprises	14.61
私营合作企业	Private Joint Venture	0.11
私营有限责任公司	Private Responsibility Co. Ltd	1909.74
私营股份有限公司	Private Share Holding Co.Ltd.	236.50
其他企业	Others	13.07
港、澳、台商投资企业	Hongkong, Macao and Taiwan Funded Enterprises	1088.47
合资经营企业(港或澳、台资)	Joint Venture with Hongkong, Macao and Taiwan	675.31
合作经营企业(港或澳、台资)	Cooperate with Hongkong, Macao and Taiwan Funded	10.11
港澳台商独资经营企业	Enterprises Solely Funded by Hongkong, Macao and Taiwan Businessmen	361.38
港澳台商投资股份有限公司	Share Holding Co.Ltd. With Hongkong, Macao and Taiwan Investment	41.67
其他港澳台投资	Others	
外商投资企业	Foreign Funded Enterprises	3170.00
中外合资经营企业	Sino – Foreign Joint Funded Enterprises	2355.98
中外合作经营企业	Sino – Foreign Cooperative Funded Enterprises	3.74
外资企业	Foreign Solely Funded Enterprises	499.47
外商投资股份有限公司	Foreign Funded Share Holding Co.Ltd.	310.81
其他外商投资	Others	
二、在总计中:亏损企业	**Of the Total: enterprises running under deficit**	**5256.15**
在总计中:国有控股企业	Of the Total: State-Owned Share Holding Enterprises	14561.69
在总计中:农村工业	Of the Total: Rural Industry	38.24
在总计中:轻工业	Of the Total: Light Industry	5106.47
重工业	Heavy Industry	19390.59
在总计中:大型企业	Of the Total: Large Scale Enterprises	17866.20
中型企业	Medium Scale Enterprises	6630.87
按行业分	Grouped by Sector	
采矿业	Mining and Qarrying	424.14

(100 million yuan)

			主营业务收入	全部从业人员年平均人数(万人)
流动资产合计 Circulating Funds	固定资产合计 Total Fined Assets	固定资产原价 Original Value of Fixed Assets	Revenue of Major Business	Average Number of Empolyment of the Curreat Year (10 000 Bersons)
10831.36	**9322.43**	**17414.38**	**25309.15**	**214.73**
8751.15	7721.01	14819.34	20152.59	176.78
1396.63	2011.42	3856.51	2662.33	25.74
1306.70	1942.34	3756.06	2571.05	23.88
89.93	69.08	100.46	91.29	1.86
7.86	6.23	14.39	32.63	0.84
0.66	0.17	0.39	0.58	0.04
0.66	0.17	0.39	0.58	0.04
3872.84	2489.68	4252.86	8945.08	73.82
962.02	633.23	1026.96	1715.91	9.78
2910.82	1856.45	3225.90	7229.17	64.04
2415.58	2351.81	3828.69	3735.08	32.08
1049.11	857.47	2861.07	4744.63	44.06
7.12	6.99	12.45	48.81	0.71
0.05	0.06	0.04	0.97	0.03
947.08	753.91	2667.31	4224.96	38.70
94.87	96.51	181.28	469.89	4.63
8.48	4.23	5.43	32.26	0.19
488.84	447.11	777.00	1368.34	14.44
321.20	264.17	471.40	808.88	7.76
4.45	1.65	4.43	4.16	0.05
142.40	172.22	286.24	531.48	6.39
20.79	9.07	14.92	23.82	0.24
1591.36	1154.31	1818.05	3788.21	23.51
1203.63	831.40	1277.14	2984.79	15.13
1.38	2.36	6.53	31.20	0.11
309.33	154.08	263.03	578.88	6.23
77.03	166.47	271.35	193.34	2.04
2104.96	**2067.52**	**3788.60**	**3977.65**	**38.10**
5677.95	5954.16	10156.03	10619.65	74.75
24.59	7.53	53.46	90.89	0.71
2709.98	1604.42	4288.73	8153.24	81.28
8121.37	7718.01	13125.65	17155.91	133.45
7479.63	6911.15	12308.40	15881.60	118.79
3351.72	2411.28	5105.98	9427.55	95.95
173.43	193.79	490.06	342.10	7.20

13-8 续表3 continued

单位: 亿元

项 目	Item	资产总计 Total Assets
煤炭开采和洗选业	Coal Mining and Processing	14.36
石油和天然气开采业	Petroleum and Natural Gas Extraction	149.26
黑色金属矿采选业	Ferrous Metals Mining and Processing	55.27
有色金属矿采选业	Non-ferrous Metals Mining and Processing	24.29
非金属矿采选业	Non-metal Minerals Mining and Processing	65.43
开采辅助活动	Mining Auxiliary Activities	115.53
其他采矿业	Other Minerals Mining and Processing	
制造业	**Manufacturing**	**20630.77**
农副食品加工业	Food Processing	662.59
食品制造业	Food Production	324.87
酒、饮料和精制茶制造业	Wine,Beverage and Refined Tea Production	862.00
烟草制品业	Tobacco Processing	399.84
纺织业	Textile Industry	546.71
纺织服装、服饰业	Textile,Garments, and Fashion Industry	277.05
皮革、毛皮、羽毛及其制品和制鞋业	Leather, Furs,Down and Related Products	39.76
木材加工和木、竹、藤、棕、草制品业	Timber Processing, Wood, Bamboo, Cane, Palm and Sraw Products	85.99
家具制造业	Furniture Manufacturing	50.32
造纸和纸制品业	Papermaking and Paper Products	183.21
印刷和记录媒介复制业	Printing and Record Processing	102.61
文教、工美、体育和娱乐用品制造业	Stationery, Education and Sports Goods	32.33
石油加工、炼焦和核燃料加工业	Petroleum Processing, Coking Products and Nuclear Fuel Processing	199.34
化学原料和化学制品制造业	Raw Chemical Material and Chemical Products	2152.59
医药制造业	Medical and pharmaceutical Products	673.22
化学纤维制造业	Chemical Fibers	38.63
橡胶和塑料制品业	Rubber and plastic products	264.69
非金属矿物制品业	Nonmetal Material Products	842.19
黑色金属冶炼和压延加工业	Smelting and Pressing of Ferrous Metals	2497.03
有色金属冶炼和压延加工业	Smelting and Pressing of Nonferrous Metals	492.15
金属制品业	Metal Products	524.06
通用设备制造业	Ordinary Machinery Manufacturing	888.16
专用设备制造业	Special Purpose Equipment Manufacturing	560.36
汽车制造业	Motor manufacturing	4582.82
铁路、船舶、航空航天和其他运输设备制造业	Railway,Watercraft,Aviation and other Transporlation Equipment manufacturing	741.48
电气机械和器材制造业	Electric Machinery and Equipment	820.49
计算机、通信和其他电子设备制造业	Telecommunication Computer,Equipment and Other Electronic Equipment Manufacturing	1564.24
仪器仪表制造业	Instruments and Meters, Manufacturing	89.92
其他制造业	Other Manufacturing	92.76
废弃资源综合利用业	Waste Comprehensive Vtilization of Resources Industry	23.03
金属制品、机械和设备修理业	Metal products,Machinery and Equipment Repairing	16.34
电力、燃气及水的生产和供应业	**Electric Power, Gas and Water Production and Supply**	**3442.16**
电力、热力生产和供应业	Electric Power, Steam and Hot Water Production and Supply	3133.73
燃气生产和供应业	Gas Production and Supply	70.25
水的生产和供应业	Tap Water Production and Supply	238.19

(100 million yuan)

流动资产合计 Circulating Funds	固定资产合计 Total Fined Assets	固定资产原价 Original Value of Fixed Assets	主营业务收入 Revenue of Major Business	全部从业人员年平均人数(万人) Average Number of Empolyment of the Curreat Year (10 000 Bersons)
7.18	5.64	6.70	26.46	0.90
39.08	96.94	311.92	40.09	1.76
21.41	29.00	57.00	121.27	1.30
7.38	5.61	13.25	15.34	0.34
32.17	15.23	37.86	71.11	1.17
66.22	41.37	63.33	67.83	1.73
10359.15	**6501.08**	**12605.21**	**23546.62**	**194.81**
281.58	323.88	1406.64	1740.58	9.56
132.73	124.50	595.49	658.58	6.34
574.41	186.57	336.26	1195.36	7.71
313.54	27.68	83.88	578.29	0.73
255.21	225.70	522.41	1253.84	17.63
154.40	85.03	173.41	526.20	11.09
17.45	18.67	25.92	54.32	2.34
29.57	35.67	77.49	119.95	1.53
16.78	12.06	19.83	43.02	0.66
100.03	62.44	246.13	264.65	2.22
62.47	29.64	67.02	131.05	1.49
17.89	5.28	32.98	49.74	0.99
73.83	117.81	191.93	694.97	0.83
810.86	1045.46	1547.35	2434.07	13.68
312.75	212.04	303.76	602.99	7.70
12.06	9.07	25.83	32.35	0.63
150.12	84.62	161.23	464.94	5.27
257.59	416.76	676.72	850.91	9.93
713.94	1197.41	2249.71	1663.62	12.15
264.47	129.52	196.00	1305.67	3.58
324.14	134.41	248.98	511.05	5.39
462.63	168.56	259.98	431.55	5.58
356.74	150.53	327.70	451.90	5.52
2442.11	938.41	1587.16	4235.07	29.70
446.58	179.61	239.04	483.26	6.34
494.95	239.50	362.86	1007.06	9.97
1172.45	240.11	486.33	1545.40	12.77
39.81	44.74	49.48	68.02	1.59
47.48	39.55	81.42	98.43	0.89
10.32	11.22	14.25	28.15	0.37
10.24	4.63	8.02	21.61	0.66
298.77	**2627.55**	**4319.11**	**1420.43**	**12.72**
197.52	2534.24	4183.78	1335.35	10.94
22.48	35.47	46.95	58.70	0.46
78.77	57.85	88.38	26.38	1.33

13-9 规模以上工业企业生产能力(2015)
OUTPUT OF MAJOR PRODUCTS OF INDUSTRY ABOVE DESIGNATED SIZE (2015)

产品名称		Item		年初生产能力 Capacity at the Beginning of the Year	年末生产能力 Capacity at the End of the Year
原煤	吨	Coal	ton	29778876.1	29858650.0
天然原油	吨	Crude Petroleum Oil	ton	772390.0	680670.0
卷烟	万支	Cigarettes	10000 pieces	19950381.0	19159875.0
棉纺锭/纺纱量	锭/吨	Knitting Spindle/Capacity	spindle/ton	10501104.1	10337481.4
气流纺锭/纺纱量	头/吨	Air Spindle/Capacity	spindle/ton	448626.5	559559.0
棉布织机/布	台/万米	Cotton Loom/Cloth	piece/10000 meters	423929.9	464692.6
原油加工能力/原油加工量	吨/吨	Crude Oil Processing Capacity	ton/ton	14003844.0	14003844.0
焦炭	吨	Coke	ton	10260000.0	9960000.0
烧碱(折100%)	吨	Caustic Soda (100%)	ton	1308000.0	1318000.0
碳化钙(电石,折300升/千克)	吨	Calcium Carbide (300 L/kg)	ton	776726.6	756596.6
农用氮、磷、钾化学肥料总计(折纯)	吨	Chemical Fertilizers	ton	16064521.0	18299545.0
初级形态塑料	吨	Primary Plastic	ton	2289783.0	2372327.0
化学纤维	吨	Chemical Fiber	ton	295805.4	282745.0
硅酸盐水泥熟料	吨	Portland Cement Clinker	ton	66522536.0	65113536.0
水泥	吨	Cement	ton	139005487.0	142633703.0
平板玻璃	重量箱	Plain Glass	weight case	110903347.7	99527427.7
生铁	吨	Pig Ion	ton	28350000.0	28354670.0
粗钢	吨	Crude Steel	ton	38286335.0	38136335.0
钢材	吨	Rolled Steel	ton	42108607.4	44043387.4
铁合金	吨	Ferroalloy	ton	484868.0	466916.0
原铝(电解铝)	吨	Electrolyzed Aluminum	ton	198000.0	198000.0
金属切削机床	台	Metal-cutting Machine Tools	piece	4545.0	3733.0
汽车	辆	Automobile	unit	2325550.0	2521950.0
其中:基本型乘用车(轿车)	辆	Cars	unit	1060000.0	1094000.0
家用电冰箱	台	Home Refrigerators	piece	4800000.0	4800000.0
房间空气调节器	台	Air Conditioners	piece	15300000.0	16600000.0
移动通信手持机(手机)	台	Mobile Phones	piece	35000000.0	165000000.0
彩色电视机	台	Color Television Sets	piece	628760.0	721782.0
发电设备容量总计/发电量	万千瓦/万千瓦小时	Generating Capacity	10000 kwh	5845.4	6027.4
其中:火电设备容量/发电量		Thermal Power	10000 kwh	2364.6	2468.9
水电设备容量/发电量		Hydropower	10000 kwh	3402.7	3420.0
风电设备容量/发电量		Wind Power	10000 kwh	31.8	95.1

13-10 规模以上工业主要产品产量(2015)
SCALE INDUSTRIAL OUTPUT OF MAIN ProduCTS (2015)

名 称	计量单位	name		产品产量
原煤	吨	Original Coal	ton	7583865.7
1.无烟煤	吨	1.Anthracite	ton	4717797.8
2.烟煤	吨	2.Bituminous Coal	ton	2866067.9
其中:一般烟煤	吨	General Bituminous Coal	ton	2866067.9
洗煤	吨	Washed Coal	ton	617626.0
其中:洗精煤	吨	Cleaned Coal	ton	617626.0
天然原油	吨	Natural Oil	ton	710012.0
天然气	万立方米	Natural Gas	10000 cu.m	13501.0
铁矿石原矿	吨	Iron Ore	ton	34923380.9
铜金属含量	吨	Copper	ton	72526.3
锌金属含量	吨	Zinc	ton	7571.0
锑金属含量	吨	Antimony	ton	443.0
钨精矿折合量(折三氧化钨 6 5 %)	吨	Tungsten Concentrate Equivalent Amount (65% of Tungsten Trioxide)	ton	316.4
钼精矿折合量(折纯钼 4 5 %)	吨	Molybdenum Concentrate Equivalent Amount (45% of Pure Mo)	ton	1149.0
硫铁矿石(折含硫35%)	吨	Pyrite Stone (35% of Sulfur)	ton	172715.0
磷矿石(折含五氧化二磷30%)	吨	Phosphate Rock (30% of Phosphorus Pentoxide)	ton	55402106.6
原盐	吨	Crude Salt	ton	4674940.0
小麦粉	吨	Wheat Flour	ton	6765206.8
大米	吨	Rice	ton	28224037.5
饲料	吨	Feed	ton	17015153.1
其中:配合饲料	吨	Compoud Feed	ton	10231926.7
混合饲料	吨	Mixed feed	ton	3043818.8
精制食用植物油	吨	Refined Edible Vegetable oil	ton	7453342.6
成品糖	吨	Sugar	ton	
鲜、冷藏肉	吨	Fresh and Chilled Meat	ton	1872716.8
冷冻水产品	吨	Frozen Seafood	ton	569460.0
糖果	吨	Candy	ton	270037.9
速冻米面食品	吨	Frozen Rice\Flour Food	ton	65033.7
方便面	吨	Instant Noodles	ton	173302.5
乳制品	吨	Dairy Products	ton	1026041.6
其中:液体乳	吨	Liquid Dairies	ton	995677.7
乳粉	吨	Milk Powder	ton	2422.0
罐头	吨	Can	ton	1230790.8
酱油	吨	Soy Sauce	ton	150204.0
冷冻饮品	吨	Frozen Drinks	ton	299606.9
食品添加剂	吨	Food Additives	ton	313335.3
发酵酒精(折96度,商品量)	千升	Fermentation of Alcohol	kl	43561.5

13-10 续表1 continued

名 称	计量单位	name		产品产量
饮料酒	千升	Alcoholic Beverage	kl	4061489.5
其中:白酒(折65度,商品量)	千升	Liquor (of 65 degrees, the amount of goods)	kl	879580.5
啤酒	千升	Beer	kl	2774824.1
葡萄酒	千升	Wine	kl	1867.8
软饮料	吨	Soft Drinks	ton	9679298.1
其中:碳酸饮料类(汽水)	吨	Carbonated Beverages (soft drinks)	ton	918209.2
包装饮用水类	吨	Packaging of Drinking Water	ton	3113639.4
果汁和蔬菜汁饮料类	吨	Fruit Juice and Vegetable Juice	ton	1098688.3
精制茶	吨	Refined Tea	ton	375213.1
卷烟	万支	Cigarette	10000 pieces	13894381.0
纱	吨	Yarn	ton	3552125.4
1、棉纱	吨	Cotton Yarn	ton	2277465.1
2、棉混纺纱	吨	Cotton Blended Yarn	ton	496803.6
3、化学纤维纱	吨	Chemical Fiber Yarn	ton	777856.7
布	万米	Fabric	10000 meters	798514.4
其中:色织布(含牛仔布)	万米	Dyed Fabric (including jean)	10000 meters	573.0
其中:1.棉布	万米	1.Cotton	10000 meters	655381.4
2.棉混纺布	万米	2.Cotton Blended Cloth	10000 meters	114958.7
3.化学纤维布	万米	3.Chemical-Fiber Cloth	10000 meters	28174.3
印染布	万米	Dyed Cloth	10000 meters	43530.3
亚麻布(含亚麻≥55%)	万米	Linen Fabric (containing linen≥ 55%)	10000 meters	315.8
苎麻布(含苎麻≥55%)	万米	Ramie fabric (containing linen ≥ 55%)	10000 meters	1810.0
蚕丝	吨	Silk	ton	1663.4
蚕丝被	万条	Silk Quilt	10000 pieces	185.2
无纺布(无纺织物)	吨	Non-woven Fabric	ton	418833.9
服装	万件	Clothing	10000 pieces	110930.3
1.梭织服装	万件	Tated Garments	10000 pieces	88317.6
其中:羽绒服	万件	Down Jacket	10000 pieces	515.5
西服套装	万件	Western-style	10000 pieces	1667.2
衬衫	万件	Shirt	10000 pieces	1695.2
2.针织服装	万件	Knitted Garments	10000 pieces	22612.7
轻革	平方米	Light Leather	sq.m	2284272.0
天然毛皮服装	万件	Leather Clothes	piece	43.0
皮革鞋靴	万双	Leather Footwear	10000 pairs	2307.5
人造板	立方米	Artificial Board	cu.m	9881457.9
其中:胶合板	立方米	Plywood	cu.m	3596909.5
纤维板	立方米	FibreBoard	cu.m	3769527.4
刨花板	立方米	Shaving Board	cu.m	192519.8
人造板表面装饰板	平方米	Artificial Board for Surface Decoration	sq.m	88620230.0

13-10 续表2 continued

名 称	计量单位	name		产品产量
复合木地板	平方米	Composite Wood Flooring	cu.m	48687849.2
家具	件	Furniture	piece	6623667.0
其中:木质家具	件	Wood Furniture	piece	2724341.0
金属家具	件	Metal Furniture	piece	498728.0
软体家具	件	Upholstered Furniture	piece	299670.0
纸浆(原生浆及废纸浆)	吨	Pulp (original pulp and waste paper pulp)	ton	123026.0
机制纸及纸板(外购原纸加工除外)	吨	Machine Made Paper and PaperBoard (excludingprocessing outsourcing base paper)	ton	2662440.2
其中:未涂布印刷书写用纸	吨	Uncoating Writing Paper	ton	567606.0
其中:新闻纸	吨	Newsprint	ton	19170.0
卫生用纸原纸	吨	Toilet Paper	ton	225154.9
箱纸板	吨	Case Board	ton	41602.5
纸制品	吨	Paper Products	ton	3246946.2
其中:瓦楞纸箱	吨	Corrugated Case	ton	1746187.4
单色印刷品	令	Monochrome Print	ream	7268930.9
多色印刷品	对开色令	Multi-color Print	folio color ream	19393931.4
原油加工量	吨	Crude Oil Processing Capacity	ton	12887860.8
汽油	吨	Gasoline	ton	3171427.0
煤油	吨	Kerosene	ton	1077465.2
柴油	吨	Diesel Fuel	ton	4504205.9
润滑油	吨	Lubricating Oil	ton	49796.7
燃料油	吨	Fuel Oil	ton	77687.1
石脑油	吨	Naphtha	ton	1445548.0
溶剂油	吨	Megilp	ton	
液化石油气	吨	LPG	ton	558440.6
石油焦	吨	Petroleum Coke	ton	972748.6
石油沥青	吨	Petroleum Pitch	ton	95018.6
焦炭	吨	Coke	ton	9200205.1
其中:机焦	吨	Organic	ton	9200205.1
硫酸(折100%)	吨	Sulfuric Acid (100% discount)	ton	7800916.1
盐酸(氯化氢,含量31%)	吨	Hydrochloric Acid (hydrogen chloride, 31%)	ton	677109.9
浓硝酸(折100%)	吨	Concentrated Nitric Acid (100% discount)	ton	4441.1
烧碱(折100%)	吨	Caustic Soda (100% discount)	ton	1068011.4
其中:离子膜法烧碱(折100%)	吨	Ionic Membrane Method(100% discount)	ton	852679.0
纯碱(碳酸钠)	吨	Soda Ash (sodium carbonate)	ton	1595050.2
精甲醇	吨	Refined Methanol	ton	394910.0
合成氨(无水氨)	吨	Anhydrous Amonia	ton	4880170.6
农用氮、磷、钾化学肥料总计(折纯)	吨	Agricultural Nitrogen, Phosphorus and Potassium Fertilizer	ton	14081253.0
1、氮肥(折含N100%)	吨	1.N (of N 100%)	ton	6257099.8
其中:尿素(折含N100%)	吨	Urea (of N 100%)	ton	1840987.0

13-10 续表3 continued

名 称	计量单位	name		产品产量
2、磷肥(折五氧化二磷100 %)	吨	2.P (of 100% phosphorus pentoxide)	ton	7824153.2
3、钾肥(折氧化钾100%)	吨	3.K (of 100% potassium hydroxide)	ton	
磷酸一铵(实物量)	吨	MAP (physical quantity)	ton	8460718.3
磷酸二铵(实物量)	吨	DAP (physical quantity)	ton	4602840.8
化学农药原药(折有效成分100%)	吨	Chemical Pesticide Active Compound	ton	253921.4
其中:杀虫剂原药	吨	Pesticide Active Compound	ton	74065.5
除草剂原药	吨	Herbicide Active Compound	ton	133653.0
涂料	吨	Paint	ton	433052.7
初级形态的塑料	吨	Primary Form Plastic	ton	2180556.0
聚丙烯树脂	吨	Polypropylene Resin	ton	715403.3
聚氯乙烯树脂	吨	PVC Resin	ton	599226.0
聚苯乙烯树脂	吨	Polystyrene Resin	ton	25531.0
ABS树脂	吨	ABS Resin	ton	22248.0
合成橡胶	吨	Synthetic Rubber	ton	98968.8
合成纤维聚合物	吨	Synthetic Fiber Polymer	ton	17467.0
化学试剂	吨	Chemical Reagent	ton	664135.7
单晶硅	千克	Single Crystal Silion	kg	
多晶硅	千克	Polycrystalline Silion	kg	5600848.0
合成洗涤剂	吨	Synthetic Detergent	ton	209940.7
其中:合成洗衣粉	吨	Synthetic Washing Powder	ton	
化学药品原药	吨	Original Drug Chemicals	ton	265156.8
中成药	吨	Chinese Patent Medicine	ton	419975.9
化学纤维用浆粕	吨	Chemical Fiber Pulp	ton	39658.0
化学纤维	吨	Chemical Fiber	ton	353508.6
其中:人造纤维(纤维素纤维)	吨	Artificid Fiber	ton	109499.0
其中:粘胶短纤维	吨	Fibranne	ton	94165.0
粘胶纤维长丝	吨	Viscose Filament	ton	15334.0
合成纤维	吨	Synthetic Fiber	ton	244009.6
其中:锦纶纤维	吨	Polyamide Fiber	ton	
涤纶纤维	吨	Polyester Fiber	ton	157434.6
丙纶纤维	吨	Polypropylene Fiber	ton	74716.0
橡胶轮胎外胎	条	Rubber Cover Tyre	piece	10164395.0
其中:子午线轮胎外胎	条	Radial Tire	piece	7832270.0
塑料制品	吨	Plastic Products	ton	6527302.4
其中:塑料薄膜	吨	Plastic Film	ton	222618.2
其中:农用薄膜	吨	Agricultural Film	ton	59780.0
泡沫塑料	吨	Foam	ton	269625.2
塑料人造革、合成革	吨	Plastic Leather and Synthetic Leather	ton	49475.0
日用塑料制品	吨	Household Plastic Products	ton	582016.4
硅酸盐水泥熟料	吨	Cement Clinker	ton	50667295.8
其中:窑外分解窑水泥熟料	吨	Cement Kiln Clinker	ton	46079285.

13-10 续表4 continued

名 称	计量单位	name		产品产量
水泥	吨	Cement	ton	112889177.8
其中:强度等级42.5水泥(含R型)	吨	Strength Grade 42.5 Cement (including R-type)	ton	13823040.7
强度等级52.5水泥(含R型)	吨	Strength Grade 52.5 Cement (including R-type)	ton	227154.0
商品混凝土	立方米	Concrete	cu.m	61651116.6
水泥混凝土排水管	千米	Concrete Drainage Pipe	km	7992.7
水泥混凝土压力管	千米	Concrete Pressure Pipe	km	6081.0
水泥混凝土电杆	根	Cement Concrete Pole	piece	602519.0
预应力混凝土桩	米	Prestressed Concrete Pile	meter	10368128.0
石膏板	万平方米	Gypsum Board	10000 sq.m	60935.4
砖	万块	Brick	10000 pieces	7484167.7
瓦	万片	Tile	10000 pieces	315976.3
瓷质砖	平方米	Porcelain Tile	sq.m	289019562.6
陶质砖	平方米	Ceramic Tile	sq.m	126742743.0
天然大理石建筑板材	平方米	Natural Marble Building Boards	sq.m	48374794.9
天然花岗石建筑板材	平方米	Natural Granite Building Boards	sq.m	21959284.0
沥青和改性沥青防水卷材	平方米	Asphalt and Modified Bitumen Sheet	sq.m	51972756.7
平板玻璃	重量箱	Plate Glass	weight case	88861430.3
钢化玻璃	平方米	Tempered Glass	sq.m	12992779.6
夹层玻璃	平方米	Laminated Glass	sq.m	1267109.4
中空玻璃	平方米	Insulating Glass	sq.m	16683146.8
日用玻璃制品	吨	Daily Glass Products	ton	741892.0
玻璃包装容器	吨	Glass Containers	ton	1780808.7
玻璃纤维纱	吨	Glass Fiber Yarn	ton	18956.5
纤维增强塑料制品	吨	Fiber Reinforced Plastic Products	ton	12258.8
卫生陶瓷制品	件	Sanitary Ceramic Products	piece	18219631.0
耐火材料制品	吨	Refractory Products	ton	1775510.0
石墨及炭素制品	吨	Graphite and Carbon Products	ton	365837.1
生铁	吨	Pig Iron	ton	22887472.3
粗钢	吨	Crude Steel	ton	29197666.8
铸铁件	吨	Iron Casting	ton	2754082.8
铸钢件	吨	Steel Casting	ton	793078.5
钢材	吨	Steel	ton	34212232.6
1.铁道用钢材	吨	1. Railway Steel	ton	579067.0
重轨	吨	Heavy Rail	ton	578548.0
2.大型型钢	吨	2. Large-scale Steel	ton	35239.0
3.中小型型钢	吨	3. Small and Medium Scale Steel	ton	1233711.0
4.棒材	吨	4. Bar	ton	2071467.5
5.钢筋	吨	5. Steel Bar	ton	6907920.9
6.线材(盘条)	吨	6. Wire (coil)	ton	2700443.0
7.特厚板	吨	7. Special Plate	ton	317906.0

13-10 续表5 continued

名 称	计量单位	name		产品产量
8.厚钢板	吨	8. Thick Steel Plate	ton	566138.0
9.中板	吨	9. Middle Plate	ton	1415245.7
10.热轧薄板	吨	10. Hot-rolled Sheet	ton	857926.9
11.冷轧薄板	吨	11. Cold-rolled Sheet	ton	1784433.7
12.中厚宽钢带	吨	12. Thick Wide Strip	ton	4202823.0
13.热轧薄宽钢带	吨	13. Hot-rolled Thin Wide Strip	ton	1742036.0
14.冷轧薄宽钢带	吨	14. Cold-rolled Wide Strip	ton	2403080.4
15.热轧窄钢带	吨	15. Hot-rolled Narrow Strip	ton	332543.0
16.冷轧窄钢带	吨	16. Cold-rolled Narrow Strip	ton	57085.0
17.镀层板(带)	吨	17. Coated Plate	ton	3192796.1
18.涂层板(带)	吨	18. Coated Plate	ton	244650.9
铁合金	吨	Ferroallory	ton	329949.3
十种有色金属	吨	10 Kinds of Nonferrous Metals	ton	962048.2
精炼铜(电解铜)	吨	Refined Copper (electrolytic copper)	ton	505235.1
铅	吨	Lead	ton	345972.0
锌	吨	Zinc	ton	2090.0
氧化铝	吨	Alumina	ton	
原铝(电解铝)	吨	Electrolytic Aluminum	ton	104167.1
黄金	千克	Gold	kg	24521.3
白银(银锭)	千克	Silver (silver bullion)	kg	1067130.8
铝合金	吨	Aluminum Alloy	ton	122196.3
铜材	吨	Copper	ton	104434.0
铝材	吨	Aluminum	ton	1162701.0
金属切削工具	万件	Metal Cutting Tools	10000 pieces	37645.2
钢丝	吨	Wire	ton	122609.0
钢丝绳	吨	Wire Rope	ton	23606.0
钢绞线	吨	Strand	ton	240392.0
锻件	吨	Forge Piece	ton	618116.1
粉末冶金零件	吨	Powder Metallurgy	ton	92681.7
工业锅炉	蒸发量吨	Industrial Boiler	ton	3345.0
发动机	千瓦	Engine	kw	123751574.0
其中:汽车用发动机	千瓦	Automotive Engine	kw	121213697.0
电站用汽轮机	千瓦	Power Plant Steam Turbine	kw	1161000.0
电站水轮机	千瓦	Turbine	kw	12950.0
金属切削机床	台	Metal Cutting Machine	piece	3938.0
其中:数控金属切削机床	台	CNC Metal Cutting Machine	piece	626.0
金属成形机床	台	Metal Forming Machine	piece	34731.0
其中: 数控金属成形机床(数控锻压设备)	台	CNC Metal Forming Machine	piece	167.0

13-10 续表6 continued

名 称	计量单位	name		产品产量
铸造机械	台	Foundry Machine	piece	57358.0
电焊机	台	Electric Welding Machine	piece	709.0
机床数控装置	套	Machine Digital Control Device	piece	5684.0
起重机	吨	Crane	piece	27490.0
电动车辆(电动叉车)	台	Electric Vehicles (electric forklift)	piece	43956.0
内燃叉车	台	Internal Combustion Forklift	piece	179.0
输送机械(输送机和提升机)	吨	Transportation Machinery (conveyors and elevators)	ton	160833.9
泵	台	Pump	piece	439469.0
其中:真空泵	台	Vacuum Pump	piece	4027.0
气体压缩机	台	Gas Compressor	piece	28539919.0
其中:制冷设备用压缩机	台	Refrigeration Equipment with Compressor	piece	28533627.0
阀门	吨	Valve	ton	56940.3
液压元件	件	Hydraulic Components	piece	886346.0
气动元件	件	Pneumatic components	piece	1831469.0
滚动轴承	万套	Roller	10000 pieces	6970.7
齿轮	吨	Gear	ton	366089.4
风机	台	Fans	piece	39116.0
包装专用设备	台	Special Equipment Package	piece	12680.0
金属密封件	万件	Metal Sealing Element	10000 pieces	2324.0
金属紧固件	吨	Metal Fastenings	ton	54239.0
弹簧	吨	Spring	ton	48617.0
减速机	台	Reducer	piece	317334.0
矿山专用设备	吨	Mining Special Equipment	ton	103751.9
挖掘、铲土运输机械	台	Digging and Scraper Transport Machinery	piece	789.0
其中:挖掘机	台	Excavator	piece	
水泥专用设备	吨	Cement Special Equipment	ton	15055.0
混凝土机械	台	Concrete Machinery	piece	1118.0
金属冶炼设备	吨	Metal Smelting Equipment	ton	7249.0
金属轧制设备	吨	Metal Rolling Equipment	ton	7804.0
炼油、化工生产专用设备	吨	Oil Refining and Chemical Production Special Equipment	ton	672683.1
塑料加工专用设备	台	Plastics Processing Special Equipment	piece	238.0
模具	套	Mold	piece	184317.0
农产品初加工机械	台	Equipment for Agricultural Products Pretreating	piece	1063254.0
饲料生产专用设备	台	Equipment for Feed Production	piece	12807.0
印刷专用设备	吨	Printing Special Equipment	ton	
中型拖拉机	台	Medium-size Tractors	piece	
小型拖拉机	台	Small Tractor	piece	60902.0
收获机械	台	Harvesting Machinery	piece	5833.0
其中:谷物收获机械	台	Cereal Harvesting Machinery	piece	5833.0

13-10 续表7 continued

名 称	计量单位	name		产品产量
收获后处理机械	台	Post-harvesting Processing Machinery	piece	47780.0
环境污染防治专用设备	台(套)	Equipment for Environmental Pollution Control	piece	89911.0
其中:大气污染防治设备	台(套)	Air Pollution Control Equipment	piece	84860.0
水质污染防治设备	台(套)	Water Pollution Control Equipment	piece	4364.0
固体废弃物处理设备	台(套)	Solid Waste Handling Equipment	piece	505.0
汽车	辆	Car	piece	1968499.0
其中:基本型乘用车(轿车)	辆	Passenger Vehicles	piece	850305.0
1升<排量≤1.6升	辆	(1) 1.0 Liter < Displacement ≤ 1.6 Liter	piece	657362.0
1.6升<排量≤2.0升	辆	(2) 1.6 Liter < Displacement ≤ 2.0 Liter	piece	184288.0
2.0升<排量≤2.5升	辆	(3) 2.0 Liter < Displacement ≤ 2.5 Liter	piece	8655.0
2.5升<排量≤3.0升	辆	(4) 2.5 Liter < Displacement ≤ 3.0 Liter	piece	
多功能乘用车(MPV)	辆	MPV	piece	156228.0
运动型多用途乘用车(SUV)	辆	SUV	piece	580339.0
客车	辆	Bus	piece	110329.0
(1)大型客车(车长>10米)	辆	(1) Large Passenger Bus (car length>10 m)	piece	134.0
(2)中型客车(7米<车长≤10米)	辆	(2) Medium Passenger Bus(7 m<car length≤10 m)	piece	3328.0
(3)轻型客车(车长≤7米)	辆	(3) light buses (car length≤ 7 m)	piece	106867.0
载货汽车	辆	Lorry	piece	270694.0
改装汽车	辆	Modified Cars	piece	252122.0
低速载货汽车	辆	Low Speed Truck	piece	6449.0
铁路货车	辆	Railway Wagon	piece	3674.0
民用钢质船舶	载重吨	Civil Steel Ships	ton	1487787.3
电动自行车	辆	Electric Bicycle	piece	885177.0
发电机组(发电设备)	千瓦	Generating Units (power equipment)	kw	1196900.0
其中:水轮发电机组	千瓦	Generator Group	kw	2400.0
汽轮发电机	千瓦	Turbonator	kw	1194500.0
交流电动机	千瓦	AC Motors	kw	1003366.7
变压器	千伏安	Transformer	kva	25335631.2
其中:电力变压器(额定容量≥8000kVA,电压≥500kV)	千伏安	Power Transformer	kva	191200.0
互感器	台	Mutual Inductor	kva	235149.0
高压开关板	面	High-voltage Switch Board	piece	182949.0
低压开关板	面	Low-voltage Switch Board	piece	246590.0
高压开关设备(11万伏以上)	台	High Voltage Switchgear (11 KV and above)	piece	34711.0
通信及电子网络用电缆	对千米	Communication and Electronic Networks Cables	km	1650747.5
电力电缆	千米	Power Cable	km	814181.0
光缆	芯千米	Optical Cable	km	61057468.7
绝缘制品	吨	Insulation Products	ton	71818.3

13-10 续表8 continued

名 称	计量单位	name		产品产量
锂离子电池	只(自然只)	Li-ion Battery	piece	147251675.0
铅酸蓄电池	千伏安时	Lead-acid Battery	kvah	24449229.7
碱性蓄电池	只(自然只)	Alkaline Battery	piece	9837500.0
原电池及原电池组(非扣式)	万只	Primary Cells and Primary Batteries	10000 pieces	
太阳能电池	千瓦	Solar Battery	kw	989401.6
家用电冰箱	台	Household Refrigerator	piece	2862000.0
家用冷柜(家用冷冻箱)	台	Household Refrigerator (household freezers)	piece	1581813.0
房间空气调节器	台	Room Air Conditioners	piece	12130356.0
家用吸排油烟机	台	Home Ventilator	piece	10451.0
家用洗衣机	台	Household Washing Machines	piece	
家用电热水器	台	Water Heater	piece	2024582.0
家用吸尘器	台	Household Vacuum Cleaner	piece	
家用燃气灶具	台	Kitchen Range	piece	1172208.0
太阳能热水器	平方米	Solar Water Heater	sq.m	326226.0
电光源	万只	Light Sources	10000 pieces	166452.3
其中:白炽灯泡	万只	Incandescent Bulb	10000 pieces	50507.0
荧光灯	万只	Fluorescent Lamp	10000 pieces	10657.1
灯具及照明装置	万套(台、个)	Lamps and Lighting Fittings	10000pieces	2612.6
电子计算机整机	台	Computers	pieces	11215247.0
微型计算机设备	台	Micro-computer Equipment	pieces	11215247.0
显示器	台	Monitor	pieces	18359604.0
程控交换机	线	SPC Exchange	line	
移动通信手持机(手机)	台	Mobile Handset (cell phone)	pieces	54756956.0
组合音响	台	Music Center	pieces	
半导体分立器件	万只	Semiconductor Discrete Devices	10000 pieces	1163524.9
集成电路	万块	IC	10000 pieces	52.0
集成电路圆片	万片	IC Wafer	10000 pieces	18.7
光电子器件	万只(片、套)	Optoelectronic Devices	10000 pieces	1043225.8
其中:发光二极管(LED)	万只	Light-emitting Diode (LED)	10000 pieces	452545.8
电子元件	万只	Electronic Component	10000 pieces	1477814.6
其中:射频元器件	万只	RF Components	10000 pieces	
印制电路板	平方米	Printed Board	sq.m	1259516.6
工业自动调节仪表与控制系统	万台(套)	Automatic Adjustment and Control System of Industrial Instrumentation	10000 piece	10.7
电工仪器仪表	台	Electric Instrument	piece	1765.0
分析仪器及装置	台(套)	Analytical Instrument	piece	689.0
汽车仪器仪表	台	Car Instrument	piece	5654388.0
光学仪器	万台(个)	Optical Instrument	10000 piece	2435.3
船舶修理	载重吨	Ship Repair	ton	
发电量	万千瓦小时	Power Generation	10000 kwh	23014332.0
其中:火力发电量	万千瓦小时	Thermal Capacity	10000 kwh	9620780.6
水力发电量	万千瓦小时	Hydroelectricity	10000 kwh	12899556.9
风力发电量	万千瓦小时	Wind Power Capacity	10000 kwh	160736.7
煤气生产量	万立方米	Coal Gas	10000 cu.m	2972019.0
自来水生产量	万立方米	Water Production	10000 cu.m	242940.7

13-11 规模以上工业企业主要经济效益指标 (2015)

项 目	Item	企业亏损面(%) Enterprises deficit (%)
总 计	**Total**	**8.8**
一、按登记注册类型分组:	**Grouped by Type of Registration**	
内资企业	Inner Funded Enterprises	8.3
国有企业	State Owned Enterprises	23.0
中央企业	Central Enterprises	26.1
地方企业	Local Enterprises	21.7
集体企业	Collective-owned Enterprise	10.2
股份合作企业	Share Holding Cooperative Enterprises	
联营企业	Joint Owned Enterprise	
国有联营企业	State Joint Ownership	
集体联营企业	Collective Joint Ownership	
国有与集体联营企业	Joint State- Collective Ownership	
其他联营企业	Other Joint Owned Enterprise	
有限责任公司	Responsibility Co. Ltd	11.6
国有独资公司	State Solely Funded Co.	24.8
其他有限责任公司	Others	11.3
股份有限公司	Share Holding Co.Ltd.	12.5
私营企业	Private - owned enterprises	5.6
私营独资企业	Solely Private - owned enterprises	3.1
私营合作企业	Private Joint Venture	6.1
私营有限责任公司	Private Responsibility Co. Ltd	5.6
私营股份有限公司	Private Share Holding Co.Ltd.	5.9
其他企业	Others	3.8
港、澳、台商投资企业	Hongkong, Macao and Taiwan Funded Enterprises	17.8
合资经营企业(港或澳、台资)	Joint Venture with Hongkong, Macao and Taiwan	19.1
合作经营企业(港或澳、台资)	Cooperate with Hongkong, Macao and Taiwan Funded	25.0
港澳台商独资经营企业	Enterprises Solely Funded by Hongkong, Macao and Taiwan Businessmen	17.2
港澳台商投资股份有限公司	Share Holding Co.Ltd. With Hongkong, Macao and Taiwan Investment	9.1
外商投资企业	Foreign Funded Enterprises	18.8
中外合资经营企业	Sino - Foreign Joint Funded Enterprises	18.1
中外合作经营企业	Sino - Foreign Cooperative Funded Enterprises	
外资企业	Foreign Solely Funded Enterprises	20.4
外商投资股份有限公司	Foreign Funded Share Holding Co.Ltd.	20.0
二、在总计中:亏损企业	**Of the Total: enterprises running under deficit**	**100.0**
在总计中:国有控股企业	Of the Total: State-Owned Share Holding Enterprises	23.8
在总计中:农村工业	Of the Total: Rural Industry	5.4
在总计中:轻工业	Of the Total: Light Industry	6.8
重工业	Heavy Industry	10.1
在总计中:大型企业	Of the Total: Large Scale Enterprises	12.3
中型企业	Medium Scale Enterprises	11.4
小型企业	Small Enterprises	8.4

MAJOR ECONOMIC INDICATORS OF INDUSTRIAL ENTERPRISES ABOVE DESIGNATED SIZE (2015)

总资产贡献率(%) Contributing Ratie of Tatal Assets(%)	资产负债率(%) Assets Liability Ratio(%)	流动资产周转率(次/年) Current Asset Tuinover (Times/year)	成本费用利润率(%) Ratio of Riofits to Industrial Cost(%)	产品销售率(%) Propovtion of Produts Sold(%)
14.16	**54.97**	**2.75**	**6.01**	**96.30**
13.59	54.20	2.79	5.74	96.71
2.23	67.53	1.86	-1.11	98.71
2.05	67.75	1.92	-1.49	98.87
5.25	64.01	1.29	4.85	96.35
20.06	60.41	4.21	4.63	97.54
9.34	67.73	2.13	4.83	95.06
20.77	44.18	4.16	5.89	97.89
25.02	38.24	2.71	15.95	96.34
7.31	64.94	0.88	2.02	91.01
21.87	37.18	36.48	0.56	100.00
15.90	58.73	2.59	5.44	96.18
33.02	60.46	1.93	6.30	94.95
12.23	58.35	2.72	5.34	96.35
11.12	45.55	1.63	10.94	96.82
19.51	46.37	4.53	5.94	96.79
33.63	36.02	8.63	5.98	98.11
29.43	50.27	7.03	5.92	98.02
18.94	46.71	4.43	5.79	96.79
23.46	44.13	4.98	7.76	96.22
21.66	39.15	6.05	5.57	98.46
11.98	50.86	2.93	5.90	89.65
10.78	55.23	2.77	5.17	85.44
1.46	42.10	1.72	-2.18	94.31
14.33	45.33	3.36	7.10	95.59
9.17	42.09	1.79	6.14	97.91
19.61	62.75	2.39	8.41	95.83
22.82	64.16	2.52	8.72	95.26
47.22	50.63	10.00	22.04	98.58
13.08	57.84	1.87	8.02	96.89
5.41	63.33	2.58	2.39	100.69
-0.66	**73.47**	**1.75**	**-6.06**	**97.07**
12.43	59.25	1.92	5.76	96.53
15.01	51.08	3.73	4.49	95.21
22.47	47.32	3.55	6.50	95.97
11.49	57.44	2.44	5.75	96.49
12.91	58.78	2.18	5.54	96.19
16.12	53.86	2.86	7.33	96.37
15.02	49.41	3.51	5.74	96.35

13-11 续表 continued

项 目	Item	企业亏损面(%) Enterprises Deficit (%)
按行业分	Grouped by Sector	
采矿业	**Mining and Qarrying**	**9.3**
煤炭开采和洗选业	Coal Mining and Processing	10.2
石油和天然气开采业	Petroleum and Natural Gas Extraction	100.0
黑色金属矿采选业	Ferrous Metals Mining and Processing	14.0
有色金属矿采选业	Non-ferrous Metals Mining and Processing	19.5
非金属矿采选业	Non-metal Minerals Mining and Processing	6.4
开采辅助活动	Mining Auxiliary Activities	25.0
其他采矿业	Other Minerals Mining and Processing	
制造业	**Manufacturing**	**8.6**
农副食品加工业	Food Processing	3.9
食品制造业	Food Production	5.5
酒、饮料和精制茶制造业	Wine,Beverage and Refined Tea Production	6.0
烟草制品业	Tobacco Processing	14.3
纺织业	Textile Industry	8.2
纺织服装、服饰业	Textile,Garments, and Fashion Industry	6.9
皮革、毛皮、羽毛及其制品和制鞋业	Leather, Furs,Down and Related Products	6.0
木材加工和木、竹、藤、棕、草制品业	Timber Processing, Wood, Bamboo, Cane, Palm and Sraw Products	3.5
家具制造业	Furniture Manufacturing	11.1
造纸和纸制品业	Papermaking and Paper Products	10.2
印刷和记录媒介复制业	Printing and Record Processing	13.2
文教、工美、体育和娱乐用品制造业	Stationery, Education and Sports Goods	7.5
石油加工、炼焦和核燃料加工业	Petroleum Processing, Coking Products and Nuclear Fuel Processing	21.3
化学原料和化学制品制造业	Raw Chemical Material and Chemical Products	8.6
医药制造业	Medical and pharmaceutical Products	8.8
化学纤维制造业	Chemical Fibers	4.2
橡胶和塑料制品业	Rubber and plastic products	5.4
非金属矿物制品业	Nonmetal Material Products	6.3
黑色金属冶炼和压延加工业	Smelting and Pressing of Ferrous Metals	15.9
有色金属冶炼和压延加工业	Smelting and Pressing of Nonferrous Metals	18.7
金属制品业	Metal Products	9.0
通用设备制造业	Ordinary Machinery Manufacturing	11.2
专用设备制造业	Special Purpose Equipment Manufacturing	9.5
汽车制造业	Motor manufacturing	12.8
铁路、船舶、航空航天和其他运输设备制造业	Railway,Watercraft,Aviation and other Transporlation Equipment manufacturing	12.7
电气机械和器材制造业	Electric Machinery and Equipment	10.0
计算机、通信和其他电子设备制造业	Telecommunication Computer,Equipment and Other Electronic Equipment Manufacturing Other Electronic Equipment Manufacturing	13.0
仪器仪表制造业	Instruments and Meters, Manufacturing	10.9
其他制造业	Other Manufacturing	8.5
废弃资源综合利用业	Waste Comprehensive Vtilization of Resources Industry	31.1
金属制品、机械和设备修理业	Metal products,Machinery and Equipment Repairing	17.4
电力、燃气及水的生产和供应业	**Electric Power, Gas and Water Production and Supply**	**18.2**
电力、热力生产和供应业	Electric Power, Steam and Hot Water Production and Supply	21.8
燃气生产和供应业	Gas Production and Supply	4.5
水的生产和供应业	Tap Water Production and Supply	21.3

总资产贡献率(%) Contributing Ratie of Tatal Assets(%)	资产负债率(%) Assets Liability Ratio(%)	流动资产周转率(次/年) Current Asset Tuinover (Times/year)	成本费用利润率(%) Ratio of Riofits to Industrial Cost(%)	产品销售率(%) Propovtion of Produts Sold(%)
12.47	**57.13**	**3.02**	**5.15**	**97.25**
26.17	43.90	4.97	9.77	98.66
-7.91	75.82	1.24	-33.40	99.43
17.32	53.21	5.98	3.69	97.64
18.52	48.60	2.45	16.94	98.02
14.84	51.22	3.10	8.29	96.51
12.25	75.91	1.04	8.27	98.20
4.11	62.95	1.13	4.04	100.00
14.64	**55.04**	**2.71**	**5.51**	**96.18**
20.10	40.46	5.79	5.48	96.45
21.65	40.63	4.76	6.53	96.44
17.82	59.60	2.42	7.48	96.82
124.57	32.35	1.98	35.20	89.97
21.25	46.22	5.29	5.08	97.01
18.00	45.30	4.00	5.00	97.32
14.63	51.99	4.38	3.46	97.76
17.37	46.43	4.32	6.41	96.54
12.53	39.49	3.65	5.72	95.62
12.70	54.22	3.01	4.97	95.25
17.58	44.25	2.89	7.39	95.12
7.79	77.09	1.85	3.46	97.74
78.92	52.92	8.87	0.41	98.67
11.86	59.21	3.45	5.09	96.94
14.99	46.95	2.34	9.08	94.79
13.94	42.24	3.24	7.87	97.70
21.57	43.87	3.67	7.36	95.89
17.00	45.31	4.02	7.00	97.49
0.50	71.45	2.56	-3.98	98.14
3.47	68.02	4.80	0.26	97.39
12.54	57.27	2.51	5.37	96.83
7.70	62.76	1.61	5.06	95.76
8.43	60.02	1.55	5.10	96.05
16.02	51.82	1.92	9.56	97.03
4.43	72.25	1.24	2.93	96.90
12.59	54.29	2.22	6.28	95.35
5.72	59.45	1.44	3.14	88.25
11.08	50.33	1.48	9.01	95.04
11.08	61.35	2.54	5.82	90.73
5.30	64.45	2.79	1.81	95.49
16.51	50.11	2.29	5.71	95.52
11.37	**53.98**	**3.83**	**19.08**	**98.55**
12.06	53.36	5.41	20.24	99.17
12.18	66.34	2.50	13.63	94.11
2.78	53.84	0.60	7.13	94.26

13-12 规模以上工业企业产销总值及主要经济指标(分地区) (2015)

单位: 亿元

地区	Region	企业单位数(个) Number of Enterprises(unit)	亏损企业 Enterprises Running under Deficit
全省	**Province**	**16413**	**1441**
武汉	Wuhan	2558	373
黄石	Huangshi	761	117
十堰	Shiyan	976	157
宜昌	Yichang	1543	118
襄阳	Xiangyang	1826	94
鄂州	Ezhou	489	35
荆门	Jingmen	1132	62
孝感	Xiaogan	1306	78
荆州	Jingzhou	1258	89
黄冈	Huanggang	1493	126
咸宁	Xianning	867	86
随州	Suizhou	688	32
恩施	Enshi	557	28
仙桃	Xiantao	386	22
潜江	Qianjiang	267	15
天门	Tianmen	296	4
神农架	Shennongjia	10	5

13-12 续表 1 continued

单位: 亿元

地区	Region	资产总计 Total Assets	流动资产合计 Circulating Funds	应收帐款净额 Net Account Received
全省	**Province**	**35399.12**	**15976.10**	**4056.46**
武汉	Wuhan	12740.05	6488.38	1924.09
黄石	Huangshi	1880.76	912.79	154.84
十堰	Shiyan	2825.17	1288.17	253.64
宜昌	Yichang	4928.59	1530.02	278.76
襄阳	Xiangyang	3199.94	1556.29	461.92
鄂州	Ezhou	578.60	208.69	55.85
荆门	Jingmen	1368.80	532.99	100.31
孝感	Xiaogan	1442.04	638.33	165.06
荆州	Jingzhou	1476.38	718.52	187.59
黄冈	Huanggang	1199.32	455.84	130.03
咸宁	Xianning	882.72	365.79	82.13
随州	Suizhou	678.76	280.66	80.36
恩施	Enshi	477.82	159.14	32.16
仙桃	Xiantao	499.12	220.79	57.38
潜江	Qianjiang	675.98	369.09	57.77
天门	Tianmen	501.77	229.63	31.51
神农架	Shennongjia	43.30	20.98	3.06

TOTAL VALUE OF PRODUCTION AND SALES AND MAJOR ECONOMIC INDICATORS OF INDUSTRIAL ENTERPRISES ABOVE DESIGNATED SIZE (BY REGIONS) (2015)

(100 million yuan)

工业总产值(当年价格) Total Output Value(current price)	工业销售产值(当年价格) Output Value of Industrial Products(current price)	出口交货值 Delivery Value for Export
45809.57	**44113.44**	**1688.02**
12862.95	12120.80	660.03
2005.91	1941.57	70.83
1822.54	1775.68	31.36
5714.37	5570.52	176.47
5879.06	5689.96	92.38
1286.41	1252.75	24.70
3089.60	3019.56	53.41
2671.40	2599.47	59.65
2368.55	2275.51	63.71
1853.61	1741.63	39.01
1734.86	1674.24	23.91
1268.89	1262.47	97.99
404.76	395.52	6.08
996.55	969.74	143.31
1010.00	1000.66	88.48
832.75	816.42	56.69
7.35	6.94	

(100 million yuan)

固定资产合计 Total Value of Fixed Assets	固定资产原价 Original Price of Fixed Assets	累计折旧 Accumulated
13328.90	**24361.81**	**11860.43**
4030.04	6997.19	3132.78
690.73	1003.92	358.59
530.62	762.16	300.67
2598.82	3862.72	1348.18
1173.95	1604.45	524.32
283.10	445.04	169.09
624.58	1529.23	954.59
629.79	2384.15	1792.73
615.87	2609.47	2129.65
498.30	625.48	162.63
353.50	472.55	148.60
282.58	324.65	67.64
257.79	345.62	106.52
242.79	379.81	145.28
253.42	528.39	285.75
249.22	466.10	226.02
13.79	20.88	7.38

13-12 续表 2 continued

单位: 亿元

地区	Region	负债合计 Total Liability	流动负债合计 Total Circulating Liability	应付账款 Account	非流动负债合计 Tatal Non-current Liability	所有者权益合计 Total Rights of Owners
全省	**Province**	**19459.99**	**14914.59**	**4363.48**	**3211.43**	**15875.33**
武汉	Wuhan	8130.64	6775.02	2389.94	1080.37	4578.18
黄石	Huangshi	1137.36	804.60	179.69	207.29	740.04
十堰	Shiyan	1208.23	990.50	287.47	156.77	1616.50
宜昌	Yichang	2668.98	1738.57	320.76	810.77	2245.82
襄阳	Xiangyang	1629.33	1149.43	354.39	237.42	1565.65
鄂州	Ezhou	332.44	269.28	58.32	51.09	246.16
荆门	Jingmen	617.83	456.29	87.56	95.76	750.66
孝感	Xiaogan	726.65	393.41	90.91	101.22	714.88
荆州	Jingzhou	673.96	549.43	141.82	81.90	800.71
黄冈	Huanggang	601.12	459.94	173.49	80.18	595.70
咸宁	Xianning	385.15	284.61	66.53	69.88	495.71
随州	Suizhou	285.39	224.83	46.04	38.55	393.36
恩施	Enshi	264.98	188.15	24.94	67.41	210.77
仙桃	Xiantao	191.39	149.74	51.01	26.81	307.73
潜江	Qianjiang	333.91	290.66	52.55	27.47	342.07
天门	Tianmen	236.26	164.12	36.58	68.16	264.47
神农架	Shennongjia	36.39	26.01	1.48	10.39	6.91

13-12 续表 3 continued

单位: 亿元

地区	Region	所有者权益合计 Total Rights of the Owners	主营业务收入 Revenue of Major Business	主营业务成本 Cost of Major Business
		外商资本 Foreign Assets		
全省	**Province**	**458.44**	**43179.21**	**36564.31**
武汉	Wuhan	266.61	11771.72	9764.15
黄石	Huangshi	66.21	2505.68	2285.59
十堰	Shiyan	3.84	1677.70	1449.40
宜昌	Yichang	21.76	5403.72	4538.81
襄阳	Xiangyang	35.79	5389.08	4514.15
鄂州	Ezhou	0.22	1189.38	1013.48
荆门	Jingmen	8.52	2965.75	2532.97
孝感	Xiaogan	11.04	2536.15	2171.71
荆州	Jingzhou	31.12	2185.88	1901.62
黄冈	Huanggang	2.93	1640.25	1429.13
咸宁	Xianning	3.90	1560.83	1315.85
随州	Suizhou	1.22	1207.48	990.47
恩施	Enshi	0.57	383.14	311.15
仙桃	Xiantao	4.04	968.67	776.83
潜江	Qianjiang	0.50	964.24	878.58
天门	Tianmen	0.17	822.68	684.87
神农架	Shennongjia		6.86	5.53

(100 million Yuan)

实收资本 Assets Recevied	国家资本 National Assets	所有者权益合计 Total Rights of Owners			
		集体资本 Collective Assets	法人资本 Corperative Assets	个人资本 Individual Assets	港澳台资本 Assets from Hongkong, Maco and Taiwan
7132.11	**2132.71**	**119.39**	**2527.84**	**1738.62**	**155.11**
1933.59	729.59	32.93	615.19	229.71	59.57
314.77	94.92	7.74	83.41	55.30	7.18
526.38	298.42	14.96	105.36	102.60	1.20
686.33	222.33	11.00	213.85	200.27	17.12
860.41	120.96	16.25	536.25	145.76	5.41
179.64	65.11	1.60	83.98	27.49	1.25
324.19	71.64	3.11	88.16	149.11	3.65
412.72	38.83	3.43	144.39	208.95	6.09
719.44	417.86	9.99	79.29	180.40	0.79
278.53	11.72	5.96	107.69	126.66	23.57
160.74	6.10	4.71	65.09	75.40	5.53
179.85	15.26	1.29	59.83	97.35	4.90
114.29	29.72	2.81	29.72	51.15	0.31
96.64	2.53	0.82	38.37	34.49	16.39
224.41	5.58	2.74	202.28	12.55	0.76
115.26	1.61	0.06	73.68	38.35	1.39
4.92	0.53		1.31	3.09	

(100 million Yuan)

主营业务税金及附加 Tax of Major Business	其他业务收入 Revenue of Other Business	其他业务利润 Profit from Other Business	销售费用 Selling Expenses	管理费用 Management Expense	
					税金 Tax
898.35	**756.81**	**37.64**	**1281.28**	**1811.39**	**105.33**
576.55	376.53	14.83	368.22	541.34	20.18
14.72	103.68	3.46	50.77	67.16	4.14
16.39	62.07	6.16	62.89	113.26	5.10
45.71	48.26	4.64	183.83	201.77	12.52
39.38	40.00	2.50	115.43	270.44	9.18
7.77	38.44	0.11	49.84	59.56	1.51
82.44	6.89	0.73	80.48	92.81	5.05
35.14	11.07	1.11	80.87	92.38	5.15
13.98	24.92	2.04	55.48	85.09	21.86
12.57	9.37	0.63	37.01	56.83	3.29
12.21	6.63	0.28	43.57	42.86	1.67
7.46	2.26	0.19	40.99	46.01	1.95
3.87	1.80	0.45	14.59	16.15	0.71
5.66	1.95	0.38	56.04	60.63	8.88
19.33	22.56	0.13	12.87	26.59	1.30
4.69	0.35	0.01	28.32	38.00	2.81
0.48	0.03		0.08	0.51	0.04

13-12 续表 4 continued

单位: 亿元

地区	Region	财务费用 Financial Expense	利息支出 Interest Expense	营业利润 Operating Profit	补贴收入 Income from Subsidy
全省	**Province**	**516.99**	**442.62**	**2313.30**	**94.38**
武汉	Wuhan	129.49	119.73	407.88	31.27
黄石	Huangshi	28.61	19.47	56.75	4.05
十堰	Shiyan	7.44	17.35	153.07	5.24
宜昌	Yichang	103.28	100.91	383.06	28.43
襄阳	Xiangyang	49.27	40.91	423.23	8.72
鄂州	Ezhou	15.03	10.65	32.36	0.35
荆门	Jingmen	27.18	22.70	143.21	1.60
孝感	Xiaogan	35.40	16.68	121.45	2.90
荆州	Jingzhou	22.91	16.55	122.26	3.99
黄冈	Huanggang	19.72	13.35	83.83	1.77
咸宁	Xianning	15.40	10.40	130.50	1.54
随州	Suizhou	17.37	12.68	105.68	1.04
恩施	Enshi	11.49	10.67	26.24	1.41
仙桃	Xiantao	8.69	7.66	61.35	0.41
潜江	Qianjiang	9.27	7.44	12.41	1.57
天门	Tianmen	15.74	14.87	50.84	0.09
神农架	Shennongjia	0.71	0.58	-0.83	

13-12 续表 5 continued

单位: 亿元

地区	Region	应交税金及附加 Tax alafor Business	本年应付工资薪酬 Wases Welfarism Payable This Year
全省	**Province**	**2565.95**	**2255.65**
武汉	Wuhan	1165.10	830.38
黄石	Huangshi	79.44	92.13
十堰	Shiyan	71.60	135.16
宜昌	Yichang	302.80	239.72
襄阳	Xiangyang	234.94	173.69
鄂州	Ezhou	48.36	36.63
荆门	Jingmen	155.26	73.07
孝感	Xiaogan	96.85	119.44
荆州	Jingzhou	95.16	87.06
黄冈	Huanggang	50.80	76.66
咸宁	Xianning	61.99	51.58
随州	Suizhou	49.69	42.22
恩施	Enshi	17.78	19.64
仙桃	Xiantao	57.36	56.33
潜江	Qianjiang	41.56	157.60
天门	Tianmen	36.23	63.57
神农架	Shennongjia	1.04	0.77

(100 million Yuan)

营业外收入 Non-operating Income	营业外支出 Non-operating Expense	利润总额 Total Profit	应交所得税 Income Tax	亏损企业亏损总额 Total Loss of Enterprises Running under Deficit	利税总额 Total Profit
207.09	**63.62**	**2456.00**	**317.47**	**310.78**	**4599.15**
90.80	16.18	481.75	101.33	185.62	1525.34
8.40	4.02	61.13	14.32	20.10	122.11
16.57	9.82	159.83	6.56	14.01	219.78
35.60	10.61	408.05	69.09	19.46	629.23
16.72	8.36	431.59	47.99	10.81	609.37
1.48	2.78	31.07	4.46	11.51	73.46
10.05	3.41	149.86	11.13	4.14	288.93
5.97	1.12	126.30	8.14	6.07	209.85
8.56	0.98	129.84	12.05	2.99	191.08
3.67	1.80	85.70	5.57	3.34	127.63
2.36	1.69	131.17	15.57	3.43	175.91
2.22	0.97	106.94	2.72	1.79	151.96
1.82	0.47	27.60	2.11	0.82	42.56
0.81	0.26	61.90	6.44	2.17	103.94
1.86	1.05	13.23	2.27	23.18	51.21
0.15	0.06	50.93	7.66	0.10	76.70
0.03	0.07	-0.87	0.04	1.24	0.09

(100 million Yuan)

本年应交增值税 Value Added Payable of the Current Year	全部从业人员年平均人数(万人) Average Number of Empolyment of the Current Year (10000 persons)
1237.80	**352.64**
464.80	86.02
46.01	18.66
43.19	19.95
175.20	36.21
136.70	36.61
34.39	8.38
56.57	17.36
48.15	24.17
47.18	19.84
28.51	19.68
32.26	12.91
37.42	10.70
11.05	5.02
36.30	12.74
18.51	11.17
21.07	13.10
0.49	0.13

13-13 分市州规模以上工业企业主要经济效益指标 (2015)

单位：%

地 区	Item	企业亏损面 Loss Making Rate of Enterprises	总资产贡献率 Contributing Rate of Total Assets
全省	**Province**	**8.8**	**14.16**
武汉市	Wuhan	14.6	12.93
黄石市	Huangshi	15.4	7.25
十堰市	Shiyan	16.1	7.88
宜昌市	Yichang	7.6	14.73
襄阳市	Xiangyang	5.1	20.27
鄂州市	Ezhou	7.2	14.48
荆门市	Jingmen	5.5	22.73
孝感市	Xiaogan	6.0	15.62
荆州市	Jingzhou	7.1	14.06
黄冈市	Huanggang	8.4	11.71
咸宁市	Xianning	9.9	20.97
随州市	Suizhou	4.7	24.29
恩施市	Enshi	5.0	10.99
仙桃市	Xiantao	5.7	22.35
潜江市	Qianjiang	5.6	8.65
天门市	Tianmen	1.4	18.25
神农架林区	Shennongjia	50.0	1.50

MAJOR INDICATORS OF ECONOMIC BENEFITS OF ABOVE DESIGNATEDSIZE INDUSTRIAL ENTERPRISES BY REGION(2015)

资产负债率 Assets Liability Ratio	流动资产周转率(次/年) Current Asset Turnover(Times/Year)	成本费用利润率 Ratio of Profits to Industrial Cost	产品销售率 Proportion of Products Sold
54.97	**2.75**	**6.01**	**96.30**
63.82	1.87	4.32	94.23
60.47	2.86	2.42	96.79
42.77	1.35	9.45	97.43
54.15	3.56	8.06	97.48
50.92	3.49	8.69	96.78
57.46	5.88	2.62	97.38
45.14	5.58	5.46	97.73
50.39	3.99	5.29	97.31
45.65	3.08	6.25	96.07
50.12	3.62	5.52	93.96
43.63	4.29	9.21	96.51
42.05	4.31	9.75	99.49
55.45	2.42	7.77	97.72
38.35	4.40	6.85	97.31
49.40	2.67	1.40	99.08
47.09	3.58	6.64	98.04
84.04	0.33	-12.76	94.47

主要统计指标解释

工业 指从事自然资源的开采，对采掘品和农产品进行加工和再加工的物质生产部门。具体包括：(1)对自然资源的开采，如采矿、晒盐等(但不包括禽兽捕猎和水产捕捞)；(2)对农副产品的加工、再加工，如粮油加工、食品加工、缫丝、纺织、制革等；(3)对采掘品的加工、再加工，如炼铁、炼钢、化工生产、石油加工、机器制造、木材加工等，以及电力、自来水、煤气的生产和供应等；(4)对工业品的修理、翻新，如机器设备的修理、交通运输工具(如汽车)的修理等。

工业统计调查单位为独立核算法人工业企业。

独立核算法人工业企业指从事工业生产经营活动的单位。独立核算法人工业企业应同时具备以下条件：①依法成立，有自己的名称、组织机构和场所，能够承担民事责任；②独立拥有和使用资产，承担负债，有权与其他单位签订合同；③独立核算盈亏，并能够编制资产负债表。

本年鉴中涉及的企业登记注册类型：

国有及国有控股企业 指国有企业加上国有控股企业。国有企业(即原全民所有制工业或国营工业)指企业全部资产归国家所有，并按《中华人民共和国企业法人登记管理条例》规定登记注册的非公司制的经济组织。包括国有企业、国有独资公司和国有联营企业。1957年以前的公私合营和私营工业，后均改造为国营工业，1992年改为国有工业，这部分工业的资料不单独分列时，均包括在国有企业内。国有控股企业是对混合所有制经济的企业进行的“国有控股”分类。它是指这些企业的全部资产中国有资产(股份)相对其他所有者中的任何一个所有者占资(股)最多的企业。该分组反映了国有经济控股情况。

集体企业 指企业资产归集体所有，并按《中华人民共和国企业法人登记管理条例》规定登记注册的经济组织。是社会主义公有制经济的组成部分。包括城乡所有使用集体投资举办的企业，以及部分个人通过集资自愿放弃所有权并依法经工商行政管理机关认定为集体所有制的企业。

股份合作企业 指以合作制为基础，由企业职工共同出资入股，吸收一定比例的社会资产投资组建，实行自主经营，自负盈亏，共同劳动，民主管理，按劳分配与按股分红相结合的一种集体经济组织。

联营企业 指两个及两个以上相同或不同所有制性质的企业法人或事业单位法人，按自愿、平等、互利的原则，共同投资组成的经济组织。联营企业包括：

国有联营企业指国有企业与国有企业间的联营；

集体联营企业指集体企业与集体企业间的联营；

国有与集体联营企业指国有企业与集体企业间的联营。

有限责任公司 指根据《中华人民共和国公司登记管理条例》规定登记注册，由两个以上，五十个以下的股东共同出资，每个股东以其所认缴的出资额对公司承担有限责任，公司以其全部资产对其债务承担责任的经济组织。

有限责任公司包括国有独资公司以及其他有限责任公司。

股份有限公司 指根据《中华人民共和国企业法人登记管理条例》规定登记注册，其全部注册资本由等额股份构成并通过发行股票筹集资本，股东以其认购的股份对公司承担有限责任，公司以其全部资产对其债务承担责任的经济组织。

私营企业 指由自然人投资设立或由自然人控股，以雇佣劳动为基础的营利性经济组织。包括按照《公司法》、《合伙企业法》、《私营企业暂行条例》规定登记注册的私营有限责任公司、私营股份有限公司、私营合伙企业和私营独资企业。

港、澳、台商投资企业 指企业注册登记类型中的港、澳、台资合资、合作、独资经营企业和股份有限公司之和。

外商投资企业 指企业注册登记类型中的中外合资、合作经营企业、外资企业和外商投资股份有限公司之和。

“三资”企业系指港、澳、台商投资企业和外资企业的简称。

轻工业 指主要提供生活消费品和制作手工工具的工业。按其所使用的原料不同，可分为两大类：(1)以农产品为原料的轻

工业,是指直接或间接以农产品为基本原料的轻工业。主要包括食品制造、饮料制造、烟草加工、纺织、缝纫、皮革和毛皮制作、造纸以及印刷等工业;(2)以非农产品为原料的轻工业,是指以工业品为原料的轻工业。主要包括文教体育用品、化学药品制造、合成纤维制造、日用化学制品、日用玻璃制品、日用金属制品、手工工具制造、医疗器械制造、文化和办公用机械制造等工业。

重工业 指为国民经济各部门提供物质技术基础的主要生产资料的工业。按其生产性质和产品用途,可以分为下列三类:(1)采掘(伐)工业,是指对自然资源的开采,包括石油开采、煤炭开采、金属矿开采、非金属矿开采等工业;(2)原材料工业,指向国民经济各部门提供基本材料、动力和燃料的工业。包括金属冶炼及加工、炼焦及焦炭、化学、化工原料、水泥、人造板以及电力、石油和煤炭加工等工业;(3)加工工业,是指对工业原材料进行再加工制造的工业。包括装备国民经济各部门的机械设备制造工业、金属结构、水泥制品等工业,以及为农业提供的生产资料如化肥、农药等工业。

根据上述划分原则,修理业中以重工业产品为修理作业对象的划为重工业,反之划为轻工业。

工业总产值

(1)定义:

工业总产值是以货币形式表现的,工业企业在一定时期内生产的工业最终产品或提供工业性劳务活动的总价值量。它反映一定时间内工业生产的总规模和总水平。

(2)计算原则:

工业生产的原则,即凡是企业在报告期生产的经检验合格的产品,不管是否在报告期销售,均包括在内。

最终产品的原则,即凡是计入工业总产值的产品,必须是本企业生产的经检验合格的,不需要再进行任何加工的最终产品。如果企业有中间产品(半成品)对外销售,则对外销售的中间产品应视为企业的最终产品。

工厂法原则,即工业总产值是以工业企业作为基本计算(核算)单位,即按企业的最终产品计算工业总产值。按这种方法计算的工业总产值,不允许同一产品价值在企业内部重复计算,不能把企业内部各个车间(分厂)生产的成果相加,但允许企业间的重复计算。

(3)内容及计算方法:

1995年全国工业普查对工业总产值(原规定)的内容及计算原则和方法做了某些修订,修订后的工业总产值(新规定)包括三项内容:即本期生产成品价值、对外加工费收入、在制品半成品期末期初差额价值三部分。

本期生产成品价值:指企业本期生产,并在报告期内不再进行加工,经检验、包装入库的全部工业成品(半成品)价值合计,包括企业生产的自制设备及提供给本企业在建工程、其他非工业部门和福利部门等单位使用的成品价值。本期生产成品价值为按自备原材料生产的产品的数量乘以本期不含增值税(销项税额)的产品实际销售平均单价计算;会计核算中按成本价格转帐的自制设备和自产自用的成品,按成本价格计算生产成品价值。生产成品价值中不包括用定货者来料加工的成品(半成品)价值。

对外加工费收入:指企业在报告期内完成的对外承接的工业品加工(包括用定货者来料加工产品)的加工费收入和对外工业修理作业所取得的加工费收入。对外加工费收入按不含增值税(销项税额)的价格计算,可根据会计“产品销售收入”科目的有关资料取得。

对于本企业对内非工业部门提供的加工修理、设备安装的劳务收入,如果企业会计核算基础较好,能取得这部分资料,而且这部分价值所占比重较大,应包括在对外加工费收入中。

自制半成品在制品期末期初差额价值:指企业报告期在制品期末减期初的差额价值,本指标一般可以从会计核算资料中取得。如果会计产品成本核算中不计算半成品、在制品的成本,则总产值中也不包括这部分价值,反之则包括。

(4)工业总产值统计范围变化和计算方法修订情况:

1984年以前工业总产值不包括村办工业,村办工业总产值划归农业。1984年以后工业总产值包括村办工业。

1995年工业普查对工业总产值计算方法做了修订,即从1995年始按新修订(新规定)方法计算工业总产值。新规定与原规定的区别如下:

全价与加工费的计算原则不同:新规定为凡自备原材料,不论其生产繁简程度如何,一律按全价计算工业总产值;凡来料加工,允许按加工费计算工业总产值。原规定则视生产加工的繁简程度不同,规定哪些行业按全价,哪些行业按加工费计算工业总产值。

自制半成品、在产品期末期初差额价值的计算原则不同：新规定要求，凡会计产品成本核算时计算了成本的差额价值，总产值中就应包括，否则可不包括；原规定则按生产周期六个月的界限区分，凡生产周期六个月以上的企业，总产值计算中应包括这部分差额价值，否则可不包括。

计算价格不同：新规定按不含增值税(销项税额)的价格计算；原规定则按含增值税(销项税额)的价格计算。

工业增加值 指工业企业在报告期内以货币表现的工业生产活动的最终成果。

工业增加值有两种计算方法：一是生产法，即工业总产出减去工业中间投入加上应交增值税；二是收入法，即从收入的角度出发，根据生产要素在生产过程中应得到的收入份额计算，具体构成项目有固定资产折旧、劳动者报酬、生产税净额、营业盈余，这种方法也称要素分配法。本年鉴中的工业增加值是以生产法计算的。

生产法工业增加值的计算方法为：

工业增加值=工业总产出-工业中间投入+应交增值税

(1)工业总产出：指工业企业在一定时期内工业生产活动的总成果。工业总产出包括：成品生产价值，对外加工费收入，自制半成品、在产品期末期初差额价值。1995年后用新规定计算的工业总产值代替。

(2)工业中间投入：指工业企业在工业生产活动中消耗的外购物质产品和对外支付的服务费用。服务费用包括支付给物质生产部门(工业、农业、批发零售贸易业、建筑业、运输邮电业)的服务费用和支付给非物质生产部门(如保险、金融、文化教育、科学研究、医疗卫生、行政管理等)的服务费用。工业中间投入的确定须遵循以下原则：必须从外部购入的，并已计入工业总产出的产品和服务价值；必须是本期投入生产，并一次性消耗掉(包括本期摊销的低值易耗品等)的产品和服务价值。

工业中间投入包括直接材料费用、制造费用中的工业中间投入、管理费用中的工业中间投入、销售费用中的工业中间投入和利息支出五部分。

资产总计 指企业拥有或控制的能以货币计量的经济资源，包括各种财产、债权和其他权利。资产按流动性分为流动资产、长期投资、固定资产、无形资产、递延资产和其他资产。该指标根据企业会计“资产负债表”中“资产总计”项目的期末数增列。

流动资产 指企业可以在一年内或者超过一年的一个生产周期内变现或者耗用的资产，包括现金及各种存款、短期投资，应收及预付款项、存货等。

流动资产平均余额 指企业在报告期内全部流动资产的平均余额。

固定资产原价 指企业在建造、购置、安装、改建、扩建、技术改造某项固定资产时所支出的全部货币总额。它一般包括买价、包装费、运杂费和安装费等。

固定资产净值年平均余额 指固定资产净值在报告期内余额的平均数。计算公式为：

$$固定资产净值年平均余额=\frac{1至12月各月月初、月末固定资产净值之和}{24}$$

该指标根据“资产负债表”中“固定资产原价”、“累计折旧”指标的期初、期末数计算填列。

固定资产净值指固定资产原价减去历年已提折旧额后的净额。计算公式为：

固定资产净值=固定资产原价-累计折旧

负债合计 指企业所承担的能以货币计量，将以资产或劳务偿付的债务，偿还形式包括货币、资产或提供劳务。负债一般按偿还期长短分为流动负债和长期负债。根据会计“资产负债表”中“负债合计”的年末数填列。

所有者权益 指企业投资人对企业净资产的所有权。企业净资产等于企业全部资产减去全部负债后的余额，包括企业投资人对企业的最初投入的实际到位的资产及资本公积金、盈余公积金和未分配利润。所有者权益合计数小于零，表示企业资不抵债。

主营业务收入 指会计“利润表”中对应指标的本年累计数。未执行2001年《企业会计制度》的企业，用“产品销售收入”的本期累计数代替。

主营业务成本 指会计“利润表”中对应指标的本年累计数。未执行2001年《企业会计制度》的企业，用“产品销售成本”的本期累计数代替。

主营业务税金及附加 指会计“利润表”中对应指标的本年累计数。未执行2001年《企业会计制度》的企业，用“产品销售税金及附加”的本期累计数代替。

利润总额 指企业生产经营活动的最终成果，是企业在一定时期内实现的盈亏相抵后的利润总额(亏损以“-”号表示)，它等于营业利润加上补贴收入加上投资收益加上营业外净收入再加上以前年度损益调整。

本年应交增值税 指企业在报告期内应交纳的增值税额。它等于本年销项税额加上出口退税加上进项税额转出数减去本年进项税额。小规模纳税企业直接按全年计税销售额乘以征收率计算取得。

从业人员平均人数 是指报告期内每天拥有的从业人员人数。其计算公式为：

$$\text{季平均人数}=\frac{\text{季内各月平均人数之和}}{3}$$

$$\text{月平均人数}=\frac{\text{报告月内每天实有人数之和}}{\text{报告月日历日数}}$$

$$\text{年平均人数}=\frac{\text{年内各月平均人数之和}}{12}$$

总资产贡献率 反映企业全部资产的获利能力，是企业经营业绩和管理水平的集中体现，是评价和考核企业盈利能力的核心指标。计算公式为：

$$\text{总资产贡献率}(\%)=\frac{\text{利润总额}+\text{税金总额}+\text{利息支出}}{\text{平均资金总额}}\times 100\%$$

公式中：税金总额为产品销售税金及附加与应交增值税之和；平均资产总额为期初期末资产之和的算术平均值。

资产负债率 该指标既反映企业经营风险的大小，也反映企业利用债权人提供的资金从事经营活动的能力。计算公式为：

$$\text{资产负债率}(\%)=\frac{\text{负债总额}}{\text{资产总额}}\times 100\%$$

资产与负债均为报告期期末数。

流动资产周转次数 指一定时期内流动资产完成的周转次数，反映投入工业企业流动资金的周转速度。计算公式为：

$$\text{流动资产周转资转次数}=\frac{\text{产品销售收入}}{\text{全部流动资产平均余额}}$$

公式中：全部流动资产平均余额为期初和期末的流动资产之和的算术平均值。

成本费用利润率 反映企业投入的生产成本及费用的经济效益，同时也反映企业降低成本所取得的经济效益。计算公式为：

$$\text{成本费用利润率}(\%)=\frac{\text{利润总额}}{\text{成本费用总额}}\times 100\%$$

公式中：成本费用总额为产品销售成本、销售费用、管理费用、财务费用之和。

全员劳动生产率 该指标反映企业的生产效率和劳动投入的经济效益。计算公式为：

$$\text{全员劳动生产率(元/人)}=\frac{\text{工业增加值}}{\text{全部从业人员平均人数}}$$

产品销售率 该指标反映工业产品已实现销售的程度，是分析工业产销衔接情况，研究工业产品满足社会需求的指标。计算公式为：

$$产品销售率(\%)=\frac{工业销售产值}{工业总产值（现价）}\times 100\%$$

Explanatory Notes on Main Statistical Indicators

Industry refers to the material production sector which is engaged in extraction of natural resources and processing and reprocessing of minerals and agricultural products, including (1) extraction of natural resources, such as mining, salt production (but not including hunting and fishing); (2) processing and reprocessing of farm and sideline produces, such as rice husking, flour milling, wine making, oil pressing, silk reeling, spinning and weaving, and leather making; (3) manufacture of industrial products, such as steel making, iron smelting, chemicals manufacturing, petroleum processing, machine building, timber processing; water and gas production and electricity generation and supply; (4)repairing of industrial products such as the repairing of machinery and means of transport (including cars).

Units of industrial statistics survey corporate industrial enterprises with independent accounting system.

Corporate industrial enterprises with independent accounting system refer to enterprises engaging in industrial production activities, which meet the following requirements: (1)They are established legally, having their own names, organizations, location, able to take civil liability; (2)They possess and use their assets independently, assume liabilities, and are entitled to sign contracts with other units; (3)They are financially independent and compile their own balance sheets.

Enterprises covered in the industrial statistics in the Yearbook include following categories by their registration:

State-owned and State-holding Enterprises refer to state-owned enterprises plus state-holding enterprises. State-owned enterprises (originally known as state-run enterprises with ownership by the whole society) are non-corporate economic entities registered in accordance with the Regulation of the People's Republic of China on the Management of Registration of Legal Enterprises, where all assets are owned by the state. Included in this category are state-owned enterprises, state-funded corporations and state-owned joint-operation enterprises. Joint state-private industries and private industries, which existed before 1957, were transformed into state-run industries since 1957, and into state-owned industries after 1992. Statistics on those enterprises are included in the state-owned industries instead of grouping them separately. State-holding enterprises is a sub-classification of enterprises with mixed ownership, referring to enterprises where the percentage of state assets (or shares by the state) is larger than any other single share holder of the same enterprise. This sub-classification illustrates the control of the state over a particular industry.

Collective-owned Enterprises refer to economic entities registered in accordance with the Regulation of the People's Republic of China on the Management of Registration of Legal Enterprises, where assets are owned by collectively. Collective enterprises constitute an integral part of the socialist economy with public ownership. They include urban and rural enterprises invested by collectives, and some enterprises registered in industrial and commercial administration agency as collective units where funds are pulled together by individuals who voluntarily give up their right of ownership.

Share-holding Cooperative Enterprises refer to economic units set up on cooperative basis, with funding partly from members of the enterprise and partly from outside investment, where the operation and management is decided by the members who also participate in the production, and the distribution of income is based both on work (labour input) and on shares (capital input).

Joint-operation enterprises refer to economic units that are established by joint investment by two or more corporate enterprises or institutions of the same or different types of ownership on voluntary, equal and mutual-beneficial basis. They include:

a) state-owned joint-operation enterprises (joint operation between state-owned enterprises);

b) collective joint–operation enterprises (joint operation between collective enterprises; and

c) state–collective joint–operation enterprises (joint operation between state and collective enterprises).

Limited Liability Corporations refer to economic units registered in accordance with the Regulation of the People's Republic of China on the Management of Registration of Corporations, with capitals from 2 to 49 investors, each investor bears limited liability to the corporation depending on his/her holding of shares, and the corporation bears liability to its debt to the maximum of its total assets.

Share–holding Corporations Ltd. refer to economic units registered in accordance with the Regulation of the People's Republic of China on the Management of Registration of Corporate Enterprises, with total registered capitals divided into equal shares and raised through issuing stocks. Each investor bears limited liability to the corporation depending on the holding of shares, and the corporation bears liability to its debt to the maximum of its total assets.

Private Enterprises refer to economic units invested or controlled (by holding the majority of the shares) by natural persons who hire labours for profit–making activities. Included in this category are private limited liability corporations, private share–holding corporations Ltd., private partnership enterprises and private sole investment enterprises registered in accordance with the Corporation Law, Partnership Enterprise Law and Tentative Regulation on Private Enterprises.

Enterprises with Funds from Hong Kong, Macao and Taiwan refers to all industrial enterprises registered as the joint–venture, cooperative, sole (exclusive) investment industrial enterprises and limited liability corporations with funds from Hong Kong, Macao and Taiwan.

Foreign Funded Enterprises refers to all industrial enterprises registered as the joint–venture, cooperative, sole (exclusive) investment industrial enterprises and limited liability corporations with foreign funds.

Enterprise with Hong Kong, Macao, Taiwan and foreign fund refer to all the enterpries with funds from Hong Kong Macao and Taiwan and foreign funded enterprises.

Light Industry refers to the industry that produces consumer goods and hand tools. It consists of two categories, depending on the materials used:

(1) Industries using farm products as raw materials. These are branches of light industry which directly or indirectly use farm products as basic raw materials, including the manufacture of food and beverages, tobacco processing, textile, clothing, fur and leather manufacturing, paper making, printing, etc.

(2) Industries using non farm products as raw materials. These are branches of light industry which use manufactured goods as raw materials, including the manufacture of cultural, educational articles and sports goods, chemicals, synthetic fiber, chemical products for daily use, glass products for daily use, metal products for daily use, hand tools, medical apparatus and instruments, and the manufacture of cultural and clerical machinery.

Heavy Industry refers to the industry which produces capital goods, and provides various sectors of the national economy with necessary material and technical basis. It consists of the following three branches according to the purpose of production or the use of products:

(1) Mining, quarrying and logging industry refers to the industry that extracts natural resources, including extraction of petroleum, coal, metal and non–metal ores.

(2) Raw materials industry refers to the industry that provides various sectors of the national economy with raw materials, fuels and power. It includes smelting and processing of metals, coking and coke chemistry, chemical materials and building materials such as cement, plywood, and power, petroleum refining and coal dressing.

(3) Manufacturing industry refers to the industry that processes raw materials. It includes machine–building industry which equips sectors of the national economy, industries of metal structure and cement products, industries producing means of agricultural production, such as chemical fertilizers and pesticides.

According to the above principle of classification, the repairing trades, which are engaged primarily in repairing products of heavy industry are classified into heavy industry while these engaged in repairing products of light industry are classified into light industry.

Gross Industrial Output Value

(1) Definition: Gross industrial output value is the total volume of final industrial products produced and industrial services provided during a given period. It reflects the total achievements and overall scale of industrial production during a given period.

(2) Principles for calculation:

Statistics on industrial production follow the principle that all products produced by the enterprises and accepted during the reference period are to be included no matter whether they are sold or not during the reference period.

Determination of final products follow the principle that all products that are included in the calculation of grow industrial output value are the final products of the enterprise which have been accepted through quality check and require no further processing. If an enterprise has intermediate (semi–finished) products to sell, these intermediate products are considered as the final products of the enterprise.

Gross industrial output value is calculated following the principle of factory approach, i.e. industrial enterprise is used as the basic accounting unit in calculating the gross industrial output value. By this approach, value of the same product is not to be double counted, and the output value of different workshops (branch factories) should not be added. However, this approach does not exclude the possibility of double counting between enterprises.

(3) Content and calculation method: The old definition of gross industrial output value was modified during the national industrial census in 1995. The revised (new) definition of gross industrial output value consists of 3 components: value of the finished products during the reference period, income from external processing, and value of change in semi–finished products at the end and at the beginning of the reference period.

Value of the finished products during the reference period: refers to the value of all finished (semi–finished) industrial products that are produced during the reference period without the need for further processing, checked for acceptance, packed and put into the warehouse of the enterprise, including the value of own–produced equipment and the value of products provided to the projects under construction of the enterprise, and to other non–industrial or welfare units. Value of finished products during the reference period is calculated by the quantity of products produced using own materials multiplied by the average unit prices at which products are sold (excluding value–added tax). Own–produced equipment and products produced for own use are value at cost prices as in the case of enterprise accounting. Value of finished products does not include the value of finished products (semi–finished products) that are produced using the materials from the clients who make the orders.

Income from external processing: refers to income from contracted external processing of industrial products (including processing of industrial products using materials from the clients), and the income from industrial repairing work provided to other units. Income from external processing is calculated using information from the item "products sales income" in the enterprise accounting at the prices excluding value–added tax.

For income from services such as processing, repairing and installation of equipment provided to non–industrial units within the enterprise, if the accounting work of the enterprise is good enough to separate it from other records, and the share of such services is significant, it should also be included in the income from external processing.

Value of change in semi–finished products at the end and at the beginning of the reference period: refers to the value of change in semi–finished products at the end and at the beginning of the reference period, which generally can be obtained from accounting records of enterprises. If the enterprise accounting excludes the cost of semi–finished products, then it should not be included in the gross industrial output value, and vice versa.

(4) Changes in the coverage and method of calculation of gross industrial output value

Prior to 1984, the value of rural industry run by villages was classified into agriculture instead of industry. Since 1984, it has been included in the gross industrial output value. Method of calculation for the gross industrial output value was modified in the industrial census in 1995. The difference in the new method as compared with the old one is outlined below:

Principle in using full value vs. processing fee: The new method stipulates that all products produced using own materials are to be calculated with full value in reporting the gross industrial output value irrespective of sophistication of production, and for external processing, it allows calculation using processing fee. In the old method, however, the use of full value or processing fee was determined by the degree of sophistication of production in different branches of industries.

Principle in determining the value of change in semi–finished products: The new method requires that value of the change in semi–finished products should be included in the gross industrial output value if it is included in the accounting record of the enterprise, otherwise it should not be included. By the old method, it is determined by the type of enterprises in terms of production cycle. If the production cycle is over 6 months, the value of change in semi–finished products is included in the gross industrial output value, otherwise it is excluded.

Difference in prices: The new method uses prices excluding value–added tax in the calculation of gross industrial output value, while the old method used prices including value–added tax.

Value–added of Industry refers to the final results of industrial production of industrial enterprises in money terms during the reference period.

Industrial value–added can be calculated by two approaches: the production approach, i.e. gross industrial output value minus intermediate input plus value–added tax, and the income approach, i.e. income for various factors used in the course of production, including depreciation of fixed assets, remuneration of labourers, net of production tax, and operating surplus. Value–added of industry in the Yearbook is calculated by production approach as following:

Value–added of industry = gross industrial output industrial intermediate input + value–added tax

(1) Gross industrial output: refers to the total achievements of industrial production during a given period. Gross industrial output includes value of finished products, income from external processing, and value of change in semi–finished products at the end and at the beginning of the reference period. Since 1995, it was substituted by the gross industrial output value by new method.

(2) Industrial intermediate input: refers to purchased goods and paid services consumed during the industrial production of enterprises. Fees paid for services include fees paid for the services provided by material production sectors (industry, agriculture, wholesale and retail trade, construction, transport, post and telecommunications) and by non–material production sectors (insurance, banking, culture, education, scientific research, health and medical care, public administration, etc.). The determination of industrial intermediate input follows the principle that the goods and services must be purchased from outside and included in the gross industrial output, and that the goods and services are inputted into production and consumed (include low–value consumables) during the reference period.

Industrial intermediate input includes 5 components, namely direct consumption of materials, industrial intermediate input in manufacturing cost, industrial intermediate input in management cost, industrial intermediate input in marketing cost and expenditure on interest.

Total Assets refer to all economic resources, in monetary terms, that is owned or controlled by enterprises, including properties, creditors equity and other economic rights of all forms. Classified by the degree of equitability, total assets include circulating assets, long–term investment, fixed assets, intangible assets and deferred assets, and other assets. Data on this indicator can be obtained by the year–end figures of total assets in the Assets and Liability Table of accounting records of enterprises.

Working Capitals refer to capitals that an enterprise can cash or use during one year or one production cycle that may exceeds one year, including cash and savings deposits of various forms, short–term investment, money receivable and prepaid money, inventories, etc.

Annual Average Value of Working Capitals refers to the average value of all working capitals of the enterprise during the reference period.

Original Value of Fixed Assets refers to the total value, in monetary terms, that an enterprise spent on fixed assets, through construction, purchase, installation, transformation, expansion or technical upgrading. Generally, it covers cost of purchase, packing, transportation and installation, etc.

Annual Average of Net Value of Fixed Assets refer to average of the net value of fixed assets during the reference period, calculated with the following formula:

Annual Average of Net Value of Fixed Assets = sum of net value of fixed assets at the beginning and at the end of each month from January to December / 24.

Information on this indicator can be obtained from the beginning and ending figures of the original value of fixed assets and cumulative depreciation from the Assets and Liability Table of enterprises.

Net value of fixed assets refers to the original value of fixed assets minus depreciation over the years, i.e.:

Net value of fixed assets = original value of fixed assets cumulative depreciation

Total Liabilities refer to payable liabilities of enterprises that have to repay in terms of money, assets or labour services. In terms of payment, it can be divided into liquid liabilities and long–term liabilities. Data on this item is obtained from the ending figures on total liabilities from theAssets and Liability Table from the enterprises.

Owner's Equity refers to the ownership of net assets of enterprise by its investors. The net assets equal the total assets minus total liabilities of the enterprise, including the actual assets invested into the enterprise by investors, accumulation of capitals and operating surplus and non–distributed profits. The enterprise's assets is less than its liabilities if the sum of owner's equity is smaller than zero.

Revenue from Principal Business refers to the annual accumulation of corresponding item in the "profit table" of the accountant. For enterprises that do not follow the 2001 Enterprise Accounting Standards, the year–end accumulation of revenue from the sales of products is used as a substitute.

Cost of Principal Business refers to the annual accumulation of corresponding item in the "profit table" of the accountant. For enterprises that do not follow the 2001 Enterprise Accounting Standards, the year–end accumulation of cost for the sales of products is used as a substitute.

Tax and Extra Charges from Principal Business refer to the annual accumulation of corresponding item in the "profit table" of the accountant. For enterprises that do not follow the 2001 Enterprise Accounting Standards, the year–end accumulation of tax and extra charges from the sales of products is used as a substitute.

Total Profits refer to the final achievements of production and operation of the enterprises, represented by the total profits after deducting losses (loss is expressed by the negative figure). It is the sum of profits from operation, income from subsidies, investment earnings, net income from activities other than operation, and adjustment of profits and losses of previous years.

Value–added Tax Payable refers to the amount of the value–added tax which should be paid by the enterprises during the reference period. It is the sum of tax on sales, export rebate, and transferred tax on purchases of the current year, minus the tax on purchases of the current year. Value–added tax payable of small–size enterprises is determined by the taxable sales of the year multiplied by the tax rate.

Average Annual Number of Employed Persons Employed persons refer to all those who are employed in enterprises and receive remunerations therefrom, including currently working employees, retirees who are re–employed, teachers of local–run schools, as well as foreigners, staff from Hong Kong, Macao and Taiwan, part–time employees and persons with second job who are employed by the enterprise, and employees of other units temporarily working in the enterprises, but excluding former employees who left the enterprise with their employment records still kept by the enterprises.

Average number of employed persons refers to the number of employees everyday during the reference period, calculated with the following formula:

Monthly average number = sum of actual employees everyday in reference month/number of calendar dates in reference month

Quarterly average number = sum of monthly average number in reference quarter/3

Annual average number = sum of monthly average number in reference year/12

Ratio of Profits, Taxes and Interests to Average Assets reflects the profit–making capability of all assets of the enterprise and is a key indicator manifesting the performance and management and evaluating the profit–making potential of the enterprise. It is calculated as follows:

Ratio of Profits, Taxes and Interests to Average Assets (%) = [(total profits + total taxes + interest payment) / average assets] × 100%

In the above formula, total taxes is the sum of tax and extra charges on the sales of products and value–added tax payable; and average assets is the arithmetic mean of the sum of beginning assets and ending assets.

Ratio of Debts to Assets reflect both the operation risk and the capability of the enterprise in making use of the capital from the creditors. It is calculated as follows:

Ratio of Debts to Assets (%) = (total debts / total assets) × 100%

Both assets and debts are figures at the end of the reference period.

Turnover of Working Capitals refers to the number of times of turnover of working capital in a given period of time, which reflects the speed of the turnover of working capital of industrial enterprises, and is calculated as follows:

Turnover of Working Capital=(sales revenue of products) / (average balance of total working capital)

In the above formula, average balance of total working capital refers to the arithmetic mean of the sum of working capital at the beginning and at the end of the reference period.

Ratio of Profits to Total Industrial Costs refers to the ratio of profits realized in a given period to the total costs in the same period, which reflects the economic efficiency of input cost and is calculated as follows:

Ratio of Profits to Total Industrial Cost (%)=(total profits/ total costs) × 100%

Total costs in the above formula is the sum of cost of products sold, marketing cost, management cost and financial cost.

Overall Labour Productivity is an indicator reflecting the production efficiency of an enterprise and the economic efficiency of its labour input, calculated by the formula:

Overall Labour Productivity (yuan/person) = industrial value–added / average of all persons engaged

Sales Ratio of Products is an indicator reflecting the actual sale of industrial products, analyzing the production–selling and supply–demand relations. It is calculated as:

Sales Ratio of Products (%) = value of industrial sales / gross industrial output value (current prices) * 100%

14 建筑业

Construction

建　筑　业

Construction

2014

建筑施工企业个数	Number of Construction Enterprises	3346	（个）
建筑施工企业职工平均人数	Average Number of Staff and Workers in Construction Enterprises	232.85	（万人）
建筑业总产值	Total Output Value of Construction Industry	10592.86	（亿元）
施工房屋面积	Construction　Area	62195.32	（万平方米）
建筑业全员劳动生产率	Overall Labor Productivity of Construction Industry	45.49	（万元/人）

建筑业总产值(亿元)

Gross Output Value of Construction Enterprises (100 million yuan)

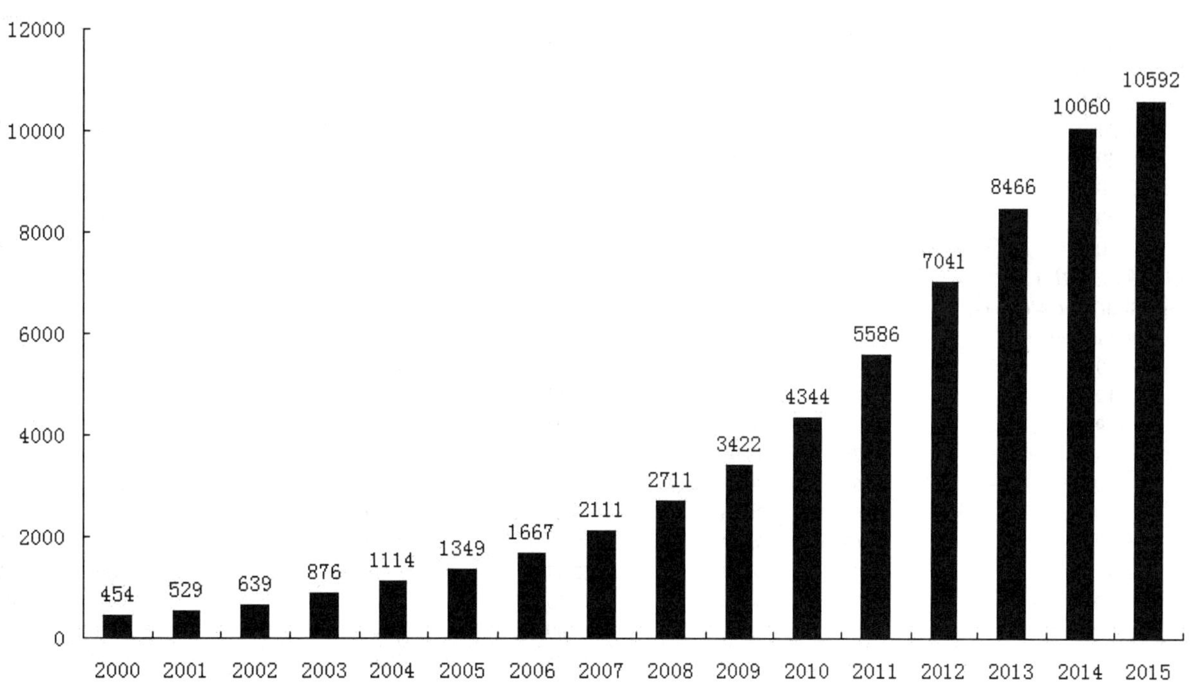

附:建筑业产值构成(%)

	2007	2008	2009	2010	2011	2012	2013	2014	2015
国有经济	50.5	49.2	47.4	52.6	52.5	48.7	46.5	47.3	44.3
城镇集体经济	3.2	2.1	2.3	1.4	1.5	1.9	0.8	0.7	0.7
乡镇企业及其他经济	46.3	51.3	50.3	45.9	45.9	49.4	52.7	52.0	55.0

14-1 建筑企业概况
BASIC STATISTICS ON CONSTRUCTION ENTERPRISES

项目 Item	总计 Total	国有经济 State-Owned	地方 Local - Owned	中央 Central- Owned	城镇集体经济 Urban Collective- Owned	其他经济 Others
企业单位个数(个) Number of Enterprises (unit)						
1992	603	184	142	42	419	
1993	898	241	208	40	642	15
1994	823	307	268	39	492	24
1995	912	323	277	46	539	50
1996	1696	403	250	53	1198	95
1997	1761	429	378	51	1207	125
1998	1838	433	379	54	1206	199
1999	2120	491	432	59	1297	332
2000	2070	488	440	48	1175	409
2001	1661	393	350	43	809	459
2002	1625	363	327	36	480	782
2003	1808	558	488	70	344	906
2004	2357	433	378	55	358	2566
2005	2114	524	448	76	268	1322
2006	2238	320	279	41	223	1695
2007	2516	449	383	66	191	1876
2008	2975	440	374	66	161	2374
2009	2878	396	331	65	152	2330
2010	2845	388	334	54	142	2315
2011	2640	376	330	46	130	2134
2012	2952	390	335	55	122	2440
2013	3376	399	334	66	98	2879
2014	3217	386	324	62	90	2741
2015	3346	384	323	61	87	2875
职工平均人数(万人) Average Staff and Workers (10000 persons)						
1992	46.13	30.92	14.89	16.03	15.21	
1993	55.75	36.41	19.65	16.76	19.15	0.19
1994	52.66	36.83	19.07	17.76	15.43	0.40
1995	57.28	38.05	18.86	19.19	16.62	2.61
1996	76.51	36.83	18.58	18.25	36.20	3.48
1997	76.09	36.36	18.60	17.76	35.96	3.77
1998	82.63	38.22	19.22	19.00	38.82	5.59
1999	85.72	39.57	22.57	17.00	36.69	9.46
2000	82.76	36.58	21.73	14.83	35.36	10.82
2001	83.11	36.16	19.99	16.44	29.30	17.65
2002	93.50	34.20	21.25	12.95	23.50	35.80
2003	108.82	50.20	30.72	19.48	16.98	41.64
2004	105.30	44.40	28.10	16.30	12.20	48.70
2005	110.09	41.70	22.85	18.85	11.60	56.79
2006	114.25	27.26	15.18	12.08	10.28	76.71
2007	136.14	39.73	19.52	20.21	9.44	86.97
2008	137.61	38.51	18.40	20.11	6.61	92.49
2009	146.02	41.68	18.76	22.92	7.22	97.12
2010	170.71	54.40	22.31	32.09	5.57	110.74
2011	141.88	42.61	15.06	27.55	4.78	94.49
2012	169.33	50.83	15.10	35.73	4.21	114.29
2013	174.18	40.50	14.83	25.67	3.04	130.64
2014	206.37	49.04	19.48	29.56	3.35	153.98
2015	232.85	55.21	19.07	36.14	3.19	174.45

14-1 续表 1 continued

项 目 Item	总 计 Total	国有经济 State-Owned	地 方 Local - Owned	中 央 Central- Owned	城镇集体经济 Urban Collective- Owned	其他经济 Others
建筑业总产值(亿元) Gross Output Value of Construction Enterprises (100 million yuan)						
1992	78.44	59.51	25.03	34.47	18.93	
1993	119.90	90.27	36.17	54.10	29.10	0.53
1994	169.28	140.29	56.95	83.34	27.75	1.24
1995	227.41	178.51	58.96	119.55	33.70	15.19
1996	284.43	187.00	60.83	126.17	79.14	18.29
1997	305.97	199.53	63.59	135.94	84.70	21.75
1998	343.65	223.80	73.98	149.82	93.15	26.70
1999	399.02	246.58	88.07	158.51	107.32	45.13
2000	454.35	266.03	106.76	159.27	123.46	64.86
2001	529.02	279.39	112.32	167.07	117.70	131.93
2002	639.11	301.93	143.90	158.03	98.90	238.29
2003	876.26	535.71	227.72	307.99	82.99	257.56
2004	1114.33	676.45	285.29	391.16	67.25	370.63
2005	1349.32	776.70	268.77	507.92	69.92	502.71
2006	1667.00	545.64	184.87	360.77	72.44	1048.92
2007	2110.80	1065.26	234.03	831.23	68.69	976.85
2008	2710.80	1333.87	241.63	1092.24	57.52	1319.41
2009	3421.89	1621.66	191.86	1429.80	77.86	1722.37
2010	4344.39	2287.08	414.78	1872.30	61.21	1996.10
2011	5586.45	2934.99	501.47	2433.52	85.04	2566.42
2012	7040.65	3428.40	627.89	2800.51	133.55	3478.70
2013	8465.50	3933.36	757.54	3175.82	66.75	4465.39
2014	10059.59	4755.30	921.65	3833.65	71.54	5232.75
2015	10591.71	4695.04	1072.67	3622.37	70.80	5825.87
施工房屋面积(万平方米) Floor Space of Buildings Under Construction (10000 sq.m)						
1992	2128.40	1190.40	829.90	360.50	938.10	
1993	2579.10	1439.30	989.10	450.20	1131.20	8.60
1994	2843.50	1894.50	1319.10	575.40	922.30	26.70
1995	3284.30	2122.80	1185.20	937.60	867.60	293.90
1996	4548.80	2224.60	1203.30	1021.30	2008.40	315.80
1997	4604.20	2330.60	1226.90	1103.70	1885.30	388.30
1998	5310.00	2488.80	1288.80	1200.00	2247.50	573.70
1999	5797.00	2703.40	1578.40	1125.00	2329.40	764.20
2000	6256.50	2889.10	1564.50	1324.60	2448.20	919.20
2001	6662.59	2792.50	1480.20	1312.30	2053.00	1817.10
2002	7215.88	2836.00	1452.00	1384.00	1742.00	2637.90
2003	8933.44	3817.50	2102.60	1714.90	1574.80	3541.10
2004	11772.31	5089.10	2522.60	2566.50	1348.90	5334.30
2005	12091.16	4568.90	1993.30	2575.60	1264.80	6257.50
2006	14478.24	3811.18	1016.18	2795.00	1021.60	9545.40
2007	16679.70	5503.80	1666.40	3837.40	1036.10	10139.80
2008	18376.50	5703.90	1060.40	4643.50	752.00	11920.60
2009	20499.30	5672.40	522.50	5149.90	799.40	14027.50
2010	25046.70	6752.80	968.80	5784.00	633.70	17660.30
2011	31023.80	9209.70	1549.00	7660.70	782.30	21031.70
2012	39112.20	10747.20	1661.70	9085.50	905.90	27459.10
2013	48937.96	14424.51	1734.33	12690.18	599.26	33914.19
2014	62227.88	22903.06	2137.75	20765.31	561.49	38763.33
2015	62195.32	21339.76	2258.52	19081.24	506.44	40349.12

14-1 续表 2 continued

项 目 Item	总 计 Total	国有经济 State-Owned	地 方 Local - Owned	中 央 Central- Owned	城镇集体经济 Urban Collective- Owned	其他经济 Others
竣工房屋面积(万平方米) Floor Space of Buildings Completed (10000 sq.m)						
1992	1002.8	508.4	378.5	129.9	494.4	
1993	1114.9	481.0	384.4	96.1	632.9	1.0
1994	1070.9	577.5	485.2	92.3	481.6	11.8
1995	1175.9	622.2	466.9	155.3	484.3	69.4
1996	1880.7	653.3	501.3	152.0	1123.5	103.9
1997	1982.3	765.3	522.1	243.2	1124.5	92.5
1998	2374.0	836.0	624.0	212.0	1298.6	239.4
1999	2873.0	1023.1	776.1	247.0	1484.3	365.6
2000	3150.1	1096.3	836.1	260.2	1572.0	481.8
2001	3673.4	1237.0	828.3	408.7	1334.1	1102.3
2002	4146.6	1261.8	889.3	372.5	1146.0	1738.8
2003	4840.8	1578.8	1143.4	435.4	993.7	2268.3
2004	6647.1	2561.3	1563.2	998.1	820.5	3265.3
2005	6896.9	2125.6	923.7	1201.9	791.5	3979.8
2006	7376.2	1137.1	450.4	686.7	678.8	5560.3
2007	8425.0	1620.9	858.6	762.3	608.8	5895.3
2008	9256.1	1386.0	537.9	848.1	476.1	7394.0
2009	10280.7	1587.1	255.9	1331.2	494.7	8198.9
2010	12813.4	2185.7	364.5	1821.2	452.8	10174.9
2011	16468.1	2593.0	600.0	1993.0	600.9	13274.2
2012	20395.2	1938.0	649.8	1288.3	705.2	17751.9
2013	22773.7	2278.0	571.7	1706.3	418.6	20077.1
2014	24867.3	2393.0	1105.0	1288.0	309.2	22165.1
2015	26825.2	3717.0	908.5	2808.5	389.3	22719.0
房屋建筑面积竣工率(%) Rate of Floor Space of Buildings Completed (%)						
1992	47.1	42.7	45.6	36.0	52.7	
1993	43.2	33.9	38.9	21.3	56.0	11.6
1994	37.7	30.5	36.8	16.0	52.2	44.2
1995	35.8	41.2	39.4	16.6	55.8	23.6
1996	41.3	29.4	41.7	14.9	55.9	32.9
1997	43.1	32.7	42.6	22.0	59.6	23.8
1998	44.7	33.6	48.4	17.7	57.8	41.7
1999	49.6	37.8	49.2	22.0	63.7	47.8
2000	50.3	37.9	53.4	19.6	64.2	52.4
2001	55.1	44.3	56.0	31.1	65.0	60.7
2002	57.5	44.5	61.2	26.9	65.8	65.9
2003	54.2	41.3	51.1	25.4	63.1	64.1
2004	56.5	50.3	62.0	38.9	60.8	61.2
2005	57.0	46.5	46.3	46.7	60.8	63.6
2006	50.9	29.8	44.3	24.6	66.4	58.3
2007	50.5	29.5	51.5	19.9	58.8	58.1
2008	50.4	24.3	50.7	18.3	63.3	62.0
2009	50.2	28.0	49.0	25.8	61.9	58.4
2010	51.2	32.4	37.6	31.5	71.5	57.6
2011	53.1	28.2	38.7	26.0	76.8	63.1
2012	52.1	18.0	39.1	14.2	77.8	64.6
2013	46.5	15.8	33.0	13.4	69.9	59.2
2014	40.0	10.4	51.7	6.2	55.1	57.2
2015	43.1	17.4	40.2	14.7	76.9	56.3

注： 本表资料包括施工总承包和专业承包企业,不含劳务分包企业(下同)。

Note: In this table, the data including general contract and specilized contract enterprises under construction, excluding labor divided contract (the same as the following tables)

14-2 分市州建筑业企业生产情况(2015)
STATISTICS ON PRODUCTION OF CONSTRUCTION ENTERPRISES OF CITIES AND PREFECTURE(2015)

单位：亿元 (100 million yuan)

项目	Item	建筑业总产值 Total Output Value of Construction Industry	建筑工程产值 Output Value of Construction Projects	安装工程产值 Output Value of Installation Projects	其他产值 Output Value of Other Projects	竣工产值 Output Value of Projects Completed
湖北省	**Hubei**	**10592.86**	**9363.58**	**889.63**	**339.65**	**5377.50**
武汉市	Wuhan	6016.26	5221.53	568.30	226.44	2542.87
黄石市	Huangshi	310.08	290.42	15.54	4.12	193.63
十堰市	Shiyan	370.19	357.00	9.91	3.27	155.72
宜昌市	Yichang	787.00	706.69	51.31	29.00	304.05
襄阳市	Xiangyang	757.84	674.09	69.25	14.51	463.39
鄂州市	Ezhou	127.59	99.82	19.55	8.22	69.76
荆门市	Jingmen	129.79	114.13	9.95	5.72	95.39
孝感市	Xiaogan	436.26	375.16	50.15	10.94	306.58
荆州市	Jingzhou	244.56	228.71	10.73	4.30	180.63
黄冈市	Huanggang	863.20	805.16	46.39	11.65	659.19
咸宁市	Xianning	133.22	122.61	6.38	4.22	103.05
随州市	Suizhou	89.08	81.11	2.39	5.57	77.10
恩施州	Enshi	123.30	111.80	8.57	2.93	93.02
仙桃市	Xiantao	44.73	43.12	1.30	0.32	33.72
潜江市	Qianjiang	89.60	73.75	13.30	3.37	56.65
天门市	Tianmen	64.17	53.60	5.98	4.59	37.48
神农架	Shennongjia	5.99	4.86	0.64	0.49	5.26

14-3 按登记注册类型分的企业数及合同情况(2015)

单位：亿元

指标名称	Item	有工作量的建筑业企业个数(个) Number of Construction Enterprises with Work (unit)
总计	**Total**	**3218**
其中:国有及国有控股企业	State-owned and State-holding Enterprises	380
一、按登记注册类型分组	Grouped by Status of Registration	
内资企业	**Domestic Funded Enterprises**	**3202**
国有企业	State-owned Enterprises	175
集体企业	Collective-owned Enterprises	85
股份合作企业	Cooperative Enterprises	4
联营企业	Joint Ownership Enterprises	2
国有联营企业	State Joint Ownership Enterprises	
集体联营企业	Collective Joint Ownership Enterprises	1
国有与集体联营企业	Joint State-collective Enterprises	1
其他联营企业	Other Joint Ownership Enterprises	
有限责任公司	Limited Liability Corporations	1393
国有独资公司	State Sole Funded Corporations	44
其他有限责任公司	Other Limited Liability Corporations	1349
股份有限公司	Share-holding Corporations Ltd.	138
私营企业	Private Enterprises	1403
私营独资企业	Private-funded Enterprises	12
私营合伙企业	Private Partnership Enterprises	2
私营有限责任公司	Private Limited Liability Corporations	1318
私营股份有限公司	Private Share-holding Corporations Ltd.	71
其他企业	Other Enterprises	2
港、澳、台商投资企业	**Enterprises with Funds from Hong Kong,Macao and Taiwan**	**13**
合资经营企业(港或澳、台资)	Joint-venture Enterprises	8
合作经营企业(港或澳、台资)	Cooperative Enterprises	
港、澳、台商独资经营企业	Enterprises with Sole Fund	4
港、澳、台商投资股份有限公司	Share-holding Corporations Ltd.	1
其他港澳台投资	Other Enterprises with Funds from Hong Kong,Macao and Taiwan	
外商投资企业	**Foreign Funded Enterprises**	**3**
中外合资经营企业	Joint-venture Enterprises	3
中外合作经营企业	Cooperative Enterprises	
外资企业	Enterprises with Sole Fund	
外商投资股份有限公司	Share-holding Corporations Ltd.	
其他外商投资	Other Foreign Funded Enterprises	

Basic Statistics on Number of Enterprises and Contracts by Status of Registration(2015)

(100 million yuan)

合同情况(亿元) Condition on Contracts (100 million yuan)		
签订的合同额 Total Value of Contracts	1.上年结转合同额 Value from Contracts Signed in Last Year	2.本年新签合同额 Value from New Contracts Signed in This Year
20751.09	**8636.89**	**12114.20**
12280.44	5914.78	6365.65
20695.06	**8621.60**	**12073.46**
518.65	200.73	317.91
74.49	12.48	62.01
7.11	0.68	6.43
0.36	0.05	0.31
0.34	0.04	0.30
0.03	0.01	0.01
15797.72	6973.72	8824.01
4172.58	1945.75	2226.83
11625.15	5027.97	6597.18
1015.97	473.34	542.63
3279.50	960.04	2319.46
10.56	2.29	8.27
0.62	0.00	0.62
2885.46	839.15	2046.31
382.86	118.60	264.26
1.26	0.56	0.70
4.59	**1.26**	**3.34**
4.08	1.01	3.07
0.30	0.03	0.27
0.21	0.21	0.00
51.44	**14.03**	**37.41**
51.44	14.03	37.41

14-4 按登记注册类型分的建筑业总产值(2015)

单位：亿元

指标名称	Item	建筑业总产值 Total Output Value
总计	**Total**	**10592.86**
其中:国有及国有控股企业	State-owned and State-holding Enterprises	4664.24
一、按登记注册类型分组	Grouped by Status of Registration	
内资企业	**Domestic Funded Enterprises**	**10552.77**
国有企业	State-owned Enterprises	341.20
集体企业	Collective-owned Enterprises	69.79
股份合作企业	Cooperative Enterprises	6.94
联营企业	Joint Ownership Enterprises	0.60
国有联营企业	State Joint Ownership Enterprises	
集体联营企业	Collective Joint Ownership Enterprises	0.31
国有与集体联营企业	Joint State-collective Enterprises	0.29
其他联营企业	Other Joint Ownership Enterprises	
有限责任公司	Limited Liability Corporations	7289.42
国有独资公司	State Sole Funded Corporations	1308.39
其他有限责任公司	Other Limited Liability Corporations	5981.03
股份有限公司	Share-holding Corporations Ltd.	596.43
私营企业	Private Enterprises	2247.55
私营独资企业	Private-funded Enterprises	8.63
私营合伙企业	Private Partnership Enterprises	0.62
私营有限责任公司	Private Limited Liability Corporations	1993.36
私营股份有限公司	Private Share-holding Corporations Ltd.	244.94
其他企业	Other Enterprises	0.84
港、澳、台商投资企业	**Enterprises with Funds from Hong Kong,Macao and Taiwan**	**3.34**
合资经营企业(港或澳、台资)	Joint-venture Enterprises	2.97
合作经营企业(港或澳、台资)	Cooperative Enterprises	
港、澳、台商独资经营企业	Enterprises with Sole Fund	0.25
港、澳、台商投资股份有限公司	Share-holding Corporations Ltd.	0.13
其他港澳台投资	Other Enterprises with Funds from Hong Kong,Macao and Taiwan	
外商投资企业	**Foreign Funded Enterprises**	**36.75**
中外合资经营企业	Joint-venture Enterprises	36.75
中外合作经营企业	Cooperative Enterprises	
外资企业	Enterprises with Sole Fund	
外商投资股份有限公司	Share-holding Corporations Ltd.	
其他外商投资	Other Foreign Funded Enterprises	

Total Output Vaule of Construction by Status of Registration(2015)

(100 million yuan)

其中：装饰装修产值 Output Value of Decoration	其中：在外省完成的产值 Output Value Completed in Other Provinces	建筑工程产值 Output Value of Construction	安装工程产值 Output Vaule of Installation	其他产值 Others
478.45	**3624.43**	**9363.58**	**889.63**	**339.65**
54.13	2751.25	4144.20	353.27	166.76
472.67	**3617.00**	**9324.06**	**889.14**	**339.57**
2.31	41.06	250.03	31.06	60.11
0.93	0.49	61.48	7.71	0.59
		5.75	1.19	
		0.56	0.02	0.01
		0.28	0.02	0.01
		0.29		
229.89	3162.81	6449.10	669.26	171.06
2.66	864.60	1204.38	98.68	5.33
227.23	2298.21	5244.72	570.58	165.73
15.50	105.67	534.59	38.52	23.32
224.03	306.95	2021.69	141.38	84.48
0.07		8.55	0.08	
0.01		0.62		
216.68	292.49	1780.99	132.04	80.33
7.27	14.46	231.53	9.26	4.15
		0.84		
2.09	**0.84**	**2.77**	**0.49**	**0.09**
1.96	0.67	2.63	0.25	0.09
0.08	0.16	0.08	0.17	
0.06		0.06	0.07	
3.69	**6.60**	**36.75**		
3.69	6.60	36.75		

14-5 按隶属关系和资质等级分的建筑业总产值的构成(2015)

单位：亿元

指标名称	Item	建筑业总产值 Total Output Value
总计	**Total**	**10592.86**
一、按隶属关系分组	**Grouped by Jurisdiction of Management**	
中央	Centre	3621.80
省(自治区、直辖市)	Province (Autonomous Region、Municipality)	444.33
地区(州、盟、省辖市)	Region (State、League、Provincial Municipality)	1305.10
县(区、市、旗)	County (District、City、Banner)	995.40
街道	Street	215.90
镇	Town	140.28
乡	Countryside	27.58
居委会	Residents' Committee	11.99
村委会	Village Committee	6.56
其他	Others	3823.92
二、按企业资质等级分组	**Grouped by Qualification Criteria**	
企业资质等级(施工总承包)	General Contracting	9893.99
特级	Special Grade	2607.13
一级	First Grade	4569.44
二级	Second Grade	1933.63
三级及以下	Third Grade and Below	783.78
企业资质等级(专业总承包)	Professional Contraction Construction	698.87
一级	First Grade	354.93
二级	Second Grade	165.63
三级及以下	Third Grade and Below	178.31

Composition of Total Output Value of Construction Enterprises by Jurisdiction of Management and Qualification Criteria (2015)

(100 million yuan)

其中：装饰装修产值 Output Value of Decoration	其中：在外省完成的产值 Output Value Completed in Other Provinces	建筑工程产值 Output Value of Construction	安装工程产值 Output Vaule of Installation	其他产值 Others
478.45	**3624.43**	**9363.58**	**889.63**	**339.65**
26.98	2562.02	3258.58	259.90	103.32
6.18	39.97	372.89	56.29	15.15
41.02	177.26	1073.57	169.89	61.64
31.80	178.11	892.07	76.72	26.61
23.89	50.55	185.04	28.85	2.01
0.71	17.14	131.80	6.41	2.06
0.08		27.47	0.10	0.01
1.05		9.31	1.77	0.91
0.23		6.36	0.14	0.06
346.51	599.37	3406.48	289.56	127.88
297.23	3420.14	8933.66	719.97	240.36
26.97	1825.72	2465.96	108.53	32.64
148.50	1456.95	4045.50	399.46	124.48
96.10	127.06	1728.97	149.36	55.30
25.66	10.40	693.23	62.62	27.93
181.22	204.30	429.91	169.66	99.30
129.45	124.20	200.31	73.13	81.49
35.62	37.53	102.51	53.51	9.62
16.15	42.57	127.09	43.02	8.20

14-6 按登记注册类型分的建筑业企业完成房屋建筑竣工面积(2015)

单位： 万平方米

指标名称	Item	合计 Total
总计	**Total**	**26828.92**
其中:国有及国有控股企业	State-owned and State-holding Enterprises	3726.81
按登记注册类型分组	Grouped by Status of Registration	
内资企业	**Domestic Funded Enterprises**	**26746.92**
国有企业	State-owned Enterprises	237.95
集体企业	Collective-owned Enterprises	386.36
股份合作企业	Cooperative Enterprises	1.48
联营企业	Joint Ownership Enterprises	2.26
国有联营企业	State Joint Ownership Enterprises	
集体联营企业	Collective Joint Ownership Enterprises	2.26
国有与集体联营企业	Joint State-collective Enterprises	0.00
其他联营企业	Other Joint Ownership Enterprises	
有限责任公司	Limited Liability Corporations	15708.92
国有独资公司	State Sole Funded Corporations	613.72
其他有限责任公司	Other Limited Liability Corporations	15095.20
股份有限公司	Share-holding Corporations Ltd.	1990.37
私营企业	Private Enterprises	8415.16
私营独资企业	Private-funded Enterprises	63.46
私营合伙企业	Private Partnership Enterprises	6.06
私营有限责任公司	Private Limited Liability Corporations	7312.32
私营股份有限公司	Private Share-holding Corporations Ltd.	1033.31
其他企业	Other Enterprises	4.41
港、澳、台商投资企业	**Enterprises with Funds from Hong Kong,Macao and Taiwan**	2.42
合资经营企业(港或澳、台资)	Joint-venture Enterprises	2.37
合作经营企业(港或澳、台资)	Cooperative Enterprises	
港、澳、台商独资经营企业	Enterprises with Sole Fund	0.05
港、澳、台商投资股份有限公司	Share-holding Corporations Ltd.	
其他港澳台投资	Other Enterprises with Funds from Hong Kong,Macao and Taiwan	
外商投资企业	**Foreign Funded Enterprises**	**79.59**
中外合资经营企业	Joint-venture Enterprises	79.59
中外合作经营企业	Cooperative Enterprises	
外资企业	Enterprises with Sole Fund	
外商投资股份有限公司	Share-holding Corporations Ltd.	
其他外商投资	Other Foreign Funded Enterprises	

Completed Floor Space of Buildings Constructed by Construction Enterprises by Status of Registration (2015)

(10 000sq.m)

住宅房屋 Residential Buildings	商业及服务用房屋 Houses for Business and Service	办公用房屋 Office Buildings	科研、教育、医疗用房屋 Houses for Scientific Research、Education and Medical Treatment	文化、体育、娱乐用房屋 Houses for Culture、Sports and Entertainment	厂房及建筑物 Workshop and Buildings	仓库 Storage	其他未列明的房屋建筑物* Others
18399.18	**1815.09**	**1649.20**	**1170.08**	**298.90**	**2744.98**	**95.04**	**652.80**
2564.73	200.56	233.23	106.31	19.75	374.51	5.60	218.49
18355.41	**1799.18**	**1632.49**	**1170.03**	**295.72**	**2742.62**	**95.04**	**652.80**
115.44	12.97	34.12	15.83	6.36	48.61	2.62	2.00
281.56	34.60	9.38	16.70	0.50	39.15	0.21	4.26
			0.56		0.92		
0.79	0.21	0.32	0.66		0.17		0.12
0.79	0.21	0.32	0.66		0.17		0.12
10555.14	1201.49	875.27	817.62	243.49	1657.29	24.39	330.60
406.94	5.94	3.82	15.82	0.00	178.74	2.47	
10148.20	1195.55	871.45	801.80	243.49	1478.55	21.92	330.60
1031.15	224.63	104.59	158.77	27.36	220.25	25.29	198.32
6366.94	325.28	608.80	159.89	18.01	776.21	42.53	117.51
56.44	0.52	3.64			1.87	0.98	
		6.06					
5540.82	302.97	427.98	155.89	16.89	721.71	41.40	104.67
769.68	21.78	171.12	4.01	1.12	52.62	0.15	12.84
4.40		0.01					
			0.05		2.37		
					2.37		
			0.05				
43.77	**15.92**	**16.71**		**3.18**			
43.77	15.92	16.71		3.18			

14-7 按隶属关系和资质等级分的建筑业企业工程完成情况(2015)

单位：万平方米

指标名称	Item	房屋建筑施工面积 Floor Space of Buildings under Construcion
一、按隶属关系分组	**Grouped by Jurisdiction of Management**	
中央	Centre	19081.2436
省(自治区、直辖市)	Province (Autonomous Region、Municipality)	1730.1382
地区(州、盟、省辖市)	Region (State、League、Provincial Municipality)	7749.5982
县(区、市、旗)	County (District、City、Banner)	7102.253
街道	Street	1371.9899
镇	Town	708.0228
乡	Countryside	138.832
居委会	Residents' Committee	87.9323
村委会	Village Committee	35.0859
其他	Others	24199.6246
四、按企业资质等级分组	**Grouped by Qualification Criteria**	
企业资质等级(施工总承包)	Enterprises Qualification Criteria (General Contracting)	61467.1207
特级	Special Grade	15475.3495
一级	First Grade	27623.0297
二级	Second Grade	13703.3034
三级及以下	Third Grade and Below	4665.4381
企业资质等级(专业总承包)	Enterprises Qualification Criteria (Professional Contraction Construction)	737.5998
一级	First Grade	181.3466
二级	Second Grade	290.2011
三级及以下	Third Grade and Below	266.05

Project Completion Situation on Construction Enterprises by Jurisdiction of Management and Qualification Criteria (2015)

(10 000 sq.m)

本年新开工面积 Floor Space of New Construction This Year	实行投标承包面积 Contracting Space of Bidding	房屋建筑竣工面积 Floor Space of Buildings Completed	住宅房屋 Residential Buildings	商业及服务用房屋 Houses for Business Use
4290.79	9728.09	2808.51	2141.98	168.22
661.35	1431.66	704.04	370.47	27.20
5092.34	6100.85	3372.05	1989.82	162.33
4654.39	3767.13	4409.27	2686.95	557.27
787.43	1111.01	980.92	515.26	78.94
576.02	489.91	516.35	317.27	14.05
107.03	125.03	127.45	107.38	0.82
72.88	71.38	66.67	42.12	12.66
23.90	13.24	32.63	28.28	
15078.11	16240.07	13811.02	10199.65	793.60
30911.07	38677.20	26385.73	18169.49	1799.59
6029.55	4929.27	4719.59	3440.20	283.30
13514.50	22509.68	10875.24	6866.48	953.12
8454.39	8634.00	7637.25	5616.89	407.16
2912.62	2604.26	3153.65	2245.93	156.02
433.17	401.15	443.19	229.69	15.50
106.35	122.54	147.90	44.51	
165.07	95.92	131.07	80.33	7.36
161.75	182.70	164.23	104.85	8.14

14-8 分市州建筑业企业工程完成情况(2015)
STATISTICS ON PROJECTS COMPLETION OF CONSTRUCTION ENTERPRISES BY CITIES AND PREFECTURES (2015)

单位：万平方米 (10 000 sq.m)

项 目	Item	房屋建筑施工面积 Floor Space of Housing Construction	本年新开工面积 Beginning projects in This Year	实行投标承包面积 Actual Floor Space by Contracts and Bids	房屋建筑竣工面积 Floor Space of Housing Projects Completed	#住 宅 Residential Buildings	#办公用房 Office Buildings
湖北省	**Hubei**	**62204.72**	**31344.24**	**39078.35**	**26828.92**	**18399.18**	**1649.20**
武汉市	Wuhan	35391.07	14427.67	20037.80	11956.87	7949.97	820.30
黄石市	Huangshi	2029.66	1136.76	1476.86	1085.35	790.72	39.78
十堰市	Shiyan	1320.17	637.66	710.56	618.16	477.35	15.65
宜昌市	Yichang	3125.40	1726.31	2647.06	1276.71	937.63	58.46
襄阳市	Xiangyang	4708.70	2709.60	3002.10	1984.41	1462.80	76.53
鄂州市	Ezhou	736.88	534.88	494.50	396.38	281.87	4.84
荆门市	Jingmen	860.76	571.27	681.48	467.35	328.34	25.01
孝感市	Xiaogan	3106.09	1903.38	1995.66	1899.35	1397.29	96.50
荆州市	Jingzhou	1521.96	849.82	933.30	816.10	496.00	46.61
黄冈市	Huanggang	5625.91	4515.32	4364.13	4033.94	2712.53	287.41
咸宁市	Xianning	736.90	532.04	444.59	582.18	505.24	29.05
随州市	Suizhou	920.80	619.89	678.56	518.85	395.16	33.16
恩施州	Enshi	709.68	411.69	464.04	432.23	210.85	73.69
仙桃市	Xiantao	331.36	251.42	280.10	222.07	165.42	16.30
潜江市	Qianjiang	663.12	285.03	576.91	265.54	114.43	10.41
天门市	Tianmen	388.74	216.52	266.10	259.61	167.88	14.77
神农架	Shennongjia	27.51	15.01	24.60	13.81	5.71	0.73

主要统计指标解释

建筑业统计单位 指从事房屋、构筑物建造和设备安装活动的法人企业。建筑业法人企业应具有建筑业资质并能够独立核算，同时其应具备以下条件：①依法成立，有自己的名称、组织机构和场所，能够承担民事责任；②独立拥有和使用资产，承担负债，有权与其他单位签订合同；③独立核算盈亏，能够编制资产负债表。

建筑业总产值 是以货币形式表现的建筑业企业在一定时期内生产的建筑业产品和提供的服务的总和。建筑业总产值包括：

(1)建筑工程产值：指列入建筑工程预算内的各种工程价值。

(2)安装工程产值：指设备安装工程价值，不包括被安装设备本身的价值。

(3)其他产值：建筑业总产值中除建筑工程、安装工程以外的产值。包括房屋构筑物修理产值、非标准设备制造产值、总包企业向分包企业收取的管理费以及不能明确划分的施工活动所完成的产值。

a.房屋构筑物修理产值：指房屋和构筑物修理所完成的产值，但不包括被修理房屋、构筑物本身价值和生产设备的修理产值。

b.非标准设备制造产值：指加工制造没有定型的非标准生产设备的加工费和原材料价值(如化工厂、炼油厂用的各种罐、槽，矿井生产统一使用的各种漏斗、三角槽、阀门等)以及附属加工厂为本企业承建工程制作的非标准设备的价值。

建筑业增加值 指建筑业企业在报告期内以货币形式表现的建筑业生产经营活动的最终成果。

从2004年第一次全国经济普查开始，建筑业现价增加值按生产法和分配法(收入法)两种方法计算，以收入法的计算结果为准，即从收入的角度出发，根据生产要素在生产过程中应得的收入份额计算。具体计算方法：经济普查年度建筑业增加值按照《经济普查年度GDP核算方案》计算，非经济普查年度建筑业增加值按照《非经济普查年度GDP核算方案》计算。

房屋建筑施工面积 指在报告期内施过工的全部房屋建筑面积，包括本期新开工的房屋面积、上期施工跨入本期继续施工的房屋面积、上期停缓建在本期恢复施工的房屋面积、本期竣工的房屋面积及本期施工后又停缓建的房屋面积。

房屋建筑竣工面积 指在报告期内房屋建筑按照设计要求全部完工，达到了使用条件，经验收鉴定合格，正式移交使用单位的房屋建筑面积。

Explanatory Notes on Main Statistical Indicators

Statistical Unit in Construction refers to corporate enterprise engaged in the construction of buildings and structures and in the installation of equipment. A corporate construction enterprise should have qualification certificates with independent accounting system, and should meet the following 3 requirements: a) being set up in line with relevant legal basis, having its full name, organization and location, and capable of taking civil liabilities; b) independently possessing and using its assets and assuming its liabilities, and entitled to sign contracts with other institutions; and c) making independent accounts of its profits and losses, and capable of compiling its own balance sheet.

Gross Output Value of Construction refers to total of construction products and services, expressed in money terms, produced or rendered by construction and installation enterprises during a given period of time. It includes:

(1) Output value of construction projects, that is the value of projects covered by the project budgets;

(2) Output value of installation projects, that is the value of the installation of equipment, (excluding the value of the equipment to be

installed);

(3) Output value of others, that is the output value of construction industry excluding that of construction projects and installation projects. It includes: output value of repair of buildings and structures; output value of non–standard equipment manufacturing; overhead expenses received by contracted enterprises to the sub–contracted enterprises and the completed output value of construction activities that have no clear definition.

a. Output value of repair of buildings and structures, that is the value created through the repairs of buildings or structures, but does not include the value of buildings or structures being repaired and the value of the repair of production equipment;

b. Output value of manufactured non–standard equipment, that is the value of non–standard production equipment including raw materials and manufacturing cost made for the construction project (i.e., chemical plant; kettles or tanks used by refineries; various fillers, triangle tanks, valves used by mines), and the output value of equipment manufactured by subsidiary workshops.

Value–added of Construction refers to the final result of the activities of production and management of construction industry in monetary terms in the reference period.

Starting from the 2004 economic census, value–added of construction is calculated by both production approach and income approach, with the income approach as the final approach, where the calculation is based on the share of production factor in the production process. Specifically, value–added of construction for census years is calculated in accordance with the Programme of Compilation of GDP and National Accounts for the Year of Economic Census, and value–added of construction for other years is calculated in accordance with the Programme of Compilation of GDP and National Accounts for the Non Economic Census Years.

Floor Space of Buildings Under Construction refers to floor space of buildings under construction during the reference period, including newly started buildings, buildings started earlier and continued during the reference period, and buildings suspended earlier but restarted during the reference period, buildings completed during the reference period, and buildings under construction and then suspended during the reference period.

Floor Space of Buildings Completed refers to the floor space of buildings that are completed in the reference period in accordance with the requirements of the design, up to the standard for putting them into use, and have been checked and accepted by concerned departments as qualified ones.

15 交通运输、邮电

Transportation, Post and Telecommunications Services

交通运输、邮电

Transportation,Post and Telecommunication Service
2015

全社会客运量	Passenger Capacity of The Whole Society	106732.59	(万人)
#公路	Public Road	89996.46	(万人)
全社会货运量	Volume of Freight Traffic	160393.06	(万吨)
#公路	Public Road	121466.43	(万吨)
邮电业务总量	Postal Service Portfolio	962.66	(亿元)
#函件	Letters	6756.5	(万件)
年末固定电话用户	Local Telephone Subscriber End of Year	872.50	(万户)
年末移动电话用户	Mobile Phone Subscriber End of Year	4650.60	(万户)

全 社 会 客 货 运 量
Passenger Capactity of The Whole Society

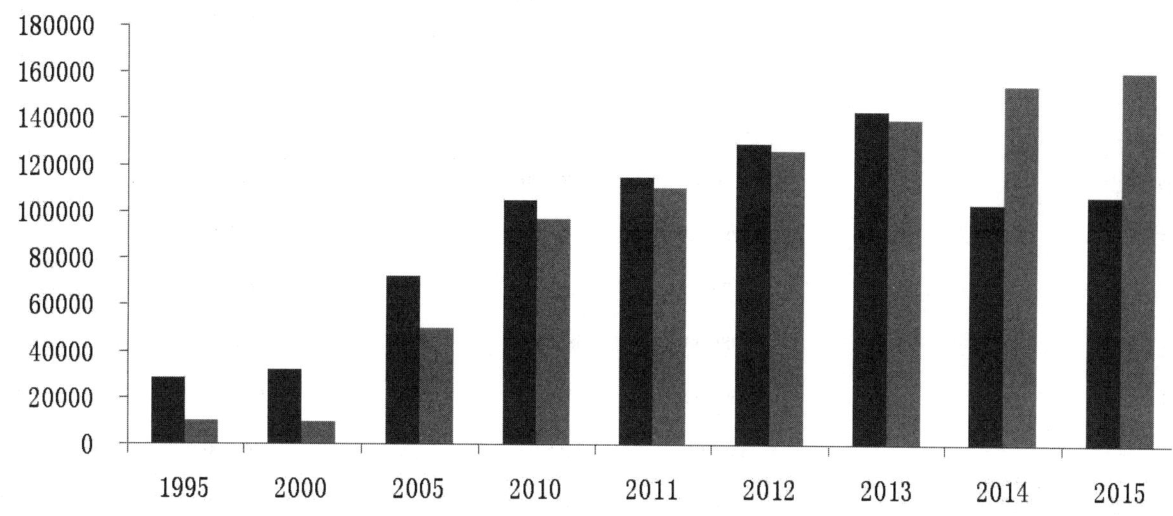

附:全社会客货运量

Passenger Capacity of The Whole Society

年份 Year	客运量(万人) Passenger Capacity (10 000 persons)	货运量(万吨) volume of freight traffic (10 000 tons)
1995	28508	10174
2000	31593	9345
2005	71892	49924
2010	105132	96938
2012	129511	126195
2013	143100	139740
2014	103672	154736
2015	106733	160393

说明: 2014年因公路运输调整统计方法,与前期数据不可比(下同)。

Note:In 2014,the statistics method of transportation has been changed, the data can not be compared by the previous(the same below).

15-1 交通运输业基本情况

指　　标	1995	2000	2005	2010
运输线路长度　(公里)				
铁路营业里程	1940	2025	2758	3032
公路通车里程	48728	57850	91131	206212
#等级公路里程	30910	48062	76075	187812
#高速公路		569	1649	3674
一级公路	641	611	1092	2210
二级公路	4967	7911	15225	16159
内河航道里程	8969	8309	8988	8988
客运量总计　(万人)	28508.20	31593.00	71892.00	105415.50
铁路	2300.00	3469.00	4615.00	7281.30
公路	24315.00	27184.00	66183.00	96873.00
水运	1745.00	679.00	601.00	375.80
民用航空	150.00	261.00	494.00	885.40
旅客周转量　(亿人公里)	285.29	398.32	803.90	1262.26
货物运输量总计　(万吨)	10173.62	9345.19	49923.52	97006.94
铁路	3986.00	3857.00	8491.00	10145.60
公路	2600.00	2228.00	33481.00	71020.00
水运	3585.00	3255.00	7944.00	15832.00
货物周转量　(亿吨公里)	776.44	831.64	1682.48	3370.37
民用车辆拥有量　(万辆)			393.90	761.11
#民用汽车拥有量	34.89	47.55	103.04	224.60
#载客汽车	14.96	24.69	53.40	151.51
载货汽车	18.61	21.72	30.96	53.29
#营运汽车			20.33	36.60
#私人汽车		41.72	59.66	165.39
民用运输船舶拥有量　(艘)		5905	5362	5502
机动船		4188	4158	4634
驳船		1717	1204	868
港口货物吞吐量　(万吨)		4113.46	13992.51	18782.67

注：2014年因公路运输统计方法调整，数据与前期不可比。

Note:From 2014, due to the statistics method of road transport has been adjusted, the data can not be compared with the previous period .

TRANSPORTATION

2011	2012	2013	2014	2015
3340	3463	4794	4059	4062
212746	218151	226912	236932	252980
196452	203145	212893	224184	240936
4006	4006	4333	5096	6204
2395	2515	2789	3344	5231
16852	17233	17576	18033	21555
8988	8988	8988	9066	9066
114736.92	129510.90	143100.28	103671.80	106732.59
8503.80	9177.40	12101.80	14302.70	15083.90
104971.00	118369.00	129533.75	87804.00	89996.46
347.60	443.50	528.00	533.80	570.10
914.52	933.50	936.73	1031.30	1082.13
1444.66	1576.97	1761.10	1458.24	1514.56
110167.83	126194.64	139740.26	154735.73	160393.06
10059.40	9177.40	9010.40	7681.30	6579.00
82741.00	97136.00	108824.21	116280.00	121466.43
17358.00	19070.00	24408.00	30765.00	32338.00
4044.45	4351.80	5036.80	5798.12	5902.19
822.68	879.01	967.23	1042.36	959.13
264.82	305.07	363.68	439.39	504.36
186.72	277.76	282.29	345.84	424.70
59.72	62.69	68.62	72.73	70.16
40.28	40.37	42.04	42.95	55.25
200.38	238.64	292.00	300.61	433.90
5505	4895	4938	4744	4357
4884	4531	4794	4500	4155
621	364	232	244	202
21662.91	23518.12	26219.00	28969.15	32949.52

15-2 客 运 量
PASSENGER TRAFFIC

单位：万人 (10 000 persons)

年份 Year	总计 Total	铁路 Railway	公路 Highway	水运 Waterway	民用航空 Civil Aviation
1978	12009.20	2854.00	7429.00	1722.00	4.20
1980	16629.26	3217.00	11282.00	2123.00	7.26
1985	28178.22	3353.00	22378.00	2433.00	14.22
1990	32145.93	2107.00	27333.00	2693.00	12.93
1991	33982.62	2016.00	29279.00	2654.00	33.62
1992	34726.00	2077.00	29635.00	2894.00	120.00
1993	30152.00	2265.00	25116.00	2665.00	106.00
1994	29607.00	2358.00	24819.00	2210.00	120.00
1995	28508.20	2300.00	24315.00	1743.00	150.00
1996	29045.40	2248.00	25180.00	1449.00	168.00
1997	29503.08	2127.00	25684.00	1538.00	154.08
1998	28208.00	2218.00	24540.00	1306.00	144.00
1999	29360.14	2545.00	25596.00	1080.00	139.14
2000	63306.00	3469.00	58897.00	679.00	261.00
2001	62696.00	3632.00	58018.00	767.00	279.00
2002	63382.00	3813.00	58623.00	638.00	308.00
2003	62880.00	3602.00	58371.00	573.00	334.42
2004	68167.00	4072.00	63127.00	522.00	446.11
2005	71892.00	4615.00	66183.00	601.00	494.00
2006	75440.00	4850.00	69335.00	706.00	549.00
2007	84088.00	5125.00	77514.00	736.00	712.70
2008	89720.00	6027.00	82532.00	388.00	774.00
2009	96219.00	6440.00	88703.00	371.00	705.00
2010	105415.50	7281.30	96873.00	375.80	885.40
2011	114736.92	8503.80	104971.00	347.60	914.52
2012	129510.90	9764.90	118369.00	443.50	933.50
2013	143100.28	12101.80	129533.75	528.00	936.73
2014	103671.40	14302.70	87804.00	533.80	1031.30
2015	106732.59	15083.90	89996.46	570.10	1082.13

注：2014年因公路运输统计方法调整，数据与前期不可比。

Note:From 2014, due to the statistics method of road transport has been adjusted, the data can not be compared with the previous period .

15-3 旅客周转量
TURNOVER VOLUME OF PASSENGER TRAFFIC

单位：亿人公里 (100 million person-kms)

年份 Year	总计 Total	铁路 Railway	公路 Highway	水运 Waterway	民用航空 Civil Aviation
1978	69.38	30.72	24.85	13.54	0.17
1980	95.88	41.79	36.20	17.52	0.37
1985	185.25	84.00	81.33	19.40	0.52
1990	225.85	82.83	112.83	29.28	0.91
1991	257.68	98.09	126.70	30.19	2.70
1992	286.35	104.89	135.61	34.72	11.13
1993	281.28	113.60	123.64	33.50	10.54
1994	283.98	121.91	121.40	28.71	11.96
1995	285.29	129.47	117.76	22.71	15.35
1996	285.04	121.17	124.97	21.09	17.81
1997	282.53	118.62	123.39	24.14	16.38
1998	278.66	126.68	118.51	18.79	14.68
1999	300.38	146.54	124.46	14.09	15.29
2000	563.78	232.00	297.46	8.84	25.48
2001	574.24	248.00	293.35	5.87	27.02
2002	633.6.9	283.00	317.02	3.60	30.07
2003	617.68	271.00	309.00	4.00	33.68
2004	703.95	322.80	334.00	3.20	43.95
2005	803.90	389.40	358.00	4.20	52.30
2006	847.42	408.10	374.80	5.10	59.42
2007	947.71	440.80	423.80	5.30	77.81
2008	1077.68	474.01	522.57	2.30	78.80
2009	1096.31	466.70	562.34	2.49	64.78
2010	1262.26	528.90	631.39	2.92	99.05
2011	1444.66	639.15	700.06	2.49	102.97
2012	1576.00	663.60	804.07	2.94	106.36
2013	1761.10	756.40	892.25	3.14	109.31
2014	1458.24	854.40	483.89	2.85	120.10
2015	1514.56	869.3	513.06	3.31	128.90

15-4 货 运 量
FREIGHT TRAFFIC

单位：万吨 (10 000 tons)

年份 Year	总计 Total	铁路 Railway	公路 Highway	水运 Waterway	#内河 Inland Waterway	#海运 Seashipping
1978	10199	3513	3556	3130		
1980	8420	3211	2199	3110		
1985	11059	2659	3852	3463		
1990	10916	3901	2941	3784		
1991	11217	3957	2999	3996		
1992	11565	4018	2828	4364		
1993	11184	4029	2734	4248		
1994	10663	3964	2666	3641		
1995	10174	3986	2600	3585		
1996	9928	3779	2537	3268		
1997	9389	3882	2280	3119		
1998	10154	3999	2009	4040		
1999	10517	3964	2141	4313		
2000	40949	6558	27863	6270	6202	68
2001	41476	7094	29851	4275	4198	77
2002	42064	7400	28777	5630	5390	240
2003	44661	7825	30348	6195	5830	365
2004	47073	7872	31584	7259	6823	436
2005	50317	8491	33481	7944	7466	478
2006	52885	8990	35361	8242	7679	536
2007	58523	9728	39568	9027	7765	1262
2008	75778	10202	52759	12681	8182	4499
2009	82714	9839	59563	13305	8108	5197
2010	97007	10145	71020	15832	9916	6082
2011	110168	10059	82741	17358	10817	6536
2012	125392	9177	97136	19070	11836	7275
2013	139740	9010	108824	21897	13575	8042
2014	154736	7681	116280	30765	21152	8476
2015	160393	6579	121466	32338	27564	6226

15-5 货物周转量
TURNOVER VOLUME OF FREIGHT TRAFFIC

单位：亿吨公里 (100 million ton-km)

年份 Year	总计 Total	铁路 Railway	公路 Highway	水运 Waterway	#内河 Inland Waterway	#沿海 Seashipping
1978	281.09	191.72	9.22	80.15		
1980	326.85	206.14	9.85	110.85		
1985	507.57	320.37	16.59	169.94		
1990	670.53	415.17	14.72	235.04		
1991	720.23	455.00	14.67	245.41		
1992	757.00	461.81	13.89	272.70		
1993	753.52	477.64	11.99	259.90		
1994	743.21	505.57	10.23	222.32		
1995	776.44	544.40	9.62	222.20		
1996	775.79	552.32	9.93	208.05		
1997	725.34	501.77	8.72	212.21		
1998	696.62	465.81	7.59	220.63		
1999	696.27	457.70	8.25	227.76		
2000	1156.57	618.37	227.16	305.29	295.07	10.22
2001	1097.60	634.90	218.97	237.31	226.15	11.16
2002	1212.82	680.00	211.49	313.60	271.30	42.29
2003	1313.13	703.80	224.00	377.00	315.38	61.61
2004	1485.76	781.83	235.60	461.08	395.75	65.33
2005	1689.86	987.60	251.00	443.20	391.05	105.00
2006	1730.93	1021.40	266.10	437.90	379.81	58.10
2007	1902.17	1138.20	302.09	458.00	361.93	95.83
2008	2699.97	1096.90	789.37	810.46	416.17	394.29
2009	2808.46	1032.40	930.10	845.18	402.82	442.36
2010	3370.37	1144.60	1079.13	1145.52	547.77	470.00
2011	4044.45	1226.80	1277.71	1538.83	625.26	609.61
2012	4693.61	1194.10	1565.45	1590.65	740.76	683.36
2013	4883.01	1195.70	1818.18	1868.08	946.02	756.69
2014	5798.12	1109.10	2340.56	2347.32	1347.07	891.82
2015	5902.19	995.70	2457.62	2447.71	1851.27	618.02

15-6 全省民用车辆拥有量(2015)
NUMBER OF CIVIL MOTOR VEHICLES OWNED BY WHOLE PROVINCE(2015)

单位：辆 (unit)

指标	Item	总计 Total	营运 Working	非营运 Non-Working
合计	**Total**	**9593480**	**681011**	**8903685**
汽车	Civil Vehicles	5043649	552549	4482316
载客汽车	Passenger Vehicles	4246956	130460	4107712
#大型	Lage Scale	52511	36888	11218
中型	Medium Scale	34553	12618	17569
小型	Small Scale	4127408	80940	4046455
#轿车	Cars	2657953	74213	2583740
载货汽车	Trucks	701571	382636	318935
#重型	Heavy Scale	154895	141211	13684
中型	Medium Scale	70021	61384	8637
轻型	Light Scale	475479	179567	295912
#普通载货	Ordinary Trucks	320522	82019	238503
其他汽车	Other Vehicles	95122	39453	55669
#三轮汽车	Tricycle Motocars	11022	4454	6568
低速汽车	Low Speed Vehicles	46285	26817	19468
摩托车	Motorear	4511464	91619	4419845
#普通	Ordinary Motor	4453831	91595	4362236
轻便	Light Motor	57633	24	57609
挂车	Freight Trailers	37829	36664	1165
其他类型车	Other Motor Vehicles	538	179	359

注：本表“其他汽车”中，包括三轮和四轮农用运输车。
Note:Tricycles and four-wheel farming vehicles are inclued in “Other Vehicles”.

15-7 私人车辆拥有量
NUMBER OF PRIVATE – OWNED VEHICLES

单位：辆 (unit)

指 标	Item	2000	2005	2010	2012	2013	2014	2015
民用汽车	Civil Vehicles	475500	596601	1653948	2386393	2919992	3566489	4338967
载客汽车	Passenger Vehicles	245500	297095	1153728	1861548	2366962	3006050	3796713
#大型	#Lage Scale	29200	3312	2939	1258	1011	951	770
轿车	Cars		177650	773727	1234812	1556798	1953696	2414210
载货汽车	Ordinary Trucks	211400	135352	327509	405060	452886	478775	473513
#重型	#Heavy Scale		8766	33281	45874	51217	59171	59388
其它汽车	Others		164154	172711	119785	100144	81664	68741
摩托车	Motors	1241000	2853113	4971619	4946723	4793599	4792901	4501871
载货挂车	Freight Trailers	4400	1714	6467	8927	10255	10893	11405

15-8 水路运输工具拥有量(2015)
NUMBER OF WATER TRANSPORT TOOLS(2015)

指 标	Item	机动船 Power Boat	客船 Passenger Ship	货船 Cargo Ship	拖船 Tugboat
数量 (艘)	Quantity (ship)	4155	721	3324	110
总载重量 (吨位)	Total Carrying Capacity (tonage)	7928786		7928786	
净载重量 (吨位)	Net Load (tonage)	7391699		7391699	
载客量 (客位)	Passenger Carrying Capacity (person)	42647	42647		
标准箱位	TEU	20869		20869	
功率 (千瓦)	Power (kw)	1913117	74104	1782776	56237

15-9 分市、州公路旅客运输完成情况(2015)
STATISTICS ON HIGHWAY PASSFNGER TRANSPORTATION OF CITIES AND PREFECTURES(2015)

地区	Region	旅客运输量(万人) Passenger Traffic (10,000 person)	旅客周转量(万人公里) Turnover Volume of Passenger Traffic (100 million person-km)	货物运输量(万吨) Freight Traffic (10 000 ton)	货物周转量(亿吨公里) Turnover Volume of Freight Traffic (100 million ton-km)
武汉市	Wuhan	11381	810885	28504	596.84
黄石市	Huangshi	2310	143943	5604	113.26
十堰市	Shiyan	3850	330712	5543	112.03
宜昌市	Yichang	10187	538429	8843	172.71
襄阳市	Xiangyang	10258	523897	20950	507.36
鄂州市	Ezhou	2456	97386	1685	35.16
荆门市	Jingmen	4116	282827	7118	144.02
孝感市	Xiaogan	6856	375743	3195	63.83
荆州市	Jingzhou	5522	275127	7361	148.93
黄冈市	Huanggang	8546	437211	7160	147.32
咸宁市	Xianning	6755	398331	4376	88.68
随州市	Suizhou	3567	187127	6365	128.78
恩施自治州	Enshi	3515	216204	4034	81.61
仙桃市	Xiantao	1893	76922	1363	28.22
潜江市	Qianjiang	1881	82738	2235	45.22
天门市	Tianmen	2075	94959	1662	34.09
神农架林区	Shennongjia	539	20788	471	9.56

15-10 邮电业务基本情况
BASIC CONDITIONS OF THE POST AND TELECOMMUNICATION SERVICES

指 标		Item	2005	2010	2013	2014	2015
邮电业务总量	**(亿元)**	**Total Volume of Post and Telecommunication Services (100 million yuan)**	**373.63**	**1028.09**	**603.67**	**720.35**	**962.66**
邮政业务总量		Postal Services	23.40	55.71	74.12	98.66	137.41
电信业务总量		Telecommunication Services	350.20	972.38	529.55	621.69	825.25
函件	(亿件)	Letters (100 million pcs)	1.30	1.00	1.05	0.67	0.68
包件	(万件)	Parcels (10 000 pcs)	320.00	210.10	170.20	141.70	105.80
快递业务量	(万件)	Special Express (10 000 pcs)	685.30	5476.60	21991.00	72570.70	50847.30
报刊期发数	(万份)	Newspaper and Magzines Circulation (10 000 pcs)	643.00	55102.50	72770.50	72570.40	70907.1
固定电话用户	(万户)	Fixed telephone subscribers (10 000 subscribers)	1236.00	1026.40	984.00	907.40	872.50
年末城市电话	(万户)	Urban Telephone Subscribers at Year-end (10 000 subscribers)	900.00	670.70	662.90	613.00	632.50
年末农村电话	(万户)	Rural Telephones (10 000 subscribers)	336.00	355.70	321.10	294.40	240.00
年末移动电话用户	(万户)	Mobile Telephone Subscribers at Year-end (10 000 subscribers)	1401.00	3454.70	4416.80	4606.80	4650.60
互联网宽带接入用户	(万户)	Internet Users (10 000 subscribers)	128.00	459.40	813.30	869.70	983.50
邮路总长度(单程)	(公里)	Length of Postal Routes and Rural Delivery (One Way) (km)		57483	57223	161205	62159
邮路线路总条数	(条)	Routes		411	578	718	653
农村投递线路条数	(条)	Highway Routes		4198	3747	3567	3562
农村投递线路长度(单程)	(公里)	Railway Routes(One Way) (km)		194656	206154	207494	205502
邮电通信工具拥有量		Telecommunication Facilities					
移动电话交换机容量	(万户)	Mobile Telephone Swicthboard Capacity (10 000 units)		5862.70	7245.20	8450.70	8748.70
固定长途电话交换机容量	(万路端)	Capacity of Long Distance Telephone Switchborad (circuit)	46.60	49.00	49.10	17.30	17.00
长途光缆线路长度	(万公里)	Length of Long Distance Optical Cable (km)		2.70	2.81	3.03	3.14

注： 邮电业务总量统计口径2011年发生变化，与以前各年份不可比。

Note:The statistic on total volume of post and telecommunication have been reconfigured from 2011.Datas of other year can not compare with the data of 2011.

15-11 邮电通信水平
LEVEL OF POST AND TELECOMMUNICATION SERVICES

指　　标	Item	2005	2010	2012	2013	2014	2015
每百人平均函件量 (件/百人)	Average Number of Letters Mailed Per 100 Persons (unit/100 person)	228.0	174.7	226.6	181.1	114.8	115.5
每百人平均订阅报刊量 (份/百人)	Average Number of Newspaper and Periodicals Subscribed Per 100 Persons (unit/100 person)	977.9	962.7	1166.0	1254.9	1247.8	1211.8
每百人平均包件 (件/百人)	Average Number of Parcels Per 100 Persons (unit/100 person)	5.6	3.4	3.0	2.9	2.4	1.8
电话普及率 (部/百人)	Rate of Popularization of Telephone (unit/100 person)	43.9	78.3	96.2	93.1	94.8	94.4
移动电话普及率 (部/百人)	Rate of Popularization of Mobile Phones (unit/100 person)	23.3	60.4	78.8	76.2	79.2	79.5

主要统计指标解释

铁路营业里程 又称营业长度(包括正式营业和临时营业里程),指办理客货运输业务的铁路正线总长度。凡是全线或部分建成双线及以上的线路,以第一线的实际长度计算;复线、站线、段管线、岔线和特殊用途线以及不计算运费的联络线都不计算营业里程。该指标可以反映铁路运输业基础设施的发展水平,也是计算客货周转量、运输密度和机车车辆运用效率等指标的基础资料。

公路里程指在一定时期内实际达到《公路工程[WTBZ]技术标准JTJ01-88》规定的等级公路,并经公路主管部门正式验收交付使用的公路里程数。包括大中城市的郊区公路以及通过小城镇街道部分的公路里程和桥梁、渡口的长度,不包括大中城市的街道、厂矿、林区生产用道和农业生产用道的里程。两条或多条公路共同经由同一路段,只计算一次,不得重复计算里程长度。该指标可以反映公路建设的发展规模,也是计算运输网密度等指标的基础资料。

内河航道里程 也称内河通航里程,指在一定时期内,能通航运输船舶及排筏的天然河流、湖泊水库、运河及通航渠道的长度。包括全年季节性通航累计三个月以上的航道,不包括仅供零散流放竹、木排的河道。该指标可以反映内河水运网的规模、水平和发展情况。

民用航空航线里程 指民航运输定期班机飞行的航线长度的总和。航线长度按机场之间的距离计算,通常有两种计算方法:一是将每条航线长度相加称为重复计算航线里程;一是将两线或两条以上航线经过同一区段里程,只计算一次航线长度称为不重复计算航线里程。一般常用的是后者,该指标可以确切反映民航运输网的规模,是表明民航事业为国民经济服务和方便人民生活程度的主要指标。

货(客)运量 指在一定时期内,各种运输工具实际运送的货物(旅客)数量。该指标是反映运输业为国民经济和人民生活服务的数量指标,也是制定和检查运输生产计划、研究运输发展规模和速度的重要指标。货运按吨计算,客运按人计算。货物不论运输距离长短、货物类别,均按实际重量统计。旅客不论行程远近或票价多少,均按一人一次客运量统计;半价票、小孩票也按一人统计。

货物(旅客)周转量 指在一定时期内,由各种运输工具运送的货物(旅客)数量与其相应运输距离的乘积之总和。该指标可以反映运输业生产的总成果,也是编制和检查运输生产计划,计算运输效率、劳动生产率以及核算运输单位成本的主要基础资料。计算货物周转量通常按发出站与到达站之间的最短距离,也就是计费距离计算。计算公式为:

货物(旅客)周转量=∑(货物(旅客)运输量×运输距离)

民用汽车拥有量 指报告期末,在公安交通管理部门按照《机动车注册登记工作规范》,已注册登记领有民用车辆牌照的全部汽车数量。汽车拥有量统计的主要分类:根据汽车结构分为载客汽车、载货汽车及其他汽车;根据汽车所有者不同分为个人(私人)汽车、单位汽车;根据汽车的使用性质分为营运汽车、非营运汽车;根据汽车大小规格不同载客汽车分为大型、中型、小型和微型,载货汽车分为重型、中型、轻型和微型。

邮电业务总量 指以价值量形式表现的邮电通信企业为社会提供各类邮电通信服务的总数量。邮电业务量按专业分类包括函件、包件、汇票、报刊发行、邮政快件、特快专递、邮政储蓄、集邮、公众电报、用户电报、传真、长途电话、出租电路、无线寻呼、移动电话、分组交换数据通信、出租代维等。计算方法为各类产品乘以相应的平均单价(不变价)之和,再加上出租电路和设备、代用户维护电话交换机和线路等的服务收入。该指标综合反映了一定时期邮电业务发展的总成果,是研究邮电业务量构成和发展趋势的重要指标。计算公式为:

邮电业务总量=∑(各类邮电业务量×不变单价)+出租代维及其他业务收入

邮政业务总量+电信业务总量

移动电话用户 指通过移动电话交换机进入移动电话网、占用移动电话号码的各类电话用户。包括签约用户和智能网预付费用户。一个移动电话号码统计为一户。

互联网上网人数 指平均每周使用互联网至少1小时的中国公民人数。

本地电话用户 指接入本地电信运营商固定电话网上的电话用户。包括:住宅用户、单位用户、公用电话用户等。按电话用户位置又分为市内电话用户和农村电话用户。1997年以前,"市内电话用户"是指接入县城及县以上城市的电话网上的电话用户;"农村电话用户"是指接入县邮电局农话台及县以下农村电话交换点,以县城为中心(除市话用户外)联通县、乡(镇)、行政村、村民小组的用户。从1997年起,电话用户数分组调整为以用户所在区域划分为"城市电话用户"和"乡村电话用户",与过去的按市内电话和农村电话划分方法不同。而电话用户总数、电话机总部数统计范围不变。

城市电话用户 指直辖市、省辖市、地级市、县级市的市区、市郊区及县城(包括县人民政府所在地的县城关区或行政建制相当于县人民政府所在地的镇)范围内接入局用交换机的电话用户数,包括分布在农村地区的独立工矿区、林区、驻军等电话用户数。

农村电话用户 指按行政区划属于城市范围以外的乡(镇)、村的电话用户数。

住宅电话用户 指安装在居民住宅或农民家里并按照住宅电话用户登记注册和收费的电话用户。包括私人付费、单位付费和按规定免费安装的住宅电话用户。

长途电话交换机容量 指用于接入长途电话网的电话交换机设备的额定容量,包括国际电话交换机容量。

局用交换机容量 指安装在电信运营企业内用于接续本地固定电话的电话交换机容量,包括现用和备用的人工或自动交换机的全部容量。不包括用户交换机容量。

移动电话交换机容量 指移动电话交换机根据一定话务模型和交换机处理能力计算出来的最大同时服务用户的数量。

Explanatory Notes on Main Statistical Indicators

Length of Railways in Operation refers to the total length of the trunk line under passenger and freight transportation (including both full operation and temporary operation). The calculation is based on the actual length of the first line even if this line has a full or partial double track or more tracks, excluding double tracks, station sidings, tracks under the charge of stations, branch lines, special-purpose lines and the non-payable connecting lines. The length of railways in operation is an important indicator to show the development of the infrastructure for the railway transport, and also the essential data to calculate volume of passenger freight transport, traffic density and utilization efficiency of the locomotives and carriages.

Length of Electrified Railways refers to the length of the section of railways in operation in which the power supply lines and other equipment are installed for the running of electrified locomotives. The proportion of the length of electrified railways to the total length of railways in operation is an important indicator to show the modernization of railways.

Automatic-blocking and Semi-automatic-blocking Length of Railways refer to length of railways installed with equipment to perform automatic or manual blocking of trains. Blocking is a spacing technique by which a section of the railway only allows one train to pass at a time in the aim of ensuring the traffic safety. the proportion of automatic/semi-automatic blocking length to the total length of railways in operation is an important indicator to show the modernization of railways.

Length of Highways refers to the length of highways which are built in conformity with the grades specified by the highway engineering standard formulated by the Ministry of Communications, and have been formally checked and accepted by the departments of highways and put into use. The length of highways includes that of the suburb highways at large and medium-sized cities, highways passing through streets at small cities and towns, and also the length of bridges and ferries. It does not include the length of streets in big and medium-sized cities and highways built for the production purpose at factories, mines, forest areas and agricultural areas. If two or more highways go the same section of the way, the length of the section is only calculated for once and no duplication is allowed. The length of highways is an important indicator to show the development of the highway construction and to provide essential information to calculate the transport network density.

Length of Navigable Inland Waterways itis an indicator reflecting the size and development of inland water network, it refers to the length of the natural rivers, lakes, reservoirs, canals, and ditches open to navigation during a given period, which enables the transport by ships and rafts. It includes the channels open to navigation for over an accumulative 3 months in a year, yet this does not include the river courses, which are only used to float odd logs and bamboo rafts. This indicator can reflect the scale, level and development situation of the inland waterway network.

Length of Civil Aviation Routes refers to the length of all routes for regular civil aviation flights. There are usually two ways to calculate the distance between airports connected by the route length: One is to put the length of all air routes together, called duplicated calculation of the length of the routes; the other is not to allow the duplication in calculation when two or more routes passing the same section of aviation routes. The latter is usually used, as it can precisely show the size of the civil aviation network and indicate the extent of civil aviation serving the national economy and the people.

Length of Oil (Gas) Pipelines used as an indicator to show the development, scale and level of the pipeline transportation, it refers to the actual transport distance of oil (or gas) products, and is in general calculated in the length of single pipeline. If the length of the double pipelines and alternate pipeline are included, it is called the extension length of the oil (gas) pipelines, which indicates the actual length of the pipelines built, excluding double pipelines.

Freight (Passenger) Traffic refers to the volume of freight (passenger) transported with various means. Freight transport is calculated in tons and passenger traffic is calculated in the number of persons. Despite the type of freight and traveling distance, the freight transport is calculated in the actual weight of the goods: and despite the traveling distance and ticket price, the passenger traffic is calculated by the principle that one person can be counted only once in one travel. The passengers who travel with a half price ticket or a child ticket is also calculated as one person. The freight (passenger) traffic provides a quantitative measure to show how the transport industry serves the national economy and people, and is also an important indicator for planning the transport industry and for studying the development scale and speed of the transport industry.

Freight (Passenger) Traffic Density refers to the freight (passenger) traffic volume carried by a particular means of transportation during a given period through one kilometer of a specific section of transportation route. The formula is as follows:

Freight (Passenger) traffic density=[freight ton-kilometers (passenger-kilometers)] / (length of route in operation)

Freight (passenger) traffic density reflects the degree of business of freight (passenger) traffic on transportation routes, and therefore provides important information for balancing transport capability, planning construction and upgrading of transport routes and studying the distribution of transport network.

Freight Ton-kilometers (Passenger-kilometers) refer to the sum of the products of the volume of transported cargo (passengers) multiplying by the transport distance. It is an important indicator to reflect the achievement of transportation industry. Normally, the shortest distance between the departure station and the destination station (i.e., the payable distance) is the basis to calculate the freight ton-kilometers. This is an important indicator to show the total results of the transport industry, to prepare and examine the transport plan and to measure the efficiency, the labour productivity and the unit cost of transport.

The formula is as follows:

Freight ton-kilometers (passenger-kilometers) = Σ {freight (passenger) traffic × distance of transportation}

Possession of Civil Motor Vehicles refer to the total numbers of vehicles that are registered and received vehicles license tags according to the Work Standard for Motor Vehicles Registration formulated by transport management office under department of public security at the end of reference period. They are divided into following categories according to the structure of motor vehicles: passenger vehicles, trucks and others; and private vehicles and vehicles for units use according to ownerships; working vehicles and non-working vehicles according to kind of usage; large passenger vehicles, medium passenger vehicles, small passenger vehicles and mini passenger vehicle, heavy trucks, light-heavy trucks, light trucks and mini trucks according to sizes of vehicles.

Business Volume of Post and Telecommunications refers to the total amount of post and telecommunication services, expressed in value terms, provided by the post and telecommunications departments for the society. Post and telecommunication services can be classified as letters, parcels, remittance, issue of newspapers and magazines, fast mail service, express mail service, savings deposits, stamps for collection, public and individual telegraph service, facsimiles, long–distance telephone service, leasing of telephone lines, urban paging service, mobile telephone service, data transfer and transmission, etc. The accounting approach is to multiply the service products of all types with their average unit price (constant price) to get sum of business value, plus income from other services such as leasing of telephone lines and equipment, maintenance of telephone switchboards and lines on behalf of customers. This indicator reflects the overall results of post and telecommunications service during a given period, and is important to study the composition of business service and the development of post and telecommunications service.

The formula is as follows:

Business volume of post and telecommunications= ∑ (Transaction of post and telecommunication service x constant price) + Income from leasing, maintenance and other services = business volume of postal service + business volume of telecommunications service

Subscribers of Wireless Paging Services Wireless paging service refers the service by which telephone users send audio, digital or character signals to persons carrying small–size pagers within the designated areas through wireless paging centers. The page carriers who have registered in paging centers are counted as paging subscribers.

Mobile Telephone Subscribers refer to the persons who own mobile telephone numbers and are connected with the mobile telephone communication network through the mobile telephone switchboards, including contracted subscribers and pre–paid subscribers for intelligent network. One mobile telephone is taken as a subscriber.

Internet Users refer to the number of Chinese citizens who use Internet at least for one hour each week.

Local Telephone Subscribers refer to subscribers that are connected to the local telecommunication service provider through fix line network, including household subscribers, institutional subscribers and public telephones. They are also classified as city subscribers and rural subscribers according to locations. Before 1997, city subscribers referred to those connected to city telephone networks in county towns and cities, while village subscribers referred to those connected to village telephone stations at and below counties. Since 1997, the classification of telephone subscribers was modified on the basis of physical location of the subscribers as urban telephone subscribers and rural telephone subscribers, which is different from the previous classification of categorizing local telephones and rural telephones, while the definition of total subscribers and total number of telephones remain unchanged.

Urban Telephone Subscribers refer to number of telephone subscribers, located at municipalities, cities under the jurisdiction of province, cities at prefecture level, downtown and suburb of city at county level town and county towns (including country towns where county government located, and towns of county level according to the administrative organizational system), that are connected to the public line telephone network, including rural mineral area, forest area, military area.

Rural Telephone Subscribers refer to telephone subscribers, located at counties (towns) and villages outside the range of cities according to administrative jurisdiction.

Household Telephone Subscribers refer to telephone sets installed in the dwelling units of urban or rural residents, and registered as residence subscribers for payment, including 3 types of payment for the service: private payment, public payment and free service.

Capacity of Long Distance Telephone Exchanges refers to the rated capacity of telephone exchanges to connect long distance telephone network, including capacity of international telephone exchanges.

Capacity of Office Telephone Exchanges refers to the capacity (measured in gate) of telephone exchanges installed in the offices of telecommunication service providers for communication between fixed telephones. It includes the capacity of both manual and automatic exchanges in use and for stand–by purpose, excluding the capacity of subscribers exchanges.

Capacity of Mobile Telephone Exchanges refers to the capacity of the maximum services provided to subscribers at one time basing on a certain model and transacting capacity of the mobile telephone exchanges.

16 国内贸易

Domestic Trade

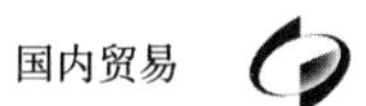

国 内 贸 易

Domestic Trade
2015

社会消费品零售总额	Total Retail Sales of Consumption Goods	14003.24	(亿元)
商品零售额	Retail Sales	12628.22	(亿元)
餐饮收入额	Amount of Food and beverage revenue	1375.02	(亿元)

社会消费品零售总额(亿元)
Total Value of Retail Sales of Consumption Goods(100 million yuan)

年份 year	1995	2000	2005	2009	2010	2011	2012	2013	2014	2015
社会消费品零售总额 Total Value of Retail of Consumption Goods	931.80	1789.35	2985.83	5929.07	7014.45	8363.34	9682.35	11035.94	12449.27	14003.24

16-1 按地区分社会消费品零售总额
TOTAL RETAIL SALES OF CONSUMER GOODS BY REGION

单位:亿元 (100 million yuan)

年份 Year	零售额 Total Retail Sales of Consumer Goods	市 City	县 County	县以下 Below County Level
1978	59.84	19.24	16.56	24.04
1980	81.91	28.98	17.01	35.92
1985	181.17	75.26	31.64	74.17
1986	200.20	81.83	35.54	82.83
1987	234.06	103.21	38.23	92.62
1988	295.80	142.49	42.08	111.23
1989	320.68	159.89	43.78	117.01
1990	326.36	166.44	45.62	114.30
1991	362.26	190.65	50.04	121.57
1992	411.52	221.59	55.04	134.89
1993	521.35	293.82	68.88	158.65
1994	723.75	411.63	101.74	210.38
1995	931.80	539.79	127.76	264.25
1996	1145.73	688.40	130.28	327.05
1997	1345.34	802.37	146.61	396.36
1998	1481.38	896.08	156.07	429.23
1999	1617.14	1019.58	150.95	446.61
2000	1789.35	1128.47	177.65	483.23
2001	1975.16	1267.09	194.21	513.86
2002	2129.38	1429.83	200.69	498.86
2003	2358.69	1603.34	222.86	587.66
2004	2619.47	1819.80	246.21	277.44
2005	2985.83	2081.31	279.43	625.09
2006	3461.09	2430.05	325.66	705.38
2007	4115.78	2889.08	393.38	833.33
2008	5109.74	3587.49	491.44	1030.80
2009	5929.07	4128.16	586.81	1213.45
2010	7014.45	(城镇)5937.80	(城区)5030.80	(乡村)1076.10
2011	8363.34	(城镇)7003.70	(城区)5954.80	(乡村)1271.50
2012	9682.35	(城镇)8112.60	(城区)6873.80	(乡村)1449.90
2013	11035.94	(城镇)9163.80	(城区)7682.40	(乡村)1722.10
2014	12449.27	(城镇)10494.82	(城区)8396.70	(乡村)1954.45
2015	14003.24	(城镇)11775.38	(城区)9412.84	(乡村)2227.85

注：1.1996年及以后社会消费品零售总额及各分组指标中不含售给城乡居民生活用住房的零售额。
2.2004、2008年为经普数据，2005-2007年为按国家统计局制定的修订方法修订数据，1993-2003年原则根据原各年环比发展速度和2004年经济普查数据调整。
3.2010年起采用国家新制定的城乡划分标准:城镇(其中:城区)、乡村

Notes:a)Since 1996, the residential house was exclued in the total retail sales of consumer goods and all the targets by groups.
b)The figures of 2004 and 2008 were from general economic Survey, that of the 2005-2007 were from statistics according to the reqirment of general economic survey; while the figures of 1993-2003 were from each year's indices (previous year =100) and readjusted according to the data of general economic survey.
c)Since 2010, a new towm and country division national standard is applied:town(including urban area), country.

16-2 分市、州社会消费品零售总额
TOTAL RETAIL SALES OF CONSUMER GOODS BY DISTRICT

单位:亿元 (100 million yuan)

地区	Region	2008	2009	2010	2011	2012	2013	2014	2015
全省	**Province**	**5109.74**	**5929.07**	**7014.45**	**8363.34**	**9682.35**	**11035.94**	**12449.27**	**14003.24**
武汉	Wuhan	1895.89	2164.09	2570.40	3031.79	3467.37	3916.60	4369.32	5102.24
黄石	Huangshi	221.60	256.09	301.63	355.05	413.50	468.86	519.71	582.36
十堰	Shiyan	217.17	254.25	308.88	364.18	424.80	491.51	548.65	639.41
宜昌	Yichang	399.41	470.41	552.72	656.00	766.19	881.93	964.53	1089.47
襄阳	Xiangyang	425.01	500.56	613.34	721.51	839.51	966.31	1030.57	1165.10
鄂州	Ezhou	107.89	126.68	135.55	159.68	182.20	208.68	230.28	261.95
荆门	Jingmen	194.26	228.82	263.08	311.25	362.85	414.68	451.78	541.43
孝感	Xiaogan	278.18	326.90	388.77	459.70	535.50	608.68	689.33	797.14
荆州	Jingzhou	381.19	445.42	505.34	595.66	688.36	781.36	831.44	946.14
黄冈	Huanggang	292.33	340.07	408.71	482.10	559.37	635.02	715.65	880.91
咸宁	Xianning	140.72	165.88	209.63	247.89	289.54	330.58	361.77	401.04
随州	Suizhou	156.67	182.05	215.21	254.09	293.51	333.86	354.37	399.57
恩施	Enshi	97.49	114.04	136.76	161.65	188.82	218.28	243.55	445.97
仙桃	Xiantao	108.87	127.87	146.79	172.64	200.81	229.00	233.58	266.17
潜江	Qianjiang	74.40	86.36	101.13	117.83	137.36	156.31	150.19	186.14
天门	Tianmen	115.42	135.21	151.57	179.04	206.91	237.50	231.05	258.90
神农架	Shennongjia	3.25	3.72	4.38	5.14	5.92	6.75	7.52	13.54

注：1.本表各市、州数据包含了"其他"部分的全口径数据；
2.2008年以前的全省的数据根据经济普查的结果进行了调整。
Notes:a)"Others " was included in the total retail sales of consumer goods in the form.
b)Before 2008,Total was adjusted accoding to the economic census data.

16-3 批发和零售业连锁经营情况
BASIC CONDITIONS OF WHOLESALES, RETAIL SALES, CATERING CHAIN STORES INDUSTRIES

指标名称	Item	合计 Total		直营店 Direct Sales Store		加盟店 League Store	
		2014	2015	2014	2015	2014	2015
一、门店总数 (个)	Number of Stores (unit)	5747	7765	5437	6808	310	957
其中:批发业 (个)	Number of Stores (unit)	488	517	488	506		11
零售业 (个)	Number of Stores (unit)	5259	7248	4949	6302	310	946
二、营业面积 (百平方米)	Floor Space of Business (100 sq.m)	71672	71820	71296	70911	376	908
其中:批发业 (百平方米)	Floor Space of Business (100 sq.m)	2760	2807	2760	2807		
零售业 (百平方米)	Floor Space of Business (100 sq.m)	68912	69013	68536	68105	376	908
三、从业人员 (人)	Person Engaged (person)	138436	136590	136287	132061	2149	4529
其中:批发业 (人)	Person Engaged (person)	11015	10473	11015	10413		60
零售业 (人)	Person Engaged (person)	127421	126117	125272	121648	2149	4469
四、商品购进总额 (亿元)	Total Value of Commodities Purchaesd (100 000 000 yuan)	1686.14	1646.21	1684.24	1613.28	1.90	32.93
#统一配送商品购进额	#Total Purchasing Value	1214.18	1178.44	1212.82	1151.48	1.36	26.96
#自有配送中心配送商品购进额	#Commodities Purchased From Dispatching Center	935.15	961.80	934.27	935.39	0.88	26.41
#非自有配送中心配送商品购进额	#Commodities Purchased From Nondispatching Center	86.32	54.80	86.05	54.68	0.28	0.12
五、商品销售额 (亿元)	Sales Amount (100 000 000 yuan)	1863.89	1882.47	1861.63	1843.67	2.26	38.80
#零售额	#Retail Sales	1590.47	1584.18	1588.40	1554.24	2.07	29.94

16-4 住宿和餐饮业连锁经营情况
BASIC CONDITIONS OF HOTELS AND CATERING SERVICES

指标名称	Item	合计 Total		直营店 Direct Sales Store		加盟店 League Store	
		2014	2015	2014	2015	2014	2015
一、门店总数 (个)	Number of Stores (unit)	670	828	669	826	1	2
二、营业面积 (百平方米)	Floor Space of Business (100 sq.m)	4483	3650	4483	3640		10
三、从业人员 (人)	Person Engaged (person)	35842	36999	35815	36899	27	100
四、客房数 (间)	Number of Hotel Rooms (unit)	6642	6590	6580	6528	62	62
五、床位数 (个)	Number of Beds (unit)	8649	8470	8551	8372	98	98
六、餐位数 (位)	Restaurant Seating Capacity (unit)	133577	135738	133577	135638		100
七、商品购进总额 (万元)	Total Value of Commodities Purchaesd (10 000 yuan)	100515	108948	100512	108746	3	202
#统一配送商品购进额	#Total Purchasing Value	83292	90436	83290	90434	3	2
#自有配送中心配送商品购进额	#Commodities Purchased From Dispatching Center	19303	18933	19300	18930	3	2
#非自有配送中心配送商品购进额	#Commodities Purchased From Nondispatching Center	39173	39557	39173	39557		
八、营业额 (万元)	Turnover (10 000 yuan)	536433	570703	536179	570164	255	539
#餐费收入	Meals Revenue	515611	552447	515611	552147		300
#商品销售额	Merchandise Sales	519092	556019	519090	555718	3	302

16-5 限额以上批发零售业基本情况(2015)
BASIC CONDITIONS OF ENTERPRISES ABOVE DESIGNATED SIZE IN WHOLESALES AND RETAILSALES TRADE (2015)

(按登记注册类型分)

(Grouped by Registration Type)

登记注册类型	Type of Registration	法人企业数(个) Number of Corperations (unit)	年末从业人数(人) Person Engaged at Year-end (person)	零售营业面积(万平方米) Floor Space of Retail Business (10 000 sq.m)
总 计	**Total**	**8178**	**528683**	**2323.61**
一、批发业	**Wholesales**	**3039**	**194098**	**595.21**
按登记注册类型分组	Grouped by Registration Type			
内资	**Domestic Funded Enterprises**	**2995**	**177382**	**520.06**
国有	State-owned Enterprises	94	14748	25.43
集体	Collective-owned Enterprises	14	815	1.91
股份合作	Cooperative Enterprises	5	201	0.51
联营企业	Joint Ownership Enterprises			
国有联营	State Joint Ownership Enterprises			
集体联营	Collective Joint Ownership Enterprises			
国有与集体联营	Joint State-collective Enterprises			
其他联营	Other Joint Ownership Enterprises			
有限责任公司	Limited Liability Corporations	1192	65462	184.34
国有独资公司	State Sole Funded Corporations	30	8560	11.65
其他有限责任公司	Other Limited Liability Corporations	1162	56902	172.69
股份有限公司	Share-holding Corporations Ltd.	73	43256	60.41
私营企业	Private Enterprises	1498	45795	226.32
私营独资	Private-funded Enterprises	67	1149	8.39
私营合伙	Private Partnership Enterprises			
私营有限责任公司	Private Limited Liability Corporations	1405	43627	210.35
私营股份有限公司	Private Share-holding Corporations Ltd.	26	1019	7.58
其他	Other Enterprises	119	7105	21.13
港澳台商投资企业	**Enterprises with Funds from Hongkong, Macao and Taiwan**	**21**	**5172**	**4.64**
合资经营	Joint-venture Enterprises	6	554	0.06
合作经营	Cooperative Enterprises			
独资经营	Enterprises with Sole Investment	14	3758	4.58
独资股份有限公司	Sole Investment Co. Ltd. With Investment	1	860	
外商投资企业	**Foreign Funded Enterprises**	**23**	**11544**	**70.51**
中外合资经营	Sino-foreign Joint-venture Enterprises	11	1886	0.23
外资企业	Enterprises with Sole Foreign Investment	8	5480	0.28
外商投资股份有限公司	Share-holding Co. Ltd. with Foreign Investment	1	14	
其他外资企业	Other Enterprises with Sole Foreign Investment	3	4164	70.00

16-5 续表 continued

登记注册类型	Type of Registration	法人企业数(个) Number of Corperations (unit)	年末从业人数(人) Person Engaged at Year-end (person)	零售营业面积(万平方米) Floor Space of Retail Business (10 000 sq.m)
二、零售业	**Retail Trade**	**5139**	**334585**	**1728.39**
按登记注册类型分组	Grouped by Registration Type			
内资	**Domestic Funded Enterprises**	**5086**	**312834**	**1647.33**
国有	State-owned Enterprises	108	8430	18.70
集体	Collective-owned Enterprises	99	11626	57.34
股份合作	Cooperative Enterprises	8	319	2.61
联营企业	Joint Ownership Enterprises	3	143	0.22
国有联营	State Joint Ownership Enterprises			
集体联营	Collective Joint Ownership Enterprises			
国有与集体联营	Joint State-collective Enterprises	2	129	0.16
其他联营	Other Joint Ownership Enterprises	1	14	0.06
有限责任公司	Limited Liability Corporations	1851	129144	637.60
国有独资公司	State Sole Funded Corporations	19	1380	3.83
其他有限责任公司	Other Limited Liability Corporations	1832	127764	633.76
股份有限公司	Share-holding Corporations Ltd.	121	55390	498.71
私营企业	Private Enterprises	2806	104652	424.82
私营独资	Private-funded Enterprises	486	8989	48.81
私营合伙	Private Partnership Enterprises	25	686	2.02
私营有限责任公司	Private Limited Liability Corporations	2249	92242	360.60
私营股份有限公司	Private Share-holding Corporations Ltd.	46	2735	13.39
其他	Other Enterprises	90	3130	7.32
港澳台商投资企业	**Enterprises with Funds from Hongkong, Macao and Taiwan**	**30**	**9383**	**26.3475**
合资经营	Joint-venture Enterprises	7	855	1.68
合作经营	Cooperative Enterprises			
独资经营	Enterprises with Sole Investment	23	8528	24.67
独资股份有限公司	Sole Investment Co. Ltd. With Investment			
外商投资企业	**Foreign Funded Enterprises**	**23**	**12368**	**54.72**
中外合资经营	Sino-foreign Joint-venture Enterprises	9	2550	11.83
外资企业	Enterprises with Sole Foreign Investment	12	9549	41.38
外商投资股份有限公司	Share-holding Co. Ltd. with Foreign Investment	1	207	1.30
其他外资企业	Other Enterprises with Sole Foreign Investment	1	62	0.20

16-6 限额以上批发零售业基本情况(2015)
BASIC CONDITIONS OF ENTERPRISES ABOVE DESIGNATED SIZE IN WHOLESALES AND RETAILSALES TRADE (2015)

(按国民经济行业分)

(Grouped by Sector)

项 目	Item	法人企业数(个) Number of Corperations (unit)	年末从业人数(人) Person Engaged at Year-end (person)	零售营业面积(万平方米) Floor Space of Retail Business (10 000 sq.m)
总 计	**Total**	**8178**	**528683**	**2323.61**
一、批发业	**Wholesales**	**3039**	**194098**	**595.21**
农、林、牧产品批发业	Wholesales of Agriculture, Forestry and Animal Husbandry Products	321	13515	104.48
食品、饮料及烟草制品批发业	Wholesales of Foods, Beverage and Tobacco	584	54948	123.28
米、面制品及食用油批发业	Wholesales of Rice, Noodles and Edible Oil	101	4342	15.23
烟草制品批发业	Wholesales of Tobacco	39	11696	2.18
纺织、服装及日用品批发业	Wholesales of Textile Products, Garments and Daily Used Articles	181	12294	78.90
服装批发业	Wholesales of Garments	54	4988	72.34
家用电器批发业	Wholesales of Home Appliances	37	2870	0.90
文化、体育用品及器材批发业	Wholesales of Cultural and Sports Goods and Equipments	47	7018	14.88
医药及医疗器材批发业	Wholesales of Medicnes and Medical Appliances	286	33624	29.24
矿产品、建材及化工产品批发业	Wholesales of Mineral Products, Building Materials and Chemical Products	1024	55354	184.25
煤炭及制品批发业	Wholesales of Coal and Coal-made Products	145	3418	22.75
石油及制品批发业	Wholesales of Petroleum Products	107	31185	73.66
非金属矿及制品批发	Wholesales of Non-metal and Non-metal Mines	41	920	4.92
金属及金属矿批发业	Wholesales of Metal and Metal Mines	271	6338	22.22
建材批发业	Wholesales of Construction Materials	175	4172	24.17
化肥批发业	Wholesales of Chemical Fertilizers	113	5425	21.58
机械设备、五金交电及电子产品批发	Wholesales of Machinery Equipment, Hardware, Transport and Electronic Products	496	14707	37.85
汽车批发业	Wholesales of Cars	85	3722	9.23
计算机、软件及辅助设备批发业	Wholesales of Computers, Softwares and Assisted Equipments	25	1504	0.11
贸易经纪与代理	Trade Agent	9	202	0.04
其他批发业	Other Wholesales	91	2436	22.30
二、零售业	**Retail Sales**	**5139**	**334585**	**1728.39**
综合零售业	Retail Sales of Department	949	151746	948.26
百货零售业	Department Stores	456	56808	576.71
超级市场零售业	Supermarkets	364	86419	341.53
食品、饮料及烟草制品专门零售业	Monopoly Retail of Foods, Beverage and Tobacco	604	26539	62.88
纺织、服装及日用品专门零售业	Monopoly Retail of Textile, Garments,and Daily Used Articles	318	20466	67.84
服装零售业	Retail Sales of Garments	180	12837	49.39
文化、体育用品及器材专门零售业	Monopoly Retail of Cultural, Sports Products and Equipments	238	10577	35.65
体育用品零售业	Retail Sales of Sports Products	10	142	1.68
图书报刊零售业	Retail Sales of Books, Newspapers and Periodicals	78	4163	9.40
医药及医疗器材专门零售业	Monopoly Retail of Medicine and Medical Appliances	297	21236	51.50
药品零售业	Retail Sales of Medicine	259	20124	50.19
汽车、摩托车、燃料及零配件专门	Monopoly Retail of Cars, and Motorcars Parts	1336	62644	289.81
汽车零售业	Retail Sales of Cars	1015	48363	233.09
机动车燃料零售业	Retail Sales of Motor Vehicles Fuels	131	10607	44.47
家用电器及电子产品专门零售业	Monopoly Retail of Home Appliances and Electronic Products	780	23604	135.29
家用视听设备零售业	Retail Sales of Home Audio-visual Equipment	170	5165	21.42
计算机、软件及辅助设备零售业	Retail Sales of Computers, Softwares and Assisted Equipments	178	3786	8.09
通讯设备零售业	Retail Sales of Communication Equipments	44	1591	3.43
五金、家具及室内装修材料专门零售业	Monopoly Retail of Hardware, Furnitures and Decorative Materials	432	10465	103.96
货摊、无店铺及其他零售业	Retail Sales of Stalls、Storeless and Others	185	7308	33.19
互联网零售	Retail Sales of Internet	32	3109	3.43

16-7 限额以上住宿和餐饮业基本情况(2015)
BASIC CONDITIONS OF ENTERPRISES ABOVE DESIGNATED SIZE IN HOTELS AND CATERING SERVICES (2015)

(按登记注册类型分)

(Grouped by Registeration Type)

项　目	Item	法人企业数(个) Number of Corperations (unit)	年末从业人数(人) Person Engaged at Year-end (person)	餐饮营业面积(万平方米) Floor Space of Catering Business (10 000 sq.m)
一、住宿业	**Hotel Trade**	**812**	**63914**	**177.07**
按登记注册类型分组	**Grouped by Registration Type**			
内资	**Domestic Funded Enterprises**	**788**	**59319**	**172.11**
国有	State-owned Enterprises	50	5389	12.69
集体	Collective-owned Enterprises	9	991	1.84
股份合作	Cooperative Enterprises	2	86	0.38
联营企业	Joint Ownership Enterprises			
国有联营	State Joint Ownership Enterprises			
集体联营	Collective Joint Ownership Enterprises			
国有与集体联营	Joint State-collective Enterprises			
其他联营	Other Joint Ownership Enterprises			
有限责任公司	Limited Liability Corporations	304	27225	72.88
国有独资公司	State Sole Funded Corporations	10	1717	2.52
其他有限责任公司	Other Limited Liability Corporations	294	25508	70.36
股份有限公司	Share-holding Corporations Ltd.	17	2421	5.14
私营企业	Private Enterprises	388	22741	77.62
私营独资	Private-funded Enterprises	43	1532	6.13
私营合伙	Private Partnership Enterprises	10	419	2.40
私营有限责任公司	Private Limited Liability Corporations	318	19740	63.38
私营股份有限公司	Private Share-holding Corporations Ltd.	17	1050	5.71
其他	Other Enterprises	18	466	1.56
港澳台商投资企业	Enterprises with Funds from Hongkong, Macao and Taiwan	19	4072	3.92
合资经营	Joint-venture Enterprises	4	846	0.63
合作经营	Cooperative Enterprises	2	342	0.54
独资经营	Enterprises with Sole Investment	10	2392	2.14
投资股份有限公司	Share-holding Co. Ltd. With Investment	3	492	0.61
外商投资企业	Foreign Funded Enterprises	5	523	1.04
中外合资经营	Sino-foreign Joint-venture Enterprises	1	235	0.20
中外合作经营	Sino-foreign Cooperative Enterprises			
外资企业	Enterprises with Sole Foreign Investment	3	256	0.54
外商投资股份有限公司	Share-holding Co. Ltd. with Foreign Investment	1	32	0.30
二、餐饮业	**Catering Trade**	**1667**	**98182**	**335.25**
按登记注册类型分组	**Grouped by Registration Type**			
内资	**Domestic Funded Enterprises**	**1643**	**85532**	**317.85**
国有	State-owned Enterprises	18	932	2.44
集体	Collective-owned Enterprises	5	235	1.22
股份合作	Cooperative Enterprises	2	226	0.24
联营企业	Joint Ownership Enterprises	1		0.50
国有联营	State Joint Ownership Enterprises			
集体联营	Collective Joint Ownership Enterprises	1		0.50
国有与集体联营	Joint State-collective Enterprises			
其他联营	Other Joint Ownership Enterprises			
有限责任公司	Limited Liability Corporations	528	39062	125.23
国有独资公司	State Sole Funded Corporations	7	1563	1.02
其他有限责任公司	Other Limited Liability Corporations	521	37499	124.21
股份有限公司	Share-holding Corporations Ltd.	16	1154	3.10
私营企业	Private Enterprises	1006	42107	175.62
私营独资	Private-funded Enterprises	308	7613	38.86
私营合伙	Private Partnership Enterprises	8	280	1.30
私营有限责任公司	Private Limited Liability Corporations	669	32775	130.47
私营股份有限公司	Private Share-holding Corporations Ltd.	21	1439	4.99
其他	Other Enterprises	67	1816	9.51
港澳台商投资企业	**Enterprises with Funds from Hongkong, Macao and Taiwan**	**14**	**3328**	**3.76**
合资经营	Joint-venture Enterprises	5	420	0.84
合作经营	Cooperative Enterprises			
独资经营	Enterprises with Sole Investment	9	2908	2.93
投资股份有限公司	Share-holding Co. Ltd. With Investment			
外商投资企业	**Foreign Funded Enterprises**	**10**	**9322**	**13.64**
中外合资经营	Sino-foreign Joint-venture Enterprises	1	420	0.60
外资企业	Enterprises with Sole Foreign Investment	9	8902	13.04
外商投资股份有限公司	Share-holding Co. Ltd. with Foreign Investment			
其他外商投资企业	Other Enterprises with Sole Foreign Investment			

16-8 限额以上住宿和餐饮业基本情况(2015)
BASIC CONDITIONS OF ENTERPRISES ABOVE DESIGNATED SIZE IN HOTELS AND CATERING SERVICES (2015)

(按国民经济行业分)

(Grouped by Sector)

行　业	Item	法人企业数 (个) Number of Corperations (unit)	年末从业人数(人) Person Engaged at Year-end (person)	餐饮营业面积 (万平方米) Floor Space of Catering Business (10 000 sq.m)
总　计	**Total**	**2479**	**162096**	**512.32**
一、住宿业	**Hotel**	**812**	**63914**	**177.07**
按国民经济行业分组	Grouped by Sector			
旅游饭店	Tourist Hotel	418	45483	115.64
一般旅馆	Regular Hotel	374	17067	56.70
其他住宿服务	Other Accomodation Service	20	1364	4.73
二、餐饮业	**Catering**	**1667**	**98182**	**335.25**
按国民经济行业分组	Grouped by Sector			
正餐服务业	Dinner	1626	85431	317.30
快餐服务业	Fast Food	24	9517	14.17
饮料及冷饮服务业	Beverage and Cold Drink Services	9	2220	1.97
其他餐饮服务业	Others	8	1014	1.81

16-9 限额以上住宿和餐饮业经营情况(2015)
BUSINESS OF ENTERPRISES ABOVE DESIGNATED SIZE OF HOTELS AND CATERING SERVICES (2015)

(按国民经济行业分)
(Grouped by Sector)

行业	Item	营业额(亿元) Turnover (100 million yuan)	客房收入 Revnue from Guest Rooms	餐费收入 Revenue from Catering Bills	商品销售收入 Revenue from Commodity Sales	其他收入 Revenue from Others	年末住宿和餐饮企业拥有床位数(万个) Number of Beds owned by Hotels and Catering Enterprises at Year-end (10 000 units)	年末住宿和餐饮企业拥有餐位数(万位) Number of Seats owned by Hotels and Catering Enterprises at Year-end (10 000 units)
总计	**Total**	**387.16**	**81.95**	**275.72**	**17.40**	**12.09**	**32.81**	**102.39**
一、住宿业	**Hotel**	**119.37**	**60.52**	**45.79**	**5.14**	**7.92**	**25.29**	**25.43**
按国民经济行业分组	Grouped by Sector							
旅游饭店	Tourist Hotel	79.64	38.50	32.34	2.23	6.57	18.86	17.79
一般旅馆	Regular Hotel	35.65	20.61	12.44	1.39	1.21	6.05	7.02
其他住宿服务	Other Accomodation Service	4.08	1.41	1.01	1.52	0.14	0.38	0.62
二、餐饮业	**Catering**	**267.78**	**21.43**	**229.94**	**12.25**	**4.17**	**7.53**	**76.96**
按国民经济行业分组	Grouped by Sector							
正餐服务业	Dinner	221.17	21.28	183.62	12.11	4.16	7.47	70.92
快餐服务业	Fast Food	35.17	0.04	35.06	0.07	0.00	0.02	4.57
饮料及冷饮服务业	Beverage and Cold Drink Services	5.81	0.02	5.73	0.06		0.01	1.14
其他餐饮服务业	Others	5.63	0.08	5.53	0.01	0.01	0.03	0.34

16-10 限额以上住宿和餐饮业经营情况(2015)

(按登记注册类型分)

单位:亿元

项　目	Item	营业额 Turnover	客房收入 Revnue from Guest Rooms
总　计	**Total**	**387.16**	**81.95**
一、住宿业	**Hotels**	**119.37**	**60.52**
按登记注册类型分组	**Grouped by Registration Type**		
内资	**Domestic Funded Enterprises**	**109.76**	**55.12**
国有	State-Owned Enterprises	6.84	3.54
集体	Collective-owned Enterprises	1.82	0.81
股份合作	Cooperative Enterprises	0.09	0.03
联营企业	Joint Ownership Enterprises		
国有联营	State Joint Ownership Enterprises		
集体联营	Collective Joint Ownership Enterprises		
国有与集体联营	Joint State-collective Enterprises		
其他联营	Other Joint Ownership Enterprises		
有限责任公司	Limited Liability Corporations	47.67	24.86
国有独资公司	State Sole Funded Corporations	5.33	1.50
其他有限责任公司	Other Limited Liability Corporations	42.33	23.36
股份有限公司	Share-holding Corporations Ltd.	4.00	1.82
私营企业	Private Enterprises	46.83	23.03
私营独资	Private-funded Enterprises	6.19	3.37
私营合伙	Private Partnership Enterprises	0.82	0.30
私营有限责任公司	Private Limited Liability Corporations	38.31	18.72
私营股份有限公司	Private Share-holding Corporations Ltd.	1.51	0.64
其他	Other Enterprises	2.52	1.03
港澳台商投资企业	**Enterprises with Funds from Hongkong, Macao and Taiwan**	8.94	5.04
合资经营	Joint-venture Enterprises	2.02	1.01
合作经营	Cooperative Enterprises	0.97	0.67
独资经营	Enterprises with Sole Investment	4.88	2.70
投资股份有限公司	Share-holding Co. Ltd. With Investment	1.07	0.67
外商投资企业	**Foreign Funded Enterprises**	**0.68**	**0.35**
中外合资经营	Sino-Foreign Joint-venture Enterprises	0.31	0.14
外资企业	Enterprises with Sole Foreign Investment	0.34	0.19
外商投资股份有限公司	Share-holding Co. Ltd. with Foreign Investment	0.03	0.03
其他外商投资企业	Other Foreign Founded Enterprises		
二、餐饮业	**Catering Trade**	**267.78**	**21.43**
按登记注册类型分组	**Grouped by Registration Type**		
内资	**Domestic Funded Enterprises**	**225.33**	**21.19**
国有	State-Owned Enterprises	2.20	0.39
集体	Collective-owned Enterprises	0.85	0.06
股份合作	Cooperative Enterprises	0.25	0.04
联营企业	Joint Ownership Enterprises	0.58	
国有联营	State Joint Ownership Enterprises		
集体联营	Collective Joint Ownership Enterprises	0.58	
国有与集体联营	Joint State-collective Enterprises		
其他联营	Other Joint Ownership Enterprises		
有限责任公司	Limited Liability Corporations	107.40	9.28
国有独资公司	State Sole Funded Corporations	1.80	0.15
其他有限责任公司	Other Limited Liability Corporations	105.60	9.12
股份有限公司	Share-holding Corporations Ltd.	2.05	0.18
私营企业	Private Enterprises	106.08	10.90
私营独资	Private-funded Enterprises	30.25	2.29
私营合伙	Private Partnership Enterprises	0.43	0.09
私营有限责任公司	Private Limited Liability Corporations	71.83	8.20
私营股份有限公司	Private Share-holding Corporations Ltd.	3.57	0.31
其他	Other Enterprises	5.92	0.33
港澳台商投资企业	**Enterprises with Funds from Hongkong, Macao and Taiwan**	**8.60**	**0.11**
合资经营	Joint-venture Enterprises	0.57	0.03
合作经营	Cooperative Enterprises		
独资经营	Enterprises with Sole Investment	8.03	0.08
投资股份有限公司	Share-holding Co. Ltd. With Investment		
外商投资企业	**Foreign Funded Enterprises**	**33.85**	**0.13**
中外合资经营	Sino-Foreign Joint-venture Enterprises	0.59	
外资企业	Enterprises with Sole Foreign Investment	33.26	0.13
外商投资股份有限公司	Share-holding Co. Ltd. with Foreign Investment		
其他外商投资企业	Other Foreign Funded Enterprises		

BUSINESS OF ENTERPRISES ABOVE DESIGNATED SIZE OF HOTELS AND CATERING SERVICES (2015)

(Grouped by Registeration Type)

(100 million yuan)

餐费收入 Revenue from Catering Bills	商品销售收入 Revenue from Commodity Sales	其他收入 Revenue from Others	年末床位数 (万个) Number of Beds at Year-end (10 000 units)	年末餐位数 (万位) Number of Seats at Year-end (10 000 units)
275.72	**17.40**	**12.09**	**32.81**	**102.39**
45.79	**5.14**	**7.92**	**25.29**	**25.43**
42.38	**5.07**	**7.18**	**24.50**	**24.45**
2.67	0.16	0.46	1.20	2.13
0.78	0.06	0.16	0.15	0.43
0.05	0.00	0.01	0.02	0.03
16.51	1.55	4.74	15.27	10.33
2.04	0.27	1.52	0.39	0.62
14.48	1.28	3.22	14.88	9.72
1.58	0.23	0.36	0.43	0.86
19.35	3.01	1.44	7.26	10.35
2.35	0.43	0.03	0.52	0.68
0.47	0.05		0.13	0.24
15.77	2.49	1.33	6.25	8.70
0.76	0.04	0.07	0.37	0.73
1.43	0.04	0.01	0.17	0.32
3.16	0.07	0.67	0.66	0.77
0.86	0.01	0.14	0.15	0.18
0.29		0.01	0.06	0.08
1.64	0.04	0.49	0.36	0.41
0.37	0.01	0.02	0.09	0.10
0.25	**0.01**	**0.07**	**0.12**	**0.21**
0.11	0.00	0.06	0.03	0.08
0.14	0.01	0.01	0.07	0.13
		0.01	0.02	0.00
229.94	**12.25**	**4.17**	**7.53**	**76.96**
188.02	**12.19**	**3.93**	**7.41**	**71.19**
1.64	0.14	0.02	0.17	0.63
0.78	0.00	0.01	0.05	0.56
0.20			0.02	0.09
0.39	0.19			0.40
0.39	0.19			0.40
89.19	6.20	2.74	3.40	32.07
1.25	0.39	0.00	0.07	0.67
87.94	5.81	2.73	3.34	31.40
1.72	0.14	0.01	0.11	0.73
89.11	4.95	1.13	3.52	34.67
25.88	1.76	0.33	0.61	8.21
0.33	0.00	0.00	0.02	0.30
59.97	2.90	0.76	2.80	25.21
2.93	0.29	0.04	0.08	0.94
4.99	0.56	0.03	0.15	2.05
8.24	**0.05**	**0.20**	**0.07**	**1.63**
0.36	0.01	0.18	0.05	0.19
7.89	0.05	0.02	0.02	1.44
33.68	**0.00**	**0.04**	**0.05**	**4.14**
0.59				0.20
33.09	0.00	0.04	0.05	3.94

16-11 限额以上批发和零售业商品购、销、存总额(2015)
TOTAL PURCHASES, SALES AND STOCK OF ENTERPRISES ABOVE DESIGNATED SIZE OF WHOLESALE AND RETAIL TRADES(2015)

(按登记注册类型分)

(Grouped by Registeration Type)

单位:亿元 (100 million yuan)

项目	Item	购进总额 Total Purchasing Value	销售总额 Total Sales Value	批发 Whole-sales	零售 Retail Sales	年末库存总额 Total Value of Inventory at Year-end
总计	**Total**	**15199.77**	**16659.26**	**10262.87**	**6396.39**	**1681.09**
一、批发业	**Wholesales**	**10001.01**	**10895.90**	**9891.99**	**1003.91**	**1039.91**
按登记注册类型分组	**Grouped by Registration Type**					
内资	Domestic Funded Enterprises	8742.07	9355.11	8477.05	878.05	989.69
国有	State-owned Enterprises	633.61	810.84	787.15	23.70	222.58
集体	Collective-owned Enterprises	12.07	12.66	11.60	1.06	1.22
股份合作	Cooperative Enterprises	2.37	2.40	1.86	0.54	0.10
联营企业	Joint Ownership Enterprises					
国有联营	State Joint Ownership Enterprises					
集体联营	Collective Joint Ownership Enterprises					
国有与集体联营	Joint State-collective Enterprises					
其他联营	Other Joint Ownership Enterprises					
有限责任公司	Limited Liability Corporations	4926.87	5143.28	4782.26	361.02	561.96
国有独资公司	State Sole Funded Corporations	1940.87	2008.73	1987.95	20.77	25.09
其他有限责任公司	Other Limited Liability Corporations	2986.00	3134.56	2794.31	340.25	536.87
股份有限公司	Share-holding Corporations Ltd.	1830.15	1942.37	1637.08	305.29	117.43
私营企业	Private Enterprises	1271.21	1367.30	1201.98	165.32	83.63
私营独资	Private-funded Enterprises	33.12	37.42	28.52	8.90	0.99
私营合伙	Private Partnership Enterprises					
私营有限责任公司	Private Limited Liability Corporations	1206.72	1295.12	1143.27	151.84	79.40
私营股份有限公司	Private Share-holding Corporations Ltd.	31.37	34.76	30.18	4.58	3.24
其他	Other Enterprises	65.79	76.25	55.13	21.11	2.78
港澳台商投资企业	**Enterprises with Funds from Hongkong, Macao and Taiwan**	**272.90**	**303.91**	**242.77**	**61.14**	**11.56**
合资经营	Joint-venture Enterprises	16.60	19.60	16.59	3.01	2.26
合作经营	Cooperative Enterprises					
独资经营	Enterprises with Sole Investment	243.44	270.51	212.39	58.13	8.89
投资股份有限公司	Share-holding Co. Ltd. With Investment	12.87	13.79	13.79		0.42
外商投资企业	**Foreign Funded Enterprises**	**986.03**	**1236.89**	**1172.17**	**64.72**	**38.66**
中外合资经营	Sino-foreign Joint-venture Enterprises	763.00	928.63	923.73	4.90	34.46
外资企业	Enterprises with Sole Foreign Investment	164.42	238.98	238.54	0.45	3.65
外商投资股份有限公司	Share-holding Co. Ltd. with Foreign Investment	0.72	0.95	0.95		
其它外商投资企业	Other Foreign Funded Enterprises	57.89	68.33	8.95	59.38	0.54
二、零售业	**Retail Trade**	**5198.75**	**5763.36**	**370.88**	**5392.48**	**641.18**
按登记注册类型分组	**Grouped by Registration Type**					
内资	**Domestic Funded Enterprises**	**4964.91**	**5481.92**	**360.42**	**5121.50**	**611.22**
国有	State-owned Enterprises	282.75	319.94	41.13	278.81	11.14
集体	Collective-owned Enterprises	178.52	186.30	11.90	174.41	12.00
股份合作	Cooperative Enterprises	4.29	4.36	0.09	4.27	0.23
联营企业	Joint Ownership Enterprises	2.76	2.76		2.76	0.03
国有联营	State Joint Ownership Enterprises					
集体联营	Collective Joint Ownership Enterprises					
国有与集体联营	Joint State-collective Enterprises	2.54	2.54		2.54	0.03
其他联营	Other Joint Ownership Enterprises	0.22	0.21		0.21	0.00
有限责任公司	Limited Liability Corporations	2079.61	2239.32	122.25	2117.07	235.68
国有独资公司	State Sole Funded Corporations	25.99	29.51	3.37	26.14	1.81
其他有限责任公司	Other Limited Liability Corporations	2053.63	2209.81	118.88	2090.93	233.87
股份有限公司	Share-holding Corporations Ltd.	1085.40	1226.40	73.43	1152.97	81.37
私营企业	Private Enterprises	1293.40	1457.59	109.21	1348.39	269.17
私营独资	Private-funded Enterprises	105.46	116.78	10.06	106.73	6.23
私营合伙	Private Partnership Enterprises	4.96	5.72	0.26	5.46	0.30
私营有限责任公司	Private Limited Liability Corporations	1135.17	1282.47	97.67	1184.79	258.47
私营股份有限公司	Private Share-holding Corporations Ltd.	47.82	52.62	1.22	51.41	4.18
其他	Other Enterprises	38.16	45.24	2.41	42.83	1.60
港澳台商投资企业	**Enterprises with Funds from Hongkong,** Macao and Taiwan	**132.78**	**163.21**	**7.57**	**155.64**	**22.33**
合资经营	Joint-venture Enterprises	11.93	12.85	6.96	5.89	0.76
合作经营	Cooperative Enterprises					
独资经营	Enterprises with Sole Investment	120.85	150.36	0.61	149.74	21.57
投资股份有限公司	Share-holding Co. Ltd. With Investment					
外商投资企业	**Foreign Funded Enterprises**	**101.06**	**118.23**	**2.89**	**115.34**	**7.64**
中外合资经营	Sino-foreign Joint-venture Enterprises	23.75	29.43	2.72	26.72	1.06
外资企业	Enterprises with Sole Foreign Investment	73.89	85.05	0.18	84.87	6.33
外商投资股份有限公司	Share-holding Co. Ltd. with Foreign Investment	1.04	1.36		1.36	0.01
其它外商投资企业	Other Foreign Funded Enterprises	2.39	2.39		2.39	0.24

16-12 限额以上批发和零售业商品购、销、存总额(2015)
TOTAL PURCHASES, SALES AND STOCK OF ENTERPRISES ABOVE DESIGNATED SIZE OF WHOLESALE AND RETAIL TRADES (2015)

(按国民经济行业分)

(Grouped by Sector)

单位:亿元 (100 million yuan)

行业	Item	购进总额 Total Purchasing Value	销售总额 Total Sales Value	批发 Whole-sales	零售 Retail Sales	年末库存总额 Total Value of Inventory at Year-end
总计	**Total**	**15199.77**	**16659.26**	**10262.87**	**6396.39**	**1681.09**
一、批发业	**Wholesales**	**10001.01**	**10895.90**	**9891.99**	**1003.91**	**1039.91**
农、林、牧产品批发业	Wholesales of Agriculture, Forestry and Animal Husbandry Products	391.25	402.16	351.22	50.94	114.31
食品、饮料及烟草制品批发业	Wholesales of Foods, Beverage and Tobacco	1633.44	1961.21	1689.62	271.59	182.17
米、面制品及食用油批发业	Wholesales of Rice, Noodles and Edible Oil	152.62	164.04	141.64	22.40	12.70
烟草制品批发业	Wholesales of Tobacco	545.25	729.89	723.29	6.61	130.96
纺织、服装及日用品批发业	Wholesales of Textile Products, Garments and Daily Used Articles	374.62	396.35	282.62	113.72	48.60
服装批发业	Wholesales of Garments	175.08	195.86	101.53	94.33	4.62
家用电器批发业	Wholesales of Home Appliances	135.11	128.28	121.22	7.06	34.75
文化、体育用品及器材批发业	Wholesales of Cultural and Sports Goods and Equipments	196.09	221.55	202.24	19.31	20.94
医药及医疗器材批发业	Wholesales of Medicnes and Medical Appliances	1007.46	1040.87	877.42	163.45	116.72
矿产品、建材及化工产品批发业	Wholesales of Mineral Products, Building Materials and Chemical Products	4930.70	5188.34	4869.31	319.03	126.18
煤炭及制品批发业	Wholesales of Coal and Coal-made Products	146.12	156.29	136.09	20.20	7.08
石油及制品批发业	Wholesales of Petroleum Products	3141.33	3323.46	3082.53	240.93	55.45
非金属及金属矿批发业	Wholesales of Non-metellic Mineral and Metal Industry	17.26	20.30	15.93	4.37	1.24
金属及金属矿批发业	Wholesales of Metal and Metal Mines	1095.52	1125.32	1112.76	12.55	38.99
建材批发业	Wholesales of Construction Materials	116.53	125.08	110.26	14.82	5.74
化肥批发业	Wholesales of Chemical Fertilizers	216.28	225.98	218.09	7.89	9.24
机械设备、五金交电及电子产品批发	Wholesales of Machinery Equipment, Hardware, Transport and Electronic Products	1355.66	1577.41	1519.08	58.32	414.28
汽车批发业	Wholesales of Cars	837.06	1001.68	979.24	22.45	38.91
计算机、软件及辅助设备批发业	Wholesales of Computers, Softwares and Assisted Equipments	198.92	221.54	209.42	12.12	2.33
贸易经纪与代理	Trade Agent	49.76	42.72	42.57	0.15	13.81
其他批发业	Other Wholesales	62.03	65.30	57.90	7.40	2.89
二、零售业	**Retail Sales**	**5198.75**	**5763.36**	**370.88**	**5392.48**	**641.18**
综合零售业	Retail Sales of Department	1629.01	1855.95	60.64	1795.32	177.80
百货零售业	Department Stores	869.56	999.10	42.37	956.72	70.43
超级市场零售业	Supermarkets	679.01	772.64	15.49	757.16	101.50
食品、饮料及烟草制品专门零售业	Monopoly Retail of Foods, Beverage and Tobacco	348.99	401.33	44.90	356.43	21.19
纺织、服装及日用品专门零售业	Monopoly Retail of Textile, Garments,and Daily Used Articles	127.55	159.78	10.90	148.88	21.43
服装零售业	Retail Sales of Garments	76.24	94.05	7.34	86.71	15.13
文化、体育用品及器材专门零售业	Monopoly Retail of Cultural, Sports Products and Equipments	100.06	117.93	6.81	111.12	13.12
体育用品零售业	Retail Sales of Sports Products	2.86	4.08		4.08	0.12
图书报刊零售业	Retail Sales of Books, Newspapers and Periodicals	29.34	32.21	2.87	29.34	4.85
医药及医疗器材专门零售业	Monopoly Retail of Medicine and Medical Appliances	300.73	341.78	44.05	297.74	39.66
药品零售业	Retail Sales of Medicine	285.58	322.89	41.02	281.87	38.59
汽车、摩托车、燃料及零配件专门零售	Monopoly Retail of Cars, and Motorcars Parts	1918.13	2051.41	142.95	1908.46	217.96
汽车零售业	Retail Sales of Cars	1468.80	1561.84	51.21	1510.63	207.24
机动车燃料零售业	Retail Sales of Motor Vehicles Fuels	386.03	422.90	77.42	345.48	5.73
家用电器及电子产品专门零售业	Monopoly Retail of Home Appliances and Electronic Products	397.75	426.10	46.56	379.54	29.03
家用视听设备零售业	Retail Sales of Home Audio-visual	93.08	97.39	6.98	90.40	7.36
计算机、软件及辅助设备零售业	Retail Sales of Computers, Softwares and Equipment Assisted Equipments	52.55	57.03	9.54	47.49	3.48
通讯设备零售业	Retail Sales of Communication Equipments	14.23	14.45	1.75	12.70	2.30
五金、家具及室内装修材料专门零售业	Monopoly Retail of Hardware, Furnitures and Decorative Materials	154.01	169.92	10.73	159.19	117.71
货摊、无店铺及其他零售业	Retail Sales of Stalls、Storeless and Others	222.53	239.16	3.35	235.81	3.29
互联网零售	Retail Sales of Internet	181.46	191.12	0.66	190.46	1.28

16-13 限额以上批发和零售业企业资产及负债(2015)
ASSETS AND LIABILITIES OF ENTERPRISES ABOVE DESIGNATED SIZE OF WHOLESALE AND RETAIL TRADES (2015)

单位:亿元 (100 million yuan)

项目	Item	流动资产合计 Total Circulating Funds	固定资产原价 Original Price of Fixed Assets	资产总计 Total Assets	负债合计 Total Liabilities	所有者权益合计 Total Creditor's Equity
总计	**Total**	**4027.54**	**1303.15**	**5776.29**	**4028.31**	**1747.98**
一、批发业	**Wholesales**	**2585.64**	**588.82**	**3415.71**	**2359.74**	**1055.97**
1. 按登记注册类型分组	Grouped by Registration Type					
内资	Domestic Funded Enterprises	2327.12	566.98	3117.58	2103.94	1013.64
国有	State-owned Enterprises	269.37	72.87	334.74	194.24	140.50
集体	Collective-owned Enterprises	9.21	1.47	10.58	9.75	0.83
股份合作	Cooperative Enterprises	0.38	0.11	0.47	0.29	0.18
联营企业	Joint Ownership Enterprises					
国有联营	State Joint Ownership Enterprises					
集体联营	Collective Joint Ownership Enterprises					
国有与集体联营	Joint State-collective Enterprises					
其他联营	Other Joint Ownership Enterprises					
有限责任公司	Limited Liability Corporations	1200.95	192.97	1507.96	1071.87	436.08
国有独资公司	State Sole Funded Corporations	89.28	61.66	174.01	127.56	46.45
其他有限责任公司	Other Limited Liability Corporations	1111.67	131.31	1333.94	944.31	389.63
股份有限公司	Share-holding Corporations Ltd.	370.48	197.58	638.52	390.46	248.05
私营企业	Private Enterprises	465.30	92.20	602.06	426.81	175.25
私营独资	Private-funded Enterprises	2.99	3.29	6.97	2.09	4.88
私营合伙	Private Partnership Enterprises					
私营有限责任公司	Private Limited Liability Corporations	454.65	85.33	583.91	418.89	165.02
私营股份有限公司	Private Share-holding Corporations Ltd.	7.66	3.58	11.18	5.83	5.35
其他	Other Enterprises	11.45	9.78	23.26	10.51	12.74
港澳台商投资企业	**Enterprises with Funds from Hongkong, Macao and Taiwan**	**47.88**	**16.88**	**67.18**	**50.15**	**17.03**
合资经营	Joint-venture Enterprises	10.33	0.29	10.62	8.47	2.15
合作经营	Cooperative Enterprises					
独资经营	Enterprises with Sole Investment	35.98	16.55	54.97	40.00	14.97
投资股份有限公司	Share-holding Co. Ltd. With Investment	1.57	0.04	1.58	1.67	-0.09
外商投资企业	**Foreign Funded Enterprises**	**210.64**	**4.96**	**230.95**	**205.65**	**25.30**
中外合资经营	Sino-foreign Joint-venture Enterprises	123.50	3.03	135.38	100.43	34.95
外资企业	Enterprises with Sole Foreign Investment	70.16	1.39	76.41	87.54	-11.13
外商投资股份有限公司	Share-holding Co. Ltd. with Foreign Investment	0.49	0.01	0.49	-0.01	0.50
其他外资企业	Other Enterprises with Sole Foreign Investment	16.49	0.53	18.67	17.70	0.97
2. 按国民经济行业分组	**Grouped by Sector**					
农、林、牧产品批发业	Wholesales of Agriculture, Forestry and Animal Husbandry Products	174.02	41.93	223.78	159.96	63.82
食品、饮料及烟草制品批发业	Wholesales of Foods, Beverage and Tobacco	570.37	155.40	744.99	400.69	344.30
米、面制品及食用油批发业	Wholesales of Rice, Noodles and Edible Oil	65.93	11.28	87.75	50.59	37.16
烟草制品批发业	Wholesales of Tobacco	154.08	63.32	205.87	75.76	130.11
纺织、服装及日用品批发业	Wholesales of Textile Products, Garments and Daily Used Articles	140.32	8.69	154.86	142.86	12.00
服装批发业	Wholesales of Garments	40.85	4.16	48.33	45.87	2.46
家用电器批发业	Wholesales of Home Appliances	75.90	0.74	77.35	76.10	1.25
文化、体育用品及器材批发业	Wholesales of Cultural and Sports Goods and Equipments	81.42	11.50	97.72	66.48	31.23
医药及医疗器材批发业	Wholesales of Medicnes and Medical Appliances	523.85	55.70	612.99	454.35	158.65
矿产品、建材及化工产品批发业	Wholesales of Mineral Products, Building Materials and Chemical Products	661.61	281.94	1089.51	738.05	351.46
煤炭及制品批发业	Wholesales of Coal and Coal-made Products	65.31	6.19	79.18	53.56	25.62
石油及制品批发业	Wholesales of Petroleum Products	140.50	225.39	445.05	251.50	193.55
非金属及金属矿批发业	Wholesales of Non-metellic Mineral and Metal Industry	9.20	2.53	13.13	10.34	2.79
金属及金属矿批发业	Wholesales of Metal and Metal Mines	317.06	21.87	380.44	308.24	72.20
建材批发业	Wholesales of Construction Materials	29.71	9.70	42.44	28.14	14.30
化肥批发业	Wholesales of Chemical Fertilizers	50.20	8.50	61.50	42.27	19.22
机械设备、五金交电及电子产品批发	Wholesales of Machinery Equipment, Hardware, Transport and Electronic Products	401.12	24.87	448.33	366.55	81.78
汽车批发业	Wholesales of Cars	158.81	6.71	179.09	138.69	40.40
计算机、软件及辅助设备批发业	Wholesales of Computers, Softwares and Assisted Equipments	92.63	0.36	93.68	85.76	7.93
贸易经纪与代理	Trade Agent	19.66	0.37	19.95	17.84	2.10
其他批发业	Other Wholesales	13.28	8.42	23.58	12.96	10.62

16-13 续表 continued

单位:亿元 (100 million yuan)

项　目	Item	流动资产合计 Total Circulating Funds	固定资产原价 Original Price of Fixed Assets	资产总计 Total Assets	负债合计 Total Liabilities	所有者权益合计 Total Creditor's Equity
二、零售业	**Retail Trade**	**1441.91**	**714.33**	**2360.59**	**1668.57**	**692.02**
1. 按登记注册类型分组	**Grouped by Registration Type**					
内资	Domestic Funded Enterprises	1329.70	671.39	2202.15	1553.48	648.67
国有	State-owned Enterprises	71.04	23.03	110.89	84.40	26.49
集体	Collective-owned Enterprises	15.58	19.15	32.09	26.01	6.07
股份合作	Cooperative Enterprises	0.68	0.73	1.44	0.61	0.84
联营企业	Joint Ownership Enterprises	0.49	0.12	0.60	0.10	0.50
国有联营	State Joint Ownership Enterprises					
集体联营	Collective Joint Ownership Enterprises					
国有与集体联营	Joint State-collective Enterprises	0.46	0.12	0.57	0.10	0.48
其他联营	Other Joint Ownership Enterprises	0.03	0.00	0.03	0.00	0.03
有限责任公司	Limited Liability Corporations	666.07	270.72	1042.24	736.69	305.55
国有独资公司	State Sole Funded Corporations	5.91	3.12	8.91	5.56	3.35
其他有限责任公司	Other Limited Liability Corporations	660.15	267.60	1033.33	731.13	302.20
股份有限公司	Share-holding Corporations Ltd.	178.08	218.80	439.96	324.54	115.42
私营企业	Private Enterprises	391.64	129.04	559.89	375.82	184.06
私营独资	Private-funded Enterprises	16.62	21.87	38.42	12.81	25.61
私营合伙	Private Partnership Enterprises	0.96	0.94	1.86	0.84	1.02
私营有限责任公司	Private Limited Liability Corporations	343.46	103.23	482.05	332.94	149.11
私营股份有限公司	Private Share-holding Corporations Ltd.	30.60	3.01	37.56	29.24	8.32
其他	Other Enterprises	6.13	9.80	15.05	5.31	9.73
港澳台商投资企业	**Enterprises with Funds from Hongkong, Macao and Taiwan**	**65.53**	**12.81**	**77.03**	**58.55**	**18.48**
合资经营	Joint-venture Enterprises	2.73	0.87	3.95	3.49	0.46
合作经营	Cooperative Enterprises					
独资经营	Enterprises with Sole Investment	62.80	11.94	73.07	55.06	18.01
投资股份有限公司	Share-holding Co. Ltd. With Investment					
外商投资企业	**Foreign Funded Enterprises**	**46.68**	**30.13**	**81.41**	**56.54**	**24.87**
中外合资经营	Sino-foreign Joint-venture Enterprises	11.78	4.68	20.44	14.51	5.94
外资企业	Enterprises with Sole Foreign Investment	34.40	23.82	58.89	39.63	19.25
外商投资股份有限公司	Share-holding Co. Ltd. with Foreign Investment	0.18	0.87	0.98	1.18	-0.19
其他外资企业	Other Enterprises with Sole Foreign Investment	0.32	0.76	1.10	1.22	-0.13
2. 按国民经济行业分组	**Grouped by Sector**					
综合零售业	Retail Sales of Department	353.98	312.08	729.60	527.71	201.89
百货零售业	Department Stores	195.68	183.24	418.60	295.97	122.63
超级市场零售业	Supermarkets	149.05	120.88	293.65	220.47	73.18
食品、饮料及烟草制品专门零售业	Monopoly Retail of Foods, Beverage and Tobacco	84.52	33.11	123.85	56.35	67.50
纺织、服装及日用品专门零售业	Monopoly Retail of Textile, Garments,and Daily Used Articles	57.95	26.92	92.24	53.54	38.69
服装零售业	Retail Sales of Garments	38.31	22.21	67.27	43.28	23.99
文化、体育用品及器材专门零售业	Monopoly Retail of Cultural, Sports Products and Equipments	43.63	22.75	74.34	43.07	31.27
体育用品零售业	Retail Sales of Sports Products	0.26	0.22	0.56	1.62	-1.06
图书报刊零售业	Retail Sales of Books, Newspapers and Periodicals	22.18	9.42	32.16	13.77	18.39
医药及医疗器材专门零售业	Monopoly Retail of Medicine and Medical Appliances	186.88	17.03	216.72	177.37	39.35
药品零售业	Retail Sales of Medicine	178.51	16.16	207.16	171.36	35.80
汽车、摩托车、燃料及零配件专门零售业	Monopoly Retail of Cars, and Motorcars Parts	550.21	216.09	847.76	649.05	198.71
汽车零售业	Retail Sales of Cars	519.50	150.04	723.61	556.34	167.27
机动车燃料零售业	Retail Sales of Motor Vehicles Fuels	13.41	60.23	98.86	76.40	22.46
家用电器及电子产品专门零售业	Monopoly Retail of Home Appliances and Electronic Products	93.06	50.15	151.42	79.37	72.05
家用视听设备零售业	Retail Sales of Home Audio-visual Equipment	17.49	9.67	28.56	14.62	13.94
计算机、软件及辅助设备零售业	Retail Sales of Computers, Softwares and Assisted Equipments	10.43	2.28	13.23	6.59	6.64
通讯设备零售业	Retail Sales of Communication Equipments	2.71	1.77	4.33	2.69	1.64
五金、家具及室内装修材料专门零售业	Monopoly Retail of Hardware, Furnitures and Decorative Materials	52.43	21.50	87.01	54.78	32.24
货摊、无店铺及其他零售业	Retail Sales of Stalls、Storeless and Others	19.24	14.69	37.65	27.34	10.31
互联网零售	Retail Sales of Internet	4.41	2.00	9.49	10.43	-0.94

16-14 限额以上批发和零售业企业主要财务指标(2015)
MAIN FINANCIAL INDICATORS OF ENTERPRISES ABOVE DESIGNATED SIZE OF WHOLESALE AND RETAIL TRADES (2015)

单位:亿元 (100 million yuan)

项 目	Item	主营业务收入 Revenue of Major Business	主营业务成本 Cost of Major Business	其他业务利润 Profits of Other Business	利润总额 Total Profits
总 计	**Total**	**13877.69**	**12396.43**	**86.83**	**422.29**
一、批发业	**Wholesales**	**9126.73**	**8282.08**	**10.18**	**269.16**
1. 按登记注册类型分组	**Grouped by Registration Type**				
内资	**Domestic Funded Enterprises**	**7956.28**	**7314.53**	**8.96**	**221.18**
国有	State-owned Enterprises	678.62	513.40	0.66	74.81
集体	Collective-owned Enterprises	12.45	11.89		0.04
股份合作	Cooperative Enterprises	2.18	1.89	-0.01	0.15
联营企业	Joint Ownership Enterprises				
国有联营	State Joint Ownership Enterprises				
集体联营	Collective Joint Ownership Enterprises				
国有与集体联营	Joint State-collective Enterprises				
其他联营	Other Joint Ownership Enterprises				
有限责任公司	Limited Liability Corporations	4309.35	4070.79	3.41	78.38
国有独资公司	State Sole Funded Corporations	1503.82	1469.43	0.08	17.24
其他有限责任公司	Other Limited Liability Corporations	2805.53	2601.37	3.33	61.15
股份有限公司	Share-holding Corporations Ltd.	1622.03	1518.74	3.35	22.88
私营企业	Private Enterprises	1259.45	1136.76	1.56	39.98
私营独资	Private-funded Enterprises	34.97	27.19	0.04	3.77
私营合伙	Private Partnership Enterprises				
私营有限责任公司	Private Limited Liability Corporations	1194.29	1081.23	1.50	35.44
私营股份有限公司	Private Share-holding Corporations Ltd.	30.20	28.34	0.03	0.78
其他	Other Enterprises	72.19	61.05	0.00	4.93
港澳台商投资企业	**Enterprises with Funds from Hongkong, Macao and Taiwan**	**108.83**	**88.64**	**0.54**	**3.81**
合资经营	Joint-venture Enterprises	17.27	15.64	0.01	0.25
合作经营	Cooperative Enterprises				
独资经营	Enterprises with Sole Investment	79.77	62.42	0.53	3.65
投资股份有限公司	Share-holding Co. Ltd. With Investment	11.79	10.58		-0.09
外商投资企业	**Foreign Funded Enterprises**	**1061.62**	**878.91**	**0.67**	**44.16**
中外合资经营	Sino-foreign Joint-venture Enterprises	788.00	680.09	0.67	34.42
外资企业	Enterprises with Sole Foreign Investment	205.78	141.39	0.00	9.61
外商投资股份有限公司	Share-holding Co. Ltd. with Foreign Investment	0.81	0.62		0.10
其他外资企业	Other Enterprises with Sole Foreign Investment	67.03	56.82		0.04
2. 按国民经济行业分组	**Grouped by Sector**				
农、林、牧产品批发业	Wholesales of Agriculture, Forestry and Animal Husbandry Products	391.53	359.84	0.16	14.28
食品、饮料及烟草制品批发业	Wholesales of Foods, Beverage and Tobacco	1517.25	1156.95	2.13	131.49
米、面制品及食用油批发业	Wholesales of Rice, Noodles and Edible Oil	151.49	138.24	0.10	4.88
烟草制品批发业	Wholesales of Tobacco	599.07	435.52	0.43	74.83
纺织、服装及日用品批发业	Wholesales of Textile Products, Garments and Daily Used Articles	351.62	320.04	0.70	2.53
服装批发业	Wholesales of Garments	177.64	159.94		1.20
家用电器批发业	Wholesales of Home Appliances	107.94	102.38	0.04	-0.26
文化、体育用品及器材批发业	Wholesales of Cultural and Sports Goods and Equipments	193.96	176.15	0.76	5.05
医药及医疗器材批发业	Wholesales of Medicnes and Medical Appliances	896.82	827.20	2.97	21.50
矿产品、建材及化工产品批发业	Wholesales of Mineral Products, Building Materials and Chemical Products	4293.73	4112.90	1.72	53.12
煤炭及制品批发业	Wholesales of Coal and Coal-made Products	143.07	127.18	0.04	3.10
石油及制品批发业	Wholesales of Petroleum Products	2570.28	2470.49	0.68	28.03
非金属及金属矿批发业	Wholesales of Non-metellic Mineral and Metal Industry	19.73	15.35		1.99
金属及金属矿批发业	Wholesales of Metal and Metal Mines	1027.23	1004.32	0.49	6.51
建材批发业	Wholesales of Construction Materials	115.69	104.33	0.05	4.23
化肥批发业	Wholesales of Chemical Fertilizers	224.07	211.56	0.34	4.54
机械设备、五金交电及电子产品批发	Wholesales of Machinery Equipment, Hardware, Transport and Electronic Products	1382.68	1235.92	1.68	39.49
汽车批发业	Wholesales of Cars	855.40	744.21	0.90	35.67
计算机、软件及辅助设备批发业	Wholesales of Computers, Softwares and Assisted Equipments	204.62	198.87	0.03	4.23
贸易经纪与代理	Trade Agent	36.69	36.65	0.01	-0.25
其他批发业	Other Wholesales	62.45	56.43	0.04	1.96

16-14 续表 continued

单位:亿元 (100 million yuan)

项 目	Item	主营业务收入 Revenue of Major Business	主营业务成本 Cost of Major Business	其他业务利润 Profits of Other Business	利润总额 Total Profits
二、零售业	**Retail Trade**	**4750.96**	**4114.35**	**76.65**	**153.13**
1. 按登记注册类型分组	**Grouped by Registration Type**				
内资	**Domestic Funded Enterprises**	**4513.06**	**3915.93**	**55.79**	**138.65**
国有	State-owned Enterprises	277.64	251.14	0.46	9.14
集体	Collective-owned Enterprises	163.89	148.09	0.31	1.93
股份合作	Cooperative Enterprises	4.28	3.73	0.00	0.24
联营企业	Joint Ownership Enterprises	2.30	2.15		0.06
国有联营	State Joint Ownership Enterprises				
集体联营	Collective Joint Ownership Enterprises				
国有与集体联营	Joint State-collective Enterprises	2.08	1.94		0.06
其他联营	Other Joint Ownership Enterprises	0.21	0.21		0.00
有限责任公司	Limited Liability Corporations	2031.71	1780.59	10.85	57.34
国有独资公司	State Sole Funded Corporations	26.23	23.53	0.05	1.01
其他有限责任公司	Other Limited Liability Corporations	2005.48	1757.06	10.80	56.33
股份有限公司	Share-holding Corporations Ltd.	695.41	580.53	40.27	15.92
私营企业	Private Enterprises	1295.52	1114.80	3.87	48.96
私营独资	Private-funded Enterprises	112.37	88.47	0.09	9.96
私营合伙	Private Partnership Enterprises	5.48	4.27	0.01	0.26
私营有限责任公司	Private Limited Liability Corporations	1131.99	981.10	3.72	37.37
私营股份有限公司	Private Share-holding Corporations Ltd.	45.68	40.96	0.04	1.37
其他	Other Enterprises	42.32	34.91	0.03	5.07
港澳台商投资企业	**Enterprises with Funds from Hongkong, Macao and Taiwan**	**140.94**	**121.91**	**19.67**	**10.64**
合资经营	Joint-venture Enterprises	12.05	10.68	0.26	0.02
合作经营	Cooperative Enterprises				
独资经营	Enterprises with Sole Investment	128.88	111.23	19.41	10.62
投资股份有限公司	Share-holding Co. Ltd. With Investment				
外商投资企业	**Foreign Funded Enterprises**	**96.96**	**76.50**	**1.19**	**3.83**
中外合资经营	Sino-foreign Joint-venture Enterprises	25.75	19.18	0.04	1.15
外资企业	Enterprises with Sole Foreign Investment	67.84	54.36	1.13	2.75
外商投资股份有限公司	Share-holding Co. Ltd. with Foreign Investment	1.33	1.04		0.02
其他外资企业	Other Enterprises with Sole Foreign Investment	2.03	1.92	0.02	-0.08
2. 按国民经济行业分组	**Grouped by Sector**				
综合零售业	Retail Sales of Department	1256.17	1032.02	66.69	46.71
百货零售业	Department Stores	642.90	542.91	61.49	31.64
超级市场零售业	Supermarkets	533.23	421.74	5.08	9.35
食品、饮料及烟草制品专门零售业	Monopoly Retail of Foods, Beverage and Tobacco	366.79	296.60	0.64	29.06
纺织、服装及日用品专门零售业	Monopoly Retail of Textile, Garments,and Daily Used Articles	142.84	109.74	0.89	6.14
服装零售业	Retail Sales of Garments	83.42	63.63	0.61	3.20
文化、体育用品及器材专门零售业	Monopoly Retail of Cultural, Sports Products and Equipments	106.85	84.00	0.69	6.81
体育用品零售业	Retail Sales of Sports Products	3.85	3.31	0.00	0.22
图书报刊零售业	Retail Sales of Books, Newspapers and Periodicals	29.46	22.03	0.38	2.27
医药及医疗器材专门零售业	Monopoly Retail of Medicine and Medical Appliances	280.75	249.20	1.10	6.56
药品零售业	Retail Sales of Medicine	263.40	236.35	1.06	5.09
汽车、摩托车、燃料及零配件专门零售业	Monopoly Retail of Cars, and Motorcars Parts	1848.97	1700.59	3.05	26.01
汽车零售业	Retail Sales of Cars	1411.91	1296.90	2.80	17.64
机动车燃料零售业	Retail Sales of Motor Vehicles Fuels	373.53	350.19	0.21	5.39
家用电器及电子产品专门零售业	Monopoly Retail of Home Appliances and Electronic Products	385.09	324.76	2.37	21.69
家用视听设备零售业	Retail Sales of Home Audio-visual Equipments	89.49	75.66	0.17	4.17
计算机、软件及辅助设备零售业	Retail Sales of Computers, Softwares and Assisted Equipments	53.54	46.96	0.17	2.20
通讯设备零售业	Retail Sales of Communication Equipments	13.24	11.11	0.01	0.59
五金、家具及室内装修材料专门零售业	Monopoly Retail of Hardware, Furnitures and Decorative Materials	151.98	123.96	0.73	7.81
货摊、无店铺及其他零售业	Retail Sales of Stalls、Storeless and Others	211.53	193.47	0.49	2.33
互联网零售	Retail Sales of Internet	163.52	154.75	0.03	-2.43

16-15 限额以上餐饮业企业资产及负债(2015)
ASSETS AND LIABILITIES OF ENTERPRISES ABOVE DESIGNATED SIZE OF CATERING SERVICES (2015)

单位:亿元 (100 million yuan)

项 目	Item	流动资产合计 Total Circulating Funds	固定资产原价 Original Price of Fixed Assets	资产总计 Total Assets	负债合计 Total Liabilities	所有者权益合计 Total Creditor's Equity
总 计	**Total**	**91.42**	**173.75**	**303.39**	**181.61**	**121.75**
1. 按国民经济行业分组	**Grouped by Sector**					
正餐服务业	Dinner	85.43	165.77	282.92	167.14	115.76
快餐服务业	Fast Food	2.89	6.07	14.73	11.36	3.37
饮料及冷饮服务业	Beverage and Cold Drink Services	0.93	1.20	3.07	1.24	1.83
其他餐饮服务业	Others	2.16	0.71	2.66	1.86	0.80
2. 按登记注册类型分组	**Grouped by Registration Type**					
内资	**Domestic Funded Enterprises**	**85.64**	**161.40**	**278.91**	**161.30**	**117.59**
国有	State-Owned Enterprises	0.62	1.76	2.05	1.08	0.97
集体	Collective-owned Enterprises	0.06	0.58	0.53	0.55	-0.02
股份合作	Cooperative Enterprises	0.02	0.08	0.10	0.01	0.09
联营企业	Joint Ownership Enterprises	0.43	0.81	1.14	0.22	0.92
国有联营	State Joint Ownership Enterprises					
集体联营	Collective Joint Ownership Enterprises	0.43	0.81	1.14	0.22	0.92
国有与集体联营	Joint State-collective Enterprises					
其他联营	Other Joint Ownership Enterprises					
有限责任公司	Limited Liability Corporations	51.66	58.31	135.89	109.52	26.34
国有独资公司	State Sole Funded Corporations	5.35	6.34	13.40	7.86	5.54
其他有限责任公司	Other Limited Liability Corporations	46.31	51.98	122.49	101.66	20.80
股份有限公司	Share-holding Corporations Ltd.	0.80	0.97	1.77	0.95	0.83
私营企业	Private Enterprises	31.14	96.31	133.63	48.16	85.47
私营独资	Private-funded Enterprises	4.22	9.68	13.56	4.31	9.25
私营合伙	Private Partnership Enterprises	0.14	0.42	0.53	0.18	0.35
私营有限责任公司	Private Limited Liability Corporations	25.65	84.59	116.05	41.73	74.31
私营股份有限公司	Private Share-holding Corporations Ltd.	1.12	1.63	3.50	1.95	1.56
其他	Other Enterprises	0.92	2.58	3.80	0.80	3.00
港澳台商投资企业	**Enterprises with Funds from Hongkong, Macao and Taiwan**	**2.27**	**4.39**	**7.27**	**5.97**	**1.30**
合资经营	Joint-venture Enterprises	0.84	2.10	2.76	3.21	-0.45
合作经营	Cooperative Enterprises					
独资经营	Enterprises with Sole Investment	1.43	2.29	4.51	2.76	1.75
投资股份有限公司	Share-holding Co. Ltd. With Investment					
外商投资企业	**Foreign Funded Enterprises**	**3.51**	**7.95**	**17.20**	**14.34**	**2.86**
中外合资经营	Sino-Foreign Joint-venture Enterprises	0.14	0.01	0.15	0.18	-0.04
外资企业	Enterprises with Sole Foreign Investment	3.37	7.95	17.06	14.16	2.90
外商投资股份有限公司	Share-holding Co. Ltd. with Foreign Investment					
其他外商投资企业	Other Enterprises with Sole Foreign Investment					

16-16 限额以上餐饮业企业主要财务指标(2015)
MAIN FINANCIAL INDICATORS OF ENTERPRISES ABOVE DESIGNATED SIZE OF CATERING SERVICES (2015)

单位:亿元 (100 million yuan)

项目	Item	主营业务收入 Revenue of Major Business	主营业务成本 Cost of Major Business	其他业务利润 Profits of Other Business	利润总额 Total Profits
总计	Total	237.04	132.14	0.98	12.20
1. 按国民经济行业分组	Grouped by Sector				
正餐服务业	Dinner	189.16	112.42	0.98	10.86
快餐服务业	Fast Food	36.65	17.22		0.44
饮料及冷饮服务业	Beverage and Cold Drink Services	5.81	1.54		0.90
其他餐饮服务业	Others	5.42	0.96	0.00	0.01
2. 按登记注册类型分组	Grouped by Registration Type				
内资	Domestic Funded Enterprises	192.83	112.84	0.98	11.24
国有	State-Owned Enterprises	2.18	1.46	0.01	0.02
集体	Collective-owned Enterprises	0.84	0.59		-0.04
股份合作	Cooperative Enterprises	0.25	0.11		0.07
联营企业	Joint Ownership Enterprises	0.50	0.41		0.03
国有联营	State Joint Ownership Enterprises				
集体联营	Collective Joint Ownership Enterprises	0.50	0.41		0.03
国有与集体联营	Joint State-collective Enterprises				
其他联营	Other Joint Ownership Enterprises				
有限责任公司	Limited Liability Corporations	78.32	41.47	0.44	1.45
国有独资公司	State Sole Funded Corporations	2.72	1.60	0.00	0.05
其他有限责任公司	Other Limited Liability Corporations	75.60	39.87	0.44	1.40
股份有限公司	Share-holding Corporations Ltd.	1.99	1.01	0.01	0.15
私营企业	Private Enterprises	102.96	63.90	0.52	8.70
私营独资	Private-funded Enterprises	29.37	19.96	0.09	3.78
私营合伙	Private Partnership Enterprises	0.42	0.26		0.05
私营有限责任公司	Private Limited Liability Corporations	69.83	41.81	0.42	4.69
私营股份有限公司	Private Share-holding Corporations Ltd.	3.33	1.87	0.02	0.18
其他	Other Enterprises	5.79	3.89		0.86
港澳台商投资企业	Enterprises with Funds from Hongkong, Macao and Taiwan	8.59	2.62		0.63
合资经营	Joint-venture Enterprises	0.57	0.19		-0.26
合作经营	Cooperative Enterprises				
独资经营	Enterprises with Sole Investment	8.02	2.43		0.89
投资股份有限公司	Sole Investment Co. Ltd. With Investment				
外商投资企业	Foreign Funded Enterprises	35.63	16.68		0.34
中外合资经营	Sino-Foreign Joint-venture Enterprises	0.59	0.51		-0.01
外资企业	Enterprises with Sole Foreign Investment	35.04	16.17		0.35
外商投资股份有限公司	Share-holding Co. Ltd. with Foreign Investment				
其他外商投资企业	Other Enterprises with Sole Foreign Investment				

16-17 限额以上住宿业企业资产及负债(2015)
ASSETS AND LIABILITIES OF ENTERPRISES ABOVE DESIGNATED SIZE OF HOTELS SERVICES (2015)

单位:亿元 (100 million yuan)

项目	Item	流动资产合计 Total Circulating Funds	固定资产原价 Original Price of Fixed Assets	资产总计 Total Assets	负债合计 Total Liabilities	所有者权益合计 Total Creditor's Equity
总 计	**Total**	**179.05**	**402.38**	**626.40**	**387.89**	**238.48**
1. 按国民经济行业分组	**Grouped by Sector**					
旅游饭店	Tourist Hotel	66	193	262.29	171.35	90.93
一般旅馆	Regular Hotel	18	30	51.00	28.46	22.54
其他住宿服务	Other Accomodation Service	3	6	9.73	6.47	3.25
2. 按登记注册类型分组	**Grouped by Registration Type**					
内资	**Domestic Funded Enterprises**	**82.65**	**205.53**	**302.39**	**189.34**	**113.05**
国有	State-Owned Enterprises	4.07	19.64	17.19	9.50	7.69
集体	Collective-owned Enterprises	1.74	5.83	4.60	2.02	2.58
股份合作	Cooperative Enterprises	0.07	0.67	0.76	0.74	0.02
联营企业	Joint Ownership Enterprises					
国有联营	State Joint Ownership Enterprises					
集体联营	Collective Joint Ownership Enterprises					
国有与集体联营	Joint State-collective Enterprises					
其他联营	Other Joint Ownership Enterprises					
有限责任公司	Limited Liability Corporations	38.55	112.85	167.15	105.81	61.35
国有独资公司	State Sole Funded Corporations	3.98	9.32	27.99	11.89	16.10
其他有限责任公司	Other Limited Liability Corporations	34.57	103.53	139.16	93.92	45.24
股份有限公司	Share-holding Corporations Ltd.	6.89	8.00	15.68	9.46	6.23
私营企业	Private Enterprises	30.98	57.75	96.03	61.52	34.50
私营独资	Private-funded Enterprises	1.75	2.53	4.31	2.47	1.84
私营合伙	Private Partnership Enterprises	0.16	0.61	0.66	0.22	0.43
私营有限责任公司	Private Limited Liability Corporations	27.58	51.55	86.44	56.70	29.74
私营股份有限公司	Private Share-holding Corporations Ltd.	1.48	3.06	4.62	2.13	2.49
其他	Other Enterprises	0.35	0.77	0.98	0.30	0.67
港澳台商投资企业	**Enterprises with Funds from Hongkong, Macao and Taiwan**	**3.70**	**20.63**	**17.32**	**14.37**	**2.96**
合资经营	Joint-venture Enterprises	0.69	11.33	7.25	4.48	2.78
合作经营	Cooperative Enterprises	0.61	2.70	1.41	2.46	-1.05
独资经营	Enterprises with Sole Investment	1.82	6.14	7.73	6.61	1.12
投资股份有限公司	Share-holding Co. Ltd. With Investment	0.59	0.46	0.93	0.83	0.11
外商投资企业	**Foreign Funded Enterprises**	**1.27**	**2.48**	**3.30**	**2.58**	**0.72**
中外合资经营	Sino-foreign Joint-venture Enterprises	1.05	1.28	2.01	1.25	0.76
外资企业	Enterprises with Sole Foreign Investment	0.21	0.29	0.51	0.43	0.09
外商投资股份有限公司	Share-holding Co. Ltd. with Foreign Investment	0.01	0.91	0.78	0.90	-0.12
其他外商投资企业	Other Enterprises with Sole Foreign Investment					

16-18 限额以上住宿业企业主要财务指标(2015)
MAIN FINANCIAL INDICATORS OF ENTERPRISES ABOVE DESIGNATED SIZE OF HOTELS SERVICES (2015)

单位:亿元 (100 million yuan)

项目	Item	主营业务收入 Revenue of Major Business	主营业务成本 Cost of Major Business	其他业务利润 Profits of Other Business	利润总额 Total Profits
总计	**Total**	**363.01**	**190.82**	**5.28**	**11.29**
1. 按国民经济行业分组	**Grouped by Sector**				
旅游饭店	Tourist Hotel	87.33	37.08	3.84	-3.31
一般旅馆	Regular Hotel	34.57	18.69	0.28	2.33
其他住宿服务	Other Accomodation Service	4.06	2.91	0.17	0.07
2. 按登记注册类型分组	**Grouped by Registration Type**				
内资	**Domestic Funded Enterprises**	**116.45**	**56.14**	**3.70**	**-0.53**
国有	State-Owned Enterprises	8.82	5.13	0.00	-0.28
集体	Collective-owned Enterprises	1.76	0.61	0.07	-0.02
股份合作	Cooperative Enterprises	0.09	0.06		
联营企业	Joint Ownership Enterprises				
国有联营	State Joint Ownership Enterprises				
集体联营	Collective Joint Ownership Enterprises				
国有与集体联营	Joint State-collective Enterprises				
其他联营	Other Joint Ownership Enterprises				
有限责任公司	Limited Liability Corporations	53.42	21.50	3.13	-1.09
国有独资公司	State Sole Funded Corporations	4.78	3.29	0.31	0.17
其他有限责任公司	Other Limited Liability Corporations	48.63	18.21	2.82	-1.26
股份有限公司	Share-holding Corporations Ltd.	3.73	1.47	0.01	0.17
私营企业	Private Enterprises	46.20	25.42	0.49	0.49
私营独资	Private-funded Enterprises	6.09	3.91	0.01	0.78
私营合伙	Private Partnership Enterprises	0.82	0.55		0.04
私营有限责任公司	Private Limited Liability Corporations	37.78	20.11	0.42	-0.37
私营股份有限公司	Private Share-holding Corporations Ltd.	1.50	0.86	0.06	0.04
其他	Other Enterprises	2.43	1.94		0.20
港澳台商投资企业	**Enterprises with Funds from Hongkong, Macao and Taiwan**	**8.88**	**2.34**	**0.59**	**-0.27**
合资经营	Joint-venture Enterprises	2.02	0.28	0.55	-0.26
合作经营	Cooperative Enterprises	0.97	0.37		-0.09
独资经营	Enterprises with Sole Investment	4.86	1.12	0.03	0.04
独资股份有限公司	Sole Investment Co. Ltd. With Investment	1.04	0.57	0.00	0.04
外商投资企业	**Foreign Funded Enterprises**	**0.63**	**0.20**		**-0.11**
中外合资经营	Sino-Foreign Joint-venture Enterprises	0.31	0.05		-0.08
外资企业	Enterprises with Sole Foreign Investment	0.29	0.12		0.01
外商投资股份有限公司	Share-holding Co. Ltd. with Foreign Investment	0.03	0.03		-0.04
其他外商投资企业	Other Enterprises with Sole Foreign Investment				

16-19 亿元以上商品交易市场基本情况(2015年)
BASIC STATISTICS ON COMMODITY EXCHANGE MARKETS OF TRANSACTION VALUE OVER 100 MILLION YUAN (2015)

单位:亿元 (100 million yuan)

市　场	Market	市场数量(个) Number of Markets (unit)	摊位数(个) Number of Booths (unit)	营业面积(万平方米) Operating Area (10 000 sq.m)	成交额(亿元) Turnover (100 million yuan)
总　计	**Total**	**157**	**78934**	**623.57**	**2030.37**
综合市场	**Integrated Markets**	**42**	**27208**	**182.74**	**504.12**
生产资料综合市场	Production Comprehensive Market	3	5952	77.02	119.81
工业消费品综合市场	Industrial Consumable Comprehensive Markets	8	7442	47.13	99.78
农产品综合市场	Farm Produce Comprehensive Markets	15	5638	20.97	120.15
其他综合市场	Other Comprehensive Markets	16	8176	37.62	164.39
专业市场	**Special Markets**	**115**	**51726**	**440.83**	**1526.25**
生产资料市场	Production Markets	19	5447	62.47	255.66
农业生产用具市场	Agricultural Production Equipment Markets				
农用生产资料市场	Agricultural Production Markets				
煤炭市场	Coal and Charcoal Markets				
木材市场	Wood Markets				
建材市场	Building Material Markets	10	2826	33.55	78.67
化工材料及制品市场	Chemical Materials and Products Markets				
金属材料市场	Metal Materials Markets	8	2313	28.32	174.16
机械设备市场	Mechanical Equipments Markets	1	308	0.60	2.83
其他生产资料市场	Others				
农产品市场	Farm Produce Markets	25	12446	85.67	492.19
粮油市场	Grain and Oil Markets	1	200	2.40	1.16
肉禽蛋市场	Meat, Poultry and Eggs Markets	2	214	0.83	2.84
水产品市场	Aquatic Products Markets	4	3690	31.91	282.43
蔬菜市场	Vegetables Markets	8	1673	15.53	45.47
干鲜果品市场	Dried and Fresh Melons and Fruits Markets	5	5103	25.98	139.79
棉麻土畜、烟叶市场	Cotton, Local & Livestock Products, and Tobacco Markets				
其他农产品市场	Others	5	1566	9.02	20.50
食品、饮料及烟酒市场	Food, Beverages, Tobacco and Liquor Markets	7	3417	18.78	59.23
食品饮料市场	Food and Beverages Markets	4	1281	15.35	18.17
茶叶市场	Tea Markets	2	1303	1.63	21.11
烟酒市场	Tobacco and Liquor Markets				
其他食品饮料及烟酒市场	Others	1	833	1.80	19.96
纺织、服装、鞋帽市场	Textiles, Clothing, Shoes and Hats Markets	21	16068	69.94	138.91
布料及纺织品市场	Cloth and Textiles Markets	2	263	0.62	2.45
服装市场	Clothing Markets	13	9408	57.92	107.46
鞋帽市场	Shoes and Hats Markets	2	697	5.00	5.14
其他纺织服装鞋帽市场	Others	4	5700	6.40	23.85
日用品及文化用品市场	Daily Use Articles and Cultural Goods Markets	6	1804	16.78	49.69

16-19 续表 continued

单位:亿元 (100 million yuan)

市 场	Market	市场数量(个) Number of Markets (unit)	摊位数(个) Number of Booths (unit)	营业面积(万平方米) Operating Area (10 000 sq.m)	成交额(亿元) Turnover (100 million yuan)
小商品市场	Merchandise Markets	1	326	0.40	2.29
箱包市场	Luggage Markets	1	370	4.70	3.33
玩具市场	Toys Markets				
文具市场	Stationary Markets				
图书、报刊杂志市场	Books, Newspapers and Magazines Markets	1	265	0.41	1.86
音像制品及电子出版物市场	Video Products and E-journal Markets				
体育用品市场	Sports Markets				
其他日用品及文化用品市场	Others	3	843	11.27	42.22
黄金、珠宝、玉器等首饰市场	Gold, Jewelry, Jade Markets				
电器、通讯器材、电子设备市场	Electrical Appliances, Communication Appliances and Electronical Appliances Markets	7	2349	13.82	39.04
家电市场	Household Appliances Markets	1	518	1.52	10.00
通讯器材市场	Communication Appliances Markets	3	892	5.10	22.07
照相、摄像器材市场	Cameras and Video Equipments Markets				
计算机及辅助设备市场	Computer and Auxiliary Equipments Markets	3	939	7.20	6.97
其他电器、通讯器材、电子设备市场	Others				
医药、医疗用品及器材市场	Medicine, Medical Materials and Medical Instruments Markets				
中药材市场	Chinese Medicine Markets				
其他医药、医疗用品及器材市场	Others				
家具、五金及装饰材料市场	Furniture, Hardware and Decoration Materials Markets	23	7031	121.46	164.60
家具市场	Furniture Markets	7	1012	20.34	15.23
装饰材料市场	Decoration Materials Markets	14	5147	95.21	144.94
灯具市场	Lamps Markets				
厨具、盥洗设备市场	Kitchen Utensils, Washing Equipments Markets				
五金材料市场	Hardware Materials Markets	1	530	3.59	2.20
其他装修市场	Others	1	342	2.32	2.23
汽车、摩托车及零配件市场	Cars, Motorcycles and Spare Parts Markets	7	3164	51.92	326.93
汽车市场	Cars Markets	5	464	24.80	176.51
摩托车市场	Motorcycles Markets				
机动车零配件市场	Vehicle Spare Parts Markets	2	2700	27.12	150.43
花、鸟、鱼、虫市场	Flower, Bird, Fish and Insects Markets				
花卉市场	Flower Markets				
鸟市场	Bird Markets				
观赏鱼市场	Fish Markets				
其他花鸟鱼虫市场	Others				
旧货市场	Second Hand Markets				
古玩、古董、字画市场	Antiques,Calligraphy and Painting Markets				
邮票、硬币市场	Stamps and Coins Markets				
其他旧货市场	Others				
其他专业市场	Others				

主要统计指标解释

社会消费品零售总额 指批发和零售业、餐饮业、新闻出版业、邮政业和其他服务业等，售予城乡居民用于生活消费的商品和社会集团用于公共消费的商品之总量。社会消费品零售总额包括：

一、批发和零售业企业(单位)：

1.售予城乡居民的各种生活消费品；

2.售予入境旅游的外国人、华侨、港澳台同胞的各类商品；

3.售予行政事业单位、社会团体、军队和武警等机构的商品，以及以零售方式售予各类企业的商品。具体包括：用于非生产和社会交往的办公用品，如通讯设备、计算器具和设备、电讯网络设备、文印设备、音像视听器材和设备、纸张、本册、文具及装订文印材料、家具、日用电器、针纺织品、清洁卫生用品、文体用品、奖品、纪念品、礼品等；供内部人员乘坐的交通工具和燃料；用于办公设施修缮的各类配件、材料、工具等；用于取暖和防暑降温的设备、燃料、材料及食品等；专用于教学的用品和设备；非营利医疗机构的中、西药品、中药材和医疗设备器材；非专用的劳动保护用品；不对外营业的内部食堂用的餐具、炊具、设备、清洁卫生工具和食品、燃料等；军队、武警用于其人员生活的衣着品和个人用品；其他各类非生产性设备和用品。

二、餐饮业出售的主食、菜肴、烟酒饮料和其他商品。

三、新闻出版业、邮政业售予城乡居民、企事业单位、军队和武警等机构的书报杂志、音像制品、邮品等。

四、其他服务业出售的食品、烟酒饮料、服装鞋帽、日常生活用品、医药保健用品、艺术品、工艺美术品、玩具、殡葬用品以及其他消费品。

批发零售业商品购、销、存总额 指各种登记注册类型的批发、零售业企业(单位)以本企业(单位)为总体的，从国内、国外市场购进的商品总量，销售和出口的商品总量、库存商品总量等情况。该指标可以反映商品流转过程中商品的购进、销售、库存之间的比例关系和存在的问题。

商品购进总额 指从本企业(单位)以外的单位和个人购进(包括从境外直接进口)作为转卖或加工后转卖的商品总额。它反映批发零售贸易业从国内、国外市场上购进商品的总量。商品购进总额包括：(1)从工农业生产者购进的商品；(2)从出版社、报社的出版发行部门购进的图书、杂志和报纸；(3)从各种登记注册类型的批发零售贸易企业(单位)购进的商品；(4)从其他单位购进的商品，如从机关、团体、企业等单位购进的剩余物资，从餐饮业、服务业购进的商品，从海关、市场管理部门购进的缉私和没收的商品，从居民手中收购的废旧商品等；(5)从国(境)外直接进口的商品。不包括企业(单位)为自身经营用和未通过买卖行为而收入的商品以及销售退回、商品升溢等。

商品销售总额 指对本企业(单位)以外的单位和个人出售(包括对境外直接出口)的商品总额。它反映批发零售贸易业在国内市场上销售商品以及出口商品的总量。商品销售总额包括：(1)售给城乡居民和社会集团消费用的商品；(2)售给工业、农业、建筑业、运输邮电业、批发零售贸易业、餐饮业、服务业等作为生产、经营使用的商品；(3)售给批发零售贸易业作为转卖或加工后转卖的商品；(4)对国(境)外直接出口的商品。不包括出售本企业(单位)自用的废旧包装用品、未通过买卖行为付出的商品、经本单位介绍，由买卖双方直接结算，本单位只收取手续费的业务、购货退出的商品以及商品损耗和损失等。

批发零售业库存 指报告期末各种登记注册类型的批发零售贸易企业(单位)已取得所有权的商品。它反映批发零售贸易企业(单位)的商品库存情况和对市场商品供应的保证程度。期末库存包括：(1)存放在批发零售贸易业经营单位(如门市部、批发站、经营处)仓库、货场、货柜和货架中的商品；(2)挑选、整理、包装中的商品；(3)已记入购进而尚未运到本单位的商品，即发货单或银行承兑凭证已到而货未到的部分;(4)寄放他处的商品,如因购货方拒绝承付而暂时存放在购货方的商品和已办完加工成品收回手续而未提回的商品;(5)委托其他单位代销(未作销售或调出)尚未售出的商品;(6)代其他单位购进尚未交付的商品。不包括所有权不属于本单位的商品、拨付除批发零售贸易业以外的其他行业所属独立核算加工厂等加工生产尚未收回成品的商品、代国家物资储备部门保管的商品等。

库存总额采用的计算价格是:农副产品采购单位按购进价计算;批发单位按进货价计算;零售单位按核算价格计算,即按什么价格核算就按什么价格计算。

住宿餐饮业营业额 指住宿和餐饮业法人企业、产业活动单位在经营活动中因提供服务或销售商品等取得的收入,包括客房收入、餐费收入、商品销售收入和其他收入。客房收入指住宿和餐饮业法人企业、产业活动单位在经营活动中因提供住宿服务取得的客房收入。餐费收入指住宿和餐饮业法人企业、产业活动单位因为顾客提供就餐服务取得的收入,包括经烹饪、调制加工后出售的各种食品,如主食、炒菜、凉拌菜等的收入。商品销售收入指住宿和餐饮业法人企业、产业活动单位伴随服务而出售商品所取得的收入。其他收入指营业收入中除客房收入、餐费收入、商品销售收入以外的其他收入,包括娱乐、健身和商务服务等。

亿元商品交易市场成交额 指年成交额达到亿元以上,经工商部门批准、专门从事商品批发、零售业务活动的市场。其市场所有摊位成交总额称为商品交易市场成交额。

连锁企业(或称连锁店、连锁公司) 指在核心企业或总店的领导下,由分散的、经营同类商品或服务的企业或活动单位,采取共同方针,实行集中采购和分散销售的有机结合,通过规范化经营,实现规模效益的经济联合组织形式。一般连锁店应由若干个分店组成。其经营特征:(1)经营同类商品;(2)使用统一商号;(3)统一采购配送,采购与销售相分离(部分商品可根据物流合理和保质保鲜原则,由供应商直接送货到门店,其余均由总部统一配送)。

连锁门店包括下列三种形式:

直营连锁:也叫正规连锁。连锁门店均由总部独资或控股开设,在总部的直接领导下统一经营。总部采取纵深似的管理方式,直接下令掌管所有的零售门店,零售门店也必须完全接受总部指挥。他是大型垄断商业资本通过吞并、兼并或独资、控股等途径,发展壮大自身实力和规模的一种形式。

特许连锁:各连锁门店(被特许人)通过合同形式,取得使用总部(特许人)商标、商号、经营技术和销售总部开发的商品的特许权,各加盟连锁门店为独立法人,在总部指导下统一经营。

自由连锁:也称自愿连锁。连锁公司的门店均为独立法人,各自的资产所有权关系不变,在公司总部的指导下共同经营。各成员店使用共同的店名,与总部订阅有关购、销、宣传等方面的合同,并按合同开展经营活动。在合同规定的范围之外,各成员店可以自由活动。根据自愿原则,各成员店可自由加入连锁体系,也可自由退出。

特许连锁加上自由连锁等于加盟连锁。

Explanatory Notes on Main Statistical Indicators

Total Retail Sales of Consumer Goods refer to the sum of retail sales of commodities sold by wholesale, retail, catering, publishing, post and telecommunications and other service industries to urban and rural households for private consumption and to social institutions for public consumption. Retail sales of consumer goods include:

1) Sales by wholesale and retail units:

a) of consumer goods sold to urban and rural households

b) of commodities sold to foreigners, overseas Chinese and Chinese compatriots from Hong Kong, Macao and Taiwan visiting in China

c)of commodities sold to government agencies, institutions, social organizations, military and armed police units, and commodities sold to enterprises in the form of retail sales. More specifically, they include: office facilities and articles for non-production purposes such as communications equipment, computing equipment and instruments, TV and network equipment, printing and copying equipment, audio–visual equipment and instruments, paper, notebooks, stationeries, furniture, electric appliances, knitwear, sanitation and cleaning articles, cultural and sport articles, articles for prizes, souvenirs, etc.; transport vehicles and fuels for employees; materials, spare parts and tools for the maintenance of office facilities; equipment, fuels, materials and food for winter heating or summer cooling purposes; articles and equipment for teaching purpose; Chinese and western medicines and medical equipment and facilities purchased by non profit–making medical institutes; non–specialized work safety articles; cooking utensils, tableware, equipment, cleaning articles, food and fuels purchased by internal cafeterias; clothes and personal articles purchased by military or armed police units for their officials and soldiers; and other equipment and articles for non–production purposes.

2) Sales of stable food, cooked dishes, beverages, tobaccos and other articles by catering units.

3) Sales of books, newspapers, magazines, audio–visual products and post products by publishing, post and telecommunications departments to urban and rural households and to enterprises, institutions, military and armed police units.

4) Sales of food, beverages, tobaccos, clothing, hats, footwear, articles for daily use, medicines, medical and health articles, work of art, handicrafts, toys, funeral articles and other articles by other service industries.

Purchase, Sales and Stock of Commodities by Wholesale and Retail Trades refer to the total volume of commodities purchased, total volume of sales and exports, and the stock of commodities by wholesale and retail enterprises (establishments) of different status of registration from domestic and overseas markets. This indictor reflects the relationship among purchase, sales and stock of commodities in the circulation of goods and reveals the existing problems.

Total Purchases of Commodities refer to the total value of purchases of commodities by the enterprises (establishments) from other establishments or individuals (including direct import from abroad) for the purpose of re–selling, either with or without further processing of the commodities purchased. This indicator is used to show the total value of purchases of commodities by wholesale and retail establishments from domestic and overseas markets. The total purchases include: (1) agricultural and industrial products purchased from producers; (2) books, magazines and newspapers purchased from distribution departments of the publishers; (3) commodities purchased from wholesale and retail establishments of different status of registration; (4) commodities purchased from other units, such as surplus materials purchased from government agencies, enterprises or institutions, commodities purchased from catering and service establishments, confiscated goods purchased from customs authorities or market management agencies, second–hand goods and wastes purchased from residents; and (5) commodities directly imported from abroad. Excluded are commodities purchased by enterprises (establishments) for use in their own business operation, commodities obtained without buying or selling procedures, rejected commodities, etc.

Total Sales of Commodities refer to value of commodities sold by the establishments to other establishments and individuals (including direct export). This indicator is used to show the total value of sales of commodities at domestic markets and export. The total sales include: (1) commodities sold to urban and rural residents and social groups for their consumption; (2) commodities sold to establishments in industry, agriculture, construction, transportation, post and telecommunications, wholesale and retail trades, catering trade and public utility for their production and operation; (3) commodities sold to wholesale and retail establishments for re selling, with or without further processing; and (4)commodities for direct export to other countries. Excluded are selling of waste packaging materials used by the establishments (units) themselves, commodities transferred without buying or selling procedures, commission income from brokerage in transactions whose settlement is directly handled by buyers and sellers, rejected commodities in the purchase, loss in commodities, etc.

Commodity Stock of Wholesale and Retail Enterprises refers to total commodities possessed by wholesale and retail enterprises (units) of various types of registration status at the end of the reference period, which reflects the commodity stock level of various wholesale and retail enterprises and the potential for market supply. It includes: (1) commodities located in storage, garages, counters, and shelves of operating units (such as sale stores, wholesale centers, and operating offices) of wholesale and retail enterprises; (2) commodities in the process of selecting, sorting, and packing; (3) commodities not arrived but recorded as purchase in the account, i.e. commodities not arrived but payment receipts for the commodities from the sellers or the banks arrived; (4) commodities deposited in other places rather than places mentioned above, for instance: commodities in the hold of purchasers temporarily due to the refusal of payment and commodities not taken back after going through the formalities; (5) commodities entrusted to other units to sell but not sold yet; (6) commodities purchased for other units but not delivered yet. Commodities not included as stock are those not owned by the enterprises (units), those allocated to financially independent factories rather than wholesale and retail enterprises for processing but not taken back yet, and finally those put in stock by wholesale and retail enterprises on behalf of the state material reserves units.

For the calculation of the value of commodities stock, the value is calculated at purchasing prices in agricultural goods purchasing units and wholesale units, and at the accounting prices in retail units.

Business Revenue of Hotels and Catering Services refer to revenue received from providing services or selling commodities by corporate enterprises and establishments engaged in hotel and catering services, including income from hotel rooms, from catering services, from selling of commodities and from other services. Income from hotel rooms refers to income of corporate enterprises and establishments by providing lodging services. Income from catering services refers to income of corporate enterprises and establishments by providing catering services, including selling of cooked or prepared foods such as stable food, cooked dishes or cold dishes. Income from selling of commodities refers to income of corporate enterprises and establishments by selling commodities that accompany the services they provide. Income from other activities refers to income received other than income from hotel rooms, catering services or selling of commodities, such as income from providing recreation, fitness or business services.

Volume of Transaction at Large Commodity Markets (with transaction value over 100 million yuan) refers to markets approved by the industrial and commercial administration departments, which specialize in wholesale and retail of commodities with an annual transaction of over 100 million yuan. The sum of sales of all sellers in the markets makes up the transaction value of the markets.

Chain Enterprises (also called chain stores or chain corporations) refer to a form of joint economic entities under which scattered enterprises or establishments engaged in providing homogeneous commodities or services, with the central leadership of core enterprise or headquarters and guided by common policies, conduct centralized purchase and distributed selling of commodities, in order to gain better efficiency through standardized operation. Consisting of a number of branch stores, the chain stores have in general following features: 1) homogeneous commodities, 2) unique name of stores, 3) centralized purchase and delivery which is separated from distributed selling operation (most commodities are delivered from the headquarters except some items which, from logistics, quality or freshness considerations, might be delivered by the suppliers directly).

Chain stores have 3 categories:

a) Chain stores under direct management: These are formal chain stores invested or controlled by the headquarters. They operate under the direct and unified management from the headquarters. Adopting a direct management approach, the headquarters give orders and control all retail stores, which follow completely the directives from the headquarters. Large monopolized commercial companies develop and expand their business through purchasing, merging, direct investment and controlling of shares.

b) Chain stores through special permit: Through contracts, chain stores (or their owners) obtain licenses from the headquarters to use designated trade marks, names, operation know-how, and to sell the commodity developed by the headquarters. Under this arrangement, each store in the chain is an independent legal entity and operates under the guidance from the headquarters.

c) Chain stores through voluntary arrangement: Under this arrangement, all stores operate together under the guidance of the headquarters, while maintaining their status of independent legal entities with full ownership of their assets. They use the same store name, sign contracts with the headquarters concerning purchase, sale, publicity, etc. and operate under the contract. They are free to engage in other activities which are not bounded in the contract. They could join or leave the chain on voluntary basis.

Chain stores through special permit and those through voluntary arrangement make up chain stores through license arrangement.

17 科技和教育

Science, Technology and Education

17-1 科技活动基本情况
BASIC STATISTICS ON PERSONEL ENGAGED IN SCIENTIFIC AND TECHNICAL ACTIVITIES

项　目	Item	2010	2011	2012	2013	2014	2015
科技活动人员 (人)	Personels Engaged in Scientific and Technical Activities (person)	282604	310240	339786	365502	388430	378828
R&D人员 (人)	R & D Personels	142683	166357	185703	205172	218094	220977
R&D经费内部支出 (万元)	Inner Expenditures of R & D Funds (10 000 yuan)	2637885	3230128	3845239	4462690	5108973	5617415
基础研究	Basic Research	102494	139256	203953	218994	186200	230593
应用研究	Practical Research	472497	471732	561485	679021	691267	705635
实验发展	Experiment Development	2062893	2619140	3079800	3564675	4231507	4681187

17-2 科技活动项目、成果与机构情况
BASIC STATISTICS ON SCIENTIFIC AND TECHNICAL PROJECTS, ACHIEVEMENT AND INSTITUTIONS

项　目	Item	2011	2012	2013	2014	2015
发表科技论文 (篇)	Scientific Research Papers Published (piece)	88826	89714	90209	93590	93190
出版科技专著数 (种)	Scientific and Techincal Books Published (kind)	2401	2672	2618	2900	2827
科技项目(课题)数 (个)	Number of Scientific Projects (unit)	45457	48669	53088	55777	56218
科技项目经费支出 (万元)	Expenses for Scientific Projects (10 000 yuan)	2440630	3208902	3433884	3768678	4504527
科学研究与开发机构数 (个)	Number of Scientific Research Institutions and Development Organizations (unit)	1471	1744	1946	2002	2245
科研机构R&D人员数 (人)	R & D Staff (person)	72747	67997	74696	68151	75338
科研机构R&D内部支出(万元)	Inner Expenditures of R & D Funds (10 000 yuan)	1237563	1464692	1938710	1901466	2111784
科研机构年末仪器设备资产原价 (万元)	Original Price of Fixed Assets of Scientific Research Institutions and Organizations at Year-end (10 000 yuan)	2037951	2293613	2553205	2591182	2635298

17-3 政府部门所属科学研究与开发机构科技活动情况
BASIC STATISTICS ON STATE-OWNED RESAEARCH AND DEVELOPMENT INSTITUTIONS

项 目	Item	机构(个) Number of Institu-tions (unit)	科技活动人员(人) Persons Engaged (person)	大学本科及以上学历 Bachelor's Degrees and Above	#R&D人员 Research and Development Persons	收费收入(万元) Revenue (10 000 yuan)	#政府拨款 Government Appropriations
2013年总计	**Total of 2013**	**268**	**9880**	**6997**	**6627**	**330002**	**262430**
一、自然科学和技术领域	Natural Science and Technology	249	8944	6240	6083	309814	244642
县级政府部门属	Department of County	135	1144	239	113	5135	3572
市、州级政府部门属	Department of Cities and Prefecture	68	1693	964	448	32952	17648
省政府部门属	Department of Province	53	3822	2958	2185	163291	98118
国务院部门属	Department of State Council	12	3221	2836	3881	210591	160783
#中科院武汉分院属	#Chinese Academy of Science Wuhan Branch	7	1876	1722	3487	112661	92969
二、社会、人文科学领域	Sosiety and Humanity	8	363	302	320	8003	7490
2014年总计	**Total of 2014**	**256**	**9938**	**7159**	**7077**	**458906**	**281806**
一、自然科学和技术领域	Natural Science and Technology	239	9038	6423	6650	433627	259948
县级政府部门属	Department of County	134	1151	234	175	14631	5443
市、州级政府部门属	Department of Cities and Prefecture	59	1617	938	717	36475	19505
省政府部门属	Department of Province	51	3800	3029	1917	171818	103203
国务院部门属	Department of State Council	12	3370	2958	4268	235982	172074
#中科院武汉分院属	#Chinese Academy of Science Wuhan Branch	6	1889	1690	3566	123589	97124
二、社会、人文科学领域	Sosiety and Humanity	7	325	274	208	10785	10601
2015年总计	**Total of 2015**	**239**	**9298**	**6975**	**6869**	**528259**	**345156**
一、自然科学和技术领域	Natural Science and Technology	223	8521	6334	6520	502541	322521
县级政府部门属	Department of County	121	988	208	95	16001	5436
市、州级政府部门属	Department of Cities and Prefecture	51	1465	870	602	37344	19126
省政府部门属	Department of Province	39	2824	2316	1420	166296	93879
国务院部门属	Department of State Council	12	3244	2940	4403	282899	204078
#中科院武汉分院属	#Chinese Academy of Science Wuhan Branch	6	1714	1559	3528	138456	111859
二、社会、人文科学领域	Sosiety and Humanity	7	312	255	182	11143	10794

17-3 续表 continued

项　目	Item	经费支出(万元) Expenditures (10 000 yuan)	*科技经费支出 Expenditure on Science & Technology	*R&D经费内部支出 Inner Expenditure of R & D	研究课题数(个) Number of Projects	课题经费投入(万元) Investment on Subject Study (10 000 Yuan)	参加课题组(人年) Number of Persons Engaged in Subjects Study (person/year)
2013年总计	**Total of 2013**	**414914**	**310410**	**158077**	**3738**	**126673**	**6523**
一、自然科学和技术领域	Natural Science and Technology	393283	292941	153014	3599	123807	6106
县级政府部门属	Department of County	15898	6576	850	49	1037	153
市、州级政府部门属	Department of Cities and Prefecture	31822	24529	5428	220	3907	542
省政府部门属	Department of Province	163291	78747	31809	936	22159	2151
国务院部门属	Department of State Council	217520	185486	119988	2533	99569	3678
*中科院武汉分院属	*Chinese Academy of Science Wuhan Branch	123903	111453	107873	1644	62085	2674
二、社会、人文科学领域	Sosiety and Humanity	8046	6545	2119	77	726	199
2014年总计	**Total of 2014**	**434547**	**326067**	**182264**	**3884**	**150800**	**7044**
一、自然科学和技术领域	Natural Science and Technology	412198	308486	174852	3817	149140	6631
县级政府部门属	Department of County	14947	7729	398	37	567	190
市、州级政府部门属	Department of Cities and Prefecture	32101	25007	7001	259	7125	702
省政府部门属	Department of Province	152770	92057	38017	881	22993	2124
国务院部门属	Department of State Council	234729	201272	136847	2707	120113	4028
*中科院武汉分院属	*Chinese Academy of Science Wuhan Branch	122286	104885	101373	1642	73891	2833
二、社会、人文科学领域	Sosiety and Humanity	10496	7896	4708	20	413	140
2015年总计	**Total of 2015**	**516130**	**394399**	**208946**	**4011**	**179430**	**6743**
一、自然科学和技术领域	Natural Science and Technology	492199	375146	201072	3931	177450	6444
县级政府部门属	Department of County	15238	7978	468	37	647	120
市、州级政府部门属	Department of Cities and Prefecture	31269	23787	7202	222	4741	589
省政府部门属	Department of Province	153526	92416	35275	813	30200	1675
国务院部门属	Department of State Council	292165	250964	158126	2859	141862	4060
*中科院武汉分院属	*Chinese Academy of Science Wuhan Branch	146046	128094	121098	1790	86273	2796
二、社会、人文科学领域	Sosiety and Humanity	11582	9118	6045	17	527	75

注：1.本表数据没有包括科技情报文献机构数据，但包括了县政府所属科技综合服务机构数。
2.科技部门的课题数包括生产性活动课题。

Notes:a)The data of intelligence literature is not included in this table.
b)The number of projects in science and technology department includes projects of production activities.

17-4 科学情报文献机构情况
STATISTICS ON SCIENTIFIC INTELLIGENCE LITERATURE ORGANIZATIONS

项目	Item	2000	2005	2010	2011	2012	2013	2014	2015
机构 (个)	Institutions (unit)	14	12	11	11	11	11	10	9
职工总数 (人)	Total Number of Employees (person)	564	546	553	560	596	610	592	513
从事科技活动人员	Persons engaged in Scientific Activities	511	456	512	521	554	573	575	465
#大学本科及以上学历	#Bachelor's degrees and Above	337	306	347	387	422	455	462	386
经费收入总额 (万元)	Funds (10 000 yuan)	2629	6677	8706	8253	11650	15472	14493	14573
#政府拨款	#Government Appropriations	1679	5210	6009	6323	8476	12131	12515	11840
经费支出总额 (万元)	Expendtitures (10 000 yuan)	2340	6778	7955	7296	10460	13584	11852	12348
#劳务费	#Service Charge	970	1179	2668	3255	4038	4105	4328	4210

17-5 高等院校科技活动情况
BASIC STATISTICS ON SCIENTIFIC AND TECHNICAL ACTIVITIES OF INSTITUTIONS OF HIGHER EDUCATION

项目	Item	2014			2015		
		合计 Total	自然科学和技术领域 Natural Science and Technology	社会、人文科学领域 Sosiety and Humanity	合计 Total	自然科学和技术领域 Natural Science and Technology	社会、人文科学领域 Sosiety and Humanity
科学研究与开发机构数 (个)	Institutions of Research and Development (unit)	542	360	182	594	405	189
科技活动人员数 (人)	Number of Personels in Scientific and Technical Activities (person)	76371	49438	26933	77421	50173	27248
研究与发展经费内部支出 (万元)	Inner Expenditures of Research and Development (10 000 yuan)	470151	395848	74303	545156	472507	72649
研究课题数 (个)	Number of Research Projects (unit)	41376	23410	17966	42709	24050	18659
项目(课题)经费投入 (万元)	Funds Invested in Research Projects (10 000 yuan)	394202	339619	54583	443381	388583	54799
项目(课题)参加人员折合全时当量 (人年)	Number of Persons Engaged in Projects (person-year)	15386	11105	4281	15275	10711	4565

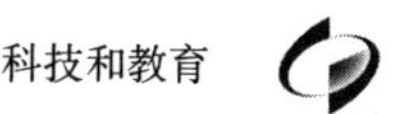

17-6 大中型工业企业科技活动情况
STATISTICS ON RESEARCH AND DEVELOPMENT ACTIVITIES OF LAREGE AND MEDIUM-SIZED INDUSTRIAL ENTERPRISES

单位:万元 (10 000 yuan)

项　目	Item	2010	2011	2012	2013	2014	2015
大中型企业个数 (个)	Large and Medium Enterprises (unit)	1421	1881	2022	2274	2277	2204
有R&D活动的企业数 (个)	Number of Enterprises with Scientific Activities (unit)	559	491	478	584	633	717
从事科技活动人员数 (人)	Number of Persons Engaged in Scientific Activities (person)	120581	136661	155116	157520	170579	163587
#大学本科以上学历	#Bachelor's Degree and Above				49624	54203	54982
研究与发展人员数 (人)	Persons Engaged in Research and Development (person)	64329	81444	93825	99563	107656	105848
企业办研发机构数 (个)	Number of Research and Development Organizations Opened by Enterprises (unit)	457	352	454	478	432	534
R&D项目数 (个)	Number of R&D Projects (unit)	4602	5222	5668	6095	6400	4954
全部R&D项目经费支出 (万元)	Expenses for Development Projects (10 000 yuan)	1193793	1331576	1978154	1892653	2172256	2627715
研究与发展经费支出 (万元)	Expenditures for Research and Development (10 000 yuan)	1429050	1835717	2287148	2521324	2978369	3272348
新产品开发费支出 (万元)	Expenditures for Developing New Products (10 000 yuan)	1760964	2113832	2488079	2606672	2896732	2856350
技术改造经费支出 (万元)	Expenditures for Technical Innovation (10 000 yuan)	1326521	891890	921059	883841	916673	835034.4
技术引进经费支出 (万元)	Expenditures for Technology Introduction (10 000 yuan)	190418	81194	153336	121278	128533	147979.3
消化吸收经费支出 (万元)	Expenditures for Technology Utilization (10 000 yuan)	29408	29911	42406	39464	38330	16046
购买国内技术经费支出 (万元)	Expenditures for Purchasing Domestic Technology (10 000 yuan)	21561	26716	38037	72594	53481	50314

17-7 有研发活动的规模以上工业企业主要分组指标

指 标	Item	有R&D活动企业(个) Number of Enterprises with R & D Activities (unit)	
		2014	2015
总 计	**Total**	**1960**	**2421**
一、按登记注册类型分	**Grouped by Type of Registration**		
内资企业	Domestic-funded Enterprises	1794	2245
国有企业	State-owned Enterprises	21	34
集体企业	Collective-owned Enterprises	2	3
股份合作企业	Cooperative Enterprises		2
联营企业	Associated Enterprises		
有限责任公司	Limited Liability Companies	817	959
股份有限公司	Share Holding Co., Ltd	215	244
私营企业	Private Enterprises	736	995
其他企业	Others	3	8
港、澳、台商投资企业	Hongkong, Maco and Taiwan-invested Enterprises	68	71
合资经营企业(港或澳、台资)	Joint Ventures (Hongkong, Maco or Taiwan Invested Enterprises)	46	46
合作经营企业(港或澳、台资)	Cooperative Ventures(Hongkong, Maco or Taiwan Invested Enterprises)	1	
港、澳、台商独资经营企业	Enterprises Solely Funded by hongkong, Maco and Taiwan Businessmen	18	23
港、澳、台商投资股份有限公司	Hongkong, Maco and Taiwan Funded Share Holding Co.Ltd.	2	2
其他港澳台投资企业	Other Hongkong, Maco and Taiwan Funded Share Holding Co., Ltd.	1	
外商投资企业	Foreign-invested Enterprises	98	105
中外合资经营企业	Sino-Foreign Joint Ventures	70	78
中外合作经营企业	Sino-Foreign Contractual Joint Ventures		
外资企业	Foreign Funded Enterprises	25	25
外商投资股份有限公司	Foreign Funded Share Holding Co., Ltd.	2	1
其他外商投资企业	Other Enterprises Invested by Foreign Businessmen	1	1
二、按行业分	**Grouped by Sector**		
煤炭开采和洗选业	Coal Mining and Processing		
石油和天然气开采业	Petroleum and Natural Gas Extraction	1	1
黑色金属矿采选业	Ferrous Metals Mining and Processing	5	8
有色金属矿采选业	Non-ferrous Metals Mining and Processing	1	1
非金属矿采选业	Non-metal Minerals Mining and Processing	16	18
开采辅助活动	Mining Auxiliary	1	1
其他采矿业	Other Mining	1	1
农副食品加工业	Primary Products and Food Processing Industry	135	176

MAJOR INDIENTORS OF INDUSTRIAL ABOVE DESIGNATED ENTERPRISES WITH RESEARCH AND DEVELOPMENT ACTIVITIES

有研发机构的企业(个) Number of Enterprises with R&D Activities (unit)		R&D人员合计 (人) R & D Personels (person)		R&D经费支出(万元) Funding for R & D Expenditure (10 000 yuan)		新产品开发经费支出(万元) Funding for New Product Development Expenditures (10 000 yuan)		新产品销售收入(万元) Revenue of New Product Sales (10 000 yuan)	
2014	2015	2014	2015	2014	2015	2014	2015	2014	2015
927	**1117**	**138562**	**140381**	**3629506**	**4072726**	**3646332**	**3644392**	**52745891**	**56769152**
874	1053	119212	122395	3042462	3402384	2967692	2981211	37352710	42560779
14	25	14487	13742	746975	578624	555910	538530	3093272	2911532
1	1	39	22	1005	755	413	1484	6510	22932
1	1		65		543	306	543	2241	7900
359	408	55138	52169	1195015	1400940	1202323	1203691	16652936	18584506
106	121	29649	30775	640818	765757	684274	687647	8039126	8815980
390	493	19867	25357	456396	651899	521617	546398	9545085	12156747
3	4	32	265	2253	3865	2850	2919	13541	61182
22	30	6542	6144	153478	168996	146152	153932	2446012	3021361
18	25	4256	4255	113908	126127	102897	114544	1867955	2352167
		9		710				8363	
4	3	1864	1722	35606	38236	40485	33572	552314	599932
	2	397	167	2943	4633	2304	5817	17380	69262
		16		311		465			
31	34	12808	11842	433566	501346	532488	509249	12947169	11187013
21	20	8452	8913	370233	415986	462848	456036	12035609	10399606
1	1					514		4657	150
8	11	2102	1683	33961	48517	61021	50827	517971	483345
1	1	2236	1222	29158	36632	7891	2387	386782	300648
	1	18	24	215	211	215		2150	3264
	1	1168	609	3386	1774	253	134		21821
1	1	66	92	1551	4020	1020	1387	4900	
1	1	21	31	1457	165	7			
8	6	240	263	9496	8846	1321	411	89067	48182
		52	58	415	914	927	432		
		53	15	191	157	111	96		
82	96	3680	4880	114861	127561	123877	112248	3559391	4490255

17-7 续表 continued

指 标	Item	有R&D活动企业(个) Number of Enterprises with R & D Activities (unit)	
		2014	2015
食品制造业	Food Production	36	51
酒、饮料和精制茶制造业	Beverage Production	37	73
烟草制品业	Tabacco Processing	3	2
纺织业	Textile Industry	43	64
纺织服装、服饰业	Textile Wearing Apparel and Accessaries	8	9
皮革、毛皮、羽毛及其制品和制鞋业	Leather, Fur, Feather and Related Products	1	
木材加工及木、竹、藤、棕、草制品业	Timber Processing and Wood, Bamboo, Rattan, Palm and Sraw Products	22	30
家具制造业	Furniture Manufacturing	4	8
造纸及纸制品业	Papermaking and Paper Products	14	15
印刷和记录媒介复制业	Printing and Record Processing	18	23
文教、工美、体育和娱乐用品制造业	Stationery, Education, Art, Sport and Entertainment Products	10	12
石油加工、炼焦及核燃料加工业	Petroleum Processing, Coking Products and Nuclear Fuel Processing	10	11
化学原料及化学制品制造业	Raw Chemical Material and Chemical Products	204	258
医药制造业	Medical and pharmaceutical Products	138	162
化学纤维制造业	Chemical Fibers	4	6
橡胶和塑料制品业	Rubber Products and Plastic Products	56	67
非金属矿物制品业	Nonmetal Material Products	98	143
黑色金属冶炼及压延加工业	Smelting and Processing of ferrous Metals	39	30
有色金属冶炼及压延加工业	Smelting and Processing of Nonferrous Metals	28	34
金属制品业	Metal Products	89	110
通用设备械制造业	Ordinaryly Machinery Manufacturing	156	197
专用设备制造业	Special Purpose Equipment Manufacturing	142	177
汽车制造业	Automobile Manufacturing	260	279
铁路、船舶、航空航天和其他运输设备制造业	Realway, Ship, Aircraft and Other Transport Equipment Manufacturing	33	41
电气机械及器材制造业	Electric Machinery and Equipment	164	200
通信设备、计算机及其他电子设备制造业	Telecommunication Equipment, Computer and Other Electronic Equipment Manufacturing	116	134
仪器仪表及文化办公用机械制造业	Instruments, Meters, Cultural and Official Machinery	45	44
其他制造业	Other Manufacturing	6	13
废弃资源和废旧材料回收加工业	Waste Resources and Junk Material Recycled	3	5
金属制品、机械和设备修理业	Repairing of Metal and Mechanical Equipment	4	5
电力、热力的生产和供应业	Electric Power, Steam and Hot Water Production and Supply	7	10
煤气生产和供应业	Gas Production and Supply	2	2
水的生产和供应业	Tap Water Production and Supply		

有研发机构的企业(个) Number of Enterprises with R & D Units (unit)		R&D人员合计(人) R & D Personels (person)		R&D经费支出(万元) Funding for R & D Expenditure (10 000 yuan)		新产品开发经费支出(万元) Funding for New Product Development Expenditures (10 000 yuan)		新产品销售收入(万元) Revenue of New Product Sales (10 000 yuan)	
2014	2015	2014	2015	2014	2015	2014	2015	2014	2015
25	31	1003	1613	23015	91012	52758	68203	475412	772453
39	39	1370	2044	32524	66964	63737	67514	607711	534672
1	1	414	206	18238	8265	17692	8157	20794	3428
36	39	2264	3846	33016	63640	51219	65454	651173	980762
9	9	642	696	11133	10077	13591	14740	96428	168437
3		11		44		44	62	9247	
11	12	745	927	15471	18096	16074	16772	290118	332304
2	4	153	59	2206	830	2536	2286	43310	30192
9	8	453	517	20137	12786	18301	12412	119305	147730
8	7	722	966	13757	16577	11408	17251	120899	215473
3	6	448	310	7174	4814	7148	6043	131240	117043
6	4	383	335	14161	32714	13458	1672	151541	300061
101	129	12530	16134	344470	499146	213064	266100	6340257	7652936
70	90	11222	10110	174454	189298	160459	173693	2589468	2959834
1	1	309	714	1916	7260	2978	7065	73495	78483
33	41	2932	3270	42282	65357	48874	61456	1279985	1295079
56	61	6278	5101	98276	125921	131652	77764	1604730	1513837
18	17	10212	6167	649274	373812	407435	311726	3030192	2692026
11	16	1830	2952	125194	172691	47292	56809	2343105	2911164
39	62	5832	4650	98378	86762	114846	97357	1460463	1412768
59	80	7192	7907	127703	146689	151769	128104	2153194	2628373
45	57	6877	6481	119318	130212	144356	128896	1390951	1511909
120	119	18683	19360	588543	703213	755655	798084	14281540	13303183
15	23	8759	9687	119242	137081	155383	151609	1415472	1622180
54	73	11550	11437	234423	286513	282361	291517	4661855	4652699
33	49	17522	15109	522336	588490	568123	621370	2993740	3295873
15	19	1346	1584	27366	34613	38487	45209	334406	397371
4	8	532	1020	16728	21236	19449	18700	204248	280256
4	3	93	114	1711	2135	518	364	87291	213484
2	1	283	255	6286	5707	903	3565	11803	15849
2	2	448	538	4950	18406	7248	9735	109540	84725
1	1	244	324	4427	8973			9623	84312

17-8 全省高新技术产业发展情况(2015)

STATISTICS ON NEW AND HIGH TECHNIC INDUSTRY DEVELOPMENT IN THE WHOLE PROVINCE(2015)

单位:亿元 (100 million yuan)

项目	Item	全省 the Whole Province	增幅(%) Increase(%)
高新技术产业增加值	**Added Value of High-tech Industry**	**5028.94**	**13.0**
"四上"高新技术产业增加值	"Four Up" Added Value of High-tech Industry	4946.79	10.9
其中:高新服务业增加值	Added Value of High-tech Service	609.04	3.8
高新制造业增加值	Added Value of High-tech Manufacturing	4337.75	12.0
1.电子信息	1.Electronic Information	531.93	16.8
2.先进制造	2.Advanced Manufacturing	1699.15	12.9
3.新材料	3.New Material	902.06	12.1
4.生物医药与医疗机械	4.Bio-medicine and Medical Instrument	353.38	7.3
"四下"高新技术产业增加值	"Four Up" Added Value of High-tech Industry	82.15	8.5
高新制造业产值*	Output Value of High-tech Manufacturing	17188.20	10.1
高新制造业产品出口交货值*	Export Value of High-tech Manufacturing	15502.84	12.6
高新制造业产品销售收入*	Revenue of High-tech Manufacturing	1147.65	7.3
高新制造业利税总额*	Tax on High-tech Manufacturing	1201.97	3.5

注:带"*"号的指标口径为规模以上工业企业。
Note:Data with "*" cover industrial enterprises above designated size(the same below).

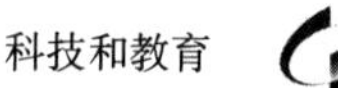
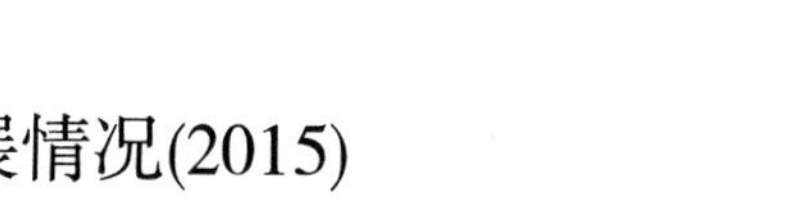

17-9 市州高新技术产业发展情况(2015)
STATISTICS ON THE DEVELOPMENT OF HIGH AND NEW TECHNOLOGY INDUSTRIE OF CITIES AND PREFECTURE (2015)

单位:亿元 (100 million yuan)

		增加值 Value Added	增加值* Value Added	增速* Increase(%)
全省合计	**Total of the Province**	**5028.94**	**4946.79**	**10.9**
武汉市	Wuhan	2246.65	2185.10	9.7
黄石市	Huangshi	156.05	155.16	4.2
十堰市	Shiyan	168.59	163.34	7.8
宜昌市	Yichang	592.32	584.03	13.0
襄阳市	Xiangyang	807.45	806.24	14.5
鄂州市	Ezhou	114.66	114.62	9.5
荆门市	Jingmen	177.18	177.00	14.2
孝感市	Xiaogan	167.45	166.57	11.4
荆州市	Jingzhou	154.68	154.10	9.1
黄冈市	Huanggang	130.46	129.90	8.3
咸宁市	Xianning	85.96	85.67	9.8
随州市	Suizhou	84.81	83.05	14.1
恩施州	Enshi	9.66	9.55	2.0
仙桃市	Xiantao	58.46	57.99	11.6
潜江市	Qianjiang	37.25	37.25	16.6
天门市	Tianmen	37.28	37.22	18.4
神农架林区	Shennongjia	0.06		

17-10 申报登记省、部级以上成果分类及经济效益
CLASSIFICATION AND ECONOMIC BENEFITS OF SCIENTIFIC ACHIEVEMENTS APPLIED AND REGISTERED ABOVE PROVINCIAL AND MINISTRIAL LEVEL

单位:项 (unit)

项目	Item	2000	2005	2010	2011	2012	2013	2014	2015
成果总类	**Total Calsses of Achievement**	**571**	**717**	**750**	**1200**	**1567**	**1621**	**1778**	**1933**
一、按成果水平分类	Grouped by Level								
国际首创/领先	International Innovation/ Leading	19	28	52	94	101	81	100	130
国际先进	Internationl Advanced Technology	97	172	195	210	254	326	353	373
国内首创/领先	Domestic Innovation/ Leading	276	394	362	559	745	751	706	743
国内先进	Domestic Advanced Technology	84	72	69	133	176	177	270	413
其它	Others	18	3	39	154	14	31	299	216
二、按成果类型分类	Grouped by Type								
基础理论研究	Basic Theory Research	37	15	15	21	24	22	13	16
应用开发研究	Applicable Development	494	669	717	1150	1507	1570	1728	1875
其它	Others	40	33	18	29	36	29	37	42
三、按成果产业属性分类	Grouped by Sector Property								
工业类成果	Industrial Achievements	145	225	226	355	532	514	560	693
农业类成果	Agricultural Achievements	79	129	124	209	197	251	371	320
医学类成果	Medical Achievements	199	291	231	385	414	441	446	394
其他类成果	Others	148	74	169	251	424	415	401	526
四、按成果完成单位分类	Grouped by Units								
高等院校完成	Institutions of Higher Education	149	169	137	168	160	246	271	198
研究单位完成	Scientific Research Institutions	92	92	64	110	86	74	116	99
厂矿企业完成	Industrial and Mineral Enterprises	137	176	303	513	1136	911	966	1233
其他单位完成	Others	193	280	246	409	185	390	425	403
五、经济效益 (亿元)	Economic Benefits (100 million yuan)								
总收入	Total Income	78.33	199.50			1212.78	331.33	462.80	379.48
本年度节约资金	Capital Saved in This Year	6.33	28.28	36.85	169.65	401.37	56.38	551.61	23.19

17-11 科学技术协会组织与活动
ORGANIZATIONS AND ACTIVITIES OF SCIENTIFIC AND TECHNOLOGICAL ASSOCIATION

项目		Item		2014	2015
一、机构与人员		**Organizations and Personels**			
1.省级学会	(个)	Provincal Institute	(unit)	133	133
会员	(人)	Members	(person)	152639	153948
高级(资深)会员	(人)	Senoir Members	(person)	21000	20349
外国会员	(人)	Foreign Members	(person)	38	5
2.市、州学会数	(个)	City and Prefecture Institute	(unit)	543	673
3.省级科协	(个)	Provincal Scientific Assosiations	(unit)	1	1
市、州科协	(个)	City and Prefecture Scientific Assosiations	(unit)	13	13
县(区)科协	(个)	County (District) Scientific Assosiations	(unit)	104	103
二、学术活动		**Academic Activities**			
省级学会及县以上科协		**Provincial Institutes and Scientific Assosiations above County level**			
国内学术会议	(次)	Domestic Academic Conference	(time)	646	757
参加人数	(人次)	Number of Person Participated	(person-time)	61440	73001
论文数	(篇)	Number of Scholary Paper	(piece)	15732	16866
境内国际学术会议	(次)	Domestic International Academic Conference	(time)	43	60
参加人数	(人次)	Number of Person Participated	(person-time)	5823	10792
论文数	(篇)	Number of Scholary Paper	(piece)	1394	3925
三、科普活动		**Science and Technology Popularization Activities**			
省级学会及县以上科协		**Provincial Institutes and Scientific Assosiations above County level**			
举办科普宣讲活动	(次)	Events of Science Popularization Lectures	(time)	9191	11471
宣讲活动受众人数	(人次)	People Participated	(person-time)	6478417	6945017
举办实用技术培训	(次)	Technical Training	(time)	10787	12058
实用技术培训人数	(人次)	People Participated	(person-time)	1980877	1887086
播放科技广播、影视节目	(分钟)	Scientific Radio and Video Programs	(mimute)	273963	439379
参加活动科技人员	(人次)	People Participated	(person-time)	96985	154045
四、青少年科技教育		**Education in Science and Technology for the Adolescents**			
省级学会及县以上科协		**Provincial Institutes and Scientific Assosiations above County level**			
举办青少年科技竞赛	(项)	Adolescent Technology Competition	(unit)	494	473
参加人数	(人次)	Number of Person Participated	(person-time)	2163083	1996254
获奖人数	(人次)	Number of Person Rewarded	(person-time)	79989	77884
举办青少年科学营	(次)	Adolescent Technology Campus		314	268
参加人数	(人次)	Number of Person Participated	(person-time)	18551	20031
举办青少年科技教育培训	(次)	Adolescent Technology Education Training		982	1101
培训人数	(人次)	Number of Person Participated	(person-time)	583166	614058
五、科普基础设施建设		**Infrastructure Construction of Science Popularization**			
县以上科协		**Scientific Assosiations above County Level**			
科技场馆	(个)	Science and Technology Museum	(unit)	64	68
建筑面积	(平方米)	Construction Area	(square metre)	185219	197956
展厅面积	(平方米)	Exhibition Area	(square metre)	73064	81454
全年参观人数	(人次)	Year-round Visitor	(person-time)	2033037	2385092
科普活动站	(个)	Science Popularization Station	(unit)	11192	12003
科普画廊建筑面积	(平方米)	Science Popularization Gallery Construction Area	(square metre)	116617	132060
省级科普教育基地	(个)	Provincial Education Base of Science Popularization	(unit)	93	145
农村科普示范基地	(个)	Rural Demonstration Base of Science Popularization	(unit)	1359	1547
六、为科技工作者服务		**Serve for Scientists**			
省级学会及县以上科协		**Provincial Institutes and Scientific Assosiations above County level**			
反映科技工作者建议	(条)	Reported Suggestions of Scientists		2048	1466
其中:获上级领导批示的建议	(条)	Answered by Leaders		420	311
答复人大政协代表(委员)提案	(件)	Replied Proposal of NPC and CPPCC Representatives(Committees)	(piece)	123	117
走访看望(慰问)科技工作者	(人次)	Visit Scientific Workers	(person-time)	2936	3757
科学道德与学风建设宣讲活动	(场次)	Preach Ethics of Science		24	9
宣讲活动受众人数	(人次)	Number of Audience	(person-time)	12110	2262
参加宣讲活动专家数	(人次)	Number of Specialists	(person-time)	316	129
技术创新方法培训班	(场次)	Technology Innovation Training Class		51	114
继续教育培训班	(场次)	Continuing Education Class		131	118
培训结业人数	(人次)	Number of People Completed Courses	(person-time)	9650	28359
宣传科技工作者人数	(人)	Propagating Scientific and Technology Workers	(person)	3432	6694
表彰奖励科技工作者	(人次)	Rewarded Scientific and Technology Workers	(person-time)	3924	3794

17-12 专利受理量、批准量及分布状况
NUMBER OF PATENT APPLICATIONS EXAMINATION, APPROVAL AND DISTRITUTION

单位:项 (unit)

项目	Item	受理量 Number of Patent Applications Examined 2005	2010	2014	2015	批准量 Number of Patent Applications Approved 2005	2010	2014	2015
合计	**Total**	**11534**	**31311**	**59050**	**74240**	**3860**	**17362**	**28290**	**38781**
发明	Creations and Inventions	2038	7410	22536	30204	733	2025	4855	7766
实用新型	Utility Models	4835	12792	27829	35676	2238	10431	19801	25298
外观设计	Designs	4661	11109	8685	8360	889	4906	3634	5717
在合计中	**Of This Total**								
个人	Individual	7400	10844	17294	18512	2189	4990	5822	8874
大专院校	Universities and Colleges	1365	3265	7972	11380	574	1972	3702	6468
科研单位	Insitutions of Scientific Research	182	1112	1537	1756	101	532	719	799
工矿企业	Industrial and Mineral Enterprises	2305	15856	28810	36702	901	9744	17746	22193
机关团体	Government Agencies and Organizations	283	234	3437	5889	98	124	301	447

17-13 按市州分三种专利申请与授权状况(2015)
THREE KINDS OF PATENT APPICATION AND AUTHORIZATION BY MUNICIPALITIES AND PREFECTURES(2015)

单位:项 (item)

市、州	Municipalities and Prefecture	申请 当年累计 Patent Application Total of year	发明 Invention	实用新型 New type of practicial Utility	外观设计 Design	授权 当年累计 Authorization Total of year	发明 Invention	实用新型 New type of practicial Utility	外观设计 Design
全省合计	**Total of the Province**	**74240**	**30204**	**35676**	**8360**	**38781**	**7766**	**25298**	**5717**
武汉	Wuhan	33565	15065	16125	2375	21679	5999	13569	2111
黄石	Huangshi	3416	1300	3455	1003	1116	102	2772	402
十堰	Shiyan	2773	814	5047	374	1417	122	1791	323
荆州	Jingzhou	7013	2555	1127	416	3715	541	1140	155
宜昌	Yichang	9297	3876	1176	940	2343	229	1014	379
襄阳	Xiangfan	1223	587	1791	168	288	45	971	443
鄂州	Ezhou	2221	761	1432	475	952	66	830	367
荆门	Jingmen	2904	997	1299	490	1586	193	654	360
孝感	Xiaogan	2484	695	1245	215	1570	156	718	168
黄冈	Huanggang	2456	913	912	418	1315	118	651	263
咸宁	Xianning	1756	426	574	248	964	50	327	144
随州	Suizhou	1256	434	266	370	495	24	237	117
恩施州	Enshi	922	447	119	333	415	61	170	130
仙桃	Xiantao	1124	443	549	132	335	35	107	160
潜江	Qianjiang	901	455	204	242	295	13	200	43
天门	Tianmen	868	416	319	156	276	9	133	149
神农架林区	Shennongjia	61	20	36	5	20	3	14	3

17-14 各类技术合同签定及执行情况
SIGNING AND IMPEMENTATION OF VARIOUS TECHNICAL CONTRACTS

项　目	Item	合同数(项) Number of Contracts (unit)	合同金额(万元) Value of Contracts (10 000 yuan)
2009	**2009**	**5694**	**779700**
技术开发合同	Technology Development Contracts	2391	337341
技术转让合同	Technology Transfer Contracts	216	239272
技术咨询合同	Technology Consultation Contracts	1144	42747
技术服务合同	Technology Service Contracts	1943	160339
2010	**2010**	**6641**	**909167**
技术开发合同	Technology Development Contracts	2390	502290
技术转让合同	Technology Transfer Contracts	199	126505
技术咨询合同	Technology Consultation Contracts	1321	71932
技术服务合同	Technology Service Contracts	2731	208439
2011	**2011**	**7799**	**1214103**
技术开发合同	Technology Development Contracts	4101	661014
技术转让合同	Technology Transfer Contracts	327	99063
技术咨询合同	Technology Consultation Contracts	1358	88232
技术服务合同	Technology Service Contracts	2013	365793
2012	**2012**	**12908**	**2345655**
技术开发合同	Technology Development Contracts	7698	1000226
技术转让合同	Technology Transfer Contracts	447	482601
技术咨询合同	Technology Consultation Contracts	1391	87457
技术服务合同	Technology Service Contracts	3372	775371
2013	**2013**	**14909**	**4187410**
技术开发合同	Technology Development Contracts	9473	1614052
技术转让合同	Technology Transfer Contracts	574	342631
技术咨询合同	Technology Consultation Contracts	1082	238981
技术服务合同	Technology Service Contracts	3780	1991746
2014	**2014**	**21696**	**6017367**
技术开发合同	Technology Development Contracts	11695	1398146
技术转让合同	Technology Transfer Contracts	518	279765
技术咨询合同	Technology Consultation Contracts	1496	389802
技术服务合同	Technology Service Contracts	7987	3949654
2015	**2015**	**22787**	**8300672**
技术开发合同	Technology Development Contracts	11318	2155738
技术转让合同	Technology Transfer Contracts	547	390390
技术咨询合同	Technology Consultation Contracts	1408	316786
技术服务合同	Technology Service Contracts	9514	5437758

17-15 全省技术买卖情况(2015)
PURCHASE AND SELLING OF TECHNOLOGY IN THE WHOLE PROVINCE (2015)

卖方类别 Type of the Seller / 买方类别 Type of the Buyer		合计 Total		机关法人 Organ Corporations		事业法人 Institutions Corporations		社团法人 Associations Corporations	
		合同数(项) Number of Contracts	成交额(万元) Contracted Value (10 000 yuan)	合同数(项) Number of Contracts	成交额(万元) Contracted Value (10 000 yuan)	合同数(项) Number of Contracts	成交额(万元) Contracted Value (10 000 yuan)	合同数(项) Number of Contracts	成交额(万元) Contracted Value (10 000 yuan)
总计	**Total**	**22787**	**8300672**	**238**	**112164**	**10013**	**1239436**	**278**	**95104**
机关法人	Departments	5021	2347027	235	111207	2521	712085	251	89437
事业法人	Institutions	3901	325369	2	570	2769	195753		
社团法人	Social Groups	62	11899			28	1185	1	378
企业法人	Corporations	13565	5544057	1	387	4632	280105	26	5289
自然人	Natural Person	23	3538			7	814		
其他组织	Other Organizations	215	68782			56	49494		

17-15 续表 continued

卖方类别 Type of the Seller / 买方类别 Type of the Buyer		企业法人 Corporations		自然人 Natural Person		其他组织 Other Organizations	
		合同数(项) Number of Contracts	成交额(万元) Contracted Value (10 000 yuan)	合同数(项) Number of Contracts	成交额(万元) Contracted Value (10 000 yuan)	合同数(项) Number of Contracts	成交额(万元) Contracted Value (10 000 yuan)
总计	**Total**	**12196**	**6831740**	**5**	**840**	**57**	**21388**
机关法人	Departments	2007	1431744	2	500	5	2053
事业法人	Institutions	1127	128565	1	10	2	471
社团法人	Social Groups	33	10336				
企业法人	Corporations	8859	5239806	1	30	46	18441
自然人	Natural Person	15	2424	1	300		
其他组织	Other Organizations	155	18865			4	423

17-16 地震观测及地方地震工作情况
STATISTICS ON EARTHQUAKE OBSERVATION AND LOCAL EFFORTS ON EARTHQUAKE WORKS

项　目	Item	2014	2015
职工总数 (人)	Total Number of Staff and Workers (person)	445	407
专业技术人员 (人)	Professtional Technical Personel (person)	309	303
高级技术人员 (人)	Senior Technical Personel (person)	75	82
市州级地震局 (个)	Number of Earthquake Agency (unit)	17	17
重点县地震办公室 (个)	Number of Earthquake Offices in Key Counties (unit)	32	32
地方地震工作人员 (人)	Local Seismologist (person)	641	641
地震观测台(网)人员 (人)	Number of Staff in Earthquake Observation Station (person)	73	73
#观测技术人员 (人)	#Technical Personel (person)	53	53
地震台站 (个)	Earthquake Observation Station (unit)	52	47
国家台	National Station	5	5
省级台	Provincial Station	47	42
GPS测量 (千米/点)	GPS Measurement (km/point)	120000/180	210000/430
流动重力测量 (千米/点)	Flow Gravity Measurement (km/point)	90000/482	70000/420

17-17 气象部门基本情况
BASIC CONDITIONS OF METEOROLOGICAL DEPARTMENT

项　目	tem	2000	2005	2010	2012	2013	2014	2015
一、气象观测人员总数 (人)	Total Number of Staff in Meteorological Depaartment (person)	333	375	378	388	415	469	446
地面观测	Groud Observation	285	320	330	340	367	410	376
高空观测	Upper Air Observation	24	18	18	16	14	24	34
雷达观测	Radar Observation	24	20	30	32	34	35	36
特种观测	Special Observation							
二、气象台站总数 (个)	Total Number of Meteorological Obervatory (unit)	85	87	87	87	89	89	89
气象台	Meteorological Obervatory	13	14	14	14	14	14	14
气象站	Weather Station	70	71	71	71	73	73	73
独立农试站	Independent Agricultural Station	2	2	2	2	2	2	2
三、卫星云图接收站点数 (个)	Number of Stations Receiving Satellite Image (unit)	11	25	15	10	17	17	17
极轨卫星	Polar Orbiting Meteorological Satellite	2	23	5	3	4	4	4
同步卫星	Geostationary Satellite	9	7	10	7	13	13	13
接收卫星云图图片数	Number of Satellite Image Pictures Received							
使用云图单位数	Number of Pictures Used	144						
四、拥有雷达数 (部)	Number of Radar Owned (unit)	11	12	15	14	17	14	14
701测风	701 Wind Sensing	4	4					
3厘米	3 cm	2	2	1	1	1	1	1
5厘米	5 cm	2	1	1		1		
10厘米	10 cm	3	5	10	10	7	10	10
l波段	1 Wave Band			3	3	8	3	3

17-18 质量技术监督检查情况
STATISTICS ON SUPERVISION AND EXAMINATION OF QUALITY TECHNOLOGY

年份 Year	机构(个) Institutions (unit)	职工人数(人) Number of Staff and Workers (person)	#专业技术人员 #Professional Technic Personel	经费收入(万元) Revenue (10 000 yuan)	经费支出(万元) Expenditures (10 000 yuan)	固定资产(万元) Fixed Assets (10 000 yuan)	#仪器设备 #Equipment and Devices	计量器具检定台(万套件) Number of Measuring Equipment Tested (10 000 units)	#衡具 #Measuring Instrument	#强制检定 #Compulsory Test
1980	88	1211	327	308	306	1667	512	60		
1985	107	1668	356	640	515	3234	1402	146	36	
1990	105	3299	1409	3063	2610	7994	3760	136	68	118
1995	167	6275	2121	10095	10374	21213	6327	150	64	140
1996	102	2265	1252	3237	3177	6985	3261	136	61	108
1997	101	2337	1337	3491	3418	6751	3680	150	62	110
1998	106	2479	1439	4 079	4034	6314	3810	126	50	100
1999	105	2531	1446	4 515	4532	6732	3713	120	43	103
2000	104	2790	1478	4 568	4853	8829	5286	150	43	105
2001	91	1632	911	3005	2899	6537	3881	132	33	65
2002	360	9583	4059	36371	34024	39461	9806	165	40	138
2003	403	9137	3960	44450	41317	47323	12114	154	45	118
2004	376	9034	4703	50520	48383	53579	14549	128	23	114
2005	398	9046	3953	59089	56152	62607	19986	120	22	98
2006	398	9050	4094	67864	64078	72440	23840	119	22	110
2007	393	9065	4072	79698	75988	81822	26984	119	19	102
2008	392	9055	3732	93140	89653	94547	27832	109	16	96
2009	395	9077	3718	111477	110965	111627	35047	128	18	107
2010	388	9133	3815	116319	109915	129113	38963	125	17	119
2011	387	8828	3693	134901	135563	150114	44143	142	15	135
2012	385	8997	3645	153332	146310	159772	45440	175	16	155
2013	383	8981	3655	197287	180390	183786	57740	199	15	188
2014	379	8420	3160	191091	177558	234080	64785	202	20	156
2015	409	8297	2996	206214	202262	248957	80114	261	20	232

17-19 标准事业基本情况
BASIC STATISTICS ON STANDARD ENTERPRISES

项　目	Item	2000	2005	2010	2012	2013	2014	2015
质量监督机构　(个)	Quality Supervision Institution　(unit)	86	99	99	99	99	99	99
固定人员　(人)	Fixed Personel　(person)	1 007						
制定标准　(项)	Standard Established　(unit)	29	36	81	101	69	77	92
修定标准　(项)	Standard Revised　(unit)			4	8	4	21	11
废止标准　(项)	Standard Abolished　(unit)							
当年采用国际标准　(项)	International Standard Adopted　(unit)	4	129	193	101	106		
受检产品质量监督　(种)	Number of Products under Quality Supervision (kind)	99						59
质量监督检测　(批次)	Quality Supervision Test　(batch)	20093	26548	40288	35117	40317	6429	4797
标准文件馆藏　(万件)	Standard Document Collection　(10 000 units)	25	22	30	57	121	160	140

17-20 档案事业基本情况
BASIC STATISTICS ON ARCHIVES

指 标		Item		2012	2013	2014	2015
各级各类档案馆数量	(个)	Number of Institutions	(unit)				
国家综合档案馆		National Comprehensive Archives		116	116	116	115
专门档案馆		National Special Archives		14	14	14	14
部门档案馆		Department Archives		7	7	7	14
各级各类档案馆馆藏		Number of Collections					
全宗	(个)	Fonds	(unit)	14628	15403	15587	15882
案卷	(万卷)	Archives	(10 000 volumes)	1527.17	1659.54	1734.76	1820.69
以件为保管单位档案	(万件)	Archives	(10 000 pieces)	490.98	678.24	632.00	712.21
照片	(万张)	Photos	(10 000 sheets)	146.00	141.00	161.00	156.72
馆藏资料	(万册)	Files	(10 000 volumes)	258.41	291.08	275.00	279.37
国家综合档案馆面积	(万平方米)	The Area of National Comprehensive Archives	(10 000 square meters)				
总建筑面积		Floor Space		18.45	20.66	21.98	23.15
库房面积		The Area of Storerooms		7.95	8.76	9.21	9.51
全省档案专业技术职称人员	(人)	Full-time Personnel	(person)				
研究馆员		Research Librarian		24	21	30	42
副研究馆员		Associate Research Librarian		274	247	250	395
馆员		Librarian		1031	940	945	909
助理馆员		Associate Librarian		882	776	630	535
全省档案馆本年度利用档案		Utilized Archives					
利用档案人数	(万人次)	Use of Material	(10 000 person-times)	28.78	30.08	37.84	42.55
利用档案卷次	(万人次)	Number of Archives Used	(10 000 person-times)	70.64	74.16	92.00	85.73
举办展览	(个)	Display Organized	(unit)	566	604	550	560
接待参观	(万人次)	Visitors	(10 000 person-times)	33.50	41.15	42.38	42.50
全省本年编研档案资料		Materials Edited This Year					
公开出版种数	(种)	Number of Materials Open Published	(kind)	85	76	90	96
公开出版字数	(万字)	Number of Words Open Published	(10 000 words)	2142.70	1929.56	1942.64	1906.21
内部参考种数	(种)	Number of Materials for Inner Reference	(kind)	172	197	224	328
内部参考字数	(万字)	Number of Words for Inner reference	(10 000 words)	1859.50	2062.96	2170.68	2778.51

17-21 各级各类学校数
NUMBER OF SCHOOLS OF VARIOUS LEVELS

单位:所 (unit)

学校分类	Type of Shool	2007	2008	2009	2010	2011	2012	2013	2014	2015
普通高等学校	Regular Institutions of Higher Education	86	87	120	120	122	122	123	123	126
#地方院校	#Local Schools	78	79	112	112	114	114	115	115	118
中等职业学校	Secondary Vocation Schools	478	462	402	413	341	332	310	301	289
普通中学	Regular Middle School	3108	3011	2897	2787	2707	2622	2576	2552	2545
#初中	#Junior High Schools	2440	2356	2275	2184	2122	2047	2013	2011	2013
城区	Urban	435	431	383	362	507	507	509	535	548
镇区	Township	539	564	622	671	929	953	945	955	968
乡村	Rural	1466	1361	1270	1151	686	587	559	521	497
高中	Senior High School	668	655	622	603	585	575	563	541	532
城区	Urban	292	295	267	243	313	318	318	314	311
镇区	Township	289	271	268	278	222	220	212	201	193
乡村	Rural	87	89	87	82	50	37	33	26	28
小学	Primary School	10210	9302	8544	7749	7415	6614	5746	5513	5398
城区	Urban	831	845	722	685	1015	1007	997	1061	1062
镇区	Township	693	715	847	937	1636	1629	1536	1556	1543
乡村	Rural	8686	7742	6975	6127	4764	3978	3213	2896	2793
特殊教育学校	Special Education School	76	76	76	76	76	77	80	83	83
幼儿园	Kindergarten	2572	2880	2995	4395	4670	5321	6011	6491	6814
技工学校	School of Technology	208	208		206				131	132

17-22 各级各类学校在校学生数
ENROLLMENT IN SCHOOLS OF VARIOUS LEVELS

单位:人 (person)

学校分类	Type of Shool	2005	2009	2010	2011	2012	2013	2014	2015
普通高等学校	Regular Institutions of Higher Education	1012665	1249061	1296920	1340298	1386086	1421434	1419699	1408738
#地方院校	#Local Schools	824960	1053341	1098570	1129010	1183416	1217155	1216228	1207217
中等职业学校	Secondary Vocation Schools	606014	1041759	903834	720915	500540	411194	372601	364893
普通中学	Regular Middle School	4466879	3650102	3418299	3208399	2652208	2471869	2294899	2241286
#初中	#Junior High Schools	3172392	2363351	2180937	2040702	1577701	1483710	1375940	1365319
城区	Urban	494739	452518	413930	561141	543902	529708	538778	547028
镇区	Township	750903	811217	848967	994830	743679	689455	627833	625858
乡村	Rural	1926750	1099616	918040	484731	290120	264547	209329	192433
高中	Senior High School	1294487	1286751	1237362	1167697	1074507	988159	918959	875967
城区	Urban	541404	512139	427334	596728	580248	555182	529827	512284
镇区	Township	553411	608803	633319	465734	435656	386923	357324	332446
乡村	Rural	199672	165809	176709	105235	58603	46054	31808	31237
小学	Primary School	4291881	3592629	3655512	3773446	3267498	3282579	3211598	3358095
城区	Urban	787812	717749	713491	1005861	1027061	1050497	1120918	1202479
镇区	Township	593090	812990	974019	1273914	1160375	1187536	1209864	1281967
乡村	Rural	2910979	2061890	1968002	1493671	1080062	1044546	880816	873649
特殊教育学校	Special Education School	9444	13959	15349	12893	10557	10576	11080	11057
幼儿园	Kindergarten	594481	831399	1118360	1324714	1355395	1473371	1538200	1625793
技工学校	School of Technology	136000		229000				93400	89400

17-23 各级各类学校招生数
NEW ENROLLMENT IN SCHOOLS OF VARIOUS LEVELS

单位:人 (person)

学校分类	Type of Shool	2005	2009	2010	2011	2012	2013	2014	2015
普通高等学校	Regular Institutions of Higher Education	315560	395929	387612	413600	406957	403860	400307	391157
#地方院校	#Local Schools	269042	346525	337621	358933	356113	352544	350391	342310
中等职业学校	Secondary Vocation Schools	273789	367161	283610	212318	143530	130995	126656	132594
普通中学	Regular Middle School	1469777	1120047	1053418	981191	838372	804312	749560	740206
#初中	#Junior High Schools	1011186	696261	657947	619213	510866	487841	454284	461592
城区	Urban	162324	139712	132571	179751	181591	177436	178772	182684
镇区	Township	241579	240542	251823	295975	237380	225227	206959	213860
乡村	Rural	607283	316007	273553	143487	91895	85178	68553	65048
高中	Senior High School	458591	423786	395471	361978	327506	316471	295276	278614
城区	Urban	187976	169309	138260	184335	178360	179553	168688	161996
镇区	Township	197496	199571	199177	144925	131519	123402	116662	106275
乡村	Rural	73119	54906	58034	32718	17627	13516	9926	10343
小学	Primary School	567411	642190	680166	692317	634766	607979	597543	625609
城区	Urban	113284	117466	126070	179176	186695	188925	203429	217723
镇区	Township	81622	144972	176073	228466	220893	211576	217982	232628
乡村	Rural	372505	379752	378023	284675	227178	207478	176132	175258
特殊教育学校	Special Education School	1038	2167	2047	1622	1483	1788	2113	2047
幼儿园	Kindergarten	396082	537579	761044	807017	785848	825253	656652	613990
技工学校	School of Technology	73000		57000				38000	34700

17–24 各级各类学校毕业生数
NUMBER OF GRADUATES FROM SCHOOLS OF VARIOUS LEVELS

单位:人 (person)

学校分类	Type of Shool	2000	2005	2010	2011	2012	2013	2014	2015
普通高等学校	Regular Institutions of Higher Education	51932	187920	331303	362991	353014	361572	390921	388621
#地方院校	#Local Schools	26461	144529	285599	312189	305545	313748	342171	339709
中等职业学校	Secondary Vocation Schools	125593	129436	335776	307701	272883	200196	147158	125735
普通中学	Regular Middle School	883828	1438503	1288944	1200425	988034	924920	826599	778302
#初中	#Junior High Schools	718015	1055083	854395	771362	575799	533709	477114	461384
城区	Urban	198402	169257	149922	203090	183511	176905	175225	179771
镇区	Township	61909	239870	326945	381043	277376	257033	224495	213005
乡村	Rural	457704	645956	377528	187229	114912	99771	77394	68608
高中	Senior High School	165813	383420	434549	429063	412235	391211	349485	316918
城区	Urban	98353	161281	147307	219472	216107	216067	197220	183878
镇区	Township	41382	164517	228146	169153	173191	157143	138866	121045
乡村	Rural	26078	57622	59096	40438	22937	18001	13399	11995
小学	Primary School	1160203	1020710	611620	583417	513818	489395	451925	466221
城区	Urban	281706	149766	120208	162925	162653	162408	162339	170042
镇区	Township	84207	134340	160359	201483	177913	180709	167271	180809
乡村	Rural	794290	736604	331053	219009	173252	146278	122315	115370
特殊教育学校	Special Education School	1310	1498	2261	1535	1292	1227	1218	1112
幼儿园	Kindergarten						572085	585677	617733
技工学校	School of Technology	24848	45000					34900	30000

17-25 各级各类学校教职工数
NUMBER OF FACULTIES AT SCHOOLS OF VARIOUS LEVELS

单位:人 (person)

学校分类	Type of Shool	2000	2005	2010	2011	2012	2013	2014	2015
普通高等学校	Regular Institutions of Higher Education	72265	107459	123491	127363	127921	128185	128878	129118
#地方院校	#Local Schools	35120	73079	89205	92721	94170	94777	95718	96039
中等职业学校	Secondary Vocation Schools	28816	36658	40985	36980	33442	30845	29809	27532
普通中学	Regular Middle School	237500	273146	263055	270838	259884	254716	250873	246443
教育部门和集体办	Run by Ministry of Education and the Collective	216338	253955	243222	249476	238671	232762	227452	222143
其他部门办	Run by Other Departments	15483	6585	646	1024	971	734	442	342
私立	Private Owned	3363				20242	21189	22967	23946
城市	Urban	97054	75581	68468	101691	104952	105801	108068	108438
县镇	Township	28889	78027	107371	119012	115008	110983	109553	106896
农村	Rural	111557	119538	87216	50135	39924	37932	33252	31109
小学	Primary Schools	299994	232888	211247	197395	193609	198262	199033	197577
城市	Urban	84877	47727	42100	51939	54139	55015	58137	60500
县镇	Township	23515	33532	51059	64920	67003	69933	71558	71355
农村	Rural	191602	151629	118088	80536	72467	73314	69338	65722
特殊教育学校	Special Education School	1676	1679	1744	1811	1826	1921	1997	1955
幼儿园	Kindergarten	40484	33094	66202	79659	92024	110376	122017	134279
技工学校	School of Technology	13070	9934					9196	9383

17-26 各级各类学校专任教师数
NUMBER OF FULL-TIME TEACHERS AT SCHOOLS OF VARIOUS LEVELS

单位：人 (person)

学校分类	Type of Shool	2000	2005	2010	2011	2012	2013	2014	2015
普通高等学校	Regular Institutions of Higher Education	30363	59009	74685	78952	80665	81784	82821	83444
#地方院校	#Local Schools	15995	43240	57264	60910	62913	64032	64908	65440
中等职业学校	Secondary Vocation Schools	15549	24036	28476	26208	23796	22555	21905	20550
普通中学	Regular Middle School	198486	233517	227962	225628	212305	205306	201758	198342
#初中	#Junior High Schools	154543	169084	156836	154295	141409	135580	133632	131325
城区	Urban	49752	31803	30409	43589	44766	44122	45998	46819
镇区	Township	13138	39851	59014	75088	69143	65457	64544	63263
乡村	Rural	91653	97430	67413	35618	27500	26001	23090	21243
高中	Senior High School	43943	64433	71126	71333	70896	69726	68126	67017
城区	Urban	27663	28330	26883	38552	39579	40383	39873	39755
镇区	Township	10336	27235	35091	26573	27221	26097	25762	24716
乡村	Rural	5944	8868	9152	6208	4096	3246	2491	2546
小学	Primary School	274979	215693	196078	194851	191699	196556	199172	200158
城区	Urban	75377	42127	37873	52716	55297	56547	60085	62736
镇区	Township	21459	30351	47480	63542	65828	68204	71378	72318
乡村	Rural	178143	143215	110725	78593	70574	71805	67709	65104
特殊教育学校	Special Education School	1231	1317	1477	1527	1560	1647	1712	1682
幼儿园	Kindergarten	29889	20018	38494	43141	49153	57736	63006	68761
技工学校	School of Technology	6182	7064					8069	7794

17-27 各级各类学校专任教师学历分类

STATISTICS ON ACADEMIC DEGREE OF FULL-TIME TEACHERS AT SCHOOLS OF VARIOUS LEVELS

单位:人 (person)

学历分类	Type of School	2011	2012	2013	2014	2015
一、中等职业学校	Secondary Vocational School	26208	23796	22555	21905	20550
高等学校本科毕业及以上	Graduated from Universities and Above	21322	19604	19172	19026	18105
高等学校专科毕业	Graduated from Colleges	4550	3861	3148	2696	2308
高中阶段及以下	Degree Below Senior High School	336	331	235	183	137
二、普通中学	Regular Secondary Schools	225628	212305	205306	201758	198342
高等学校本科毕业及以上	Graduated from Universities and Above	154668	156745	156715	158575	158861
高等学校专科毕业	Graduated from Colleges	66739	52938	47284	41857	38500
中专、高中毕业的	Graduated from Secondary and High Schools	4132	2521	1257	1266	981
三、小学	Primary School	194851	191699	196556	199172	200158
中师、高中毕业及以上的	Graduated from Teacher Schools and Degrees Above	194079	191282	196300	199012	199969
四、幼儿园(不包括园长)	Kindergarten (President is Excluded)	43141	49153	57736	63006	68761
中师、高中毕业及以上的	Graduate from Teacher Schools and Degrees Above	41455	47040	55669	61096	66395

17-28 高等学校分类别情况

单位:所、人

学校分类	Type of School	2000 学校数 Number of Colleges and Universities	2000 在校生数 Students Enrollment in Schools	2000 招生数 New Enroll-ment	2000 毕业生数 Graduates	2005 学校数 Number of Colleges and Universities	2005 在校生数 Students Enrollment in Schools	2005 招生数 New Enroll-ment	2005 毕业生数 Graduates
总 计	Total	54	346568	139666	51932	85	989754	306775	184706
综合大学	Comprehensive Universities	6	79303	28489	13871	10	196454	48591	48617
理工院校	Colleges and Universities of Science	11	124501	47724	18603	49	545277	181361	92857
农业院校	Colleges and Universities of Agriculture	2	13111	4311	1775	1	15715	3999	2763
林业院校	Colleges and Universities of Forestry	4	10770	4095	1068	1	1678	1062	121
医药院校	Colleges and Universities of Medicine	7	39694	17186	5950	3	26534	7686	5238
师范院校	Colleges and Universities of Teacher-Training	4	26218	9923	4466	5	52581	15687	12960
语文院校									
财经院校	Colleges and Universities of Finance	1	2482	974	448	6	93524	30319	12771
政法院校	Colleges and Universities of Politics and Law	1	2787	915	515	3	12389	3416	2369
体育院校	Colleges and Universities of Physical Education	2	2255	749	318	1	8837	2735	1154
艺术院校	Colleges and Universities of Art	2	12719	4298	2584	4	8834	4378	814
民族院校	Colleges and Universities of Minority Groups	14	32728	21002	2334	2	27931	7539	5042

CLASSIFICATION OF HIGHER EDUCATION INSTITUTIONS

(unit, person)

2010				2014				2015			
学校数 Number of Colleges and Universities	在校生数 Students Enrollment in Schools	招生数 New Enroll-ment	毕业生数 Graduates	学校数 Number of Colleges and Universities	在校生数 Students Enrollment in Schools	招生数 New Enroll-ment	毕业生数 Graduates	学校数 Number of Colleges and Universities	在校生数 Students Enrollment in Schools	招生数 New Enroll-ment	毕业生数 Graduates
120	1290243	386984	327208	123	1417860	399771	389985	126	1408738	391157	388621
8	166008	44736	39434	8	180625	43613	43250	8	175368	41640	45686
74	773095	238873	202148	76	853331	252772	243807	79	848861	243049	239337
1	18239	4600	3892	1	18670	4613	4333	1	18796	4607	4241
1	5721	2051	1461	1	9752	3505	2378	1	10132	3031	2651
4	38173	10979	10031	4	41237	10231	10259	4	40827	10258	10428
7	78905	24018	18007	8	89299	24982	24325	8	91256	27337	24750
				1	8973	1905	3089	1	8057	2145	3004
12	123204	37315	30366	11	127495	33988	35882	11	124607	34449	36217
4	11698	2877	4157	4	12788	4501	3991	4	14224	4790	3289
2	14826	4298	2855	3	16437	4101	4115	3	16234	4240	4128
5	26179	8000	6898	4	17667	5231	4736	4	18388	5602	4663
2	34195	9237	7959	2	41586	10329	9820	2	41988	10009	10227

17-29 大学、中专专任教师职称情况
STATISTICS ON RANKS AND TITLES OF FULL-TIME TEACHERS AT SCHOOLS OF VARIOUS LEVELS

单位:人 (person)

职称	Ranks and Titles	2000	2005	2009	2010	2011	2012	2013	2014	2015
普通高等学校专任教师数	**Number of Full-Time Teachers of Regular Higher Education Institutions**	**30363**	**59009**	**73159**	**74685**	**78952**	**80665**	**81784**	**82821**	**83444**
正高级	Senoir	3253	6434	8297	8674	9378	9998	10217	10622	10901
副高级	Associate Senoir	9448	17843	21608	22047	23013	24373	24959	25927	26572
中　级	Junior	9847	19169	24978	26077	29013	30244	31147	31273	30983
初　级	Primary	5741	10311	13817	13656	13475	11883	11242	10544	9981
无职称	No Title	2074	5252	4459	4231	4073	4167	4219	4455	5007
中等职业学校专任教师数	**Number of Full-Time Teachers of Specialized Schools**	**15549**	**24036**	**29148**	**28476**	**26208**	**23796**	**22555**	**21905**	**20550**
正高级	Senoir									97
副高级	Associate Senoir	3523	5152	6541	6441	5958	5644	5495	5507	5262
中　级	Junior	7229	11467	13366	12935	11960	10760	10187	10040	9258
初　级	Primary	4399	5889	7403	7229	6856	6082	5762	5289	4961
无职称	No Title	398	1528	1838	1871	1434	1310	1111	1069	972

17-30 各级各类学校校舍建筑面积情况(2015)
STATISTICS ON FLOOR SPACE OF SCHOOL HOUSES UNDER CONSTRUCTION IN SCHOOLS OF VARIOUS LEVELS(2015)

单位:万平方米 (10 000 sq.m)

项 目	Item	学校占地面积	校舍建筑面积	其中:教学及辅助用房
普通中学	Regular Middle School	9946.33	4159.74	1411.16
城区	Urban	3707.20	1739.24	672.50
镇区	Township	4744.22	1879.14	570.46
乡村	Rural	1494.92	541.37	168.19
其中:初中	#Junior High Schools	6191.75	2371.23	831.70
城区	Urban	1526.49	688.89	302.51
镇区	Township	3344.75	1224.97	382.21
乡村	Rural	1320.50	457.37	146.99
其中:高中	Senior High School	3754.58	1788.51	579.46
城区	Urban	2180.71	1050.35	369.99
镇区	Township	1399.46	654.16	188.26
乡村	Rural	174.41	84.00	21.21
小学	Primary School	9151.91	2791.92	1377.92
城区	Urban	1584.28	701.00	399.87
镇区	Township	3031.19	982.65	464.41
乡村	Rural	4536.44	1108.27	513.64
特殊学校	Special Education School	83.95	34.62	15.48
城区	Urban	53.78	21.14	9.17
镇区	Township	24.52	11.30	5.28
乡村	Rural	5.66	2.18	1.03

17-31 初中毕业生升入高中和小学毕业生升入初中的升学率

STATISTICS ON PROPORTION OF MIDDLE-SCHOOL STUDENTS ENTERING HIGH SCHOOL AND PROPORTION OF PRIMARY-SCHOOL STUDENTS ENTERING MIDDLE SCHOOL

年份 Year	初中毕业生升入高中升学率 Proportion of Middle-School Students Entering High-School			小学毕业生升学率 Proportion of Primary-School Students Entering Middle-School		
	初中毕业生数(万人) Number of Middle-School Graduates (10 000 persons)	高中招生数(万人) Number of High-School Graduates (10 000 persons)	升学率(%) Proportion of Students Entering Schools of Higher Level(%)	小学毕业生数(万人) Number of Primary School Graduates (10 000 persons)	初中招生数(万人) Number of Middle-School Graduates (10 000 persons)	升学率(%) Proportion of Students Entering Schools of Higher Level(%)
1965	7.60	3.75	49.4	29.60	24.95	84.3
1975	49.25	31.26	63.5	116.05	110.11	94.9
1978	98.80	43.33	43.9	132.37	119.46	90.3
1980	52.23	25.04	47.7	107.64	88.93	82.6
1985	49.92	19.13	38.3	104.89	69.21	66.0
1990	51.71	16.78	32.5	89.96	66.63	74.1
1995	57.85	19.88	34.4	90.76	80.53	88.7
1996	59.33	19.86	33.5	90.19	83.59	92.7
1997	64.70	21.29	32.9	95.35	89.30	93.7
1998	69.23	24.53	35.4	103.75	96.10	92.6
1999	69.60	27.20	39.1	111.24	101.40	91.2
2000	71.80	31.43	43.8	116.02	109.06	94.0
2001	76.34	35.31	46.3	121.00	113.49	93.8
2002	82.93	42.45	51.2	122.17	120.07	98.3
2003	91.61	39.61	43.2	118.70	117.83	99.3
2004	99.32	42.97	43.3	109.93	109.69	99.8
2005	105.51	45.86	43.5	102.07	101.85	99.8
2006	106.18	45.55	42.9	94.66	97.07	102.6
2007	99.77	43.98	44.1	83.29	87.27	104.8
2008	96.10	43.91	45.7	71.51	77.75	108.7
2009	92.38	42.38	45.9	64.68	69.63	107.7
2010	85.44	39.55	46.3	61.16	65.79	107.6
2011	77.14	36.20	46.9	58.34	61.92	106.1
2012	57.58	32.75	56.9	51.38	51.09	99.4
2013	53.37	31.65	59.3	48.94	48.78	99.7
2014	47.71	29.53	61.9	45.19	45.43	100.5
2015	46.14	27.86	60.39	46.62	46.16	99.01

17-32 小学学龄儿童入学率

STATISTICS ON PROPORTION OF CHILDREN AT SCHOOLING AGE ENTERING PRIMARY SCHOOLS

年份 Year	学龄儿童数(万人) Number of Children at Schooling Age (10 000 person)	已入学学龄儿童数(万人) Number of Children Entering School (10 000 persons)	入学率(%) Proportion of Students Entering Schools of Higher Level (%)
1975	629.50	611.00	97.1
1978	616.86	597.73	96.9
1980	594.80	576.86	97.0
1985	496.69	489.38	98.5
1990	485.00	480.32	99.0
1991	556.39	549.35	98.7
1992	571.44	563.44	98.6
1993	574.54	566.84	98.7
1994	599.47	593.88	99.1
1995	637.12	632.34	99.2
1996	661.72	658.38	99.5
1997	681.52	678.95	99.6
1998	685.87	682.53	99.5
1999	669.16	665.88	99.5
2000	641.60	638.57	99.5
2001	585.99	583.29	99.5
2002	538.02	535.98	99.6
2003	490.29	488.68	99.7
2004	440.03	438.66	99.7
2005	397.52	396.11	99.7
2006	363.99	362.14	99.5
2007	345.49	344.77	99.8
2008	340.59	340.08	99.9
2009	343.63	342.74	99.7
2010	350.95	350.82	99.96
2011	362.77	362.74	99.96
2012	317.15	317.06	99.97
2013	320.48	320.41	99.98
2014	315.77	315.72	99.99
2015	330.72	330.69	99.99

17-33 各级各类学校服务的人口及每万人口中在校学生数
STATISTICS ON THE NUMBER OF POPULATION SERVED BY SCHOOLS OF VARIOUS LEVELS AND THE NUMBER OF STUDENTS AT SCHOOL PER 10000 PERSONS

项 目	Item	2000	2005	2009	2010	2011	2012	2013	2014	2015
每一学校服务的人口数 (万人)	**Number of Population Served by Each School (10 000 persons)**									
普通高等学校	Regular Institutions of Higher Education	111.63	70.95	47.67	47.70	47.20	47.37	47.15	47.28	46.44
成人高等学校	Adults Higher Education	188.37	354.76	408.57	408.86	411.29	412.79	414.21	415.43	417.96
普通中等专业学校	Specialized Secondary School	29.69	13.80	14.23	13.86	16.89	17.41	18.71	19.32	20.25
普通高中	RegualrHigh-School									11.00
普通初中	Regualr Middle-School									2.91
小学	Primary School	0.26	0.48	0.67	0.74	0.78	0.87	1.01	1.05	1.08
幼儿园	Kindergarten	1.61	2.58	1.91	1.30	1.23	1.09	0.96	0.90	0.86
每万人口中的学生数 (人)	**Number of Students at School per 10 000 Persons (person)**									
普通高等学校	Regular Institutions of Higher Education	57.49	167.91	218.37	226.58	232.77	239.85	245.12	244.10	240.75
成人高等学校	Adults Higher Education	35.94	37.05	48.27	45.79	46.19	47.59	48.77	47.31	40.78
普通中等专业学校	Specialized Secondary School	46.22	100.48	182.13	157.90	125.20	86.61	70.91	64.06	62.36
普通高中	RegualrHigh-School									149.70
普通初中	Regualr Middle-School									233.33
小学	Primary School	1107.77	711.64	628.08	638.63	655.34	565.41	566.06	552.20	573.89
幼儿园	Kindergarten	120.56	98.57	145.35	195.38	230.06	234.54	254.07	264.48	277.84

17-34 各级各类学校每个专任教师负担的学生数
STATISTICS ON STUDENT-TEACHER RATIO BY LEVELS OF SCHOOL

单位:人 (person)

项　目	Item	2000	2005	2007	2008	2009	2010	2011	2012	2013	2014	2015
普通高等学校	Regular Institutions of Higher Education	11.41	15.86	15.35	15.29	15.7	17.37	16.98	17.18	17.35	17.14	15.73
中等职业学校	Secondary Vocation School	17.92	25.21	31.89	33.8	35.74	31.74	27.51	21.03	18.23	17.01	17.76
普通中学	Regular High School	17.68	19.13	17.66	16.82	15.77	15.00	14.22	12.49	12.04	11.37	11.30
#初中	#Junior Middle Schools	18.19	18.76	17.06	15.96	14.71	13.91	13.23	11.16	10.94	10.30	10.40
高中	Senior High School	15.89	20.09	19.11	18.83	18.18	17.40	16.37	15.16	14.17	13.49	13.07
小学	Primary School	24.28	19.90	18.07	17.92	12.09	18.64	20.46	17.04	16.7	16.12	16.78
幼儿园	Kindergarten	24.31	29.70	29.45	29.95	18.13	29.05	30.71	27.58	25.52	24.41	23.64

17-35 各级学校女学生和女教师数
NUMBER OF FEMALE STUDENTS AND FEMALE TEACHERS AT SCHOOL OF VARIOUS LEVELS

单位:万人 (10 000 persons)

项 目	Item	2000	2005	2009	2010	2011	2012	2013	2014	2015
一、女学生数	Number of Female Students	506.17	473.27	436.92	426.07	416.40	360.95	350.98	337.8	341.05
普通高等学校	Regular Institutions of Higher Education	11.93	44.11	58.90	62.25	65.13	67.70	69.12	69.04	68.46
中等专业学校	Specialized Secondary School	14.33	29.14	49.73	44.22	34.96	24.58	19.84	17.90	16.96
普通中学	Regualr High School	155.66	203.98	166.26	154.98	145.44	119.94	112.14	104.22	102.39
小学	Primary School	317.45	194.85	161.82	164.62	170.87	148.73	149.88	146.64	153.24
二、女学生占学生总数 %	Percentage of Female Students in School	46.2	45.5	45.8	46.2	46.1	46.2	46.3	46.3	46.2
普通高等学校	Regular Institutions of Higher Education	34.4	43.6	47.2	48.0	48.6	48.8	48.6	48.6	48.5
中等专业学校	Specialized Secondary School	51.4	48.1	47.7	48.9	48.5	49.1	48.3	48.0	46.5
普通中学	Regualr High School	44.4	45.7	45.6	45.3	45.3	45.2	45.4	45.4	45.7
小学	Primary School	47.5	45.4	45.0	45.0	45.3	45.5	45.7	45.7	45.6
三、女教师数	Number of Female Teachers	20.33	21.58	22.35	22.43	22.61	22.4	22.81	23.43	22.87
普通高等学校	Regular Institutions of Higher Education	1.02	2.34	3.07	3.16	3.42	3.51	3.59	3.65	3.72
中等专业学校	Specialized Secondary School	0.60	0.94	1.19	1.17	1.07	0.99	0.94	0.92	0.83
普通中学	Regualr High School	6.26	7.94	8.37	8.4	8.43	8.22	8.15	8.21	8.26
小学	Primary School	12.07	10.32	9.71	9.7	9.69	9.68	10.13	10.65	10.06
四、女教师占教师总数 %	Percentage of Female Teachers in School	38.3	40.4	41.9	42.5	43.0	44.0	45.1	46.3	47.1
普通高等学校	Regular Institutions of Higher Education	33.6	39.7	42.0	42.3	43.3	43.5	43.9	44.1	44.6
中等专业学校	Specialized Secondary School	38.5	39.1	40.7	41.0	40.8	41.5	41.5	41.8	42.3
普通中学	Regualr High School	31.5	34.0	36.1	36.9	37.4	38.7	39.7	40.7	41.7
小学	Primary School	43.9	47.9	49.0	49.5	49.7	50.5	51.5	53.5	54.5

17-36 各级各类成人学校在校学生数
NUMBER OF ADULT STUDENTS ENROLLED AT SCHOOLS OF VARIOUS LEVELS

单位:万人 (10 000 persons)

各类学校	Items	2000	2005	2009	2010	2011	2012	2013	2014	2015
成人高等学校	Adult Higher Education	21.66	22.34	27.61	26.21	26.60	27.5	28.28	27.51	23.86
广播电视大学	Radio and TV Universities	2.78	2.52	0.76	0.54	0.61	0.45	0.43	0.33	0.35
职工大学	Schools of Higher Education for Staff	1.36	0.22	0.30	0.04	0.01	0.01	0.004		
管理干部学院	Colleges for Management and Caders	0.90	0.60	0.48	0.35	0.20	0.06	0.04	0.02	0.004
教育学院	Pedagogical College	0.94	0.89	0.42	0.37	0.26	0.24	0.24	0.23	0.18
普通高等学校办函授部、夜大学	Correspondence and Evening College Run by Regualr High Education	15.16	18.11	25.64	24.91	25.52	26.74	27.57	26.93	23.33
成人中等学校	Secondary Schools for Adults	139.75	35.90	64.40	81.77	49.27	43.85	45.06	39.46	28.16
中学	Middle School	0.61	2.42	3.00	3.69	2.64	4.57	4.24	3.67	3.36
技术培训学校	Technical Training Schools	131.86	33.48	55.28	78.08	46.63	39.28	40.82	35.79	24.8
成人初等学校	Primary Schools for Adults	12.50	2.20	0.81	0.73	0.86	0.15	0.05	0.17	
*扫盲班	*Class for Illiteracy	6.43	0.82	0.34	0.39	0.03	0.01	0.03	0.02	

注:成人高等学校学生数是本、专科学生数。
Note:The number of students in Adults Higher Education refers to the number of students in vocational schools.

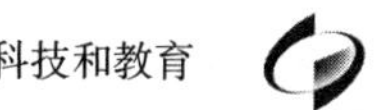

17-37 研究生基本情况
BASIC CONDTIONS ABOUT POST-GRADUATES

单位:人 (person)

项 目	Item	2011	2012	2013	2014	2015
高等学校在校研究生数	Number of Post-graduates at School in Institutions of Higher Education	104879	108528	112707	114260	117085
攻读博士学位研究生	Post-graduate Studying for Doctor's Degree	19905	20927	22367	21509	22049
攻读硕士学位研究生	Post-graduate Studying for Master's Degree	84974	87601	90340	92751	95036
招收研究生数	New Students Enrollment	36358	37371	39027	38867	39785
攻读博士学位研究生	Post-graduate Studying for Doctor's Degree	4706	4766	5070	4891	4940
攻读硕士学位研究生	Post-graduate Studying for Master's Degree	31652	32605	33957	33976	34845
毕业研究生数	Number of Graduates	30510	32201	34585	31992	34116
攻读博士学位研究生	Post-graduate Studying for Doctor's Degree	3763	3692	3948	4038	3520
攻读硕士学位研究生	Post-graduate Studying for Master's Degree	26747	28509	30637	27954	30596
科研单位在学研究生数	Number of Post-graduates Studying in Research Institutions	2288	2328	2362	2399	2812
攻读博士学位研究生	Post-graduate Studying for Doctor's Degree	721	760	819	845	883
攻读硕士学位研究生	Post-graduate Studying for Master's Degree	1567	1568	1543	1554	1929
招收研究生数	New Students Enrollment	760	777	779	790	778
攻读博士学位研究生	Post-graduate Studying for Doctor's Degree	212	220	229	246	237
攻读硕士学位研究生	Post-graduate Studying for Master's Degree	548	557	550	544	541
毕业研究生数	Number of Graduates	652	646	650	624	615
攻读博士学位研究生	Post-graduate Studying for Doctor's Degree	196	174	160	208	196
攻读硕士学位研究生	Post-graduate Studying for Master's Degree	456	472	490	416	419

主要统计指标解释

科技活动 指在自然科学、农业科学、医药科学、工程与技术科学、人文与社会科学领域(简称科学技术领域)中,与科技知识的产生、发展、传播和应用密切相关的有组织的活动。可分为研究与试验发展(R&D)、研究与试验发展成果应用及相关的科技服务三类活动。该定义是联合国教科文组织考虑成员国特别是发展中国家开展科技统计工作的需要,而对科技活动所作的统计界定。

科技活动人员 指直接从事科技活动、以及专门从事科技活动管理和为科技活动提供直接服务,累计的实际工作时间占全年制度工作时间10%及以上的人员。(1)直接从事科技活动的人员包括:在独立核算的科学研究与技术开发机构、高等学校、各类企业及其他事业单位内设的研究室、实验室、技术开发中心及中试车间(基地)等机构中从事科技活动的研究人员、工程技术人员、技术工人及其它人员;虽不在上述机构工作,但编入科技活动项目(课题)组的人员;科技信息与文献机构中的专业技术人员;从事论文设计的研究生等。(2)专门从事科技活动管理和为科技活动提供直接服务的人员,包括:独立核算的科学研究与技术开发机构、科技信息与文献机构、高等学校、各类企业及其他事业单位主管科技工作的负责人,专门从事科技活动的计划、行政、人事、财务、物资供应、设备维护、图书资料管理等工作的各类人员,但不包括保卫、医疗保健人员、司机、食堂人员、茶炉工、水暖工、清洁工等为科技活动提供间接服务的人员。该指标用来反映投入科技活动人力的规模。

科学家与工程师 指科技活动人员中具有高、中级技术职称(职务)的人员和不具有高、中级技术职称(职务)的大学本科及以上学历人员。该指标用来反映投入科技活动人力的素质。

研究与试验发展(R&D) 指在科学技术领域,为增加知识总量,以及运用这些知识去创造新的应用进行的系统的创造性的活动,包括基础研究、应用研究、试验发展三类活动。国际上通常采用R&D活动的规模和强度指标反映一国的科技实力和核心竞争力。

专业技术人员 指从事专业技术工作和专业技术管理工作的人员,即企事业单位中已经聘任专业技术职务从事专业技术工作和专业技术管理工作的人员,以及未聘任专业技术职务,现在专业技术岗位上工作的人员。包括工程技术人员,农业技术人员,科学研究人员,卫生技术人员,教学人员,经济人员,会计人员,统计人员,翻译人员,图书资料、档案、文博人员,新闻出版人员,律师、公证人员,广播电视播音人员,工艺美术人员,体育人员,艺术人员及企业政治思想工作人员,共十七个专业技术职务类别。用来反映科技人力资源情况。

科技活动经费筹集 指从各种渠道筹集到的计划用于科技活动的经费,包括政府资金、企业资金、事业单位资金、金融机构贷款、国外资金和其他资金等。反映各社会经济主体对促进科技进步所做的努力。

新产品 指采用新技术原理、新设计构思研制、生产的全新产品,或在结构、材质、工艺等某一方面比原有产品有明显改进,从而显著提高了产品性能或扩大了使用功能的产品。既包括政府有关部门认定并在有效期内的新产品,也包括企业自行研制开发,未经政府有关部门认定,从投产之日起一年之内的新产品。用来反映科技产出及对经济增长的直接贡献。

专利 是专利权的简称,是对发明人的发明创造经审查合格后,由专利局依据专利法授予发明人和设计人对该项发明创造享有的专有权。包括发明、实用新型和外观设计。反映拥有自主知识产权的科技和设计成果情况。

发明 指对产品、方法或者其改进所提出的新的技术方案。是国际通行的反映拥有自主知识产权技术的核心指标。

普通高等学校 指按照国家规定的设置标准和审批程序批准举办的,通过全国普通高等学校统一招生考试,招收高中毕业生为主要培养对象,实施高等教育的全日制大学、独立设置的学院和高等专科学校、高等职业学校和其他机构。

大学、独立设置的学院主要实施本科层次以上教育,高等专科学校、高等职业学校实施专科层次教育,其他机构是承担国家普通招生计划任务不计校数的机构。包括普通高等学校分校和批准筹建的普通高等学校等。

成人高等学校 指按照国家规定的设置标准和审批程序批准举办的,通过全国成人高等学校统一招生考试,招收具有高中毕业或同等学历的在职从业人员为主要培养对象，利用函授、业余、脱产等多种形式对其实施高等学历教育的学校。包括职工高等学校、农民高等学校、管理干部学院、教育学院、独立函授学院、广播电视大学、其他机构等。其他机构是承担国家成人招生计划任务不计校数的机构。

小学学龄儿童净入学率 指调查范围内已入小学学习的学龄儿童占校内外学龄儿童总数(包括弱智儿童，不包括盲聋哑儿童)的比重。计算公式为：

$$\text{小学学龄儿童净入学率}=\frac{\text{已入学的小学学龄儿童数}}{\text{校内外小学学龄儿童总数}}\times 1000‰$$

Explanatory Notes on Main Statistical Indicators

Scientific and Technological Activities (S&T Activities) refer to organized activities which are closely related with the creation, development, dissemination and application of the scientific and technical knowledge in the fields of natural sciences, agricultural science, medical science, engineering and technological science, humanities and social sciences (referred to as scientific and technological fields). S&T activities can be classified in to 3 categories: research and development (R&D) activities, application of R&D results, and related S&T services. This statistical definition is made by UNICHIEF for scientific and technological activities to meet the need of carrying out statistical work in this field for its member countries in particular those developing countries.

Personnel Engaged in S&T Activities efer to personnel directly engaged in S&T activities, in the management of S&T activities, and in providing direct service to S&T activities, who spend over 10% of the total working hours in a year in S&T activities. (1) Personnel directly engaged in S&T activities include researchers, engineers, technicians and other related personnel engaged in S&T activities in independent-accounting R&D institutions, institutions of higher learning, and in research institutes, laboratories, technology development centers and central experiment workshops under enterprises and institutions. Also included are people working in S&T research project teams, professional and technical personnel working in S&T information archiving institutes, and graduate students working on the design of their thesis. (2) Personnel engaged in the management of S&T activities and in providing direct service to S&T activities include senior management people responsible for S&T activities in independent-accounting R&D institutions, S&T information archiving institutes, institutions of higher learning, and in enterprises and institutions where S&T activities are undertaken. Also included are people responsible for the planning, administration, personnel management, financial management, logistics supply, equipment maintenance, information and library management that are related with S&T activities. People providing indirect services are excluded, such as security, medical service, drivers, plumbers, cleaners and those providing catering and related service. This indicator reflects the size of personnel engaged in S&T activities.

Scientists and Enginee rsrefer to persons engaged in S&T activities who have obtained titles of senior and middle level professional positions, and those without such position but have completed university or higher education. This indicator reflects the quality of personnel engaged in S&T activities.

Research and Development (R&D) refers to systematic and creative activities in the field of science and technology aiming at increasing the knowledge and using the knowledge for new application. R&D includes 3 categories of activities: basic research, applied research and experiments and development. The scale and intensity of R&D are widely used internationally to reflect the strength of S&T and the core competitiveness of a country in the world.

Professional and Technical Personnel refer to persons engaged in professional and technical work or in the management of professional and technical activities, i.e., people with professional or technical positions who are engaged in professional and technical work or in the management of professional and technical activities, and people without professional or technical positions but are working on professional or technical posts. They include professionals and technicians working in 17 categories of technical occupations including engineering, agriculture, scientific researches, medical service, teaching, economic research and application, accounting, statistics, translation, libraries, archives, cultural and museum service, journalism and publication, lawyers, notarization service, radio and television broadcasting, handicraft and fine arts, sports, performing art, and political workers in enterprises. This indicator reflects the condition of human resources in S&T.

Funding for S&T Activities refers to funds obtained from various sources for S&T activities, including government funds, self-raised funds by enterprises, self-raised funds by institutions, loans from financial institutions, foreign funds and other funds. This indicator reflects the efforts made by various social economic entities in promoting the development of S&T.

New Products refer to new products produced with new technology and new design, or products that represent noticeable improvement in terms of structure, material, or production process so as to improve significantly the character or function of the older versions. They include new products certified by relevant government agencies within the period of certification, as well as new products designed and produced by enterprises within a year without certification by government agencies. This indictor reflects the direct contribution of S&T output to economic growth.

Patentis an abbreviation for the patent right andrefers to the exclusive right of ownership by the inventors or designers for the creation or inventions, given from the patent offices after due process of assessment and approval in accordance with the Patent Law. Patents are granted for inventions, utility models and designs. This indicator reflects the achievements of S&T and design with independent intellectual property.

Inventions refer to the new technical proposals to the products or methods or their modifications. This is universal core indicator reflecting the technologies with independent intellectual property.

Regular Institutions of Higher Learning refer to educational establishments set up according to the government evaluation and approval procedures, enrolling graduates from senior secondary schools and providing higher education courses and training for senior professionals. They include full-time universities, colleges, high professional schools, high professional vocational schools and others.

Universities and colleges are mainly providing undergraduate courses; those high professional schools and high professional vocational schools are mainly providing professional trainings; and others refer to educational establishments, which are responsible for enrolling students but not covered in the total number of schools, including: branch schools of universities and colleges, and universities and colleges that have been proved and prepared to construct.

Institutions of Higher Learning for Adults refer to educational establishments, set up in line with relevant rules approved by the government, enrolling staff and workers with senior secondary school or equivalent education, and providing higher education courses in many forms of correspondence, spare time, or full time for adults. Professionals thus trained receive a qualification equivalent to graduates studying regular courses at regular universities, colleges and professional colleges. Institutions of higher learning for adults include schools of high education for staff and workers, schools of high education for peasants, colleges for management cadres, pedagogical colleges, independent correspondence colleges, Radio and TV universities and other educational establishments. Other educational establishments are responsible for enrolling adult students but not covered in the number of schools.

Enrollment Rate of Primary School Age Children refers to the proportion of school age children enrolled at schools to the total number of school age children both in and outside schools (including retarded children, but excluding blind, deaf and mute children). The formula is:

Enrollment Rate of Primary School-age Children = (Total Primary School-age Children at Schools)/(TotalPrimary School age Children Both at and OutsideSchools) x 100%

18 卫生和社会服务

Public Health and Social Services

18-1 卫生机构数
NUMBER OF HEALTH CARE INSTITUTIONS

单位：个 (unit)

年 份 Year	总计 Total	医 院 Hospitals	综合医院 General Hospitals	中医医院 Hosptials Specialized in Traditional Chinese Medicine	专科医院 Specialized Hosptials	基层医疗卫生机构 Basic Medical Institutions	社区卫生服务中心(站) Community Health Service Centers	街道卫生院 Urban Health Centers	乡镇卫生院 Township Health Centers
2006	10052	575	401	82	82		664	55	1140
2007	11093	580	393	83	93		1089	53	1160
2008	10305	593	389	86	106		1115	48	1155
2009	32790	614	409	86	105		1142	48	1134
2010	34269	602	394	87	107		1294	44	1149
2011	35625	608	393	91	111	34509	1278	34	1161
2012	35240	650	414	95	126	34063	1220	34	1165
2013	35631	711	444	98	153	34042	1231	36	1152
2014	36077	771	483	102	169	34503	1175	36	1150
2015	36173	869	532	109	208	34569	1189	29	1140

注：卫生事业机构数从2009年起包含村卫生室数量。
Note: The statistics of health care units, hospital beds and health care professionals started to include the village clinics since 2012.

18-1 续表 continued

单位：个 (unit)

年 份 Year	村卫生室 Village Clinices	门诊部(所) Outpatient Department	专业公共卫生机构 Specialized Public Health Institutions	疾病预防控制中心 Center for Disease Control and Prevention	专科疾病防治院(所/站) Specialized Disease Prevention & Treatment Institution	妇幼保健院(所/站) Women and Children Care Agencies	卫生监督所(中心) Health Inspection Institution (center)
2006		7116		114	116	95	72
2007		7677		113	118	100	83
2008		6871		110	109	99	93
2009	22405	6936		112	87	99	97
2010	24112	6729		115	84	100	98
2011	25204	6832	425	112	83	100	98
2012	24976	6668	438	111	83	100	109
2013	24941	6682	779	113	75	101	102
2014	24919	7223	696	112	76	100	103
2015	24796	7415	577	113	76	103	107

18-2 卫生机构人员数
NUMBER OF PERSONS ENGAGED IN HEALTH CARE INSTITUTIONS

单位：万人 (10 000 persom)

年份 Year	总计 Total	卫生技术人员 Medical Technical Personel	执业(助理)医师 Licensed (Assistant) Doctors	执业医师 Licensed Doctors	注册护士 Pegistertered Nurses	药师(士) Pharmacist	乡村医生和卫生员 Village Doctors and Assistants	每千人口医生数(人) Number of Doctors per 1000 Population (person)
1970	10.30	8.33	4.15		1.83			1.03
1975	15.05	11.85	4.91		2.05			1.11
1980	19.94	15.59	6.32		3.09			1.35
1985	23.58	18.48	7.27		3.77			1.47
1990	26.75	20.92	8.68		5.66			1.62
1991	27.51	21.55	8.79		5.97			1.62
1992	28.24	22.15	9.02		6.25			1.64
1993	28.91	22.46	9.16		6.49			1.64
1994	29.31	22.84	9.38		6.64			1.66
1995	29.55	23.20	9.58		6.83			1.68
1996	29.65	23.47	9.72		7.00			1.67
1997	30.38	23.90	9.96		7.21			1.70
1998	30.31	23.96	10.11		7.29			1.71
1999	30.40	24.05	10.31		7.41			1.74
2000	30.14	23.88	10.30		7.53			1.74
2001	29.48	23.41	10.21		7.51			1.72
2002	25.30	20.59	8.63		6.35			1.43
2003	25.62	20.83	8.72		6.38			1.45
2004	26.06	21.38	8.99		6.62			1.49
2005	26.22	21.50	8.98		6.94			1.49
2006	26.53	21.80	9.01		7.06			1.49
2007	27.80	22.70	9.20	7.65	7.69			1.52
2008	28.48	23.38	9.20	7.7	8.06			1.51
2009	33.71	24.70	9.79	8.22	8.73		3.86	1.59
2010	34.95	25.58	9.95	8.37	9.38	1.77	4.15	1.62
2011	36.52	26.81	10.21	8.53	10.21	1.77	4.41	1.66
2012	38.64	28.87	10.91	9.01	11.57	1.74	4.30	1.89
2013	41.12	30.93	11.72	9.65	12.79	1.77	4.29	1.90
2014	43.82	33.55	12.61	10.39	14.40	1.78	4.22	2.17
2015	47.55	36.76	13.60	11.22	16.51	1.82	4.09	2.32

注：卫生人员数从2009年起包含村卫生室卫生人员数量。
Note: The statistics of health care units, hospital beds and health care professionals started to include the village clinics since 2012.

18-3 卫生机构床位数
NUMBER OF BEDS IN HEALTH CARE INSTITUTIONS

单位：万张 (10 000 beds)

年 份 Year	总 计 Total	医 院 Hospitals	基层医疗卫生机构 Basic Medical Institutions	乡镇卫生院 Township Health Centers	专业公共卫生机构 Specialized Public Health Institutions	每千人口卫生机构床位数(张) Beds of Medical InstitutionsPer 1000Population (bed)
1970	6.14	5.56				1.38
1975	9.90	9.02				2.05
1980	12.59	11.22				2.40
1985	14.70	11.52				2.34
1990	16.34	13.16				2.45
1991	16.52	13.43				2.47
1992	16.62	13.46				2.44
1993	16.30	13.48				2.41
1994	16.13	13.40				2.36
1995	15.78	13.08				2.29
1996	14.42	13.08				2.24
1997	15.30	13.08				2.24
1998	15.09	13.03				2.21
1999	14.90	12.91				2.07
2000	14.96	12.99				2.18
2001	14.62	12.91				2.18
2002	12.72	8.53				2.12
2003	13.59	9.39				2.26
2004	13.78	9.52				2.29
2005	13.96	9.67				2.31
2006	14.24	9.81				2.35
2007	15.06	10.36				2.48
2008	16.73	11.32				2.75
2009	18.72	12.66		4.33		2.82
2010	20.04	13.50		4.64		3.26
2011	22.40	15.20	6.23	5.05	0.96	3.63
2012	25.30	17.38	6.83	5.58	1.09	4.38
2013	28.82	20.05	7.47	6.18	1.32	4.97
2014	31.83	22.20	8.15	6.77	1.48	5.47
2015	34.38	24.66	8.39	6.90	1.57	5.87

18-4 分等级医疗卫生机构情况(2015)
HEALTH CARE INSTITUTIONS BY LEVEL(2015)

单位:个 (Unit)

项目	Iem	合计 Total	三级 Thrid-level	二级 Second-level	一级 First-level	其他 Others
医院	Hospitals	869	121	266	235	247
其中:综合医院	General Hospitals	532	68	150	154	160
中医医院	Hosptials Specialized in Traditional Chinese Medicine	109	20	63	15	11
中西医结合医院	Hospitals of Traditional Chinese Medicine and Western Medicine	17	1	3	8	5
民族医院	Minortiy Hospitals	3	0	3	0	0
专科医院	Specialized Hosptials	208	32	47	58	71
妇幼保健院	Women and Children Care Agencies	96	12	79	1	4
专科疾病防治院	Specialized Prevention & Treatment Centers	14	0	2	3	9

18-5 医院业务工作开展情况
BASIC STATISTICS ON HOSPITAL BUSINESS

项 目	Item	2000	2005	2010	2013	2014	2015
机构数 (个)	Number of Institutions (unit)	507	574	603	713	771	869
诊疗总人次数 (万人次)	Number of Clients (10 000 person-times)	4616.20	5452.11	7710.20	10056.28	11399.93	12111.16
#门、急诊人次数 (万人次)	#Number of Outpacients and Emergency (10 000 person-times)	4396.10	5107.19	7533.44	9859.71	10976.72	11721.98
出院人数 (万人)	Number of discharged Patients (10 000 persons)	158.93	219.45	423.28	647.55	735.70	780.05
死亡 (万人)	Dead (10 000 persons)	1.59	2.28	3.13	2.93	3.29	3.81
病死率 (%)	Rate of Death from Illness (%)	1.08	1.04	0.74	0.45	0.45	0.49
病床平均周转次数 (次)	Average times of Beds Usage (time)	18.66	23.99	32.50	34.90	35.40	33.98
病床平均工作日 (日)	Average Day of Beds Usage (day)	218.79	268.24	350.40	353.30	350.90	337.40
病床使用率 (%)	Utilization Rate of Beds (%)	59.94	73.49	96.01	99.52	96.14	92.44
出院者平均住院日 (日)	Average Days for Hospitalization Discharged (day)	11.12	10.71	10.50	9.90	9.70	9.83

18-6 农村村级卫生组织情况

STATISTICS ON HEALTH CARE INSTITUTIONS AT VILLAGE LEVEL

项 目	Item	2000	2005	2010	2013	2014	2015
行政村数 (个)	Number of Villages (unit)	32400	26678	26018	25452	25448	25109
村设置的医疗点数 (个)	Medical care Station Set by Villages (unit)	26879	21136	24057	24953	24918	24795
#村或集体办	#Set by Villages or Collective Set	14666	11207	15395	15410	15551	15495
联合办	Set with Village Doctors	4640	3777	2815	2449	2445	2984
医院设点	Set by Hospital	2403	2410	3348	4027	4085	3559
私人办	Set by Individual	4344	2907	1833	2164	1998	1922
其他	Others	826	835	666	903	839	835
乡村医生和卫生员人数 (人)	Number of Village Doctors and Medical Working Personel (person)	57511	34417	41473	43840	42304	40897
#乡村医生	#Village Doctors	44490	33375	40425	40833	40502	38970
卫生员	Medical Working Personel	1301	1042	1048	3007	1802	1927

主要统计指标解释

卫生机构 包括医疗机构、疾病预防控制中心(防疫站)、采供血机构、卫生监督及监测(检验)机构、医学科研和在职培训机构、健康教育所等。

医疗机构 包括医院、社区卫生服务中心(站)、疗养院、卫生院、门诊部、诊所(卫生所、医务室)、妇幼保健院(所、站)、专科疾病防治院(所、站)、急救中心(站)和临床检验中心。医疗机构分为非赢利性医疗机构和赢利性医疗机构。

医院 包括综合医院、中医医院、中西医结合医院、民族医院、各类专科医院和护理院。

卫生技术人员 指卫生机构中医生、护理人员 、药剂人员、检验人员等卫生技术人员。

医生 指在医疗、预防保健机构工作且取得《执业医师证书》的执业医师和执业助理医师。

Explanatory Notes on Main Statistical Indicators

Health Care Institutions include medical institutions, disease prevention and control centers (epidemic prevention stations), blood gathering and supplying institutions, health supervision and inspection (check up) institutions, medicinal scientific research and on–job training institutions, health education and so on.

Medical Organizations include hospitals, health service centers (stations) of communities, nursing homes, health centers, clinics, clinics (health stations and infirmaries), maternity and child care agencies (centers and stations), special disease prevention and curing agencies (centers and stations), first aid centers (stations) and clinical inspection centers. Medical organizations are grouped by two types: profit–making and non–profit–making medical organizations.

Hospitals include polyclinics, traditional Chinese medical hospitals, hospitals integrated with traditional Chinese therapeutics and western therapeutics, ethical hospitals, various specialties hospitals and nursing hospitals.

Medical Technical Personnel refers to doctors, assistant nurses, pharmacists, and laboratory technicians working in medical institutions.

Doctors refer to certified physicians and certified assistant physicians with certifications working in medical and health care and prevention agencies.

19 文化和体育

Culture and Sports

19-1 文化事业机构、人员数
NUMBER OF CULTURAL INSTITUTIONS AND PERSONEL

单位：个、人 (unit, person)

项 目	Item	2009	2010	2011	2012	2013	2014	2015
艺术业机构	Art Performing Institution			239	295	363	328	340
#剧团	#Troupes			172	226	307	273	282
#剧场	#Theater			65	66	53	52	58
文物事业机构	Historical Relics Institutions	171	166	175	214	291	300	302
#博物馆	#Museums	114	121	125	161	170	174	175
图书馆事业机构	Library Institutions	104	107	109	111	112	112	112
群众文化事业机构	Public Culture Institutions	1367	1378	1378	1379	1382	1390	1399
群众艺术馆	Public Art Center	17	13	13	13	13	13	13
文化馆(站)	Art Center	1350	1365	1365	1366	1369	1377	1386
艺术业人员数	Number of People Engaged in Art Performing			5018	10976	10384	9774	10596
#剧团人员	#Staff in Troupes			4580	9216	9005	8520	8999
#剧场人员	#Staff in Theater			437	1750	1367	1241	1597
文物事业人员数	Number of Historical Relics Staffs	3915	3297	3596	4334	4713	4928	5025
#博物馆人员	#Number of staff in Library	2281	2298	2380	3078	3360	3380	3449
图书馆事业人员数	Number of People Engaged in Library	2178	2151	2149	2219	2226	2231	2212
群众文化事业人员数	Number of People Engaged in Public Art	4951	4943	5022	5044	4912	5045	4869
群众艺术馆人员	Number of People in Public Art Center	610	481	489	448	494	479	478
文化馆(站)人员	Number of People in Cultural Station	4341	4462	4533	4596	4418	4566	4391
#乡镇文化站	#Township Cultural Stations	2181	2175	2221	2256	2046	2234	2109

19-2 公共图书馆发展情况
DEVELOPMENT STATISTICS ON PUBLIC LIBRARIES

项 目		Item		2005	2010	2011	2012	2013	2014	2015
机构数	(个)	Number of Library	(unit)	102	107	109	111	112	112	112
藏书数	(万册)	Total Collections	(10 000 volumes)	1923	2361	2410	2521	2648	2822	3003
书架单层总长度	(万米)	Total Length of Bookshelves	(10 000 m)	101	111	108	51	53	53	54
有效借书证数	(万个)	Valid Library card number	(10 000 units)	72	104	95	138	108	128	144
图书流通情况		Number of Circulation								
公共图书馆流通人次	(万人次)	The public library circulation	(10 000 person-times)	1145	1516	1342	1516	1763	1868	1955
册次	(万册数)	Volume-time	(10 000 volume-times)	927	1846	1114	1386	1570	1755	1816
为读者服务举办各种活动		Service for Readers								
次数	(次)	Times	(time)	1621	1790	2258	2928	3098	3498	3615
参加人数	(万人次)	Number of Readers Involved	(10 000 person-times)	176	105	120	128	178	173	163
当年新购图书	(万册)	New Books Purchaesd in 2012	(10 000 volume-times)	43	60	82	111	138	161	185
图书费	(万元)	Purchase Expenses	(10 000 yuan)	1296	1847	2138	4210	5076	5713	7302

19-3 公共图书馆藏书及分类情况
STATISTICS ON BOOKS AND TYPE OF BOOKS IN PUBLIC LIBRARIES

单位：万册 (10 000 volumes)

年份 Year	合计 Total	#外文 #Foreign	#古籍 #Ancient	#图书 #New Books	其它藏量 Other Reserves
1996	1472	82	97		
1997	1533	81	97		
1998	1599	81	96		
1999	1643	81	96		
2000	1678	82	97		
2001	1709	83	98		
2002	1759	81	99		
2003	1819	83	98		
2004	1867		94		
2005	1923		97		
2006	1981		100		
2007	2037		96		
2008	2106		97		
2009	2181		96		
2010	2361		95		
2011	2410		98	1860	453
2012	2521		98	2008	415
2013	2648		99	2156	393
2014	2822		101	2295	426
2015	3003		101	2462	441

注：其它藏量包括报刊、视听文献、缩微制品、电子图书和其它
Note: Other reserves include newspapers, audiovisual documents, microform, electronic books and other materials.Contains a total electronic books

19-4 图书、报纸、期刊出版情况
STATISTICS ON PUBLICATION OF BOOKS, NEWSPAPERS AND PERIODICALS

项 目	Item	2000	2005	2010	2012	2013	2014	2015
一、图书出版种数 (种)	Category of Library Books Published (kind)	4529	6535	10464	14256	13900	16043	15543
新出版 (种)	New Publications (kind)	2443	3739	6328	8476	8445	9662	8932
总印数 (千册)	Total Prints (1 000 volume)	288416	345510	275330	259720	262740	271933	262997
总印张 (千印张)	Total Number of Paper Printed (1 000 pages)	1552128	2495183	1997639	2045531	2088169	2288053	2250020
二、杂志出版种数 (种)	**Category of Magazines Published** (kind)	391	407	407	408	408	409	412
总印数 (千册)	Total Prints (1000 volume)	220280	196800	300770	341410	309375	280895	251249
总印张 (千印张)	Total Number of Paper Printed (1 000 pages)	746145	745526	1482345	1865793	1781708	1662398	1458924
三、报刊出版种数 (种)	Category of Newspapers and Periodicals Published (kind)	164	193	130	130	130	130	129
总印数 (千份)	Total Prints (1 000 copies)	1342282	1956980	1816720	2060760	1982020	1910667	1539203
总印张 (万印张)	Total Number of Paper Printed (10 000 pages)	339434	520833	889514	931133	858508	826749	538040

19-5 电影、艺术活动、群众文化活动、图书馆及博物馆活动情况 STATISTICS ON MOVIE, ART ACTIVITIES, PUBLIC CULTURE ACTIVITIES, LIBRARY AND MUSEUM

项 目	Item	2000	2005	2010	2012	2013	2014	2015
城市电影活动	Movie of city							
放映场次数 (万场)	Times Projected (10 000 times)				95.40	128.09	162.47	231.71
观众人数 (千人次)	Number of the audience (1000 person-times)				24496	33168	43905	66425
艺术活动	Art Activities							
年表演场次 (场)	Annual Times of Performing (time)	15000	16000	22850	35920	37230	39000	38490
观众人数 (千人次)	Number of Spectators (1000 person-times)	21211	16939	28454	30144	28801	33444	29017
年人均观看次数 (次)	Annual Times of Watching Per Capita (time)	0.36	0.28	0.50	0.52	0.50	0.57	0.50
群众文化活动	Public Culture Activities							
举办展览个数 (个)	Number of Expo Displayed (unit)	2785	2653	4276	3427	4045	4467	4399
举办训练班结业人数(万人次)	Number of Training Activities (10 000 person-times)	9.90	13.00	10.80	83.80	87.8	95.1	97.6
图书馆活动	Library Activities							
书刊外借人次 (千人次)	Number of Circulation (1000 person-times)						10525	9918
图书流通册次 (千册)	Number of Circulation (1000 volumes)	9485	9267	18462	13865	15701	17554	18164
人均年借阅册数 (册)	Number of Books Borrowed Per Capita Annually (volume)	0.16	0.15	0.32	0.24	0.27	0.30	0.31
人均年借阅人数(次)	Number of People Borrowing Annually (person)	0.12	0.19	0.27	0.15	0.16	0.18	0.17
博物馆活动	Museum Activities							
现有陈列展览个数 (个)	Number of Display at Present (unit)	210	218	686	937	796	857	964
参观人数 (千人次)	Visitors (1000 persons)	1819	2194	19212	22297	23576	25996	26239
人均年参观次数 (次)	Number of Visit Per Capia Annually (time)	0.03	0.04	0.34	0.39	0.41	0.45	0.45

19-6 艺术表演团体、群众艺术馆、文化馆经费情况
STATISTICS ON EXPENSES OF ART TROUPES, PUBLIC ART CENTERS AND CULTURE ACTIVITIES CENTERS

单位：万元 (10 000 yuan)

项 目	Item	2011	2012	2013	2014	2015
艺术表演团体 (个)	**Art Troupes (unit)**					
补贴团体	Subsidized Troupes	4	1	2	2	2
国家经费补贴	National Subsidy	8915	2868	2625	3219	3562
业务及其他收入	Revenue from Business and From Others	2154	831	462	441	381
#演出收入	#From Performing	842	243	243	149	164
总支出	Total Expenditure	11168	3406	3239	3734	3726
第三产业增加值	Value Added of Tertiary Industry	8636	2186	2343	3074	3039
经费自给率 (%)	Percentage of Self-supply Expenses (%)	19.2	24.0	14.0	11.8	10.0
群众艺术馆、文化馆(站)	**Mass Art Galleries and Culture Galleries**					
总支出	Total Expenditure	2079	1985	2476	3068	3481
#预算	#Budget	1320	1344	1959	2110	2518
#项目支出	#Project spending	759	1144	1452	1714	2160
修缮费	Maintainace Fees					
第三产业增加值	Value Added of Tertiary Industry	732	869	1207	1416	1893

注：本表各项指标口径为文化厅系统内。
Note: Items in this table refer to those within culture bureau system.

19-7 文化、文物事业经费支出及基本建设情况
BASIC CONDITIONS ABOUT EXPENDITURES ON CULTURE AND HISTORICAL RELICS AND ITS CONSTRUCTION

单位：万元 (10 000 yuan)

项 目	Item	2011	2012	2013	2014	2015
文化、文物事业经费支出总计	**Total Expenditures on Culture and Historical Relics**	**244474**	**286344**	**333675**	**357361**	**450545**
文化事业	Culture	194222	218712	249298	270471	338057
艺术表演团体	Art Performing Groups	43000	43492	52952	54940	63525
艺术表演场所	Art Performing Places	12807	5245	9233	10163	9784
图书馆	Library	35003	34313	43633	45054	50295
群众文化	Public Culture	29273	36247	39667	43503	51708
中等专业学校	Secondary Vocation School	5533	3511	3276	2972	12412
干部训练	Cadre Taining					
其他文化事业	Others	74136	95833	100466	113768	150333
文物事业	Historical Relics	44719	67632	84377	86890	112488
博物馆	Museum	29256	38330	54176	56199	59126
文物事业机构	Institutions of Historical Relics	8567	19254	16912	12956	21621
其它文物事业	Others	6896	10048	13290	17735	31741
文化、文物基本建设完成投资	Investment in Culture & Historical Relics Cause Construction	83371	31446	83300	64377	35872
文化事业	Culture Cause	26533	21360	52887	39263	17955
文物事业	Historical Relics Cause	56838	10086	30413	25114	17917

19-8 广播电视从业人员基本情况(2015)
BASIC STATISTICS ON PERSONEL ENGAGED IN BROADCASTING AND TELEVISION (2015)

单位：人 (person)

		全省合计 Total of the Province	省级 Provincial Level	市州级 Municiple and Prefecture Level	县级 County Level
从业人员	Personel	40513	24282	6597	9634
其中：长期职工	#Long-term Staff and Workers	38672	22979	6450	9243
党员	Party Members(Communists)	15969	8231	2964	4774
按岗位分：	Classified by Job Division:				
管理人员	Management Personel	7097	3819	1260	2018
专业技术人员	Professional Technical Personel	21248	11732	4258	5258
编辑、记者	Editors and Reporters	6951	2394	2222	2335
播音员、主持人	Announcers and Hosts	1244	337	448	459
按学历分：	Classified by Academic Qualifications:				
研究生及以上	#Graduate and Above	957	629	272	56
本科及大专	Undergraduate and Post-secondary	25856	14546	5341	5969
高中及以下	High School and Below	13700	9107	984	3609
按职称分：	Classified According to Occupation:				
正高	Senior	361	282	75	4
副高	Vice-senior	1464	825	534	105
中级	Medium	7610	3294	2024	2292
初级及以下	Primary and Below	21052	13862	2984	4206
按年龄分：	Classified by Age:				
35岁以下	35 and Below	13649	8866	2330	2453
36岁至50岁	36-50	20421	12016	3098	5307
50岁以上	50 and Above	6443	3400	1169	1874

19-9 广播电视传输覆盖与经济效益
STATISTICS ON BROADCASTING AND TV COVERAGE RATING AND ECONOMIC BENEFITS

项 目	Item	2010	2012	2013	2014	2015
广播覆盖率 (%)	Broadcasting Coverage Rate (%)	98.10	98.72	98.80	98.90	99.08
电视覆盖率 (%)	TV Coverage Rate (%)	98.11	98.75	98.81	98.89	98.98
有线电视用户 (万户)	Cable Television Users (10 000 household)	894.07	1048.38	1045.31	1070.89	1067.80
中短波发射转播台/机 (座/部)	Medium and Short-Wave Transmitting Stations (set)	26/76	28/82	28/86	28/86	28/88
中短波发射转播台功率 (千瓦)	Power of Medium and Short-Wave Transmitters (kw)	1256.00	1331.00	1371	1371	1391
调频电视发射转播台 (座/部)	FM and TelevisionTransmitting Stations (set)					835/716
调频发射机 (部)	FM Transmitters (set)	584	604	609	611	716
调频发射机功率 (千瓦)	Power of FM Transmitters (kw)	520.31	551.51	558.91	564.91	623.69
电视发射转播台 (座/部)	Television Transmitting Station (set)	991/1275	991/1273	908/1191	885/1170	835/888
电视发射转播台功率 (千瓦)	Power of Television Transmitters (kw)	592.22	590.43	583.88	586.70	598.69
微波线路站数/长度 (座/公里)	Length of Micro-Wave Route Per Station (set/km)	121/2961.05	119/2936.05	116/2906.05	116/2906.05	126/2875.05
创收收入 (亿元)	Revenue (100 million yuan)	48.57	63.09	73.12	89.02	89.40
固定资产原值 (亿元)	Original Price of Fixed Assets(100 million yuan)	90.43	116.90	95.31	104.43	110.89

19-10 广播电视宣传和节目制作
BROADCASTING PUBLICITY AND PROGRAM PRODUCTION

项 目	Item	2005	2010	2013	2014	2015
广播电台 (座)	Broadcasting Station (unit)	11	11	7	6	6
电视台 (座)	TV Station (unit)	12	12	8	8	8
广播电视台 (座)	Radiated TV Station (unit)	71	71	75	76	81
广播节目套数 (套)	Number of Radio Programs (unit)	81	85	87	87	87
广播平均日播音时间 (小时)	Average Broadcasting Hour per Week (h)	1040.40	1225.65	1289.00	1296.97	1308.36
广播节目年制作能力 (万小时)	Annual Capacity of Radio Program Production (10 000 h)	20.59	23.54	24.29	24.29	24.63
电视节目套数 (套)	Number of TV Programs (unit)	113	114	117	117	114
电视平均周播出时间 (万小时)	Average TV Hour per Week (10 000 h)	1.05	1.26	1.32	1.32	1.31
电视节目年制作能力 (万小时)	Annual Capacity of TV program Production (10 000 h)	7.93	9.48	10.65	10.92	10.77
电视剧制作 (部/集)	Production of TV Series (episode)	11/ 208	11/314	5/151	20/854	19/835

19-11 分单位类型、分人员类型体育系统从业人员数(2015)
NUMBER OF STAFF AND WORKERS IN SPORTS COMMISSIONS(2015)

单位：人 (person)

		合计 Total	公务员 Civilian	管理人员 Adminis-trator	专业技术人员				运动员 Athlete	工勤人员 Worker	其他 Others
					小计 Subtotal	其中：教练员 Coach	其中：科研人员 Scientific research personnel	其中：卫生技术人员 Health technical personnel			
合计	Total	6478	971	1299	2161	840	28	44	1008	514	525
体育行政机关	Sports Administrative Authority	1174	971							49	154
运动项目管理部门(优秀运动队)	Sports Management Department	1167		149	234	214		9	728	47	9
本科院校	Undergraduate School	1315		171	824	36		32	268	52	
体育运动学校	Sports School for athelets	501		64	381	150	5	2		42	14
少年儿童体育学校	Sports School for Kids	643		203	388	300	2	1	12	26	14
体育中学	Middle School for Athelets	59		18	37	21				4	
训练基地	Training Base	146		76	43	31				17	10
体育场馆	Stadium	865		372	203	84				249	41
体育科研机构	Sports Science Reaserch Institution	48		9	39		21				
其他事业单位	Other Institution	514		200	12	4				26	276
其它	Others	46		37						2	7

19-12 等级裁判员、运动员情况
NUMBER OF ATHLETES AND REFEREES IN GRADES

单位：人 (person)

项 目	Item	2000	2005	2009	2010	2011	2012	2013	2014	2015
等级裁判员合计	**Number of Referees in Grades**	**1195**	**787**	**1438**	**1504**	**1870**	**1667**	**2335**	**1725**	**3021**
国家级裁判	**National Referees**	29	25	6	24	23	15	27		4
一级裁判	**First Grade**	143	115	467	352	378	403	377	394	317
二级裁判	**Second Grade**	1023	647	965	1128	1469	1249	1931	1331	2700
等级运动员合计	**Number of Athletes in Grade**	**418**	**1149**	**1503**	**1639**	**1570**	**1723**	**2109**	**2111**	**1556**
国际运动健将	**International Master of Sports**	6		1	1	5	8		4	4
运动健将	**Master of Sports**	36	36	51	21	54	54	61	41	68
一级运动员	**First Grade**	10	247	180	180	227	328	214	359	316
二级运动员	**Second Grade**	366	866	1271	1437	1284	1333	1834	1707	1168

19-13 体育竞赛成果情况
STATISTICS ON ACHIEVEMENT IN SPORTS COMPETITION

项 目	Item	2000	2005	2009	2010	2011	2012	2013	2014	2015
世界比赛获奖牌数 (枚)	**Number of Medals Won in International Games (unit)**	**13**	**5**	**34**	**12**	**80**	**64**	**51**	**86**	**66**
金牌	Gold Medal	4	3	12	2	48	30	25	41	29
银牌	Silver Medal	6	2	10	3	19	21	9	23	32
铜牌	Bronze Medal	3		12	7	13	13	17	22	5
亚洲比赛获奖牌数 (枚)	**Number of Medals Won in Asia Games (unit)**	**5**	**7**	**23**	**13**	**17**	**24**	**11**	**26**	**35**
金牌	Gold Medal	4	5	5	8	13	15	5	17	17
银牌	Silver Medal		2	9	4	4	7	4	3	9
铜牌	Bronze Medal	1		9	1		2	2	6	9
全国比赛获前六名 (人)	**Top Six Places in National Games (person)**		**155**	**315**	**134**	**524**	**461**	**356**	**356**	**502**
第一名	First Place	35	24	49	21	99	82	57	48	75
第二名	Second Place	22	23	53	21	71	74	72	53	78
第三名	Third Place	21	27	51	17	90	76	82	69	85
第四名	Fourth Place	35	24	44	23	92	68	48	55	76
第五名	Fifth Place	29	31	66	30	103	86	65	87	109
第六名	Sixth Place	26	26	52	22	69	75	32	44	79

19-14 新建健身场地设施情况(2015)
SITUATION OF NEW-BUILT FITNESS FACILITIES(2015)

			合计 Total	村级农民体育健身工程 Town-based Peasant Fitness Project	乡镇体育健身工程 County-based Fitness Project	全民健身路径工程 Citizen "Fitness Path" Project	全民健身活动中心 Citizen Fitness Center
数量 (个)	Number	(unit)	6418	2517	119	3299	9
器材件数 (件)	Number of Instrument	(piece)	21107			20617	
场地面积 (平方米)	Area	(sq. m)	2643508	1791938	121898	384757	43178
场地长度 (米)	Length	(m)	106900				
投资总额 (万元)	Total Invenstment	(10 000 Yuan)	77383	4541	1416	38006	784

19-14 续表

			户外健身场地设施 Outdoor Fitness Facilities					其他场地设施 Other Fitness Facilities
			体育公园 Fitness Park	全民健身广场 Citizen Fitness Square	户外体育营地 Outdoor Fitness Center	社区运动场地 Community-based Fitness Square	健身步道 Fitness Path	
数量	(个)Number	(unit)	2	13	1	91	14	353
器材件数	(件)Number of Instrument	(piece)						490
场地面积	(平方米)Area	(sq. m)	51500	54300	3000	124881		68056
场地长度	(米)Length	(m)					106900	
投资总额	(万元)Total Invenstment	(10 000 Yuan)	25023	520	80	2381	2427	2205

19-15 分市州文化及相关产业"三上"法人单位数(2015)
NUMBER OF LEGAL PERSONS OF CULTURE AND RELAVANT INDUSTRY ABOVE DESIGNATED BY REGION(2015)

单位：个 (unit)

地 区	Region	"三上"法人单位数 Legal Persons	规上文化制造业 Cultual Manufacturing	限上文化批发和零售业 Wholesale and Rerail of Culture	规上文化服务业 Services of Culture
全 省	**Province**	**1652**	**540**	**445**	**667**
武汉市	Wuhan	459	77	91	291
黄石市	Huangshi	46	20	6	20
十堰市	Shiyan	41	6	19	16
宜昌市	Yichang	290	97	64	129
襄阳市	Xiangyang	334	96	104	134
鄂州市	Ezhou	15	4	6	5
荆门市	Jingmen	48	23	20	5
孝感市	Xiaogan	101	64	28	9
荆州市	Jingzhou	67	29	29	9
黄冈市	Huanggang	80	33	34	13
咸宁市	Xianning	59	32	9	18
随州市	Suizhou	30	21	7	2
恩施州	Enshi	43	12	21	10
仙桃市	Xiantao	15	12	2	1
潜江市	Qianjiang	9	6	2	1
天门市	Tianmen	11	8	3	
神农架	Shennongjia	4			4

19-16 分市州规模以上文化制造业企业基本情况(2015)
BASIC CONDITIONS CULTURAL MANUFACTURING ENTERPRISES ABOVE DESIGNATED SIZE BY REGION(2015)

单位：万元 (10 000 yuan)

地 区	Region	企业单位数(个) Number of Enterprises (unit)	年末从业人员(人) Engaged Person at Year-end (person)	资产总计 Total Assets	营业收入 Business Revenue	营业税金及附加 Taxes and Extra Charges on Business	营业利润 Operating Profit	应交增值税 Value-added Tax Payable
全 省	**Province**	**540**	**99744**	**7588280.4**	**11587526**	**77268.4**	**553191.1**	**257828.6**
武汉市	Wuhan	77	16300	3079111.7	2906287.5	7225.7	94657.2	43072.1
黄石市	Huangshi	20	4164	117656.9	175588.4	1388.3	3721.7	3012
十堰市	Shiyan	6	725	19171	28853.8	1095.6	1745.5	826.9
宜昌市	Yichang	97	20995	1642132.6	2301584.2	14169	132655.7	73438.4
襄阳市	Xiangyang	96	19985	1034212.4	2348977.8	12980.7	128531	50251
鄂州市	Ezhou	4	541	27883.2	181015.5	1410.6	7158.5	9034.5
荆门市	Jingmen	23	2640	133754.8	312854.7	5385.8	26110.1	3949.9
孝感市	Xiaogan	64	8810	432779	1168785.5	22074.6	56385.9	29121.1
荆州市	Jingzhou	29	6755	323670.1	807864.1	1224.6	16641.3	11003.9
黄冈市	Huanggang	33	4092	218398.1	203705	1702.9	10743.7	3019.9
咸宁市	Xianning	32	4835	253116.6	517092.1	3323.6	30163.6	7663
随州市	Suizhou	21	3078	100000.9	187331.2	983.2	11078.4	9881.6
恩施州	Enshi	12	1514	24330.2	48603.2	524.5	2513.3	640.1
仙桃市	Xiantao	12	1832	93055.2	207930.5	2325.3	19231.5	8689.1
潜江市	Qianjiang	6	670	17761.5	81364.6	823.4	4257.8	851
天门市	Tianmen	8	2808	71246.2	109688.3	630.6	7595.9	3374.1
神农架	Shennongjia							

19-17 分市州限额以上文化批发和零售企业基本情况(2015)
BASIC CONDITIONS OF ENTERPRISES OF WHOLESALE AND RETAIL OF CULTURE ABOVE DESIGNATED SIZE BY REGION(2015)

单位：万元 (10 000 yuan)

地区	Region	企业单位数(个) Number of Enterprises (unit)	年末从业人员(人) Engaged Person at Year-end (person)	资产总计 Total Assets	营业收入 Business Revenue	营业税金及附加 Taxes and Extra Charges on Business	营业利润 Operating Profit	应交增值税 Value-added Tax Payable
全省	**Province**	**445**	**23512**	**2090419**	**4107613.3**	**25678.4**	**178715.2**	**52135.9**
武汉市	Wuhan	91	11156	1164410.4	2220248.2	6615.3	33770.7	14210.3
黄石市	Huangshi	6	266	14981.1	16798.2	183.2	1685.9	194.7
十堰市	Shiyan	19	666	25689.8	44695.1	933.8	3074.6	800.2
宜昌市	Yichang	64	3584	293754.6	458650	3414.2	16335.1	16390.4
襄阳市	Xiangyang	104	2514	137937.5	478188.3	9412.8	49340.6	12351.3
鄂州市	Ezhou	6	300	9374.6	56169.2	40.5	2062.3	82
荆门市	Jingmen	20	401	17570.9	27087.4	583.2	3152.2	738.2
孝感市	Xiaogan	28	978	65298.5	168153.3	336.7	24638.3	1535.8
荆州市	Jingzhou	29	721	40988	72020.4	1146.9	4303.1	580.5
黄冈市	Huanggang	34	1091	74818.8	85606.6	412.6	5667.6	589.3
咸宁市	Xianning	9	172	13770.7	35863.1	350	5708.8	321.4
随州市	Suizhou	7	218	19687.7	24402.6	341	3242.4	535.1
恩施州	Enshi	21	508	28026.1	42889.4	155.4	2814	182.3
仙桃市	Xiantao	2	96	10073.9	10002.9	158.1	981.7	141
潜江市	Qianjiang	2	654	35921.9	182273.5	28.4	172.5	15.6
天门市	Tianmen	3	187	138114.5	184565.1	1566.3	21765.4	3467.8
神农架	Shennongjia							

19-18 分市州规模以上文化服务业企业基本情况(2015)
BASIC CONDITIONS OF ENTERPRISES OF SERVICES OF CULTURE ABOVE DESIGNATED BY REGION(2015)

单位：万元 (10 000 yuan)

地 区	Region	企业单位数(个) Number of Enterprises (unit)	年末从业人员(人) Engaged Person at Year-end (person)	资产总计 Total Assets	营业收入 Business Revenue	营业税金及附加 Taxes and Extra Charges on Business	营业利润 Operating Profit	应交增值税 Value-added Tax Payable
全 省	**Province**	**667**	**121985**	**13473922**	**5713247.2**	**129686**	**600335.3**	**141169.4**
武汉市	Wuhan	291	96294	11463787	4966683.4	107012.2	498733.5	127819.2
黄石市	Huangshi	20	1240	43314	28048.7	674.8	1957.7	389.7
十堰市	Shiyan	16	2266	376922.1	75993.4	1196.4	13632.7	932.7
宜昌市	Yichang	129	9096	559259.9	320617.7	8797	51836.1	6350.6
襄阳市	Xiangyang	134	6605	518642.2	153740.4	7747	23485.9	4017.4
鄂州市	Ezhou	5	444	13874.8	8582	38.7	-288.5	12
荆门市	Jingmen	5	534	18131.9	7779.8	72.6	910.9	226.6
孝感市	Xiaogan	9	713	52643.7	11451.3	389.8	2398.1	348.3
荆州市	Jingzhou	9	445	12864.1	13962.7	47.4	176.8	113.8
黄冈市	Huanggang	13	1070	46429.1	28376.1	1098	4013.4	705.6
咸宁市	Xianning	18	1571	132171.3	56334.8	988.7	243.1	-129.5
随州市	Suizhou	2	157	517.3	1636.1	63.6	51	
恩施州	Enshi	10	1266	187684.4	29530.4	1225.9	2336.9	378.5
仙桃市	Xiantao	1	34	90	47.8	2.7	1.3	
潜江市	Qianjiang	1	22	563.1	976.3	4.9	7.3	2.5
天门市	Tianmen							
神农架	Shennongjia	4	228	47026.9	9486.3	326.3	839.1	2

主要统计指标解释

文化事业机构 指从事专业文化工作和为专业文化工作服务的独立建制的单位。不包括这些单位另外举办独立核算的其他机构和各部门的业余文化组织。该指标主要反映文化事业机构发展规模水平。

艺术表演团体 指从事戏曲、音乐、舞蹈、杂技等专业艺术表演,有独立帐户的单位,不包括半工半艺、半农半艺和民间职业剧团。该指标主要反映全国专业艺术表演团体发展规模水平。

艺术表演观众人数(人次) 指售票、包场演出或民族地区免费演出的艺术表演观众人次数,不包括彩排审查和内部观摩演出的观看人次数。该指标主要反映全国观看专业艺术表演团体演出的效益规模。

等级运动员 是指经考核正式批准授予运动员称号的运动员,等级称号由高到低依次为国际级运动健将、运动健将、一级运动员、二级运动员、三级运动员。

广播节目综合人口覆盖率 指根据国家广电总局制定的《广播电视人口覆盖率统计技术标准和方法》进行统计调查的,在对象区能接收到由中央、省、地区或县通过无线、有线或卫星等技术方式传播的各级广播节目的人口数占全国总人口数的百分比。

电视节目综合人口覆盖率 指根据国家广电总局制定的《广播电视人口覆盖率统计技术标准和方法》进行统计调查的,在对象区能接收到由中央、省、地区或县通过无线、有线或卫星等技术方式传播的各级电视节目的人口数占全国总人口数的百分比。

Explanatory Notes on Main Statistical Indicators

Cultural Institutions refer to units, which have their own organizational system and independent accounting system and specialize in or serve cultural development. They exclude other establishments run by these cultural institutions and amateur cultural groups established by various departments. This indicator reflects the development of cultural units.

Art Troupe refers to the troupe which is engaged in drama, opera, music, dance, acrobatics or other art performance, opens independent accounts with banks and has self-supporting accounting system; excluding the troupes which are engaged partly in industrial or agricultural activities, partly in art performance and the professional troupes organized by the people. This indicator reflects the development of national professional art troupes.

Number of Audience at Art Performance refers to the number of attendants at commercial shows, completely booked shows or free shows given in minority national areas, and does not include the number of spectators at rehearsals for examination and internal shows for study.

Certified Grade Athletes refer to those who are awarded the title of athletes through assessment. The titles rank from high to low as: international level athletes, national level athletes, first grade athletes, second grade athletes and third grade athletes.

Radio Coverage of Population refers to the percentage of population, which can receive central, provincial, city, prefecture, and county radio programs relayed by wireless, cable, satellite and other technical means, in the surveying area, to national total population, according to Statistical Standard and Method on Television and Radio Coverage of Population established by the State Administration of Broadcasting, Film and Television.

Television Coverage of Population refers to the percentage of population, which can receive central, provincial, city, prefecture, and county television programs relayed by wireless, cable, satellite and other technical means, in the surveying area, to national total population, according to Statistical Standard and Method on Television and Radio Coverage of Population established by the State Administration of Broadcasting, Film and Television.

20 公共管理及其他

Public Management and Other

20-1 工会组织情况
BASIC STATISTICS ON LABOR UNION

年 份 Year	工会基层组织数（个） Number of Grassroot Labor Union Organizations (unit)	全省已建工会的基层单位职工与会员人数(万人) Number of Grassroot Staff and Workers and Members of Established Labor Union in the Province(10 000 persons)				工会专职工作人员人数(万人) Number of Full-time Workers in Labor Union (10 000 persons)
		职工人数 Number of Staff and Workers	#女职工 #Women Workers	会员人数 Number of Members	#女会员 #Women Members	
1975	18872	280.22	83.18	174.72	56.24	0.87
1980	22802	387.95	139.20	299.41	94.91	1.04
1985	25286	484.68	192.32	404.58	156.62	2.76
1990	33990	559.00	227.00	498.00	198.00	3.40
1995	28461	564.34	230.90	511.11	207.49	1.81
1996	28459	584.30	238.16	527.09	213.08	2.88
1997	20151	472.60	192.65	419.72	168.89	2.68
1998	17488	445.80	183.90	400.90	163.90	2.30
1999	18976	442.97	178.21	396.90	155.03	3.18
2000	45251	532.31	197.81	475.57	176.87	2.45
2001	111309	728.94	218.68	660.82	198.25	2.45
2004	50391	755.90	276.69	721.46	262.74	2.95
2005	54893	856.07	298.78	771.95	279.94	3.09
2006	61627	904.15	314.67	856.95	296.39	3.76
2007	69886	1004.92	358.44	972.30	345.64	3.94
2008	79048	1099.78	382.72	1073.22	377.43	4.48
2009	83436	1160.45	418.82	1127.68	411.12	4.75
2010	88647	1220.52	437.50	1184.88	429.00	5.80
2011	107995	1319.08	462.18	1267.28	453.11	6.10
2012	120561	1336.09	491.49	1292.06	481.87	6.44
2013	130513	1348.45	494.94	1312.16	487.57	6.36
2014	130326	1325.35	495.91	1285.13	487.36	6.67
2015	130118	1355.78	505.27	1301.52	490.43	6.61

注：因文革期间工会统计中断，表中1975年数据根据年平均增长值推算

Note:The data in 1975 were calculated by the average growth rate because Labor Union statistics had been suspended in the period of "The Great Cultural Revolution".

20-2 基层政权和村(居)委会情况
BASIC STATISTICS ON GRASSROOT REGIME AND VILLAGE COMMITTEES

单位:个 (unit)

年份 Year	镇 Township	乡 Villages	街道办事处 Regional Office	居委会个数 Number of Committees	村委会个数 Number of Village Committees
1986	859	3700	178	3257	32796
1987	836	1257	186	3394	32738
1988	828	1260	215	3483	32354
1989	840	1143	298	3545	32094
1990	849	1123	293	3573	32703
1991	849	1121	307	3709	32595
1992	852	1117	297	3830	32716
1993	857	1097	214	3921	32674
1994	864	1092	218	3998	32636
1995	865	1038	236	4110	32547
1996	823	567	252	4170	32486
1997	840	552	252	4287	32393
1998	847	543	253	4364	32293
1999	850	488	271	4425	32187
2000	860	466	283	3619	32001
2001	735	228	250	3468	31191
2002	738	224	272	3265	27667
2003	735	224	273	3351	27127
2004	738	224	274	3356	26470
2005	733	217	277	3465	29534
2006	737	210	277	3545	25828
2007	734	210	279	3653	25722
2008	735	207	285	3794	25551
2009	740	204	283	3882	25517
2010	741	199	290	3983	25763
2011	742	194	297	4051	25643
2012	746	188	298	4032	25575
2013	757	175	300	4208	25452
2014	761	170	302	4187	25448
2015	761	168	304	4294	25109

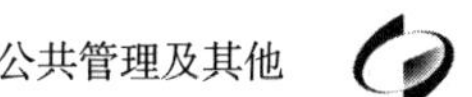

20-3 社会福利事业、企业单位机构及人员数
BASIC STATISTICS ON NUMBER OF SOCIAL WELFARE ENTERPRISES AND PERSONS ENGAGED

单位：个 (unit)

项目	Item	机构数 Number of Institutions					
		2010	2011	2012	2013	2014	2015
全省合计	**Total of the Province**	**6149**	**6807**	**8251**	**12000**	**12453**	**16451**
一、事业单位	Institution	5395	6084	7545	11375	11919	15973
(一)收养性事业单位	Adoptive Institutions	2520	2528	2545	2213	2008	1658
1.优抚休(疗)养院	Special Care Nursing Home	97	97	102	105	101	74
2.社会福利收养院	Welfare Homes	2423	2431	2443	2108	1816	1492
(二)非收养性事业单位	Non-Adoptive Institutions	2875	3556	5000	9162	9917	12931
1.烈士纪念建筑物管理单位	Managing Organizations on Martyrs Memorials	46	51	52	55	56	56
2.军队离退休干部管理机构	Managing Organizations on Veterans	106	107	106	108	107	108
3.军供站	Military Supply Station	9	9	9	9	9	9
4.社区服务机构	Community Service Centre	2315	2887	4330	8466	9216	12165
5.救助管理站	Home for Beggers and Vagrants	63	81	87	86	87	86
6.未成年人救助保护中心	Protection Centre for Street Children	13	81	78	66	65	55
7.殡葬事业单位	Funeral Units	132	136	147	172	178	175
#殡仪馆	#Funeral Home	83	82	84	88	85	84
8.福利彩票发行单位	Lottery Tickets Issuing Units	52	53	54	54	54	53
9.婚姻登记服务单位	Marriage Registration Service Center	97	108	93	99	97	95
10.救灾储备单位	Relief Unit	42	43	44	47	48	45
二、社会福利企业	Social Welfare Enterprises	754	723	706	625	534	478

20-3 续表 continued

单位：人 (person)

项 目	Item	人员数 Number of Persons Engaged in					
		2010	2011	2012	2013	2014	2015
全省合计	**Total of the Province**	**74891**	**76524**	**84733**	**95296**	**99577**	**111933**
一、事业单位	Institution	33401	37222	44100	56987	64951	80785
(一)收养性事业单位	Adoptive Institutions	18835	20017	19754	19871	23511	26183
1.优抚休(疗)养院	Special Care Nursing Home	2723	2700	2776	3088	3790	3457
2.社会福利收养院	Welfare Homes	16112	17317	16978	16783	19721	14820
(二)非收养性事业单位	Non-Adoptive Institutions	14566	17205	24346	37116	41440	54602
1.烈士纪念建筑物管理单位	Managing Organizations on Martyrs Memorials	597	618	670	695	690	682
2.军队离退休干部管理机构	Managing Organizations on Veterans	871	848	882	879	859	874
3.军供站	Military Supply Station	247	246	247	236	229	218
4.社区服务机构	Community Service Centre	7919	9851	16586	28863	33648	44384
5.救助管理站	Home for Beggers and Vagrants	553	818	805	871	886	863
6.未成年人救助保护中心	Protection Centre for Street Children	183	324	547	541	335	289
7.殡葬事业单位	Funeral Units	3152	3349	3440	3761	3695	3631
#殡仪馆	#Funeral Home	2552	2641	2575	2592	2449	2499
8.福利彩票发行单位	Lottery Tickets Issuing Units	430	492	488	536	380	439
9.婚姻登记服务单位	Marriage Registration Service Center	487	538	549	603	591	589
10.救灾储备单位	Relief Unit	127	121	132	131	127	134
二、社会福利企业	Social Welfare Enterprises	41490	39302	40633	38309	34626	31148

20-4 社会保险基本情况
BASIC CONDITIONS ABOUT SOCIAL INSURANCE

年 份 year	失业保险 Unemployment Insurance		城镇职工基本养老保险 Basic Endowment Insurance for Urban and Rural Employees		工伤保险年末参保人数（万人） Participants at Year-end (10 000 persons)	年末参加生育保险人数（万人） Number of People Participated in Maternity Insurance at Year-end (10 000 persons)
	年末参保人 数（万人） Participants at Year-end (10 000 persons)	全年发放失业保险金（亿元） Unemployed Relief Released (100 million yuan)	年末参保职工人数（万人） Participants at Year-end (10 000 persons)	年末参保离退休人数（万人） Retirees (10 000 persons)		
1996	392.9	0.4	353.2		177.6	137.8
1997	381.2	0.5	355.8		188.5	165.5
1998	378.2	0.5	413.1	107.4	190.0	168.8
1999	517.6	0.6	455.3	122.4	183.8	189.0
2000	459.6	1.6	465.6	130.4	185.0	191.3
2001	420.8	3.2	474.4	136.6	182.3	182.1
2002	416.1	5.4	532.7	154.5	183.2	182.7
2003	390.1	5.6	554.5	167.5	189.2	182.1
2004	391.3	4.0	586.1	194.7	187.2	179.9
2005	391.5	4.0	597.6	206.4	230.3	175.9
2006	395.5	3.7	630.2	220.5	275.5	194.5
2007	405.4	3.8	651.4	235.3	328.0	225.0
2008	422.6	3.6	671.7	252.4	350.7	315.4
2009	437.0	3.6	701.9	273.7	396.5	350.6
2010	464.5	3.9	749.1	301.3	444.5	388.7
2011	496.0	3.7	766.0	341.4	467.3	412.9
2012	501.4	3.8	801.4	367.3	505.8	444.7
2013	511.9	4.2	822.0	396.0	541.0	457.9
2014	520.9	5.1	847.0	419.3	576.7	480.6
2015	531.2	5.8	874.9	440.6	640.1	500.2

20-5 参加基本养老保险人数
NUMBER OF PRESONS PARTICIPATED IN BASIC ENDOEMENT INSURANCE

年份 Year	合计 Total	职工 Number of Employees	企业(含其他) Enterprises (including others)	离退休人员 Number of Retirees	企业(含其他) Enterprises (including others)
1996	353.2	353.2	353.2		
1997	355.8	355.8	355.8		
1998	520.5	413.1	413.1	107.4	107.4
1999	577.7	455.3	455.3	122.4	122.4
2000	596.0	465.6	465.6	130.4	130.4
2001	611.0	474.4	474.4	136.6	136.6
2002	687.2	532.7	481.5	154.5	147.2
2003	722.0	554.5	501.1	167.5	158.6
2004	780.8	586.1	530.6	194.7	184.5
2005	804.0	597.6	539.8	206.4	195.1
2006	850.7	630.2	570.0	220.5	207.5
2007	886.7	651.4	602.6	235.3	223.0
2008	924.1	671.7	628.7	252.4	238.7
2009	975.6	701.9	660.5	273.7	259.2
2010	1050.4	749.1	690.9	301.3	258.3
2011	1107.4	766.0	725.5	341.4	325.6
2012	1168.7	801.4	757.8	367.3	351.2
2013	1217.9	822.0	779.1	396.0	379.7
2014	1266.2	847.0	802.5	419.3	402.1
2015	1315.5	874.9	830.7	440.6	422.9

20-6 城乡各种福利院基本情况
BASIC CONDITIONS OF WELFARE HOUSES IN URBAN AND RURAL AREAS

年份 Year	单位数(个) Number of Units (unit)	职工人数(人) Number of Staff and Workers (person)	床位数(张) Number of Beds (unit)	收养人数(人) Number of People Adopted (person)
1986	3955	12373	52912	46818
1987	3655	12360	57698	49356
1988	3300	11901	57356	47448
1989	3285	11759	57022	47075
1990	3252	11854	57878	48017
1991	3130	11966	57839	47684
1992	3114	12361	61878	50885
1993	3101	12955	61389	51638
1994	3066	13280	63451	52866
1995	2977	13607	64417	53662
1996	2907	13664	65853	54987
1997	2715	14163	69970	57471
1998	2650	14392	72284	59753
1999	2603	14552	76203	63326
2000	2459	14203	77871	63901
2001	2191	14173	78119	62590
2002	2145	14414	79522	65564
2003	2123	14856	117511	103320
2004	2359	16344	156461	144042
2005	2755	18132	189486	168800
2006	2770	17705	198458	179385
2007	2616	17157	206049	188308
2008	2553	18395	210342	180286
2009	2504	18190	216211	185933
2010	2596	19571	228375	189782
2011	2690	21159	233503	190917
2012	2710	21106	240985	193466
2013	2365	21283	241671	183140
2014	2265	21970	277345	183173
2015	1884	20451	318453	176931

20-7 婚姻登记和离婚情况
STATISTICS ON MARRIAGE REGISTERATION AND DIVORCE

年份 Year	准予登记结婚(对) Marriage Registeration Granted (couple)	初婚(人) First Marriage (person)	再婚(人) Digamist(person)	离婚(对) Divorce (couple)	离婚率(‰) Rate of Divorce (‰)
1986	402315	785319	19311	6322	0.25
1987	417552	809808	25296	6660	0.26
1988	362654	698447	26861	7389	0.29
1989	413460	801171	25749	9203	0.35
1990	408688	790477	26899	9477	0.35
1991	424708	820092	29324	9584	0.35
1992	463279	897899	28659	10793	0.39
1993	425276	822044	28508	11937	0.43
1994	457324	884817	29831	12910	0.46
1995	482063	930832	33294	13340	0.46
1996	442532	851577	33487	14590	0.50
1997	426460	820615	32305	21260	0.72
1998	399900	763163	36637	24711	0.84
1999	376961	716175	37747	19519	0.66
2000	353781	673294	34268	21255	0.71
2001	335421	632188	38654	22077	0.74
2002	321517	605055	37979	24003	0.80
2003	329256	614244	44268	29375	0.98
2004	381472	710633	52311	46369	1.54
2005	394093	717495	70691	53394	1.77
2006	445672	822294	69050	57682	1.91
2007	485278	896768	73788	65876	2.17
2008	542251	1025496	59006	76003	2.49
2009	565400	1058851	71949	81133	2.84
2010	570810	1068715	72905	89549	3.11
2011	626912	1169771	84053	98874	3.18
2012	615861	1155365	76357	109862	3.81
2013	645767	1201344	90190	127604	4.40
2014	621946	1182271	61621	133723	4.60
2015	572954	1079852	66056	144684	4.90

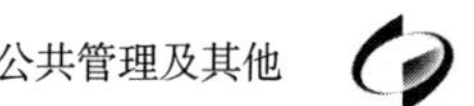

20-8 残疾人基本情况
BASIC STATISTICS ON THE DISABLED

单位：人 (10 000 persons)

项目		Item		2014	2015
康复		Rehabilitation			
视力残疾康复		Rehabilitation of Persons with Visual Disability			
白内障复明手术	(例)	Sight-restoring Surgeries for Cataract Patients	(cases)	30337	26409
低视力者配用助视器	(人)	Persons with Low-vision Fitted with Vision-aids	(persons)	5420	5753
盲人定向行走训练	(人)	Blind Persons Receiving Orientation Skill Training	(persons)	6000	5762
听力语言残疾康复		Rehabilitation of Persons with Hearing and Speech Disability			
新收训聋儿	(人)	Deaf Children Newly Trained in the year	(persons)	829	922
培训聋儿家长	(人)	Parents Trained	(persons)	1128	1155
肢体残疾康复		Rehabilitation of Persons with Physical Disability			
肢体残疾(脑瘫)儿童机构康复训练	(人)	Rehabilitation Training Institutions for Children with Mobility Impairment(Cerebral Palsy)	(persons)	2651	2492
肢体残疾人社区、家庭康复训练	(人)	Persons with Mobility Impairment Receiving Rehabilitation Training in Communities and Families	(persons)	9891	9749
智力残疾康复		Rehabilitation of Persons with Intellectual Disability			
智力残疾儿童康复训练	(人)	Children with Intellectual Disability Receiving Rehabilitation Training	(persons)	4588	6687
成年智力残疾人社区、家庭康复	(人)	Adults with Intellectual Disability Trained in Communities and Families	(persons)	893	957
精神病防治康复		Prevention and Rehabilitation of Mental Illness(PRMI)			
监护精神病人	(人)	Peoplw with Mental Illness under Guardianship	(persons)	227545	220738
显好率	(%)	Significant Improvement Rate	(%)	61.9	62
社会参与率	(%)	Social Involvement Rate	(%)	47.8	46.1
孤独症儿童机构训练	(人)	Children with Autism Trained in Institutions	(person)	820	819
残疾人辅助器具供应服务		Provision of Assistive Devices			
辅助器具供应	(件)	Assistive Devices Provided	(pieces)	32002	32573
残疾人假肢装配	(件)	Prosthesis Installed for the Disabled	(pieces)	1597	1305
残疾人矫形器装配	(例)	Orthotic Devices for the Disabled	(cases)	735	843
教育		Education			
未入学学龄残疾儿童少年	(人)	School-age Disabled Children Unable to Enter School	(persons)	2017	3243
特殊教育普通高中在校生	(人)	Students at Special Education Senior High Schools	(persons)	420	320
残疾人中等职业教育在校生	(人)	Students at Secondary Vocational Schools for PWDs	(persons)	262	145
高等院校录取残疾考生	(人)	Disabled Students Admitted to Higher Education Institutions	(persons)	369	351
就业		Employment			
城镇残疾人新增安排就业	(人)	Newly Employed PWDs in Urban Areas in the Year	(persons)	10865	10537
集中就业		Employed in Collective Form		51181	44310
按比例就业		Employed by Quota Scheme		56502	52213
个体及其他形式就业		Self-employed or Employed in Other Forms		107828	108175
社会保障	(人)	Social Security	(persons)		
城镇残疾职工参加养老保险		Urban Worker with Disabilities Covered by Social Pension Insurance		140056	146033
城镇残疾职工参加医疗保险		Urban Worker with Disabilities Covered by Medical Insurance		151301	156589
残疾居民参加城乡社会养老保险		Disabled residents in Urban and Rural Social endowment Insurance		1046080	1088793
城乡残疾人纳入最低生活保障托养残疾人		PWDs Covered by the Basic Living Allowance System Fostered PWDs		703107	660135
扶贫		Poverty Alleviation			
扶持农村贫困残疾人	(人次)	Impoverished PWDs Assited in Rural Areas	(persons-times)	129103	133611
农村残疾人实用技术培训	(人次)	Vocational Skills Training for PWDs	(persons-times)	29896	29744
农村贫困残疾人危房改造	(户)	Dilapidated House Renovation for Poor PWDs	(households)	513	290
受益残疾人	(人)	PWDs Benefited	(persons)	582	334
维权		Rights Protection			
贫困残疾人家庭无障碍改造	(户)	Barrier Free Home Renovation for Poor PWDs	(households)	2034	1880
残疾人机动轮骑车燃油补贴	(人)	Fuel Subsidy for Motor Wheelchairs of PWDs	(persons)	19835	49043
组织建设		Organization Development			
残疾人人口库持证残疾人	(万人)	PWDs with Disability Certificate in the PWD Database	(10 000 persons)	119	125.8

20-9 刑事案件发、破案情况
STATISTICS ON OCCURANCE AND CLEARING UP OF CRIMINAL CASES

指 标	Item	2000	2005	2010	2011	2012	2013	2014	2015
刑事案件发案总数 (件)	Number of Criminal Cases Occurred (case)	114866	147004	221735	243521	335813	279638	265260	299522
刑事案件破案总数 (件)	Number of Criminal Cases Cleared (case)	72796	71455	76401	63849	139738	118092	90652	77355
刑事案件破案率 (%)	Rate of Criminal Cases Cleared (%)	63.4	48.6	34.5	26.2	41.6	42.2	34.2	25.8

20-10 城市交通事故与火灾情况
BASIC STATISTICS ON TRAFFIC ACCIDENTS AND FIRE ACCIDENTS

指 标	Item	2000	2005	2010	2011	2012	2013	2014	2015
交通事故处理发生件数 (起)	Number of Traffic Accidents (case)	20148	9585	6465	6490	6007	5798	5268	4627
死亡人数 (人)	Deaths (person)	3792	2417	1967	1909	1822	1801	1771	1694
受伤人数 (人)	Injuries (person)	16492	10555	7684	7609	6818	6353	5468	4638
折合经济损失 (万元)	Losses Converted into Money (10 000 yuan)	7041	4958	3294	4029	5391	4473	5071	5176
火灾发生数 (起)	Number of Fire Accsidents (case)	6780	9356	9333	8262	4951	2695	2322	2121
死亡人数 (人)	Deaths (person)	54	56	17	38	11	22	2	3
受伤人数 (人)	Injuries (person)	106	47	7	4	10	72	10	3
折合经济损失 (万元)	Losses Converted into Money (10 000 yuan)	1754	1945	3565	6014	4927	4791	5520	4142

20-11 审查批捕、起诉情况
STATISTICS ON EXAMINATION, ARREST AND PROSECUTION

项 目	Item	2000	2005	2010	2011	2012	2013	2014	2015
受理批捕件数 (件)	Number of Cases (case)	20378	19846	9120	23175	28905	27194	28267	28860
受理批捕人数 (人)	Number of People Arrested (person)	31245	29427	13391	33822	43040	37801	38379	38400
批准逮捕 (人)	Number of Arrests Granted (person)	25114	27063	12081	30633	38468	31813	32398	32400
不批捕人数 (人)	Number of Non-Arrest (person)	4329	1522	1001	2473	3725	5616	5305	5388
受理审查起诉件数 (件)	Number of Cases Received (case)	17660	21966	10028	28574	46382	36882	39980	42337
受理审查起诉人数 (人)	Number of Prosecution Accepted (person)	25416	33410	15280	43393	75876	52541	55410	57002
起诉人数 (人)	Prosecutor (person)	22396	26926	11600	35501	47348	44947	45740	46609
不起诉人数 (人)	Non-prosecutor (person)	1019	982	329	1173	1343	1806	2115	2235

20-12 检察机关查办职务犯罪情况
STATISTICS ON CRIMES COMMITTED BY TAKING ADVANTAGE OF DUTY BY PROCURATORIAL ORGAN

项 目	Item	2000	2005	2010	2011	2012	2013	2014	2015
受理案件件数 (件)	Number of Cases Dealt (case)	8343	3125	1074	1733	1840	2168	2703	2947
立案件数 (件)	Registered Cases (case)	2034	1552	988	1525	1651	1935	2438	2542
立案人数 (人)	Registered Offenders (person)	2312	1682	1228	1877	2127	2374	2897	3021
贪污贿赂件数 (件)	Number of Corruption and Bribe Cases (case)	1821	1363	801	1232	1290	1508	1864	1947
渎职侵权件数 (件)	Number of Malversation Cases (case)	213	189	187	1515	361	427	574	595
查办大案件数 (件)	Large Cases (case)	882	887	1039	1000	1120	1429	1972	2127
#5万元以上件数	#Money Involved Above 50000 yuan	850	839	936	884	911	1319	1580	1722
查办要案人数 (人)	Number of Offender Involved in Large Cases (person)	108	139	133	144	152	173	267	218
#厅局级人数	#Number of Offenders at Bureau Level	11	17	10	16	16	15	55	218
提起公诉人数 (人)	Number of People Prosecuted (person)	1490	1265	1725	1535	1871	2053	2145	1841

20-13 律师、公证、调解工作基本情况
BASIC STATISTICS ON LAWYERS, NOTARIZATION AND MEDIATION

项 目	Item	2005	2010	2011	2012	2013	2014	2015
一、律师工作	**Lawyers**							
律师事务所 (个)	Number of Lawyer Office (person)	387	466	490	512	549	595	665
专职律师	Number of Full-Time Lawyer	3722	5869	6602	7300	7805	8502	9419
兼职律师	Number of Part-Time Lawyer	165	252	278	306	334	351	363
担任法律顾问 (家)	Number of Units with Legal Advisors (unit)	9565	12059	12706	14046	14339	16973	34772
民事案件诉讼代理 (件)	Agent of Civil Cases (case)	27079	45403	47831	61052	63917	64479	79913
经济案件诉讼代理 (件)	Agent of Economic Cases (case)	13799						
刑事诉讼辩护及代理 (件)	Defender and Agent of Criminal Cases (case)	11341	17724	17964	17095	19043	18155	19076
非诉讼法律事务 (件)	Agent of Non-Litigious Legal Affairs (case)	34674	37521	37940	38011	24310	24928	26276
解答法律咨询 (万人次)	Agent of Legal Advisory Services (10 000 (person-times)	15.23	11.01	12.70	12.58	11.12	12.12	14
代写法律事务文件 (万件)	Agent of Legal Document Written on Behalf of Clients (10 000 cases)	3.49	1.59	1.61	2.09	2.3	1.8	2.45
二、公证工作	**Notarization**							
公证机构 (个)	Number of Notary Offices (unit)	118	116	117	117	117	117	117
公证人员 (人)	Notarial Pesonel (person)	689	643	687	739	830	807	850
#公证员	#Notaries	455	353	378	367	387	397	424
公证员助理	Assistant Notaries	62	167	309	372	244	236	254
办理公证文件 (万件)	Number of Domestic Notarized Document (10 000 cases)	31.04	32.65	32.82	33.79	28.6	35.84	42.04
#涉外公证 (件)	#Foreign Notarized Documents (case)	65498	79723	80818	88877	91467	107445	113143
三、人民调解工作	**People's Mediation**							
人民调解委员会 (万个)	Number of People's Mediation Committees (10 000 units)	3.70	3.62	3.43	3.43	3.44	3.36	3.37
调解人员 (万人)	Number of Mediators (10 000 persons)	17.20	20.43	16.20	15.81	15.87	14.51	14.73
调解纠纷总数 (万件)	Number of Disputes Mediated (10 000 cases)	21.62	22.85	27.20	28.33	30.00	32.13	32.15
调解成功总数 (万件)	Number of Successful Mediation (10 000 cases)	21.13	22.14	26.33	27.60	29.33	31.50	31.44

20-14 涉外公证文书分类情况
FOREIGN-RELATED NOTARIAL DOCUMENTS BY TYPE

单位：件 (case)

分类	Item	2005	2008	2009	2010	2011	2012	2013	2014	2015
合 计	**Total**	**65498**	**71672**	**70482**	**79723**	**80818**	**88877**	**91467**	**107445**	**113143**
出生	Births	7243	8254	6874	11567	12956	14791	10812	12074	15972
学历	Academic Degree	10078	16682	9078	7181	6138	5367	6754	8555	10140
经历	Personal Experience	806	347	289	863	875	1068	294	775	2222
生存和居住	Survival and Residence	102	48	61	67	54	62	88	127	110
死亡	Death	109	139	126	103	82	106	137	146	173
收养子女	Children Adoption	539	929	707	692	591	470	269	271	321
亲属关系	Kinship	3962	7665	6598	6605	7811	8562	7247	9322	11665
婚姻状况	Marital Status	3691	5979	5274	5774	5464	6670	3072	2795	2555
继承权	Rights of Inheritance	28	52	1003	94	81	35	122	788	100
遗嘱	Testament	18	35	43	82	75	38	48	19	21
职称	Title	141	231	21	172	239	131	15	7	67
身份	Identity	150	73	58	719	697	546	82	36	417
组织资格	Qualification of Organization	16	18	44	31	12	13	14	24	4
委托书	Trust Deed	293	298	31	643	948	1184	1916	3385	2313
公司章程	Chapter of Company	24	21	159	39	31	38	15	5	6
副本与原本相符	Confirmation of Copy and Photo-offset Copies to Originals	7861	4389	3954	12982	11230	16069	19897	24379	26754
证书(执照)	Operation Document	186	32	202	285	264	1035	2392	6672	13767
声明书	Declaration	3972	1039	33	1140	1526	1649	1255	1486	820
合同(协议)	Contract(Agreement)	372	43	37	46	36	18	28	37	20
受、未受刑事处分	Criminal Record & Uncriminal Record	6126	7857	6470	10359	11279	12788	7770	10078	12704
其他	Others	9916	9059	14868	11943	12339	9799	24622	20528	12992

20-15 履行法律监督情况
SUPERVISION ON LAW ENFORCEMENT

单位：人、件 (person, case)

项 目		2000	2005	2010	2011	2012	2013	2014	2015
监督公安机关立案件数	Number of Cases Registered by Public Security	247	554	1088	1150	2218	3243	2429	1412
监督追捕人数	Number of Criminals Hunted under Supervision	300	204	903	1387	2166	3063	2253	1985
监督追诉人数	Number of People Being Prosecuted	61	78	1130	1309	2103	3746	2347	1484
刑事抗诉件数	Number of Cases Against Crimnal Prosecutions	192	123	119	187	274	357	470	433
监督刑罚执行纠错人次	Person-times of Error Correction of Execution of Punishment	3546	51	499	319	1587	4635	4362	3700
民事行政监督抗诉件数	Number of Counterappeal Civil Cases	894	514	432	404	435	303	218	155

20-16 调解民间纠纷分类
CIVIL DISPUTES MEDIATION BY TYPE

项 目	Item	调解纠纷(件) Number of Disputes Mediated (case)				各种纠纷所占比重(%) Proportion (%)			
		2012	2013	2014	2015	2012	2013	2014	2015
合计	**Total**	**196093**	**102052**	**63013**	**71671**	**100.0**	**100.0**	**100.0**	**100.0**
婚姻	Marriage	28264	22568	21441	18596	14.4	22.1	34.0	26.0
继承	Rights of Inheritance	685	613	505	658	0.3	0.6	0.8	0.9
房地产开发	Real Estate Development	3038	1229	964	1158	1.5	1.2	1.5	1.6
运输合同	Transportation Contracts	261	210	293	257	0.1	0.2	0.5	0.4
买卖合同	Selling and Purchasing Contracts	8856	6096	6416	6083	4.5	6.0	10.2	8.5
借款合同	Loans Contracts	22761	14684	15128	12740	11.6	14.4	24.0	17.8
劳动争议	Labor Disputes	5990	3337	3484	2727	3.1	3.3	5.5	3.8
人身权	Personal Rights	44355	13297	12005	15487	22.6	13.0	19.1	21.6
所有权	Right of Ownership	10302	3067	1845	1378	5.3	3.0	2.9	1.9
其他	Others	71581	36951	932	12587	36.5	36.2	1.5	17.6

20-17 人民法院审理一审案件情况
STATISTICS ON FIRST INSTANCE CASES IN PEOPLE'S COURT

单位：件 (case)

年份 Year	收案 Cases Received	刑事 Criminal Cases	民商事 Civil Cases	海事海商 Maritime	行政 Administration
1985	63079	12709	40660	26	
1990	227618	29086	166960		568
1995	257312	21391	174908	456	4359
1998	252403	17763	171025	606	6368
1999	238715	19598	151191	647	6247
2000	228804	19204	146838	618	6754
2001	251003	21741	222702	745	6560
2002	211464	19548	188163	525	3753
2003	193780	18943	171282	488	3555
2004	172889	18833	150682	592	3374
2005	155478	19672	132585	745	3221
2006	156885	19914	133584	606	3387
2007	161728	21719	137328	459	2681
2008	165099	22364	140072	746	2663
2009	173032	23481	147319	710	2232
2010	179631	22963	154299	781	2369
2011	280572	25074	249792	1458	5706
2012	395414	31489	354789	1501	9136
2013	422427	31621	387593	1914	3213
2014	344515	33931	306601	1951	3983
2015	316619	37034	272384	2022	7201

注：一审案件指人民法院按照诉讼级别管辖按第一审程序审理的案件。
Note: First instance cases refer to cases in the first instance process in People's Court.

20-18 人民法院刑事一审案件收结案情况
END OF FIRST INSTANCE CASES IN PEOPLE'S COURT OF CRIMINAL LAWSUITS

单位：件 (case)

项 目	Item	收案 Cases Received				结案 Cases Closed			
		2012	2013	2014	2015	2012	2013	2014	2015
合 计	**Total**	**31489**	**31621**	**33931**	**37034**	**30912**	**31188**	**33183**	35766
危害公共安全罪	Crimes Harming Public Security	5009	5564	6520	8187	4964	5455	6381	8094
破坏社会主义市场经济秩序罪	Crimes Harming Socialism Market Economy Order	1319	1590	1415	1409	1261	1566	1358	1320
侵害公民人生权利民主权利罪	Crimes against Rights in Human Life and Democratic Rights	7011	6650	6844	6521	6919	6518	6784	6312
侵犯财产罪	Property Violation	10435	9086	9453	9936	10164	9134	9271	9677
妨害社会管理秩序罪	Crimes Harming Social Management Order	6296	7233	8105	9453	6187	7097	7929	9286
危害国防利益罪	Crimes Harimg National Defense Interests	10	6	19	10	9	7	17	14
贪污贿赂罪	Corruption and Bribe	1190	1242	1305	1319	1186	1188	1194	893
渎职罪	Malversation	214	235	259	195	218	211	236	168
其他	Others	5	15	11	4	4	12	13	2
合计中含自诉案件	Self-Suing Cases	271	184	155	217	281	184	151	199

20-19 人民法院刑事案件中青少年犯罪情况
STATISTICS ON JUVENILE DELINQUENCY IN PEOPLE'S COURT OF CRIMINAL LAWSUITS

单位：人 (person)

年份 Year	刑事犯罪总数 Total Number of Criminal Cases	青少年犯罪（25岁以下） Juvenile Delinquency (Under the age of 25)	不满18岁 Juvenile Age under 18	18-25岁 Age 18-25	青少年罪犯刑事罪犯率% Percentage of Juvenile Delinquency in Criminal Cases %
1999	20534	6836	1302	5534	33.3
2000	20076	5922	1279	4643	29.5
2001	22911	6597	1774	4823	28.8
2002	20868	5669	1901	3768	27.2
2003	20908	6207	2328	3879	29.7
2004	20429	5838	2633	3205	28.6
2005	21669	6283	2939	3344	29.0
2006	22876	6933	2945	3988	30.3
2007	17368	7459	3131	4328	43.0
2008	26682	6810	3030	3780	25.5
2009	28507	7700	2930	4770	27.0
2010	27928	7058	2287	4771	25.3
2011	29280	7263	2229	5034	24.8
2012	35419	7327	2050	5277	20.7
2013	33871	5398	1365	4033	15.9
2014	34599	4721	1170	3551	13.6
2015	43918	6011	1084	4927	13.7

20-20 人民法院民事一审案件收结案情况(2015)
STATISTICS ON END OF FIRST INSTANCE CASES IN PEOPLE'S COURT OF CIVIL LAWSUITS (2015)

单位：件 (case)

项 目	Item	收案 Cases Received	结案 Cases Ended	调解 Mediated	判决 Judgement	驳回 Cases Rejected	撤诉 Cases Withdraw	其他 Others
合 计	**Total**	**272384**	**246061**	**71671**	**99234**	**3985**	**53078**	**18093**
婚姻家庭	Marriage	52667	50998	18596	20204	329	11536	333
继承	Rights of Inheritance	1605	1406	658	474	15	246	13
知识产权	Intelligence Property Rights	5111	5243	1417	2166	184	1443	33
房地产开发	Real Estate Development	5021	4045	1158	1926	100	796	65
运输合同	Transportation Contracts	825	780	257	381	9	127	6
买卖合同	Selling and Purchasing Contracts	21711	19179	6083	7635	314	4793	354
借款合同	Loans Contracts	56536	47543	12740	22131	680	10488	1504
劳动争议	Labor Disputes	12083	10590	2727	5435	390	1773	265
海事海商	Martial Commerce	2022	1755	612	678	3	420	42
人身权	Personal Right	42256	37782	15487	17466	160	4391	278
特别程序	Special Procedure	17434	17496		1490	724	1117	14165
破产	Bankruptcy	90	142		66	2	7	67
所有权及与其相关合同	Rights of Ownership and Relevant Contracts	7601	6498	1378	2738	323	1916	143
其他	Others	47422	42604	10558	16444	752	14025	825

注：结案中含上年旧存。
Note: The statistics of ended cases include statistics of last year.

20-21 人民法院行政一审案件收结案情况(2015)
STATISTICS ON END OF FIRST INSTANCE CASES IN PEOPLE'S COURT OF ADMINISTRATION (2015)

单位：件 (case)

项 目	Item	收案 Cases Received	结案 Cases Ended	维持 Cases Maintained	撤消 Cases Cancled	驳回 Cases Rejected	撤诉 Cases Withdraw	单独赔偿 Sole Compensation	其他 Others
合 计	**Total**	**7201**	**5853**	**190**	**470**	**1193**	**1543**	**9**	**2448**
土 地	Land	874	727	8	30	200	108	3	378
公 安	Public Security	797	716	43	15	128	216		314
城 建	City Construction	1559	1167	24	89	334	282	3	435
交通运输	Transportation	43	40	2	3	2	20		13
工 商	Industry and Commerce	146	120	1	14	13	35		57
环 保	Environment	40	33	1		2	12		18
林 业	Forestry	136	125	4	46	11	23		41
税 务	Taxes	13	11			1	7	1	2
卫 生	Sanitary and Hygiene	33	30	1	4	8	8		9
其 他	Others	3560	2884	106	269	494	832	2	1181

注：结案中含上年旧存。
Note: The statistics of ended cases include statistics of last year.

主要统计指标解释

社会福利事业单位 指集中收养社会孤老、残、幼的机构，包括由民政部门管理的社会福利院、儿童福利院、精神病人福利院和城镇集体举办的福利院及农村集体举办的敬老院以及优抚医院和具有收养能力的社区服务中心等。该指标主要反映我国在社会福利性单位投入的水平。

社会福利事业单位收养人数 包括民政部门管理和城镇、农村集体举办的社会福利事业单位中收养的老人、少年儿童、缺乏生活自理能力的残疾人员和精神病人。该指标主要反映收养性社会福利单位的收养能力。

社会福利企业单位 指以安置城镇有一定劳动能力的盲、聋、哑和肢体残疾人员就业为目的，享受国家减免税待遇的国有或集体企业。包括福利工厂、福利商业和服务业、假肢厂和安置农场等单位。该指标主要反映我国对残疾人照顾的特殊政策。

粗离婚率 指当年离婚对数占年平均人口的比重，计算公式为：

$$粗离婚率=\frac{当年离婚对数}{年平均人口数}\times 1000‰$$

基本养老保险

1.(参保)职工人数：指报告期末按照国家法律、法规和有关政策规定参加基本养老保险并在社保经办机构已建立缴费记录档案的职工人数，包括中断缴费但未终止养老保险关系的职工人数，不包括只登记未建立缴费记录档案的人数。

2.(参保)离退休人员人数：指报告期末参加基本养老保险的离休、退休和退职人员的人数。

3.基本养老保险基金收入：指根据国家有关规定，由纳入基本养老保险范围的缴费单位和个人按国家规定的缴费基数和缴费比例缴纳的养老保险基金，以及通过其他方式取得的形成基金来源的收入。包括单位和职工个人缴纳的基本养老保险费、基本养老保险基金利息收入、上级补助收入、下级上解收入、转移收入、财政补贴和其他收入。

4.基本养老保险基金支出：指按照国家政策规定的开支范围和开支标准从养老保险基金中支付给参加基本养老保险的离休、通休、退职人员个人的养老金、丧葬抚恤补助，以及由于保险关系转移、上下级之间调剂资金等原因而发生的支出。包括离休金、退休金、退职金、各种补贴、医疗费、死亡丧葬补助费、抚恤救济费、社会保险经办机构管理费、补助下级支出、上解上级支出、转移支出、其他支出等。

5.基本养老保险基金累计结余：指截止报告期末基本养老保险基金收支相抵后的累计余额。

离休、退休、退职人员 指正式办理了离休、退休、退职手续，并享受相应的离休、退休、退职待遇的人员。

基本医疗保险

1.参保人数：指报告期末按国家有关规定参加基本医疗保险的人数。包括参加保险的职工人数和退休人员人数。

2.基金收入：指根据国家有关规定，由纳入基本医疗保险范围的缴费单位和个人，按国家规定的缴费基数和缴费比例缴纳的基金，以及通过其他方式取得的形成基金来源的款项，包括：单位缴纳的社会统筹基金收入、个人缴纳的个人账户基金收入、财政补贴收入、利息收入、其他收入。

3.基金支出：指按照国家政策规定的开支范围和开支标准从社会统筹基金中支付给参加基本医疗保险的职工和退休人员的医疗保险待遇支出，和从个人帐户基金中支付给参加基本医疗保险的职工和退休人员的医疗费用支出，以及其他支出。包括：住院医疗费用支出、门急诊医疗费用支出、个人账户基金支出、其他支出。

4.基金累计结余：指截止报告期末基本医疗保险的社会统筹和个人帐户基金累计结余金额。包括银行存款、财政专户、债券投资和其他。

失业保险

1.参保人数：指报告期末按照国家法律、法规和有关政策规定参加了失业保险的城镇企业事业单位的职工及地方政府规定参加失业保险的其他人员的人数。

2.失业保险基金收入:指按照规定从企业、事业及其他单位筹集的失业保险费及其他并入失业保险基金收入的总额。包括单位和个人缴纳的失业保险费、失业保险基金利息收入、上级补助收入、下级上解收入、转移收入、财政补贴和其他收入。

3.失业保险基金支出:指报告期内为保障失业人员和下岗职工基本生活、促进其再就业等支出的基金总额。包括失业救济金、医疗费、死亡丧葬补助费、抚恤救济费、转业训练费支出、失业保险经办机构管理费、补助下级支出、上解上级支出、转移支出和其他支出。

4.基金累计结余:指截止报告期末失业保险基金收支相抵后的累计余额。

工伤保险

1.参加保险人数: 指报告期末依据国家有关规定参加工伤保险的职工人数。

2.享受保险待遇人数: 指劳动者因工负伤致残、死亡或因患职业病致残,根据有关规定享受工伤保险待遇职工或供养直系亲属人数。包括伤残人数、职业病人数、因工死亡人数、供养直系亲属人数。

3.基金收入: 指根据国家有关规定,由参加工伤保险的单位按国家规定的缴费基数和缴费比例缴纳的工伤保险基金,以及通过其他形式取得的形成基金来源的款项。包括:单位缴纳的社会统筹基金收入、财政补贴收入、利息收入、其他收入。

4.基金支出: 指按照国家政策规定的开支范围和开支标准从工伤保险基金中支付给参加工伤保险的人员及供养直系亲属工伤保险待遇支出及其他支出。包括工伤医疗费、伤残补助金、工亡补助金、护理费、丧葬补助费、工伤预防费用、职业康复费用和其他支出。

5.基金累计结余: 指截止报告期末工伤保险基金累计结余金额。包括银行存款、财政专户、债券投资和其他。

生育保险

1.参保人数: 指报告期末依据有关规定参加生育保险的职工人数。

2.基金收入: 指根据国家有关规定,由参加生育保险的单位按照国家规定的缴费基数和缴费比例缴纳的生育保险基金,以及通过其他方式取得的形成基金来源的款项,包括:单位缴纳的基金收入、利息收入和其他收入。

3.基金支出: 指按照国家政策规定的开支范围和开支标准,从生育保险基金中支付给参加生育保险的职工,因妊娠、分娩和计划生育手术而享受的待遇及其他支出。包括:生育津贴、医疗费用支出及其他支出。

4.基金累计结余: 指截止报告期末生育保险基金累计结余金额。包括银行存款、财政专户、债券投资和其他。

离休、退休、退职人员保险福利费用 指离休、退休、退职人员实际得到的生活费用总额,包括从社会保险经办机构和单位得到的费用。

1.离休金:指按规定支付给离休人员的生活费用。

2.退休金:指按规定支付给退休人员的生活费用。

3.退职生活费:指按规定支付给退职人员的生活费用。

4.医疗卫生费:指单位直接支付给离休、退休、退职人员的医疗费、住院费以及住院伙食补助等费用。

5.其他:指离休金、退休金、退职生活费和医疗卫生费以外的其他保险福利费用,如丧葬抚恤救济费、生活补贴、物价补贴、冬季取暖补贴等。

律师 指依法取得律师执业证书,担任法律顾问,民事(刑事、行政)案件代理人、刑事案件辩护人、办理非诉讼业务,解答法律询问,代写法律事务文书等,为社会提供法律服务的人员。

公证人员 指在公证处工作的人员总称,包括公证处主任、副主任、公证员、公证员助理(助理公证员)和其他从事辅助性工作的人员。

公证文书 指公证处根据当事人申请,依照事实和法律,按照法定程序制作的,具有法律效力的司法证明文书。根据公证书用途和使用地,公证书分为国内公证书、国内经济公证书、涉外民事公证书、涉外经济公证书四类。

调解员 指在人民调解委员会担负调解民间纠纷工作的人员,包括调解委员会的委员和调解小组的调解员。该指标主要反映从事人民调解工作的人员数量。

调解民间纠纷 指调解委员会按照法律规定,根据自愿原则,用说服教育的方法调解民间发生的有关民事权利和义务争执的件数,包括调解成功数和调解未成功数。该指标主要反映人民调解委员会的工作量。

立案 指人民检察院对受理的报案、控告、举报或自首及自行发现的犯罪线索、犯罪嫌疑人进行初步调查后,认为存在职务犯罪事实和应追究刑事责任,并决定作为刑事案件进行侦查的诉讼活动,是追究犯罪的开始。该指标主要反映人民检察院依法将职务犯罪线索作为刑事案件进行侦查的诉讼活动。

大案 指贪污、贿赂案数额在5万元以上,挪用公款案数额在10万元以上,集体私分、巨额财产来源不明、隐瞒境外存款案数额在50万元以上以及按照《人民检察院直接受理的渎职、侵权重、特大案件标准(试行)》认定的案件。该指标主要反映人民检察院立案查办的职务犯罪案件中经济损失大、社会危害严重的案件。

要案 指县、处级以上干部的犯罪案件。该指标主要反映国家工作人员中县、处级以上干部因职务犯罪被人民检察院依法立案侦查的情况。

决定逮捕 指人民检察院对直接受理、自行侦查的案件,认为需要逮捕犯罪嫌疑人时,依据法律做出的逮捕决定。该指标主要反映人民检察院对直接受理的案件行使决定逮捕权的情况。

批准逮捕 指人民检察院对公安机关、国家安全机关、监狱管理机关提出逮捕的犯罪嫌疑人进行审查,根据事实,依法做出逮捕决定。该指标主要反映人民检察院对提请逮捕机关提请逮捕犯罪嫌疑人进行审查后依法做出批准逮捕决定的情况。

决定起诉 指人民检察院对公安机关、国家安全机关、监狱管理机关和检察机关内设机构反贪污贿赂部门等移送起诉的案件进行审查,根据事实,做出提起公诉的案件。该指标主要反映人民检察院对各种刑事案件向人民法院提起公诉的情况。

申诉 指经检察机关信访部门审查处理后,移送到检察机关申诉部门的申诉案件,包括不服检察机关处理决定和不服法院刑事判决和裁定的申诉的案件。

受理劳动争议案件数 指劳动争议仲裁委员会根据国家有关规定,对劳动争议当事人的申请予以审查,符合受理条件而正式立案、准备处理的劳动争议案件数。

Explanatory Notes on Main Statistical Indicators

Social Welfare Institutions refer to institutions taking care of old people without children, handicapped people and orphans. They include social welfare institutions run by civil affairs departments, children welfare institutions, social welfare institutions for mental patients, collective-owned old people's homes in rural areas, convalescent homes and community service centers with the capacity of receiving those people. This indicator reflects the input in social welfare institutions.

Number of People Taken in by Social Welfare Institutions refers to the number of old people, children, totally dependent handicapped people and mental patients taken in by social welfare institutions run by civil affairs departments and those run by collective units in urban and rural areas. This indicator reflects the capacity of social welfare institutions.

Social Welfare Enterprises are collective owned enterprises which employ the blind, deaf-mute, and other handicapped people who are able to work in cities and towns and enjoy exemption from state taxes, including welfare plants, welfare commercial services, artificial limb plants and farms, etc. This indicator reflects the preferential policies toward disabled persons.

Crude Divorce Rate refers to proportion of divorced people to the annual average population for the reference year, the formula is:

Crude Divorce rate= number of couples divorced for the reference year/annual average population x 1000 per thousand

Basic Medical Care Insurance:

1. Number of people participating in the insurance programme refers to people participating in the basic medical care insurance programme according to related regulations by the end of reference period, including number of staff and workers and retirees participating in this insurance programme.

2. Revenue of insurance programme refer to payments made by employers and individuals participating in medical care insurance programs in accordance with the basis and proportion stipulated in state regulations, and income from other sources that become source of medical insurance fund, including income of social comprehensive funds paid by employers, income from individual accounts, government

financial subsidies, interest income and other income.

3. Expenses of insurance programme refer to payment made from social comprehensive funds to those retired and resigned people covered in basic medical care insurance within the scope and standards of expenditure according to related national policies, and medical care payment made from individual accounts to staff and workers and retirees, and other expenses, including medical expenses of hospital inpatients, medical expenses for outpatients and emergency patients, payment from individual accounts and other expenditure.

4. Balance of basic medical care insurance refer to the balance of medical care insurance of social comprehensive funds and individual accounts at the end of the reference period, including bank savings, special fiscal accounts, investment in bonds and others.

Unemployment Insurance

1. Number of people covered refers to staff and workers in urban enterprises or institutions who have participated in unemployment insurance programme in line relevant policies and regulations, and other people who have participated according to local government regulations, by the end of reference period.

2. Revenue of unemployment insurance refer to payments made by employers and individuals participating in unemployment insurance programme in accordance with relevant regulations and other income contributed to this programme, including unemployment insurance premium made by employers and individuals, interest income, subsidies from higher level agencies, income as transfer from subordinate agencies, transferred income, government financial subsidies and other income.

3. Expenses of unemployment insurance refer to total expenses during the reference period to guarantee the basic livelihood of unemployed people and laid-off staff and workers and to encourage their re-employment. Included are unemployment relief, medical fees, funeral subsidies, compensation pension, training expenses, management fees for unemployment insurance agencies, subsidies to lower level agencies, expenses as transfer to higher level agencies, transferred expenditure and other expenditure.

4. Balance of unemployment insurance refer to the balance of unemployment revenue deducting unemployment expenses at the end of the reference period.

Work Injury Insurance

1. Number of people covered refers to staff and workers who have participated in work injury insurance programme in line with relevant national regulations.

2. Number of beneficiaries refers to staff and workers and their direct dependents who can, in line with relevant regulations, benefit from work injury insurance, as a result of work injury leading to disability or death of the staff/worker, or occupational disease leading to disability. Included in this category are number of injured and disabled people, number of people with occupational diseases, number of deaths at work places, and number of direct dependents.

3. Revenue of work injury insurance refer to payments made by employers participating in work injury insurance programs in accordance with the basis and proportion stipulated in state regulations, and income from other sources that become source of work injury insurance fund, including income of social comprehensive funds paid by employers, government financial subsidies, interest income and other income.

4. Expenses of work injury insurance refer to payments made from work injury insurance funds to those who participated in the work injury insurance programme and their direct dependents within the scope and standards of expenditure according to related national policies, and other expenditure, including medical fees for work injury, injury and disability subsidies, death subsidies, nursing fees, funeral subsidies, injury prevention fees, rehabilitation fees for occupational diseases and other expenditure.

5. Balance of work injury insurance refer to the balance of the work injury funds at the end of the reference period, including bank savings, special fiscal account, investment in bonds and others.

Maternity Insurance

1. Number of people covered refers to staff and workers who have participated in maternity insurance programme according to relevant regulation at the end of the reporting period.

2. Revenue of maternity insurance refers to payments made by employers participating in maternity insurance programs in accordance with the basis and proportion stipulated in state regulations, and income from other sources that become source of maternity insurance fund, including income of funds paid by employers, interest income and other income.

3. Expenses of maternity insurance refer to payments made from maternity insurance funds to staff and workers who participated in maternity insurance programme within the scope and standards of expenditure according to related national policies, expenses paid for pregnancy, child delivery or surgeries related to family planning, and other expenditure, including allowance for child bearing, medical fees and other expenditure.

4. Balance of the maternity insurance refers to the balance of the maternity insurance funds at the end of reference period, including bank savings, special fiscal account, investment in funds and others.

Insurance and Welfare Funds for Retirees refer to the total payment for living expenses actually received by retirees, including payment received from social insurance management agencies and units.

1. Pensions for retired veteran cadres refer to living expenses paid to retired veteran cadres according to related regulations.

2. Pensions for retirement refer to living expenses paid to retired staff and workers according to related regulations.

3. Living allowances for resigned staff and workers refer to living expenses paid to resigned staff and workers according to related regulation.

4. Medical care expenses refer to medical fees, hospitalization cost and per diem subsidies during hospitalizations paid by employers directly to retirees.

5. Others refer to insurance and welfare payments other than the above-mentioned payments, including funeral subsidies, living allowances, price subsidies and heating subsidies during winter.

Lawyers are certified legal workers according to law, and who are employed by legal counseling firms to act as legal advisers, agents in criminal or civil lawsuits, or defenders in criminal lawsuits, or to handle non-litigious legal affairs, to advise on matters of law or to write legal papers for others, and provide service to the public.

Notary Personnel refers to people working for notary offices including: directors, deputy director, notaries, assistant notaries, and other people providing assistance.

Notary Documents refer to the judicatory notary documents drawn up by the request of the party and are in accordance with facts and laws and following certain legal proceedings. According to usage and locality, the notary documents are divided into following 4 types: domestic notary documents, domestic economic notary documents, foreign-related civil notary documents and foreign-related economic notary documents.

Mediators refer to workers on peoples mediation committees responsible for mediating in civil disputes and cases of slight infraction of the law. They include members of the mediation committees and mediators of mediation groups. This indicator reflects the number of people engaged in meditation.

Mediation of Civil Disputes refers to number of cases made by mediation committees in mediating in civil disputes concerning civil rights and duties through persuasion and education in accordance with the provisions of law on a voluntary basis, so as to solve disputes by helping the parties involved come to an agreement and understanding, including those unsuccessful ones. This indicator reflects the workload of the mediation committees.

Acceptance of Case refers to the decision made by the people's procuratorate office on reported cases, prosecution, impeachment, surrender, self-found criminal clues or suspects after initial investigation to confirm the act of crime and to start legal proceedings of the case as criminal case.

Large Cases refer to cases involving a corruption or bribery of over 50,000 yuan, or a misappropriation of over 100,000 yuan. Cases of collectively illegal possession of public funds, unstated sources of large properties, or disguised overseas savings deposits involving 500,000 yuan, or a case that has been defined by the "Standard on Serious and Large Cases of Misconduct and Tortious that Directly Accepted by People's Procurators Office (trial)". This indicator mainly reflects number of accepted cases of job–related criminals that caused serious economic losses or extremely harmful to the society.

Key Cases refer to cases committed by government officials with a ranking of division director or county administrator. This indicator mainly reflects the recorded and spied on cases by the people's procurators offices toward government official with a ranking of division director or county administrator.

Decision on Arrest refers to decision made by people's procurators office, in accordance with laws, to arrest the suspect(s) in the cases that are accepted and to be investigated by procurators office. This indicator mainly reflects the implementation of the decision on arrest by people's procurators office.

Approval for Arrest refers to the decision made by people's procurators office, in accordance with laws and relevant facts, to approve the arrest of the suspect(s) that is proposed by the public security departments, state security departments or authority of prisons. This indicator reflects approved arrests made by people's procurators office that are proposed by related departments.

Decision on Prosecution refers to the decision made by people's procurators office, in accordance with laws and relevant facts, to institute proceedings to the people's court against the suspect(s) of criminal cases handed over by the public security departments, state security departments or authority of prisons, or by the anti–corruption departments within the procurators office. This indicator reflects the condition of the prosecutions made by people's procurators office toward the people's court.

Appeals refer to cases transferred to the appeal departments of procurator's offices after initial review by departments dealing with complaint letters and calls of the public. Included are appeals against decisions made by procurator's offices and appeals against court rules and verdicts.

Number of Labor Dispute Cases Accepted refers to the number of cases of labor dispute submitted that, after being reviewed by the labor dispute arbitration committees in line with the relevant national regulations, are accepted and registered for treatment.

Basic Pension Insurance

1.Number of staff and workers covered refer to staff and workers participating in basic pension insurance programme in line with national laws, regulations and related policies by the end of reference period, who have already had payment records in social security management agencies, including those who interrupt payment without terminating the insurance programme. Those who have registered in the programme with no payment records are not included.

2. Number of retirees participating in basic pension insurance programme refer to number of retirees participating in basic pension insurance programme by the end of reference period.

3. Revenue of basic pension insurance refer to payments made by employers and individuals participating in pension insurance programs in accordance with the basis and proportion stipulated in state regulations, and income from other sources that become source of pension insurance fund, including the premium paid by employers and staff and works, interest income, subsidies from higher level agencies, income as transfer from subordinate agencies, transferred income, government financial subsidies and other income.

4. Expenses of basic pension insurance refer to payment made to those retired and resigned people covered in pension insurance program in terms of pension or compensation within the scope and standards of expenditure according to related national policies, and expenditure occurred due to shift of the insurance relationship or adjustment of funds among agencies, including pension for resigned people, pension for retired people, pension for people quitting jobs, various subsidies, medical fees, funeral subsidies, compensation pension, management fees for social security agencies, expenses on subsidies to lower subordinates, expenses as transfer to agencies at higher level, transferred expenditure and other expenditure.

5. Balance of basic pension insurance refers to the balance of basic pension insurance at the end of the reference period after deducting expenses from revenue.

Retired or Resigned Personnel refers to people who have formally completed formalities for their retirement or quitting work and enjoy the corresponding retirement treatments.

21 开发区主要经济指标

Major Economic Indicators of Development Zone

21-1 湖北省开发区经济发展基本情况(2015)

BASIC INDICATORS OF ECONOMIC DEVELOPMENT OF DEVELOPMAENT ZONE IN HUBEI PROVINCE(2015)

指标	Item	2014	2015	增幅(%) Percentage of Increase (%)
基本情况	**Basic condition**			
开发区批准规划面积 (平方公里)	Floor Areas Approved in Development Zone (sq.km.)	4586.53	4780.69	4.2
开发区实际占地面积 (平方公里)	Actual Land Areas of Development Zone (sq.km.)	1844.26	1972.72	7.0
企业个数 (个)	Number of Enterprises (unit)	105731	120376	13.9
其中:工业企业 (个)	#Those Belong to Industrial Enterprises (unit)	27508	29646	7.8
其中:规模以上 (个)	#Enterprises above Designated Scale (unit)	8856	9667	9.2
高新技术企业 (个)	High and New Technological Enterprises (unit)	2523	3072	21.8
外商投资企业 (个)	Foreign Invested Enterprises (unit)	1759	1839	4.5
从业人员 (万人)	Population of Employment (10 000 persons)	384.42	398.95	3.8
其中:工业企业 (万人)	#Those Belong to Industrial Enterprises (10 000 persons)	282.81	293.00	3.6
其中:规模以上 (万人)	#Those Engaged in Enterprises above Designated Scale (10 000 persons)	227.93	237.87	4.4
主要经济指标	**Major Economic Indicators**			
规模以上工业总产值 (亿元)	Total Output Value of Enterprises above Designated Scale (100 million Yuan)	30190.78	33368.48	10.5
规模以上工业增加值 (亿元)	Value-added of Enterprises above Designated Scale (100 million Yuan)	8650.36	9490.61	8.7
其中:高新技术产业 (亿元)	#Value-added of High and New Technological Enterprises (100 million Yuan)	3670.74	4146.54	13.0
规模以上工业主营业务收入 (亿元)	Total Income From Major Business of Enterprises above Designated Scale (100 million Yuan)	29120.04	32562.66	11.8
固定资产投资总额 (亿元)	Total Value of Investment in Fixed Assets (100 million Yuan)	10452.81	10718.05	2.5
其中:基础设施建设投资 (亿元)	#Infrastructure Investment (100 million Yuan)	2018.28	2476.82	22.7
施工项目个数 (个)	Number of Projects under Construction (unit)	9472	9848	4.0
其中:亿元以上项目 (个)	#the Value of the Projects is Worth More Than 100 million Yuan (unit)	4002	4231	5.7
新开工项目 (个)	Newly Opened Projects (unit)	5188	5478	5.6
外商投资项目 (个)	Foreign Invested Projects (unit)	391	358	-8.4
省外内资项目 (个)	Foreign-funded Projects (unit)	3164	3238	2.3
开发区税收总额 (亿元)	Total Tax Revenue of Development Zone (100 million Yuan)	1502.06	1741.07	15.9
招商引资总额 (亿元)	The Total Investment (100 million yuan)	7896.06	9155.95	16.0
其中:外商投资金额 (亿美元)	#Total Value of Foreign Investment (100 million dollars)	55.02	51.34	-6.7
出口总额 (亿美元)	Total Value of Export (100 million dollars)	185.87	203.35	9.4

21-2 湖北省131家开发区主要指标(2015)

开发区名称	Name of Development Zone	实际开发面积(平方公里) Actual Land Areas of Development Zone (sq. km)	
		2014	2015
湖北省	**Hubei Province**	**1844.26**	**1972.72**
武汉市	**Wuhan**	**333.72**	**348.57**
武汉江岸经济开发区	Wuhan Jiang'an Economic Development Zone	3.31	3.31
武汉江汉经济开发区	Wuhan Jianghan Economic Development Zone	1.56	1.56
武汉硚口经济开发区	Wuhan Qiaokou Economic Development Zone	1.14	1.14
武汉汉阳经济开发区	Wuhan Hanyang Economic Development Zone	12	12
武汉武昌经济开发区	Wuhan Wuchang Economic Development Zone	2.34	2.34
武汉青山经济开发区	Wuhan Qingshan Economic Development Zone	10	10
武汉洪山经济开发区	Wuhan Hongshan Economic Development Zone	0.7	0.7
武汉临空港经济技术开发区	Wuhan Linkonggang Economic and Technology Development Zone	121	125.49
武汉汉南经济开发区	Wuhan Hannan Economic Development Zone	15.13	15.13
武汉蔡甸经济开发区	Wuhan Caidian Economic Development Zone	23.9	44.5
武汉江夏经济开发区	Wuhan Jiangxia Economic Development Zone	105	108
武汉盘龙城经济开发区	Wuhan Panlongcheng Economic Development Zone	20	20
武汉阳逻经济开发区	Wuhan Yangluo Economic Development Zone	30.88	31.85
武汉经济技术开发区	Wuhan Economic and Technology Development Zone	79.5	79.5
武汉东湖新技术产业开发区	Wuhan East Lake New Technology Industrial Development Zone	60.24	68.32
黄石市	**Huangshi**	**113.89**	**126.77**
湖北黄石港工业园区	Hubei Huangshi Port Industrial Park	2.2	2.2
湖北黄石新港工业园区	Hubei Huangshi New Port Industrial Park	12.2	15.3
湖北西塞山工业园区	Hubei Xisaishan Industrial Park	11	15.06
湖北下陆长乐山工业园区	Hubei Xialu Changleshan Industrial Park	12	12.6
黄石经济技术开发区	Huangshi Economic and Technology Development Zone	55	55
湖北阳新经济开发区	Hubei Yangxin Economic Development Zone	12	15
湖北大冶经济开发区	Hubei Daye Economic Development Zone	31.89	32.51
大冶灵成工业园	Daye Lingcheng Industrial Park	6.3	7
十堰市	**Shiyan**	**87.59**	**88.46**
十堰经济技术开发区	Shiyan Economic and Technology Development Zone	40	40
湖北郧阳区经济开发区	Hubei Yunyang County Economic Development Zone	18.76	19.13
湖北郧西工业园区	Hubei West Yun Industrial Park	1.53	1.53
湖北竹山经济开发区	Hubei Zhushan Economic Development Zone	10	10
湖北竹溪工业园区	Hubei Zhuxi Industrial Park	2.1	2.4
湖北房县工业园区	Hubei Fang County Industrial Park	4.2	4.2
湖北丹江口经济开发区	Hubei Danjiangkou Economic Development Zone	11	11.2
宜昌市	**Yichang**	**109.95**	**122.05**
湖北西陵经济开发区	Hubei Xiling Economic Development Zone	4	4
湖北伍家岗工业园区	Hubei Wujiagang Industrial Park	4	4
湖北点军工业园区	Hubei Dianjun Industrial Park	5.4	5.4
湖北夷陵经济开发区	Hubei Yiling Economic Development Zone	28	28
湖北远安工业园区	Hubei Yuan'an Industrial Park	15	18
湖北兴山经济开发区	Hubei Xingshan Economic Development Zone	2.6	2.64
湖北秭归经济开发区	Hubei Zigui Economic Development Zone	6	6
湖北长阳经济开发区	Hubei Changyang Economic Development Zone	2.8	2.8
湖北五峰工业园区	Hubei Wufeng Industrial Park	2.3	2.3
湖北五峰民族工业园	Hubei Wufeng National Industrial Park	0.79	0.87
宜昌高新技术产业开发区	Yichang High-tech Industrial Development Zone	71.2	77.5
湖北宜都工业园区	Hubei Yidu Industrial Park	10.6	12.25
湖北当阳经济开发区	Hubei Dangyang Economic Development Zone	26	26
湖北枝江经济开发区	Hubei Zhijiang Economic Development Zone	25.52	29.57
枝江安福寺工业园	Zhijiang Anfu Temple Industrial Park	1.84	1.86

MAIN INDICATORS OF 131 DEVELOPMENT ZONE IN HUBEI(2015)

企业个数(个) Number of Enterprises (unit)		其中:规模以上工业企业(个) Among which, Industrial Enterprises above Designated Size (unit)		高新技术企业(个) Number of High and New Technological Enterprises (unit)		从业人员(万人) Population of Employment (10 000 persons)	
2014	2015	2014	2015	2014	2015	2014	2015
105731	**120376**	**8856**	**9667**	**2523**	**3072**	**384.42**	**398.95**
59301	**67588**	**1396**	**1411**	**1086**	**1312**	**104.07**	**99.84**
183	242	28	15	11	7	1.08	0.90
399	399	15	11	3	3	2.36	2.36
344	408	29	27	9	9	4.46	4.00
921	921	61	68	24	25	3.77	3.89
293	216	29	16	15	11	2.04	1.85
321	323	98	99	15	15	3.67	3.68
151	157	15	13	24	18	0.84	0.87
24398	29626	262	273	61	62	25.85	29.04
489	493	131	136	12	13	3.59	3.70
326	479	79	85	12	18	3.15	3.30
717	738	168	168	45	53	6.05	6.20
629	673	39	41			4.71	5.04
136	147	66	85	12	15	2.75	2.90
6480	216	203	216	89	89	19.90	11.70
26735	35982	662	683	832	1063	43.85	45.28
6862	**8085**	**487**	**547**	**128**	**136**	**23.86**	**24.94**
43	43	11	12	12	12	0.49	0.43
30	33	13	13	2	2	0.20	0.21
310	338	71	72	10	10	3.60	3.75
158	163	26	23	8	7	2.02	2.01
4487	5608	145	180	53	56	8.96	9.67
392	417	54	63	12	12	3.41	3.42
1569	1612	180	187	35	39	6.24	6.32
61	67	26	23	6	7	1.16	1.35
4740	**5386**	**605**	**624**	**110**	**133**	**18.97**	**19.78**
3423	3957	254	233	67	81	9.49	10.20
235	251	82	95	12	17	2.76	2.93
52	53	30	30	3	3	0.36	0.28
198	199	28	28	5	6	0.62	0.62
103	105	34	35	3	3	1.80	1.80
186	198	71	70	11	11	1.10	0.98
543	623	106	133	9	12	2.84	2.97
4241	**5041**	**709**	**812**	**118**	**240**	**23.61**	**26.22**
476	546	12	11	6	9	0.90	0.86
92	92	27	32	10	11	1.55	1.50
18	18	16	16	7	9	0.48	0.32
835	1120	143	150	23	25	4.81	5.23
166	181	90	94	16	18	2.91	3.27
46	49	17	19	3	3	0.74	1.01
208	223	70	75	8	10	2.01	2.03
82	112	49	49	9	13	1.14	1.28
285	300	20	20	5	5	1.20	0.75
10	14	4	9		1	0.40	0.50
2765	3485	330	390	120	170	12.10	13.90
347	358	172	204	41	46	3.24	3.62
851	964	171	175	37	39	5.53	5.84
1068	1125	173	177	16	20	6.65	6.98
51	59	30	32	1	3	1.22	1.22

21-2 续表 1 continued

开发区名称	Name of Development Zone	实际开发面积(平方公里) Actual Land Areas of Development Zone (sq. km)	
		2014	2015
襄阳市	**Xianyang**	**196.5**	**211.6**
襄阳高新技术产业开发区	Xiangyang High-tech Industrial Development Zone	37.8	42.8
襄阳鱼梁州经济开发区	Xiangyang Yuliangzhou Economic Development Zone	2.0	2.0
襄阳经济技术开发区	Xiangyang Economic Development Zone	70.0	76.0
湖北襄城经济开发区	Hubei Xiangcheng Economic Development Zone	16.0	16.0
湖北樊城经济开发区	Hubei Fancheng Economic Development Zone	7.4	8.1
湖北襄州经济开发区	Hubei Xiangzhou Economic Development Zone	22.0	24.6
襄州双沟工业园	Xiangyang Industrial Park	3.0	3.0
湖北南漳经济开发区	Hubei Nanzhang Economic Development Zone	19.2	21.2
湖北谷城经济开发区	Hubei Gucheng Economic Development Zone	20.0	20.0
谷城石花经济开发区	Gucheng Shihua Economic Development Zone	10.0	10.0
湖北保康经济开发区	Hubei Baokang Economic Development Zone	10.0	10.5
湖北老河口经济开发区	Hubei Laohekou Economic Development Zone	27.0	29.0
湖北枣阳经济开发区	Hubei Zaoyang Economic Development Zone	6.5	6.5
枣阳吴店工业园	Zaoyang Wudian Industrial Park	3.5	3.9
湖北宜城经济开发区	Hubei Yicheng Economic Development Zone	12.1	16.0
鄂州市	**E'zhou**	**28.9**	**30.4**
湖北鄂州花湖经济开发区	Hubei E'Zhou Huahu Economic Development Zone	12.8	14.0
鄂州葛店经济技术开发区	E'Zhou Gedian Economic and Technology Development Zone	28.9	30.4
湖北鄂州经济开发区	Hubei E'Zhou Economic Development Zone	20.0	21.0
荆门市	**Jingmen**	**95.7**	**120.7**
湖北东宝工业园区	Hubei Dongbao Industrial Park	13.6	15.5
荆门高新技术产业开发区	Hubei Jingmen High-tech Industrial Development Zone	24.0	45.5
湖北荆门化工循环产业园	Hubei Jingmen Chemical Recycling Development Zone	10.4	13.0
湖北京山经济开发区	Hubei Jingshan Economic Development Zone	14.0	23.5
湖北屈家岭经济开发区	Hubei Qujialing Economic Development Zone	7.0	7.0
湖北沙洋经济开发区	Hubei Shayang Economic Development Zone	30.5	31.5
湖北钟祥经济开发区	Hubei Zhongxiang Economic Development Zone	20.0	22.0
钟祥胡集经济开发区	Zhongxiang Huji Economic Development Zone	9.0	10.0
孝感市	**Xiaogan**	**135.0**	**135.9**
孝感高新技术产业开发区	Xiaogan high-tech Industrial Development Zone	12.0	12.0
湖北孝南经济开发区	Hubei Xiaonan Economic Development Zone	30.5	35.5
湖北孝昌经济开发区	Hubei Xiaochang Economic Development Zone	12.0	12.0
湖北大悟经济开发区	Hubei Dawu Economic Development Zone	17.3	17.3
湖北云梦经济开发区	Hubei Yunmeng Economic Development Zone	17.6	17.6
湖北应城经济开发区	Hubei Yingcheng Economic Development Zone	20.0	21.0
湖北安陆经济开发区	Hubei Anlu Economic Development Zone	36.6	36.6
湖北汉川经济开发区	Hubei Hanchuan Economic Development Zone	20.5	21.5
荆州市	**Jingzhou**	**199.8**	**214.2**
湖北沙市经济开发区	Hubei Shashi Economic Development Zone	38.0	38.0
湖北荆州城南经济开发区	Jingzhou Chengnan Economic Development Zone	14.1	14.0
荆州经济技术开发区	Jingzhou Economic and Technology Development Zone	55.7	55.7
湖北公安经济开发区	Hubei Gong'an Economic Development Zone	17.6	20.5
湖北监利经济开发区	Hubei Jianli Economic Development Zone	49.2	51.1
湖北江陵经济开发区	Hubei Jiangling Economic Development Zone	14.8	14.8
湖北石首经济开发区	Hubei Shishou Economic Development Zone	28.4	34.2
湖北洪湖经济开发区	Hubei Honghu Economic Development Zone	13.1	15.9
洪湖府场经济开发区	Honghu Fuchang Economic Development Zone	15.0	16.0
湖北松滋经济开发区	Hubei Songzi Economic Development Zone	6.0	6.0
黄冈市	**Huanggang**	**244.4**	**263.5**
黄冈高新技术产业开发区	Hubei Huanggang Economic Development Zone	212.6	226.1

企业个数(个) Number of Enterprises (unit)		其中:规模以上工业企业(个) Among which, Industrial Enterprises above Designated Size (unit)		高新技术企业(个) Number of High and New Technological Enterprises (unit)		从业人员(万人) Population of Employment (10 000 persons)	
2014	2015	2014	2015	2014	2015	2014	2015
11375	**12554**	**1205**	**1268**	**295**	**347**	**50.76**	**53.44**
7546	9225	330	351	147	181	14.80	15.90
67	50					0.12	0.12
785	912	155	155	33	35	10.52	10.79
250	256	35	40	7	7	2.60	2.60
345	372	113	122	24	26	4.09	4.26
546	602	121	125	38	42	7.52	8.37
273	346	18	19	2	3	2.90	3.50
112	120	82	87	5	7	1.67	1.69
1358	1534	100	112	22	25	6.94	7.28
280	285	52	51	12	14	2.90	2.98
49	51	32	32	8	9	1.21	1.50
358	453	192	198	24	26	3.98	4.32
489	537	151	157	42	45	4.25	4.38
302	337	66	73	4	5	2.87	3.08
145	151	77	84	6	9	2.83	3.02
2945	**3037**	**261**	**283**	**28**	**44**	**8.58**	**9.40**
327	365	54	53	15	13	1.45	1.47
2945	3037	261	283	28	44	8.58	9.40
308	327	71	82	21	11	1.12	1.14
1434	**1578**	**667**	**781**	**78**	**150**	**21.50**	**22.09**
148	165	92	92	13	13	3.20	3.29
482	873	292	364	52	76	7.72	8.26
50	57	27	29	5	10	0.63	0.84
381	393	88	125	18	19	2.69	3.52
42	51	17	19	1	1	0.20	0.20
159	181	73	83	15	17	2.70	3.00
328	336	122	128	16	19	6.30	6.46
69	76	34	36	5	7	1.85	1.92
3266	**3971**	**799**	**936**	**150**	**169**	**25.74**	**28.01**
1880	2208	394	508	95	107	10.62	11.30
362	318	131	145	17	26	5.10	5.18
236	258	35	37	5	6	2.22	2.25
60	61	28	27	3	5	1.50	1.50
285	302	113	135	17	17	8.13	8.22
160	165	134	139	18	18	3.41	3.41
352	359	61	65	28	31	4.26	4.33
738	1085	281	299	19	20	7.14	8.63
2331	**2675**	**619**	**696**	**84**	**98**	**26.83**	**30.39**
184	193	89	95	5	5	3.30	3.41
712	805	132	140	6	6	6.51	6.89
1213	1456	157	152	34	38	7.88	9.46
132	157	73	87	7	11	3.15	3.55
85	98	85	90	4	4	1.70	1.73
99	116	35	43	7	7	1.13	1.01
78	83	76	77	7	7	1.52	1.53
208	215	43	54	6	8	2.71	2.84
352	361	48	50	6	7	3.53	3.68
164	189	102	143	13	16	5.21	6.59
2716	**3031**	**593**	**678**	**164**	**183**	**23.86**	**26.77**
2444	2758	506	574	125	139	20.58	22.99

21-2 续表 2 continued

开发区名称	Name of Development Zone	实际开发面积(平方公里) Actual Land Areas of Development Zone (sq. km)	
		2014	2015
湖北黄州火车站经济开发区	Hubei Huangzhou Railway Station Economic Development Zone	8.5	8.5
黄州工业园	Huangzhou Industrial Park	20.0	21.3
湖北龙感湖工业园区	Hubei Longganhu Industrial Park	8.2	8.5
湖北团风经济开发区	Hubei Tuanfeng Economic Development Zone	8.0	8.5
湖北红安经济开发区	Hubei Hong'an Economic Development Zone	30.0	35.0
湖北罗田经济开发区	Hubei Luotian Economic Development Zone	9.0	10.0
湖北英山经济开发区	Hubei Yingshan Economic Development Zone	14.6	18.9
湖北浠水经济开发区	Hubei Xishui Economic Development Zone	28.0	28.0
湖北蕲春李时珍医药工业园区	Hubei Qichun Li Shizhen Pharmaceutical Industrial Park	18.0	20.0
蕲春经济开发区	Qichun Economic Development Zone	17.0	18.0
湖北黄梅经济开发区	Hubei Huangmei Economic Development Zone	24.6	26.8
湖北麻城经济开发区	Hubei Macheng Economic Development Zone	35.0	35.0
湖北武穴经济开发区	Hubei Wuxue Economic Development Zone	14.5	14.7
咸宁市	**Xianning**	**99.4**	**104.4**
湖北咸安经济开发区	Hubei Xian'an Economic Development Zone	9.9	10.9
湖北嘉鱼经济开发区	Hubei Jiayu Economic Development Zone	14.5	15.0
湖北通城经济开发区	Hubei Tongcheng Economic Development Zone	6.0	6.0
湖北崇阳工业园区	Hubei Chongyang Industrial Park	8.4	9.2
湖北通山经济开发区	Hubei Tongshan Economic Development Zone	18.0	19.3
咸宁高新技术产业开发区	Xianing high-tech Industrial Development Znoe	16.6	16.6
湖北赤壁经济开发区	Hubei Chibi Economic Development Zone	18.0	19.1
湖北赤壁蒲纺工业园区	Hubei Chibi Puqi Textile Industrial Park	8.0	8.0
随州市	**Suizhou**	**58.9**	**60.4**
随州高新技术产业开发区	Suizhou high-tech Industrial Development Znoe	58.9	60.4
湖北曾都经济开发区	Hubei Zengdu Economic Development Zone	20.0	20.0
湖北随县经济开发区	Hubei Sui County Economic Development Zone	4.8	4.8
湖北广水经济开发区	Hubei Guangshui Economic Development Zone	9.1	9.6
恩施自治州	**Enshi Autonomous Prefecture**	**49.6**	**53.5**
湖北恩施经济开发区	Hubei Enshi Economic Development Zone	14.7	14.7
湖北恩施州经济开发区	Hubei Enshi Prefecture Economic Development Zone	5.1	5.1
湖北利川经济开发区	Hubei Lichuan Economic Development Zone	5.0	5.0
湖北建始工业园区	Hubei Jianshi Industrial Park	4.2	4.2
湖北巴东经济开发区	Hubei Badong Economic Development Zone	5.0	6.0
湖北宣恩工业园区	Hubei Xuan'en Industrial Park	2.1	2.5
湖北咸丰工业园区	Hubei Xianfeng Industrial Park	6.1	8.5
湖北来凤经济开发区	Hubei Laifeng Economic Development Zone	5.5	5.5
湖北鹤峰经济开发区	Hubei Hefeng Economic Development Zone	2.0	2.0
仙桃市	**Xiantao**	**27.5**	**28.5**
仙桃高新技术产业开发区	Xiantao high-tech Industrial Development Znoe	27.5	28.7
仙桃彭场工业园	Xiantao Pengchang Industrial Park	6.0	6.5
潜江市	**Qianjiang**	**23.9**	**26.4**
湖北潜江经济开发区	Hubei Qianjiang Economic Development Zone	6.5	7.0
潜江张金经济开发区	Qianjiang Zhangjin Economic Development Zone	2.4	2.4
潜江园林经济开发区	Qianjiang Yuanlin Economic Development Zone	15.0	17.0
天门市	**Tianmen**	**33.3**	**35.8**
湖北天门经济开发区	Hubei Tianmen Economic Development Zone	33.3	35.8
神农架盘水生态产业园区		1.8	2.0

企业个数(个) Number of Enterprises (unit)		其中:规模以上工业企业(个) Among which, Industrial Enterprises above Designated Size (unit)		高新技术企业(个) Number of High and New Technological Enterprises (unit)		从业人员(万人) Population of Employment (10 000 persons)	
2014	2015	2014	2015	2014	2015	2014	2015
47	47	12	13	4	6	0.29	0.27
58	55	26	23	10	7	0.91	0.72
111	120	24	31	4	4	1.07	1.24
81	85	28	31	10	8	1.21	1.02
381	416	79	93	7	13	2.20	3.00
73	95	33	40	15	19	0.69	0.85
88	98	30	33	20	21	1.52	1.69
500	526	47	56	28	29	3.40	3.60
138	165	30	34	5	6	1.63	1.71
97	128	25	30	2	3	1.56	1.78
186	218	63	68	12	13	2.85	3.19
128	156	57	75	28	32	2.34	2.67
213	265	104	105	12	13	2.44	2.76
1037	**1078**	**514**	**571**	**70**	**84**	**12.36**	**12.29**
151	172	79	89	11	14	1.63	1.74
143	145	115	137	9	15	1.80	1.82
87	88	54	57	6	6	3.25	2.95
128	138	65	68	3	6	1.45	1.56
60	67	33	35	5	7	0.81	0.83
290	299	59	63	18	18	2.20	2.20
120	123	84	102	18	15	0.62	0.65
58	46	25	20		3	0.60	0.54
1503	**1852**	**317**	**323**	**63**	**65**	**11.45**	**11.85**
1503	1852	317	323	63	65	11.45	11.85
265	302	78	71	21	26	2.80	2.73
39	42	25	28	5	7	0.43	1.51
241	252	45	52	11	12	1.28	1.41
881	**940**	**250**	**281**	**19**	**24**	**10.89**	**11.57**
338	340	39	40	7	10	2.20	2.22
39	42	4	6	1	1	1.21	1.22
60	65	21	25	1	1	0.52	10.52
32	39	24	25	3	3	0.58	0.62
156	178	29	31	2	2	1.34	1.59
69	85	23	29		1	1.45	1.57
86	87	48	55	3	3	1.28	1.50
76	77	43	43	1	2	1.68	1.71
25	27	19	27	1	1	0.63	0.62
874	**1222**	**258**	**280**	**41**	**48**	**8.11**	**8.43**
874	1222	258	280	41	48	8.11	8.43
230	228	55	46	2	8	4.85	4.51
1871	**1914**	**54**	**52**	**14**	**21**	**5.77**	**5.55**
88	83	21	21	6	13	1.46	1.21
122	125	15	14	4	4	2.12	2.12
1661	1706	18	17	4	4	2.19	2.22
331	**356**	**117**	**119**	**13**	**16**	**8.01**	**8.26**
331	356	117	119	13	16	8.01	8.26
23	28	5	5	2	2	0.05	0.12

21-2 续表 3 continued

开发区名称	Name of Development Zone	其中:规模以上工业企业(万人) Among which, Industrial Enterprises above Designated Size (10 000 persons)	
		2014	2015
湖北省	**Hubei Province**	**227.93**	**237.87**
武汉市	**Wuhan**	**55.79**	**55.80**
武汉江岸经济开发区	Wuhan Jiang'an Economic Development Zone	0.60	0.30
武汉江汉经济开发区	Wuhan Jianghan Economic Development Zone	0.53	0.54
武汉硚口经济开发区	Wuhan Qiaokou Economic Development Zone	1.34	1.28
武汉汉阳经济开发区	Wuhan Hanyang Economic Development Zone	1.58	2.00
武汉武昌经济开发区	Wuhan Wuchang Economic Development Zone	1.09	0.92
武汉青山经济开发区	Wuhan Qingshan Economic Development Zone	3.06	3.06
武汉洪山经济开发区	Wuhan Hongshan Economic Development Zone	0.28	0.25
武汉临空港经济技术开发区	Wuhan Linkonggang Economic and Technology Development Zone	5.76	5.68
武汉汉南经济开发区	Wuhan Hannan Economic Development Zone	1.56	1.60
武汉蔡甸经济开发区	Wuhan Caidian Economic Development Zone	1.78	1.76
武汉江夏经济开发区	Wuhan Jiangxia Economic Development Zone	4.00	3.53
武汉盘龙城经济开发区	Wuhan Panlongcheng Economic Development Zone	0.82	0.95
武汉阳逻经济开发区	Wuhan Yangluo Economic Development Zone	2.15	2.30
武汉经济技术开发区	Wuhan Economic and Technology Development Zone	11.70	11.70
武汉东湖新技术产业开发区	Wuhan East Lake New Technology Industrial Development Zone	31.02	32.14
黄石市	**Huangshi**	**14.24**	**14.58**
湖北黄石港工业园区	Hubei Huangshi Port Industrial Park	0.26	0.24
湖北黄石新港工业园区	Hubei Huangshi New Port Industrial Park	0.17	0.17
湖北西塞山工业园区	Hubei Xisaishan Industrial Park	1.52	1.50
湖北下陆长乐山工业园区	Hubei Xialu Changleshan Industrial Park	1.93	1.90
黄石经济技术开发区	Huangshi Economic and Technology Development Zone	4.18	4.45
湖北阳新经济开发区	Hubei Yangxin Economic Development Zone	2.81	2.86
湖北大冶经济开发区	Hubei Daye Economic Development Zone	4.72	4.74
大冶灵成工业园	Daye Lingcheng Industrial Park	0.75	0.79
十堰市	**Shiyan**	**10.65**	**11.45**
十堰经济技术开发区	Shiyan Economic and Technology Development Zone	5.37	5.85
湖北郧阳区经济开发区	Hubei Yun County Economic Development Zone	2.38	2.48
湖北郧西工业园区	Hubei West Yun Industrial Park		
湖北竹山经济开发区	Hubei Zhushan Economic Development Zone	0.28	0.28
湖北竹溪工业园区	Hubei Zhuxi Industrial Park	0.40	0.40
湖北房县工业园区	Hubei Fang County Industrial Park	0.76	0.55
湖北丹江口经济开发区	Hubei Danjiangkou Economic Development Zone	1.46	1.80
宜昌市	**Yichang**	**19.64**	**22.26**
湖北西陵经济开发区	Hubei Xiling Economic Development Zone	0.20	0.15
湖北伍家岗工业园区	Hubei Wujiagang Industrial Park	1.00	0.40
湖北点军工业园区	Hubei Dianjun Industrial Park	0.36	0.30
湖北夷陵经济开发区	Hubei Yiling Economic Development Zone	2.90	3.27
湖北远安工业园区	Hubei Yuan'an Industrial Park	2.32	2.51
湖北兴山经济开发区	Hubei Xingshan Economic Development Zone	0.51	0.62
湖北秭归经济开发区	Hubei Zigui Economic Development Zone	1.29	1.30
湖北长阳经济开发区	Hubei Changyang Economic Development Zone	0.79	1.00
湖北五峰工业园区	Hubei Wufeng Industrial Park	0.40	0.30
湖北五峰民族工业园	Hubei Wufeng National Industrial Park	0.31	0.37
宜昌高新技术产开发区	Yichang High-tech Industrial Development Zone	11.00	13.00
湖北宜都工业园区	Hubei Yidu Industrial Park	2.89	3.22

规模以上工业增加值(亿元) Above-scale Industrial Added Value (100 million Yuan)		规模以上工业主营业务收入(亿元) Scale Industrial Core Business Revenue (100 million Yuan)		固定资产投资总额(亿元) Total Investment In Fixed Assets (100 million Yuan)		施工项目个数(个) Number of Construction Project (unit)	
2014	2015	2014	2015	2014	2015	2014	2015
8650.36	**9490.61**	**32562.66**	**29120.04**	**14052.81**	**10718.15**	**9472**	**9848**
2739.67	**3063.73**	**9075.15**	**10314.98**	**1847.06**	**2303.87**	**1102**	**1031**
9.60	9.03	23.41	42.01	12.23	15.35	3	2
8.79	9.38	32.88	34.49	5.52	7.1	6	7
24.70	26.40	90.00	95.15	15	12	10	7
558.50	616.44	765.10	827.90	71.9	72	25	29
44.52	47.98	189.46	195.01	1.22		1	1
36.73	29.14	135.78	132.89	29.31	27.16	36	18
7.21	6.49	27.05	24.05	4.5	4	5	2
330.90	255.53	599.63	664.94	418.22	498.53	213	186
32.72	355.53	114.03	119.73	30.53	53.59	25	27
187.00	203.00	531.00	571.00	212	150	68	79
81.05	161.00	273.40	524.42	335.06	362.19	127	136
36.13	33.88	122.41	120.90	49.67	57.5	36	85
136.18	130.76	418.65	489.55	220.2	245	122	117
755.60	679.30	2310.20	2257.40	461.7	661.6	292	322
1486.00	1778.00	5562.00	6512.00	626.13	749.48	451	375
547.60	**542.69**	**2216.17**	**2237.70**	**789.02**	**918.49**	**532**	**648**
2.26	2.30	5.86	6.50	4.85	4	24	13
6.31	5.56	19.47	17.54	21.06	15.12	18	11
74.00	61.00	248.00	270.00	43	58.01	52	54
123.00	107.00	1067.00	1053.00	41	37	20	18
243.03	242.11	1293.13	1264.90	442.36	519.64	221	285
31.81	34.56	93.18	101.11	62.4	67	45	49
162.08	177.60	468.68	509.47	178.22	207.52	171	175
34.42	25.12	107.32	85.72	58.19	32.32	19	72
392.86	**436.00**	**1254.12**	**1461.95**	**566.79**	**679.33**	**686**	**620**
268.02	290.99	858.17	1025.16	312.03	386.51	232	243
39.32	42.95	127.82	131.72	58.91	61.37	107	119
5.50	4.45	17.33	11.76	13.23	10.78	13	16
12.81	12.38	35.93	34.17	35.81	37.2	40	30
8.47	8.58	27.77	27.64	19	19.4	16	16
16.30	19.66	41.60	46.70	78.57	91.65	189	129
42.44	57.07	145.50	184.80	49.24	72.42	89	67
974.53	**1067.89**	**3277.95**	**3850.70**	**1106.52**	**1343.21**	**863**	**1002**
6.70	7.60	18.30	22.04	26.6	35.18	52	19
14.02	15.68	4.50	32.50	30	0.56	5	6
15.52	15.32	64.48	40.49	4.02	20.63	5	15
200.11	248.96	706.16	785.86	201.4	254.2	140	210
84.93	98.03	225.69	244.23	90.35	113.83	93	98
12.54	14.05	59.51	65.92	11.7	13.4	34	13
30.35	34.98	77.58	96.21	33.01	36.55	60	62
23.28	25.69	62.93	70.72	49.95	56.77	74	92
4.88	5.64	16.43	18.89	21.36	30	44	55
2.53	4.13	9.54	15.57	10.51	4051	7	10
505.00	530.00	1950.00	2220.00	582	4.51	396	404
275.61	315.45	728.25	912.78	273.69	364.47	315	423

21-2 续表 4 continued

开发区名称	Name of Development Zone	其中:规模以上工业企业(万人) Among which, Industrial Enterprises above Designated Size (10 000 persons)	
		2014	2015
襄阳市	**Xianyang**	**31.44**	**33.60**
襄阳高新技术产业开发区	Xiangyang High-tech Industrial Development Zone	12.60	13.60
襄阳鱼梁州经济开发区	Xiangyang Yuliangzhou Economic Development Zone		
襄阳经济技术开发区	Xiangyang Economic Development Zone	6.03	6.13
湖北襄城经济开发区	Hubei Xiangcheng Economic Development Zone	1.40	1.40
湖北樊城经济开发区	Hubei Fancheng Economic Development Zone	2.80	2.90
湖北襄州经济开发区	Hubei Xiangzhou Economic Development Zone	4.32	4.41
襄阳工业园	Xiangyang Industrial Park	0.63	0.72
湖北南漳经济开发区	Hubei Nanzhang Economic Development Zone	1.52	1.53
湖北谷城经济开发区	Hubei Gucheng Economic Development Zone	2.20	2.60
谷城石花经济开发区	Gucheng Shihua Economic Development Zone	1.70	1.81
湖北保康经济开发区	Hubei Baokang Economic Development Zone	0.55	0.63
湖北老河口经济开发区	Hubei Laohekou Economic Development Zone	2.13	2.41
湖北枣阳经济开发区	Hubei Zaoyang Economic Development Zone	2.41	2.48
枣阳吴店工业园	Zaoyang Wudian Industrial Park	1.11	1.19
湖北宜城经济开发区	Hubei Yicheng Economic Development Zone	1.74	1.85
鄂州市	**E'zhou**	**3.34**	**3.42**
湖北鄂州花湖经济开发区	Hubei E'Zhou Huahu Economic Development Zone	0.59	0.57
鄂州葛店经济技术开发区	E'Zhou Gedian Economic and Technology Development Zone	3.34	3.42
湖北鄂州经济开发区	Hubei E'Zhou Economic Development Zone	0.71	0.74
荆门市	**Jingmen**	**14.78**	**15.29**
湖北东宝工业园区	Hubei Dongbao Industrial Park	2.41	2.40
荆门高新技术产业开发区	Hubei Jingmen High-tech Industrial Development Zone	7.41	7.83
湖北荆门化工循环产业园	Hubei Jingmen Chemical Recycling Development Zone	0.44	0.51
湖北京山经济开发区	Hubei Jingshan Economic Development Zone	1.71	3.05
湖北屈家岭经济开发区	Hubei Qujialing Economic Development Zone	0.18	0.18
湖北沙洋经济开发区	Hubei Shayang Economic Development Zone	1.70	1.90
湖北钟祥经济开发区	Hubei Zhongxiang Economic Development Zone	3.85	4.00
钟祥胡集经济开发区	Zhongxiang Huji Economic Development Zone	1.35	1.42
孝感市	**Xiaogan**	**16.49**	**17.32**
孝感高新技术产业开发区	Xiaogan high-tech Industrial Development Zone	8.21	8.60
湖北孝南经济开发区	Hubei Xiaonan Economic Development Zone	1.40	1.47
湖北孝昌经济开发区	Hubei Xiaochang Economic Development Zone	1.31	1.31
湖北大悟经济开发区	Hubei Dawu Economic Development Zone	1.00	1.00
湖北云梦经济开发区	Hubei Yunmeng Economic Development Zone	3.02	3.15
湖北应城经济开发区	Hubei Yingcheng Economic Development Zone	2.51	2.51
湖北安陆经济开发区	Hubei Anlu Economic Development Zone	1.29	1.32
湖北汉川经济开发区	Hubei Hanchuan Economic Development Zone	4.68	5.09
荆州市	**Jingzhou**	**11.17**	**11.71**
湖北沙市经济开发区	Hubei Shashi Economic Development Zone	2.20	2.44
湖北荆州城南经济开发区	Jingzhou Chengnan Economic Development Zone	1.91	2.10
荆州经济技术开发区	Jingzhou Economic and Technology Development Zone	3.28	3.05
湖北公安经济开发区	Hubei Gong'an Economic Development Zone	1.17	1.37
湖北监利经济开发区	Hubei Jianli Economic Development Zone	1.70	1.71
湖北江陵经济开发区	Hubei Jiangling Economic Development Zone	0.58	0.59
湖北石首经济开发区	Hubei Shishou Economic Development Zone	1.51	1.52
湖北洪湖经济开发区	Hubei Honghu Economic Development Zone	0.67	0.76
洪湖府场经济开发区	Honghu Fuchang Economic Development Zone	0.47	0.53
湖北松滋经济开发区	Hubei Songzi Economic Development Zone	1.79	2.18
黄冈市	**Huanggang**	**13.80**	**14.84**
湖北黄冈经济开发区	Hubei Huanggang Economic Development Zone	11.71	12.48

规模以上工业增加值(亿元) Above-scale Industrial Added Value (100 million Yuan)		规模以上工业主营业务收入(亿元) Scale Industrial Core Business Revenue (100 million Yuan)		固定资产投资总额(亿元) Total Investment In Fixed Assets (100 million Yuan)		施工项目个数(个) Number of Construction Project (unit)	
2014	2015	2014	2015	2014	2015	2014	2015
1129.75	**1205.00**	**3840.78**	**4258.00**	**1655.3**	**200.36**	**1017**	**1049**
661.20	769.70	1970.30	2280.80	666.7	801	305	344
				0.18	0.3	1	2
285.56	315.07	878.91	995.63	229.2	291.7	101	108
46.00	44.00	94.00	101.00	21.4	26	21	15
68.00	73.00	213.00	227.00	86	92	77	81
130.64	156.42	407.77	488.05	229.2	285.31	101	108
25.80	33.20	101.36	105.20	48.65	45	14	11
51.86	52.81	146.92	151.35	90.03	88.94	64	46
87.79	89.83	243.89	264.84	105.21	116.73	118	119
86.90	82.70	277.60	173.90	57	59.64	56	47
23.12	26.20	43.71	49.97	37.56	39.95	35	40
127.65	137.34	487.35	556.85	178.67	221.85	148	160
112.00	155.31	428.00	515.00	199.4	252	110	108
49.02	56.85	162.51	177.13	68.6	100.5	29	48
90.62	104.69	290.68	356.00	60.49	68	86	69
179.90	**200.05**	**653.30**	**726.40**	**333**	**407**	**245**	**248**
26.79	30.49	98.22	108.20	66.9	55.2	34	29
179.90	200.05	653.30	726.40	333	407	245	248
23.13	28.01	91.40	92.69	41.4	51.79	24	40
498.90	**557.87**	**1990.00**	**2125.34**	**711**	**854**	**1183**	**1271**
71.05	87.24	257.11	324.93	153.22	218.16	223	231
255.20	285.70	906.50	1016.40	305.83	370.32	382	426
7.69	8.95	25.68	29.10	26.6	40.58	48	56
89.75	116.30	301.14	408.98	62	122.9	177	189
4.84	5.34	18.05	19.25	12.53	14.97	24	23
47.46	51.47	165.32	182.50	94.19	120.86	78	86
138.00	155.00	469.00	527.00	124.77	140.1	184	184
48.58	55.87	172.54	195.27	44.86	56.38	67	76
502.34	**559.55**	**1771.33**	**1993.76**	**787.02**	**956.09**	**595**	**628**
280.00	310.00	952.00	1104.00	428	518	311	335
39.50	45.20	162.00	170.00	227	265	342	277
10.32	10.32	38.60	38.80	35	51.4	52	50
9.34	9.64	26.30	28.70	32.4	34.2	20	26
78.92	83.48	289.88	306.37	162.2	197.9	118	147
114.42	120.02	422.76	422.78	42.3	44.15	291	294
46.10	52.30	112.00	126.80	85.6	105	93	96
156.58	177.29	642.43	695.46	206.02	247.49	119	121
349.37	**377.40**	**1205.64**	**1325.34**	**555.89**	**637.19**	**886**	**918**
45.32	55.34	137.16	158.78	127.51	148	55	57
84.38	72.04	292.67	285.19	90.24	89.95	42	62
76.10	72.30	255.70	243.96	204.48	225.24	385	372
52.84	57.97	186.26	200.39	90.61	114.57	43	44
61.26	61.30	197.19	207.20	32	36.45	45	43
16.68	19.32	59.60	69.68	40.06	37.41	53	56
47.97	53.51	179.33	201.57	42.11	50.4	43	48
35.38	40.56	142.61	168.75	39.44	50.72	90	98
15.24	16.74	50.06	55.35	36.73	40.58	110	115
43.90	55.70	134.89	178.26	70.46	81.82	117	142
274.48	**303.83**	**743.93**	**848.03**	**610.28**	**707.3**	**700**	**699**
240.16	265.11	661.82	746.02	555.88	642.35	558	539

21-2 续表 5 continued

开发区名称	Name of Development Zone	其中:规模以上工业企业(万人) Among which, Industrial Enterprises above Designated Size (10 000 persons)	
		2014	2015
湖北黄州火车站经济开发区	Hubei Huangzhou Railway Station Economic Development Zone	0.08	0.06
黄州工业园	Huangzhou Industrial Park	0.70	0.54
湖北龙感湖工业园区	Hubei Longganhu Industrial Park	0.55	0.65
湖北团风经济开发区	Hubei Tuanfeng Economic Development Zone	0.75	0.62
湖北红安经济开发区	Hubei Hong'an Economic Development Zone	1.00	1.10
湖北罗田经济开发区	Hubei Luotian Economic Development Zone	0.63	0.73
湖北英山经济开发区	Hubei Yingshan Economic Development Zone	0.91	0.98
湖北浠水经济开发区	Hubei Xishui Economic Development Zone	1.30	0.35
湖北蕲春李时珍医药工业园区	Hubei Qichun Li Shizhen Pharmaceutical Industrial Park	1.18	0.21
蕲春经济开发区	Qichun Economic Development Zone	1.08	1.11
湖北黄梅经济开发区	Hubei Huangmei Economic Development Zone	2.30	2.58
湖北麻城经济开发区	Hubei Macheng Economic Development Zone	1.03	1.34
湖北武穴经济开发区	Hubei Wuxue Economic Development Zone	1.68	1.71
咸宁市	**Xianning**	**11.03**	**11.04**
湖北咸安经济开发区	Hubei Xian'an Economic Development Zone	1.43	1.50
湖北嘉鱼经济开发区	Hubei Jiayu Economic Development Zone	1.64	1.68
湖北通城经济开发区	Hubei Tongcheng Economic Development Zone	3.12	2.90
湖北崇阳工业园区	Hubei Chongyang Industrial Park	1.13	1.25
湖北通山经济开发区	Hubei Tongshan Economic Development Zone	0.77	0.79
湖北咸宁高新技术产业开发区	Xianning high-tech Industrial Development Znoe	1.80	1.80
湖北赤壁经济开发区	Hubei Chibi Economic Development Zone	0.56	1.62
湖北赤壁蒲纺工业园区	Hubei Chibi Puqi Textile Industrial Park	0.58	0.50
随州市	**Suizhou**	**5.08**	**5.17**
湖北随州高新技术产业开发区	Suizhou high-tech Industrial Development Znoe	5.08	5.17
湖北曾都经济开发区	Hubei Zengdu Economic Development Zone	2.10	2.05
湖北随县经济开发区	Hubei Sui County Economic Development Zone	0.37	0.43
湖北广水经济开发区	Hubei Guangshui Economic Development Zone	0.86	0.93
恩施自治州	**Enshi Autonomous Prefecture**	**5.85**	**6.31**
湖北恩施经济开发区	Hubei Enshi Economic Development Zone	1.00	1.02
湖北恩施州经济开发区	Hubei Enshi Prefecture Economic Development Zone	0.04	0.05
湖北利川经济开发区	Hubei Lichuan Economic Development Zone	0.33	0.40
湖北建始工业园区	Hubei Jianshi Industrial Park	0.55	0.56
湖北巴东经济开发区	Hubei Badong Economic Development Zone	0.30	0.33
湖北宣恩工业园区	Hubei Xuan'en Industrial Park	0.86	0.92
湖北咸丰工业园区	Hubei Xianfeng Industrial Park	0.81	0.96
湖北来凤经济开发区	Hubei Laifeng Economic Development Zone	1.43	1.45
湖北鹤峰经济开发区	Hubei Hefeng Economic Development Zone	0.53	0.62
仙桃市	**Xiantao**	**5.78**	**5.91**
仙桃高新技术产业园区	Xiantao high-tech Industrial Development Znoe	5.78	5.91
仙桃彭场工业园	Xiantao Pengchang Industrial Park	3.19	2.97
潜江市	**Qianjiang**	**2.79**	**2.57**
湖北潜江经济开发区	Hubei Qianjiang Economic Development Zone	0.78	0.55
潜江张金经济开发区	Qianjiang Zhangjin Economic Development Zone	1.10	1.10
潜江园林经济开发区	Qianjiang Yuanlin Economic Development Zone	0.91	0.92
天门市	**Tianmen**	**6.04**	**6.55**
湖北天门经济开发区	Hubei Tianmen Economic Development Zone	6.04	6.55
神农架盘水生态产业园区		0.02	0.05

规模以上工业增加值(亿元) Above-scale Industrial Added Value(100 million Yuan)		规模以上工业主营业务收入(亿元) Scale Industrial Core Business Revenue (100 million Yuan)		固定资产投资总额(亿元) Total Investment In Fixed Assets(100 million Yuan)		施工项目个数(个) Number of Construction Project (unit)	
2014	2015	2014	2015	2014	2015	2014	2015
2.25	6.26	5.70	20.99	16.6	8	27	7
13.60	12.26	35.63	31.08	12.6	14.72	12	16
10.60	11.50	34.20	38.50	22.3	26.14	38	39
17.78	15.03	58.65	48.25	20.51	13.76	23	14
13.90	14.64	35.00	36.60	91	101.4	98	100
14.30	15.50	34.32	45.86	11.6	13.1	36	42
9.42	11.72	13.79	17.65	20.5	25.71	68	79
11.31	13.08	28.74	36.23	66	80.2	75	79
26.92	32.89	86.18	101.50	51.64	69.24	53	55
17.86	20.98	59.10	69.80	46.23	58.23	56	56
22.83	25.16	73.60	80.38	86.9	95.6	108	96
32.47	38.14	81.56	95.42	77.74	94.06	18	23
62.43	65.04	145.11	165.80	57.02	70.07	55	53
319.69	**360.86**	**887.30**	**1008.90**	**526.07**	**568.37**	**424**	**378**
40.06	46..17	122.08	138.98	61.11	74.02	60	68
75.43	81.12	267.38	285.50	91.05	103.65	127	92
37.90	38.10	85.20	86.70	28.6	19.5	30	12
21.54	24.60	63.50	72.00	30.4	38.6	50	45
15.60	17.21	49.80	58.03	12.8	18.86	26	32
28.00	29.50	88.19	105.40	145.86	126	58	58
91.88	114.85	180.43	229.15	151.11	181.73	60	61
9.28	9.31	30.72	33.14	5.14	6.01	13	10
217.90	**238.16**	**482.64**	**525.04**	**223.05**	**264.01**	**306**	**371**
217.90	238.16	482.64	525.04	223.05	264.01	306	371
71.00	95.34	208.00	225.23		134.53	123	186
21.27	27.27	53.63	67.48	39.67	41.95	20	21
24.82	26.16	72.58	74.26	18.35	21.39	28	23
97.05	**108.66**	**245.08**	**277.53**	**206.48**	**237.21**	**460**	**479**
37.58	40.60	73.50	78.50	97.27	106.1	150	110
0.89	0.97	3.78	3.80	10.54	10.55	25	25
9.00	10.77	22.61	26.45	11.53	12	14	14
8.78	10.55	22.66	26.79	17.23	21.84	44	62
6.05	6.92	19.56	22.87	27.65	37.13	76	103
4.56	5.54	12.78	15.49	10.32	10.54	48	42
14.05	15.48	45.56	51.81	11.11	13.28	51	56
9.26	10.67	25.60	29.17	16.8	22.24	42	45
6.88	7.16	19.03	22.65	4.03	3.53	10	15
208.37	**229.46**	**713.11**	**798.19**	**208.64**	**258.77**	**151**	**143**
208.37	229.46	713.11	798.19	208.64	258.77	151	143
33.45	32.86	125.35	124.21	28.16	29.75	24	32
99.52	**110.39**	**369.43**	**375.05**	**142.65**	**193.7**	**143**	**189**
34.95	42.66	148.19	149.91	55.54	83.8	44	63
49.00	50.00	168.50	166.30	19	24.9	18	21
15.57	17.73	52.74	58.84	68.11	85	81	105
117.63	**128.17**	**393.61**	**434.87**	**153.34**	**185.85**	**157**	**146**
117.63	128.17	393.61	434.87	153.34	185.85	157	146
0.8	0.9	0.5	0.8	3.2	3.4	22	28

21-2 续表 6 continued

开发区名称	Name of Development Zone	其中:亿元以上项目(个) Number of Projects above 100 million yuan (unit)	
		2014	2015
湖北省	**Hubei Province**	**4002**	**4231**
武汉市	**Wuhan**	**446**	**443**
武汉江岸经济开发区	Wuhan Jiang'an Economic Development Zone	3	2
武汉江汉经济开发区	Wuhan Jianghan Economic Development Zone		1
武汉硚口经济开发区	Wuhan Qiaokou Economic Development Zone	7	5
武汉汉阳经济开发区	Wuhan Hanyang Economic Development Zone	18	22
武汉武昌经济开发区	Wuhan Wuchang Economic Development Zone	1	1
武汉青山经济开发区	Wuhan Qingshan Economic Development Zone	15	7
武汉洪山经济开发区	Wuhan Hongshan Economic Development Zone	2	1
武汉临空港经济技术开发区	Wuhan Linkonggang Economic and Technology Development Zone	171	154
武汉汉南经济开发区	Wuhan Hannan Economic Development Zone	15	21
武汉蔡甸经济开发区	Wuhan Caidian Economic Development Zone	59	44
武汉江夏经济开发区	Wuhan Jiangxia Economic Development Zone	101	110
武汉盘龙城经济开发区	Wuhan Panlongcheng Economic Development Zone	6	1
武汉阳逻经济开发区	Wuhan Yangluo Economic Development Zone	51	44
武汉经济技术开发区	Wuhan Economic and Technology Development Zone	48	48
武汉东湖新技术产业开发区	Wuhan East Lake New Technology Industrial Development Zone	113	122
黄石市	**Huangshi**	**237**	**261**
湖北黄石港工业园区	Hubei Huangshi Port Industrial Park	4	5
湖北黄石新港工业园区	Hubei Huangshi New Port Industrial Park	12	7
湖北西塞山工业园区	Hubei Xisaishan Industrial Park	22	20
湖北下陆长乐山工业园区	Hubei Xialu Changleshan Industrial Park	9	8
黄石经济技术开发区	Huangshi Economic and Technology Development Zone	115	131
湖北阳新经济开发区	Hubei Yangxin Economic Development Zone	36	39
湖北大冶经济开发区	Hubei Daye Economic Development Zone	51	52
大冶灵成工业园	Daye Lingcheng Industrial Park	9	14
十堰市	**Shiyan**	**281**	**261**
十堰经济技术开发区	Shiyan Economic and Technology Development Zone	112	115
湖北郧阳区经济开发区	Hubei Yun County Economic Development Zone	43	49
湖北郧西工业园区	Hubei West Yun Industrial Park	5	4
湖北竹山经济开发区	Hubei Zhushan Economic Development Zone	28	21
湖北竹溪工业园区	Hubei Zhuxi Industrial Park	7	7
湖北房县工业园区	Hubei Fang County Industrial Park	49	38
湖北丹江口经济开发区	Hubei Danjiangkou Economic Development Zone	37	27
宜昌市	**Yichang**	**495**	**545**
湖北西陵经济开发区	Hubei Xiling Economic Development Zone	16	9
湖北伍家岗工业园区	Hubei Wujiagang Industrial Park	2	3
湖北点军工业园区	Hubei Dianjun Industrial Park	3	7
湖北夷陵经济开发区	Hubei Yiling Economic Development Zone	111	165
湖北远安工业园区	Hubei Yuan'an Industrial Park	53	60
湖北兴山经济开发区	Hubei Xingshan Economic Development Zone	6	3
湖北秭归经济开发区	Hubei Zigui Economic Development Zone	15	14
湖北长阳经济开发区	Hubei Changyang Economic Development Zone	26	22
湖北五峰工业园区	Hubei Wufeng Industrial Park	10	9
湖北五峰民族工业园	Hubei Wufeng National Industrial Park	3	2
宜昌高新技术产开发区	Yichang High-tech Industrial Development Zone	250	271
湖北宜都工业园区	Hubei Yidu Industrial Park	140	185
湖北当阳经济开发区	Hubei Dangyang Economic Development Zone	143	128
湖北枝江经济开发区	Hubei Zhijiang Economic Development Zone	92	71
枝江安福寺工业园	Zhijiang Anfu Temple Industrial Park	10	16

新开工项目(个) Number of Newly Opened Projects (unit)		开发区税收总额(万元) Total Tax Revenue of Development (10 000 yuan)		外商投资金额(万美元) Total Value of Foreign Investment (10 000 US dollors)		出口总额(万美元) Total Value of Export (10 000 US dollors)	
2014	2015	2014	2015	2014	2015	2014	2015
5188	**5478**	**15020620**	**17410766**	**550158**	**513423**	**1858739**	**2033525**
371	**330**	**8393254**	**9545911**	**252019**	**232405**	**857414**	**998791**
1		32398	30124	751		2932	1245
4	6	129500	139900			7867	7511
3		119911	112716			17514	16172
12	12	300467	330513			1028	512
		51390	43225	120		1600	1750
26	5	99196	981043	1397	1700	8532	1703
3		35750	28360			500	260
118	120	1228198	1371248	28944	36762	36731	42279
20	23	60849	35149	3238	3859	10137	9400
37	63	132441	115869	13000	16167	44126	50028
58	28	291100	431821	15100	19322	14337	24560
5	50	157285	143136			3450	3800
96	58	104540	115175	13327	15500	13080	14537
75	75	2689997	2954799	27086	2689997	126902	160211
113	107	3944510	4573618	128904	149253	656898	752314
312	**392**	**779402**	**861503**	**27788**	**21789**	**131093**	**126486**
12	5	3150	2600			400	350
8	3	15858	16315			200	350
29	21	87364	96100	20		48423	32549
15	10	52356	76472			39489	14080
110	155	338514	377172	22044	15426	56894	62014
20	23	31459	34127	724	863	16331	17470
131	135	303115	338964	5000	5500	7485	13636
10	53	15800	12540			1560	467
292	**330**	**520145**	**605041**	**25639**	**25562**	**56747**	**62130**
107	116	398749	478499	13982	18688	45164	47451
61	68	33175	35805	3417	3902	2874	2904
6	8	3801	4393	1000	500	229	
7	5	13558	14112			1350	2459
9	8	7500	8000	800	800	800	500
59	97	15871	14551	1615		4300	5000
43	28	47491	49681	4825	1692	2030	3780
516	**643**	**949665**	**1194912**	**37877**	**39909**	**114924**	**127264**
40	10	28000	28598			6744	8504
3		11957				13936	14526
3	12	6745	6904	1800	396	4780	5190
86	108	155387	112055	11058	12800	1597	1037
56	60	85247	88343	400	500	11636	13400
7	4	37080	41500			20700	23100
40	49	47710	50597	400		5988	6867
51	53	15078	15681			6258	640
35	31	12404	14885			748	823
6	8	2750	5380			612	323
220	224	470886	595443	30270	31025	54926	60024
207	276	248083	342242	3400	4800	25939	29830
86	128	59707	59503	4100	4641	5952	5845
70	116	221651	244986	3712	3846	22099	27425
13	19	6295	6861	495	238	11347	9644

21-2 续表 7 continued

开发区名称	Name of Development Zone	其中:亿元以上项目(个) Number of Projects above 100 million yuan (unit)	
		2014	2015
襄阳市	**Xianyang**	**695**	**685**
襄阳高新技术产业开发区	Xiangyang High-tech Industrial Development Zone	232	245
襄阳鱼梁州经济开发区	Xiangyang Yuliangzhou Economic Development Zone		
襄阳经济技术开发区	Xiangyang Economic Development Zone	85	83
湖北襄城经济开发区	Hubei Xiangcheng Economic Development Zone	12	9
湖北樊城经济开发区	Hubei Fancheng Economic Development Zone	46	50
湖北襄州经济开发区	Hubei Xiangzhou Economic Development Zone	85	83
襄阳工业园	Xiangyang Industrial Park	14	11
湖北南漳经济开发区	Hubei Nanzhang Economic Development Zone	36	34
湖北谷城经济开发区	Hubei Gucheng Economic Development Zone	98	89
谷城石花经济开发区	Gucheng Shihua Economic Development Zone	22	12
湖北保康经济开发区	Hubei Baokang Economic Development Zone	35	40
湖北老河口经济开发区	Hubei Laohekou Economic Development Zone	65	73
湖北枣阳经济开发区	Hubei Zaoyang Economic Development Zone	92	82
枣阳吴店工业园	Zaoyang Wudian Industrial Park	24	30
湖北宜城经济开发区	Hubei Yicheng Economic Development Zone	41	37
鄂州市	**E'zhou**	**129**	**135**
湖北鄂州花湖经济开发区	Hubei E'Zhou Huahu Economic Development Zone	19	18
鄂州葛店经济技术开发区	E'Zhou Gedian Economic and Technology Development Zone	129	135
湖北鄂州经济开发区	Hubei E'Zhou Economic Development Zone	21	17
荆门市	**Jingmen**	**437**	**507**
湖北东宝工业园区	Hubei Dongbao Industrial Park	68	89
荆门高新技术产业开发区	Hubei Jingmen High-tech Industrial Development Zone	95	116
湖北荆门化工循环产业园	Hubei Jingmen Chemical Recycling Development Zone	30	37
湖北京山经济开发区	Hubei Jingshan Economic Development Zone	82	87
湖北屈家岭经济开发区	Hubei Qujialing Economic Development Zone	12	13
湖北沙洋经济开发区	Hubei Shayang Economic Development Zone	43	52
湖北钟祥经济开发区	Hubei Zhongxiang Economic Development Zone	78	80
钟祥胡集经济开发区	Zhongxiang Huji Economic Development Zone	29	33
孝感市	**Xiaogan**	**274**	**276**
孝感高新技术产业开发区	Xiaogan high-tech Industrial Development Zone	123	136
湖北孝南经济开发区	Hubei Xiaonan Economic Development Zone	61	72
湖北孝昌经济开发区	Hubei Xiaochang Economic Development Zone	30	10
湖北大悟经济开发区	Hubei Dawu Economic Development Zone	15	16
湖北云梦经济开发区	Hubei Yunmeng Economic Development Zone	73	62
湖北应城经济开发区	Hubei Yingcheng Economic Development Zone	31	31
湖北安陆经济开发区	Hubei Anlu Economic Development Zone	63	66
湖北汉川经济开发区	Hubei Hanchuan Economic Development Zone	45	46
荆州市	**Jingzhou**	**256**	**271**
湖北沙市经济开发区	Hubei Shashi Economic Development Zone	37	35
湖北荆州城南经济开发区	Jingzhou Chengnan Economic Development Zone	11	27
荆州经济技术开发区	Jingzhou Economic and Technology Development Zone	46	36
湖北公安经济开发区	Hubei Gong'an Economic Development Zone	43	42
湖北监利经济开发区	Hubei Jianli Economic Development Zone	21	26
湖北江陵经济开发区	Hubei Jiangling Economic Development Zone	35	46
湖北石首经济开发区	Hubei Shishou Economic Development Zone	34	35
湖北洪湖经济开发区	Hubei Honghu Economic Development Zone	37	38
洪湖府场经济开发区	Honghu Fuchang Economic Development Zone	12	14
湖北松滋经济开发区	Hubei Songzi Economic Development Zone	28	34
黄冈市	**Huanggang**	**230**	**288**
湖北黄冈经济开发区	Hubei Huanggang Economic Development Zone	188	234

新开工项目(个) Number of Newly Opened Projects (unit)		开发区税收总额(万元) Total Tax Revenue of Development (10 000 yuan)		外商投资金额(万美元) Total Value of Foreign Investment (10 000 US dollors)		出口总额(万美元) Total Value of Export (10 000 US dollors)	
2014	2015	2014	2015	2014	2015	2014	2015
583	**617**	**1391738**	**1627184**	**47974**	**53657**	**169055**	**195723**
182	192	639051	784431	25000	30120	74620	81820
1	2	980	1500				
62	41	415987	437517	7159	8263	19531	19623
12	2	80858	79541	1853	1895	1289	1215
41	55	81575	89732	1524	1615	3738	4071
61	41	189958	8767	7159	8767	12900	15620
8	4	4269	11000	27000	29000	2436	3109
29	35	16228	17363			2206	2433
114	95	68559	72459	1450	1614	7862	8801
20	35	48168	50576	67	125	3143	4915
8	10	8444	8905	1520	2030	4657	5597
56	75	59879	82375	9887	6432	28675	31256
49	75	65472	92683	3673	5103	16178	27100
		27438	35120			983	1436
59	33	58915	62323	2000	5000	15600	18339
138	**174**	**182171**	**221524**	**5900**	**7500**	**7213**	**8152**
25	20	30262	25003			2697	2470
138	174	182171	221524	5900	7500	7213	8512
21	33	26567	27729	2286		1925	900
763	**848**	**387035**	**452057**	**28156**	**32396**	**76794**	**88149**
194	203	43439	5359			1699	1881
267	294	270113	523244	12622	15735	40206	57112
24	26	7400	187380			3060	4142
101	128	73869	77160	6164	8949	13248	15428
6	7	828	1124	328	400	1764	1530
46	48	27786	29028	3455	3890	11395	13500
107	120	50625	56819	7890	8635	9570	10815
18	22	29676	32643			11083	13889
273	**298**	**662106**	**824614**	**23482**	**27752**	**89633**	**95841**
110	135	457125	550565	15971	19521	33113	44825
301	185	186382	196261	3000	3500	7394	8400
15	8	11572	45200			3310	5579
7	8	27500	29500			1280	2128
84	113	83100	106300	4359	5458	12000	15500
25	25	91002	91004	10012	10012	1008	1009
58	62	28963	29023	1100	1100	9232	985
83	85	136946	170326	6411	7131	42698	33459
625	**627**	**400670**	**483522**	**32659**	**33080**	**91594**	**53207**
42	44	30416	31516			15446	17228
8		42557	52000			14557	13550
370	352	174599	222581	2811		56804	25000
24	27	38573	45659		2153	662	815
16	32	16800	16700	28600	29560	5500	5950
24	14	5617	6576			662	815
23	11	35663	47835			17410	10183
48	52	21098	22132	1248	1367	4023	3088
50	54	16558	19465				
70	85	91762	102574				1100
426	**383**	**328840**	**360098**	**47912**	**20933**	**49292**	**52275**
325	271	294624	319225	46762	47902	44455	46762

21-2 续表 8 continued

开发区名称	Name of Development Zone	其中:亿元以上项目(个) Number of Projects above 100 million yuan (unit)	
		2014	2015
湖北黄州火车站经济开发区	Hubei Huangzhou Railway Station Economic Development Zone	7	7
黄州工业园	Huangzhou Industrial Park	10	11
湖北龙感湖工业园区	Hubei Longganhu Industrial Park	18	24
湖北团风经济开发区	Hubei Tuanfeng Economic Development Zone	10	9
湖北红安经济开发区	Hubei Hong'an Economic Development Zone	35	38
湖北罗田经济开发区	Hubei Luotian Economic Development Zone	13	18
湖北英山经济开发区	Hubei Yingshan Economic Development Zone	11	12
湖北浠水经济开发区	Hubei Xishui Economic Development Zone	25	27
湖北蕲春李时珍医药工业园区	Hubei Qichun Li Shizhen Pharmaceutical Industrial Park	14	16
蕲春经济开发区	Qichun Economic Development Zone	16	18
湖北黄梅经济开发区	Hubei Huangmei Economic Development Zone	25	32
湖北麻城经济开发区	Hubei Macheng Economic Development Zone	12	15
湖北武穴经济开发区	Hubei Wuxue Economic Development Zone	28	33
咸宁市	**Xianning**	**160**	**164**
湖北咸安经济开发区	Hubei Xian'an Economic Development Zone	17	19
湖北嘉鱼经济开发区	Hubei Jiayu Economic Development Zone	37	31
湖北通城经济开发区	Hubei Tongcheng Economic Development Zone	13	5
湖北崇阳工业园区	Hubei Chongyang Industrial Park	18	33
湖北通山经济开发区	Hubei Tongshan Economic Development Zone	5	5
湖北咸宁经济开发区	Hubei Xianning Economic Development Zone	47	39
湖北赤壁经济开发区	Hubei Chibi Economic Development Zone	21	30
湖北赤壁蒲纺工业园区	Hubei Chibi Puqi Textile Industrial Park	2	2
随州市	**Suizhou**	**92**	**99**
湖北随州经济开发区	Hubei Suizhou Economic Development Zone	92	99
湖北曾都经济开发区	Hubei Zengdu Economic Development Zone	36	34
湖北随县经济开发区	Hubei Sui County Economic Development Zone	10	11
湖北广水经济开发区	Hubei Guangshui Economic Development Zone	5	4
恩施自治州	**Enshi Autonomous Prefecture**	**89**	**90**
湖北恩施经济开发区	Hubei Enshi Economic Development Zone	30	23
湖北恩施州经济开发区	Hubei Enshi Prefecture Economic Development Zone	13	12
湖北利川经济开发区	Hubei Lichuan Economic Development Zone	7	13
湖北建始工业园区	Hubei Jianshi Industrial Park	5	5
湖北巴东经济开发区	Hubei Badong Economic Development Zone	12	13
湖北宣恩工业园区	Hubei Xuan'en Industrial Park	6	9
湖北咸丰工业园区	Hubei Xianfeng Industrial Park	6	6
湖北来凤经济开发区	Hubei Laifeng Economic Development Zone	9	9
湖北鹤峰经济开发区	Hubei Hefeng Economic Development Zone	1	
仙桃市	**Xiantao**	**88**	**100**
仙桃高新技术产业园区	Hubei Xiantao Economic Development Zone	88	100
仙桃彭场工业园	Xiantao Pengchang Industrial Park	8	5
潜江市	**Qianjiang**	**50**	**63**
湖北潜江经济开发区	Hubei Qianjiang Economic Development Zone	17	19
潜江张金经济开发区	Qianjiang Zhangjin Economic Development Zone	7	13
潜江园林经济开发区	Qianjiang Yuanlin Economic Development Zone	26	31
天门市	**Tianmen**	**39**	**43**
湖北天门经济开发区	Hubei Tianmen Economic Development Zone	39	43
神农架盘水生态产业园区		2	2

新开工项目(个) Number of Newly Opened Projects (unit)		开发区税收总额(万元) Total Tax Revenue of Development (10 000 yuan)		外商投资金额(万美元) Total Value of Foreign Investment (10 000 US dollors)		出口总额(万美元) Total Value of Export (10 000 US dollors)	
2014	2015	2014	2015	2014	2015	2014	2015
23	7	3132	3410			441	480
4	5	5284	3120	21200		3169	1790
20	20	7793	8572	10		498	200
5	6	12500	12850			1235	950
28	30	11532	11840	2950	3000	267	283
32	37	9123	10491			4126	5018
49	55	17303	21801			213	295
38	20	18000	19860	2000	780	12100	12921
36	37	27541	29580	8630	8665	6020	6983
34	35	24753	25061	131	500	3317	3715
95	75	28100	29800			3739	4500
12	13	56919	63749	3400		1077	1198
38	28	52348	56858	2500	20	8700	8927
255	**241**	**355559**	**417903**	**2659**	**2188**	**34708**	**35518**
46	50	28519	31386			4328	4654
62	52	18826	19700	518	550	7886	8500
15	6	25995	27869			5211	5324
36	34	11800	13102	529		2100	2360
12	16	14815	16100			560	575
29	28	194200	230385	19	543	7360	9081
46	50	55172	78355	948	1095	4780	5024
9	5	1232	1006	645		2483	
150	**135**	**109449**	**120531**	**5146**	**5847**	**80808**	**79462**
150	135	109449	120531	5146	5847	80808	79462
58	61	38127	34769			29449	18162
11	12	5887	7245			16589	12668
12	8	9600	11800	2680	2910	4200	4400
240	**209**	**255247**	**288640**	**200**	**395**	**17571**	**19564**
82	21	155682	163150			2600	3410
10	11	6000	6300				
9	7	45549	64176			202	496
34	57	6067	7263			2775	2786
34	35	10840	13734		1	6800	7710
15	13	3896	4325		153	367	1019
29	35	12600	13620	200	240	2912	3179
26	22	10783	12422			425	
1	5	3830	3650			1490	458
71	**43**	**172400**	**203358**	**8303**	**4384**	**38948**	**55508**
71	43	172400	203358	8303	4384	38948	55508
23	7	18765	17536			21700	22653
100	**151**	**120038**	**139906**	**3520**	**4610**	**35946**	**27457**
22	61	22806	30159		1000	5914	5094
17	14	10090	9000	3520	3610	11502	8155
61	76	87142	100747			18530	14208
68	**52**	**57845**	**61273**	**924**	**1015**	**6999**	**7637**
68	52	57845	61273	924	1015	6999	7637
5	5	2000	2800				

主要统计指标解释

规划面积:指国土部门核定的开发区规划面积。

实际开发面积:指开发区实际开发并已完成基础设施建设的面积。

企业个数:指报告期末已在工商行政管理机关登记注册、并在开发区管理机构进行统计登记的法人单位数,包括内资企业、港澳台投资企业和外商投资企业。不含个体企业。

工业企业:包括采矿业、制造业、电力、燃气及水的生产和供应业。

规模以上工业企业:是指企业所在地在开发区内的全部年主营收入2000万元及以上的法人工业企业。即无论企业是否在开发区注册,也无论企业隶属何行政级别或部门,只要所在地在开发区的所有规模以上企业都在本制度规定的统计范围以内。反之,所在地不在开发区,尽管其在开发区注册的规模以上企业也不在本制度规定的统计范围之内。

高新技术企业:指生产高新技术产品经省科学技术厅授牌的企业。

外商投资企业:指企业注册登记类型中的中外合资、合作经营企业、外资企业和外商投资股份有限公司之和。(含港、澳、台商投资企业: 指企业注册登记类型中的港、澳、台资合资、合作、独资经营企业和股份有限公司之和。)

第三产业:除第一、第二产业以外的其他各业。由于第三产业包括的行业多、范围广,根据我国的实际情况,第三产业可分为两大部分;一是流通部门,二是服务部门。具体又可分为四个层次:

第一层次:流通部门,包括交通运输、仓储及邮电通信业,批发和零售贸易、餐饮业。

第二层次:为生产和生活服务的部门,包括金融、保险业,地质勘查业、水利管理业,房地产业,社会服务业,农、林、牧、渔服务业,交通运输辅助业,综合技术服务业等。

第三层次:为提高科学文化水平和居民素质服务的部门,包括教育、文化艺术及广播电影电视业,卫生、体育和社会福利业,科学研究业等。

第四层次:为社会公共需要服务的部门,包括国家机关、政党机关和社会团体以及军队、警察等。

从业人员:指报告期末在开发区企业、行政和事业单位中工作,取得工资或其他形式的劳动报酬的全部人员数。包括在岗职工,再就业的离退休人员、民办教师及在企业工作的外方人员和港澳台方人员、兼职人员、借用的外单位人员和第二职业者。不包括离开本单位但仍保留劳动关系的职工。

开发区生产总值: 即按市场价格计算的国内生产总值的简称。指开发区内所有常住单位在一定时期内生产活动的最终成果。国内生产总值有三种表现形态,即价值形态、收入形态和产品形态。

从价值形态看,它是所有常住单位在一定时期内生产的全部货物和服务价值超过同期投入的全部非固定资产货物和服务价值的差额,即所有常住单位的增加值之和;从收入形态看,它是所有常住单位在一定时期内创造并分配给常住单位和非常住单位的初次分配收入之和;从产品形态看它是最终使用的货物和服务减去进口货物和服务。在实际核算中,国内生产总值的三种表现形态表现为三种计算方法,即生产法、收入法和支出法。三种方法分别从不同的方面反映国内生产总值及其构成。

(1) 生产法是从生产的角度衡量常住单位在一定时期新创造价值的方法。即从生产的全部货物和服务总产品价值中,扣除生产过程中投入的中间货物和服务价值得到增加价值。国民经济各产业部门生产法增加值计算公式如下:

增加值 = 总产出 - 中间投入 将国民经济各产业部门生产法增加值相加,得到生产法GDP。

总产出:指常住单位在一定时期内生产的所有货物和服务的价值,既包括新增价值,也包括转移价值。它反映常住单位生产活动的总规模。总产出按生产者价格计算。

中间投入:指常住单位在一定时期内生产过程中消耗和使用的非固定资产货物和服务的价值。中间投入也称为中间消耗,反映用于生产过程中的转移价值,一般按购买者价格计算。计入中间投入的货物和服务必须具备两个条件,一是与总产出的计

算范围保持一致;二是本期一次性使用的。

(2)收入法也称为分配法。按收入法计算国内生产总值是从生产过程创造收入的角度,对常住单位的生产活动成果进行核算。按照这种计算方法,增加值由劳动者报酬、生产税净额、固定资产折旧和营业盈余四个部分组成。计算公式为:增加值=劳动者报酬+生产税净额+固定资产折旧+营业盈余。国民经济各部门的增加值之和等于国内生产总值。

(3)支出法是从最终使用的角度反映国内生产总值最终使用去向的一种方法。最终使用包括货物和服务的最终消费支出、资本形成总额、货物和服务净出口三部分,计算公式为:国内生产总值=最终消费支出+资本形成总额+货物和服务净出口。

按三种方法计算的国内生产总值反映的是同一经济总体在同一时期的生产活动成果,因此,从理论上讲,三种计算方法所得到的结果应该是一致的。但是,在实践中,由于受资料来源的口径范围的限制和计算方法的影响,要保证这三种计算方法所得的结果完全相等几乎是不可能的。

工业总产值(现价):是以货币形式表现的,工业企业在一定时期内生产的工业最终产品或提供工业性劳务活动的总价值量。

工业总产值包括本期生产成品价值、对外加工费收入,在制品半成品期末期初差额价值三部分。

①本期生产成品价值:是指企业本期生产,并在报告期内不再进行加工,经检验、包装入库的全部工业成品(半成品)价值合计,包括企业生产的自制设备及提供给本企业在建工程、其他非工业部门和生活福利部门等单位使用的成品价值,本期生产成品价值按自备原材料生产的产品的数量乘以本期不含增值税(销项税额)的产品实际销售平均单价计算;会计核算中按成本价格转帐的自制设备和自产自用的成品,按成本价格计算生产成品价值。生产成品价值中不包括用定货者来料加工的成品(半成品)价值。

②对外加工费收入:是指企业在报告期内完成的对外承接的工业品加工(包括用定货者来料加工产品)的加工费收入和对外工业修理作业所取得的加工费收入。对外加工费收入按不含增值税(销项税额)的价格计算,可根据会计“产品销售收入”科目的有关资料取得。

对于本企业对内非工业部门提供的加工修理、设备安装的劳务收入,如果企业会计核算基础比较好,能取得这部分资料,而且这部分价值所占比重较大,应包括在对外加工费收入中。

③自制半成品在制品期末期初差额价值:是指企业报告期自制半成品、在制品期末减期初的差额价值,本指标一般可从会计核算资料中取得。如果会计产品成本核算中不计算半成品、在制品的成本,则总产值中也不包括这部分价值,反之则包括。

工业增加值:指工业企业在报告期内以货币形式表现的工业生产活动的最终成果,是企业全部生产活动的总成果扣除了在生产过程中消耗或转移的物质产品和劳务价值后的余额,是企业生产过程中新增加的价值。

计算工业增加值通常采用两种方法。一是“生产法”,二是“收入法”,目前工业统计主要采用“生产法”计算工业增加值。

“生产法”,即从工业生产过程中产品和劳务价值形成的角度入手,剔除生产环节中间投入的价值,从而得到新增价值的方法。公式为:

工业增加值=工业总产值—工业中间投入+本期应交增值税

上述公式中,本期应交增值税的企业为负数时,综合部门汇总时按零处理。

“收入法”,即从工业生产过程中创造的原始收入初次分配的角度,对工业生产活动最终成果进行核算的一种方法,其计算公式为:

工业增加值=固定资产折旧+劳动者报酬+生产税净额+营业盈余

工业中间投入:1. 定义:指企业在报告期内用于工业生产活动所一次性消耗的外购原材料、燃料、动力及其他实物产品和对外支付的服务费用。

2. 计算原则:计算工业中间投入须遵循以下三条原则:(1)必须是从企业外部购入的产品和服务的价值,不包括生产过程中回收的废料以及自制品的价值。(2)必须是本期投入生产,并一次性消耗的产品和服务的价值,不包括固定资产转移价值;(3)中间投入的计算口径必须与总产值的计算口径相一致:即计入工业中间投入的产品和服务价值必须已经计入了工业总产值中。

3. 分类:工业中间投入按企业支付对象可以分为中间物质投入和中间劳务投入。中间物质投入是指生产过程中所消耗的外购原材料、燃料、动力以及其它实物产品和支付给物质生产部门(工业、农业、批发零售贸易业、建筑业、货物运输及邮电业)的服务费用,中间劳务投入指支付给非物质生产部门(如金融、保险、文化教育、科学研究、医疗卫生、行政管理)的服务费用。

工业中间投入按照具体内容分为直接材料、制造费用中的中间投入、管理费用中的中间投入、销售费用中的中间投入和利息支出五大项。

日常统计中计算中间投入是按第二种分类计算的。

4. 计算方法:计算工业中间投入的具体方法可以分为二种。一是正算法,即将制造费用、管理费用、销售费用中属于中间投入的部分分别相加,再加上直接材料和利息支出,得出工业中间投入合计。二是倒算法,即分别用制造费用、管理费用、销售费用合计减去其中属于增加值的项目(大体包括工资、福利费、折旧、劳动保险费、职工待业保险费等),倒算出三项费用中的中间投入,再加上直接材料和利息支出,得出工业中间投入合计。在实算操作过程中,采用倒算法计算比较简便易行。

5. 资料来源:计算中间投入的资料来源,可分别根据企业“产品成本表”、“管理费用”、“财务费用”、“销售费用”明细表归纳整理填报。

高新技术增加值:增加值是指报告期内企业在生产活动中新创造的价值。

高新技术增加值指报告期省科技厅认定的高新技术企业的增加值和非高新技术企业中的高新技术产品的增加值两部分。高新技术产品指高新技术领域的产品。即满足下列条件之一的产品:①首次应用新科学原理生产的最新产品;②首次应用最新工艺生产并使产品质量、成本和劳动效率有显著改进的产品;③技术水平达到90年代国际先进水平的产品。

有两种计算方法:一是“生产法”;二是“收入法”,亦称要素分配法。计算方法为:

(1)按生产法计算的工业增加值=工业总产值—工业中间投入+本期应交增值税;(2)按分配法计算的工业增加值=固定资产折旧+劳动者报酬+生产税净额+营业盈余。

主营业务收入:指企业经常性的、主要业务所产生的收入。不同行业的企业主营业务收入包括的内容不同。工业企业的主营业务收入主要包括销售产品、自制半成品、提供工业性劳务等收入;商品流通企业的主营业务收入主要包括销售商品取得的收入。主营业务收入一般占企业收入的比重较大,对企业的经济效益产生较大的影响。在会计核算中单独设置“主营业务收入”科目核算经常性的、主要业务所产生的收入。

固定资产投资总额:指开发区各单位报告期内500万元以上(含500万元)项目完成的投资额(包括实际完成的建筑安装工程价值,设备、工具、器具的购置费,以及实际发生的其他费用),是以货币表示的建造和购置固定资产活动的工作量以及与此有关的费用总称。

基础设施建设投资:指报告期内开发区基础公用设施:包括供水排水、供气、供热、供电、环卫设施、排污系统、固体废弃物收集和处理系统、电信及道路、桥梁、平整土地等施工建设投资。

施工项目个数:指报告期内曾进行建筑或安装工程施工活动的建设项目个数,包括报告期内新开工项目、报告期以前开工跨入报告期继续施工的项目以及报告期施过工并在报告期内全部建成投产或停缓建的项目个数。

税收总额:指开发区全口径税收收入。包含国税收入、地税收入。主要有增值税、营业税、所得税、城市维护建设税、城镇土地使用税、房产税、印花税、资源税、土地增值税等。

招商引资总额:指报告期内除本行政区划以外的国内外投资者在开发区的投资金额之和。

外商投资金额:指外国企业和经济组织或个人(包括华侨、港澳台胞以及我国在境外注册的企业)按我国有关政策、法规,用现汇、实物、技术等在我国境内开办外商独资企业、与我国境内的企业或经济组织共同举办中外合资经营企业、合作经营企业或合作开发资源的投资(包括外商投资收益的再投资),以及经政府有关部门批准的项目投资总额内企业从境外借入的资金。

省外境内投资额:指报告期内除湖北省以外的国内投资者(不包括港、澳、台)在开发区的投资金额。

出口总额:指实际出口的货物总金额。我国规定出口货物按离岸价格统计。

高新产品出口交货值:指企业生产的交给外贸部门或自营(委托)出口(包括销往香港、澳门、台湾),用外汇价格结算的批量销售,在国内或在边境批量出口等的高新产品价值,还包括外商来样、来料加工、来件装配和补偿贸易等生产的产品价值。

Explanatory Notes on Main Statistical Indicators

Land Area Approved for Development Zone refers to the land area of development zone ratified for program by the state department of territory.

Floor Area of Development Zone refers to the land area of development zone that is practically exploited and occupied.

The Number of Enterprise refers to the number of impersonal entity that has registered at industrial organs and commerce administration at the end of report period and that has been counted and registered. Included in this catogary are domestic—funded enterprises, enterprises with funds from Hong kong,Macao,Taiwan and foreign—funded enterprises. Private enterprises are excluded.

Enterprises of High and New Technology refer to enterprises verified by provincial office of science and technology that produce hi-tech products.

Industrial Enterprises include mining,manufacturing, and manufacturing and supply of power, gas and water.

Industrial enterprises above designated size refer to entity industrial enterprises whose main annual turnover exceeds 5 million in the circle of development zone where enterpriese are located. That is to say,no matter enterprises has registered or not, what department enterprises belong to, all the enterprises whose location are in the development zone are counted which are above designated size. Otherwise, enterprises above designated size whose location is not in the development zone are not counted although they have registered at development zone.

Employees refer to all the workers working in enterprises in development zone,administrative unit and public institution who have got their income or payment of labour in other forms at the end of report period. Included in this category are workers on guard, re—employed laid—off workers and retirees, citizen-managed teachers; foreign workers in enterprises,workers of Hong Kong, Macao and Taiwan, part—time workers, borrowed workers from external enterprises and second—job workers. Workers having left enterprises who reserve labour relations are excluded.

Total turnover of technology, industry and trade refers to the total sum of product sales proceeds, technological gain and goods sales proceeds that are related to our products,other business gain,external—business gain in one year,and the like.

Technological turnover refers to the gain of technology transferrance, technology contract, technology advisory and service, technology share,products of pilotscale experiment and the gain of external-entrusted scientific research.

Technology contract turnover refers to the gain from contract of technology program design,design and contract of technology project.

Technology advisory and service turnover refers to the income from technical intellegence, technilcal information,technical advisory and test analysis provided availing enterprises themselves of human resources,physical resources and data system, and other kinds of technical service.

Revenue of entrusted reserch and development refers to the revenue from reserch and development of new products contracted provided to various social units.

Gross Industrial Output Value (at current price) refers to the total volum of final industrial products produced and industrial services provided in money terms during a given period .

Gross Industrial Output Value consists of 3 components: value of the finished products during the reference period, income from external processing, and value of change in semi-finished products at the end of and at the beginning of the reference period.

①**value of the finished products during the reference period** refers to the value of all finished(semi-finished) industrial products that are produced during the reference period without the need for further processing, checked for accepatance, packed and put into the warehouse of the enterprise, including the value of own–produced equipment and the value of products provided to the projects under construction of the enterprise, and to other non–industrial or welfare units. Value of finished products during the reference period is calculated by the quantity of products produced using own materials multiplied by the average unit prices at which products are sold(exculding value–added tax). Own–produced equipment and products for own use are value at cost prices as in the case of enterprise accounting. Value of finished products does not include the value of finished products(semi–finished products) that are produced using the materials from the clients who make the ordres.

②**Income from external processing** refers to income from contracted external processing of industrial products(including processing of industrial products using materials from the clients), and the income from industrial repairing work provided to other units. Income from external processing is calculated using information from the item "products sales income" in the enterprise accounting at the prices excluding value–added tax.For income from external services such as processing, repairing and installation of equipment provided to non–industrial units within the enterprise, if the accounting work of the enterprise is good enough to separate it from other records, and the share of such services is significant, it should also be included in the income from external processing.

③**value of change in semi–finished products at the end of and at the beginning of the reference period** refers to the value of change in semi–finished products at the end and at the beginning of the reference period, which generally can be obtained from accounting records of enterprises. If the enterprise accounting excludes the cost of semi–finished products, then it should not be inculded in the gross industrial output value,and vice versa.

Highandnew technology value High and new technology products refer to products in the area of high and new technology, namely any kind of products meeting following standars: ① the latest products using latest scientific principles the first time; ②the products that are produced by the latest technology and have noticeably improved the quality, cost and work efficiency; ③ products whose technical merit has reached advanced international standards of 1990s. High and new technology value refers to 2 components: the value of high and new technology enterprises designated by provincial Science and Technology Office in reference period, and value of high and new technology products of non–high–and–new technology enterprises.

Industrial value added refers to the final results of industrial production enterprises in money terms during the the reference period.

Industrial value added can be usually calculated by two approaches:the production approach,and the income approach.Industrial stastics mainly adopts the production approach to calculate the industrial value added at present.

The production approach is the approach that newly–increased value is gained by eliminating the value indulged in the production link in terms of value formation of products and labor in the process of industrial prodution. The formula is: Industrial value added= total industrial value–industrial intermediate input

+current value added tax receivable

In this formula,when current value added tax receivale is minus, the Integration Department will treat it as zero.

The income approach is an approach that final results of industrial production activities are checked in terms of the primary distribution of original income created in the indusrial production. Here is its formula: Industrial value added=depreciation of fixed assets+remuneration of labourers+net of produce tax+operating surplus

Industrial intermediate input:

1.Definition: It refers to the service cost for purchased raw material,gas,power and other physical products,and external–paid services consumed during the reference period for the industrial production of enterprises.

2.Calculating principles:Calculating industrial intermediate input must follow the three principles:(1)The value must be the value of goods and services that are purchased from outside,exculding the value of reclaimedwaste materials in the production and that of own products.(2) The value must be the value of goods and services that are inputted into production consumed during the reference period,ex–

cluding transfer value of fixed assets.(3)The calculating units of the intermediate input must be in correspondence with that of total value, namely the value of products and service reckoned in industrial intermediate input has been reckoned in industrial value.

3.Category: Industrial intermediate input in terms of pay objectcan be classified as intermediate material input and intermediate labor input . Intermediate material input refers to the the purchased raw material, gas,power and other physical products consumed in the production, and the cost of service paid to departments of material production(industry,agriculcuture, wholesales and retail trade,construction goods transportation and post). Intermediate labor input refers to cost of service paid todepartments of nonmaterial production(finance, insurance,cultural education,scientific research,medical health and administration)

Industrial intermediate input in terms of concrete content can be classified into 5 components , namely direct consumption of materials,industrial intermediate input in manufacturing cost, industrial intermediate input in management cost, industrial intermediate input in marketing cost and expenditure on interest.

Intermediate input in common calculating is calculated by the second category.

4.Calculating approaches:the calculating approaches to industrial intermediate input have two approaches. Positive calculating, namely add respectively the manufacuring cost, management cost,sales cost that belong to intermediate input, then add direct material and interest expense.The final result is reconed into the total.Negative calculating, namely manufacturing cost, management cost, sale cost that belong to value-added items(generally included are sallary, welfarism, depreciation,labor insurance, employee's job-waiting insurance,ect)is substracted respectively from the total.The result is the its intermediate input respectively. Then direct material and interest expense are added. The final result is reconed into the total. Negative calculating is easier to carry out in pratical calculating.

5.Information source: The information source in calculating intermediate input can be obtained from product Cost Table, tables of Management Cost, Financial Expense and Sales Cost.

Value added of high and new technology value added refers to the newly created value in the production in the reference period. There are two approaches to calculting, the production approach, and the income approach,also factor distribution approach. The calculation methods are: (1)industrial value added by the production approach=total industrial value-industrial intermediate input+ current value added tax receivable; (2) industrial value added by distribution approach=depreciation of fixed assets+ remuneration of labourers+net of produce tax+operating surplus

Value added of high and new technology refers to the value added of high and new technology enterprises designated by provincial Science and Technology Office in reference period, and value added of high and new technology products of non-high-and-new technology enterprises.

Income from major business refers to the income of regular and major bussiness of enterprises. The content of the income from major business differs from enterprise to enterprise. The income from major business of industrial enterprises mainly includes the income from product sales,own semi-finished products,industrial labor; the income from major business of commodity circulation enterprises mainly includes the incoome from commodity sales.Income from major business generally takes a big share in the income of enterprise, and has a great influence on the economic benefit.The "income from major business" item is set individually to check income from regular and major business in accounting.

Total investment in fixed assets refers to the generic term for operation capacity of building up and purchasing fixed assets in money terms during the reference period and related cost. Total investment in fixed assets in reference period is calculated by actual investment(including value of actual finish constructive installation engineering,purchasing cost of equipment,tools and devices,and other actual cost)

The number of projects under construction:refers to number of projects that has carried out construction or installation engineering in reference period, including the number of newly-opened projects during reference period,projects opened before reference period and constructed over reference period,and projects that have been constructed in reference period and completed or delayed within reference period.

Total tax revenue refers to tax revenue in all units of development zone.Included in this category are national and local tax revenue.They are mainly value added tax, turnover tax, income tax, city maintenance construction tax, use tax of town land, house tax, stamp tax, resource tax, land value increment tax, ect.

Value of foreign investment refers to the investment made by the soley foreign–owned enterprises opened according to the relevant policies and regulations and by means of convertible foreign exchange, physical goods,and technology,ect ; sino–foreign joint venture run by foreign enterprises,ecnomic organizations or individuals(including overseas Chinese,fellow citizens of Hongkong,Macao and Taiwan and Sino–enterprises registered in foreign countries) with Chinese enterprises or Chinese ecnomic organizations. And capital borrow from abroad and within the total value of investment in projects approved by the relevant department of Government.

Total value of export refers to total value of pratical outward cargoes. Our country stipulates that outward cargoes are calculated on FOB basis.

22 “两圈”主要经济指标

Major Economic Indicators of “Twice”

22-1 武汉城市圈主要经济指标(2015)
MAIN ECONOMIC INDICATORS OF WUHAN URBAN CIRCLE(2015)

指标	Item	土地面积(平方公里) Land Area (sq.km)	常住人口(万人) Total Population (year-end) (10 000 persons)	地区生产总值(亿元) Gross Regional Product(100 million yuan)	第一产业(亿元) Primary Industry (100 million yuan)	第二产业(亿元) Secondary Industry (100 million yuan)	#工业(亿元) #Industry (100 million yuan)	第三产业(亿元) Tertiary Industry (100 million yuan)	人均地区生产总值(元) Per Capita Gross Regional Prduct (yuan/person)
合计	**Total**	**58052**	**3120.62**	18535.51	1605.48	8753.28	7385.90	8176.75	59699
武汉市	Wuhan Municipality	8494	1060.77	10905.60	359.81	44981.554	4081.91	5564.25	104132
黄石市	Huangshi Municipality	4583	245.80	1228.11	108.56	679.88	600.99	439.67	50053
鄂州市	Ezhou Municipality	1594	105.95	730.01	84.66	422.44	383.26	22.91	68921
孝感市	Xiaogan Municipality	8910	487.80	1457.20	259.45	705.76	618.36	491.99	29924
黄冈市	Huanggang Municipality	17446	629.10	1589.24	379.62	618.42	477.01	591.20	25321
咸宁市	Xianning Municipality	9861	250.70	10300.07	178.59	500.47	447.38	351.01	41234
仙桃市	Xiantiao Municipality	2538	115.50	597.60	87.99	318.14	291.32	191.48	51496
潜江市	Qianjiang Municipality	2004	95.80	557.57	69.88	305.17	284.00	182.52	58201
天门市	Tianmen Municipality	2622	129.20	440.10	76.90	221.46	201.67	141.72	34069

22-1 续表 1 continued

指标	Item	固定资产投资总额(亿元) Investment in Fixed Assets (100 million yuan)	地方公共财政预算收入(亿元) Revenue of Local Governments (100 million yuan)	#各项税收(亿元) #Taxes (100 million yuan)	地方财政支出(亿元) Expenditures of Local Governments (100 million yuan)	农村居民人均可支配收入(元) Annual Per Capita Disposable Income of Rural Households (yuan)	城镇居民人均可支配收入(元) Annual Per Capita Disposable Income of Urban Households (yuan)
合计	**Total**	**16163.83**	**1779.17**	**1369.89**	**2731.19**	**13954**	**28477**
武汉市	Wuhan Municipality	7680.89	1245.63	1015.91	1338.05	17722	36436
黄石市	Huangshi Municipality	1351.93	100.53	68.28	225.94	12004	27536
鄂州市	Ezhou Municipality	806.21	47.17	29.83	86.80	13812	24774
孝感市	Xiaogan Municipality	1762.35	122.77	79.04	290.38	12655	25753
黄冈市	Huanggang Municipality	1958.41	112.82	75.35	401.03	10252	22620
咸宁市	Xianning Municipality	1349.62	80.12	50.29	190.85	11940	23505
仙桃市	Xiantiao Municipality	445.50	27.69	22.07	69.30	14422	24641
潜江市	Qianjiang Municipality	435.52	22.85	15.45	64.11	14076	24721
天门市	Tianmen Municipality	373.41	19.59	13.67	64.73	13178	22618

22-1 续表 2 continued

指标	Item	农林牧渔业总产值(亿元) Gross Output Value of Agriculture (100 million yuan)	粮食产量(万吨) Output of Grain (10 000 tons)	棉花产量(万吨) Output of Cotton (tons)	油料产量(万吨) Output of Oil-bearing Crops (10 000 tons)	工业企业单位数(个) Number of Enterprises (unit)	房屋建筑竣工面积(万平方米) Floor Space Completed of Buildings (10 000 sq.m)	社会消费品零售总额(亿元) Total Retail Sales(100 million yuan)
合计	**Total**	**2696.61**	**1114.62**	**14.33**	**160.49**	**8423**	**7991.78**	**8736.83**
武汉市	Wuhan Municipality	620.28	127.00	1.65	18.33	2558	3123.90	5102.24
黄石市	Huangshi Municipality	158.75	65.94	0.41	9.47	761	142.03	582.36
鄂州市	Ezhou Municipality	149.83	36.74	0.39	6.22	489	310.95	261.95
孝感市	Xiaogan Municipality	476.88	231.02	2.35	23.92	1306	2022.21	797.14
黄冈市	Huanggang Municipality	593.01	331.99	3.75	55.70	1493	1365.55	880.91
咸宁市	Xianning Municipality	301.15	109.43	0.28	10.64	867	406.43	401.04
仙桃市	Xiantiao Municipality	147.49	83.71	1.76	14.26	386	93.16	266.17
潜江市	Qianjiang Municipality	119.24	53.49	1.40	10.22	267	46.94	186.14
天门市	Tianmen Municipality	129.98	75.30	2.34	11.73	296	480.61	258.90

22-1 续表 3 continued

指标	Item	实际外商直接投资(万美元) Actually Foreign Direct Investments (USD 10 000)	入境旅游者人数(万人次) Number of International Tourists (10 000 person-times)	国际旅游外汇收入(万美元) Foreign Exchange Earnings (USD 10 000)	金融机构人民币存款(亿元) State Bank Deposits (100 million yuan)	金融机构人民币贷款(亿元) State Bank Loans(100 million yuan)
合计	**Total**	**701825**	**206.03**	**134987.24**	**27542.28**	**20284.21**
武汉市	Wuhan Municipality	599126	202.36	133736.19	19057.17	16018.30
黄石市	Huangshi Municipality	12453	0.05	18.85	1341.81	926.67
鄂州市	Ezhou Municipality	24450	0.14	38.02	507.91	328.98
孝感市	Xiaogan Municipality	34501	0.08	28.49	1856.60	915.28
黄冈市	Huanggang Municipality	10357	0.92	189.33	2320.97	991.08
咸宁市	Xianning Municipality	6474	2.13	788.49	1035.44	628.97
仙桃市	Xiantiao Municipality	4424	0.21	159.60	488.32	182.30
潜江市	Qianjiang Municipality	5832	0.02	3.75	487.27	158.18
天门市	Tianmen Municipality	4208	0.12	24.52	446.78	134.46

22-2 鄂西生态文化旅游圈主要经济指标(2015)
MAIN ECONOMIC INDICATORS OF WUHAN URBAN CIRCLE(2015)

指标	Item	土地面积(平方公里) Land Area (sq.km)	常住人口(万人) Total Population (year-end) (10 000 persons)	地区生产总值(亿元) Gross Regional Product(100 million yuan)	第一产业 Primary Industry	第二产业 Secondary Industry	#工业 #Industry	第三产业 Tertiary Industry	人均地区生产总值(元) Per Capita Gross Regional Prduct (yuan/person)
合计	**Total**	**127909**	**2730.88**	**12523.03**	**1753.02**	**6598.54**	**5966.29**	**4171.47**	**45874**
宜昌市	Yichang Municipality	21084	411.50	3384.80	361.40	1986.37	1807.11	1037.03	82359
荆州市	Jingzhou Municipality	14067	570.59	1590.50	3530.1	695.12	625.33	542.37	27781
襄阳市	Xiangyang Municipality	19724	561.40	3382.12	402.14	1922.92	1748.85	1057.06	60319
荆门市	Jingmen Municipality	12404	289.63	1388.46	200.86	729.66	678.86	457.947	47999
十堰市	Shiyan Municipality	23680	338.30	1300.12	157.48	636.11	574.11	506.53	38431
随州市	Suizhou Municipality	9636	219.08	785.26	132.31	376.20	330.20	276.75	35844
恩施州	Enshi Prefecture	24061	332.70	670.81	143.86	244.42	197.32	282.53	20191
神农架	Shennongjia	3253	7.68	20.95	1.96	7.74	4.51	11.25	27280

22-2 续表 1 continued

指标	Item	固定资产投资总额(亿元) Investment in Fixed Assets (100 million yuan)	地方公共财政预算收入(亿元) Revenue of Local Governments (100 million yuan)	#地方税收(亿元) #Taxes (100 million yuan)	地方财政支出(亿元) Expenditures of Local Governments (100 million yuan)
合计	**Total**	**11935.98**	**1070.39**	**691.23**	**2508.53**
宜昌市	Yichang Municipality	2921.38	339.10	200.00	537.53
荆州市	Jingzhou Municipality	1853.59	103.95	74.95	346.48
襄阳市	Xiangyang Municipality	2921.78	339.10	210.67	584.50
荆门市	Jingmen Municipality	1404.58	80.43	56.47	225.90
十堰市	Shiyan Municipality	1225.51	93.38	66.30	307.65
随州市	Suizhou Municipality	907.68	43.34	29.25	153.10
恩施州	Enshi Prefecture	666.11	67.23	51.26	332.59
神农架	Shennongjia	35.35	3.86	2.33	20.78

农村居民人均可支配收入(元) Annual Per Capita Disposable Income of Rural Households (yuan)	城镇居民人均可支配收入(元) Annual Per Capita Disposable Income of Urban Households (yuan)	农林牧渔业产值(现价)(亿元) Gross Output Value of Agriculture (100 million yuan)	粮食产量(万吨) Output of Grain (10 000 tons)	棉花产量(万吨) Output of Cotton (10 000 tons)	油料产量(万吨) Output of Oil-bearing Crops (10 000 tons)	工业企业单位数(个) Number of Enterprises (unit)
12193	**25224**	**3123.12**	**1815.76**	**14.86**	**179.11**	**7990**
12990	27275	617.68	170.79	1.62	24.19	1543
13728	25382	631.45	410.74	7.71	59.93	1258
13650	26282	725.55	505.32	2.58	24.08	1826
14716	26731	365.84	278.18	2.14	40.04	1132
7779	24057	286.78	117.64	0.01	13.35	976
13022	22791	244.36	163.42	0.80	6.98	688
7969	22198	247.39	167.41		10.50	557
7578	21404	4.07	2.26		0.04	10

22-2 续表 2 continued

指标	Item	房地产企业房屋竣工面积合计(万平方米) Floor Space of Building Completed of the Real Enterprises Estate (10 000 sq.m)	房地产企业房屋竣工价值(亿元) Value of Building Completed of the Real Enterprises Estate (100 million yuan)	社会消费品零售总额(亿元) Total Retail Sales(100 million yuan)
合计	**Total**	**1029.97**	**233.50**	**5240.62**
宜昌市	Yichang Municipality	189.34	48.63	1089.47
荆州市	Jingzhou Municipality	72.82	18.37	946.14
襄阳市	Xiangyang Municipality	237.83	58.83	1165.10
荆门市	Jingmen Municipality	240.49	45.13	541.43
十堰市	Shiyan Municipality	89.16	20.37	639.41
随州市	Suizhou Municipality	92.91	20.06	399.57
恩施州	Enshi Prefecture	107.42	22.11	445.97
神农架	Shennongjia			13.54

实际使用外资(万美元) Actually Foreign Direct Investments (USD 10 000)	入境旅游者人数(万人次) Number of International Tourists (10 000 person-times)	国际旅游外汇收入(万美元) Foreign Exchange Earnings (USD 10 000)	金融机构(含外资)本外币贷款余额(亿元) Financial Institutions Local & Foreign Currency Balance of Loans (100 million yuan)
192976	**105.73**	**32292.79**	**7839.77**
34044	39.32	12430.52	2133.19
13295	2.00	507.53	1070.63
72779	5.27	3692.28	1683.60
34000	1.79	846.51	793.90
23805	18.27	5908.31	1030.92
11398	1.04	507.79	453.58
3655	33.91	7542.42	659.42
	4.12	857.43	14.53

23 县域经济主要指标

Economy of Cities and Counties

23-1 县市主要经济指标
MAIN ECONOMIC INDICATORS OF COUNTIES

指标名称	Item	土地面积(平方公里) Land Area(Sq. km)	常住人口(万人) The Resident (10 000 persons)		#城镇人口(万人) #Urban Population (10 000 persons)		#乡村人口(万人) #Rural Population (10 000 persons)	
		2015	2014	2015	2014	2015	2014	2015
蔡甸区	Caidian District	1108	43.90	45.10	24.00	24.89	19.90	20.21
江夏区	Jiangxia District	2010	84.65	87.70	43.72	45.41	40.93	42.29
黄陂区	Huangpi District	2261	91.10	94.51	38.55	41.74	52.55	52.77
新洲区	Xinzhou District	1500	86.00	88.27	43.05	44.32	42.95	43.95
汉南区	Hannan District	288	12.90	13.10	7.54	7.67	5.36	5.43
阳新县	Yangxin County	2783	82.34	82.75	28.07	28.94	54.27	53.81
大冶市	Daye City	1566	90.13	90.54	48.59	49.23	41.54	41.31
郧阳区	Yun County	3863	56.31	56.36	20.78	23.68	35.53	32.68
郧西县	Yunxi County	3509	45.11	45.21	15.56	16.07	29.55	29.14
竹山县	Zhushan County	3299	41.29	41.38	14.79	15.25	26.50	26.13
竹溪县	Zhuxi County	3585	31.08	31.15	10.64	10.98	20.44	20.17
房县	Fang County	5110	39.44	39.58	14.22	14.70	25.22	24.88
丹江口市	Danjiangkou City	3121	39.65	39.80	19.21	19.90	20.44	19.90
夷陵区	Yiling District	3425	52.29	52.41	24.93	26.26	27.36	26.15
远安县	Yuanan County	1752	18.67	18.73	8.46	8.81	10.21	9.92
兴山县	Xingshan County	2328	17.07	17.10	7.42	7.62	9.65	9.48
秭归县	Zigui County	2427	36.13	36.17	13.20	13.63	22.93	22.54
长阳县	Changyang Tujia A.C.	3430	38.60	38.64	11.59	12.13	27.01	26.51
五峰县	Wufeng Tujia A.C.	2072	18.77	18.82	6.65	6.84	12.12	11.98
宜都市	Yidu City	1357	38.90	39.00	20.63	21.32	18.27	17.68
当阳市	Dangyang City	2159	46.77	46.86	22.27	23.13	24.50	23.73
枝江市	Zhijiang City	1310	50.05	50.15	26.26	27.18	23.79	22.97
襄州区	Xiangzhou District	2306	83.00	83.50	43.58	45.19	39.42	38.31
南漳县	Nanzhang County	3859	53.92	54.05	20.97	21.74	32.95	32.31
谷城县	Gucheng County	2553	50.21	50.65	22.08	23.32	28.13	27.33
保康县	Baokang County	3225	22.17	22.50	8.73	9.20	13.44	13.30
老河口市	Laohekou City	1032	48.47	48.53	24.52	25.48	23.95	23.05
枣阳市	Zaoyang City	3277	98.95	99.10	50.72	51.33	48.23	47.77
宜城市	Yicheng City	2115	52.02	52.16	23.51	24.62	28.51	27.54
梁子湖区	Liangzihu District	500	14.42	14.43	5.49	5.69	8.93	8.74
华容区	Huarong District	493	23.98	24.01	11.62	11.82	12.36	12.19
鄂城区	Echeng District	600	67.48	67.51	50.21	50.62	17.27	16.89
东宝区	Dongbao District	1645	34.13	34.67	24.74	23.65	12.39	11.02
京山县	Jingshan County	3520	54.70	55.01	28.08	29.68	26.62	25.33
沙洋县	Shayang County	2044	57.41	57.44	20.75	21.55	36.66	35.89

23-1 续表 1 continued

指标名称	Item	土地面积(平方公里) Land Area(Sq. km)	常住人口(万人) The Resident (10 000 persons)		#城镇人口(万人) #Urban Population (10 000 persons)		#乡村人口(万人) #Rural Population (10 000 persons)	
		2015	2014	2015	2014	2015	2014	2015
钟祥市	Zhongxiang City	4488	91.22	92.10	46.89	49.69	44.33	42.41
孝南区	Xiaonan District	1020	91.77	92.20	64.48	65.63	27.29	26.57
孝昌县	Xiaochang County	1217	59.45	59.63	22.16	23.16	37.29	36.47
大悟县	Dawu County	1979	61.90	62.05	25.88	26.93	36.02	35.12
云梦县	Yunmeng County	604	52.84	53.00	25.54	26.52	27.30	26.48
应城市	Yingcheng City	1103	59.81	60.01	34.12	35.05	25.69	24.96
安陆市	Anlu City	1355	57.72	57.92	27.82	28.84	29.90	29.08
汉川市	Hanchuan City	1632	102.64	102.99	54.00	55.33	48.64	47.66
荆州区	Jingzhou District	1046	57.27	57.47	42.78	43.18	14.49	14.29
江陵县	Jiangling County	981	33.25	33.16	11.44	11.95	21.81	21.21
公安县	Gongan County	2258	89.99	88.01	37.62	38.90	52.37	49.11
监利县	Jianli County	3460	107.93	106.99	43.42	43.30	64.51	63.69
石首市	Shishou City	1424	57.64	57.12	25.42	26.15	32.22	30.97
洪湖市	Honghu City	2221	85.90	84.90	35.13	36.28	50.77	48.62
松滋市	Songci City	2235	77.36	77.46	35.12	36.61	42.24	40.85
黄州区	Huangzhou District	353	37.22	37.68	28.14	28.62	9.08	9.06
团风县	Tuanfeng County	833	34.06	34.26	12.14	12.62	21.92	21.64
红安县	Hongan County	1789	60.19	60.45	23.29	24.18	36.90	36.27
罗田县	Luotian County	2129	54.69	54.94	21.14	21.89	33.55	33.05
英山县	Yingshan County	1449	35.92	36.10	13.55	14.05	22.37	22.05
浠水县	Xishui County	1949	87.76	88.15	32.28	33.59	55.48	54.56
蕲春县	Qichun County	2398	77.36	77.66	29.83	30.97	47.53	46.69
黄梅县	Huangmei County	1246	86.37	86.47	34.23	35.29	52.14	51.18
麻城市	Macheng City	1701	82.54	82.70	34.83	36.41	47.71	46.29
武穴市	Wuxue City	3599	60.14	60.50	29.65	30.56	30.49	29.94
咸安区	Xian'an District	1504	51.95	52.41	35.42	35.79	16.53	16.62
嘉鱼县	Jiayu County	1017	31.67	31.40	14.08	14.46	17.59	16.94
通城县	Tongcheng County	1141	40.72	41.04	15.98	16.77	24.74	24.27
崇阳县	Chongyang County	1968	39.80	40.14	16.95	17.53	22.85	22.61
通山县	Tongshan County	2680	36.38	37.08	13.97	14.96	22.41	22.12
赤壁市	Chibi City	1723	48.40	48.63	24.78	25.83	23.62	22.80
曾都区	Zengdu District	1425	58.57	58.60	39.02	39.74	19.55	18.86
随县	Sui Country	5673	79.34	79.54	25.05	26.57	54.29	52.97
广水市	Guangshui City	2641	76.37	76.56	34.75	35.66	41.62	40.90
恩施市	Enshi City	3972	76.58	76.87	38.37	39.76	38.21	37.11
利川市	Lichuan City	4603	65.95	66.20	24.84	26.00	41.11	40.20
建始县	Jianshi County	2666	41.54	41.64	14.22	14.99	27.32	26.65
巴东县	Badong County	3354	42.44	42.50	14.12	14.64	28.32	27.86
宣恩县	Xuanen County	2730	30.19	30.26	9.40	9.99	20.79	20.27
咸丰县	Xianfeng County	2520	30.42	30.48	11.24	11.62	19.18	18.86
来凤县	Laifeng County	1344	24.50	24.55	8.78	9.32	15.72	15.23
鹤峰县	Hefeng County	2872	20.15	20.20	6.36	6.68	13.79	13.52
仙桃市	Xiantiao City	2520	115.30	115.50	61.40	63.06	53.90	52.44
潜江市	Qianjiang City	1930	95.44	95.80	49.82	51.25	45.62	44.55
天门市	Tianmen City	2528	129.16	129.20	63.59	65.25	65.57	63.95

23-1 续表 2 continued

指标名称	Item	地区生产总值(亿元) Gross RegionalProduct (100million yuan)		人均地区生产总值(元) Per CapitaGDP(yuan)		固定资产投资(亿元) Investment inFixed Assets(100 million yuan)		社会消费品零售总额(亿元) Total Retail Sales (100 million yuan)	
		2014	2015	2014	2015	2014	2015	2014	2015
蔡甸区	Caidian District	345.27	377.59	79082	84852	398.12	348.93	82.18	98.05
江夏区	Jiangxia District	583.37	637.93	69429	74027	487.85	590.90	135.74	173.60
黄陂区	Huangpi District	506.51	563.76	56005	60747	545.97	627.22	204.89	223.83
新洲区	Xinzhou District	501.57	559.78	58468	64243	400.64	502.28	177.03	158.47
汉南区	Hannan District	112.05	120.67	87607	92823	128.39	94.66	21.07	21.85
阳新县	Yangxin County	184.10	190.08	22381	23027	229.78	274.25	93.37	103.95
大冶市	Daye City	500.12	509.98	55541	56454	528.71	645.52	179.13	184.76
郧阳区	Yun County	82.82	91.25	14727	16198	135.92	160.38	56.24	61.66
郧西县	Yunxi County	59.04	61.39	13095	13594	62.30	73.21	37.79	41.40
竹山县	Zhushan County	74.19	79.75	17974	19294	117.77	138.50	36.93	42.73
竹溪县	Zhuxi County	62.02	66.61	19975	21408	64.95	76.05	26.81	30.32
房县	Fang County	66.08	71.04	16766	17980	112.28	131.60	41.18	45.85
丹江口市	Danjiangkou City	165.81	182.04	42127	45825	159.51	188.39	65.28	69.13
夷陵区	Yiling District	441.24	486.93	84424	93014	392.72	491.03	98.37	111.71
远安县	Yuanan County	172.02	190.09	92211	101652	184.50	225.11	35.06	40.12
兴山县	Xingshan County	86.47	95.06	50687	55639	33.77	41.89	24.66	28.53
秭归县	Zigui County	100.53	110.09	27831	30454	92.26	111.74	33.34	38.40
长阳县	Changyang Tujia A.C.	109.88	120.46	28473	31191	71.04	86.24	38.71	43.25
五峰县	Wufeng Tujia A.C.	55.28	60.23	29477	32046	43.01	52.41	16.75	19.19
宜都市	Yidu City	454.93	501.00	117023	128626	439.68	550.48	87.40	98.79
当阳市	Dangyang City	395.48	435.04	84568	92927	339.75	425.68	106.46	120.53
枝江市	Zhijiang City	389.63	429.70	77839	85768	335.62	442.49	103.52	119.07
襄州区	Xiangzhou District	501.53	550.92	60465	66177	447.90	504.63	142.67	159.85
南漳县	Nanzhang County	192.86	212.02	35745	39274	172.11	230.61	79.45	89.34
谷城县	Gucheng County	265.58	290.82	53000	57668	210.43	252.08	80.38	93.90
保康县	Baokang County	92.15	100.79	41342	45126	126.63	121.73	38.71	43.40
老河口市	Laohekou City	268.46	293.74	55450	60565	217.87	260.99	95.62	107.76
枣阳市	Zaoyang City	479.57	527.09	48532	53228	211.00	430.58	121.38	171.33
宜城市	Yicheng City	259.90	283.66	50058	54456	209.97	221.11	83.37	93.18
梁子湖区	Liangzihu District	56.36	59.65	39125	41352	46.11	62.25	16.67	18.06
华容区	Huarong District	217.23	230.29	90664	95974	299.60	361.62	42.15	66.61
鄂城区	Echeng District	416.38	441.40	61755	65397	340.50	382.34	174.39	173.45
东宝区	Dongbao District	262.91	284.20	70818	82616	274.55	365.16	137.15	161.78
京山县	Jingshan County	291.02	307.51	53218	56059	297.58	424.95	116.82	142.93
沙洋县	Shayang County	213.96	224.68	37279	39126	139.66	174.58	66.92	74.92

23-1 续表 3 continued

指标名称	Item	地区生产总值(亿元) Gross RegionalProduct (100million yuan)		人均地区生产总值(元) Per CapitaGDP(yuan)		固定资产投资(亿元) Investment inFixed Assets(100 million yuan)		社会消费品零售总额(亿元) Total Retail Sales (100 million yuan)	
		2014	2015	2014	2015	2014	2015	2014	2015
钟祥市	Zhongxiang City	361.83	382.46	39807	41726	330.13	453.00	133.64	169.42
孝南区	Xiaonan District	248.70	268.56	27124	29196	296.42	361.63	123.38	149.06
孝昌县	Xiaochang County	97.31	104.28	16383	17514	110.53	131.78	45.47	56.54
大悟县	Dawu County	110.25	118.84	17825	19175	161.64	192.46	61.15	74.79
云梦县	Yunmeng County	185.19	196.67	35077	37164	198.32	122.53	88.55	100.89
应城市	Yingcheng City	220.60	239.08	36914	39907	214.94	252.09	112.80	124.65
安陆市	Anlu City	157.26	172.22	27269	29786	163.19	226.26	89.50	99.47
汉川市	Hanchuan City	386.15	416.13	37655	40474	294.59	360.61	171.71	188.50
荆州区	Jingzhou District	216.72	226.99	37958	39565	261.58	288.93	128.19	136.85
江陵县	Jiangling County	62.21	68.32	18511	20575	57.68	75.52	31.16	40.13
公安县	Gongan County	194.89	210.00	21701	23595	206.18	249.59	112.24	127.27
监利县	Jianli County	214.78	229.33	19726	21341	154.72	188.06	108.81	132.39
石首市	Shishou City	136.29	149.77	23868	26101	143.06	171.68	87.72	91.75
洪湖市	Honghu City	182.42	196.44	21362	23003	120.00	104.57	93.52	100.37
松滋市	Songci City	200.81	218.72	25960	28255	203.89	244.80	106.39	109.36
黄州区	Huangzhou District	173.97	188.69	46936	50385	220.12	283.41	94.09	117.59
团风县	Tuanfeng County	71.76	75.45	21042	22087	68.46	73.00	22.61	31.25
红安县	Hongan County	120.76	130.05	20031	21560	143.23	169.06	51.50	61.72
罗田县	Luotian County	105.66	112.75	19321	20569	139.79	164.66	49.23	60.99
英山县	Yingshan County	78.55	82.89	21870	23019	73.79	87.00	25.67	32.75
浠水县	Xishui County	183.18	199.28	20886	22657	163.20	192.39	97.08	118.35
蕲春县	Qichun County	180.44	193.50	23376	24965	210.90	249.41	88.07	107.16
黄梅县	Huangmei County	163.43	174.22	18924	20160	172.50	190.79	94.52	114.31
麻城市	Macheng City	226.21	244.31	27492	29570	267.15	301.37	103.63	124.57
武穴市	Wuxue City	224.59	240.72	34484	39907	207.24	247.30	96.44	115.79
咸安区	Xian'an District	225.15	240.34	43465	46060	307.11	334.21	92.24	105.41
嘉鱼县	Jiayu County	189.03	201.06	59735	63758	198.03	235.83	47.69	51.72
通城县	Tongcheng County	103.84	108.97	25460	26656	116.54	137.66	47.75	52.65
崇阳县	Chongyang County	96.95	102.23	24378	25577	119.35	142.23	44.71	50.00
通山县	Tongshan County	90.10	95.23	24780	25927	133.40	182.18	41.29	86.96
赤壁市	Chibi City	316.39	341.36	65437	70362	309.18	467.51	111.95	149.16
曾都区	Zengdu District	334.15	360.91	53447	61605	314.98	390.65	162.43	179.89
随县	Sui Country	164.82	178.13	23055	22423	217.95	257.40	103.45	115.77
广水市	Guangshui City	228.01	246.22	29885	32200	235.89	278.33	91.70	103.55
恩施市	Enshi City	157.28	171.39	20453	22338	128.81	157.78	78.25	139.93
利川市	Lichuan City	90.97	98.86	13729	14962	82.89	102.89	35.64	79.04
建始县	Jianshi County	71.30	77.78	17105	18702	66.11	81.65	22.98	49.78
巴东县	Badong County	81.45	88.85	19208	20921	74.52	91.74	26.86	50.63
宣恩县	Xuanen County	50.26	55.01	16596	18200	33.21	40.51	15.08	34.00
咸丰县	Xianfeng County	60.66	66.20	19866	21741	46.54	57.47	22.54	36.56
来凤县	Laifeng County	53.01	57.86	21584	23592	50.12	62.02	19.67	32.29
鹤峰县	Hefeng County	43.62	47.72	21630	23653	37.35	45.56	18.87	26.03
仙桃市	Xiantiao City	552.27	597.61	47387	51786	374.73	445.50	233.58	266.17
潜江市	Qianjiang City	540.22	557.57	56662	58310	369.34	435.52	150.19	186.14
天门市	Tianmen City	401.86	440.10	31145	34069	316.78	373.41	231.05	258.90

23-1 续表 4 continued

指标名称	Item	财政总收入(亿元) TotalFiscal Revenue (100 million yuan)		地方公共财政预算收入(亿元) Revenue of LocalGovernments (100 million yuan)		#税收(亿元) Taxes(100 million yuan)	
		2014	2015	2014	2015	2014	2015
蔡甸区	Caidian District	41.33	46.19	26.79	30.62	16.83	18.25
江夏区	Jiangxia District	87.23	99.41	62.82	70.19	47.03	52.89
黄陂区	Huangpi District	64.35	64.52	46.74	48.32	32.82	31.61
新洲区	Xinzhou District	43.08	49.50	28.60	32.82	19.04	22.40
汉南区	Hannan District	22.58	24.01	13.11	14.58	11.69	13.22
阳新县	Yangxin County	15.10	18.08	10.24	12.58	6.80	7.56
大冶市	Daye City	67.34	71.73	40.48	45.18	28.30	31.05
郧阳区	Yun County	9.85	10.67	6.00	7.07	4.42	5.05
郧西县	Yunxi County	4.13	4.66	3.00	3.43	2.14	2.35
竹山县	Zhushan County	6.08	7.17	4.56	5.22	3.28	3.56
竹溪县	Zhuxi County	5.14	5.89	3.80	4.35	2.77	2.95
房县	Fang County	5.49	6.18	4.02	4.64	2.89	3.07
丹江口市	Danjiangkou City	17.22	19.46	11.53	13.21	8.02	8.80
夷陵区	Yiling District	48.62	57.65	33.89	42.36	22.01	25.42
远安县	Yuanan County	14.72	17.02	11.74	14.69	8.00	8.80
兴山县	Xingshan County	10.62	12.72	7.57	9.50	4.81	6.08
秭归县	Zigui County	9.67	11.63	7.84	9.84	5.39	6.03
长阳县	Changyang Tujia A.C.	9.03	10.73	7.28	9.11	4.43	5.49
五峰县	Wufeng Tujia A.C.	3.82	4.62	2.91	3.64	2.13	2.25
宜都市	Yidu City	41.50	50.29	36.62	44.97	24.14	27.39
当阳市	Dangyang City	32.78	39.19	25.03	31.29	16.87	19.85
枝江市	Zhijiang City	32.37	38.05	25.32	31.68	18.45	20.45
襄州区	Xiangzhou District	28.99	38.58	23.81	33.55	17.22	21.44
南漳县	Nanzhang County	12.24	16.38	10.37	14.12	7.83	9.83
谷城县	Gucheng County	20.02	25.39	15.98	21.77	10.71	13.65
保康县	Baokang County	11.44	13.64	9.13	11.51	5.52	6.94
老河口市	Laohekou City	24.12	31.16	21.00	28.60	13.85	17.29
枣阳市	Zaoyang City	29.43	39.34	26.25	35.76	17.34	21.54
宜城市	Yicheng City	21.37	28.98	19.08	25.97	11.56	14.19
梁子湖区	Liangzihu District	3.05	3.54	2.45	2.79	1.79	1.91
华容区	Huarong District	6.66	7.58	4.97	5.88	3.53	4.04
鄂城区	Echeng District	17.64	16.24	13.09	12.21	9.42	8.07
东宝区	Dongbao District	23.14	27.26	17.19	20.05	15.67	18.18
京山县	Jingshan County	16.99	18.14	12.75	14.79	9.06	9.78
沙洋县	Shayang County	7.52	8.40	5.81	6.70	3.99	4.65

23-1 续表 5 continued

指标名称	Item	财政总收入(亿元) TotalFiscal Revenue (100 million yuan)		地方公共财政预算收入(亿元) Revenue of Local Governments (100 million yuan)		*税收(亿元) Taxes(100 million yuan)	
		2014	2015	2014	2015	2014	2015
钟祥市	Zhongxiang City	19.56	22.35	15.15	17.58	9.46	11.03
孝南区	Xiaonan District	23.78	26.89	16.56	19.24	11.07	12.83
孝昌县	Xiaochang County	10.19	11.49	8.01	8.90	4.86	5.35
大悟县	Dawu County	11.83	13.29	7.93	8.81	4.77	5.31
云梦县	Yunmeng County	14.41	16.59	10.98	12.75	7.04	8.21
应城市	Yingcheng City	20.08	21.48	14.17	15.82	9.08	10.31
安陆市	Anlu City	12.13	13.36	8.75	10.27	6.25	7.20
汉川市	Hanchuan City	26.90	29.60	17.50	20.26	12.18	14.63
荆州区	Jingzhou District	19.90	22.02	13.20	14.41	11.11	12.32
江陵县	Jiangling County	3.54	4.26	2.44	3.02	1.60	1.90
公安县	Gongan County	12.33	14.21	9.20	10.30	6.22	7.03
监利县	Jianli County	7.49	9.78	5.42	7.32	4.58	5.56
石首市	Shishou City	9.64	11.95	6.19	7.34	4.31	5.27
洪湖市	Honghu City	8.94	10.61	6.62	8.03	4.77	5.80
松滋市	Songci City	18.81	21.51	10.80	12.66	7.27	8.42
黄州区	Huangzhou District	14.18	18.53	10.58	12.70	7.83	9.66
团风县	Tuanfeng County	5.80	6.65	4.32	4.98	2.90	3.35
红安县	Hongan County	20.47	23.83	10.37	13.11	7.27	9.28
罗田县	Luotian County	7.33	8.37	5.37	6.29	3.55	4.19
英山县	Yingshan County	4.54	5.17	3.34	3.93	2.34	2.78
浠水县	Xishui County	10.18	11.45	7.52	8.65	4.93	5.69
蕲春县	Qichun County	13.66	15.40	10.02	11.56	6.36	7.20
黄梅县	Huangmei County	11.72	12.98	8.84	10.19	5.62	6.52
麻城市	Macheng City	17.62	19.86	13.03	14.99	8.51	9.84
武穴市	Wuxue City	16.79	19.80	12.82	15.24	8.52	9.70
咸安区	Xian'an District	15.41	19.57	11.51	14.42	9.09	10.83
嘉鱼县	Jiayu County	11.18	11.32	8.80	9.35	6.27	6.12
通城县	Tongcheng County	8.11	8.41	5.83	6.04	3.72	3.63
崇阳县	Chongyang County	6.81	7.60	5.30	6.19	3.52	3.88
通山县	Tongshan County	7.32	7.19	5.81	5.90	4.01	3.67
赤壁市	Chibi City	20.63	23.87	15.75	17.02	10.48	10.86
曾都区	Zengdu District	19.97	22.92	14.91	16.96	11.93	13.12
随县	Sui Country	6.42	8.00	4.11	5.20	2.90	3.61
广水市	Guangshui City	17.80	20.82	8.73	10.60	6.26	6.97
恩施市	Enshi City	23.50	27.01	18.33	21.44	15.94	17.51
利川市	Lichuan City	15.18	15.97	8.76	9.74	6.63	7.05
建始县	Jianshi County	8.48	8.90	4.62	5.15	3.57	4.01
巴东县	Badong County	7.72	8.17	5.42	5.86	4.05	4.31
宣恩县	Xuanen County	3.69	4.20	2.59	2.98	2.21	2.48
咸丰县	Xianfeng County	5.77	6.14	3.41	3.68	2.45	2.65
来凤县	Laifeng County	6.86	7.35	3.14	3.73	2.56	3.01
鹤峰县	Hefeng County	3.57	4.58	2.36	3.03	2.01	2.34
仙桃市	Xiantiao City	36.51	41.89	24.16	27.69	19.41	22.07
潜江市	Qianjiang City	34.05	33.97	22.69	22.85	16.63	15.45
天门市	Tianmen City	22.25	25.24	17.35	19.59	12.10	13.67

23-1 续表 6 continued

指标名称	Item	外贸出口(万美元) Total Exports(USD 10 000)		城镇居民人均可支配收入(元) Annual Per Capita Disposable Income of Urban(yuan)		农村居民人均可支配收入(元) Annual Per Capita Disposable Income of RuralHouseholds(yuan)	
		2014	2015	2014	2015	2014	2015
蔡甸区	Caidian District	47271	51555	24735	27060	15021	16502
江夏区	Jiangxia District	16933	24560	24309	26716	15101	16641
黄陂区	Huangpi District	9073	18163	24103	26562	14713	16228
新洲区	Xinzhou District	18382	20037	22503	24798	14410	15894
汉南区	Hannan District	13016		24496	26946	15292	16653
阳新县	Yangxin County	25129	32108	17900	19960	8379	9267
大冶市	Daye City	32826	46659	28473	30848	14523	15861
郧阳区	Yun County	6516	7461	20247	21867	7038	7783
郧西县	Yunxi County	1654	2417	19193	20853	6805	7509
竹山县	Zhushan County	1928	3927	18894	20549	6900	7628
竹溪县	Zhuxi County	1603	2149	18507	20076	6818	7550
房县	Fang County	3889	4758	19888	21622	6878	7592
丹江口市	Danjiangkou City	3008	4072	21002	22827	7728	8553
夷陵区	Yiling District	8651	10110	25778	28202	14389	15793
远安县	Yuanan County	11639	13425	23587	25817	13401	14715
兴山县	Xingshan County	28517	44684	20552	22478	8757	9610
秭归县	Zigui County	5971	6926	19937	21810	7336	8062
长阳县	Changyang Tujia A.C.	5552	6410	20580	22525	7448	8148
五峰县	Wufeng Tujia A.C.	926	1065	18761	20508	7164	7880
宜都市	Yidu City	37006	43281	26213	28651	15035	16449
当阳市	Dangyang City	10384	11958	24716	27068	15114	16512
枝江市	Zhijiang City	25158	31088	23675	25955	15285	16697
襄州区	Xiangzhou District	30726	40954	22354	24330	13585	14808
南漳县	Nanzhang County	9475	12159	22160	24265	11351	12350
谷城县	Gucheng County	13646	18668	22484	24710	11620	12651
保康县	Baokang County	4690	5597	19817	21710	8376	9165
老河口市	Laohekou City	26489	33815	23975	26301	13401	14607
枣阳市	Zaoyang City	21649	27184	24665	27040	13100	14280
宜城市	Yicheng City	18734	22442	22243	24367	13263	14430
梁子湖区	Liangzihu District	172	201	17380	18930	9704	10563
华容区	Huarong District	6505	8287	20428	22284	13273	14476
鄂城区	Echeng District	13705	14451	23836	25936	13766	14959
东宝区	Dongbao District	7399	8700	26498	28756	13622	14872
京山县	Jingshan County	17183	20572	23649	25780	13495	14731
沙洋县	Shayang County	11395	14003	23465	25576	13255	14469

23-1 续表 7 continued

指标名称	Item	外贸出口(万美元) Total Exports(USD 10 000)		城镇居民人均可支配收入(元) Annual Per CapitaDisposable Income of Urban(yuan)		农村居民人均可支配收入(元) Annual Per CapitaDisposable Income of RuralHouseholds(yuan)	
		2014	2015	2014	2015	2014	2015
钟 祥 市	Zhongxiang City	21903	25035	23681	25821	13839	15106
孝 南 区	Xiaonan District	16769	18156	25155	27580	13153	14420
孝 昌 县	Xiaochang County	4207	4792	20620	22567	7774	8540
大 悟 县	Dawu County	1880	2131	20846	22803	7957	8742
云 梦 县	Yunmeng County	13385	15904	23710	26083	13605	14931
应 城 市	Yingcheng City	8505	10354	24047	26483	13923	15177
安 陆 市	Anlu City	6111	7173	23050	25364	11731	12796
汉 川 市	Hanchuan City	43039	38376	23760	26131	13308	14664
荆 州 区	Jingzhou District	10629	7096	25846	28397	14158	15431
江 陵 县	Jiangling County	974	963	20644	22652	11258	12244
公 安 县	Gongan County	7645	7414	21991	24155	13182	14410
监 利 县	Jianli County	6525	4887	20609	22579	12308	13327
石 首 市	Shishou City	17041	9626	21621	23850	12476	13600
洪 湖 市	Honghu City	6836	1828	21414	23630	12364	13400
松 滋 市	Songci City	10745	16003	21995	24255	12678	13850
黄 州 区	Huangzhou District	9714	6477	23242	25538	11566	12573
团 风 县	Tuanfeng County	1160	1276	18988	20699	8635	9428
红 安 县	Hongan County	1523	1680	19516	21202	8057	8826
罗 田 县	Luotian County	4878	5662	19206	21027	7790	8493
英 山 县	Yingshan County	1418	1697	18840	20502	8364	9072
浠 水 县	Xishui County	5317	6044	20284	22172	9965	10899
蕲 春 县	Qichun County	8462	9768	20013	21848	9424	10341
黄 梅 县	Huangmei County	3739	4527	20738	22733	10453	11413
麻 城 市	Macheng City	4496	5079	21209	23279	9038	9841
武 穴 市	Wuxue City	12705	15417	22005	24003	10927	12011
咸 安 区	Xian'an District	10962	12749	23758	25896	12080	13243
嘉 鱼 县	Jiayu County	7888	8843	21286	23245	12551	13760
通 城 县	Tongcheng County	5238	3907	20547	22375	10661	11679
崇 阳 县	Chongyang County	2139	2393	19422	21131	10253	11247
通 山 县	Tongshan County	1079	1270	18073	19654	8050	8851
赤 壁 市	Chibi City	8551	9968	22273	24248	12400	13616
曾 都 区	Zengdu District	71026	64659	22939	24985	12535	13785
随 县	Sui Country	48447	45128	18897	20733	12067	13109
广 水 市	Guangshui City	7976	7973	20769	22581	11743	12877
恩 施 市	Enshi City	12601	14109	22142	24226	7453	8274
利 川 市	Lichuan City	7201	8475	20092	22108	7091	7839
建 始 县	Jianshi County	3992	4819	19018	20767	7145	7920
巴 东 县	Badong County	6819	7711	19123	21058	7140	7893
宣 恩 县	Xuanen County	2779	3219	18870	20606	7048	7805
咸 丰 县	Xianfeng County	4797	5505	18919	20775	7077	7856
来 凤 县	Laifeng County	2220	2696	19398	21388	7050	7794
鹤 峰 县	Hefeng County	5265	5933	19231	21118	7546	8372
仙 桃 市	Xiantiao City	52134	68922	22503	24641	13193	14422
潜 江 市	Qianjiang City	43778	29353	22609	24721	12862	14076
天 门 市	Tianmen City	7054	10472	20622	22618	12086	13178

23-1 续表 8 continued

指标名称	Item	农业总产值(亿元) Total Value of Agricultural Output(100 million yuan)		农产品加工业产值(亿元) Value of Agricultural Product Processing(100 million yuan)		常用耕地面积(千公顷) Area of Cultivated Land (1000 hectare)		粮食产量(万吨) Output of Grain (10 000 tons)	
		2014	2015	2014	2015	2014	2015	2014	2015
蔡甸区	Caidian District	61.19	67.69	199.60	218.77	24.35	24.13	13.34	13.31
江夏区	Jiangxia District	138.68	153.77	100.56	113.25	35.69	35.69	29.24	29.21
黄陂区	Huangpi District	170.97	190.21	187.47	213.44	52.44	52.35	46.11	46.05
新洲区	Xinzhou District	127.18	138.83	106.28	125.40	50.47	50.35	32.51	32.40
汉南区	Hannan District	22.28	23.22	26.77	55.38	10.05	10.05	3.41	3.40
阳新县	Yangxin County	73.92	81.00	41.44	50.02	51.64	52.11	35.37	35.44
大冶市	Daye City	65.69	69.93	162.44	177.94	35.67	35.61	28.51	29.40
郧阳区	Yun County	43.41	45.51	41.33	54.78	35.25	35.69	23.73	23.23
郧西县	Yunxi County	41.32	43.33	7.10	6.31	26.84	26.83	19.05	19.50
竹山县	Zhushan County	41.40	43.29	20.40	19.20	32.71	32.87	23.53	22.98
竹溪县	Zhuxi County	43.11	44.99	15.35	15.26	29.53	28.92	24.11	23.57
房县	Fang County	46.57	49.27	27.44	32.53	28.14	27.62	14.90	15.40
丹江口市	Danjiangkou City	49.71	52.55	60.75	82.93	21.19	21.16	12.01	12.40
夷陵区	Yiling District	87.37	92.90	531.25	637.78	33.65	33.70	21.73	21.87
远安县	Yuanan County	28.53	30.35	61.04	71.90	11.98	11.99	10.38	10.47
兴山县	Xingshan County	18.90	20.12	19.50	18.48	16.21	16.21	5.99	6.03
秭归县	Zigui County	34.43	37.83	50.45	61.19	23.70	24.10	9.19	9.28
长阳县	Changyang Tujia A.C.	56.00	59.57	51.17	55.30	40.65	40.65	11.03	11.45
五峰县	Wufeng Tujia A.C.	32.22	34.28	23.49	24.71	20.43	20.41	8.44	8.91
宜都市	Yidu City	67.92	71.31	258.17	279.48	15.84	15.73	11.43	11.64
当阳市	Dangyang City	121.26	128.65	262.01	302.26	54.64	55.79	53.74	54.73
枝江市	Zhijiang City	117.42	124.92	341.26	435.62	45.52	45.60	34.82	35.46
襄州区	Xiangzhou District	164.46	170.27	255.19	281.88	110.35	110.69	136.14	136.46
南漳县	Nanzhang County		76.41	107.79	124.43	40.90	41.13	45.04	45.17
谷城县	Gucheng County	56.79	60.04	222.57	241.46	28.53	28.53	27.88	28.05
保康县	Baokang County	35.36	36.30	37.39	35.67	22.80	22.61	14.30	14.58
老河口市	Laohekou City	72.34	75.24	263.82	302.08	40.46	40.61	37.23	37.42
枣阳市	Zaoyang City	161.00	165.18	352.54	383.52	111.00	110.91	136.49	136.81
宜城市	Yicheng City	87.09	90.76	306.72	363.03	62.32	62.88	69.59	69.75
梁子湖区	Liangzihu District	41.55	43.50	7.10	7.70	14.61	15.16	10.99	10.44
华容区	Huarong District	43.93	45.99	138.90	155.91	14.11	16.07	11.67	11.05
鄂城区	Echeng District	57.64	60.34	40.69	44.44	12.15	15.74	13.72	12.65
东宝区	Dongbao District	27.14	28.23	73.08	66.74	20.26	20.63	17.32	17.41
京山县	Jingshan County	91.04	95.45	430.88	471.68	69.64	69.61	73.40	74.94
沙洋县	Shayang County	97.98	100.75	220.09	227.99	78.44	78.45	83.80	85.59

23-1 续表 9 continued

指标名称	Item	农业总产值(亿元) Total Value of Agricultural Output(100 million yuan)		农产品加工业产值(亿元) Value of Agricultural Product Processing(100 million yuan)		常用耕地面积(千公顷) Area of Cultivated Land (1000 hectare)		粮食产量(万吨) Output of Grain (10 000 tons)	
		2014	2015	2014	2015	2014	2015	2014	2015
钟祥市	Zhongxiang City	114.50	119.53	319.92	368.00	83.01	84.55	89.03	90.82
孝南区	Xiaonan District	54.11	54.77	142.18	149.46	34.10	34.10	21.87	22.15
孝昌县	Xiaochang County	54.15	54.74	15.06	20.88	32.71	32.72	26.92	27.50
大悟县	Dawu County	55.24	55.88	24.64	25.92	36.68	36.61	28.95	29.35
云梦县	Yunmeng County	60.88	61.62	153.86	114.77	25.52	25.53	22.05	22.53
应城市	Yingcheng City	79.28	80.17	131.61	127.02	38.56	38.59	36.90	37.32
安陆市	Anlu City	61.19	61.98	143.91	157.14	33.32	33.62	34.60	35.10
汉川市	Hanchuan City	104.40	106.51	582.44	644.87	65.98	65.73	55.69	56.63
荆州区	Jingzhou District	64.98	66.13	173.23	172.34	34.98	34.98	22.77	23.11
江陵县	Jiangling County	35.34	36.23	51.38	66.24	37.99	37.99	28.63	29.64
公安县	Gongan County	102.33	103.24	138.28	162.54	80.38	80.38	67.12	69.88
监利县	Jianli County	155.88	160.31	210.77	230.19	137.69	137.69	143.59	146.20
石首市	Shishou City	59.07	60.23	87.31	100.87	41.47	41.70	23.22	23.69
洪湖市	Honghu City	109.03	114.00	152.90	175.69	64.19	64.19	71.33	73.40
松滋市	Songci City	63.68	64.38	173.01	203.80	59.63	59.64	35.65	37.00
黄州区	Huangzhou District	20.98	22.30	68.41	61.68	10.75	10.71	5.70	5.82
团风县	Tuanfeng County	23.00	24.50	26.84	24.82	17.63	17.61	13.03	13.51
红安县	Hongan County	36.09	38.61	47.07	58.84	37.78	37.53	23.22	23.65
罗田县	Luotian County	38.71	42.04	23.60	26.72	26.35	26.35	25.60	25.98
英山县	Yingshan County	46.10	48.56	33.25	37.67	17.28	17.27	14.01	14.50
浠水县	Xishui County	90.16	94.02	89.53	89.27	44.63	44.86	51.07	51.62
蕲春县	Qichun County	68.05	71.90	117.82	128.51	40.96	40.95	52.96	53.67
黄梅县	Huangmei County	67.89	72.34	142.71	117.25	54.63	54.63	50.01	50.31
麻城市	Macheng City	86.33	91.42	73.57	127.00	53.05	58.05	55.36	56.14
武穴市	Wuxue City	73.77	78.32	80.35	87.61	36.77	38.66	32.38	33.66
咸安区	Xian'an District	44.25	48.30	205.04	226.43	35.16	35.22	19.38	19.59
嘉鱼县	Jiayu County	69.63	72.90	195.29	213.03	31.75	31.76	18.37	18.72
通城县	Tongcheng County	35.49	38.85	30.64	28.95	21.29	21.28	18.72	19.09
崇阳县	Chongyang County	39.25	41.38	19.27	15.56	23.21	22.87	20.26	20.68
通山县	Tongshan County	25.86	28.06	30.15	52.33	23.52	23.27	8.75	9.11
赤壁市	Chibi City	65.81	71.66	198.44	231.38	32.97	32.97	21.72	22.25
曾都区	Zengdu District	42.75	45.90	164.41	177.57	25.99	25.99	26.28	26.69
随县	Sui Country	105.01	115.61	158.22	167.62	78.30	78.33	92.62	93.74
广水市	Guangshui City	78.17	82.85	179.02	183.43	39.10	39.07	42.01	42.99
恩施市	Enshi City	42.56	44.26	66.40	85.49	47.08	46.48	23.39	23.72
利川市	Lichuan City	50.98	53.12	33.42	34.94	58.33	57.94	36.96	37.28
建始县	Jianshi County	30.39	31.85	13.98	16.50	34.35	34.27	23.40	23.66
巴东县	Badong County	28.52	29.83	19.89	24.77	36.32	36.32	22.59	22.96
宣恩县	Xuanen County	24.71	25.98	19.00	21.25	24.73	24.80	13.20	13.70
咸丰县	Xianfeng County	23.45	24.38	22.87	26.91	27.23	27.78	23.38	23.61
来凤县	Laifeng County	19.19	20.09	12.32	17.69	17.01	17.01	12.79	13.08
鹤峰县	Hefeng County	17.21	17.88	35.55	38.98	16.28	15.77	9.14	9.38
仙桃市	Xiantiao City	142.59	147.49	493.10	480.40	90.54	90.33	82.58	83.71
潜江市	Qianjiang City	114.24	119.24	473.80	512.53	72.18	72.19	53.27	53.49
天门市	Tianmen City	113.73	129.98	353.70	361.43	110.16	109.93	73.42	75.30

23-1 续表 10 continued

指标名称	Item	棉花产量(吨) Output of Cotton Cotton (ton)		油料产量(万吨) Output of Oil-bearing Crops(10 000 tons)		肉类产量(万吨) Output of Meat (10 000 tons)	
		2014	2015	2014	2015	2014	2015
蔡甸区	Caidian District	4278	4144	1.53	1.54	1.45	1.38
江夏区	Jiangxia District	196	160	4.27	4.05	8.09	8.08
黄陂区	Huangpi District	2450	2510	6.41	6.50	8.32	8.35
新洲区	Xinzhou District	9672	8233	5.47	5.48	3.72	3.24
汉南区	Hannan District	2794	812	0.14	0.13	1.91	1.57
阳新县	Yangxin County	2646	2099	4.84	4.85	4.26	4.14
大冶市	Daye City	2552	1960	4.36	4.37	4.62	4.44
郧阳区	Yun County	56	48	2.04	1.90	5.45	5.34
郧西县	Yunxi County	14		1.63	1.64	2.63	2.58
竹山县	Zhushan County			4.27	4.35	2.22	2.21
竹溪县	Zhuxi County			2.57	2.61	2.67	2.63
房县	Fang County	28	32	1.72	1.72	2.90	2.85
丹江口市	Danjiangkou City	22	27	1.08	1.07	2.54	2.51
夷陵区	Yiling District		8	2.86	3.06	8.44	7.54
远安县	Yuanan County			1.36	1.39	2.57	2.44
兴山县	Xingshan County			0.82	0.84	3.07	2.91
秭归县	Zigui County			1.40	1.42	4.80	5.07
长阳县	Changyang Tujia A.C.			1.35	1.33	7.55	7.60
五峰县	Wufeng Tujia A.C.			0.54	0.52	3.09	2.97
宜都市	Yidu City	25	28	2.13	2.17	6.83	6.72
当阳市	Dangyang City	5207	4733	7.54	7.55	9.22	9.16
枝江市	Zhijiang City	15126	11400	5.51	5.58	9.03	9.12
襄州区	Xiangzhou District	10283	8270	8.14	7.57	15.37	14.53
南漳县	Nanzhang County	343	138	0.94	0.99	10.37	10.48
谷城县	Gucheng County			1.45	1.46	6.59	6.28
保康县	Baokang County			1.06	1.08	3.17	3.06
老河口市	Laohekou City	4345	4220	2.17	2.12	6.76	6.34
枣阳市	Zaoyang City	6425	5849	1.47	1.49	12.07	12.47
宜城市	Yicheng City	6850	6600	7.35	7.28	8.57	8.98
梁子湖区	Liangzihu District	1281	416	1.68	1.72	2.56	2.79
华容区	Huarong District	2450	1891	2.31	2.12	2.42	2.79
鄂城区	Echeng District	1101	1593	2.16	2.33	9.71	2.80
东宝区	Dongbao District	850	909	3.20	3.25	5.27	4.58
京山县	Jingshan County	7927	3690	5.14	5.35	9.64	9.49
沙洋县	Shayang County	7017	3347	13.84	13.69	9.36	9.14

23-1 续表 11 continued

指标名称	Item	棉花产量(吨) Output of Cotton Cotton (ton)		油料产量(万吨) Output of Oil-bearing Crops(10 000 tons)		肉类产量(万吨) Output of Meat (10 000 tons)	
		2014	2015	2014	2015	2014	2015
钟祥市	Zhongxiang City	13621	13022	12.92	13.21	10.56	10.31
孝南区	Xiaonan District	5044	3721	2.98	3.02	2.56	2.41
孝昌县	Xiaochang County	1276	1039	3.73	3.79	4.38	4.58
大悟县	Dawu County	256	216	5.92	5.94	4.17	4.19
云梦县	Yunmeng County	2686	2018	2.10	2.12	3.74	3.56
应城市	Yingcheng City	3363	2516	3.23	3.19	3.84	3.77
安陆市	Anlu City	890	750	2.00	2.02	8.83	8.94
汉川市	Hanchuan City	17669	13218	3.82	3.70	5.57	5.62
荆州区	Jingzhou District	7130	5292	5.63	4.54	2.94	2.82
江陵县	Jiangling County	7068	5202	7.49	7.57	2.85	2.76
公安县	Gongan County	29815	24509	12.56	11.80	6.47	6.09
监利县	Jianli County	16787	13040	12.15	11.94	8.35	8.02
石首市	Shishou City	13841	11950	7.13	7.45	5.10	4.86
洪湖市	Honghu City	6798	5468	9.01	8.58	3.58	3.59
松滋市	Songci City	11200	7979	7.41	7.14	10.14	9.74
黄州区	Huangzhou District	5800	4508	0.60	0.64	1.02	0.70
团风县	Tuanfeng County	3532	2466	2.38	2.37	1.97	1.19
红安县	Hongan County	1062	818	10.06	9.73	4.92	5.33
罗田县	Luotian County	368	280	2.98	2.73	3.08	2.74
英山县	Yingshan County	506	399	1.74	1.82	1.88	1.90
浠水县	Xishui County	8046	6028	7.84	8.04	8.16	7.19
蕲春县	Qichun County	5008	3564	5.39	5.78	7.64	7.02
黄梅县	Huangmei County	9580	6886	6.64	6.82	5.48	5.16
麻城市	Macheng City	7500	5689	9.84	10.04	11.90	9.85
武穴市	Wuxue City	7703	6301	8.06	7.69	7.68	7.79
咸安区	Xian'an District	150	226	4.44	4.43	4.59	4.82
嘉鱼县	Jiayu County	1177	658	1.08	1.16	1.70	1.55
通城县	Tongcheng County	200	282	0.54	0.56	6.09	5.85
崇阳县	Chongyang County	560	532	1.16	1.20	5.47	5.47
通山县	Tongshan County			0.53	0.55	2.03	1.92
赤壁市	Chibi City	1500	1087	2.70	2.73	2.66	2.40
曾都区	Zengdu District	2000	1550	0.79	0.79	5.92	5.71
随县	Sui County	5356	4050	2.42	2.43	9.56	9.31
广水市	Guangshui City	3000	2356	3.76	3.76	6.65	6.43
恩施市	Enshi City	7	13	1.81	1.85	9.29	9.16
利川市	Lichuan City			1.29	1.31	7.17	6.92
建始县	Jianshi County			1.58	1.60	6.57	6.33
巴东县	Badong County	8		2.09	2.19	7.10	6.85
宣恩县	Xuanen County			0.55	0.56	5.29	5.11
咸丰县	Xianfeng County			1.71	1.76	5.90	5.67
来凤县	Laifeng County			0.72	0.75	2.59	2.55
鹤峰县	Hefeng County			0.50	0.48	2.24	2.16
仙桃市	Xiantiao City	22858	17567	13.46	14.26	9.12	8.54
潜江市	Qianjiang City	20874	14018	10.96	10.22	9.03	8.69
天门市	Tianmen City	30548	23438	11.74	11.73	8.44	8.03

附录 全国分省主要指标

Major Indicators by Region

附录1-1 各地区年末常住人口
THE END OF THE TOTAL POPULATION OF ALL REGIONS

单位:万人 (10 000 persons)

地 区	Region	2009	2010	2011	2012	2013	2014	2015
全 国	**National Total**	**133450**	**134091**	**134735**	**135404**	**136072**	**136782**	**137462**
北 京	Beijing	1860	1962	2019	2069	2115	2152	2171
天 津	Tianjin	1228	1299	1355	1413	1472	1517	1547
河 北	Hebei	7034	7194	7241	7288	7333	7384	7425
山 西	Shanxi	3427	3574	3593	3611	3630	3648	3664
内蒙古	Inner Mongolia	2458	2472	2482	2490	2498	2505	2511
辽 宁	Liaoning	4341	4375	4383	4389	4390	4391	4382
吉 林	Jilin	2740	2747	2749	2750	2751	2752	2753
黑龙江	Heilongjiang	3826	3833	3834	3834	3835	3833	3812
上 海	Shanghai	2210	2303	2347	2380	2415	2426	2415
江 苏	Jiangsu	7810	7869	7899	7920	7939	7960	7976
浙 江	Zhejiang	5276	5447	5463	5477	5498	5508	5539
安 徽	Anhui	6131	5957	5968	5988	6030	6083	6144
福 建	Fujian	3666	3693	3720	3748	3774	3806	3839
江 西	Jiangxi	4432	4462	4488	4504	4522	4542	4566
山 东	Shangdong	9470	9588	9637	9685	9733	9789	9847
河 南	Henan	9487	9405	9388	9406	9413	9436	9480
湖 北	**Hubei**	**5720**	**5728**	**5758**	**5779**	**5799**	**5816**	**5852**
湖 南	Hunan	6406	6570	6596	6639	6691	6737	6783
广 东	Guangdong	10130	10441	10505	10594	10644	10724	10849
广 西	Guangxi	4856	4610	4645	4682	4719	4754	4796
海 南	Hainan	864	869	877	887	895	903	911
重 庆	Chongqing	2859	2885	2919	2945	2970	2991	3017
四 川	Sichuan	8185	8045	8050	8076	8107	8140	8204
贵 州	Guizhou	3537	3479	3469	3484	3502	3508	3530
云 南	Yunnan	4571	4602	4631	4659	4687	4714	4742
西 藏	Tibet	296	300	303	308	312	318	324
陕 西	Shaanxi	3727	3735	3743	3753	3764	3775	3793
甘 肃	Gansu	2555	2560	2564	2578	2582	2591	2600
青 海	Qinghai	557	563	568	573	578	583	588
宁 夏	Ningxia	625	633	639	647	654	662	668
新 疆	Xinjiang	2159	2185	2209	2233	2264	2298	2360

注:1.全国数据包括中国人民解放军现役军人数,但不包括香港、澳门特别行政区和台湾省数据;分省数据中未包括中国人民解放军现役军人数。

2.2010年数据为第六次全国人口普查初步汇总数。

Notes:a)The number of national data including military personnel, but not including Hong Kong and Macao Special Administrative Region and Taiwan Province; provincial data does not include active duty PLA.

b)2010 years of data for the sixth national census preliminary summary number.

附录1-2　各地区按三次产业分法人单位数(2014)
REGIONS BY THE NUMBER OF UNITS THREE INDUSTRIES CORPORATE UNITS(2014)

单位:个　　(unit)

地区	Region	法人单位数 Corporate Units	第一产业 Primary Industry	第二产业 Secondary Industry	#工业 #Industry	第三产业 Tertiary Industry
全　国	**National Total**	**13701440**	**773414**	**3244154**	**2779179**	**9683872**
北　京	Beijing	660703	8949	53433	34414	598321
天　津	Tianjin	264151	5155	62959	50544	196037
河　北	Hebei	530948	34108	135975	118489	360865
山　西	Shanxi	304890	61120	39551	30800	204219
内蒙古	Inner Mongolia	208636	22892	29682	24083	156062
辽　宁	Liaoning	500312	17652	122603	98364	360057
吉　林	Jilin	172127	12662	34021	27536	125444
黑龙江	Heilongjiang	209042	17734	37463	30632	153845
上　海	Shanghai	434106	6321	97354	81104	330431
江　苏	Jiangsu	1344793	22794	469994	407431	852005
浙　江	Zhejiang	1235667	57578	454354	421624	723735
安　徽	Anhui	467775	37105	108915	86596	321755
福　建	Fujian	566075	30243	146990	129271	388842
江　西	Jiangxi	326563	26282	72526	61624	227755
山　东	Shangdong	1042834	34118	258436	213474	750280
河　南	Henan	623772	34473	139984	124474	449315
湖　北	**Hubei**	**567795**	**35773**	**107631**	**84000**	**424391**
湖　南	Hunan	424939	15675	82262	73431	327002
广　东	Guangdong	1295271	23233	394595	362972	877443
广　西	Guangxi	334563	45757	41540	34025	247266
海　南	Hainan	63619	9122	7796	3827	46701
重　庆	Chongqing	378003	55400	65200	54953	257403
四　川	Sichuan	462084	27765	81202	69146	353117
贵　州	Guizhou	209860	30956	40490	35521	138414
云　南	Yunnan	279007	31186	39945	28898	207876
西　藏	Tibet	26143	568	3693	1500	21882
陕　西	Shaanxi	310150	18798	54308	39820	237044
甘　肃	Gansu	173848	23298	22514	18962	128036
青　海	Qinghai	52074	8954	7302	5575	35818
宁　夏	Ningxia	54607	6678	7953	6513	39976
新　疆	Xinjiang	177083	11065	23483	19576	142535

附录1-3 各地区按行业分法人单位数(2014)
REGION NUMBER OF CORPORATE UNITS BY SECTOR(2014)

单位:个 (unit)

地 区	Region	法人单位数 Corporate Units	#农、林、牧、渔业 Agriculture, Forestry, Animal husbandry, Fishery	#采矿业 Mining Industry	#制造业 Manufacturing	#电力、热力、燃气及水的生产和供应业 Electricity, Gas and Water Production and Supply	#建筑业 Construction	#交通运输、仓储及邮政业 Traffic, Transport, Storage and Postal Industry
全国总计	**National Total**	**13701440**	**951045**	**101673**	**2616671**	**79679**	**464975**	**323044**
北 京	Beijing	660703	9474	126	34084	640	19019	14437
天 津	Tianjin	264151	5739	136	50541	589	12415	13246
河 北	Hebei	530948	44777	7081	110020	2140	17486	11511
山 西	Shanxi	304890	66666	5938	23769	1552	8751	6731
内蒙古	Inner Mongolia	208636	31322	5097	17424	1905	5599	5622
辽 宁	Liaoning	500312	27981	6039	91540	2169	24239	14438
吉 林	Jilin	172127	20467	1452	24865	1441	6485	4290
黑龙江	Heilongjiang	209042	28504	1965	27546	1510	6831	4912
上 海	Shanghai	434106	6689	1	81777	185	16250	15560
江 苏	Jiangsu	1344793	37928	743	405636	2953	62563	34062
浙 江	Zhejiang	1235667	62483	1387	417132	4633	32730	20161
安 徽	Anhui	467775	51112	2595	81904	2674	22319	12573
福 建	Fujian	566075	33397	3101	119932	6860	17719	13425
江 西	Jiangxi	326563	31064	4114	53806	4042	10902	10462
山 东	Shangdong	1042834	48678	3759	208334	2947	44962	27638
河 南	Henan	623772	45427	6353	116185	2402	15510	11185
湖 北	**Hubei**	**567795**	**44612**	**4757**	**76294**	**3553**	**23631**	**14207**
湖 南	Hunan	424939	22396	7154	61075	5506	8831	6605
广 东	Guangdong	1295271	32259	3731	351166	9906	31623	32194
广 西	Guangxi	334563	49601	3386	28087	2750	7515	6647
海 南	Hainan	63619	9897	341	3148	390	3969	1355
重 庆	Chongqing	378003	59258	2557	50578	2161	10247	6615
四 川	Sichuan	462084	32780	5445	57888	6248	12056	9609
贵 州	Guizhou	209860	32131	6917	26912	1877	4969	3300
云 南	Yunnan	279007	36078	6492	20034	2561	11047	5210
西 藏	Tibet	26143	615	230	1148	150	2193	337
陕 西	Shaanxi	310150	21203	4027	35125	2056	14488	6290
甘 肃	Gansu	173848	25308	2162	15466	1567	3552	2989
青 海	Qinghai	52074	9446	967	4135	528	1727	879
宁 夏	Ningxia	54607	7846	738	5477	359	1440	1115
新 疆	Xinjiang	177083	15907	2882	15643	1425	3907	5439

附录1-3 续表1 continued

单位:个 (unit)

地 区	Region	*信息传输、信息技术服务和软件业 Information Transmission, Computer Services and Software	*批发和零售业 Wholesale and Retail Trade	*住宿和餐饮业 Accommodation and Catering Services	*房地产业 Real Estate	*租赁和商务服务业 Leasing and Business Services
全国总计	**National Total**	**289162**	**3513338**	**235337**	**419618**	**1161947**
北 京	Beijing	46848	197293	16649	18244	140269
天 津	Tianjin	9386	80350	3781	7256	29363
河 北	Hebei	5233	131451	5101	15593	29344
山 西	Shanxi	2955	62599	3885	8035	16412
内蒙古	Inner Mongolia	2427	48765	3137	6885	13677
辽 宁	Liaoning	11279	137479	7500	18170	41114
吉 林	Jilin	2933	36877	2019	5400	10231
黑龙江	Heilongjiang	3350	45135	2499	6753	11440
上 海	Shanghai	14876	148697	12958	16068	55448
江 苏	Jiangsu	30926	392798	14353	36490	109728
浙 江	Zhejiang	25388	335289	17271	28067	98892
安 徽	Anhui	8843	107659	7192	15438	39947
福 建	Fujian	11738	155845	9158	14794	48347
江 西	Jiangxi	4287	63083	4085	9457	24079
山 东	Shangdong	16620	310631	14296	28633	74033
河 南	Henan	6306	118451	12223	17160	29737
湖 北	**Hubei**	**10810**	**151599**	**12083**	**19929**	**44965**
湖 南	Hunan	5984	90441	9435	12376	24417
广 东	Guangdong	32964	354617	22232	51159	152560
广 西	Guangxi	3851	84623	4103	11513	25498
海 南	Hainan	976	12427	1655	5526	5819
重 庆	Chongqing	8239	104519	16608	10814	29351
四 川	Sichuan	6047	71240	9310	13620	30079
贵 州	Guizhou	1907	36267	5043	7367	12131
云 南	Yunnan	5318	66547	4915	9591	21345
西 藏	Tibet	172	2253	537	214	1158
陕 西	Shaanxi	5163	70968	7128	11233	17573
甘 肃	Gansu	1210	31611	2936	4439	7123
青 海	Qinghai	532	8169	948	1477	2920
宁 夏	Ningxia	521	12454	765	1529	2994
新 疆	Xinjiang	2073	43201	1532	6388	11953

附录1-3　续表2 continued

单位:个 (unit)

地区	Region	#科学研究和技术服务 Research and Technical Service	#水利、环境和公共设施管理业 Water, Environment and Public Facilities Management	#居民服务、修理和其他服务业 Resident Services、Repair and Other Services	#教育 Education	#卫生和社会工作 Health, and Social Wark	#文化、体育和娱乐业 Culture, Sports and Entertainment	#公共管理、社会保障和社会组织 Public Management、Social Security and Social Organization
全国总计	**National Total**	**544309**	**97522**	**242251**	**444038**	**265537**	**263384**	**1596327**
北京	Beijing	75727	3989	19429	11260	3885	27309	17187
天津	Tianjin	18593	1703	7663	4254	1654	3179	10959
河北	Hebei	15365	3707	7695	20277	9762	7901	81924
山西	Shanxi	7966	2705	4778	10345	5487	6073	58110
内蒙古	Inner Mongolia	6379	2362	3697	6894	4999	3357	36824
辽宁	Liaoning	20888	4186	9339	14196	12909	8745	44530
吉林	Jilin	5601	1606	3528	6313	3874	3142	30173
黑龙江	Heilongjiang	6729	1820	3001	8092	5855	4133	36929
上海	Shanghai	19994	2061	12302	5895	3289	6864	13163
江苏	Jiangsu	52997	8711	20725	20279	16153	18371	73537
浙江	Zhejiang	35096	6565	15590	22464	8041	17680	81300
安徽	Anhui	15405	3709	7797	15349	8994	11029	49519
福建	Fujian	17502	3975	9326	16174	8201	9927	63119
江西	Jiangxi	8546	2755	5517	14149	10130	6084	56925
山东	Shangdong	48629	5898	16531	24931	18638	13593	128569
河南	Henan	27150	4614	8029	42309	37933	15757	103815
湖北	**Hubei**	**24724**	**5573**	**13000**	**19842**	**12353**	**11787**	**70884**
湖南	Hunan	13860	3965	7789	21751	16014	14328	90708
广东	Guangdong	42616	6789	21772	39650	11075	16988	74744
广西	Guangxi	12613	3129	4709	20043	5745	7302	51127
海南	Hainan	1835	475	1073	3435	1141	1605	8050
重庆	Chongqing	8777	2181	10199	10854	5744	6896	29163
四川	Sichuan	17782	4091	6620	25604	18868	15232	116370
贵州	Guizhou	4756	1510	4451	11290	4537	3476	39258
云南	Yunnan	9847	2655	5289	10521	5376	6212	46947
西藏	Tibet	540	81	210	1042	467	485	14204
陕西	Shaanxi	11219	3116	5652	15706	14651	6322	55777
甘肃	Gansu	4144	1290	2275	10410	4222	3774	47615
青海	Qinghai	1581	507	746	1876	1118	1056	13086
宁夏	Ningxia	1325	436	794	1867	934	1149	11389
新疆	Xinjiang	6123	1358	2725	6966	3488	3628	40422

附录1-4 地区生产总值
GROSS DOMESTIC PRODUCT

单位:亿元 (100 million yuan)

地 区	Region	2009	2010	2011	2012	2013	2014年	2015
北 京	Beijing	12153.0	14113.6	16251.9	17879.4	19800.8	21330.8	22968.6
天 津	Tianjin	7521.9	9224.5	11307.3	12893.9	14442.0	15726.9	16538.2
河 北	Hebei	17235.5	20394.3	24515.8	26575.0	28443.0	29421.2	29806.1
山 西	Shanxi	7358.3	9200.9	11237.6	12112.8	12665.3	12761.5	12802.6
内蒙古	Inner Mongolia	9740.3	11672.0	14359.9	15880.6	16916.5	17770.2	18032.8
辽 宁	Liaoning	15212.5	18457.3	22226.7	24846.4	27213.2	28626.6	28743.4
吉 林	Jilin	7278.8	8667.6	10568.8	11939.2	13046.4	13803.1	14274.1
黑龙江	Heilongjiang	8587.0	10368.6	12582.0	13691.6	14454.9	15039.4	15083.7
上 海	Shanghai	15046.5	17166.0	19195.7	20181.7	21818.2	23567.7	24965.0
江 苏	Jiangsu	34457.3	41425.5	49110.3	54058.2	59753.4	65088.3	70116.4
浙 江	Zhejiang	22990.4	27722.3	32318.9	34665.3	37756.6	40173.0	42886.5
安 徽	Anhui	10062.8	12359.3	15300.7	17212.1	19229.3	20848.7	22005.6
福 建	Fujian	12236.5	14737.1	17560.2	19701.8	21868.5	24055.8	25979.8
江 西	Jiangxi	7655.2	9451.3	11702.8	12948.9	14410.2	15714.6	16723.8
山 东	Shangdong	33896.7	39169.9	45361.9	50013.2	55230.3	59426.6	63002.3
河 南	Henan	19480.5	23092.4	26931.0	29599.3	32191.3	34938.2	37010.3
湖 北	**Hubei**	**12961.1**	**15967.6**	**19632.3**	**22250.5**	**24791.8**	**27379.2**	**29550.2**
湖 南	Hunan	13059.7	16038.0	19669.6	22154.2	24621.7	27037.3	29047.2
广 东	Guangdong	39482.6	46013.1	53210.3	57067.9	62474.8	67809.9	72812.6
广 西	Guangxi	7759.2	9569.9	11720.9	13035.1	14449.9	15672.9	16803.1
海 南	Hainan	1654.2	2064.5	2522.7	2855.5	3177.6	3500.7	3702.8
重 庆	Chongqing	6530.0	7925.6	10011.4	11409.6	12783.3	14262.6	15719.7
四 川	Sichuan	14151.3	17185.5	21026.7	23872.8	26392.1	28536.7	30103.1
贵 州	Guizhou	3912.7	4602.2	5701.8	6852.2	8086.9	9266.4	10502.6
云 南	Yunnan	6169.8	7224.2	8893.1	10309.5	11832.3	12814.6	13717.9
西 藏	Tibet	441.4	507.5	605.8	701.0	815.7	920.8	1026.4
陕 西	Shaanxi	8169.8	10123.5	12512.3	14453.7	16205.5	17689.9	18171.9
甘 肃	Gansu	3387.6	4120.8	5020.4	5650.2	6330.7	6836.8	6790.3
青 海	Qinghai	1081.3	1350.4	1670.4	1893.5	2122.1	2303.3	2417.1
宁 夏	Ningxia	1353.3	1689.7	2102.2	2341.3	2577.6	2752.1	2911.8
新 疆	Xinjiang	4277.1	5437.5	6610.1	7505.3	8443.8	9273.5	9324.8

注：本表按当年价格计算。本表数据为国家统计局最终核实数。

Note:The table at current prices.National Bureau of Statistics data for this table is to verify the final number.

附录1-5　地区生产总值指数
INDICES OF GROSS DOMESTIC PRODUCT

(上年=100) (last year=100)

地 区	Region	2009	2010	2011	2012	2013	2014	2015
北 京	Beijing	110.2	110.3	108.1	107.7	107.7	107.3	106.9
天 津	Tianjin	116.5	117.4	116.4	113.8	112.5	110.0	109.3
河 北	Hebei	110.0	112.2	111.3	109.6	108.2	106.5	106.8
山 西	Shanxi	105.4	113.9	113.0	110.1	108.9	104.9	103.1
内蒙古	Inner Mongolia	116.9	115.0	114.3	111.5	109.0	107.8	107.7
辽 宁	Liaoning	113.1	114.2	112.2	109.5	108.7	105.8	103.0
吉 林	Jilin	113.6	113.8	113.8	112.0	108.3	106.5	106.5
黑龙江	Heilongjiang	111.4	112.7	112.3	110.0	108.0	105.6	105.7
上 海	Shanghai	108.2	110.3	108.2	107.5	107.7	107.0	106.9
江 苏	Jiangsu	112.4	112.7	111.0	110.1	109.6	108.7	108.5
浙 江	Zhejiang	108.9	111.9	109.0	108.0	108.2	107.6	108.0
安 徽	Anhui	112.9	114.6	113.5	112.1	110.4	109.2	108.7
福 建	Fujian	112.3	113.9	112.3	111.4	111.0	109.9	109.0
江 西	Jiangxi	113.1	114.0	112.5	111.0	110.1	109.7	109.1
山 东	Shangdong	112.2	112.3	110.9	109.8	109.6	108.7	108.0
河 南	Henan	110.9	112.5	111.9	110.1	109.0	108.9	108.3
湖 北	**Hubei**	**113.5**	**114.8**	**113.8**	**111.3**	**110.1**	**109.7**	**108.9**
湖 南	Hunan	113.7	114.6	112.8	111.3	110.1	109.5	108.6
广 东	Guangdong	109.7	112.4	110.0	108.2	108.5	107.8	108.0
广 西	Guangxi	113.9	114.2	112.3	111.3	110.2	108.5	108.1
海 南	Hainan	111.7	116.0	112.0	109.1	109.9	108.5	107.8
重 庆	Chongqing	114.9	117.1	116.4	113.6	112.3	110.9	111.0
四 川	Sichuan	114.5	115.1	115.0	112.6	110.0	108.5	107.9
贵 州	Guizhou	111.4	112.8	115.0	113.6	112.5	110.8	110.7
云 南	Yunnan	112.1	112.3	113.7	113.0	112.1	108.1	108.7
西 藏	Tibet	112.4	112.3	112.7	111.8	112.1	110.8	111.0
陕 西	Shaanxi	113.6	114.6	113.9	112.9	111.0	109.7	108.0
甘 肃	Gansu	110.3	111.8	112.5	112.6	110.8	108.9	108.1
青 海	Qinghai	110.1	115.3	113.5	112.3	110.8	109.2	108.2
宁 夏	Ningxia	111.9	113.5	112.1	111.5	109.8	108.0	108.0
新 疆	Xinjiang	108.1	110.6	112.0	112.0	111.0	110.0	108.8

注：本表按不变价格计算。本表数据为国家统计局最终核实数。
Note:At constant prices, this table.National Bureau of Statistics data for this table is to verify the final number.

附录1-6　地区生产总值构成(2015)
COMPOSITION OF GROSS DOMESTIC PRODUCT(2015)

(地区生产总值=100)

(GDP=100)

地 区	Region	第一产业 Primary Industry	第二产业 Secondary Industry	工 业 Industry	建筑业 Contruction	第三产业 Tertiary Industry
北 京	Beijing	0.6	19.7	15.9	4.2	79.7
天 津	Tianjin	1.3	46.5	42.2	4.5	52.2
河 北	Hebei	11.5	48.3	42.4	6.0	40.2
山 西	Shanxi	6.2	40.8	34.3	6.6	53.0
内蒙古	Inner Mongolia	9.0	51.0	44.0	7.0	40.0
辽 宁	Liaoning	8.3	46.6	40.5	6.5	45.1
吉 林	Jilin	11.2	51.4	45.1	6.5	37.4
黑龙江	Heilongjiang	17.5	31.8	26.9	5.6	50.7
上 海	Shanghai	0.4	31.8	28.5	3.4	67.8
江 苏	Jiangsu	5.7	45.7	39.9	5.8	48.6
浙 江	Zhejiang	4.3	46.0	40.1	6.0	49.8
安 徽	Anhui	11.2	51.5	43.9	7.7	37.3
福 建	Fujian	8.2	50.9	42.2	8.7	41.0
江 西	Jiangxi	10.6	50.7	41.8	9.0	38.6
山 东	Shangdong	7.9	46.8	41.1	5.8	45.3
河 南	Henan	11.4	49.1	43.5	5.8	39.5
湖 北	**Hubei**	**11.2**	**45.7**	**39.0**	**6.9**	**43.1**
湖 南	Hunan	11.5	44.6	38.2	6.5	43.9
广 东	Guangdong	4.6	44.7	41.4	3.4	50.8
广 西	Guangxi	15.3	45.8	37.7	8.1	38.9
海 南	Hainan	23.1	23.6	13.1	10.5	53.3
重 庆	Chongqing	7.3	45.0	35.4	9.6	47.7
四 川	Sichuan	12.2	47.5	40.1	7.7	40.3
贵 州	Guizhou	15.6	39.5	31.6	7.9	44.9
云 南	Yunnan	15.0	40.0	28.6	11.5	45.0
西 藏	Tibet	9.4	36.7	6.8	29.8	53.9
陕 西	Shaanxi	8.8	51.5	42.0	9.8	39.7
甘 肃	Gansu	14.1	36.7	26.2	10.8	49.2
青 海	Qinghai	8.6	49.9	37.0	13.0	41.4
宁 夏	Ningxia	8.2	47.4	33.6	13.7	44.4
新 疆	Xinjiang	16.7	38.2	28.8	10.3	45.0

注：本表按当年价格计算。本表数据为国家统计局最终核实数。
Note:At present year price,this table.National Bureau of Statistics data for this table is to verify the final number.

附录1-7 人均地区生产总值
PER CAPITA GROSS DOMESTIC PRODUCT

单位:元　　本表按当年价格计算(At current price)　　(yuan)

地 区	Region	2009	2010	2011	2012	2013	2014	2015
北 京	Beijing	66940	73856	81658	87475	94648	99995	106284
天 津	Tianjin	62574	72994	85213	93173	100105	105231	107960
河 北	Hebei	24581	28668	33969	36584	38909	39984	40255
山 西	Shanxi	21522	26283	31357	33628	34984	35070	35017
内蒙古	Inner Mongolia	39735	47347	57974	63886	67836	71046	71903
辽 宁	Liaoning	35149	42355	50760	56649	61996	65201	65524
吉 林	Jilin	26595	31599	38460	43415	47428	50160	51852
黑龙江	Heilongjiang	22447	27076	32819	35711	37697	39226	39462
上 海	Shanghai	69165	76074	82560	85373	90993	97370	103141
江 苏	Jiangsu	44253	52840	62290	68347	75354	81874	87995
浙 江	Zhejiang	43842	51711	59249	63374	68805	73002	77644
安 徽	Anhui	16408	20888	25659	28792	32001	34425	35997
福 建	Fujian	33437	40025	47377	52763	58145	63472	67966
江 西	Jiangxi	17335	21253	26150	28800	31930	34674	36724
山 东	Shangdong	35894	41106	47335	51768	56885	60879	64168
河 南	Henan	20597	24446	28661	31499	34211	37072	39131
湖 北	**Hubei**	**22677**	**27906**	**34197**	**38572**	**42826**	**47145**	**50654**
湖 南	Hunan	20428	24719	29880	33480	36943	40271	42968
广 东	Guangdong	39436	44736	50807	54095	58833	63469	67503
广 西	Guangxi	16045	20219	25326	27952	30741	33090	35190
海 南	Hainan	19254	23831	28898	32377	35663	38924	40818
重 庆	Chongqing	22920	27596	34500	38914	43223	47850	52330
四 川	Sichuan	17339	21182	26133	29608	32617	35128	36836
贵 州	Guizhou	10971	13119	16413	19710	23151	26437	29847
云 南	Yunnan	13539	15752	19265	22195	25322	27264	29015
西 藏	Tibet	15008	17027	20077	22936	26326	29252	31999
陕 西	Shaanxi	21947	27133	33464	38564	43117	46929	48023
甘 肃	Gansu	13269	16113	19595	21978	24539	26433	26165
青 海	Qinghai	19454	24115	29522	33181	36875	39671	41252
宁 夏	Ningxia	21777	26860	33043	36394	39613	41834	43805
新 疆	Xinjiang	19942	25034	30087	33796	37553	40648	40036

附录1-8 各地区全社会固定资产投资
REGIONAL TOTAL INVESTMENT IN FIXED ASSETS

单位:亿元 (100 million yuan)

地 区	Region	2009	2010	2011	2012	2013	2014	2015
全国总计	**National Total**	**224598.8**	**278121.9**	**311485.1**	**374694.7**	**446294.1**	**512020.7**	**561999.8**
北 京	Beijing	4616.9	5403.0	5578.9	6112.4	6847.1	6924.2	7496.0
天 津	Tianjin	4738.2	6278.1	7067.7	7934.8	9130.2	10518.2	11832.0
河 北	Hebei	12269.8	15083.4	16389.3	19661.3	23194.2	26671.9	29448.2
山 西	Shanxi	4943.2	6063.2	7073.1	8863.3	11031.9	12354.5	14074.2
内蒙古	Inner Mongolia	7336.8	8926.5	10365.2	11875.7	14217.4	17591.8	13702.3
辽 宁	Liaoning	12292.5	16043.0	17726.3	21836.3	25107.7	24730.8	17917.9
吉 林	Jilin	6411.6	7870.4	7441.7	9511.5	9979.3	11339.6	12705.3
黑龙江	Heilongjiang	5028.8	6812.6	7475.4	9694.7	11453.1	9829.0	10183.0
上 海	Shanghai	5043.8	5108.9	4962.1	5117.6	5647.8	6016.4	6352.7
江 苏	Jiangsu	18949.9	23184.3	26692.6	30854.2	36373.3	41938.6	46246.9
浙 江	Zhejiang	10742.3	12376.0	14185.3	17649.4	20782.1	24262.8	27323.3
安 徽	Anhui	8990.7	11542.9	12455.7	15425.8	18621.9	21875.6	24385.9
福 建	Fujian	6231.2	8199.1	9910.9	12439.9	15327.4	18177.9	21301.4
江 西	Jiangxi	6643.1	8772.3	9087.6	10774.2	12850.3	15079.3	17388.1
山 东	Shangdong	19034.5	23280.5	26749.7	31256.0	36789.1	42495.5	48312.5
河 南	Henan	13704.5	16585.9	17769.0	21450.0	26087.5	30782.2	35660.4
湖 北	**Hubei**	**7866.9**	**10262.7**	**12557.3**	**15578.3**	**19307.3**	**22915.3**	**26563.9**
湖 南	Hunan	7703.4	9663.6	11880.9	14523.2	17841.4	21242.9	25045.1
广 东	Guangdong	12933.1	15623.7	17069.2	18751.5	22308.4	26293.9	30343.1
广 西	Guangxi	5237.2	7057.6	7990.7	9808.6	11907.7	13843.2	16227.7
海 南	Hainan	988.3	1317.0	1657.2	2145.4	2697.9	3112.2	3451.2
重 庆	Chongqing	5214.3	6688.9	7473.4	8736.2	10435.2	12285.4	14353.2
四 川	Sichuan	11371.9	13116.7	14222.2	17040.0	20326.1	23318.6	25525.9
贵 州	Guizhou	2412.0	3104.9	4235.9	5717.8	7373.6	9025.8	10945.5
云 南	Yunnan	4526.4	5528.7	6191.0	7831.1	9968.3	11498.5	13500.6
西 藏	Tibet	378.3	462.7	516.3	670.5	876.0	1069.2	1295.7
陕 西	Shaanxi	6246.9	7963.7	9431.1	12044.5	14884.1	17191.9	18582.2
甘 肃	Gansu	2363.0	3158.3	3965.8	5145.0	6527.9	7884.1	8754.2
青 海	Qinghai	798.2	1016.9	1435.6	1883.4	2361.1	2861.2	3210.7
宁 夏	Ningxia	1075.9	1444.2	1644.7	2096.9	2651.1	3173.8	3505.4
新 疆	Xinjiang	2725.5	3423.2	4632.1	6158.8	7732.3	9447.7	10813.0
不分地区	**Irrespective of region**	**5779.7**	**6759.1**	**5651.3**	**6106.4**	**5655.4**	**6268.4**	**5552.4**

附录1-9 各地区固定资产投资
REGIONAL INVESTMENT IN FIXED ASSET

单位:亿元 (100 million yuan)

地 区	Region	2009	2010	2011	2012	2013	2014	2015
全国总计	**National Total**	**193920.39**	**241430.89**	**302396.06**	**364854.15**	**435747.43**	**501264.87**	**551590.04**
北 京	Beijing	4149.63	4916.53	5519.84	6064.86	6797.54	6873.44	7446.02
天 津	Tianjin	4446.57	5896.52	7040.68	7913.26	9103.01	10490.37	11814.57
河 北	Hebei	10476.50	12922.66	15780.26	19104.63	22629.77	26147.20	28905.74
山 西	Shanxi	4509.56	5526.60	6837.69	8584.85	10745.35	12035.46	13744.59
内蒙古	Inner Mongolia	7143.84	8687.99	10252.97	11749.77	14072.39	17437.85	13529.15
辽 宁	Liaoning	11605.12	15106.33	17431.46	21535.37	24791.40	24426.83	17640.37
吉 林	Jilin	5958.95	7395.23	7226.65	9262.23	9725.76	11107.94	12508.59
黑龙江	Heilongjiang	4695.74	6292.67	7157.92	9375.44	11121.28	9537.88	9884.28
上 海	Shanghai	4618.91	4630.47	4959.93	5114.64	5644.13	6012.97	6349.39
江 苏	Jiangsu	14266.80	17416.47	26313.46	30473.74	35982.52	41552.75	45905.17
浙 江	Zhejiang	7454.33	8438.08	13651.65	17095.96	20194.07	23554.76	26664.72
安 徽	Anhui	7945.50	10281.29	12007.87	14943.81	18091.21	21256.29	23803.93
福 建	Fujian	5548.61	7385.78	9677.09	12182.52	15045.81	17869.76	20973.98
江 西	Jiangxi	6008.12	7856.94	8753.93	10378.37	12434.95	14646.31	16993.90
山 东	Shangdong	15439.10	18844.41	25907.38	30319.76	35875.86	41599.13	47381.46
河 南	Henan	11454.89	13934.82	16934.32	20558.61	25188.06	30012.28	34951.28
湖 北	**Hubei**	**7183.67**	**9405.63**	**12195.39**	**15148.71**	**18796.85**	**22441.67**	**26086.42**
湖 南	Hunan	6880.00	8617.98	11407.74	13966.26	17225.19	20548.55	24324.17
广 东	Guangdong	10230.05	12599.26	16599.16	18250.13	21795.52	25843.06	29950.48
广 西	Guangxi	4689.88	6383.26	7580.90	9345.18	11383.93	13287.61	15654.95
海 南	Hainan	942.68	1257.50	1599.14	2064.44	2625.59	3039.46	3355.40
重 庆	Chongqing	4855.11	6170.61	7366.95	8610.37	10290.95	12140.83	14208.15
四 川	Sichuan	9090.09	11061.38	13687.75	16530.31	19755.29	22662.13	24965.56
贵 州	Guizhou	2049.83	2609.36	4026.47	5504.95	7102.78	8778.40	10676.70
云 南	Yunnan	4117.51	5052.61	5932.75	7553.51	9621.83	11073.81	13069.39
西 藏	Tibet	327.64	404.98	516.31	670.52	876.00	1069.23	1295.68
陕 西	Shaanxi	5888.37	7569.90	9108.98	11705.83	14533.51	16840.27	18231.03
甘 肃	Gansu	2076.36	2808.55	3870.08	5040.03	6407.20	7759.63	8626.60
青 海	Qinghai	689.09	840.01	1365.91	1808.67	2285.30	2788.91	3144.17
宁 夏	Ningxia	964.16	1292.80	1589.14	2033.03	2577.79	3093.92	3426.42
新 疆	Xinjiang	2434.15	3065.13	4444.99	5857.98	7371.24	9067.79	10525.42
不分地区	**Irrespective of region**	**5779.66**	**6759.14**	**5651.29**	**6106.38**	**5655.37**	**6268.38**	**5552.35**

注：2010年前为城镇固定资产投资口径；2011年起为固定资产投资(不含农户)。
Note: Datas of the table are urban fixed asset investment before 2011, and are investment in fixed assets in 2011.

附录1-10 各地区房地产开发企业(单位)房屋施工、竣工面积和商品房销售面积

REGIONAL REAL ESTATE DEVELOPMENT ENTERPRISES(UNITS) HOUSING CONSTRUCTION, COMPLETION AND SALES OF COMMERCIAL SPACE AREA

单位:万平方米 (10 000 sqm)

地区	Region	房屋施工面积 Housing Construction Area		房屋竣工面积 Housing Completed Area		商品房销售面积 Sales of Commercial Area	
		2014	2015	2014	2015	2014	2015
全国总计	**National Total**	**726482**	**735693**	**107459**	**100039**	**120649**	**128495**
北 京	Beijing	13588	12993	3054	2631	1454	1554
天 津	Tianjin	10652	10230	2925	2904	1613	1771
河 北	Hebei	31628	30435	4038	4039	5706	5855
山 西	Shanxi	15477	15734	2182	2114	1576	1593
内蒙古	Inner Mongolia	18474	17641	2012	1697	2457	2369
辽 宁	Liaoning	38617	29283	6147	3238	5755	3916
吉 林	Jilin	12268	11566	1574	1287	1582	1492
黑龙江	Heilongjiang	14218	12410	3001	2924	2476	1997
上 海	Shanghai	14690	15095	2313	2647	2085	2431
江 苏	Jiangsu	57638	58118	9620	10297	9847	11414
浙 江	Zhejiang	42144	41687	6390	5893	4677	5985
安 徽	Anhui	33479	34245	5196	5538	6202	6174
福 建	Fujian	30052	30891	3584	3437	4119	4038
江 西	Jiangxi	13333	15294	1872	1908	3067	3478
山 东	Shangdong	54508	57206	7787	8278	9180	9727
河 南	Henan	38858	40994	7324	5390	7880	8556
湖 北	**Hubei**	**26322**	**28296**	**3431**	**2785**	**5602**	**6245**
湖 南	Hunan	27748	28322	4023	3970	5440	6363
广 东	Guangdong	53977	57942	7328	6044	9316	11681
广 西	Guangxi	17472	18608	1866	1675	3157	3523
海 南	Hainan	7557	8317	1204	1069	1004	1052
重 庆	Chongqing	28624	28986	3718	4630	5100	5381
四 川	Sichuan	36499	38981	5334	4546	7142	7671
贵 州	Guizhou	20369	20878	2842	2583	3178	3560
云 南	Yunnan	20035	20722	1789	2547	3194	3145
西 藏	Tibet	273	381	52	92	59	51
陕 西	Shaanxi	19466	20752	2189	1682	3094	2979
甘 肃	Gansu	7660	8586	813	962	1326	1435
青 海	Qinghai	2546	2586	559	454	416	393
宁 夏	Ningxia	7019	7046	1204	1169	1129	839
新 疆	Xinjiang	11289	11465	2086	1609	1816	1825

注:商品房销售面积包括期房。
Note:Sales of Commercial, including Forward House.

附录1-11　各地区房地产开发企业(单位)投资和商品房销售额

REGIONAL REAL ESTATE DEVELOPMENT COMPANY(UNITS) OF INVESTMENT AND COMMERCIAL HOUSING SALES

单位:亿元　　(100 million yuan)

地 区	Region	房地产开发投资额 Real Estate Development Investment		商品房销售额 Commercial Housing Sales		#住 宅 #Residential	
		2014	2015	2014	2015	2014	2015
全国总计	**National Total**	**95035.6**	**95978.8**	**76292.4**	**87280.8**	**62411.0**	**72753.0**
北 京	Beijing	3715.3	4177.0	2738.7	3517.6	2102.5	2512.9
天 津	Tianjin	1699.6	1871.5	1486.9	1790.0	1309.7	1646.4
河 北	Hebei	4059.7	4285.3	2928.0	3371.6	2501.6	2854.2
山 西	Shanxi	1403.6	1494.9	746.1	775.6	639.8	702.3
内蒙古	Inner Mongolia	1370.9	1081.1	1064.8	1052.2	765.0	766.1
辽 宁	Liaoning	5301.3	3558.6	3092.1	2255.0	2518.9	1907.6
吉 林	Jilin	1030.1	924.2	808.6	816.9	667.6	680.3
黑龙江	Heilongjiang	1324.1	992.1	1208.5	1027.1	962.7	824.2
上 海	Shanghai	3206.5	3468.9	3499.5	5093.5	2923.4	4319.9
江 苏	Jiangsu	8240.2	8153.7	6898.4	8396.2	5969.6	7374.9
浙 江	Zhejiang	7262.4	7111.9	4923.0	6299.5	4172.6	5519.3
安 徽	Anhui	4339.0	4424.9	3345.2	3369.4	2691.8	2714.3
福 建	Fujian	4567.4	4469.6	3763.5	3585.8	2939.6	2839.8
江 西	Jiangxi	1322.5	1520.1	1621.8	1863.7	1379.5	1606.7
山 东	Shangdong	5818.0	5892.2	4879.7	5408.0	4009.5	4510.8
河 南	Henan	4375.7	4818.9	3440.6	3945.6	2739.7	3300.3
湖 北	**Hubei**	**3983.8**	**4249.2**	**3088.3**	**3661.4**	**2543.8**	**3198.5**
湖 南	Hunan	2883.6	2613.7	2299.1	2738.9	1858.6	2253.8
广 东	Guangdong	7638.5	8538.5	8461.8	11442.8	6960.3	9967.3
广 西	Guangxi	1838.5	1909.1	1532.1	1747.8	1274.6	1459.4
海 南	Hainan	1431.7	1704.0	935.2	982.8	873.2	908.6
重 庆	Chongqing	3630.2	3751.3	2815.0	2952.2	2253.3	2244.4
四 川	Sichuan	4380.1	4813.0	3997.4	4199.8	3145.0	3269.5
贵 州	Guizhou	2187.7	2205.1	1370.3	1571.7	1000.0	1068.1
云 南	Yunnan	2846.7	2669.0	1596.4	1666.9	1165.4	1236.8
西 藏	Tibet	52.9	50.0	34.3	21.1	28.6	16.7
陕 西	Shaanxi	2426.5	2494.3	1598.0	1597.4	1368.1	1381.3
甘 肃	Gansu	721.5	768.1	602.3	704.9	513.5	603.1
青 海	Qinghai	308.3	336.0	211.3	206.0	155.8	139.8
宁 夏	Ningxia	654.8	633.6	465.0	370.3	352.0	284.0
新 疆	Xinjiang	1014.8	998.9	840.5	849.2	625.3	641.6

附录1-12 各地区货物进出口总额
TOTAL IMPORT AND EXPORT REGIONS

(按经营单位所在地分)

(Location of Points by Business Units)

单位:亿美元 (100 million US dollors)

地 区	Region	2009	2010	2011	2012	2013	2014	2015
全国总计	**National Total**	**22075.4**	**29740.0**	**36418.6**	**38671.2**	**41589.9**	**43015.3**	**39569.0**
北 京	Beijing	2147.3	3017.2	3895.6	4081.1	4290.0	4155.2	3196.2
天 津	Tianjin	638.3	821.0	1033.8	1156.3	1285.0	1338.9	1143.5
河 北	Hebei	296.3	420.6	536.0	505.6	549.1	598.8	514.8
山 西	Shanxi	85.7	125.8	147.4	150.4	157.9	162.3	147.2
内蒙古	Inner Mongolia	67.7	87.3	119.3	112.6	119.9	145.6	127.5
辽 宁	Liaoning	629.3	807.1	960.4	1040.9	1144.8	1140.0	959.6
吉 林	Jilin	117.4	168.5	220.6	245.6	258.3	263.8	189.4
黑龙江	Heilongjiang	162.3	255.2	385.2	375.9	388.8	389.0	209.9
上 海	Shanghai	2777.1	3689.5	4375.5	4365.9	4412.7	4664.0	4492.4
江 苏	Jiangsu	3387.4	4658.0	5395.8	5479.6	5508.0	5635.5	5456.1
浙 江	Zhejiang	1877.3	2535.3	3093.8	3124.0	3357.9	3550.4	3473.4
安 徽	Anhui	156.8	242.7	313.1	392.8	455.2	491.8	479.7
福 建	Fujian	796.5	1087.8	1435.2	1559.4	1693.2	1774.1	1693.6
江 西	Jiangxi	127.8	216.2	314.7	334.1	367.5	427.3	424.7
山 东	Shangdong	1390.5	1891.6	2358.9	2455.4	2665.3	2769.3	2417.5
河 南	Henan	134.8	178.3	326.2	517.4	599.6	649.7	738.4
湖 北	**Hubei**	**172.5**	**259.3**	**335.9**	**319.6**	**363.8**	**430.4**	**456.0**
湖 南	Hunan	101.5	146.6	189.4	219.5	251.8	308.3	293.3
广 东	Guangdong	6110.9	7849.0	9134.7	9840.2	10915.8	10765.8	10228.7
广 西	Guangxi	142.5	177.4	233.6	294.8	328.3	405.5	512.6
海 南	Hainan	48.8	86.5	127.6	143.2	149.9	158.6	139.6
重 庆	Chongqing	77.1	124.3	292.1	532.0	686.9	954.3	744.8
四 川	Sichuan	241.7	326.9	477.2	591.4	645.7	702.0	514.7
贵 州	Guizhou	23.0	31.5	48.9	66.3	82.9	107.7	122.2
云 南	Yunnan	80.5	134.3	160.3	210.1	253.0	296.1	245.2
西 藏	Tibet	4.0	8.4	13.6	34.2	33.2	22.5	9.1
陕 西	Shaanxi	84.1	121.0	146.5	148.0	201.3	273.6	305.0
甘 肃	Gansu	38.7	74.0	87.3	89.0	102.4	86.4	80.0
青 海	Qinghai	5.9	7.9	9.2	11.6	14.0	17.2	19.3
宁 夏	Ningxia	12.0	19.6	22.9	22.2	32.2	54.4	37.9
新 疆	Xinjiang	139.5	171.3	228.2	251.7	275.6	276.7	196.8

附录1-13　各地区货物出口、进口额(2015)
TOTAL IMPORT AND EXPORT REGIONS(2015)

单位:亿美元　　(100 million yuan)

地 区	Region	按经营单位所在地分 Location of Points by Business Units	
		出口额 Exports	进口额 Imports
全国总计	**National Total**	**22749.5**	**16819.5**
北 京	Beijing	546.7	2649.5
天 津	Tianjin	511.8	631.6
河 北	Hebei	329.4	185.4
山 西	Shanxi	84.2	62.9
内蒙古	Inner Mongolia	56.5	71.0
辽 宁	Liaoning	507.1	452.5
吉 林	Jilin	46.5	142.8
黑龙江	Heilongjiang	80.3	129.6
上 海	Shanghai	1959.4	2533.0
江 苏	Jiangsu	3386.7	2069.5
浙 江	Zhejiang	2766.0	707.5
安 徽	Anhui	322.8	156.9
福 建	Fujian	1130.2	563.4
江 西	Jiangxi	331.3	93.4
山 东	Shangdong	1440.6	976.9
河 南	Henan	430.7	307.7
湖 北	**Hubei**	**292.1**	**163.8**
湖 南	Hunan	191.4	101.9
广 东	Guangdong	6435.1	3793.6
广 西	Guangxi	280.3	232.4
海 南	Hainan	37.4	102.2
重 庆	Chongqing	551.9	192.9
四 川	Sichuan	332.3	182.4
贵 州	Guizhou	99.5	22.7
云 南	Yunnan	166.2	79.0
西 藏	Tibet	5.9	3.3
陕 西	Shaanxi	147.9	157.2
甘 肃	Gansu	58.1	21.8
青 海	Qinghai	16.4	2.9
宁 夏	Ningxia	29.8	8.1
新 疆	Xinjiang	175.1	21.7

附录1-14　各地区居民消费价格指数
REGIONAL CONSUMER PRICE INDEX

(上年=100) (Previous Year = 100)

地 区	Region	2009	2010	2011	2012	2013	2014	2015
全 国	**National Total**	**99.3**	**103.3**	**105.4**	**102.6**	**102.6**	**102.0**	**101.4**
北 京	Beijing	98.5	102.4	105.6	103.3	103.3	101.6	101.8
天 津	Tianjin	99.0	103.5	104.9	102.7	103.1	101.9	101.7
河 北	Hebei	99.3	103.1	105.7	102.6	103.0	101.7	100.9
山 西	Shanxi	99.6	103.0	105.2	102.5	103.1	101.7	100.6
内蒙古	Inner Mongolia	99.7	103.2	105.6	103.1	103.2	101.6	101.1
辽 宁	Liaoning	100.0	103.0	105.2	102.8	102.4	101.7	101.4
吉 林	Jilin	100.1	103.7	105.2	102.5	102.9	102.0	101.7
黑龙江	Heilongjiang	100.2	103.9	105.8	103.2	102.2	101.5	101.1
上 海	Shanghai	99.6	103.1	105.2	102.8	102.3	102.7	102.4
江 苏	Jiangsu	99.6	103.8	105.3	102.6	102.3	102.2	101.7
浙 江	Zhejiang	98.5	103.8	105.4	102.2	102.3	102.1	101.4
安 徽	Anhui	99.1	103.1	105.6	102.3	102.4	101.6	101.3
福 建	Fujian	98.2	103.2	105.3	102.4	102.5	102.0	101.7
江 西	Jiangxi	99.3	103.0	105.2	102.7	102.5	102.3	101.5
山 东	Shangdong	100.0	102.9	105.0	102.1	102.2	101.9	101.2
河 南	Henan	99.4	103.5	105.6	102.5	102.9	101.9	101.3
湖 北	**Hubei**	**99.6**	**102.9**	**105.8**	**102.9**	**102.8**	**102.0**	**101.5**
湖 南	Hunan	99.6	103.1	105.5	102.0	102.5	101.9	101.4
广 东	Guangdong	97.7	103.1	105.3	102.8	102.5	102.3	101.5
广 西	Guangxi	97.9	103.0	105.9	103.2	102.2	102.1	101.5
海 南	Hainan	99.3	104.8	106.1	103.2	102.8	102.4	101.0
重 庆	Chongqing	98.4	103.2	105.3	102.6	102.7	101.8	101.3
四 川	Sichuan	100.8	103.2	105.3	102.5	102.8	101.6	101.5
贵 州	Guizhou	98.7	102.9	105.1	102.7	102.5	102.4	101.8
云 南	Yunnan	100.4	103.7	104.9	102.7	103.1	102.4	101.9
西 藏	Tibet	101.4	102.2	105.0	103.5	103.6	102.9	102.0
陕 西	Shaanxi	100.5	104.0	105.7	102.8	103.0	101.6	101.0
甘 肃	Gansu	101.3	104.1	105.9	102.7	103.2	102.1	101.6
青 海	Qinghai	102.6	105.4	106.1	103.1	103.9	102.8	102.6
宁 夏	Ningxia	100.7	104.1	106.3	102.0	103.4	101.9	101.1
新 疆	Xinjiang	100.7	104.3	105.9	103.8	103.9	102.1	100.6

附录1-15 各地区全体居民人均收入与支出

REGIONAL PER CAPITA INCOME AND CONSUMPTION EXPENDITURE OF URBAN AND RURAL HOUSEHOLDS

单位:元 (yuan)

地 区	Region	可支配收入 Disposable Income		消费支出 Expenses on Consumption	
		2014	2015	2014	2015
全国总计	**National Total**	**20167.1**	**21966.2**	**14491.4**	**15712.4**
北 京	Beijing	44488.6	48458.0	31102.9	33802.8
天 津	Tianjin	28832.3	31291.4	22343.0	24162.5
河 北	Hebei	16647.4	18118.1	11931.5	13030.7
山 西	Shanxi	16538.3	17853.7	10863.8	11729.1
内蒙古	Inner Mongolia	20559.3	22310.1	16258.1	17178.5
辽 宁	Liaoning	22820.2	24575.6	16068.0	17199.8
吉 林	Jilin	17520.4	18683.6	13026.0	13763.9
黑龙江	Heilongjiang	17404.4	18592.7	12768.8	13402.5
上 海	Shanghai	45965.8	49867.2	33064.8	34783.6
江 苏	Jiangsu	27172.8	29538.9	19163.6	20555.6
浙 江	Zhejiang	32657.6	35537.1	22552.0	24116.9
安 徽	Anhui	16795.5	18362.6	11727.0	12840.1
福 建	Fujian	23330.9	25404.4	17644.5	18850.2
江 西	Jiangxi	16734.2	18437.1	11088.9	12403.4
山 东	Shangdong	20864.2	22703.2	13328.9	14578.4
河 南	Henan	15695.2	17124.8	11000.4	11835.1
湖 北	**Hubei**	**18283.2**	**20025.6**	**12928.3**	**14316.5**
湖 南	Hunan	17621.7	19317.5	13288.7	14267.3
广 东	Guangdong	25685.0	27858.9	19205.5	20975.7
广 西	Guangxi	15557.1	16873.4	10274.3	11401.0
海 南	Hainan	17476.5	18979.0	12470.6	13575.0
重 庆	Chongqing	18351.9	20110.1	13810.6	15139.5
四 川	Sichuan	15749.0	17221.0	12368.4	13632.1
贵 州	Guizhou	12371.1	13696.6	9303.4	10413.8
云 南	Yunnan	13772.2	15222.6	9869.5	11005.4
西 藏	Tibet	10730.2	12254.3	7317.0	8245.8
陕 西	Shaanxi	15836.7	17395.0	12203.6	13087.2
甘 肃	Gansu	12184.7	13466.6	9874.6	10950.8
青 海	Qinghai	14374.0	15812.7	12604.8	13611.3
宁 夏	Ningxia	15906.8	17329.1	12484.5	13815.6
新 疆	Xinjiang	15096.6	16859.1	11903.7	12867.4

注：本表按当年价格计算。
Note:The table at current prices.

附录1-16　各地区城镇居民人均可支配收入与支出
REGIONAL PER CAPITA INCOME AND CONSUMPTION EXPENDITURE OF URBAN HOUSEHOLDS

单位：元　　　　(yuan)

地区	Region	可支配收入 Disposable Income		消费支出 Expenses on Consumption	
		2014	2015	2014	2015
全国总计	**National Total**	**28843.9**	**31194.8**	**19968.1**	**21392.4**
北京	Beijing	48531.8	52859.2	33717.5	36642.0
天津	Tianjin	31506.0	34101.3	24289.6	26229.5
河北	Hebei	24141.3	26152.2	16203.8	17586.6
山西	Shanxi	24069.4	25827.7	14636.9	15818.6
内蒙古	Inner Mongolia	28349.6	30594.1	20885.2	21876.5
辽宁	Liaoning	29081.7	31125.7	20519.6	21556.7
吉林	Jilin	23217.8	24900.9	17156.1	17972.6
黑龙江	Heilongjiang	22609.0	24202.6	16466.6	17152.1
上海	Shanghai	48841.4	52961.9	35182.4	36946.1
江苏	Jiangsu	34346.3	37173.5	23476.3	24966.0
浙江	Zhejiang	40392.7	43714.5	27241.7	28661.3
安徽	Anhui	24838.5	26935.8	16107.1	17233.5
福建	Fujian	30722.4	33275.3	22204.1	23520.2
江西	Jiangxi	24309.2	26500.1	15141.8	16731.8
山东	Shangdong	29221.9	31545.3	18322.6	19853.8
河南	Henan	23672.1	25575.6	16184.5	17154.3
湖北	**Hubei**	**24852.3**	**27051.5**	**16681.4**	**18192.3**
湖南	Hunan	26570.2	28838.1	18334.7	19501.4
广东	Guangdong	32148.1	34757.2	23611.7	25673.1
广西	Guangxi	24669.0	26415.9	15045.4	16321.2
海南	Hainan	24486.5	26356.4	17513.8	18448.4
重庆	Chongqing	25147.2	27238.8	18279.5	19742.3
四川	Sichuan	24234.4	26205.3	17759.9	19276.8
贵州	Guizhou	22548.2	24579.6	15254.6	16914.2
云南	Yunnan	24299.0	26373.2	16268.3	17675.0
西藏	Tibet	22015.8	25456.6	15669.4	17022.0
陕西	Shaanxi	24365.8	26420.2	17546.0	18463.9
甘肃	Gansu	21803.9	23767.1	15942.3	17450.9
青海	Qinghai	22306.6	24542.3	17492.9	19200.6
宁夏	Ningxia	23284.6	25186.0	17216.2	18983.9
新疆	Xinjiang	23214.0	26274.7	17684.5	19414.7

注：本表按当年价格计算。
Note: The table at current prices.

附录1-17　各地区农村居民人均可支配收入与支出

REGIONAL PER CAPITA INCOME AND CONSUMPTION EXPENDITURE OF RURAL HOUSEHOLDS

单位:元　　(yuan)

地 区	Region	可支配收入 Disposable Income		消费支出 Expenses on Consumption	
		2014	2015	2014	2015
全国总计	**National Total**	**10488.9**	**11421.7**	**8382.6**	**9222.6**
北 京	Beijing	18867.3	20568.7	14535.1	15811.2
天 津	Tianjin	17014.2	18481.6	13738.6	14739.4
河 北	Hebei	10186.1	11050.5	8248.0	9022.8
山 西	Shanxi	8809.4	9453.9	6991.7	7421.2
内蒙古	Inner Mongolia	9976.3	10775.9	9972.2	10637.4
辽 宁	Liaoning	11191.5	12056.9	7800.7	8872.8
吉 林	Jilin	10780.1	11326.2	8139.8	8783.3
黑龙江	Heilongjiang	10453.2	11095.2	7830.0	8391.5
上 海	Shanghai	21191.6	23205.2	14820.1	16152.3
江 苏	Jiangsu	14958.4	16256.7	11820.3	12882.5
浙 江	Zhejiang	19373.3	21125.0	14497.8	16107.7
安 徽	Anhui	9916.4	10820.7	7980.8	8975.2
福 建	Fujian	12650.2	13792.7	11055.9	11960.8
江 西	Jiangxi	10116.6	11139.1	7548.3	8485.6
山 东	Shangdong	11882.3	12930.4	7962.2	8747.6
河 南	Henan	9966.1	10852.9	7277.2	7887.4
湖 北	**Hubei**	**10849.1**	**11843.9**	**8680.9**	**9803.1**
湖 南	Hunan	10060.2	10992.5	9024.8	9690.6
广 东	Guangdong	12245.6	13360.4	10043.2	11103.0
广 西	Guangxi	8683.2	9466.6	6675.1	7582.0
海 南	Hainan	9912.6	10857.6	7029.0	8210.3
重 庆	Chongqing	9489.8	10504.7	7982.6	8937.7
四 川	Sichuan	9347.7	10247.4	8301.1	9250.6
贵 州	Guizhou	6671.2	7386.9	5970.3	6644.9
云 南	Yunnan	7456.1	8242.1	6030.3	6830.1
西 藏	Tibet	7359.2	8243.7	4822.1	5579.7
陕 西	Shaanxi	7932.2	8688.9	7252.4	7900.7
甘 肃	Gansu	6276.6	6936.2	6147.8	6829.8
青 海	Qinghai	7282.7	7933.4	8235.1	8566.5
宁 夏	Ningxia	8410.0	9118.7	7676.5	8414.9
新 疆	Xinjiang	8723.8	9425.1	7365.3	7697.9

注:本表按当年价格计算。
Note:The table at current prices.

附录1-18 各地区农林牧渔业总产值及增长速度(2015)
REGIONAL FORESTYR,ANIMAL HUSBANDDRY AND FISHERY OUTPUT VALUE GROWTH RATE(2015)

地 区	Region	农林牧渔业总产值(亿元) Forestry, Animal Husbandry Fishery (million)	#农业 #Agriculture	#林业 #Forestry	#牧业 #Livestock	#渔业 #Fishing	农林牧渔业总产值比上年增长(%) Previous Year (%)
全国总计	**National Total**	**107056.4**	**57635.8**	**4436.4**	**29780.4**	**10880.6**	**3.9**
北 京	Beijing	368.2	154.5	57.3	135.9	11.9	-11.7
天 津	Tianjin	467.4	238.0	7.7	130.2	80.4	2.6
河 北	Hebei	5978.9	3441.4	121.5	1904.1	198.7	2.7
山 西	Shanxi	1522.6	969.5	97.4	359.0	9.9	1.1
内蒙古	Inner Mongolia	2751.6	1418.3	99.4	1160.9	30.8	2.4
辽 宁	Liaoning	4686.7	2068.6	166.1	1561.4	689.8	3.8
吉 林	Jilin	2880.6	1400.4	109.8	1244.9	39.9	4.3
黑龙江	Heilongjiang	5044.9	2911.9	204.2	1704.8	117.6	5.2
上 海	Shanghai	302.6	162.0	12.2	65.6	51.8	-6.7
江 苏	Jiangsu	7030.8	3722.1	129.1	1262.1	1517.5	2.6
浙 江	Zhejiang	2933.4	1434.7	151.6	426.2	855.9	1.2
安 徽	Anhui	4390.8	2174.6	290.1	1259.0	475.1	4.2
福 建	Fujian	3717.9	1618.6	314.3	571.3	1082.3	3.9
江 西	Jiangxi	2859.1	1326.9	293.7	719.8	420.0	4.0
山 东	Shangdong	9549.6	4929.9	139.9	2523.2	1524.7	4.3
河 南	Henan	7641.3	4610.7	134.3	2445.3	123.6	4.6
湖 北	**Hubei**	**5728.6**	**2780.4**	**180.6**	**1503.3**	**922.8**	**5.4**
湖 南	Hunan	5630.7	3043.5	317.4	1601.7	366.9	3.7
广 东	Guangdong	5520.0	2793.8	296.7	1117.1	1117.2	3.1
广 西	Guangxi	4197.1	2146.4	313.9	1140.3	429.8	3.7
海 南	Hainan	1323.9	613.9	99.2	238.5	324.9	5.5
重 庆	Chongqing	1738.1	1033.7	60.4	542.9	74.9	4.6
四 川	Sichuan	6377.8	3335.5	205.8	2515.6	210.5	3.6
贵 州	Guizhou	2738.7	1772.6	137.7	665.2	55.9	6.8
云 南	Yunnan	3383.1	1841.5	317.1	1031.0	81.7	6.0
西 藏	Tibet	149.5	68.0	2.1	75.3	0.2	4.5
陕 西	Shaanxi	2813.5	1910.7	75.8	665.5	23.6	5.0
甘 肃	Gansu	1722.1	1252.5	28.6	279.4	2.2	5.7
青 海	Qinghai	319.3	145.0	7.4	158.4	2.8	1.8
宁 夏	Ningxia	483.0	311.0	11.6	122.9	15.8	4.4
新 疆	Xinjiang	2804.4	2005.4	53.2	649.5	21.8	6.3

注：本表绝对数按当年价格计算，增长速度按可比价格计算。
Note:In this table are at current prices, growth rates at constant prices.

附录1-19 各地区主要农产品产量(2015)
MAJOR AGRICULTURAL PRODUCTION REGIONS(2015)

单位:万吨 (10 000 tons)

地 区	Region	粮 食 Food	油 料 Oil feed	棉 花 Cotton	糖 料 Sugar	蔬 菜 Vegetables	水 果 Fruit
全国总计	**National Total**	**62143.9**	**3537.0**	**560.3**	**12500.0**	**78526.1**	**27375.0**
北 京	Beijing	62.6	0.6	0.01		205.1	87.9
天 津	Tianjin	181.7	0.4	2.6		441.5	62.7
河 北	Hebei	3363.8	151.5	37.3	89.2	8243.7	2117.2
山 西	Shanxi	1259.6	15.3	1.4	5.5	1302.2	842.6
内蒙古	Inner Mongolia	2827.0	193.6	0.02	230.1	1445.3	296.7
辽 宁	Liaoning	2002.5	46.1	0.02	5.2	2932.8	882.0
吉 林	Jilin	3647.0	76.4		1.3	860.0	209.0
黑龙江	Heilongjiang	6324.0	18.3		7.3	957.4	213.5
上 海	Shanghai	112.1	1.2	0.02	0.6	364.5	61.5
江 苏	Jiangsu	3561.3	143.1	11.7	9.5	5595.7	914.8
浙 江	Zhejiang	752.2	31.3	2.0	62.2	1806.9	740.9
安 徽	Anhui	3538.1	227.9	23.4	20.3	2714.2	1029.8
福 建	Fujian	661.1	30.7	0.01	43.6	1903.6	837.0
江 西	Jiangxi	2148.7	124.0	11.5	65.8	1359.1	663.4
山 东	Shangdong	4712.7	324.1	53.7		10272.9	3218.6
河 南	Henan	6067.1	599.7	12.6	24.3	7456.5	2665.1
湖 北	**Hubei**	**2703.3**	**339.6**	**29.8**	**32.0**	**3852.0**	**966.3**
湖 南	Hunan	3002.9	242.9	14.5	66.0	3996.9	981.0
广 东	Guangdong	1358.1	110.3		1452.9	3438.8	1648.5
广 西	Guangxi	1524.8	64.7	0.3	7504.9	2786.4	1720.0
海 南	Hainan	184.0	11.3		264.8	572.2	405.9
重 庆	Chongqing	1154.9	59.9		9.8	1780.5	375.9
四 川	Sichuan	3442.8	307.6	1.0	54.2	4240.8	934.2
贵 州	Guizhou	1180.0	101.3	0.1	156.1	1731.9	224.9
云 南	Yunnan	1876.4	65.9	0.01	1930.1	1873.9	726.5
西 藏	Tibet	100.6	6.4			69.6	1.5
陕 西	Shaanxi	1226.8	62.7	3.9	0.2	1822.5	1930.9
甘 肃	Gansu	1171.1	71.6	4.3	16.0	1823.1	679.0
青 海	Qinghai	102.7	30.5		0.03	166.4	3.6
宁 夏	Ningxia	372.6	15.3			575.8	298.9
新 疆	Xinjiang	1521.3	62.9	350.3	448.3	1933.9	1635.0

注:水果产量含果用瓜。
Note:Fruit production with fruit with a melon.

附录1-19 续表 continued

单位:万吨 (10 000 tons)

地区	Region	肉类 Meat	#猪肉 #Pork	#牛肉 #Beef	#羊肉 #Sheep Meat	奶类 Dairy
全国总计	**National Total**	**8625.0**	**5486.5**	**700.1**	**440.8**	**3870.3**
北京	Beijing	36.4	22.5	1.5	1.2	57.2
天津	Tianjin	45.8	29.2	3.4	1.6	68.0
河北	Hebei	462.5	275.0	53.2	31.7	480.9
山西	Shanxi	85.6	60.3	5.9	6.9	92.7
内蒙古	Inner Mongolia	245.7	70.8	52.9	92.6	812.2
辽宁	Liaoning	429.4	227.1	40.3	8.5	142.6
吉林	Jilin	261.1	136.0	46.6	4.8	52.8
黑龙江	Heilongjiang	228.7	138.4	41.6	12.3	574.4
上海	Shanghai	20.3	16.1	0.1	0.6	27.7
江苏	Jiangsu	369.4	225.8	3.2	8.1	59.6
浙江	Zhejiang	131.1	103.3	1.2	1.8	16.5
安徽	Anhui	419.4	259.1	16.2	16.6	30.6
福建	Fujian	216.6	134.5	3.1	2.4	15.4
江西	Jiangxi	336.5	253.5	13.6	1.2	13.0
山东	Shangdong	774.0	397.4	67.9	37.1	284.9
河南	Henan	711.1	468.0	82.6	25.9	352.3
湖北	**Hubei**	**433.3**	**331.5**	**23.0**	**8.8**	**16.9**
湖南	Hunan	540.1	448.0	19.9	11.6	9.7
广东	Guangdong	424.2	274.2	7.0	0.9	12.9
广西	Guangxi	417.3	258.8	14.4	3.2	10.1
海南	Hainan	78.0	45.8	2.6	1.0	0.2
重庆	Chongqing	213.8	156.2	8.8	3.8	5.4
四川	Sichuan	706.8	512.4	35.4	26.3	67.5
贵州	Guizhou	201.9	160.7	16.8	4.2	6.2
云南	Yunnan	378.3	288.6	34.3	15.0	62.5
西藏	Tibet	28.0	1.5	16.5	8.2	35.0
陕西	Shaanxi	116.2	90.4	7.9	7.8	189.9
甘肃	Gansu	96.3	50.8	18.8	19.6	39.9
青海	Qinghai	34.7	10.3	11.5	11.6	32.7
宁夏	Ningxia	29.2	7.1	9.7	10.1	136.5
新疆	Xinjiang	153.2	33.1	40.4	55.4	163.8

附录1-20 各地区规模以上工业企业主要经济指标(2015)
REGIONAL-SCALE INDUSTRIAL ENTERPRISES MAIN ECONOMIC INDICATORS (2015)

单位:亿元

地区	Region	主营业务收入 Main Business Income	主营业务成本 Main Business Costs	销售费用 Selling expenses	管理费用 Overhead expenses	财务费用 Finance expenses	利润总额 Total Profit
全国总计	**National Total**	**1103300.7**	**945359.2**	**28740.0**	**41135.4**	**13371.2**	**63554.0**
北京	Beijing	19026.0	15915.1	925.5	938.3	209.2	1580.3
天津	Tianjin	27958.9	23937.3	626.0	854.1	193.7	2002.9
河北	Hebei	44843.9	39487.5	809.3	1278.0	568.3	2181.4
山西	Shanxi	14393.7	12569.6	502.9	745.1	593.5	-68.1
内蒙古	Inner Mongolia	18522.7	15648.6	430.3	686.3	441.2	940.5
辽宁	Liaoning	37123.7	32264.5	882.8	1484.4	595.6	1191.1
吉林	Jilin	22045.9	18626.8	857.3	952.5	242.6	1171.5
黑龙江	Heilongjiang	11384.5	9649.7	288.0	597.1	145.4	409.9
上海	Shanghai	33468.0	27025.0	1303.4	2169.8	148.4	2635.4
江苏	Jiangsu	148283.8	127321.0	3634.1	5458.9	1300.5	9617.1
浙江	Zhejiang	62740.5	53198.9	1678.2	2998.0	941.6	3717.7
安徽	Anhui	38364.4	33626.2	934.6	1287.0	454.9	1852.7
福建	Fujian	39106.6	33728.7	988.5	1376.4	428.1	2208.7
江西	Jiangxi	32459.4	28591.1	551.3	736.9	198.8	2128.0
山东	Shangdong	146886.7	128905.0	2896.1	3720.1	1663.8	8617.2
河南	Henan	72381.4	63351.3	1324.5	1568.3	758.8	4840.6
湖北	**Hubei**	**42470.2**	**36326.7**	**1278.0**	**1625.7**	**508.2**	**2233.1**
湖南	Hunan	35152.2	29644.3	1011.8	1447.8	413.0	1548.6
广东	Guangdong	117461.7	99329.8	4020.1	5573.9	716.8	7208.8
广西	Guangxi	20078.4	17076.3	468.1	761.4	235.2	1175.4
海南	Hainan	1660.6	1314.8	66.1	63.5	37.7	89.6
重庆	Chongqing	20370.3	17241.4	587.1	843.3	218.9	1396.8
四川	Sichuan	37876.3	32039.4	1120.1	1492.6	702.8	2044.0
贵州	Guizhou	9221.4	7440.6	295.6	398.1	233.6	606.5
云南	Yunnan	9823.3	7614.3	269.0	423.0	362.6	462.0
西藏	Tibet	130.9	104.7	6.1	9.5	4.7	6.4
陕西	Shaanxi	18336.3	14822.0	478.8	811.6	312.3	1339.7
甘肃	Gansu	8155.8	7351.5	129.4	268.4	230.4	-72.3
青海	Qinghai	2130.1	1777.6	78.2	71.7	105.6	68.8
宁夏	Ningxia	3403.9	2936.2	69.5	127.7	127.7	79.3
新疆	Xinjiang	8039.1	6493.3	229.4	365.9	277.1	340.5

注:本表为2015年1-11月快报数据(下表同)。
Note:This table is from January to November 2014, Express Data (the same).

附录1-20 续表 continued

单位:亿元 (100 million yuan)

地区	Region	亏损企业亏损总额 Total Loss of Enterprises Running under Deficit	应收账款 Account Received	存货 Inventory	产成品 Finished Products	资产总计 Total Assets	负债合计 Total Liability
全国总计	**National Total**	**9115.5**	**114546.9**	**100107.2**	**38700.1**	**999741.1**	**561560.3**
北京	Beijing	209.5	3835.5	2186.9	776.2	38788.9	17943.5
天津	Tianjin	215.3	3325.5	2707.5	966.8	24349.0	14910.0
河北	Hebei	492.1	3373.0	3789.5	1423.3	41809.4	23419.7
山西	Shanxi	613.2	2358.9	1925.3	831.8	31508.4	23826.4
内蒙古	Inner Mongolia	520.2	1670.1	1497.3	643.1	28380.8	17722.5
辽宁	Liaoning	612.7	3764.4	3823.0	1340.2	38085.9	22430.7
吉林	Jilin	242.0	1369.8	1741.1	569.5	17399.8	9361.7
黑龙江	Heilongjiang	220.7	1281.3	1368.7	463.7	14556.9	8261.5
上海	Shanghai	335.0	6203.0	4363.6	1453.9	36238.2	17288.6
江苏	Jiangsu	730.2	17445.9	11854.2	4540.7	106814.7	56733.0
浙江	Zhejiang	372.1	10413.4	7935.7	3309.7	66515.7	38078.9
安徽	Anhui	277.2	3887.7	3100.6	1257.0	30487.3	17592.7
福建	Fujian	255.7	3840.0	3539.5	1428.9	29285.5	15609.3
江西	Jiangxi	65.5	1779.6	1775.7	778.8	18971.6	9400.7
山东	Shangdong	496.2	8310.0	10373.2	4481.6	99610.3	53804.2
河南	Henan	413.0	4899.6	4141.9	1572.2	54227.5	25352.8
湖北	**Hubei**	**259.8**	**3815.7**	**3803.0**	**1549.2**	**33540.3**	**18188.7**
湖南	Hunan	186.4	2787.2	2645.2	891.9	22732.2	11876.7
广东	Guangdong	507.6	16478.0	12122.3	4533.0	93808.1	53474.6
广西	Guangxi	165.9	1357.0	1626.4	731.7	14692.4	9120.5
海南	Hainan	23.3	172.7	205.7	90.4	2723.9	1482.6
重庆	Chongqing	149.0	2100.0	1558.8	710.9	17006.4	10430.5
四川	Sichuan	343.9	3766.4	3442.7	1283.3	38999.5	23498.6
贵州	Guizhou	123.6	813.3	1052.1	306.2	12100.3	7720.1
云南	Yunnan	296.4	1047.2	2154.2	566.9	18096.1	11705.7
西藏	Tibet	17.7	19.5	23.7	7.7	883.8	424.7
陕西	Shaanxi	194.4	1969.2	1862.3	795.0	25905.2	14470.4
甘肃	Gansu	297.8	763.6	1376.6	545.1	11160.0	7113.7
青海	Qinghai	72.0	257.3	295.1	111.0	5553.1	3847.4
宁夏	Ningxia	89.0	453.2	713.9	268.8	7701.4	5203.4
新疆	Xinjiang	318.1	988.8	1101.3	471.7	17808.1	11266.4

附录1-21 各地区主要工业产品产量(2015)
MAJOR INDUSTRIAL PRODUCTS BY REGION(2015)

地 区	Region	原油(万吨) Crude Oil (10 000 tons)	天然气(亿立方米) Natural gas (100 million cu.m)	布(亿米) Cloth (100 million meters)	农用化肥(万吨) Agricultural Fertilizers (10 000 Tons)	水泥(万吨) Cement (10 000 tons)	生铁(万吨) Pig Iron (10 000 tons)	粗钢(万吨) Crude steel (10 000 tons)
全国总计	**National Total**	**21455.6**	**1346.1**	**892.6**	**7432.0**	**235939.6**	**69141.3**	**80382.5**
北 京	Beijing		16.9	0.02		553.5		1.5
天 津	Tianjin	3496.8	20.5	2.5	13.1	777.6	1953.2	2068.9
河 北	Hebei	580.1	10.4	78.4	215.8	9126.2	17382.3	18832.0
山 西	Shanxi		43.1	0.8	465.0	3777.1	3576.4	3847.0
内蒙古	Inner Mongolia	45.8	9.2		293.0	5830.8	1461.4	1735.1
辽 宁	Liaoning	1037.1	6.6	3.5	64.7	4567.7	6059.0	6071.3
吉 林	Jilin	665.5	20.3	0.4	57.1	3325.0	974.9	1066.8
黑龙江	Heilongjiang	3838.6	35.8	0.1	49.4	3111.9	408.9	418.5
上 海	Shanghai	6.8	1.9	1.0	1.5	433.6	1686.7	1783.8
江 苏	Jiangsu	190.5	0.4	140.5	205.3	18056.1	7044.8	10995.2
浙 江	Zhejiang			239.6	38.8	11330.9	1072.5	1594.9
安 徽	Anhui			15.3	309.8	13207.9	2092.5	2506.0
福 建	Fujian			79.2	52.2	7787.5	980.1	1586.5
江 西	Jiangxi		0.4	10.8	141.5	9458.1	2083.2	2211.0
山 东	Shangdong	2608.0	4.6	126.0	584.0	15249.1	6747.9	6619.3
河 南	Henan	412.1	4.2	33.5	558.9	16676.2	2903.6	2897.4
湖 北	**Hubei**	**71.0**	**1.4**	**88.2**	**1171.8**	**11145.5**	**2288.7**	**2919.8**
湖 南	Hunan			4.4	112.7	11680.1	1762.8	1852.8
广 东	Guangdong	1572.6	96.6	33.9	72.0	14560.0	1146.3	1761.7
广 西	Guangxi	50.5	0.2	0.4	114.3	11144.5	1220.3	2146.0
海 南	Hainan	30.0	1.9		64.2	2225.2		23.9
重 庆	Chongqing		33.3	5.8	222.4	6840.2	366.6	689.5
四 川	Sichuan	15.4	267.2	19.7	507.2	14091.0	1747.4	1947.7
贵 州	Guizhou		0.9	0.5	603.6	9940.9	407.6	466.4
云 南	Yunnan				354.5	9436.2	1235.4	1418.1
西 藏	Tibet					467.9		
陕 西	Shaanxi	3736.7	415.9	7.6	187.1	8578.7	800.9	1027.3
甘 肃	Gansu	66.6	0.1		48.0	4764.3	690.5	852.1
青 海	Qinghai	223.0	61.4		520.2	1767.9	112.6	120.6
宁 夏	Ningxia	13.4			82.5	1749.8	175.3	181.8
新 疆	Xinjiang	2795.1	293.0	0.7	321.5	4278.5	759.5	739.6

附录1-21　续表 continued

地区	Region	钢材(万吨) Steel (10 000 tons)	汽车(万辆) Car (10 000)	家用电冰箱(万台) Household Refrigerators (10 000 units)	程控交换机(万线) PBX (10 000 lines)	移动通信手持机(万台) Mobile Handset (10 000 units)	微型计算机设备(万台) Micro-computer Equipment (10 000 units)	发电量(亿千瓦小时) Power generation (Billion kilowatt hours)
全国总计	**National Total**	**112349.6**	**2450.4**	**7992.8**	**1880.3**	**181261.4**	**31418.7**	**58105.8**
北京	Beijing	175.0	202.4		266.5	9540.8	885.6	420.9
天津	Tianjin	8186.2	52.9	58.4		7315.6	1029.7	622.8
河北	Hebei	25244.3	112.9		13.4			2497.8
山西	Shanxi	4267.3				2038.4		2449.3
内蒙古	Inner Mongolia	1897.2	2.6					3928.8
辽宁	Liaoning	6321.6	109.0	147.1	60.8	1614.5	0.2	1665.2
吉林	Jilin	1152.5	208.1					731.3
黑龙江	Heilongjiang	403.8	8.0				1.7	873.6
上海	Shanghai	2202.7	243.0	140.4	95.3	6747.5	3652.0	792.7
江苏	Jiangsu	13560.8	115.8	844.6	0.8	4691.0	5911.6	4360.8
浙江	Zhejiang	4047.7	41.1	710.5	187.3	4036.0	151.4	3010.8
安徽	Anhui	3334.7	117.0	2703.2		64.3	1801.5	2061.9
福建	Fujian	2820.7	19.2			2133.6	818.8	1901.0
江西	Jiangxi	2577.6	42.1	85.9		4195.3		982.1
山东	Shangdong	9003.2	81.9	872.1		6732.6	24.3	4684.6
河南	Henan	4766.8	32.9	184.4		19841.8		2624.6
湖北	**Hubei**	**3421.2**	**196.4**	**286.2**		**5475.7**	**1121.5**	**2301.4**
湖南	Hunan	1951.3	36.3	8.9	3.5	34.2	33.9	1314.0
广东	Guangdong	3271.0	239.4	1523.6	1246.9	83795.4	3241.7	4034.9
广西	Guangxi	3545.4	229.4				3.1	1299.9
海南	Hainan	34.7	7.0					261.0
								679.8
重庆	Chongqing	1411.4	260.9	179.8		17605.1	6180.8	
四川	Sichuan	2702.5	42.3	73.6		3375.3	6342.7	3129.6
贵州	Guizhou	463.0		174.1		2015.2	218.2	1814.9
云南	Yunnan	1695.4	11.7		5.8			2553.4
西藏	Tibet	2.5						44.8
								1623.1
陕西	Shaanxi	1655.6	34.1			9.1		
甘肃	Gansu	847.8	2.4					1242.2
青海	Qinghai	113.6						565.6
宁夏	Ningxia	201.6						1154.7
新疆	Xinjiang	1070.5	1.6					2478.5

附录1-22 各地区电力消费量

REGIONAL ELECTRICITY CONSUMPTION

单位:亿千瓦时 (10 000 KW/h)

地 区	Region	2009	2010	2011	2012	2013	2014
北 京	Beijing	739.1	809.9	821.7	874.3	913.1	937.1
天 津	Tianjin	550.2	645.7	695.2	722.5	774.5	794.4
河 北	Hebei	2343.8	2691.5	2984.9	3077.7	3251.2	3314.1
山 西	Shanxi	1267.5	1460.0	1650.4	1765.8	1832.3	1822.6
内蒙古	Inner Mongolia	1287.9	1536.8	1864.1	2016.8	2181.9	2416.7
辽 宁	Liaoning	1488.2	1715.3	1861.5	1899.9	2008.5	2038.7
吉 林	Jilin	515.3	577.0	630.2	637.0	653.8	667.8
黑龙江	Heilongjiang	688.7	747.8	801.9	827.9	845.2	859.4
上 海	Shanghai	1153.4	1295.9	1339.6	1353.4	1410.6	1369.0
江 苏	Jiangsu	3314.0	3864.4	4281.6	4580.9	4956.6	5012.5
浙 江	Zhejiang	2471.4	2820.9	3116.9	3210.6	3453.1	3506.4
安 徽	Anhui	952.3	1077.9	1221.2	1361.1	1528.1	1585.2
福 建	Fujian	1134.9	1315.1	1515.9	1579.5	1700.7	1855.8
江 西	Jiangxi	609.2	700.5	835.1	867.7	947.1	1018.5
山 东	Shangdong	2941.1	3298.5	3635.3	3794.6	4083.1	4223.5
河 南	Henan	2081.4	2354.0	2659.1	2747.7	2899.2	2919.6
湖 北	**Hubei**	**1135.1**	**1330.4**	**1450.8**	**1507.9**	**1629.8**	**1656.5**
湖 南	Hunan	1010.6	1171.9	1293.4	1346.5	1423.1	1430.9
广 东	Guangdong	3609.6	4060.1	4399.0	4619.4	4830.1	5235.2
广 西	Guangxi	856.4	993.2	1112.2	1153.9	1237.7	1308.0
海 南	Hainan	133.8	159.0	185.3	210.3	232.0	251.9
重 庆	Chongqing	533.8	626.4	717.0	723.5	813.3	867.2
四 川	Sichuan	1324.6	1549.0	1751.4	1830.7	1949.0	2014.8
贵 州	Guizhou	750.3	835.4	944.1	1046.7	1126.3	1173.7
云 南	Yunnan	891.2	1004.1	1204.1	1315.9	1459.8	1529.4
西 藏	Tibet	17.7	20.4	23.8	27.8	30.7	34.0
陕 西	Shaanxi	740.1	859.2	982.5	1066.7	1152.2	1226.0
甘 肃	Gansu	705.5	804.4	923.4	994.6	1073.2	1095.5
青 海	Qinghai	337.2	465.2	560.7	602.2	676.3	723.2
宁 夏	Ningxia	463.0	546.8	724.5	741.8	811.2	848.8
新 疆	Xinjiang	547.9	662.0	839.1	1151.5	1539.8	1900.2

附录1-23 各地区社会消费品零售总额
REGIONAL TOTAL RETAIL SALES OF CONSUMER GOODS

单位:亿元 (100 million yuan)

地 区	Region	2009	2010	2011	2012	2013	2014	2015
全国总计	**National Total**	**132678.4**	**158008.0**	**187205.8**	**214432.7**	**242842.8**	**271896.1**	**300930.8**
北 京	Beijing	5309.9	6340.3	7222.2	8123.5	8872.1	9638.0	10338.0
天 津	Tianjin	2430.8	2860.2	3395.1	3921.4	4470.4	4738.7	5257.3
河 北	Hebei	5764.9	6821.8	8035.5	9254.0	10516.7	11820.5	12990.7
山 西	Shanxi	2809.0	3318.2	3903.4	4506.8	5139.3	5717.9	6033.7
内蒙古	Inner Mongolia	2855.3	3384.0	3991.7	4572.5	5114.2	5657.6	6107.7
辽 宁	Liaoning	5812.6	6887.6	8095.3	9304.2	10581.4	11857.0	12787.2
吉 林	Jilin	2957.3	3504.9	4119.8	4772.9	5426.4	6080.9	6651.9
黑龙江	Heilongjiang	3401.8	4039.2	4750.1	5491.0	6251.2	7015.3	7640.2
上 海	Shanghai	5173.2	6186.6	7185.8	7840.4	8557.0	9303.5	10131.5
江 苏	Jiangsu	11484.1	13606.3	16058.3	18411.1	20878.2	23458.1	25876.8
浙 江	Zhejiang	8622.3	10387.0	12532.8	14199.6	15970.8	17835.3	19784.7
安 徽	Anhui	3527.8	4300.5	5288.2	6142.8	7044.7	7957.0	8908.0
福 建	Fujian	4481.0	5310.0	6276.2	7256.5	8275.3	9346.7	10505.9
江 西	Jiangxi	2484.4	2971.0	3560.5	4123.3	4696.1	5292.6	5925.5
山 东	Shangdong	12363.0	14620.3	17155.5	19651.9	22294.8	25111.5	27761.4
河 南	Henan	6746.4	8004.2	9453.6	10915.6	12426.6	14005.0	15740.4
湖 北	**Hubei**	**5928.4**	**7014.4**	**8363.3**	**9682.4**	**11035.9**	**12449.3**	**14003.2**
湖 南	Hunan	4913.7	5952.6	7209.0	8318.7	9509.5	10723.5	12024.0
广 东	Guangdong	14891.8	17458.4	20297.5	22677.1	25453.9	28471.1	31517.6
广 西	Guangxi	2790.7	3312.0	3908.2	4516.6	5133.1	5772.8	6348.1
海 南	Hainan	537.5	663.8	822.5	950.2	1090.9	1224.5	1325.1
重 庆	Chongqing	2479.0	3051.1	3782.3	4403.0	5055.8	5710.7	6424.0
四 川	Sichuan	5758.7	6884.8	8290.8	9622.0	11001.0	12393.0	13877.7
贵 州	Guizhou	1247.3	1531.6	1899.9	2266.3	2601.2	2936.9	3283.0
云 南	Yunnan	2051.1	2555.8	3105.9	3597.9	4112.6	4632.9	5103.2
西 藏	Tibet	156.6	192.4	237.5	277.9	322.2	364.5	408.5
陕 西	Shaanxi	2699.7	3257.5	3900.6	4581.6	5245.0	5918.7	6578.1
甘 肃	Gansu	1183.0	1435.5	1772.9	2064.4	2368.8	2668.3	2907.2
青 海	Qinghai	300.5	351.0	413.4	480.3	549.6	620.8	691.0
宁 夏	Ningxia	339.3	418.5	515.5	590.5	668.5	737.2	789.6
新 疆	Xinjiang	1177.5	1386.1	1662.4	1916.1	2179.5	2436.5	2606.0

附录1-24 各地区客运量和旅客周转量(2015年)
REGIONAL PASSENGER TRAFFIC AND TURNOVER VOLUME OF PASSENGER TRAFFIC(2015)

地区	Region	客运量 (万人) Passenger Traffic (10 000 Persons)	*铁路 Railway	*公路 Highway	*水运 Waterway	旅客周转量 (亿人公里) Turnover Volume of Passenger Traffic (100 million person-kms)	*铁路 Railway	*公路 Highway	*水运 Waterway
全国总计	**National Total**	**1941444**	**251657**	**1619097**	**27072**	**30059**	**11961**	**10743**	**73**
北京	Beijing	62752	12821	49931		279.4	149.3	130.1	
天津	Tianjin	18345	4054	14219	72	252.3	170.5	81.7	0.1
河北	Hebei	53274	9706	43563	5	1213.2	944.4	268.4	0.3
山西	Shanxi	29587	7393	22085	109	380.0	215.4	164.5	0.1
内蒙古	Inner Mongolia	16125	5108	11017		371.1	210.8	160.3	
辽宁	Liaoning	73685	12912	60269	504	923.8	604.7	313.1	6.0
吉林	Jilin	36359	7158	29013	188	430.3	252.2	177.8	0.3
黑龙江	Heilongjiang	42713	9709	32632	372	487.5	257.6	229.6	0.4
上海	Shanghai	13844	9692	3766	386	215.2	89.0	125.5	0.8
江苏	Jiangsu	138308	16116	119800	2392	1453.7	625.5	825.5	2.7
浙江	Zhejiang	110951	14806	92304	3841	1092.5	541.9	544.8	5.8
安徽	Anhui	86810	8553	78072	185	1218.2	642.9	574.9	0.4
福建	Fujian	51646	9256	40394	1996	575.5	305.3	267.3	2.8
江西	Jiangxi	62418	8458	53687	273	953.8	668.7	284.7	0.3
山东	Shangdong	60142	11183	46960	1999	1147.3	664.3	471.4	11.6
河南	Henan	124981	12166	112535	280	1630.6	886.1	743.9	0.5
湖北	**Hubei**	**101659**	**13132**	**87953**	**574**	**1218.7**	**726.1**	**489.3**	**3.3**
湖南	Hunan	131311	10511	119266	1534	1527.5	888.8	635.6	3.1
广东	Guangdong	123709	22932	98050	2727	1796.5	751.1	1034.9	10.5
广西	Guangxi	49101	7046	41522	533	731.8	318.2	410.8	2.7
海南	Hainan	13728	1651	10363	1714	112.9	30.2	79.3	3.5
重庆	Chongqing	62282	3994	57556	732	533.6	151.0	376.4	6.1
四川	Sichuan	135969	9207	124014	2748	987.8	313.5	671.6	2.6
贵州	Guizhou	87541	4901	80621	2019	658.2	229.9	422.8	5.5
云南	Yunnan	48513	3668	43688	1157	456.6	123.9	330.2	2.5
西藏	Tibet	1092	221	871		38.3	14.1	24.2	
陕西	Shaanxi	69680	7866	61436	378	758.3	464.4	293.2	0.6
甘肃	Gansu	40453	3123	37240	90	619.7	370.7	248.7	0.2
青海	Qinghai	5602	936	4596	70	119.2	74.4	44.6	0.1
宁夏	Ningxia	9300	661	8444	195	115.5	47.4	68.0	0.1
新疆	Xinjiang	35948	2719	33229		477.3	228.0	249.3	
不分地区		43618				7282.6			

注：不分地区合计为民航完成数。
Note: The total passenyer traffil not classified by region lefers to thut completed by civil aviation